T0311675

Export–Import Theory, Practices, and Procedures

This book remains the sole export–import textbook aimed squarely at the academic audience. Discussing theoretical issues in depth, while maintaining a practical approach, it offers a comprehensive exploration of import procedures and export regulations.

In addition to updated cases, this new edition includes:

- New major developments in bilateral and regional trade agreements
- Changes to INCOTERMS 2010
- Coverage of the role of e-commerce
- Expanded updates on methods of payment, export pricing, and government export finance

This clearly written and comprehensive textbook will ground students in theory and prepare them for the realities of a career in this fast-moving field. Suitable for upper-level undergraduates and postgraduates of international trade, the book stands alone in its blend of conceptual frameworks and cogent analysis. A related website, filled with export–import resources, opinion pieces, cases, and the latest news is located at: www.export-importtradecenter.com.

Belay Seyoum is Professor of International Business Studies at Nova Southeastern University, USA. Dr. Seyoum has published two books as well as numerous articles in the area of international trade in several prestigious academic journals such as the *International Business Review*, *European Business Review*, *The Thunderbird International Business Review*, *The Asia Pacific Business Review*, and the *Journal of Economic Studies*.

Fourth Edition

EXPORT–IMPORT THEORY, PRACTICES, AND PROCEDURES

Belay Seyoum

Routledge
Taylor & Francis Group

NEW YORK AND LONDON

Fourth edition published 2022
by Routledge
605 Third Avenue, New York, NY 10158

and by Routledge
2 Park Square, Milton Park, Abingdon, Oxon OX14 4RN

Routledge is an imprint of the Taylor & Francis Group, an informa business

© 2022 Taylor & Francis

First edition published by Routledge 2000
Third edition published by Routledge 2013

Library of Congress Cataloging-in-Publication Data
Names: Seyoum, Belay, 1953– author.
Title: Export–import theory, practices, and procedures / Belay Seyoum.
Description: Fourth edition. | New York, NY : Routledge, 2021. |
Includes bibliographical references and index.
Subjects: LCSH: Exports. | Imports. | Export marketing. | International trade.
Classification: LCC HF1414.4 .S49 2021 (print) | LCC HF1414.4 (ebook) | DDC 382–dc23
LC record available at https://lccn.loc.gov/2020055600
LC ebook record available at https://lccn.loc.gov/2020055601

ISBN: 978-0-367-89681-2 (hbk)
ISBN: 978-0-367-89678-2 (pbk)
ISBN: 978-1-003-02050-9 (ebk)

DOI: 10.4324/9781003020509

Typeset in Times New Roman
by Newgen Publishing UK

CONTENTS

Introduction
A Brief History of International Trade

ANCIENT PERIOD

International trade based on the free exchange of goods started as early as 2500 BC. Archaeological discoveries indicate that the Sumerians of Northern Mesopotamia enjoyed great prosperity based on trade by sea in textiles and metals. The Greeks profited by the exchange of olive oil and wine for grain and metal somewhere before 2000 BC.

By around 340 BC, many devices of modern commerce had made their appearance in Greece and its distant settlements: banking and credit, insurance, trade treaties, and special diplomatic and other privileges.

With the decline of Greece, Rome became powerful and began to expand to the East. In the first century AD the Romans traded with the Chinese along the Silk Road and developed many trade routes and complex trading patterns by sea. However, the absence of peace made traveling unsafe and discouraged the movement of goods, resulting in the loss of distant markets.

By the time of the breakup of the Roman Empire in the fifth century, the papacy (papal supremacy) had emerged as a strong institution in a new and unstable world. The church's support (sponsorship) for the crusades (eleventh century) revived international trade in the West through the latter's discovery and introduction of new ideas, customs, and products from the East. New goods such as carpets, furniture, sugar, and spices brought from Egypt, Syria, India, and China stimulated the markets and the growing commercial life of the West. This helped Italian cities such as Venice and Genoa to prosper and to replace Constantinople as the leading center of international commerce. Letters of credit and bills of exchange and insurance of goods in transit were extensively used to accommodate the growing commercial and financial needs of merchants and travelers.

By the end of the fifteenth century, the center of international commerce had moved from the Mediterranean to Western Europe. Spain, Portugal, and later Holland became the focal points of international commercial activity. The more developed areas of Europe were changing from a subsistence economy to one relying heavily on imports paid by money or letters of credit.

COLONIAL PERIOD (1500–1900)

With the discovery of America in 1492, and sea routes to India in 1498, trade flourished and luxury goods and food products such as sugar, tobacco, and coffee became readily available in the markets of Europe.

The principal motivations behind global expansion (colonization) in the fifteenth century had been to enhance national economic power (mercantilist policy) by exploiting the colonies for the exclusive benefit of the mother country. Colonies were regarded as outposts of the home economy that would reduce trade dependence on rival nations and augment national treasure through exports as well as discoveries of precious metals. This first phase of colonization, which lasted until the advent of the Industrial Revolution in England (1750), was characterized by the following general elements with respect to commerce:

1. All commerce between the colonies and the mother country was a national monopoly, meaning all merchandise exports/imports had to be carried by ships of the mother country and pass through specified ports.
2. Little encouragement was provided toward the development or diversification of indigenous exports. For example, in 1600, precious metals constituted 90 percent of colonial exports to Spain. In the mid-1650s, British imports from its colonies were mainly concentrated in three primary products: sugar, tobacco, and furs. To protect domestic producers, competing colonial exports were restricted or subject to special duties. The patterns of economic relations were fashioned on the basis of dissimilarity, that is, non-competitiveness of colonial and metropolitan production.
3. Certain enumerated products could only be exported to the mother country or another colony. The policy ensured a supply of strategic foodstuffs and raw materials.
4. Private companies in the metropolis received a charter from the government that granted them (i.e., the companies) a monopoly of trade in the colonies. In most cases, the charter also granted complete local administrative authority, ranging from the making of laws and administration of justice to the imposition of taxes. Examples of this include the British East India Company (1600), the Dutch West India Company (1621), and Hudson's Bay Company (1670).

The second historical phase of overseas expansion (1765–1900) was dictated more by commercial considerations than by mere territorial gains. Britain emerged as the dominant colonial power and by 1815 had transformed its empire into a worldwide business concern. By the 1860s, the Industrial Revolution had transformed the social and economic structure of England, and mass production dictated an expansion of the market for goods on an international scale. The political economy of mercantilism that had proliferated over the preceding century was gradually replaced by that of free trade. By 1860, Britain had unilaterally repealed the Corn Laws and had abolished the Navigation Act restrictions (foreign ships were permitted to take colonial goods anywhere), as well as the commercial monopolies given to particular companies. Preferential duties on empire goods were gradually abolished. In trade, as in foreign policy, Britain led the free trade ideology based on non-discrimination. At the time, Britain was most likely to benefit from free trade because of its industrial and commercial lead over other nations.

1900 TO THE PRESENT

The major characteristics of economic relations from 1900 until the outbreak of World War I were the further development of trade and the emergence of a world economy. These were also the result of the international migration of people and capital from Europe, particularly Britain, since the 1850s, to other countries such as the United States, Australia, Argentina, Brazil, and Canada. This pattern of world economy provided the industrial economies with new sources of food and raw materials and new markets for exports of manufactures. For example, by 1913, Brazil was the source of two-thirds of German coffee imports, whereas North Africa supplied over half of French imports of wine. However, much of the import trade in Europe was subject to trade restrictions, such as tariffs, to secure home markets for local producers. Even within Britain, there were mounting pressures for the abolition of free trade.

The post-World War I recovery was further delayed by the disruption of trading links, as new nations were created and borders were redrawn. State intervention and restrictive economic policies had been consolidated in Europe and other countries by the end of the war. The U.S. government introduced the Fordney-McCumber Tariff, which imposed high tariffs on agricultural imports in 1922, and later, the Smoot-Hawley Tariff in 1930, which provoked widespread retaliation. Britain imposed high duties on various industrial products, such as precision instruments and synthetic organic chemicals, to encourage domestic production under the Safeguarding of Industries Act 1921. The volume of world trade in manufactures fell by 35 percent between 1929 and 1932, and prices also fell by a similar amount. The volume of trade in primary products fell by 15 percent, but prices fell by about 50 percent. To alleviate the worst effects of the Depression, countries resorted to more protectionism. This wave of protectionism produced a massive contraction of international trade and further aggravated the Depression. Many of the barriers placed on trade included tariffs and quotas, a variety of price maintenance schemes, as well as arbitrary currency manipulation and foreign exchange controls and management.

To avoid a repetition of the economic situation of the previous two decades, Allied countries met even before the outbreak of World War II to discuss the international financial arrangements that should govern trade and capital movements in the postwar world. In 1944, they established the International Monetary Fund (IMF) and the International Bank for Reconstruction and Development (IBRD). The IMF was to be concerned with facilitating the growth and expansion of global trade through the system of fixed exchange rates, while IBRD was established to promote long-term investment. This was followed by an agreement (the General Agreement on Tariffs and Trade, or the GATT) in 1948 to permit the free flow of goods among nations.

PART I

Overview of International Trade

CHAPTER 1

Growth and Direction of International Trade

LEARNING OBJECTIVES:

1.1 Describe international trade

1.2 Learn about the growth of world trade in goods and services

1.3 Learn about the importance of trade to the global economy

1.4 Understand the major determinants of trade

1.5 Learn about the volume and direction of world trade

1.6 Describe important developments in trade

International Trade in Practice

Covid-19 and Its Effects on International Trade

The Covid-19 pandemic has had a devastating human toll in many parts of the world where it has killed thousands of people. It has also brought the world economy into a depression with serious adverse effects on trade worse than the global financial crisis. Efforts to contain the pandemic resulted in lockdowns and other restrictions that impacted trade.

- Seaports such as Rotterdam and Shanghai witnessed a significant drop in container throughput volumes.
- Cargo volumes declined as many countries began to change port protocols ranging from port closure and quarantine measures to additional documentation requirements.
- Lockdowns also impacted the availability of labor to unload ships. It also raised costs due to increased protective equipment for workers. Additional costs were incurred by firms due to the introduction of health and safety measures for participants.
- The additional measures implemented to prevent transmission resulted in higher transaction costs for firms engaged in international trade.

The economic contraction in China was smaller than the global average as the country managed to control the outbreak relatively quickly and reopened its economy. The economic effects of the pandemic were particularly severe in the USA, Japan, and the European Union. Latin America and the Caribbean was the most affected developing region. The effects of the virus were transmitted through global supply chains. For example, when China implemented a lockdown on the affected region and its national borders, exports of intermediate goods for autos, electronics, and medical supplies were suspended, forcing importing firms in other countries to shut down for several months. The initial supply shock was compounded by a demand shock which occurred as a result of measures adopted in North America, Europe, and other countries. It also resulted in increased automation, e-commerce, and teleworking.

One of the major casualties of the pandemic was trade in services. Tourism, for example, which generally accounts for a quarter of global exports of services, registered a steep decline. In many countries, arrivals dropped by 60–80 percent.

Viable measures to alleviate adverse effects include:

* Maintenance of open supply chains for essentials
* Avoidance of export restrictions that would exacerbate the problem.
* Rejection of protectionist policies that distort trade.

Opportunities include:

* Pursuance of paperless trade
* Preparation of advance measures to reduce vulnerability to external shocks
* Promotion of regional value chains to take advantage of economies of scale.

International trade is the exchange of goods and services across national boundaries. It is the most traditional form of international business activity and has played a major role in shaping world history. It is also the first type of foreign business operation undertaken by most companies because importing or exporting requires the least commitment of, and risk to, the company's resources. For example, a company could produce for export by using its excess production capacity. This is an inexpensive way of testing a product's acceptance in the market before investing in foreign production facilities. A company could also use intermediaries, who will take on import–export functions for a fee, thus eliminating the need to commit additional resources to hire personnel or maintain a department to carry out foreign sales or purchases (Daniels, Radebaugh, and Sullivan, 2017).

World merchandise trade volume declined by 0.1 percent in 2019 (compared to 2.9 percent growth in 2018), the first contraction since the global financial crisis in 2008–2009. This is well below the average annual growth rate of (by volume) 2.3 percent since the financial crisis. In US dollar value terms, world merchandise exports fell by 3 percent to 19 trillion in 2019. Global service exports also declined to 5.89 trillion (2019) showing a mere growth of 2 percent from the 9 percent recorded in 2018 (WTO, 2020). During the past few years (2014, 2015, 2019), the growth of world trade has lagged behind global GDP. The overall decline in the growth of world trade can be attributed to persistent trade tensions as well as weaker global GDP growth. Furthermore, the Covid-19 pandemic has contributed to a significant contraction in trade and economic growth in 2020. Table 1.1 presents a breakdown of global trade figures alongside GDP growth, while Table 1.2 shows world export values in 2019.

IMPORTANCE OF INTERNATIONAL TRADE TO THE GLOBAL ECONOMY

International trade allows manufacturers and distributors to seek out products and services produced in foreign countries. Companies acquire them because of cost advantages or in order to learn about advanced technical methods used abroad, for example, methods that help reduce the cost of production, lower prices and in turn, induce more consumption, thus producing increased profit. Trade also enables firms to acquire resources that are not available at home. Besides providing consumers with a variety of goods and services, international trade increases incomes and employment. In 2016, the number of U.S. jobs supported by exports ($2.3 trillion) to all foreign markets reached 10.7 million (Rasmussen, 2017). Many studies show the positive role of international trade in raising employment and wages.

- Case studies reviewing the experience of the twelve most rapidly growing countries over the past sixty years shows the important contribution of trade in raising employment and incomes (OECD, 2012).
- Trade represents about 30 percent of the US economy. In 2017, nearly 20 percent of US jobs were linked to international trade (Trade Partnership Worldwide, 2019).

Even though imports are associated with loss of jobs due to plant closings or production cut-backs of domestic industries, the export job-generation effect is about 7.5 percent larger than the import job-loss effect (Belous and Wyckoff, 1987). Most occupations show a net job gain from an equal amount of exports and imports except for blue-collar occupations, which are shrinking in most developed countries due to increasing pressure from low-wage imports.

Exports create high wage employment. Exporters in the United States, for example, on average pay wages that are some 6 percent higher than non-exporters (Bernard et al., 2007). A study by the International Trade Commission (Riker, 2015) shows that export-intensive industries pay more on average and that the export earnings premium is larger for blue-collar workers in production and support occupations than white-collar workers in management and professional occupations. The general export earnings premium in 2014 was estimated at 16.3 percent (manufactures) and 15.5 percent (service industries). Imports are also found to have a strong positive effect on wages through their positive effects on productivity. An OECD-led study on a broad sample of countries (1970–2000) shows that workers in the manufacturing sector in open economies benefitted from pay rates that were between 3 and 9 times greater than those in closed economies (depending on the region) (Flanagan and Khor, 2012). Another study on wages and trade also finds a strong positive correlation between export intensity and wages. This could be partly explained by the fact that export-intensive sectors tend to show higher levels of productivity than other

TABLE 1.1 GDP and Trade (Goods and Services) by Value, 2016–2019 (Annual % change)

	GDP growth				Export (import) growth*			
	2016	2017	2018	2019	2016	2017	2018	2019
World	2.59	3.26	3.04	2.48	2.68 (2.28)	5.09 (6.02)	4.27 (4.19)	1.46 (1.61)
North America	1.51	2.31	2.84	2.27	0.28 (1.67)	3.05 (4.63)	3.03 (4.08)	2.92 (1.70)
USA	1.57	2.22	2.93	2.33	-0.01 (1.99)	3.48 (4.71)	3.02 (4.37)	-1.1 (-1.7)
Canada	1.00	3.17	2.01	1.66	1.41 (0.05)	1.41 (4.24)	3.08 (2.60)	1.28 (0.56)
Latin America & Caribbean	-0.34	1.77	1.57	0.83	2.43 (-1.17)	3.79 (6.31)	4.09 (5.04)	0.67 (-0.82)
European Union	2.05	2.73	2.15	1.52	3.39 (4.38)	5.72 (5.43)	3.68 (3.56)	2.65 (3.78)
Central Europe & Baltics	3.05	4.79	4.42	3.69	7.00 (6.32)	7.60 (8.17)	5.42 (6.86)	3.93 (3.92)
Middle East & N. Africa	4.96	1.72	2.38	1.81	5.41 (-3.08)	2.45 (6.83)	6.29 (6.10)	7.2 (5.5)
East Asia & Pacific	4.09	4.76	4.17	3.76	2.04 (1.47)	6.41 (6.72)	4.69 (5.04)	-2.5 (3.5)
South Asia	7.78	6.83	6.10	4.83	4.35 (4.38)	4.12 (16.54)	11.81 (9.96)	-0.51 (-4.40)
Africa	1.24	2.55	2.41	2.28	2.42 (-2.76)	6.51 (1.92)	2.16 (6.19)	2.01 (1.03)

*Based on constant 2010 US dollars

Source: WTO, 2019

TABLE 1.2 World Exports of Merchandise and Commercial Services, 2019 (US$ trillions)

Trade	Value	Trade	Value
Merchandise trade	**19.05**	**Services trade**	**5.89**
Agriculture	1.8	Transportation	1.12
Fuels/minerals	3.0	Travel	1.42
Manufactures	13.0	Other commercial services	3.17

Source: WTO, 2019

firms. It is also consistent with economic theory which states that industries in which a nation enjoys comparative advantage are likely to be those where workers are more productive and therefore receive higher wages. It also shows that greater import penetration is associated with greater demand elasticity, which reduces workers' bargaining power (Harless, 2006).

DETERMINANTS OF TRADE

Why do some countries trade more than others? Several studies have been conducted to establish major factors that influence exports. The trade and exchange rate regime (import tariffs, quotas, and exchange rates), the presence of an entrepreneurial class, efficiency-enhancing government policy, as well as secure access to transport (and transport costs) and marketing services are considered to be important influential factors of export behavior (Kaynak and Kothavi, 1984; Fugazza, 2004). A study on the nature, composition, and determinants of Singapore's technology exports suggests that the country's open trade and investment regime, and development-oriented economic policy have been the key factors in enhancing the country's exports. Singapore's economy has shown continued and remarkable growth in exports for over thirty years with only three brief and mild recessions in the mid-1970s, mid-1980s and July 2020 during the pandemic. Its total trade as a proportion of GDP remains one of the highest in the world, approximately 319 percent in 2019 (World Bank, 2020). A recent study on the determinants of export performance underlines the importance of foreign direct investment (FDI) and the general quality of the institutional framework. Foreign direct investment contributes to capital formation and helps promote the development and export of knowledge-based industries (Fugazza, 2004).

Much of the research literature on imports underlines the importance of high per capita incomes, price of imports, and the exchange rate in determining import levels (Lutz, 1994). For developing countries, however, determinants of import demand also include factors such as government restrictions on imports and availability of foreign exchange. A study examining the factors influencing import demand in South Korea (Kim et al., 2017) shows that i) the growth of exports is associated with imports of intermediate goods and raw materials used as production inputs for exports, ii) imports of intermediate goods and raw materials are positively associated with inward foreign investment.

VOLUME AND DIRECTION OF TRADE

In 1990, the world reached a milestone when the value of international trade in goods and services measured in current dollars surpassed $4 trillion. By 2019, the value of exports of goods and services was over six times the 1990 levels, approaching $25 trillion. The dollar value of total world trade in 2020 was greater than the gross national product of every nation in the world including the United States (US GDP estimated at $22 trillion in 2020). Another measure of the significance of world trade is that one fourth of everything grown or made in the world is now exported.

The rapid increase in the growth of world trade after World War II can be traced to increased consumption of goods and services as more people joined the middle class in many countries of the world. Trade liberalization, both at the regional and international level, has also created a global environment that is conducive to the growth and expansion of world trade. New technologies such as computers, telecommunications, and other media also assisted in the physical integration of world markets.

Small countries tend to be more dependent on international trade than larger ones because they are less able to produce all that they need. Larger countries (in terms of population) import fewer manufactured goods on a per capita basis because such countries tend to have a diversified economy that enables them to produce most of their own needs. The above statement can be exemplified by the case of the United States, Japan, India, and China, which have low import propensities compared to countries such as Belgium or the Netherlands.

Merchandise trade currently accounts for about four-fifths of world trade. The top ten exporters accounted for just over one-half of world merchandise exports (China, United States, Germany, Japan, Netherlands, France, South Korea, Italy, United Kingdom, and Mexico) (Table 1.3). Merchandise trade includes three major sectors: agriculture, mining and manufactures. Trade in manufactured goods has been the most dynamic component of world merchandise trade. In 2019, the value

TABLE 1.3 Leading exporters and importers of merchandise and commercial services, 2019 ($ billions)

Merchandise exporters		Merchandise importers		Service exporters		Service importers	
Country	Value	Country	Value	Country	Value	Country	Value
China	2499	USA	2568	USA	824	USA	571
USA	1646	China	2077	UK	412	China	497
Netherlands	709	Germany	1234	Germany	331	Germany	360
Japan	706	Japan	721	China	282	Ireland	320
France	570	UK	692	France	280	UK	278
South Korea	542	France	651	Netherlands	262	France	256
Hong Kong	535	Netherlands	636	Ireland	238	Netherlands	246
Italy	533	Hong Kong	578	India	214	Japan	202
UK	469	South Korea	503	Singapore	205	Singapore	199
Mexico	461	India	484	Japan	201	India	178

Source: WTO, 2020

of world merchandise exports was estimated at US$19 trillion compared to that of US$5.89 trillion for services (WTO, 2020).

Industrial market economies account for the largest part of world trade. Trade among these countries is estimated to be approximately 47 percent of global merchandise trade. Over the last few decades, one observes shifting patterns of trade as evidenced by a steady growth in the role of developing countries especially that of emerging economies and increasing levels of trade among developing nations.

IMPORTANT DEVELOPMENTS IN TRADE

Multilateral and Regional Trade Agreements

- In June 2016 the United Kingdom held a referendum to determine whether the United Kingdom should leave or remain in the European Union (EU). Fifty two percent of the people voted in favor of leaving the EU. The decision to leave was not popular in some parts of the United Kingdom. For example, 62 percent of people in Scotland, 56 percent in N. Ireland and 60 percent in London voted in favor of remaining in the EU. The withdrawal negotiations began in March 2017 and attempted to deal with the United Kingdom's exit conditions such as financial matters and the rights of EU citizens in the United Kingdom as well as the modalities of the United Kingdom's future relationship with the EU.

- After the implementation of the Uruguay Round, WTO members launched a subsequent Round in Doha, Qatar in 2001 to further reduce trade barriers. The focus of this Round has been on the reduction of trade-distorting agricultural subsidies provided by developed countries and the introduction of equitable trade rules for developing nations. The negotiations are at a complete stalemate with no prospect of success in spite of considerable progress on specific issues. In a multi-polar world, there are a number of power centers and a proliferation of national interests that erode international consensus across many areas. This is going to impede the development of international trade rules and standards and undermine the role of the WTO as a forum for trade negotiations.

- The current irreconcilable deadlock in the Doha Round has provided additional motivation for countries to engage in bilateral and regional trade agreements. Bilateral and regional agreements require less time to negotiate and provide opportunities for deeper trade policy integration. The United States, for example, has recently launched trade agreements with Japan and the United Kingdom. Many developing countries also perceive such agreements to be the most feasible means for gaining market access as the prospects for completing the Doha negotiations seem more remote. The share of trade among bilateral and regional trade partners is likely to grow in the next few decades.

- Many scholars believe that such bilateral/regional agreements are inferior to the multilateral, non-discriminatory approach of the WTO. Bilateral/regional trade arrangements discriminate against non-members and create a maze of trade barriers that vary for every exporting country: rules of origin, tariff schedules, non-tariff barriers such as quotas, etc. There are concerns that such agreements also work in favor of powerful nations that will sneak in reverse preferences such as protection of intellectual property rights or labor standards.

Global Trade Imbalances

- The U.S. current account deficit reached 2.87 percent of GDP in the last quarter of 2019. Imports exceed exports by about $616 billion (2019). At the same time, the East Asian economies (including Japan) held about US$5.0 trillion in official foreign exchange reserves out of a global total of $11 trillion in 2019. China's foreign currency reserves alone are estimated at US$3.11 trillion at the end of 2019. The Southeast Asian countries' heavy reliance on exports as a way of sustaining domestic economic growth, weak currencies, and high savings has resulted in unsustainable global imbalances. Global imbalances cannot diminish without, inter alia, reducing such excess savings through currency adjustments and/or increased imports in the surplus countries.

- Export-led growth in surplus countries feeds (and is dependent on) debt-led growth in deficit countries. It is impossible for all countries to run surpluses, just as it is impossible for all to run deficits. A country's trade balance is a reflection of what it spends minus what it produces. In surplus countries income exceeds their spending, so they lend the difference to countries where spending exceeds income, accumulating international assets in the process. Deficit countries are the flipside of this. They spend more than their income, borrowing from surplus countries to cover the difference, in the process accumulating international liabilities or debts.

- So long as trade deficits remain modest and economies invest the corresponding capital inflows in ways that boost productivity growth, such imbalances are sustainable. But the imbalances we see today are of a different character. First, they are much bigger. The most egregious is that between China and the United States, where China is running a huge trade surplus with the United States ($616 billion in 2019). Many of the other imbalances are between countries of broadly similar levels of economic development, such as those between members of the euro-zone, or that between Japan and the United States.

- Trade imbalances lead to destabilizing capital flows between economies. For example, the global financial crisis of 2007 and the subsequent euro-zone crisis were basically the result of capital flows between countries. Over-leveraged banks amplified the problem, but the underlying cause was outflows of capital from economies with excess savings in search of higher returns. The deficit countries that attracted large-scale capital inflows struggled to find productive uses for them: rather than boosting productivity, the inflows pumped up asset prices and encouraged excessive household borrowing.

Developing Countries in World Trade

- There has been a steady growth in the role of developing countries in world trade. Between 2000 and 2019, the value share of developed nations in world merchandise trade declined from 62 to 47 percent while that of developing nations increased from 29 percent to 53 percent. Over this period, China's share alone increased from 2.6 percent to 12 percent. The share of Latin America and the Caribbean also increased from 4.5 percent to 4.7 percent (WTO, 2020).

- China joined the WTO in 2001. Within three years, its exports doubled and the country is now the world's largest merchandise exporter ($2.5 trillion in 2019) and second largest importer of goods ($2.07 trillion in 2011).
- Only a few developing nations have managed to climb up the value chain and diversify their export base to cater to the expanding global market. About 83 percent of the increase in the share of developing countries' total trade (2010–2019) accrued to a small number of emerging economies: The BRICs (Brazil, Russia, India, and China), Mexico, and South Korea. India, China, and South Korea accounted for about one-third of world exports and about two-thirds of developing country exports in 2019.
- Such shifting patterns of trade and the increased demand for primary commodities from rapidly growing economies have strengthened South–South trade (trade among developing countries) and economic cooperation. South–South trade increased at a rate of 14 percent per year between 2010 and 2019 compared to the world average of 9 percent. During the same period, merchandise exports from the developing countries to the developed nations increased by 10 percent per year.

Transportation and Security

- About 60 percent (by value) of total world merchandise trade is carried by sea. In volume terms, 75 percent of world merchandise trade is carried by sea, whereas 16 percent is by rail and road (9 percent by pipeline, and 0.3 percent by air). Increases in fuel prices could act as a disincentive to exports by raising transportation costs. In air transportation (more fuel sensitive than shipping), rising oil prices could severely damage trade in time-sensitive products such as fruit and vegetables, or parts in just-in time production, etc. Faster economic growth in emerging economies is also putting pressure on the limited supply of other raw materials such as copper or coal.
- World air cargo traffic has grown during the past decade due to an increased trade in high-value-low-weight cargo, globalization, and associated just-in time production and distribution systems.
- In light of increasing threats of terrorism, countries have put in place procedures to screen cargo across the entire supply chain. There is an overall attempt to facilitate international trade without compromising national security.

CHAPTER SUMMARY

Major benefits of international trade	To acquire a variety of goods and services, to reduce cost of production, to increase incomes and employment, to learn about advanced technical methods used abroad and to secure raw materials.

Determinants of trade	Major determinants of exports: Presence of an entrepreneurial class, access to transportation, marketing, and other services, exchange rates, and government trade and exchange rate policies. Major determinants of imports: Per capita income, price of imports, exchange rates, government trade and exchange rate policies, and availability of foreign exchange.
Value and volume of trade	1. World trade approached US$25 trillion in 2019. 2. Services trade accounts for about 20 percent of total trade. 3. Merchandise trade accounts for 80 percent of world trade. 4. The industrial market economies account for 47 percent of world merchandise trade.
Major developments in trade	1. The absence of any meaningful progress in the Doha negotiations of the WTO. 2. Proliferation of bilateral and regional trade agreements 3. Growing role of developing countries in world trade 4. The increasing US current account deficit and global imbalances. 5. Fast economic growth in many countries and pressure on limited resources. 6. Business adjustment to security costs after 9/11.

REVIEW QUESTIONS

1. Discuss the importance of international trade to national economies.
2. What are the major determinants of exports? Why do some countries trade more than others?
3. What is the volume and dollar value of world trade today?
4. What are some of the major developments in trade over the last few decades?
5. What are the implications of the increasing U.S. trade deficit for global production and exports?
6. What is the reason behind the increase in common markets and free trade areas over the last few decades?
7. What are the limitations of export-led growth?
8. Why are small countries more dependent on international trade than larger ones?

REFERENCES

Belous, R. and Wyckoff, A. (1987). Trade has job winners too. *Across The Board* (September): 53–55.

Bernard, B., Jensen, J., Redding, J., and Schott, P. (2007). Firms in international trade. *Journal of Economic Perspectives*, 21(3): 105–130.

Daniels, J., Radebaugh, L., and Sullivan, D. (2017). *International Business*. New York: Pearson.

Flanagan, J. and Khor, N. (2012). *Policy Priorities for International Trade and Jobs*. Paris: OECD.

Fugazza, M. (2004). *Export Performance and Its Determinants: Supply and Demand Constraints*. Study no. 26. Geneva: UNCTAD.

Harless, A. (2006). *Exports, Imports and Wages: What Trade Means for US Job Quality*. Washington, DC: Center for National Policy.

Kaynak, E. and Kothavi, V. (1984). Export behavior of small and medium-sized manufacturers: Some policy guidelines for international marketers. *Management International Review* 24: 61–69.

Kim, Y., Park, H., Keum, H., and Lee, S. (2017). *Determinants of Korea's Imports and Its Effects on Distribution of Firms*. KIEP Research paper, World Economy Brief: 17–21.

Lutz, J. (1994). To import or to protect? Industrialized countries and manufactured products. *Journal of World Trade,* 28(4): 123–145.

OECD (2012). *Trade, Growth and Jobs*. Paris: OECD.

Rasmussen, C. (2017). *Jobs Supported by Exports 2016: An Update*. Washington, DC: International Trade Administration (ITA).

Riker, D. (2015). *Export-intensive Industries Pay More on Average: An Update*. Washington, DC: USITC.

Trade Partnership Worldwide (2019). *Trade and American Jobs: The Impact of Trade on US and State-level Employment.* Washington, DC: Business Roundtable.

World Bank (2020). *World Development Indicators.* Washington, DC: World Bank.

WTO (2019, 2020). *International Trade Statistics*. Geneva: WTO.

World Wide Web Sources

Growth of international trade/trade data/developments:
www.wto.org/english/res_e/statis_e/wts2020_e/wts20_toc_e.htm
www.census.gov/foreign-trade/balance/c4239.html#2013
https://unctad.org/webflyer/trade-and-development-report-2020

International Trade Closing Cases and Discussions

1. The Limitations of Export-led Growth

International trade played an important role in the economic development of North America and Australia in the nineteenth century and that of East Asian economies in the second half of the twentieth century. East Asia's growth contributed to increased living standards and reduced inequality as the new prosperity was widely shared among its population. In Malaysia and Thailand, for example, the level of poverty was reduced from almost 50 percent in the 1960s to less than 20 percent by 2000.

Central to the success of these countries is the promotion of exports. Governments provided credits, restricted competing imports, and developed export marketing institutions. As they increased their exports to wealthy countries, their economies grew at 7 to 8 percent per year.

The export-led model may have worked for a few countries during the time when most developing countries pursued import substitution policies—substituting domestic production for imports of manufactured goods. There are a number of limitations to export-led growth when many countries including China begin to use it. Here are some of its potential limitations.

- It is difficult for all countries to increase exports by 8–10 percent per year when the world economy grows at 2 or 3 percent per year. It is not possible for every country to have a trade surplus. Every item that is exported by one country has to be imported by another. If every country adopts an export-led strategy, economic growth will be difficult to achieve since many countries try to export (attempt to reduce their imports) thus leading to a zero-sum game.

- The major importing nation, the United States, cannot continue to run large trade deficits. Its economy is debt saturated, Europe is constrained by fiscal austerity and Japan continues to suffer from weak internal demand and an aging population while also hooked on export-led growth. Other potential destinations for global exports, South Korea, Japan, and Germany, also rely on an export promotion policy to sustain economic growth and are not willing to run large deficits.
- China and other East Asian economies have not taken measures to open their markets in order to absorb increasing exports from the rest of the world. In the absence of other sources of economic growth, focusing on the U.S. market is unsustainable in the long run.
- Export-led growth is a strategy that is highly dependent on foreign demand. The satisfaction of this demand is contingent on access to foreign markets which may be impeded by various tariff and non-tariff barriers. Furthermore, if the products are geared primarily toward the foreign market, the country will be left with products or services that cannot be applied to domestic needs if the export market shrinks or closes off.
- In order to sustain export-led growth and remain competitive in foreign markets, countries must keep labor costs down. This curtails wage growth in export industries, thus exacerbating income inequality.
- Export-led growth exposes countries to commodity price volatility.

Questions

1. Do you agree with the author's view regarding the limitations to export-led growth?
2. What other alternatives are available to export-led growth?

2. The Impact of the Financial Crisis on International Trade

The world economy has experienced several financial crises over the last few decades: The European monetary crisis (1992–1993), the Mexican crisis (1994–1995), the Asian financial crisis (1997–1998) and the global financial crisis (2007–2008). Even though the pathology of these crises may vary, the adverse effects on international trade is not disputed.

There are two types of financial crisis: banking and currency crises. A banking crisis occurs when a large number of customers withdraw their deposits from a financial institution at one time due to lack of confidence in the bank. Banks play an important role in a country's economy, primarily through investment and lending. After a banking crisis, businesses that depend on loans struggle to raise the capital required to maintain and expand their businesses. The fall in liquidity and investment reduces employment, lowers state revenues, and reduces overall investor and consumer confidence. A banking crisis affects trade in a couple of ways:

- In the case of a bank run, depositors suffer losses and investments are often liquidated before maturity (lack of liquidity, lower demand for goods/services), leading to an overall decrease in exports and imports. As aggregate investment decreases, demand for foreign inputs drops, thus creating a negative long-term effect on imports.
- The reduction in trade finance, i.e., "the oil that lubricates the machinery of international trade," makes it difficult for businesses to finance their export–import businesses. Firms engaged in international trade are likely to be more reliant than domestic firms on working-capital financing to cover the costs of goods that have been produced but not yet delivered. Over 90 percent of trade transactions involve some form of credit, insurance, or guarantee issued by a bank or other financial institution. Given that banks are the principal suppliers of trade finance, the supply of such financing is likely to be closely tied to the health of the banks. In particular, as the health of banks deteriorates, these financial institutions find it increasingly difficult to raise funds either through interbank borrowing or through the issuance of new bonds or equity. In the 2008 crisis, the standard measure of the risk premium charged to banks (the difference between interbank offer rates charged to banks and the overnight indexed swap rate (OIS)) jumped sharply, reflecting higher bank borrowing costs. Eighty-eight banks in forty-four countries revealed that the average spreads on letters of credit, export credit insurance, and short- to medium-term trade-related lending rose by 70, 107, and 99 basis points, respectively in the second quarter of 2009 relative to the fourth quarter of 2007.

A currency crisis can occur in two ways. If a country is unable to control its budget deficit and prints money to finance its spending, it could trigger a currency depreciation (as in the case of Argentina, Brazil, and Mexico). Secondly, an external shock (in some cases, a currency crisis in another country) causes demand for local products to fall in the international markets (leading to price deflation in Thailand and Malaysia, for example). This affects trade in several ways. One is the adverse effect on exports and imports triggered by the lack of demand for local products in foreign markets. Consumers may also substitute local products for foreign ones (if the relative price of local products decreases).

Question

1. What is the effect of a financial crisis on exports?

CHAPTER 2

International and Regional Agreements Affecting Trade

LEARNING OBJECTIVES:

2.1 Describe the principles of GATT/WTO

2.2 Learn about the various GATT trade negotiations since 1947

2.3 Learn about the Uruguay Round negotiations and its significance

2.4 Understand regional trade agreements

2.5 Learn about the US–Mexico–Canada trade agreement (USMCA)

2.6 Describe the European Union and its institutions

International Trade in Practice

Likely Impact of USMCA on the U.S. Economy

The US–Mexico–Canada free trade agreement entered into force in July 2020. The US International Commission (USITC) recently made an assessment of the likely impact of the USMCA on the U.S. economy and industry sectors. The model estimates that, if fully implemented and enforced, USMCA would have a positive impact on U.S. real GDP and employment. Here are some of the significant highlights of the study.

• Parts of the agreement that have significant effects on the U.S. economy are:

a. provisions that reduce policy uncertainty about digital trade; and

b. certain new rules of origin applicable to the automotive sector.

In the services sector, USMCA's new international data transfer provisions, including provisions that largely prohibit forced localization of computing facilities and restrictions on cross-border data flows will help reduce policy uncertainty.

- Given the fact that the North American Free Trade Area (NAFTA) has already eliminated duties on most qualifying goods and significantly reduced non-tariff measures, USMCA's emphasis will be on reducing remaining non-tariff measures on trade. It also addresses other issues that affect trade such as workers' rights, harmonizing regulations from country to country and deterring certain potential future trade and investment barriers, all leading to a positive effect on GDP and employment.
- USMCA strengthens rules of origin in the auto sector and increases regional value content (RVC) requirements. Even though there is likely to be a small increase in prices and a slight decrease in auto purchases in the United States, the new rules will enhance production and employment in the sector.
- USMCA prohibits restrictions on transfers of data, which will have a positive effect on a wide range of industries that rely on such transfers.
- The changes in the investor-state dispute settlement (ISDS) mechanism will probably reduce U.S. investment in Mexico but will increase domestic investment in manufacturing and mining.
- USMCA is likely to enhance labor standards and strengthen workers' rights in terms of collective bargaining and could lead to higher wages and better working conditions in Mexico.
- New intellectual property rights are likely to increase U.S. trade in technology-intensive industries.
- The Commission's model estimates that USMCA would raise U.S. real GDP by $68.2 billion (0.35 percent) and U.S. employment by 176,000 jobs (0.12 percent). The model estimates that USMCA will likely have a positive impact on U.S. trade, both with USMCA partners and with the rest of the world.
- U.S. exports to Canada and Mexico will increase by $19.1 billion (5.9 percent) and $14.2 billion (6.7 percent), respectively. United States imports from Canada and Mexico would increase by $19.1 billion (4.8 percent) and $12.4 billion (3.8 percent), respectively. The model estimates that the agreement will likely have a positive impact on all broad industry sectors within the U.S. economy. Manufacturing will experience the largest percentage gains in output, exports, wages, and employment, while in absolute terms, services will experience the largest gains in output and employment.

THE GATT AND THE WTO

The General Agreement on Tariffs and Trade (GATT) was established in 1945 as a provisional agreement pending the creation of an International Trade Organization (ITO). The ITO draft charter, which was the result of trade negotiations at the Havana Conference of 1948, never came into being due to the failure of the U.S. Congress to approve it. Other countries also declined to proceed with the ITO without the participation of the United States. Thus, the GATT continued to fill the vacuum as a de facto trade organization, with codes of conduct for international trade but with almost no basic constitution designed to regulate its international activities and procedures. The GATT, in theory, was not an "organization" and participating nations were called "Contracting Parties" (CPs) and not members (Jackson, 1992; Hoekman and Kostecki, 1995).

Since its inception, the GATT has used certain policies to reduce trade barriers between CPs:

- *Non-discrimination*: All CPs must be treated in the same way with respect to import–export duties and charges. According to the most favored nation treatment, each CP must grant to every other CP the most favorable tariff treatment (MFN) that it grants to any country with respect to imports and exports of products. Certain exceptions, however, are allowed, such as free trade areas, customs unions or other preferential arrangements in favor of developing nations. Once imports have cleared customs, a CP is required to treat foreign imports the same way as it treats similar domestic products (the national treatment standard).

- *Trade Liberalization*: The GATT has been an important forum for trade negotiations. It has sponsored periodic conferences among CPs to reduce trade barriers (see International Perspective 2.1). The Uruguay Round (1986–1994) gave rise to the establishment of a permanent trade organization (World Trade Organization or WTO). The most recent round (Doha Round) hopes to reach agreement on other trade distortions such as agricultural subsidies and trade barriers imposed by developing countries on imports of manufactured goods.

- *Settlement of Trade Disputes*: The GATT/WTO has played an important role in resolving trade disputes between CPs. In certain cases where a party did not follow GATT's recommendations, it ruled for trade retaliation that is proportional to the loss or damage sustained. It is fair to state that the existence of the GATT/WTO has been a deterrent to damaging trade wars between nations.

- *Trade in Goods*: The GATT rules apply to all products both imported and exported, although most of the rules are relevant to imports. It was designed primarily to regulate tariffs and related barriers to imports such as quotas, internal taxes, discriminatory regulations, subsidies, dumping, discriminatory customs procedures, and other non-tariff barriers. The Uruguay Round (1994) resulted in a new general agreement on trade in services, trade-related aspects of intellectual property (TRIPS), and trade-related investment measures (TRIMS). Thus, CPs have moved beyond the original purpose of the GATT to achieve unrestricted trade in goods, to reduce barriers to trade in services and investment, and to protect intellectual property (Collins and Bosworth, 1994).

INTERNATIONAL PERSPECTIVE 2.1

GATT Negotiations (1947–2001)

GATT Round	Explanation
Geneva (1947)	Twenty-three countries participated in establishing the GATT in 1947. Average tariff cut of 35% on trade estimated at $10 billion.
Annecy, France (1949)	Thirty-three countries participated in tariff reductions.

GATT Round	Explanation
Torquay, UK (1951)	Thirty-four countries participated in tariff reductions.
Geneva (1956)	Twenty-two countries participated in tariff reductions on trade estimated at $2.5 billion.
Dillon (1960–1961)	Forty-five countries participated in tariff reductions on trade estimated at $5 billion.
Kennedy (1962–1967)	Forty-eight countries participated in tariff reductions on trade estimated at $40 billion.
Tokyo (1973–1979)	Ninety-nine countries participated in reductions of tariff and non-tariff barriers on trade valued at $155 billion.
Uruguay (1986–1994)	Broadening of the GATT to include services, intellectual property, and investment. It also resulted in the establishment of the WTO. One hundred and twenty-four countries participated in reductions of tariff and non-tariff barriers on trade valued at $300 billion.
Doha (2001–)	Reduction of agricultural subsidies and other trade barriers on agricultural exports, broadening of international rules in services, lowering trade barriers by developing nations. More than 124 countries participate in this Round.

The Uruguay Round and WTO

In 1982, the United States initiated a proposal to launch a new round of GATT talks. The major reasons behind the U.S. initiative were 1) to counter domestic pressures for protectionism precipitated by the strong dollar and rising trade deficit, 2) to improve market access for U.S. products by reducing existing tariff and non-tariff barriers to trade, 3) to reverse the erosion of confidence in the multilateral trading system, 4) to extend GATT coverage to important areas such as services, intellectual property, and investment, and 5) to bring developing nations more effectively into the international trading system.

Despite the initial reluctance of many developing nations, the effort culminated in the conclusion of a successful trade negotiation (the Uruguay Round) in 1994. The results of the Uruguay Round can be summarized as follows.

Trade Liberalization

Significant progress was made toward reducing trade barriers in the areas of agriculture and textiles that had long been resistant to reform. Tariff reductions of about 40 percent were achieved. The agreement also opened access to a broad range of government contracts (Government Procurement Agreement). It also provided for the liberalization of the textiles and apparel sector by the end of 2004. Textile quotas have been removed except for occasional safeguards used to protect a sudden increase in imports.

Trade Rules

The Uruguay Round added new rules relating to unfair trade practices (dumping, subsidies) and the use of import safeguards.

New Issues

The agreement broadened the coverage of the GATT to include areas such as trade in services (General Agreement on Trade in Services, GATS), trade-related aspects of intellectual property (TRIPS), and trade-related investment measures (TRIMS). The GATS established rules to liberalize trade in services, which in 2019 was estimated to be almost $6.0 trillion (WTO, 2019). The TRIPS agreement established new trade disciplines with regard to the protection and enforcement of intellectual property rights. TRIMS provided for the elimination of trade distorting investment requirements such as local content, limitation of ownership, or exports of certain shares of domestic production.

Institutional Reforms

In the area of institutional reform, the Uruguay Round strengthened the multilateral dispute settlement mechanism and established a new and permanent international institution, the World Trade Organization, responsible for governing the conduct of trade relations among its members. The new dispute settlement procedure instituted an appeals procedure, expedited decision making and encouraged compliance with GATT decisions. Members of the WTO are required to comply with the GATT rules as well as various agreements (rounds) negotiated under GATT auspices.

REGIONAL INTEGRATION AGREEMENTS (RIAS)

Members of the WTO are permitted to enter into RIAs under specific conditions. These agreements must be consistent with the WTO rules, which require that the parties to the agreement 1) establish free trade on most goods in the regional area within ten years and 2) refrain from raising their tariffs against countries outside the agreement.

The number of RIAs and their share in global trade has been steadily rising over the last decade (Table 2.5). As of September 2020 about 306 RIAs are in effect. A large percentage of these agreements (over 80 percent) are mostly bilateral free trade deals (free trade agreements) intended for market access and do not require a high degree of policy coordination between participating countries. Less than 10 percent of the agreements provide for high levels of integration as well as harmonization of trade policies (a customs union). Recent notifications of RIAs to the WTO include USMCA (2020), an EU–Vietnam trade agreement (2020), a Peru–Australia trade agreement (2020) and a Chile–Indonesia trade agreement (2020).

Small countries enter into RIAs not only for market access but also to deal more effectively with larger economies in multilateral trade talks and other areas. Although RIAs are not often considered a potential threat to multilateralism, some scholars believe that 1) they lead to large volumes of trade diversion often resulting in substantial welfare losses, 2) they create lobbies and interest groups against multilateral trade liberalization, and 3) their differing regulatory regimes including rules of origin pose a challenge to the multilateral trading system (Das, 2004).

The major drivers of RIAs are stated to be as follows:

- Consolidation of peace, regional security, and free market reforms in many countries.
- Promotion of deeper levels of economic integration than what is available under the WTO (issues pertaining to competition, investment, labor, and the environment).
- Market access and a means of attracting FDI. Discriminatory liberalization in favor of partner countries is likely to provide firms (from these countries) with competitive advantages.
- Sluggish progress in multilateral trade talks.

THE UNITED STATES–MEXICO–CANADA AGREEMENT (USMCA)

The free trade agreement between the United States, Mexico, and Canada came into effect on July 1, 2020 after ratification by the US Congress and approval by the Canadian and Mexican legislatures. The USMCA constitutes the largest free trade zone with a population of nearly 500 million people and a GDP of over US$24 trillion in 2020. It is also the first reciprocal free trade pact between a developing nation and industrial countries. Upon entry into force of the USMCA, the North American Free Trade Area (NAFTA) ceased to exist. The new agreement updates some of the existing NAFTA provisions and covers new areas such as digital trade, labor, and small enterprises (summarized in Table 2.1). Some of the NAFTA provisions have also been incorporated with limited or no modifications.

Negotiating Objectives

The United States

It was logical to embark on a free-trade arrangement with Canada and Mexico not only due to their geographical proximity but also because they are the most important trading partners of the United States. The United States is the destination for over 75 percent of Canadian and Mexican exports. Both countries also import about one-third of U.S. exports. The United States is also the largest investor in both countries. It was in the interests of the United States to maintain and expand existing trade and investment opportunities through a regional trade arrangement. However, the reasons behind the renegotiation of NAFTA stem from the U.S. government's concern over its rising trade deficit with the partner countries. Even though there was a sizable trade deficit with Mexico, the U.S. had a trade surplus, albeit small, with Canada. However, there was mistaken belief by the Trump Administration that there was a trade imbalance in favor of Canada at the time. The United States also wanted to tighten up the existing 62.5 percent auto rules of origin (to increase U.S. and regional content), reform NAFTA rules on safeguards and government procurement, and introduce free trade on e-commerce, improve protections for intellectual property

TABLE 2.1 Key USMCA modifications/upgrades from NAFTA

Agricultural trade	• Expands market access for certain agricultural products: dairy products, poultry etc.; Canada will eliminate discriminatory grading of U.S. wheat and wines • Creates new and enforceable rules to ensure that sanitary and photo-sanitary measures are science based
Auto and auto parts	• Establishes regional value content of 75% (versus 62.5% under NAFTA) to qualify for preferential treatment under USMCA • USMCA requires that at least 70% of a producer's steel and aluminum purchases originate in North America • Requires that a certain percentage of qualifying vehicles must be produced by employees making an average of $16 per hour
Digital trade	• Creates free trade (no tariffs and other restrictions) on digital products • Facilitates data transfer across borders and digital transactions by permitting use of electronic signatures, open access to public data • Guarantees enforceable consumer protections
Intellectual property	• Full national treatment for copyrights and related rights • Extends terms for the protection of copyright, industrial designs, and data protection for agriculture chemicals • Criminal penalties and civil remedies for satellite and cable theft • Enforcement measures for the digital environment
Energy and energy products	• Free trade (zero tariff) on energy exports • Creates new rules of origin certification requirements for oil and gas moving between the parties
Labor and environment	• Adoption of core labor standards • Prohibits importation of products using forced or child labor • Commits parties to enforce their environmental laws, protect coastal and marine environments, and improve air quality
Non-market practices	• Expands the definition of state-owned enterprises (SOEs) to include cases where the state owns a minority equity but exercises control • Prohibits distorting subsidies to SOEs • Prohibits competitive devaluations • Criminalizes acts of corruption by domestic and foreign government officials
Textiles and apparel	• Incentives for use of regional inputs • Updates rules of origin to provide flexibility • New enforcement procedures to prevent circumvention and fraud
Monitoring and enforcement	• Closes loopholes in the NAFTA state-to-state dispute settlement mechanism that allowed parties to block the formation of panels • Creates a labor rapid response mechanism to enforce labor rights in Mexico at particular facilities • Creates interagency monitoring committee to ensure that parties are living up to their environmental obligations

rights as well as incorporate labor and environment issues into the core text of the agreement to make them enforceable and subject to dispute resolution.

Canada and Mexico

The USMCA permits Canadian and Mexican firms to achieve economies of scale by operating larger and more specialized plants. It also provides secure access to a large consumer market. Even though tariff rates between the United States, Canada, and Mexico have declined over time, there had been an increase in protectionist sentiment and use of aggressive trade remedies to protect domestic industries in the United States. These measures created uncertainty for producers with respect to investment in new facilities. A free trade agreement reduces this uncertainty since it provides rules and procedures for the application of trade remedies and the resolution of disputes. For Mexico, trade liberalization has been considered as an effective means of fostering domestic reform and consolidating its export-led growth strategy by improving secure access to the U.S. market. Furthermore, both countries wanted to address issues pertaining to security, narcotics, and immigration. Canada was also interested in amending the provisions dealing with binational panel arbitration given its involvement in several trade disputes with the United States over the years.

Overview of the USMCA

Market Access for Goods

The USMCA incorporates the basic national treatment obligation of the GATT. This means that goods imported from any member country will not be subject to discrimination in favor of domestic products. The 1994 NAFTA provided for a gradual elimination over fifteen years of tariffs for trade between Mexico and Canada as well as Mexico and the United States except for certain agricultural products. Under the Canada–U.S. Free Trade Agreement (1989), tariffs between the two countries were eliminated in January 1998.

Free trade in goods had been largely achieved under NAFTA. It is fair to state that almost all North American trade in goods became duty free by 2008. The USMCA also prohibits the use of export duties, taxes, and other charges and the waiver of specific customs processing fees. It adds new provisions for transparency in import and export licensing procedures, prohibits parties from requiring the use of local distributors for importation and from applying restrictions on the importation of commercial goods that contain cryptography.

To qualify for preferential market access, however, goods must be wholly or substantially made or produced within the member countries. For example, farm goods wholly grown or substantially processed within the USMCA region would qualify for duty-free treatment. The rules of origin under NAFTA have been largely retained except for autos and auto parts, which require a regional value content of 75 percent (versus 62.5 percent under NAFTA). It also requires that at least 70 percent of a producer's steel and aluminum purchases must originate in partner countries. It also promotes greater use of USMCA fibers, yarns, and fabrics in the production of apparel and other finished products to qualify for trade benefits.

Services

The USMCA covers trade in services in general and devotes certain chapters to the regulation of specific services such as telecommunications and financial services. It retains the principle of national treatment (services and service providers must be extended a treatment no less favorable than that provided to its own services and service providers) and most-favored nation treatment (services and service providers of another party to be accorded no less favorable treatment than that extended to services or service providers of another party or non-party) found in NAFTA. The market access provision prohibits any party from imposing limitations on the number of service providers including the total number of employees as well as the total value or number of service transactions. It also prohibits requirements for local presence in order to provide a service. An important provision relating to the movement of labor encourages parties to recognize the experience and education of foreign service providers which may be achieved by harmonization and other agreements. The agreement attempts to enhance commercial opportunities in services for small and medium-sized enterprises (SMEs) such as direct selling and protect them from fraudulent practices. There are annexes that deal with specific services: delivery services, transportation services, professional services, programming services, and guidelines for mutual recognition of professional services.

The chapter on financial services updates the NAFTA provisions. It recognizes the importance of maintaining regional macroeconomic stability through market-determined exchange rates (such as refraining from competitive devaluations). It requires parties to provide access to payment and clearance systems operated by public agencies, allow for transfer of information and data into and out of the host country, and refrain from requiring local presence as a condition for conducting computing services.

The USMCA also covers telecommunications services. It retains the NAFTA provisions that commit members to impose no conditions (i.e., reasonable and non-discriminatory terms) on access to, or use of, public telecommunication networks unless they are necessary to safeguard the public service responsibilities of the network operators or the technical integrity of the networks. It contains provisions applicable to mobile service providers, major suppliers of public telecommunications services, value-added services, and technology neutrality (prohibiting requirements that force technology choices). It requires major suppliers of public telecommunications services to extend the national and most-favored nation standard to suppliers of such services from other parties.

The agreement also restricts Mexican-based carriers from operating beyond the border commercial zones. It creates a review process to identify and remove Mexican-based operators that cause material harm to U.S. truckers (by not being subject to the same U.S. safety regulations and receiving lower wages, which could have a negative impact on wages in the U.S. trucking industry).

Investment

Investment includes majority-controlled or minority interests, portfolio investments, and investments in real property from member countries. The USMCA retains NAFTA provisions that 1) provide national and most-favored treatment to investors from member countries throughout the lifecycle of the investment; 2) prohibit the imposition and enforcement of certain performance requirements in connection with the conduct or operation of investments, such as export requirements or domestic content; 3) require each party to give investments "treatment in accordance with customary international law," i.e., fair and equitable treatment within the minimum standard accorded to aliens under customary international law; 4) limits expropriation only for a public purpose and requires it to be done in a non-discriminatory manner with prompt, adequate, and effective compensation.

Canada and the United States removed the availability of arbitrations to resolve investor–state disputes. United States and Canadian investors alleging a violation of the USMCA by their host government would only have recourse to domestic courts or other dispute resolution mechanisms. The USMCA retains investor–state dispute settlement under NAFTA but investors could only bring claims alleging breach of national or MFN treatment or for direct expropriation. Such claims could still be undertaken through USMCA state-to-state dispute settlement measures. Breaches of national treatment dealing with respect to establishment, acquisition, or indirect expropriation will no longer be covered.

Intellectual Property and Digital Trade

With regard to intellectual property and digital trade, NAFTA had become outdated since the agreement was negotiated during the time when the Internet was in its infancy and trade secrets had limited importance. The USMCA retains some of the NAFTA provisions but also makes significant innovations. It extends the terms for copyright (seventy years after the author's death or publication plus seventy-five years for companies who own these rights), trade marks (initial registration to be for a term of at least ten years), and industrial designs. It mandates patent term extensions for unreasonable patent office and regulatory delays. In the area of digital trade, the USMCA prohibits the imposition of tariffs and other measures on digital products (e-books, videos, software, and games) and facilitates digital transactions by promoting the use of e-signatures while safeguarding confidential personal and business information. It provides for enforcement procedures including civil and criminal penalties.

Agriculture

NAFTA did not eliminate all tariffs on agricultural trade between parties. Under the USMCA, parties agreed to reduce the use of trade-distorting policies such as subsidies, strengthen disciplines for science-based sanitary and photo-sanitary measures, and prohibit barriers for the sale and distribution of wines and spirits. The agreement will open up the market for dairy, poultry, and sugar products in partner countries.

Government Procurement

Purchase of goods and services by government entities in member countries is estimated at over one trillion dollars. NAFTA extended the national treatment standard (equal treatment to all member country providers) for all goods and services procured by federal government entities above a set monetary threshold (unless specifically exempted). It allowed parties to provide preferential treatment for small and medium-sized enterprises. The USMCA provisions only apply to US–Mexico procurement, while Canada remains covered by the recent WTO rules, which have a higher monetary threshold.

Labor and the Environment

Unlike NAFTA, the labor and environment provisions constitute part of the core agreement, fully enforceable and subject to dispute resolution. With regard to labor, the USMCA requires parties to adopt and maintain core labor standards as recognized by the International Labor Organization (freedom of association, right to strike, etc.), restrict importation of products using forced or child labor, and ensure that migrant workers are protected under these laws.

The environmental provisions require parties to promote air quality, protect coastal and marine environments, and ensure market access for environmental technologies.

Dispute Settlement

Disputes arising over the implementation of the agreement may be resolved through 1) consultations; 2) mediation, conciliation, or other means of dispute resolution that might facilitate an amicable resolution; or 3) a panel (if consultations fail to resolve the matter). Once a panel report determines that the responding party has violated the agreement, the parties are expected to resolve the dispute within forty-five days or compensation or retaliation may result. The USMCA essentially retains NAFTA's provisions on trade remedies pertaining to antidumping, countervailing duty determinations (binational panels), and safeguard actions. Unlike NAFTA, each side cannot block the process by refusing to name panelists.

Preliminary Assessment of USMCA

Overall Increase in Trade between Members

There has been a marked increase in trade among the three member countries since the first trade agreement went into effect in January 1994 (Table 2.2). Intra-USMCA trade jumped from $304 billion in 1993 to $1.3 trillion in 2019 compared to USMCA's trade with the rest of the world, which increased from $536 billion to $2.24 trillion during the same period. An increasing portion of Canadian and Mexican trade is conducted with the United States. The United States accounted for 75 percent of Canadian exports (64 percent of its imports) and 76 percent of Mexican exports (55 percent of its imports) in 2019. During the same year, the two countries accounted for about 33 percent of U.S. exports (18 percent for Canada and 15 percent for Mexico).

Increase in the U.S. Trade Deficit

The U.S. merchandise trade deficit with Canada and Mexico has quadrupled since the establishment of NAFTA. United States merchandise (services) exports to

TABLE 2.2 Merchandise Exports, 1993 and 2019 (US$ billion)

Source	Destination	1993	2019
US exports to	Canada	100	292
	Mexico	42	256
Canadian exports to	USA	117	337
	Mexico	0.64	5.5
Mexican exports to	USA	42	358
	Canada	1.57	14.3
Total intra-NAFTA trade		303.82	1257
NAFTA trade with rest of world		535.68	2237

Source: U.S. Census Bureau (1993–2020)

Canada and Mexico grew from $142 (27) billion in 1993 to $548 (101) billion in 2019. However, this was not sufficient to offset the growing merchandise trade deficit with both countries. The U.S. merchandise trade deficit with Canada and Mexico stands at US$45 and 106 billion, respectively, in 2019. A substantial part of the deficit is attributed to imports of mineral fuels, vehicles, machinery, and equipment from Canada and Mexico. In services, the United States has a trade surplus of $38 billion (with Canada) and $3 billion with Mexico.

The Trade Agreement's Impact on Jobs is Uncertain

There is no conclusive evidence on the effect of NAFTA/USMCA on jobs. There are certain indications, however, that the agreement may have had a negative effect on jobs. Between 1994 and 2002, the U.S. Department of Labor certified 525,000 workers for income support and training due to loss of jobs arising from shifts in production to Mexico or Canada. In view of its narrow eligibility criteria, the program covers a small number of workers who lost their jobs due to NAFTA/USMCA. The Economic Policy Institute contends that 682,900 U.S. jobs have been lost or displaced due to NAFTA/USMCA and the resulting trade deficit (Scott, 2011). Most of the job dislocations appear to be concentrated in the apparel and electronic industries. This may be attributed to the growing trade deficit with both countries that often leads to declines in production and employment. There are also some studies that show its negative effects on agricultural employment and real wages in manufacturing in Mexico. The Canadian Center for Policy Alternatives states that the Canadian government reduced social spending (such as the qualification for unemployment insurance) to enhance competitiveness (Campbell, 2006).

A U.S. Chamber of Commerce 2012 study, however, showed that trade with the two countries supported nearly 14 million jobs of which 5 million are attributed to the increase in trade generated by NAFTA/USMCA. The U.S. International Trade Commission's report (ITC, 2019) on the likely impact of USMCA on the U.S. economy indicates that the agreement will have a positive effect on real GDP and employment.

Substantial Increase in Foreign Investment in all Countries

Since NAFTA, there has been a substantial growth in inward FDI in member countries (Table 2.3).

TABLE 2.3 Gross Inward FDI Flows 1994 and 2019 (US$ billion)

Country	1994	% of world FDI flows	2019	% of world FDI flows
Canada	8.2	3.2	50.33	3.26
Mexico	10.64	4.2	33.00	2.14
USA	45.1	17.6	246.22	15.97

Source: UNCTAD, 2020

INTERNATIONAL PERSPECTIVE 2.2

Stages of Economic Integration

Preferential Trade Arrangements: Agreement among participating nations to lower trade barriers. *Example*: British Commonwealth preference scheme, 1934.

Free Trade Area: All barriers are removed on trade among members but each nation retains its own barriers on trade with nonmembers. *Example*: The European Free Trade Area (EFTA) formed in 1960 by Austria, Denmark, Norway, Portugal, The United Kingdom, Sweden, and Switzerland.

Customs Union: In addition to an agreement to lower or remove trade barriers, members establish a common system of tariffs against nonmembers (common external tariff). *Example*: The Andean Common Market, MERCOSUR.

Common Market: A common market includes all the elements of a customs union and allows free movement of labor and capital among member nations. *Example:* The European Union achieved common market status in 1968.

Economic Union: Economic Union goes beyond a common market and requires members to harmonize and/or unify monetary and fiscal policies of member states. *Example*: Benelux, which includes Belgium, The Netherlands, and Luxembourg, formed in the 1920s and also forms part of the EU; the European Union.

THE EUROPEAN UNION

The EU is the oldest and most significant economic integration scheme involving twenty-seven Western and Eastern European countries: Austria, Belgium, Bulgaria, Croatia, Cyprus, Czech Republic, Denmark, Estonia, Finland, France, Germany, Greece, Hungary, Ireland, Italy, Latvia, Lithuania, Luxembourg, Malta, The Netherlands, Poland, Portugal, Romania, Slovakia, Slovenia, Spain, and Sweden. The United Kingdom left in January 2020. One of the most important developments was the EU enlargement from fifteen to twenty-five countries in May 2004 with the admission of Cyprus, Malta, and eight East European countries. In January 2007 Bulgaria and Romania also joined the EU, increasing the number to twenty-eight countries until the United Kingdom's departure. Turkey and other East European countries will be considered for admission in the coming years based on certain criteria such as stable democratic institutions, free markets, and their ability to assume EU treaty obligations (Van Oudenaren, 2002; Poole, 2003).

Although European economic integration dates back to the Treaty of Rome in 1957, the EU is the outcome of the Maastricht treaty in 1992. The European Union has an aggregate population of about 447 million and a total economic output (GDP) of US$18.8 trillion in 2019, and involves the largest transfer of national sovereignty to a common institution (see International Perspective 2.3). In certain designated areas, for example, international agreements can only be made by the EU on behalf of member states (Wild, Wild, and Han, 2006).

The pursuit of such integration was party influenced by the need to create a lasting peace in Europe as well as to establish a stronger Europe that could compete economically against the United States and Japan (Table 2.4). Since the countries were not large enough to compete in global markets, they had to unite in order to exploit economies of large-scale production.

The objectives of European integration as stated in the Treaty of Rome (1957) are as follows:

- To create free trade among member states and provide uniform customs duties for goods imported from outside the EU (common external tariff).
- To abolish restrictions on the free movement of all factors of production, that is, labor, services, and capital. Member states are required to extend the national treatment standard to goods, services, capital, etc. from other member countries with respect to taxation and other matters (non-discrimination).
- To establish a common transport, agricultural, and competition policy.

A number of the objectives set out in the Treaty of Rome were successfully accomplished. The Common Agricultural Policy (CAP) was established in 1962 to maintain common prices for agricultural products throughout the community and to stabilize farm incomes. Tariffs between member nations were eliminated and a common external tariff established in 1968. However, efforts to achieve the other objectives, such as a single internal market (elimination of non-tariff barriers), the free movement of services or capital, and so forth, was slow and difficult. Coordinated or common policies in certain areas such as transport simply did not exist (Archer and Butler, 1992).

The European Commission presented a proposal in 1985 to remove existing barriers to the establishment of a genuine common market. The proposal, which was

TABLE 2.4 USMCA and EU: Major Differences

USMCA	EU
USMCA does not provide for a common external tariff	EU has a common external tariff
USMCA has no provision for economic assistance or economic/monetary union	EU provides for economic assistance to members and economic/monetary union
USMCA does not provide for free movement of labor	EU allows for free movement of labor

adopted and entitled The Single European Act (SEA), constitutes a major revision to the Treaty of Rome. The Single European Act set the following objectives for its members:

- To complete the single market by removing all the remaining barriers to trade such as customs controls at borders, harmonization of technical standards, liberalization of public procurement, provision of services, removal of obstacles to the free movement of workers, and so on. In short, efforts involved the removal of physical, technical, and fiscal (different excise and value-added taxes) barriers to trade.
- To encourage monetary cooperation leading to a single European currency. The Maastricht Treaty of 1992 further reinforced this and defined plans for achieving economic and monetary union.
- To establish cooperation on research and development (R&D) and create a common standard on environmental policy.
- To harmonize working conditions across the community and improve the dialogue between management and labor.

The Single European Act established a concrete plan and timetable to complete the internal market by 1992. It is fair to state that most of the objectives set out under the SEA were accomplished: border checks are largely eliminated, free movement of workers has been achieved through mutual recognition of qualifications from any accredited institution within the EU, free movement of capital (banks, insurance, and investment services) has been made possible with certain limitations and the single currency (the euro) was introduced in 1999. The euro has helped reduce transaction costs by eliminating the need to convert currencies and made prices between markets more transparent. There still exists a number of challenges in completing and sustaining the single market, expanding EU policy responsibilities in certain controversial areas such as energy policy, and undertaking appropriate structural reforms to take advantage of the economic and monetary union.

INTERNATIONAL PERSPECTIVE 2.3

Institutions of the European Union

The European Council: Composed of representatives (Ministers) of member states, the council sets out the general direction of the union. The council approves legislation and international agreements, acting on a proposal from the commission and after consulting with the European Parliament.

The European Commission: Members of the commission are chosen by the mutual agreement of national governments and serve four-year terms. Larger nations appoint two while smaller nations appoint one commissioner. They neither represent nor take orders from member states. The commission initiates policies and ensures members' compliance with the EU treaty.

The European Parliament: Composed of 732 representatives directly elected, the European Parliament supervises the commission, adopts the community budget, and influences the legislative process. Any agreement concerning international cooperation must be reviewed and accepted by parliament before it is concluded. The parliament, however, does not have express legislative powers.

The Court of Justice: Settles disputes arising from the EU treaty (i.e. interprets and applies the treaty). The judges are appointed by mutual agreement of member states and serve six-year terms. The court ensures uniform interpretation and application of community law, evaluates the legality of legislation adopted by the council and the commission, and provides rulings on community law when requested by national courts in member states.

TABLE 2.5 Other Major Regional Trade Agreements

Africa Continental Free Trade Area (AfCFTA, 2019)	*Members:* 30 African countries have ratified the agreement that allows for free trade in goods, services, and dispute settlement. It will also include agreements on investment, intellectual property, and competition
The European Free Trade Association (EFTA, 1960)	*Members:* Iceland, Liechtenstein, Norway, Switzerland *Objectives:* Removal of customs barriers and differing technical standards. Free trade with EU strictly limited to commercial matters
The Preferential Area for Eastern and Southern American Common Market (MERCOSUR, 1991)	*Members:* Argentina, Brazil, Paraguay, Uruguay, Venezuela. Chile and Bolivia joined as associate members *Objectives:* Free trade and industrial cooperation
The Central American Common Market (CACM, 1960)	*Members:* Costa Rica, El Salvador, Guatemala, Honduras, Nicaragua *Objectives:* Free trade and a common external tariff
The Andean Pact, 1969	*Members:* Bolivia, Colombia, Ecuador, Peru, Venezuela *Objectives:* Free trade and industrial development
The Association of Southeast Asian Nations (ASEAN, 1967)	*Members:* Brunei, Cambodia, Indonesia, Laos, Malaysia, Mynamar, Philippines, Singapore, Thailand, Vietnam *Objectives:* Reduction of trade barriers, industrial cooperation
The Caribbean Common Market (CARICOM, 1973)	*Members:* Antigua and Barbuda, The Bahamas, Barbados, Belize, Dominica, Grenada, Haiti, Guyana, Jamaica, Montserrat, St. Kitts and Nevis, St. Lucia, St. Vincent and the Grenadines, Trinidad and Tobago, Suriname *Objectives:* Political unity, economic cooperation
The Southern African Customs Union (SACU, 1969)	*Members:* Botswana, Lesotho, Namibia, South Africa, Swaziland *Objectives:* Free movement of goods, common external tariff

(continued)

TABLE 2.5 Cont.

The Economic Community of West African States (ECOWAS, 1974)	*Members:* Benin, Burkina Faso, Cape Verde, Cote d'Ivoire, the Gambia, Ghana, Guinea, Guinea-Bissau, Liberia, Mali, Niger, Nigeria, Senegal, Sierra Leone, Togo *Objectives:* Economic and monetary union
Asia Pacific Economic Cooperation (APEC, 1989)	*Members:* Australia, Brunei, Canada, Chile, China, Japan, South Korea, Malaysia, Mexico, New Zealand, Papua New Guinea, Philippines, Peru, Russia, Singapore, Taiwan, Thailand, USA, Vietnam *Objectives:* Strengthen the multilateral trading system, simplify and liberalize trade and investment procedures among members

CHAPTER SUMMARY

The GATT/WTO	*Principal objectives of the GATT:* Non-discrimination, trade liberalization, and settlement of trade disputes between members
The Uruguay Round of the GATT and the birth of WTO	*Important results of the Uruguay Round trade negotiations (1986–1994):* Reductions in tariffs, adoption of new trade rules on unfair trade practices, GATT coverage extended to trade in services, intellectual property, and trade-related investment measures, the birth of WTO.
The United States–Mexico–Canada Free Trade Agreement (USMCA)	*Scope of coverage:* Market access for goods, services, investment, protection of intellectual property, government procurement, safeguards, standards, dispute settlement
USMCA: Preliminary assessment	*Benefits:* Increases in overall trade between members, increase in the U.S. trade deficit on merchandise trade with members, and a rise in foreign investment
The European Union (EU)	*Major objectives of the EU:* To create free trade and a common external tariff between members, to abolish restrictions on the free movement of all factors of production, to establish common policies in the area on transport, agriculture, competition, etc. *Institutions of the EU:* The European Council, the European Commission, the European Parliament, the Court of Justice
Other Regional Trade Agreements	Africa Continental Free Trade Area (AfCFTA, 2019), The European Free Trade Association (EFTA), MERCUSOR, The Central American Common Market (CACM),The Andean Pact, The Association of Southeast Asian Nations (ASEAN),The Caribbean Common Market (CARICOM), The Southern African Customs Union (SACU), The Economic Community of West African States (ECOWAS), Asia Pacific Economic Cooperation (APEC, 1989)

REVIEW QUESTIONS

1. What were the major achievements of the Uruguay Round of the GATT/WTO?
2. Distinguish between the most-favored nation and the national treatment standard in international trade.
3. Discuss the major drivers of regional trade agreements.
4. Compare and contrast the negotiating objectives of Canada and Mexico behind the USMCA.
5. Discuss the USMCA pertaining to services and investment. Has it increased trade between the member countries?
6. What are the various stages of economic integration?
7. What are the objectives of European integration? Which countries joined the EU in 2004?
8. Discuss the major differences between the USMCA and the EU.
9. What were the major achievements of the Single European Act?
10. What is the role of the EU Commission?

REFERENCES

Archer, C. and Butler, F. (1992). *The European Community*. New York: St. Martin's Press.

Campbell, B. (2006). NAFTA's broken promises (July issue). http://policyalternatives.ca/monitor issues/2006/.

Collins, S. and Bosworth, B. (eds.) (1994). *The New GATT*. Washington, DC: Brookings Institution.

Das, D. (2004). *Regionalism in Global Trade*. Northampton, MA: Praeger.

Hoekman, B. and Kostecki, M. (1995). *The Political Economy of the World Trading System*. New York: Oxford University Press.

Jackson, J. (1992). *The World Trading System*. Cambridge, MA: MIT Press.

Poole, P. (2003). *Europe: The EU's Eastern Enlargement*. London, UK: Praeger.

Scott, R. (2011). *Heading South: US-Mexico trade and job displacement after NAFTA*. Washington, DC: Economic Policy Institute.

UNCTAD (2020). *World Investment Report*. Geneva: United Nations.

U.S. Census Bureau (1993–2020). *U.S. Trade Statistics*. http://census.gov.

U.S. Chamber of Commerce (2012). *NAFTA Triumphant: Assessing Two Decades of Gains in Trade, Growth and Jobs*. New York: U.S. Chamber of Commerce.

U.S. International Trade Commission (USITC, 2019). *U.S.-Mexico-Canada Trade Agreement: Likely Impact on the U.S. Economy and on Specific Industry Sectors*. Washington, DC: USITC.

Van Oudenaren, J. (2002). *Uniting Europe: European Integration and the Post-Cold War World*. New York: Rowman & Littlefield Publishers.

Weintraub, S. (2004). *NAFTA's Impact on North America: The First Decade*. Washington, DC: Center for Strategic and International Studies.

Wild, J., Wild, K., and Han, J. (2006). *International Business: The Challenges of Globalization*. Upper Saddle River, NJ: Prentice Hall.

WTO (2019). *Annual Report*. Geneva: WTO. www.wto.org.

World Wide Web Resources

The European Union
Information on the EU and its institutions: https://europa.eu/european-union/index_en

NAFTA: Economic and Commercial Information
NAFTA: the complete agreement: www-tech.mit.edu/Bulletins/nafta.html

USMCA
https://ustr.gov/trade-agreements/free-trade-agreements/united-states-mexico-canada-agreement

World Trade Organization

Basic information about the WTO, its agreements and activities: www.wto.org

International Trade Closing Cases and Discussions

1. The Euro Crisis and Implications

Serious intraregional divergences in competitiveness and the related build-up of regional imbalances have been the root cause of the crisis in the euro zone. The Maastricht treaty of 1992, which created the European Union and led to the creation of a single European currency (the euro), established criteria for EU member states that included the following conditions: Inflation rates below 1.5 percent, budget deficits not to exceed 3 percent of GDP, and public debt not to exceed 60 percent of GDP. Since wages are an important determinant of prices, wage rates corrected for productivity growth (unit labor costs) were expected to remain aligned to keep the union in a sustainable position.

While Germany restrained wages, other member countries such as Greece and Portugal failed to limit the continued rise in wages and inflation which affected their overall competitiveness. Trade imbalances built up as low inflation countries began to gain in competitiveness over those with high wage price inflation. Trade deficits in crisis affected countries were financed by debt as banks in surplus countries such as Germany lent to borrowers and spenders in deficit countries. Borrowed funds were used to finance consumption and speculation (house building) and not to improve productivity or competitiveness.

When the investors who bought the bonds to finance the loans to these countries realized that these countries were unable to repay the loans, they became nervous and started to sell off the bonds. Government bonds that were considered risky were subject to speculative attack and their risk premiums rose dramatically. This rendered commercial banks whose balance sheets were loaded with these bonds insolvent. The banking crisis morphed into a sovereign debt crisis. Banks began to demand higher interest rates to lend to weaker countries. *Rising borrowing costs for weaker countries and trouble for banks that loaned money to these countries constitute the root causes of the crisis.*

In essence, all new initiatives continue to follow the old blueprint. Measures are mainly focused on strengthening the so-called Stability and Growth Pact and aligning policies with the latest version of the EU's long-standing structural reform agenda—the Europe 2020 strategy. Europe continues to ignore the vital issues of domestic demand management and proper policy coordination for internal balance including the need for upward adjustment of wages and prices in surplus countries.

Questions

1. What are the major causes of the euro crisis?
2. To what extent does international trade play a role in the crisis?

2. BREXIT: Withdrawal of the United Kingdom from the EU

In a referendum held in June 2016, the United Kingdom voted in favor of leaving the EU. It was a close vote and those who voted to leave the EU won by a thin margin since the option to leave was not popular in some parts of the country. While England (53.4%) and Wales (52.5%) voted to leave, Scotland and N. Ireland voted to remain in the EU (62% and 55.8% respectively). The parties (United Kingdom and EU) have negotiated the exit conditions and the United Kingdom's future relations with the EU. The UK and EU have now concluded a Trade and Cooperation Agreement which has entered a period of provisional application in January, 2021. Free trade between the parties will continue with new rules of origin set out in the agreement. There will be new customs, border, and immigration rules. Separate provisions apply to trade with N. Ireland.

Observers provide a number of reasons that gave rise to the United Kingdom's decision to leave the Union:

*   The United Kingdom is one of the biggest contributors to the EU budget (US$11–17 billion a year). Even though it does reap some benefits from its financial contributions, some people feel that they pay more than they receive in tangible benefits. They believe that these contributions could be better used to build schools, hospitals, and other infrastructure that is sorely needed than providing it to the EU.
*   The EU countries are highly regulated from Brussels and withdrawal gives the country an opportunity to take back control of its laws and policies such as immigration. Leaving allows the United Kingdom to deregulate its economy and strike agreements with other countries. It is not clear whether the existing arrangement within the EU prevents the United Kingdom from undertaking further deregulation. It remains to be seen whether the new trade arrangements with the United States and other countries compensate for lower U.K.–EU trade.

There are potential consequences for such a decision. The United Kingdom will be a new actor in international economic relations. It has to establish a new framework for its bilateral and international relations. There will be substantial costs involved to settle financial obligations arising from its withdrawal that are estimated at US$43–51 billion. It also entails further costs relating to replacing all existing EU laws and undertaking further negotiations to define its future status with the EU.

The United Kingdom's economic performance since joining the European Common Market in 1973 has been quite impressive. Since 1973, its GDP per capita has doubled and the Human Development Index that measures overall standards of living shows the United Kingdom outperforming other member countries (except Germany). Presently, the EU accounts for 44 percent of U.K. exports and 53 percent of its imports. Exports from the United Kingdom to the EU account for 12 percent of U.K. GDP while U.K. imports from the EU account for 3 percent of EU GDP. Furthermore, U.K.–EU trade is 3.2 times larger than the United Kingdom's trade with the United States, its second-largest trading partner. There are concerns that withdrawal from the EU will weaken its economic position (lower trade, lower FDI inflows) and social cohesion (for example, Scotland seeking independence from the union).

PART II

Export Planning and Strategy

CHAPTER 3

Setting Up the Business

LEARNING OBJECTIVES:

3.1 Describe the different ownership structures of export organizations
3.2 Learn about the use of trade names, location, and use of professional services
3.3 Identify the organizational structures of export firms
3.4 Learn about taxation of export–import transactions
3.5 Understand transfer pricing and its use in international trade

International Trade in Practice

Export Restrictions: Do They Make Sense?

Export restrictions (ER) are tariffs and other restrictions (export taxes, export bans, regulated exports) imposed by governments on the export of goods and services delivered to non-residents. They are less common than import restrictions. Nonetheless, fifty-three countries imposed ER as of 2014. Most developed countries do not have ER (though Norway has ERs on fish and fish products). Other than a few middle-income countries such as China, Russia, or Turkey that impose ERs on certain goods, most ERs are imposed by developing nations. In the United States, the Federal Constitution prohibits taxes on exports. Export restrictions are also prohibited in many bilateral (EU–Mexico; Canada–Chile) and regional trade agreements (EU, MERCOSUR, USMCA). However, such restrictions are not prohibited under the WTO.

Export restrictions are often imposed on food exports to ensure domestic availability of food and to dampen growing public discontent about food prices. China's use of ERs on the rare earth elements tungsten and molybdenum, which are extensively used for producing electronics (China accounts for 97 percent of global production), were challenged at the WTO by the United States, EU, and Japan due to its adverse effects on downstream producers.

Export restrictions can lead to global welfare losses if the country is the sole or major supplier of the product (with limited substitution), leading to higher prices. In the 1970s, the Philippines imposed export taxes on copra and coconut oil to improve its terms of trade. However, this did not provide the expected benefits because importers bought lower-priced substitutes and the measure led to reduced incomes for domestic producers and lower wages (Warr, 2002). Indonesia (palm oil) and Thailand (rice) imposed export taxes in the 1990s (mainly to reduce price inflation), which had the adverse effect of reducing producers' incomes and the incomes of low-skilled labor. In the case of Indonesia, studies show that some benefits accrued to consumers although most of the benefits of export taxes were appropriated by distributors.

There are several arguments in favor of ERs:

a. ERs can improve the country's terms of trade, i.e., it will increase the world price of the taxed commodity and thus increase the relative price of exports compared to imports.
b. ERs stabilize domestic prices and reduces inflationary pressures. The increasing world price is redistributed from domestic producers to both the government and domestic consumers.
c. ERs encourage high domestic value-added production: ERs on raw materials could encourage domestic firms to establish domestic manufacturing or processing industries with high value-added exports. In the 1990s, Pakistan imposed export taxes on raw cotton to encourage the development of the yarn industry. This led to a transfer of income from cotton to yarn producers. However, additional growth in the yarn industry was not realized partly because new technologies were not adopted that would have led to efficiency gains (Zambersky and Cajka, 2015).

Whether it is a new or existing export–import business, the legal form, or structure, will determine how the business is to be conducted, its tax liability, and other important considerations. Each form of business organization has its own advantages and disadvantages, and the entrepreneur has to select the one that best fulfills the goals of the entrepreneur and the business (for questions to consider before starting a business, see Table 3.1).

Selection of an appropriate business organization is a task that requires accounting and legal expertise and should be done with the advice of a competent attorney or accountant.

OWNERSHIP STRUCTURE

In this section, we examine different forms of business organizations: sole proprietorships, partnerships, corporations, and limited liability companies.

Sole Proprietorships

A sole proprietorship is a firm owned and operated by one individual. No separate legal entity exists. There is one principal in the business who has total control over all export–import operations and who can make decisions without consulting anyone. The major advantages of sole proprietorships are as follows:

1. They are easy to organize and simple to control. Establishing an export–import business as a sole proprietorship is simple and inexpensive and requires little or no government approval. In the United States, at the state level, registration of the business name is required, while at the federal level, sole proprietors need to keep accurate accounting records and attach a profit or loss statement for the business when filing individual tax returns (schedule C, Internal Revenue Service Form 1040). They must operate on a calendar year and can use the cash or accrual method of accounting.
2. They are more flexible to manage than partnerships or corporations. The owner makes all operational and management decisions concerning the business. The owner can remove money or other assets of the business without legal or tax consequences. He/she can also easily transfer or terminate the business.
3. Sole proprietorships are subject to minimal government regulations versus other business concerns.
4. The owner of a sole proprietorship is taxed as an individual, at a rate lower than the corporate income tax rate. Losses from the export–import business can be applied by the owner to offset taxable income from other sources. Sole proprietors are also allowed to establish tax-exempt retirement accounts (Cheeseman, 2019; Mallor et al., 2013).

The major disadvantage of running an export–import concern as a sole proprietorship is the risk of unlimited liability. The owner is personally liable for the debts and other liabilities of the business. Insurance can be bought to protect against these liabilities; however, if insurance protection is not sufficient to cover legal liability for defective products, or debts, judgment creditors' next recourse is the personal assets of the owner. Another disadvantage is that the proprietor's access to capital is limited to personal funds plus any loans that can be obtained. In addition, very few individuals have all the necessary skills to run an export–import business, and the owner may lack certain skills. The business may also terminate upon the death or disability of the owner.

Partnerships

A partnership is an association of two or more persons to carry on as co-owners of a business for profit. "Persons" is broadly interpreted to include corporations, partnerships, or other associations. "Co-ownership" refers to a sharing of ownership of the business and is determined by two major factors: share of the business profits and management responsibility. The sharing of profits creates a rebuttable presumption that a partnership exists. The presumption about the existence of a partnership is disproved if profits are shared as payment of a debt, wages to an employee, interest on a loan, or rent to a landlord.

Example: Suppose Gardinia export company owes Kimko Realty $10,000 in rent. Gardinia promises to pay Kimko 20 percent of its business profits until the rent is fully paid. Kimko realty is sharing profits from the business but is not presumed to be a partner in the export business.

Although a written agreement is not required, it is advisable for partners to have some form of written contract that establishes the rights and obligations of the parties. Since partnerships dissolve upon the death of any partner that owns more than 10 percent interest, the agreement should ascertain the rights of the deceased partner's spouse and that of surviving partners in a way that is least disruptive of the partnership.

A partnership is a legal entity only for limited purposes, such as the capacity to sue or be sued, to collect judgments, to have title of ownership of partnership property, or to have all accounting procedures in the name of the partnership. Federal courts recognize partnerships as legal entities in such matters as lawsuits in federal courts (when a federal question is involved), bankruptcy proceedings, and the filing of informational tax returns (the profit and loss statement that each partner reports on individual returns). The partnership, however, has no tax liability. A partner's profit or loss from the partnership is included in each partner's income tax return and taxed as income to the individual partner (Cooke, 1995; Cheeseman, 2019 Mallor et al., 2013).

Partners are personally liable for the debts of the partnership. However, in some states, the judgment creditor (the plaintiff in whose favor a judgment is entered by a court) must exhaust the remedies against partnership property before proceeding to execute against the individual property of the partners.

What are the duties and powers of partners? The fiduciary duty that partners owe the partnership and the other partners is a relationship of trust and loyalty. Each partner is a general agent of the partnership in any business transaction within the scope of the partnership agreement. For example, when a partner in an import business contracts to import merchandise, both the partner and the partnership share liability unless the seller knows that the partner has no such authority. In the latter case, the partner who signed the contract will be personally liable but not the partnership. A partner's action can bind the partnership to third parties if his or her action is consistent with the scope of authority, that is, expressed or implied authority provided in the partnership agreement (Cheeseman, 2019; Mallor et al., 2013).

Limited Partnerships

A limited partnership is a special form of partnership that consists of at least one general (investor and manager) partner and one or more limited (investor) partners. The general partner is given the right to manage the partnership and is personally liable for the debts and obligations of the limited partnership. The limited partner, however, does not participate in management and is liable only to the extent of his or her capital contribution. Any person can be a general or limited partner, and this includes natural persons, partnerships, or corporations. Limited partners have no right to bind the partnership in any contract and owe no fiduciary duty to that partnership or the other partners due to the limited nature of their interest in the partnership.

Whereas a general partnership may be formed with little or no formality, the creation of a limited partnership is based on compliance with certain statutory requirements. The certificate of limited partnership must be executed and signed by the parties. It should include certain specific information and be filed with the secretary of state and the appropriate county to be legal and binding. The limited partnership is taxed in exactly the same way as a general partnership. A limited partner's losses from an export–import business could be used to offset income generated only by other passive activities, that is, investments in other limited partnerships (passive loss rules). They cannot be used against salaries, dividends, interest, or other income from portfolio investments.

Both types of partnership can be useful in international trade. They bring complimentary assets needed to distribute and/or commercialize the product or service. The combination of skills of different partners usually increases the speed with which the product/service enters a market and generally contributes to the success of the business. Limited partners may also be useful when capital is needed by exporters or importers to prepare a marketing plan, expand channels of distribution, increase the scope and volume of goods or services traded, and so on. However, potential exists for conflict among partners unless a partnership agreement exists that eliminates or mitigates any sources of conflict. If limited partners become involved in marketing or other management decisions of the export–import firm, they are considered general partners and, hence, assume unlimited risk for the debts of the partnership (Cheeseman, 2019; Mallor et al., 2013).

Corporations

A corporation is a legal entity separate from the people who own or operate it and created pursuant to the laws of the state in which the business is incorporated. Many export–import companies prefer this form of business organization due to the advantage of limited liability of shareholders. This means that shareholders are liable only to the extent of their investments. These companies could be sued for any harm or damage they cause in the distribution of the product, and that incorporation limits the liability of such companies to the assets of the business. Other advantages of incorporation are *free transferability of shares, perpetual existence, and the ability to raise additional capital by selling shares in the corporation.* However, most of these companies are closely held corporations; that is, shares are owned by few shareholders who are often family members, relatives, or friends and not traded on national stock exchanges.

Export–import corporations as legal entities have certain rights and obligations: they can sue or be sued in their own names, enter into or enforce contracts, and own or transfer property. They are also responsible for violation of the law. Criminal liability includes loss of a right to do business with the government, a fine, or any other sanction.

If an export–import company that is incorporated in one state conducts intrastate business (transacts local business in another state), such as selling merchandise or services in another state, it is required to file and qualify as a "foreign corporation" to do business in the other state. Conducting intrastate business usually includes maintaining an office to conduct such business. Using independent contractors for sales, soliciting orders to be accepted outside the state, or conducting isolated business transactions do not require qualification to do business in another state. The qualification procedure entails filing certain information with the secretary of state, payment of the required fees, and appointing a registered agent that is empowered to accept service of process on behalf of the corporation.

Forming a corporation (incorporating) can be expensive and time consuming. A corporation comes into existence when a certificate of incorporation, signed by one or more persons, is filed with the secretary of state. The corporation code in every state describes the types of information to be included in the articles of incorporation. Generally, they include provisions such as the purpose for which the corporation is organized, its duration, and powers of the corporation.

Many businesses incorporate their companies in the state of Delaware even when it is not the state in which the corporation does most of its business. This is because Delaware has laws that are very favorable to businesses' internal operations and management. It is even more ideal for companies that plan to operate with little or no surpluses or have a large number of inaccessible shareholders, making obtaining their consent difficult when needed.

One of the main disadvantages of a corporation as a form of business organization is that its profits are subject to double taxation. Tax is imposed by federal and state governments on profits earned by the company, and later, those profits are taxed as income when distributed to shareholders. Companies often avoid this by increasing salaries and bonuses for their owners and reporting substantially reduced profits. In this way, the income will be subject to tax when the owners or shareholders receive it rather than at the corporate level.

It is important that export–import companies maintain a separate identity from that of their owners. This includes having a separate bank account and export/distributor contracts in the name of the company, holding stockholders' meetings, and so on. In circumstances in which corporations are formed without sufficient capital or when there is a non-separation of corporate and personal affairs, courts have disregarded the corporate entity. The implication of this is that shareholders may be found personally liable for the debts and obligations of the company. The corporate entity is also disregarded in cases in which the corporation is primarily used to defraud others and for similar illegitimate purposes, such as money laundering, trade in narcotics, or funneling money to corrupt officials (bribery).

Directors and officers of export–import companies owe a duty of trust and loyalty to the corporation and its shareholders. Directors and officers must act within their scope of authority (duty of obedience) and exercise honest and prudent business judgement (duty of care) in the conduct of the affairs of the corporation. In the absence of these, they could be held personally liable for any resultant damages to the corporation or its shareholders. Breach of duty of obedience and care by directors and officers of an export–import company could include one or more of the following:

- *Investment of profits*: Investment of profits from export–import operations in a way that is not provided in the articles of incorporation or corporate bylaw.
- *Corporate decisions:* Making export–import decisions without being adequately informed, in bad faith, or at variance with the goals and objectives of the company.

S Corporations

The Subchapter S Revision Act of 1982 divides corporations into two categories: S corporations and C corporations, that is, all other corporations. If an export company elects to be an S corporation, it has the best of advantages of a corporation and a partnership. Similar to a corporation, it offers the benefits of limited liability, but still permits the owner to pay taxes as an individual, thereby avoiding double taxation. One advantage of paying taxes at the level of the individual shareholder is that export–import companies' losses could be used to offset shareholders' taxable income from other sources. It is also beneficial when the corporation makes a profit and when a shareholder falls within a lower-income tax bracket than the corporation. However, the corporation's election to be taxed as an S corporation is based on the following preconditions (Mallor et al., 2013):

1. *Domestic entity:* The corporation must be a domestic entity, that is, it must be incorporated in the United States.
2. *No membership in an affiliated group*: The corporation cannot be a member of an affiliated group (not part of another organization).
3. *Number of shareholders:* The corporation can have no more than seventy-five shareholders.
4. *Shareholders:* Shareholders must be individuals or estates. Corporations and partnerships cannot be shareholders. Shareholders must also be citizens or residents of the United States.
5. *Classes of stock:* The corporation cannot have more than one class of stock.
6. *Corporate income:* No more than 20 percent of the corporation's income can be from passive investment income (dividends, interest, royalties, rents, annuities, etc.).

Failure to maintain any one of these conditions will lead to cancellation of the S corporation status. Another election after cancellation of status cannot be made for five years.

Limited Liability Companies

This form of business organization combines the best of all the other forms. It has the advantages of limited liability and no restrictions on the number of owners or their nationalities (as in the case of S corporations). It is taxed as a partnership, and, unlike limited partnerships, it does not grant limited liability on the condition that the members refrain from active participation in the management of the company. To be taxed as a partnership, a limited liability company (LLC) can possess any of the following attributes: two or more persons as associates, objectives to carry on business and divide gains, limited liability, centralized management and continuity, and free transferability of interests (Cheeseman, 2019; Mallor et al., 2013). Such a company can be formed by two or more persons (natural or legal) and its articles of incorporation filed with the appropriate state agency. Limited liability companies provide the advantage of limited liability, management structure (participation in management without being subject to personal liability), and partnership tax status. It has become a popular form of business for subsidiaries of foreign corporations as well as small scale and medium-sized businesses (August, 2004) (Table 3.1).

TABLE 3.1 Forms of Business

	Formation	Duration	Management	Owner Liability	Transferability of Owners' Interest	Federal Income Taxation
Sole Proprietorship	One person owns business. No Corporation or LLC formed	Terminates on death or withdrawal of owner	By sole proprietor	Unlimited	None	Only sole proprietor taxed
Partnership	By agreement of owners or by default when two or more owners conduct business together without creating another business form	Usually unaffected by death or withdrawal of partner	By partners	Unlimited	Limited	Only partners taxed
Limited Liability Partnership	By agreement of owners; must comply with limited liability partnership statute	Usually unaffected by death or withdrawal of partner	By partners	Limited to capital contribution, except for owners' individual torts	Limited	Usually only partners taxed; may elect to be taxed like a corporation
Limited Partnership	By agreement of owners; must comply with limited partnership statute	Unaffected by death or withdrawal of partner	By general partners	Unlimited for general partners; limited to capital contribution for limited partners	Limited, unless agreed otherwise	Usually only partners taxed; may elect to be taxed like a corporation

	Creation	Continuity	Management	Liability	Transferability	Taxation
Limited Liability Limited Partnership	By agreement of owners; must comply with limited liability limited partnership statute	Unaffected by death or withdrawal of partner	By general partners	Limited to capital contribution, except for owner's individual torts	Limited, unless agreed otherwise	Usually only partners taxed; may elect to be taxed like a corporation
Corporation	By agreement of owners; must comply with corporation statute	Unaffected by death or withdrawal of shareholder	By board of directors	Limited to capital contribution, except for owners' individual torts	Freely transferable, although shareholders may agree otherwise	Corporation taxed; shareholders taxed on dividends (double tax)
S Corporation	By agreement of owners; must comply with corporation statute; must elect S Corporation status under Internal Revenue Code	Unaffected by death or withdrawal of shareholder	By board of directors	Limited to capital contribution, except for owners' individual torts	Freely transferable, although shareholders usually agree otherwise	Only shareholders taxed
Limited Liability Company	By agreement of owners; must comply with limited liability company statute	Usually unaffected by death or withdrawal of member	By members, unless choose to be manager-managed	Limited to capital contribution, except for owners' individual torts	Limited, unless agreed otherwise	Usually only members taxed; may elect to be taxed like a corporation

BUSINESS OR TRADE NAME

A sole proprietorship or partnership that is engaged in an export–import business can operate under the name of the sole proprietor or one or more of the partners. There are no registration requirements with any government agency. However, if the sole proprietorship or partnership operates under a fictitious name, it must file a fictitious business name statement with the appropriate government agency. Most states also require publication of the trade name in a local newspaper serving the area where the business is located.

> Example: Suppose John Rifkin wants to operate an export–import business (sole proprietorship) under the name "Global." This is commonly stated as: "John Rifkin doing business as Global."

Corporations are required to register their business name with the state. It is important to obtain permission to use a trade name before incorporation. This is intended to ensure that 1) the trade name does not imply a purpose inconsistent with that stated in the articles of incorporation, and 2) the trade name is not deceptively similar to registered and reserved names of other companies incorporated to do business in the state. The secretary of state or other designated agency will do a search before authorizing the party to use the name (Cheeseman, 2019; Mallor et al., 2013).

Unlike the effect of corporate name registration, registration of fictitious names does not prevent the use of the same name by others. This is because most states do not have a central registry of fictitious business names and that registration of such names is simply intended to indicate the person doing business under the trade name. To avoid registration of a similar trade name, it is advisable to check records of counties as well as local telephone directories for existing fictitious business names (McGrath, Elias, and Shena, 1996).

Another important issue is the potential problems that ensue when such names are used as trademarks to identify goods or services. Suppose John Rifkin intends to use the trade name "Global" to market his perfume imports. It is important to ensure that the same or similar name is not being used or registered with the U.S. Patent and Trademarks Office by another party prior to Rifkin's use of "Global" as a mark. The basic principles also apply in the case of corporations. If Rifkin used "Global" as a trademark in connection with his trade or business for some time, he acquires exclusive use of the mark regardless of the previous registration of the same or similar mark by others. Once a trader acquires a reputation in respect of his mark, then it becomes part of his goodwill, which is regarded by law as part of personal property that may be sold or licensed.

BANK ACCOUNTS, PERMITS, AND LICENSES

An export–import firm must open a bank account with an international bank that can accommodate specialized transactions such as letters of credit, foreign exchange payments, forfeiting, and so on. Some international banks have subsidiaries in importing countries that can verify the creditworthiness of foreign buyers. Sole proprietors and partnerships can open a bank account by submitting an affidavit of the fictitious business name statement to the bank with the initial deposit. In the case of a corporation, banks often require articles of incorporation, an affidavit that the company exists and its tax identification number. It is important to check with the city or county to determine if permits or business licenses are required.

LOCATION AND USE OF PROFESSIONAL SERVICES

When the export–import business is small, it is economical to use one's home as an office during the early phase of the operations. Besides saving money and travel time, using a portion of a home provides opportunities for deduction of expenses related to the business. All of the direct expenses for the business part of the home, for example, painting or repairs, are deductible expenses. The business use of a home may, however, provide the wrong impression to credit-rating agencies or clients who may decide to pay an impromptu visit. Another problem with using one's home is that it may violate a city's bylaws that prohibit the conduct of any trade or business in an area that is zoned strictly for residential purposes. Homeowner's insurance coverage may not cover business equipment, merchandise, or supplies. It may be advisable to rent from a company with extra space or rent an office with basic services.

The use of professional services (use of attorneys, accountants, and consultants) is important not only during the early stages of the business but throughout its operation as an informal source of guidance on liability, expansion, taxes, and related matters. If the entrepreneur does not have sufficient resources to pay for such services, many professionals are willing to reduce rates, defer billing, or make other arrangements.

ORGANIZATION FOR EXPORT: INDUSTRY APPROACH

The U.S. government agency, Small Business Administration (SBA) states that, besides multinational firms such as General Motors or IBM, there are many small-scale industries that export their output. For many of these companies, there are a number of organizational issues that need to be addressed to achieve an optimal allocation of resources. Some of the issues include 1) the level at which export decisions should be made, 2) the need for a separate export department, and 3) if the decision is made to establish a separate department, its organization within the overall structure of the firm including coordination and control of several activities. Such organizational issues involve three related areas:

1. *Subdivision of line operations based on certain fundamental competencies*: This relates to functional (production, finance, etc.), product, and geographical variables. A firm's organizational structure is often designed to fit its corporate strategy, which is in turn responsive to environmental realities (Cavusgil, Knight, and Riesenberger, 2020).
2. *Centralization or decentralization of export tasks and functions*: Centralization is generally advantageous for firms with highly standardized products, product usage, buying behavior, and distribution outlets. Advantages from centralization also tend to accrue to firms 1) with few customers and large multinational competitors, and 2) with a high R&D-to-sales ratio and rapid technological changes.

3. *Coordination and control*: Coordination and control of various activities among the various units of the organization is determined by the information-sharing needs of central management and foreign units.

Conventional business literature suggests that the choice of organizational structure determines export performance. The development of formal structures becomes important as the firm grows in size and complexity and in order to respond to internal and external changes. The adoption of a flexible organizational structure can partly offset the disadvantage arising from a formal organizational structure (Enderwick and Ranayne, 2004).

A study by Beamish et al. (1999) shows that the organizational structure within which a firm manages its exports has a significant impact on export performance. It also suggests that management commitment to internationalize by establishing a separate export department increases firms' export performance.

In the United States, small and medium-sized firms (employing less than 500 workers) account for about 33 percent of export value while the rest is undertaken by large firms. A separate export department within a firm may become necessary as overseas sales volume increases. However, the provision of additional resources for a separate department is not warranted at the early phase of market entry, since such activities can often be handled by domestic marketing units. Firms selling to a few markets or responding to a handful of foreign orders often use the existing marketing department within the firm to handle exports. This requires one person or a few people to manage all export activities. As the firm begins to internationalize and sell to more markets, its organizational structure will change. The coordination of its growing foreign market activities requires the deployment of specialized personnel and a separate export department.

For many firms, the exporting function is often a byproduct of different modes of market entry. Exporting firms may be wholly owned or joint ventures and manufacturing may take place within the home country or overseas.

Organizational Structures

As the firm's exports and other international business activities grow, it becomes imperative to create a separate unit within the firm (an international division accountable to the CEO) to handle international operations. This marks an important shift in resource allocation and increased focus on international operations. Under this arrangement, functional staff located at the head office (marketing, finance, etc.) serve all regions in their specialties. Such a structure is easy to supervise and provides access to specialized skills. However, it could lead to coordination problems among various units as well as duplication of tasks and resources. An international division is generally suitable for companies that produce standardized products during the early stages of international operations.

An international company can organize its export–import activities along product, geographical, or functional lines. Organization of export operations along product lines is suitable for firms with diversified product lines and extensive R&D activities. Under this structure, product division managers become responsible for the production and marketing of their respective product lines throughout the world. Even though this structure poses limited coordination problems and promotes cost efficiency in existing markets, it leads to duplication of resources and facilities in various countries and inconsistencies in divisional activities and procedures.

Organization along geographical lines is essentially based on the division of foreign markets into regions that are, in turn, subdivided into areas/subsidiaries. The regions are self-contained and obtain the necessary resources for marketing and research. This structure is suitable for firms with homogenous products that need efficient distribution and product lines that have similar technologies and common end-use markets (Albaum, Duerr, and Josiassen, 2016). It allows firms to respond to the changing demands of the market. This organizational approach makes coordination of tasks difficult when new and diverse products are involved. It also leads to duplication of certain tasks at the regional level. Certain companies adopt a mixed structure to manage international marketing activities. This structure combines two or more competencies on a worldwide basis. Companies can also organize along functional lines such as production or marketing. This requires a high level of functional expertise and works well when the firm has few product lines that require limited coordination.

GENERAL PRINCIPLES OF TAXATION

The United States levies taxes on the worldwide income of its citizens and residents. The United States, the Netherlands, and Germany are some of the few countries that impose taxes on the basis of worldwide income; most other countries tax income only if it is earned within their territorial borders. For U.S. tax purposes, an individual is considered a U.S. resident if the person 1) has been issued a resident alien card (green card), 2) has been physically present in the United States for 183 days or more in the calendar year, or 3) meets the cumulative presence test: this test may be met if the foreign individual was present in the U.S. for at least 183 days for the three-year period ending in the current year. In establishing cumulative presence, one must be physically present in the United States on at least a) 31 days during the current year and b) 183 days during the three-year period that includes the current year and the two years immediately before that, i.e., counting all the days you were present in the current year added to one third of the days present in the preceding year and one sixth of the days in the second preceding year. An alien is treated as a resident if the total equals or exceeds 183 days.

> *Example 1*: If Jim (a U.K. citizen) was in California for sixty-six days in 2018, thirty-three days in 2019 and 162 days in 2020, he would be considered a U.S. resident for 2020 (162 + 33/3 + 66/6 = 184 days). Jim may, however, rebut this presumption by showing that he has a closer connection to the United Kingdom than the United States, or that his regular place of business is in the United Kingdom. Exempt individuals include those temporarily present (foreign government-related), teachers/trainees, and professional athletes.

A company incorporated in the United States is subject to tax on its worldwide income, as in the case of U.S. citizens and residents. A partnership is not treated as a separate legal entity, and, hence, it does not pay taxes. Such income is taxed in the hands of the individual partners, whether natural or legal entities.

Example 2: Suppose Joan, a U.S. citizen, has an export–import business as a sole proprietor and also works as manager in a fast-food restaurant. The profit from the business is added on to her employment income. If the business operates at a loss, the loss will be subtracted from her employment or other income, thus reducing the tax payable.

EXAMPLE 2A Joan's Income Tax Liability as Sole Proprietor (US$)

	Year 1	Year 2
Joan's salary	30,000	31,500
Export–import profit (loss)	12,000	(8,500)
Total income	42,000	23,000
Itemized deduction	(10,000)	(10,000)
Taxable income	32,000	13,000

EXAMPLE 2B Joan's Income Tax Under a Corporation (US$)

Taxable income of export–import company	48,000
Less corporate income tax (21%)	(10,080)
Distributed dividend to Joan	37,920
Dividend tax on Joan's individual tax return	(11,376)
Total corporate and individual income tax	21,456

As illustrated in example 1B, a corporation's income is subject to double taxation, first at the corporate level and then on the individual income tax return. Such incidences of double taxation are often reduced when deductions and other allowances are applied against taxable income. If earnings are left in the business, the tax rate may be lower than what would be paid by a sole proprietor. If the export–import business is incorporated as an S corporation, earnings are taxed only once at the owner's individual tax rate. Payment of social security tax is also avoided by withdrawing profits as dividends.

TAXATION OF EXPORT–IMPORT TRANSACTIONS

Taxation of U.S. Resident Aliens or Citizens

United States citizens and resident aliens are taxed on their worldwide income. In general, the same rules apply irrespective of whether the income is earned in the United States or abroad. Foreign tax credits are allowed against U.S. tax liability to mitigate the effects of taxes by a foreign country on foreign income. It also avoids double taxation of income earned by a U.S. citizen or resident, first in a foreign country where the income is earned (foreign source income) and in the United States. Such benefits are available mainly to offset income taxes paid or accrued to a foreign country and may not exceed the total U.S. tax due on such income.

Example 3: Nicole, who is a U.S. resident, has a green card. She exports appliances (washers, dryers, stoves, etc.) to Venezuela and occasionally receives service fees for handling the maintenance and repairs at the clients' locations in Caracas and Valencia. Last year, she received $9,000 in export revenues (taxable income) and $3,500 in service fees (taxable income). No foreign tax was imposed on Nicole's export receipt of $9,000. However, she paid $2,200 in taxes to Venezuela on the service fees. Nicole also received $15,000 from her part-time teaching job at a community school (taxable income). Assume a 30 percent U.S. tax rate.

Source of Income	Taxable Income	Tax Liability
Venezuela	9,000	2,700
Venezuela	3,500	2,200
United States	15,000	4,500
Total income	**27,500**	**9,400**

Foreign tax limit = US tax liability X

Taxable income from all foreign sources/total taxable worldwide income

The credit is the lesser of creditable taxes paid ($2,200) or accrued to all foreign countries (and U.S. possessions) or the overall foreign tax credit limitation ($3,750). The foreign tax credit limitation = 30 percent (27,500) x 12,500/ 27,500 = $3,750.

If the foreign tax credit limitation is lower than the foreign tax owed (i.e., suppose the foreign tax was greater than $3,750), the excess amount can be carried back one year and forward five years to a tax year in which the taxpayer has an excess foreign credit limitation.

Taxation of Foreign Persons in the U.S. (Non-resident Aliens, Branches, or Foreign Corporations)

Foreign firms (foreign corporations, non-resident aliens) use different channels when marketing their products in the United States. They often commence to sell goods through independent distributors until they gain sufficient resources and experience. As their export volume grows, they may wish to directly export to their U.S. customers and market their products by having their employees occasionally travel to the United States in order to contact potential clients, identify growing markets, or negotiate sales contracts. As the company becomes more successful in the market, it may decide to establish a branch or subsidiary in the United States.

Foreign persons engaged in U.S. trade or business are subject to U.S. taxation on the income that is "efficiently connected" with the conduct of U.S. trade or business. This includes U.S. source income derived by a non-resident alien, a foreign corporation, or U.S. branch from the sale of goods or provision of services.

"Effectively connected income" may be extended beyond U.S.-source income to include certain types of foreign-source income that was facilitated by use of a fixed place of business or office in the United States.

> *Example 4*: Amin, a Brazilian software exporter opens a small sales office in Hammond, Indiana in order to sell in the United States and Canada. Canadian sales (foreign source income) are generally considered "effectively connected" since income is produced through the U.S. sales office in Indiana. Amin's sales in the United States (through a U.S. branch or subsidiary) are also subject to U.S. tax due to permanent establishment in the U.S. or income from U.S. trade or business.

A foreign corporation or non-resident alien that exports goods or services to the United States through a fixed place of business or office can claim deductions for expenses, losses, and foreign taxes or claim a tax credit for any foreign income taxes, i.e., foreign and U.S.-source effectively connected income. The credits are not used to offset U.S. withholding or branch profits tax and are allowable only against U.S. taxes on "effectively connected income." While a tax deduction reduces taxable income by the amount of a given expense, tax credits are a dollar-for-dollar reduction of U.S. income tax by the amount of the foreign tax.

Model tax treaties that the U.S. has entered into with many trading nations contain the following common provisions:

- Foreign person's (non-resident alien, foreign corporation, U.S. branch) export profits are exempt from U.S. tax unless such profits are attributable to a permanent establishment maintained in the United States, i.e., a fixed place of business or when U.S. dependent agents have authority to conclude sales contracts on behalf of the company.

Example 5: Donga Inc., a trading company incorporated in Monaco, exports ceiling fans to the United States. Its sales agents spend two months every year traveling across the United States to market/promote sales with major clients. When they receive orders, they forward them to the home office for final approval. The agents do not sign purchase orders or sales contracts.

Donga Inc. is not subject to U.S. taxes since a) the agents do not have contracting authority and b) the company does not have permanent establishment in the United States.

- Marketing products in the United States through independent agents or distributors does not create a permanent establishment and thus no tax liability in the United States.
- Income from personal services provided by non-resident aliens in the United States are normally exempt unless the employee is present in the United States for over 183 days or paid by a U.S. resident. Income derived by professionals (accountants, doctors, etc.) are exempt unless attributable to a fixed place of business in the United Sates.

Taxation of U.S. Exports

In general, U.S. companies that export their goods overseas will incur no tax liability in the importing country if:

1. They undertake their exports through independent distributors (they have non-taxable presence in the importing country).
2. Their agents/employees overseas do not have authority to conclude sales contracts on behalf of the U.S. exporter.
3. The services performed are not attributable to a fixed place of business in the host country.

An export–import firm may enter a foreign market by establishing a branch in a foreign country. Branches are often used to retain exclusive control of overseas operations or to deduct losses on initial overseas activities. A branch is not a separate corporation; it is considered an extension of the domestic corporation. One of the major disadvantages of operating a branch is that it exposes the domestic firm to liability in a foreign country. The foreign branch is subject to the tax laws of the host country. The income, deductions, and credits of the foreign branch are taken into account in calculating the tax liability of the parent corporation. Branch losses reduce the taxable income of the parent firm and the U.S. taxes paid on foreign source branch income are reduced with foreign tax credits.

An export–import firm can enter a foreign market by establishing a separate corporation (subsidiary) to conduct business. The parent corporation and subsidiary are separate legal entities and their individual liabilities are limited to the capital investment of each respective firm. Prior to 2017, foreign income earned by a foreign subsidiary of a U.S. corporation was not subject to tax in the United States until the income was distributed as a dividend to the U.S. corporation. The new rules impose a transition tax on untaxed foreign earnings of the foreign subsidiary by deeming those earnings to be repatriated. The tax on repatriated earnings (15.5 percent on cash and cash equivalents) can be paid in installments over an eight-year period. In 2015, it was estimated that US companies held over US$2.6 trillion in untaxed income in their foreign subsidiaries.

The Tax Cuts and Jobs Act of 2017 (TCJA) reduces tax rates on individual and business income and provides incentives for domestic investment. Corporate tax rates are lowered from 35 percent to a flat rate of 21 percent. Sole proprietorships and other pass-through entities pay a lower tax with deductions available for non-service-related operations (reduced from 39.6 to 29.6 percent). The TCJA limits the amount of business losses that can be deducted against other income. Unused losses can be carried forward and used in future years. The TCJA introduces major changes in the area of international taxation of U.S. corporations, as follows.

a. The TCJA exempts foreign profits from domestic tax, and profits paid to U.S. parent companies in the form of dividends are fully deductible against taxable income. To benefit from this deduction, the U.S. corporation must own 10 percent of the value of the controlled foreign corporation.
b. In order to prevent companies from making investments in intangible assets overseas, the TCJA imposes a minimum tax of 10.5 percent on global intangible low-taxed income (GILTI) on profits earned abroad that exceed a firm's "normal" return (without deferral) (normal return: 10 percent on the adjusted basis in tangible property held abroad). Under the Act, a U.S. parent corporation will generally have to pay an immediate U.S. income tax (at a 10.5 percent rate, increasing to 13.1 percent after 2025) on a big part of the profits of its non-U.S. subsidiaries.

GILTI is supposed to reduce the incentive to shift corporate profits out of the United States by using intellectual property (IP) (August, 2018).

c. A lower tax rate (13.13 percent) is provided for income from the use of IP in the United States to generate exports. This foreign-derived intangible income (FDII) is intended to encourage U.S. corporations to keep IP within the country.

d. In order to prevent U.S. domestic corporations from avoiding domestic liability by shifting profits overseas to related corporations, the TCJA imposes a minimum tax on large corporations with gross receipts of $500 million or more (August, 2018).

Deductions and Allowances

Export–import businesses may deduct ordinary and necessary expenses. Ordinary and necessary expenses are defined by the Internal Revenue Service as follows:

> An ordinary expense is one that is common and accepted in your industry. A necessary expense is one that is helpful and appropriate for your trade or business. An expense does not have to be indispensable to be considered necessary.
>
> (IRS, 2019a)

When one starts an export–import business, all costs are treated as capital expenses. These expenses are a part of the investment in the business and generally include:

1. The cost of getting started in the business before beginning export–import operations such as market research, expenses for advertising, travel, utilities, repairs, employees' wages, salaries, and fees for executives and consultants; and
2. Business assets such as building, furniture, trucks, etc., and the costs of making any improvements to such assets, for example, a new roof, new floor, and so on. The cost of the improvement is added to base value of the improved property.

The cost of specific assets can be recovered through depreciation deductions. Other start-up costs can be recovered through amortization; that is, costs are deducted in equal amounts over sixty months or more. Organizational costs for a partnership (expenses for setting up the partnership) or corporation (costs of incorporation, legal and accounting fees etc.) can be amortized over sixty months and must be claimed on the first business tax return. Once the business has started operations, standard business deductions are applied against gross income. Standard business deductions include the following:

1. *General and administrative expenses:* Office expenses such as telephones, utilities, office rent, legal and accounting expenses, salaries, professional services, dues, and so forth. These also include interest payments on debt related to the business, taxes (real estate and excise taxes, estate and employment taxes), insurance, and amortization of capital assets (IRS, 2019a).
2. *Personal and business expenses:* If an expense is incurred partly for business and partly for personal purposes, only the part that is used for business is deductible. If the export–import business is conducted from one's home, part of the expense of maintaining the home could be claimed as a business expense. Such expenses include mortgage interest, insurance, utilities, and repairs. To successfully claim

such limited deductions, part of the home must be used exclusively and regularly as the principal place of business for the export–import operation or as a place to meet customers or clients. Similarly, automobile expenses to conduct the business are deductible. If the car is used for both business and family transportation, only the miles driven for the business are deductible as business expenses. Automobile-related deductions also include depreciation on the car; expenses for gas, oil, tires, and repairs; and insurance and registration fees (IRS, 2019c).

3. *Entertainment, travel, and related business expenses:* Expenses incurred entertaining clients for promotional purposes, travel expenses (the cost of air, bus, and taxi fares), as well as other related expenses (dry cleaning, tips, subscriptions to relevant publications, convention expenses) are tax deductible (IRS, 2019c).

International Transfer Pricing

Transactions between unrelated parties and prices charged for goods and services tend to reflect prevailing competitive conditions. Such market prices cannot be assumed when transactions are conducted between related parties, such as a group of firms under common control or ownership. If a parent company sells its output to a foreign marketing subsidiary at a higher price, it moves overall gains to itself. It if charges a lower price, it will shift more of the overall gains to the subsidiary. Even though transfer prices do not affect the combined income or absolute amount of gain or loss among related persons or "controlled group of corporations," they do shift income among related parties in order to take advantage of differences in tax rates (International Perspective 3.1).

In the example below, the combined income remains at $1,000 for the steel export regardless of the transfer price used to allocate income between the parent and subsidiary. If the tax rate is 30 percent in the United States and 40 percent in Spain, the U.S. parent company can use a higher transfer price for its controlled sale (Option B) to reduce its worldwide taxes:

Option A: 1000 × 40% = $400 (Spain's rate)
Option B: 1000 × 30% = $300 (U.S. rate)

In cases where U.S. companies operate in low-tax jurisdictions, income can be shifted to a low-tax subsidiary. This has the advantage of U.S. tax deferral until the foreign subsidiary repatriates its earnings through dividend distribution.

Example

	U.S. Parent Co. (Steel Co.) in Detroit, Michigan	U.S. Subsidiary in Madrid, Spain
Option A	Production Cost = 1000	Cost of sales = 1000
		Selling expense = 200
	Sale to subsidiary − 1000	Sales revenue − 2200
	Net Profit = $0	Net Profit = $1000

	U.S. Parent Co. (Steel Co.) in Detroit, Michigan	U.S. Subsidiary in Madrid, Spain
Option B	Production cost = 1000	Cost of sales = 2000
		Selling expense = 200
	Sales to subsidiary = 2000	Sales revenue = 2200
	Net Profit = $1000	Net Profit = $0

Regulation in the United States (Section 482) on transfer pricing is largely intended to ensure that taxpayers report and pay taxes on their actual share of income arising from controlled transactions. The appropriateness of any transfer price is evaluated on the basis of the arm's-length or market value standard. For example, in the case of loans extended by a U.S. parent company to its overseas subsidiary, the Internal Revenue Service has successfully imposed an arm's-length interest charge (a charge that would be paid by unrelated parties under similar circumstances).

INTERNATIONAL PERSPECTIVE 3.1

Transfer Pricing Methods

A number of factors are considered in the determination of comparable prices between parties dealing in arm's-length transactions: contractual terms, such as provisions pertaining to volume of sales, warranty, duration or extension of credit, functions performed such as marketing, R&D, etc., and risks assumed including responsibility for currency fluctuations, credit collection, or product liability. Other factors include economic market conditions (similarly of geographical market, competitive conditions in industry and market) as well as the nature of property or services transformed.

In the case of the sale of tangible goods between related parties, the arm's-length charge is determined by using the following methods:

- The comparable uncontrolled price method: prices on the sale of similar goods to unrelated parties.
- Resale price method: resale price to unrelated parties using gross profit margin.
- Cost plus method: cost plus method is used in situations in which products are manufactured and sold to related parties.
- Comparable profits method: this method uses profit level indicators such as rate of return on operating assets, etc. of uncontrolled parties to adjust profit levels of each group.
- Profit split method: allocation of profit between related parties based on the relative value of the contribution to the profit of each party.

In the performance of services to related parties, the regulations do not require that a profit be made on the charge for services unless the services are an integral part of the business activity of the providing party, that is, the principal activity of the service provider is that of rendering such services to related or unrelated parties.

Tax Treaties

Income tax treaties are entered into by countries to reduce the burden of double tax-ation on the same activity and to exchange information to prevent tax evasion. Tax treaty partners generally agree on rules about the types of income that a country can tax and the provision of a tax credit for any taxes paid to one country against any taxes owed in another country.

The United States has entered into tax treaties with about sixty countries. They include Canada, China, EU countries, India, Japan, South Korea, Mexico, New Zealand, South Africa, and many transition economies of Central and Eastern Europe. In most countries, the treaty prevails over domestic law. In the United States, if there is a conflict between a treaty provision and domestic law, whichever is most recently enacted will govern the transaction.

The following are some of the common treaty provisions with regard to business profits.

- The export profits of an enterprise of one treaty country shall be taxable only in that country unless the enterprise carries on business in the other treaty country through a permanent establishment situated therein. The importing country may tax the enterprise's profits that are attributable to that permanent establishment (U.S. Model Income Tax Treaty, 7.1).
- Permanent establishment is meant to describe a fixed place of business through which the business of an enterprise is wholly or partially discharged. It includes a place of management, a branch, an office, a factory, a workshop, a mine, or any other place of extraction of natural resources. It is assumed to be a permanent establishment only if it lasts or the activity continues for a period of more than twelve months (U.S. Model Income Tax Treaty, 5.3).
- Permanent establishment shall not include certain auxiliary functions such as pur-chasing, storing, or delivering inventory (U.S. Model Income Tax Treaty, 5.4).
- An enterprise is deemed to have a permanent establishment in a treaty country if its employees conclude sales contracts in its name. If a Canadian exporter sends its sales agents to enter into a contract with a U.S. firm in New York, the Canadian company shall be deemed to have a permanent establishment in the United States even if it does not have an office in the United States (U.S. Model Income Tax Treaty, 5.5).
- Permanent establishment is not imputed in cases where a product is exported through independent brokers or distributors, regardless of whether these inde-pendent agents conclude sales contracts in the name of the exporter (U.S. Model Income Tax Treaty, 5.6).

CHAPTER SUMMARY

Ownership structure	The forms of business organizations are sole proprietorship, partnership, and corporation.
Business or trade name	Corporations are required to register their trade name with the state. Sole proprietorships and partnerships are required to register with the appropriate government agency if they operate under a fictitious name.

Bank accounts, permits, and licenses	1. Opening a bank account: It is advisable to open an account with an international bank. 2. An export/import firm can be operated from a home during the early phase of the business. All direct expenses related to the business are tax deductible. 3. The use of professional services is important as a source of guidance on liability, taxes, expansion, and related matters. 4. Permits and licenses: It is important to check with the city or county to determine if permits or business licenses are required.
Organizational issues	Considerations include the level at which export decisions should be made, the need for a separate export department, coordination and control of various activities, organizational structure of the export–import department.
Common organizational structures	Organized along functional lines, along geographical lines, or based on product or market.
Taxation of export–import business	Foreign persons' export profits are exempt from U.S. tax unless such profits are attributable to a permanent establishment maintained in the United States. Similarly, U.S exports will not be subject to tax in the importing country unless the firm has a fixed place of trade or business in the importing country or its agents in the latter country have authority to conclude contracts on behalf of the U.S. exporter. *Deductions and allowances*: organizational costs, general and administrative expenses, personal and business expenses, entertainment, travel, and other related business expenses. *Transfer pricing* is intended to ensure that taxpayers report and pay tax on their actual share of income arising from controlled transactions. There are several methods used to estimate an arm's-length charge for transfers of tangible property: the comparable uncontrolled price method, the resale price method, the cost plus method, the comparable profits method, and the profit split method.

REVIEW QUESTIONS

1. What are the major disadvantages of running an export–import business as a partnership?
2. Are partnerships recognized as legal entities? Discuss.
3. Both general and limited partnerships may be useful forms of organization for export–import businesses. Why/why not?
4. What is an S corporation?
5. What types of professional services are needed when you start an export–import business?
6. State three typical organizational structures of firms that are engaged in international trade. Is a separate export department necessary for a manufacturing firm with limited exports?

7. ABC Co. is incorporated in Florida although all its business activities are done in France. Its management office is located in Amsterdam where the board of directors holds their regular meeting. The shareholders are from the U.K and Denmark and hold their annual meeting in Vienna. What is ABC's residence for tax purposes?

8. Are U.S. exporters subject to income tax in importing countries? What are the tax implications of establishing a trading firm as a branch (as opposed to a subsidiary) in foreign countries?

REFERENCES

Albaum, G., Duerr, E., and Josiassen, A. (2016). *International Marketing and Export Management*. New York: Pearson.

August, J. (2018). Tax Cuts and Jobs Act of 2017 introduces major reforms to the international taxation of US corporations. *The Practical Tax Lawyer*, Winter: 43–54.

August, R. (2004). *International Business Law*. Upper Saddle River, NJ: Prentice Hall.

Beamish, P., Karavis, L., Goerzon, A., and Lane, C. (1999). The relationship between organizational structure and export performance. *Management International Review*, 39(1): 37–55.

Cavusgil, S. T., Knight, G., and Riesenberger, J. (2020). *International Business*. Boston, MA: Pearson.

Cheeseman, H. (2019). *Business Law*. New York: Pearson.

Cooke, R. (1995). *Doing Business Tax-Free*. New York: John Wiley and sons.

Enderwick, P. and Ranayne, E. (2004). Reconciling entrepreneurship and organizational structure in international operations: Evidence from New Zealand specialist food exporters. *Journal of Asia Pacific Marketing*, 3(2): 53–69.

Internal Revenue Service (IRS, 2019a). *Business Expenses*. Department of the Treasury, Publication 535.

Internal Revenue Service (IRS, 2019b). *Business Use of your Home*. Department of the Treasury, Publication 587.

Internal Revenue Service (IRS, 2019c). *Travel, Entertainment, Gift and Car Expenses*. Department of the Treasury, Publication 463.

Mallor, J., Barnes, A., Bowers, T., and Langvardt, A. (2013). *Business Law: The Ethical, Global and E-commerce Environment*. New York: McGraw-Hill/Irwin.

McDaniel, P., Ault, H., and Repetti, J. (1981). *Introduction to United States International Taxation*. Boston, MA: Kluwer.

McGrath, K., Elias, S. with Shena, S. (1996). *Trademark: How to Name a Business or Product*. Berkeley, CA: Nolo Press.

U.S. Government (1996). *Convention between the US and ---- for the avoidance of double taxation and the prevention of fiscal evasion with respect to taxes on income* (1004). Washington, DC: USGPO (U.S. Model Tax Treaty).

Warr, P. (2002). Export taxes and income distribution: The Philippines coconut levy. *Weltwirtschaftliches Archiv*, 138: 437–458.

Zambersky, P. and Cajka, R. (2015). Taxation of exports—theory and practice. *Agricultural Economics*, 4: 158–165.

World Wide Web Resources

Fictitious Business Names

Information on filing fictitious business names: www.sba.gov/content/register-your-fictitious-or-doing-business-dba-name

Tips on choosing a business name: www.sba.gov/content/how-name-business
Seven secrets of great business names: www.entrepreneur.com/article/223694

Starting a Business
Answers to frequently asked questions about starting a business: www.irs.gov/businesses/ small-businesses-self-employed/starting-operating-or-closing-a-business

International Trade Closing Cases and Discussions

Trade-related Global Financial Flows

Illicit financial flows (IFFs) are illegal movements of money or capital from one country to another. One of the ways in which illegal movements of capital take place is through trade mis-invoicing. Trade mis-invoicing occurs when importers and exporters deliberately falsify the stated prices for goods they are importing or exporting in order to illicitly launder the proceeds of criminal activity, transfer value across international borders, circumvent currency controls, evade tax and/or customs duties, and hide profits offshore. Using bilateral trade data, Global Financial Integrity (GFI) reports trade mis-invoicing between various countries by identifying value gaps (mismatches) in reporting countries' export and import data. For example, if Ethiopia reported $20 million of coffee exports to the United Kingdom in 2018 but the United Kingdom reported $38 million in coffee imports from Ethiopia for the year, there is a value gap which indicates an illicit movement of $18 million to the United Kingdom. Trade mis-invoicing takes place in the following ways:

Trade mis-invoicing	Motivating factors
Under-invoicing of exports	To shift money overseas; evade exchange controls; shift wealth into convertible currency; lower taxable income; lower or evade export taxes.
Over-invoicing of exports	Prices of export goods are falsified to benefit from government rebates or drawbacks as well as subsidies for exports.
Over-invoicing of imports	To shift money overseas; evade exchange controls; shift wealth into convertible currency; lower taxable income; avoid anti-dumping duties.
Under-invoicing of imports	To evade value-added taxes or customs duties; circumvent regulatory requirements on imports over a given value.

Much of the trade mis-invoicing is driven by the need to shift capital and evade taxes. The shifting of capital maybe due to unstable political and economic conditions in host countries as well as the need to shift wealth into hard currency. It is estimated that about 80 percent of all import invoices in many developing countries are mis-invoiced.

Largest value gaps with other trading partners	Ranked by size in US$ million (2008–2017)	Largest average value gaps between 135 developing countries and 35 advanced nations	US$ million 2008–2017
China	482.4	Electrical machinery	153.7
Russia	92.6	Mineral fuels	113.2
Mexico	81.5	Machinery	111.7
India	78.0	Vehicles	66.4
Malaysia	64.1	Precious stones and metals	31.8
Poland	53.9	Plastics	31.7
Brazil	53.2	Pharmaceuticals	22.0
Thailand	49.6	Optical products	20.2
UAE	45.2	Iron and steel products	19.6
Indonesia	43.4	Knitted apparel	18.9

Many developing countries face foreign currency shortages because import growth is not matched with growth in exports, thus leading to persistent trade deficits. The widening trade deficits will further push down already declining levels of reserves. Trade mis-invoicing will further reduce the foreign currency earnings that most developing countries need to finance imports and promote economic growth. Dollar shortages have become food shortages in countries such as Egypt and Venezuela, as well as much of Sub-Saharan Africa, which rely heavily on food imports. For many of the least developed countries, duties and other taxes account for about 45 percent of government revenue and trade mis-invoicing reduces the resources they need for various development projects.

In order to reduce this problem of trade mis-invoicing and IFFs, countries can take various measures:

- Adopt legislation outlawing such practices. South Korea criminalized trade mis-invoicing in 2013.
- Strengthen customs enforcement.
- Share information between exporting and importing countries.
- Adopt bilateral and multilateral agreements on trade mis-invoicing.

Questions

1. What are the ways in which trade mis-invoicing takes place?
2. What is the impact of trade mis-invoicing on developing countries?

CHAPTER 4

Planning and Preparations for Export

LEARNING OBJECTIVES:

4.1 Describe the two major approaches to selecting a product for export

4.2 Understand the purpose of international market research and important data sources

4.3 Identify the techniques used for international market assessment

4.4 Learn the various components of an international business plan

4.5 Identify the types of government counseling and assistance available to U.S. exporters

International Trade in Practice

Understanding Your Foreign Customers

Too many businesses think of the foreign market as an extension of the domestic market and believe that products can be exported with minimal adjustments. This may be the case where customers are geographically homogeneous and have similar cultures or buying habits. In most cases, customers are different and a proper evaluation of the market is required to identify the needs of foreign customers. In the home market, customers are familiar with the company and its product and there is a certain level of goodwill that has been established over the years. None of these conditions exist in a foreign market and the firm has to acquire the requisite resources and extra time and effort to satisfy its new customers.

It is helpful to consider approaches that were adopted by some firms in order to suit the needs of their foreign customers.

- Focus on potential customers that are similar to the ones you have in your home market. The global furniture rental market (commercial and residential) was estimated at over US$20 billion in 2020. It is big business in Europe and the United States and firms such as CORT and JMT have been engaged in the provision of such services for several years. Rapid urbanization and growth in the hospitality industry account for a substantial part of this growth. In spite of this, the idea of renting furniture is not popular in many countries. Home Essentials, a U.S. furniture rental company, focused on expatriates in Dubai, Iraq, Hong Kong, Malaysia, and Singapore as well as local landlords who rent apartments to them. It has been quite popular with expatriates in these countries because it eliminates the need to buy or ship furniture to the expatriate's next destination.

• Modify products for different markets. An important benefit of standardization is the cost savings in production and marketing. Regional and global integration is also driving firms to standardize their approaches to marketing in terms of branding and packaging. Industrial products (steel, chemicals) and technology-intensive goods (medical equipment) tend to be less culturally grounded and require less adaptation than consumer goods. Consumer goods need to be adapted to local tastes and preferences and economic conditions (less expensive packaging in low-income countries). Firms may also design and introduce a new product for the export market. Most studies show that the majority of products have to be modified for the international market (Czinkota, Ronkainen, and Buonafina, 2004). Factors affecting export product adaptation decisions include government regulations (product testing, certification requirements, and other barriers), customer characteristics (consumption patterns, attitudes toward the product or brand), influence of culture, product characteristics (durability, brand, packaging, after-sales service), and firm considerations (organizational capabilities and level of adaptation needed to justify the effort).

• If the product is new to the export market, work with local partners to get ideas about customer needs. Two U.S. pioneers formed a partnership (Eno) to make casual wear for young people in China. Their success is largely attributed to allowing local designers to come up with design concepts that are popular with Chinese youth. In some cases, you can identify the attributes of the product in one country that appeal to consumers in other markets. Tokypop, a U.S. firm located in California, created a U.S. market for manga (Japanese novels depicting superhero tales, love stories for teen girls, business dramas for adults) by picking product segments that appeal to U.S. customers.

• Provide superior value by offering a lower price than the competition or a superior product at a higher price. ResMed, a U.S. medical technology company designs humidifiers, masks, ventilators, and air pumps. As the global innovator in breathing technology, its market leadership comes from its high R&D expenditure, superior products, and ability to meet the needs of customers by offering a range of sizes and styles.

Questions

1. Discuss some of the ways in which a firm can meet the needs of its customers in foreign markets.
2. What circumstances require adaptation of a product for an export market?

ASSESSING AND SELECTING THE PRODUCT

Although the basic functions of exporting and domestic selling are the same, international markets differ widely because of great variations in certain uncontrollable environmental forces. These include currency exchange controls/risks, taxation, tariffs, and inflation, which originate outside the business enterprise. Such variations require managers to be aware of global threats and opportunities.

If a company already manufactures a product or service, it is reasonable to assume that the same product or service is what will be exported. However, companies must first determine the export potential of a product or service before they invest their resources into the business of foreign trade. To establish the export potential of a product, firms must consider the following: *the success of the product in domestic markets, participation in overseas trade shows, advertising, and market data.*

If a product is successful in the domestic market, there is a good chance that it will be successful in markets abroad. However, a careful analysis of a product's overseas market potential is needed. One could start by assessing the demand for similar products domestically and abroad, as well as determining the need for certain adaptations or improvements. Trade statistics provide a preliminary indication of markets for a particular product in most countries. For products or services that are not new, low-cost market research is often available that can help determine market potential. Products that are less sophisticated and that have a declining demand in developed countries' markets often encounter a healthy demand in developing nations because the goods are less expensive and easy to handle (Weiss, 2007).

Participation in overseas trade shows is a good way to test the export potential of products or services. A study commissioned by America Business Media found that seven out of ten business executives purchased or recommended the purchase of a product or service after looking at an advertisement or promotion at a trade show (Schwartz, 2006). Alternatively, if an assessment of the actual and potential uses of the product or service indicates that it satisfies certain basic needs in the marketplace, initial sales can be made to establish demand as well as to determine potential improvements.

To achieve success, there must be a strong and lasting management commitment to the export business. Long-term commitment is necessary to ensure the recovery of high market entry costs related to product modification, legal representation, and advertising, as well as the development of an agent/distributor network (see Table 4.1).

Companies already operating in the domestic market need to consider the development of export markets through the allocation of financial and personnel resources or through the use of outside experts. In the absence of sufficient knowledge about exporting, it is often advisable for companies to hire consultants who can be engaged in the establishment of the department and the training of personnel.

An individual entrepreneur acting as a middleman between the manufacturer and importer can pick any product or service. The following are two approaches to selecting a product or service.

Systematic Approach

The systematic approach involves selection of a product or service based on overall market demand. An individual entrepreneur often selects a product line or service

TABLE 4.1 The Export Decision: Management Issues

Experience
- *With what countries is trade being conducted?*
- *Which product lines are most in demand and who are the buyers or likely buyers?*
- *What is the trend in sales?*
- *Who are the main domestic and international competitors?*
- *What lessons have been learned from past experience?*

Management and Personnel
- *Who will be responsible for the export department's organization and staff?*
- *How much management time should or could be allocated?*
- *What organizational structure is suitable?*

Production Capacity
- *What is the firm's production capacity?*
- *What is the effect of exports on domestic sales and production capacity and cost?*
- *Is a minimum order quantity required?*
- *What are the design and packaging requirements for exports?*

Financial Capacity
- *What amount of capital is tied up in exports?*
- *What level of export department operating costs can be supported?*
- *What are the initial expenses of export efforts to be allocated?*
- *When should the export effort pay for itself?*

based on demand and growth trends by observing trade flows. A variety of statistical sources provide data (for products and services) pertaining to the major export markets, projected total demand, and U.S. exports in each market, along with a ranking of countries based on the projected import value. This process of collecting and analyzing information will enable the potential exporter to draw conclusions on the best line of products or services as well as promising markets. It is important, however, to select products or services based on familiarity and skill. A computer technician is in a more advantageous position to export computers, computer parts, software, and computer services than a graphic designer because of the former's prior knowledge about the product or service. This individual is more likely to be familiar with product- and/or service-specific issues such as quality, technical specifications, adaptability to overseas requirements, and maintenance or after-sales service.

Other important factors to consider in product/service selection include proximity of the producer or manufacturer to one's home or office in order to maintain close personal contact and closely monitor/discuss product quality, production delays, order processing, and other pertinent matters. Once a potential product (or service) for export has been identified, the individual must undertake market research to select the most promising markets based on import value and growth trends. Both in the case of manufacturing companies and individuals, one must consider if a given product has export potential before substantial time, effort, and capital are invested (Geringer, McNett, and Ball, 2020).

Reactive Approach

The reactive approach involves selecting a product based on immediate market need. Even though it is quite common to select the product and identify possible markets, certain exporters initially identify the consumer need and then select a product or service to satisfy the given market demand. A plethora of publications advertise products and services that are needed in foreign countries by public-or private-sector importers, and exporters can also advertise. The first step would be to contact potential importers to indicate one's interest in supplying the product and to obtain other useful information. Once there is a reasonable basis to proceed (based on the importer's response), potential suppliers of the product/service can be identified from the various directories of manufacturers. In the United States, for example, the *Thomas Register of Manufacturers* is considered to be a comprehensive source of U.S. manufacturers.

In both cases (systematic or reactive), selection of the manufacturer depends on a number of factors including price, quality, proximity to home or office, as well as the manufacturer's commitment to export sales. There must be a long-term commitment from management to encourage the development of export markets, and this cannot be motivated by the occasional need to dispose of surplus merchandise. It is also important to consider the existence of export restrictions that limit the sale of these products to specific countries and their implications for sales and profits. Manufacturers may also impose certain restrictions when they have an agent/distributor or a subsidiary producing the goods in the market (International Perspective 4.1).

The reactive approach to selecting a product has certain disadvantages for the individual entrepreneur who acts as an intermediary between the manufacturer and importer:

1. *Lack of focus on a given product or market*: Chasing product orders in different markets impedes the development of a systematic export strategy. This approach ignores the idea of niche exporting, which is critical to the success of any export–import enterprise. It leads to exports of unfamiliar products and/or sales to difficult markets, which hampers the long-term growth and profitability of export businesses.
2. *Absence of a long-term relationship with the importer:* Selling different products to different markets impedes the development of a long-term relationship with importers. It also creates suspicion on the part of importing firms about the long-term reliability and commitment of the firm to exporting. (See Table 4.3 to check your readiness to enter the export-import business".)

INTERNATIONAL PERSPECTIVE 4.1

Important Factors to Consider in Selecting the Export Product

Shifting spending patterns: Basic determinants of how much a consumer buys of a product are the person's taste and preference, as well as the price of the product (relative to the price of other products). Another major influence is the consumer's income. If the consumer's income increases, demand for most goods will rise. However, the demand for goods that people regard as necessities, such as fuel, tobacco, bread, or meat, tends to decline and exporters of such products are not likely to greatly benefit from rising consumer incomes in other countries. The demand for luxuries, such as new cars or expensive food, expands rapidly. Therefore, exporters should generally put more emphasis on goods that consumers regard as "luxuries" as spending patterns shift in response to rising incomes.

Products to be excluded from the list: Individuals starting an export–import trade should initially work with small to medium-sized manufacturers because large companies, such as GE, have their own export departments or overseas subsidiaries that produce the goods in those markets. Products that compete with such large companies should not be considered at this stage. It is also important to avoid product/services that require too many export/licensing requirements as a condition of executing an international business transaction. Also, the fashion-oriented market is too volatile and unpredictable to warrant a full commitment until a later stage. This also extends to multimillion-dollar contracts for overseas government projects, as well as sophisticated products that often require the development of training facilities and a network of technicians for after-sales service.

Emphasis on quality and niche marketing: Several studies on export–import trade indicate that firms that have shown a sustained increase in their sales and overall profits have often emphasized quality and concentrated on niches. In this age of diversity, marketers are being awakened to the erosion of the mass market. Traditional marketing methods are no longer as effective as they used to be and a new emphasis on quality and niche marketing is proving successful. Even after the elimination of textile quotas in 2005, many European textile producers have maintained steady growth in their exports because of their emphasis on high fashion items with special brand identity.

INTERNATIONAL MARKET RESEARCH

International market research deals with how business organizations engaged in international trade make decisions that lead to the allocation of resources in markets with the greatest potential for sales (Geringer et al., 2020). This process of market screening helps to maximize sales and profits by identifying and selecting the most desirable markets.

Why Conduct International Market Research?

International market research is needed because export/investment decisions are often made without a careful and objective assessment of foreign markets and with a limited appreciation for different environments abroad. This is often a result of the perception of other markets as an extension of the domestic market and that methods and practices that work at home also work abroad. The cost of conducting international research is seen as prohibitively high and managers make export decisions based on short-term and changing market needs (a reactive approach). Environmental scanning is viewed as a prerequisite for the successful alignment of competitive strategies (Subramanian, Fernandes, and Harper, 1993; Beal, 2000).

The purpose of international marketing research is to: 1) identify, evaluate, and compare the size and potential of various markets and select the most desirable market(s) for a given product or service, and 2) reassess market changes that may require a change in a company's strategy. A firm may research a market by using either primary or secondary data sources.

Primary research (using primary data) is conducted by collecting data directly from the foreign marketplace through interviews, focus groups, observation, surveys, and experimentation with representatives and/or potential buyers. It attempts to answer certain questions about specific markets such as sales potential or pricing. Primary research has the advantage of being tailored to the company's market and therefore provides specific information. However, collection of such data is often expensive and time-consuming.

Secondary market research is based on data previously collected and assembled for a certain project other than the one at hand. Such information can often be found inside the company or in the library, or it can be purchased from public or private organizations that specialize in providing information, such as overseas market studies, country market surveys, export statistics profiles, foreign trade reports, or competitive assessments of specific industries. Although such data are readily available and inexpensive, certain limitations apply to using secondary sources:

1. The information often does not meet one's specific needs. Because these materials are collected by others for their own purpose, they may be too broad or too narrow in terms of their scope to be of much value for the research at hand. Also, such information is often out of date.
2. There could be differences in definition of terms or units of measurement that make it difficult to categorize or compare the research data.
3. It is difficult to assess the accuracy of the information because little is known about the research design or techniques used to gather the data.

INTERNATIONAL MARKET ASSESSMENT

International market assessment is a form of environmental scanning that permits a firm to select a small number of desirable markets on the basis of broad variables. Companies must determine where to sell their products or services because they seldom have enough resources to take advantage of all opportunities. Not using scanning techniques may create the tendency to overlook growing markets. For example, European companies have often neglected the fastest growing markets in Southeast Asia while expanding their traditional markets in North America. Assessment of foreign markets involves subjecting countries to a series of environmental analyses with a view to selecting a handful of desirable markets for exports. In the early stages of assessment, secondary data are used to establish market size, level of trade, as well as investment and other economic and financial information.

Preliminary Screening (Basic Need and Potential)

The first step in market assessment is the process of establishing whether there is a basic need for the company's products or services in foreign markets. Basic need potential is often determined by environmental conditions such as climate, topography, or natural resources. In situations in which it is difficult to determine potential need, firms can resort to foreign trade and investment data to establish whether the product and/or service has been previously imported, its volume, its dollar value, and the exporting countries.

After establishing basic need potential, it is important to determine whether the need for the product or service has been satisfied. Needs may be met by local production or imports. If there are plans for local production by competitors, imports may cease or be subject to high tariffs or other barriers. Market opportunities still exist for competitive firms if a growing demand for the product cannot be fully met by local production insofar as governments do not apply trade restrictions in favor of local producers or imports from certain countries. If the research indicates that market opportunities exist, it is pertinent to consider the market's overall buying power by examining country-specific factors such as population, gross domestic product, per capital income, distribution of wealth, exports, and imports. While considering these factors, one should note that 1) per capita income might not be a good measure of buying power unless the country has a large middle class and no profound regional disparities, and 2) imports do not always indicate market potential. Availability of foreign currency, as well as changes in duties and trade policies should be monitored to ensure that they are conducive to the growth of imports in the country.

Secondary Screening (Financial and Economic Conditions)

Secondary screening involves financial and economic conditions such as trends in inflation, interest rates, exchange rate stability, and availability of credit and financing. Countries with high inflation rates (as well as controlled and low interest rates) should be carefully considered because they may limit the volume of imports by restricting the availability of foreign exchange. There is also a need to verify the availability of commercial banks that can finance overseas transactions and handle collections, payments, and money transfers.

Economic data are also used to measure certain indicators such as market size (relative size of each market as a percentage of the total world market), market intensity (degree of purchasing power), and growth of the market (annual increase in sales). Countries with advanced economies, such as the United States or Germany, account for a large percentage of the world market for automobiles, computers, and televisions. Their high per capita incomes reflect the attractiveness of the market and the degree of purchasing power. Such information will help in selecting countries with rapidly growing markets and high concentrations of purchasing power.

Third Screening (Political and Legal Forces)

It is important to assess the type of government (democratic/nondemocratic) and its stability. Countries with democratic governments tend to be politically stable, favor open trade policies, and are less likely to resort to measures that restrict imports or impede companies' abilities to take certain actions. Political instability may lead to damage to property and/or disruption of supplies or sales. It could be as a result of wars, insurrections, takeover of property and/or a change of rules. Consideration should also be given to legal forces that affect export/import operations. These include the following:

- *Entry barriers*: Product restrictions, high import tariffs, restrictive quotas, import licenses, special taxes on imports, product labeling, and other restrictive trade laws.
- *Limits on profit remittances and/or ownership*: Imposition of strict limits on capital outflows in foreign currencies, restrictions on or delays in remittance of profits, and ownership requirements to establish a business.
- *Taxes and price controls and protection of intellectual property rights*: The existence of high taxes, price controls, and a lack of adequate protection for intellectual property rights should be considered.

Fourth Screening (Sociocultural Forces)

This involves consideration of sociocultural forces such as customs, religion, and values that may have an adverse effect on the purchase or consumption of certain products. Examples include sales of pork and its derivatives and alcohol in Muslim countries.

Fifth Screening (Competitive Forces)

It is important to appraise the level and quality of competition in potential markets. The exporter has to identify companies competing in the markets, and the level of their technology, the quality and price of the products and/or services, and their estimated market shares, as well as other pertinent matters.

Final Selection (Field Trip)

This stage involves a visit to the markets that appear to be promising in light of the market assessment technique. Such visits could be in the form of trade missions (a group of business and government officials that visit a market in search of business opportunities) or trade fairs (a public display of products and services by firms of several countries to prospective customers). The purpose of such a visit is to:

- corroborate the facts gathered during the various stages of market assessment; and
- supplement currently available information by doing research in the local market, including face-to-face interviews with potential consumers, distributors, agents, and government officials.

This will facilitate the final selection of the most desirable markets as well as the development of a marketing plan, product modification, pricing, promotion, and distribution.

STUDYING THE MARKET COMPETITION

As you explore opportunities in a foreign market, it is important to view the competition in the context of specific customers you intend to target in that market. You can focus on weaknesses that you can exploit and consider whether this will provide a reasonable market share that is worthwhile. As you study the foreign market competition, it is critical to note the following:

- *Market segments and competitor positions*: It is important to examine the customers (significant customer segments) for the product in the market and the growth rate of these segments. Among the promising market segments (with high growth rates), you identify segments with incumbent competitors versus those that are either unoccupied or have weak incumbents. Explore unmet customer needs in the latter two categories, the market share, and how these needs can be met. French Gourmet, the Hawaiian dough maker, has been supplying frozen dough to customers operating hotels, restaurants, and cruise lines in Hawaii since 1984. It decided to expand to foreign markets in Asia and the Middle East. It realized that there was limited competition in these markets as existing competitors could not make "frozen dough that is still baked fresh." The company met potential customers and conducted baking demonstrations using on-site ovens. It enjoyed first-mover advantages and competed on superior quality. Competitors attempted to take away the firm's market share by providing a low-quality product at lower prices. The company continues to win foreign markets and over 70 percent of its sales are now generated from exports. This underscores the need to pick the right market segment and focus on providing superior value to customers to fend off competitors.
- *Study export leaders and laggards and their value chains*: It is important to identify market leaders (with increasing market share) and those that are falling behind in your market segment as well as key differences in their value chain activities. Studies show that market leaders know their customers well and often have a unique brand that distinguishes their product. They build a value chain network that supports the brand and often difficult to imitate. Ikea, the Swedish firm, designs and sells ready-to-assemble furniture, kitchen appliances, home accessories, and other goods and services and operates 433 stores in 52 countries. Its success is largely attributed to providing a unique customer experience (a distinct store layout), lower prices than the competition, designing inexpensive and appealing products tailored to each market, and building of an efficient supply chain (it has over 2,000 suppliers in about 50 countries that design and manufacture products for its stores).
- *A checklist for evaluating foreign competition*: Find out unmet needs in the market that your product can satisfy by talking to foreign customers, distributors, or wholesalers.
- *Evaluate imitation capabilities*: Assess whether local competitors can easily imitate your product or service, appraise their strategies and capabilities, and evaluate whether your firm can achieve a sustainable competitive advantage over the competition.
- *Close the capability gap*: It is important to identify core capabilities that will help the firm succeed in foreign markets (manufacturing, distribution, marketing) and close existing deficiencies. This may require establishing partnerships with other firms with expertise in a given market. Brew Dog, a U.K.-based brewer, expanded its export sales in the United States and other foreign markets through distributor partnerships that helped to establish export beachheads in these countries.

BRIDGING THE CULTURAL GAP

Culture is a cognitive frame of reference and a pattern of behavior transmitted from one generation to another. It is not "innate" but learned, shared, and defines the boundaries of different groups. The influence of culture is more prominent on firm activities that require direct interaction with the public. For example, direct exporting to host countries is the most affected by sociocultural influences compared to indirect exporting through foreign distributors or exporting trading companies. Different cultural settings may require unique marketing strategies involving product design, packaging, promotion, and pricing to reflect variations in cultural attitudes and values. The greater the export firm's involvement in the host country, the greater the need for management to understand the sociocultural environment.

We outline some elements of the cultural environment that potential exporters need to appreciate.

- *Business style and punctuality*: In many countries, personal relationships are valued in business and indulging in small talk is standard business practice. In some cultures, it is not considered appropriate to discuss business at a meal until the food has been ordered. It is important to establish a good rapport and reach a level of trust needed before discussing business. In countries such as Japan or Germany, it is considered rude to arrive late for business meetings. However, in other countries, standards are less stringent and meetings can start anywhere from 15 minutes to 45 minutes late.
- *Dress and gift-giving*: In the absence of specific guidance, it is advisable to dress formally for the first meeting. Questions can be raised with the hosts for subsequent meetings. In some cultures ceremonial gifts are expected to be exchanged such as pens or popular books as a sign of respect for the other party.
- *Negotiation*: The purpose of business negotiations often varies based on the parties' cultural background. While businesses from Western countries view negotiations as a means of concluding a contract, Asian negotiators see it as a way of creating a rewarding long-term relationship. For example, Japanese businesses approach negotiations as a win–win process while others see it as a win–lose strategy (one side wins, the other side loses). Appropriate formalities must be followed during negotiations such as use of titles, first or last names, or dress. Culture impacts styles of communication (direct versus indirect). For example, Americans value directness and often provide a clear and unambiguous response to business proposals while the Japanese respond using indirect methods, which often means decoding seemingly vague comments and gestures. Culture also impacts the ways in which business negotiations are organized. Some countries have a small negotiating team with a supreme leader with authority to decide important matters (e.g., the United States) while others use team negotiation and consensus decision making (e.g., China, Japan).
- *Language and color*: Language is the primary means of communication and indicates social and cultural differences among groups. Export–import firms must be aware of not only language barriers but also tone and body language. Effective communication requires an understanding of and a sensitivity to all these contextual elements. Misunderstandings during contract negotiations could lead to costly mistakes and future conflicts. Some of the critical elements in the negotiations may be lost in translation. The original contract must be translated by a native speaker to his own language and then translated back

to the original language of the contract by a foreigner to compare with the original. Trade names or labels on export goods should be examined to ensure that they do not violate host countries' cultural norms. The Series 44 computer exported by IBM to Japan had to be renamed because "4" is similar to the word "death" in Japanese (Karimian, 2007). Selection of colors should reflect the aesthetic sense and culture of the foreign customer. For example, in China white and yellow symbolize death and pornography, respectively, and should not be used in packaging or marketing goods.

- *Religion*: Religion has an impact on a host of sociocultural factors and also shapes the behaviors of individuals and groups in society. It influences attitudes and values among people, which, in turn impacts consumption and purchasing patterns. Religious holidays may bring an increase or decrease in the consumption of certain items (Christmas: increases in gift-giving and food consumption; Ramadan: a decline in sale of cigarettes). Religious dietary restrictions can affect consumption of certain foods (pork in the case of Jews and Muslims; alcohol for Muslims; beef for Hindus). Organized religious groups can encourage or block the introduction or sale of certain products and technologies based on religious law or doctrine. It is important to consider the impact of religious beliefs on the sale and marketing of export products.

DEVELOPING AN INTERNATIONAL BUSINESS PLAN

A business plan involves a process in which an entity puts together a given set of resources (people, capital, materials) to achieve defined goals and objectives over a specific period of time. In addition to providing the direction necessary for success, a sound business plan should be flexible to take advantage of new opportunities or to allow adjustments when certain assumptions or conditions change. This plan should be reviewed and progress assessed (perhaps once every three or four months) to ensure that implementation is consistent with overall goals and objectives laid out in the business plan.

Developing a business plan is an important factor for success regardless of the size, type, or time of establishment of the business. Even though some export–import companies start a business plan after they have reached a certain stage, planning is needed at all stages of business development from inception to maturity (Williams and Manzo, 1983; Hisrich, Peters, and Shepherd, 2012). It is a roadmap to one's targeted destination. By allowing for critical evaluation of different alternatives, a business plan forces entrepreneurs to set realistic goals, predict resource allocation, and project future earnings. Such a practice assists in avoiding costly mistakes and enhances the decision-making abilities of businesses (Silvester, 1995; Hisrich, Peters, and Shepherd, 2012). A written business plan is the basis upon which other parties (e.g., bankers, potential partners, etc.) assess the overall business concern. It is used for obtaining bank financing, seeking investment funds, obtaining large contracts to supply governments or companies, or arranging strategic alliances to conduct joint marketing and other activities.

The structure of a typical business plan includes the following components (see Figure 4.1): executive summary, description of the industry and company, target market, present and future competition, marketing plan and sales strategy, management and organization, long-term development and exit plan, as well as the financial plan (Cohen, 1995; Hisrich, Peters, and Shepherd, 2012). Some plans also include critical risks/problems and community benefits.

FIGURE 4.1 Structure of an International Business Plan

Executive Summary: Company background, market potential, product /service, sales and profit projections, etc.

General Description of Industry and Company: General company description, current status and prospect for industry, description of product /service

Target Market: Market description, market size, market share and trends, competition

Marketing Plan and Sales Strategy: Marketing strategy, sales tactics and distribution, advertising and promotion

Management and Organization: Compensation and ownership, organization and key management

Long-Term Development Plan: Basic strategy, potential risks

Financial Plan: Cash flow projections for three years, pro forma income statement and balance sheet

EXPORT COUNSELING AND ASSISTANCE

A number of sources are able to give assistance to U.S. exporters.

The U.S. Department of Commerce

Through the local district office, the exporter has access to assistance available through the International Trade Administration (ITA) and to trade information gathered overseas by the U.S. and foreign commercial services. The U.S. Trade Information Center serves as a single source of research support, trade information, counseling, and industry consultation. A valuable source of trade information while conducting foreign market research is the National Trade Data Bank (NTDB). The

NTDB provides specific product and country information as well as a list of foreign importers in specific product areas. United States exporters can also advertise in *Commercial News USA*, a bi-monthly magazine that promotes U.S. products and services overseas. It is distributed throughout the U.S. embassies and consulates in over 140 countries (International Perspective 4.2).

The following is a list of some of the major programs offered by the Department of Commerce (U.S. Department of Commerce, 2015).

- *Market Access and Compliance (MAC)*: MAC specialists monitor foreign country trade practices and help U.S. exporters deal with foreign trade barriers.
- *U.S. and Foreign Commercial Service (U.S. & FCS)*: U.S. commercial officers in foreign countries provide important trade and investment information on foreign companies. This includes but is not limited to conducting market research and finding foreign representatives.
- *Trade Development*: This unit offers extensive support to U.S. exporters by providing critical information on market and trade practices overseas, including industry analysis and trade policy. Industry-specific trade development includes aerospace, automotive, consumer goods, e-commerce, energy, and so on. Industry officers identify trade opportunities by product or service, develop export marketing plans, and conduct trade missions.
- *Gold Key Service*: This helps U.S. exporters by prescreening potential distributors, professional associations, etc. It is available in many countries.
- *Trade events*: The Department of Commerce organizes various trade events (trade fairs, trade missions, international catalog exhibitions, etc.) in order to help market U.S. products or locate representatives abroad.

Small Business Administration (SBA)

The SBA provides free export counseling services to potential and current small business exporters (through its field offices) throughout the United States.

- *SCORE/ACE programs*: Members of the Service Corps of Retired Executives (SCORE) and the Active Corps of Executives (ACE), with years of practical experience in international trade, assist small firms in evaluating export potential, developing and implementing export marketing plans, identifying problem areas, etc. "SCORE" has a new acronym, Counselors to America's Small Business "CASB." Since its inception, the organization has worked with over seven million entrepreneurs.
- *Small Business Development Centers (SBDCs)*: Additional export counseling and assistance is offered through the Small Business Development Centers (SBDCs), which are located within some colleges and universities. The centers are intended to offer technical help to exporters by providing, for example, an export marketing feasibility study, and an analysis for the client firms. There is also an initial legal assistance program for small exporters on the legal aspects of exporting.
- *U.S. Export Assistance Centers (EACs)*: These are intended to deliver a comprehensive array of export counseling and trade finance services to U.S. firms. They integrate the export marketing know-how of the Department of Commerce with the trade finance expertise of the Small Business Administration and Export–Import Bank. Trade specialists from EACs help U.S. firms enter new

markets and increase market share by identifying the best markets for their products; developing an effective marketing strategy; advising on distribution channels, market entry, promotion, and export procedures; and assisting with trade finance. They are generally located with state promotion agencies, local Chambers of Commerce, and other local export promotion organizations.

U.S. Department of Agriculture

The U.S. Department of Agriculture (USDA) provides a wide variety of programs to promote U.S. agricultural exports. Some of the trade assistance programs include promotion of U.S. farm exports in foreign markets, services of commodity and marketing specialists, trade fairs, and information services. Programs are available to, for example, expand dairy product exports and provide technical assistance for specialty crops.

State Government and City Agencies

Many states, cities, and counties have special programs to assist their own exporters. Such programs generally include export education, marketing assistance, trade missions, and trade shows.

Private Sources of Export Assistance

Commercial banks, trading companies, trade clubs, Chambers of Commerce and trade associations, as well as trade consultants provide various forms of export assistance (see Table 4.2).

TABLE 4.2 Private Sources of Export Assistance

Private Sources	Services
Commercial banks	Advice on export regulations, exchange of currencies, financing exports, collections, credit information and assistance.
Trading companies	Market research and promotion, shipping and documentation, financing sales, facilitating prompt payment, appointing overseas distributors, etc.
World trade clubs	Education programs on international trade and organization of promotional events.
Chambers of Commerce and trade associations	Chambers of Commerce provide the following services: Export seminars, trade promotion, contacts with foreign companies and distributors, issuance of certificates of origin, transportation routing and consolidating shipments. U.S. Chambers of Commerce abroad are also a valuable source of marketing information. Trade associations provide information on market demand and trends and other information on pertinent trade issues through newsletters.
Trade consultants	Advise on all aspects of exporting ranging from domestic/foreign regulations to market research and risk analysis.

INTERNATIONAL PERSPECTIVE 4.2

Programs for U.S. Exporters

The United States government provides several services to U.S. exporters. The business contact programs provided by the Department of Commerce include the following:

- **International Partner Search (IPS):** The US Commercial Service's IPS program will use its resources in different countries to find U.S. businesses the most suitable strategic partners (pre-qualified partners). U.S. businesses can obtain

    a. information on the marketability and sales potential for their products and services;
    b. contact information for key officers of each potential partner along with data on, for example, company size, sales, and number of employees.

- **Commercial News USA (CNUSA):** The CNUSA program allows U.S. firms to receive global exposure through its catalogs, magazines, and electronic resources. The catalog and magazines are distributed throughout the U.S. embassies and consulates among 152 countries, specifically for business readers. All published products must be at least 51 percent U.S. made (parts), with 51 percent U.S. labor. The leads obtained by the program are redirected to the U.S. exporting firms and include detailed contact information, including sales, representation, distributorships, and joint ventures or licensing agreements that help these firms identify potential markets. Inquiries from abroad do not go through the CNUSA channels but go directly to the exporting firms.
- **Gold Key Service:** The Gold Key Service is a matching service that sets appointments in foreign markets with prescreened partners for U.S. exporters. The service provides an orientation briefing, market research, a debriefing with trade professionals after meetings, and also offers assistance in generating follow-up strategies for exporting firms. The service is offered by the Commercial Service for a fee.
- **International Company Profiles (ICP):** The commercial officers of the ICP prepare background reports of foreign firms who are interested in working with U.S. exporters. Each report includes information on a foreign organization's bank and trade references, principles, key officers and managers, product lines, number of employees, financial data, sales volume, reputation, and market outlook. The ICP is only offered to countries that are in need of providers who offer background information on local companies in the private sector. Credit reports from private sector resources are generally available on nearly all foreign firms.
- **Trade Events Program (TEP):** The Department of Commerce organizes trade shows, fairs, and trade missions overseas. It also has the International Buyer Program (IBP) under which it recruits qualified foreign buyers, sales representatives, and business partners to U.S. trade shows each year providing U.S. exhibitors good opportunities to expand business globally.

> • **BuyUSA.GovMatchmaking:** This is a convenient online program that matches U.S. exporters with buyers in overseas markets. When an importer registers with a profile that matches a U.S. exporter's activities, the service will automatically notify the U.S. exporter.

OVERSEAS TRAVEL AND PROMOTION

Once market research is conducted and the target countries are selected, the next step is to visit the countries in order to locate and cultivate new customers or to develop and maintain relationships with foreign distributors. The world has become one market, and this has naturally given rise to more intercultural encounters. The exporter has to be aware of certain important factors before embarking on a trip, not only to avoid embarrassment but also to be able to conclude a successful business arrangement (International Perspective 4.3).

Planning and Preparing for the Trip

Making Prior Arrangements

The most important meetings should be confirmed before leaving the United States. One should avoid traveling during national holidays, or political elections in the host countries. Contacts can be made with the Department of Commerce country desk officers in Washington, D.C. and/or U.S. embassies abroad to obtain current and reliable information about the target countries.

Acquiring Basic Knowledge of the Host Country

Exporters should know some basic facts about the history, culture, and customs of the host countries. Several books and magazines cover business manners, customs, dietary practices, humor, and acceptable dress in various countries. It is essential to exercise flexibility and cultural sensitivity when doing business abroad. The exporter should also obtain prior information on such important areas such as weather conditions, healthcare, exchanging currency, and visa requirements. Various travel publications provide such information (for export procedures, see International Perspective 4.4).

Obtaining the ATA Carnet

For exporters who take product samples, duties and burdensome customs formalities can be avoided by obtaining the ATA (Admission Temporaire) carnet. The United States is a member of the ATA carnet system, which permits U.S. commercial and professional travelers to take material to member countries of the ATA carnet system for a temporary period of time without paying duty. An exporter should check whether a host country is a member of the ATA convention. The U.S Council for International Business handles applications for carnets. A bond, a letter of credit, or a cash equivalent, (as guarantee for 40 percent of the value) will, however, be required to cover outstanding duties in case the samples are not returned to the United States.

Business Negotiations

Negotiations should be entered into with sufficient planning and preparation. The exporter should establish the line or boundary below which he or she is not willing to concede. It is also advisable to draft the agreements since it will enable the exporter to include terms and conditions with important implications into the contract.

Documentation

The exporter should document the various meetings at the end of the day to avoid confusing one market with another. It also provides a record for company files. Once the trip is over and the exporter returns home, there should be an immediate follow-up, with a letter confirming the commitments and timetable for implementation of these commitments.

Overseas Promotion

Overseas promotion of exports is often designed to open new markets, maintain and increase existing market share, and obtain market intelligence. Such efforts must meet strategic marketing goals and achieve the greatest impact at the lowest possible cost. Effective promotion should go beyond enabling the potential buyer to receive the desired information. It must be strong enough to motivate him/her to react positively. This requires the conveying of a message that does not offend cultural sensibilities and one that is uniquely designed for each market. The exporter can choose one or a combination of promotional tools: Direct mail, advertising, trade fairs/missions, and publicity. The choice will depend on the target audience, company objectives, the product or service exported, the availability of internal resources, as well as the availability of the tool in a particular market (Czinkota, Ronkainen, and Moffett, 2020). Exporters may use the same promotional strategy in different foreign markets if the target markets vary little with respect to product use and consumer attitudes. In some cases, the product and/or promotional strategy must be adapted to foreign market conditions. For example, Tang sold in Latin America is especially sweetened and promoted as a drink for mealtimes. In the United States, people drink it in the morning and the product is promoted as a drink for breakfast (Ball et al.,2020).

In certain developing countries where the rate of illiteracy is high, advertising in periodicals does not reach a broad audience. However, if the marketed product or service is intended for a small part of the population, such as middle-or high-income consumers, using periodicals could be an effective way of reaching the target market. For products that are intended for a broader audience, such as soap or cooking oil, radios or billboards could be an effective way of reaching many consumers in these countries.

It is often stated that adapting a product to local conditions and accentuating the local nature of a certain aspect of the product in the promotional material tend to create a favorable image among the public and stimulate product sales. This means that exporters should consider ways and means of localizing a certain part of their activity, such as product adaptation to local conditions or assembly of parts, in the host countries. Such activities not only increase product sales, but also create employment opportunities in the local economy. For less sophisticated products a firm could export the necessary ingredients or components into a host country, preferably into a free trade zone, and use local labor to produce or assemble the final product. In addition to being a good promotional tool for the product, such localization will enhance the competitiveness of the product by reducing cost.

Advertising

Advertising is any paid form of nonpersonal presentation and promotion of ideas, goods, or services by an identified sponsor. Typically, no one vehicle reaches an entire target audience and, hence, exporters must evaluate the many alternatives so as to meet their desired objectives. One or a combination of vehicles can be used (magazines, newspapers, TV, radio, direct mail, or billboards) to carry the advertisements to target audiences.

Exporters should be aware of regulations in various countries that govern advertising. In some European countries, for example, television stations allow only a certain percentage (12 to 18 percent) of advertising per hour. In many developed countries, the advertising of tobacco and alcoholic beverages is heavily regulated. In some Latin American countries, such as Peru, commercial advertising on national television should be domestically produced.

The advertising process involves: 1) budgeting: how much it will cost and how much the exporter can afford, 2) determining the most effective and least expensive media to reach the potential customer, and 3) preparing the appropriate advertising package that emphasizes the few most important points.

Small exporters often use direct mail (correspondence and brochures) to reach their overseas customers. In Southeast Asian markets, direct mail is the most effective way of promoting the sale of industrial goods. Brochures have to be translated into the local language and accurate mailing lists have to be obtained. Mailing lists can be purchased from private firms and most libraries have various resources, such as trade publications and journals of various trade associations, from which a list of potential overseas customers can be obtained. In addition, such lists are available from the directory and catalog of trade shows and other government publications, such as *Foreign Trades Index*, *The Export Contact List Service* and the *World Traders Data Reports* (WTDR).

The exporter can use one or a combination of the following media to advertise a product or service.

Foreign media: A product can be advertised in an overseas retailers or distributors catalog, or a trade publication. Cooperative advertising, that is, a group advertising program can be arranged by business associations and local chambers of commerce. Cooperative advertising is more effective for noncompeting and/or complementary products. The advantage of such advertising is that it reduces expenses, especially for small exporters, and also enables exporters to combine advertising budgets to reach a larger audience than is normally possible individually.

Government-supported advertising. There are many federal- and state-supported promotional programs for U.S. exporting firms that facilitate the marketing of U.S. products overseas.

Commercial publications. Many U.S. trade publications are widely read around the globe. Advertising in such journals or magazines will enable the exporter to reach a broader market. Some of these publications include *Showcase U.S.A.*, *Export*, and *Automobile and Truck International.*

The Internet. The Internet provides the exporter with an additional global medium. Potential consumers can be reached through websites in key languages and by email. A number of products are being made available online. Data collected from customers can also be used for future marketing efforts.

INTERNATIONAL PERSPECTIVE 4.3

The Twelve Most Common Mistakes of Potential Exporters

- Failing to obtain qualified export counseling and to develop a master international marketing plan before starting an export business
- Insufficient commitment by top management to overcome the initial difficulties and financial requirements of exporting
- Insufficient care in selecting overseas distributors
- Chasing orders from around the world instead of establishing a basis for profitable operations and orderly growth
- Neglecting export business when the U.S. market booms
- Failing to treat international distributors on an equal basis with domestic counterparts
- Assuming that a given market technique and product will automatically be successful in all countries
- Unwillingness to modify products to meet regulations or cultural preferences of other countries
- Failure to print service, sale, and warranty messages in locally understood languages
- Failure to consider use of an export management company
- Failure to consider licensing or joint venture agreements
- Failure to provide readily available servicing for the product

---

Personal Selling

Personal selling is often used during the first stages of internationalization. It is also used for the marketing of industrial, especially high-priced goods. Personal selling entails oral presentations by sales personnel of the organization or agents to prospective overseas purchasers. Salespeople also collect information on competitive products, prices, services, and delivery problems that assist exporters in improving quality and service. In short, such media are used in cases in which advertising does not provide an effective line to target markets, the price is subject to negotiation, and the product/service needs customer application assistance. Avon and Unilever, for example, use personal sellers in rural villages in many developing countries to market their products.

Sales Promotion

Sales promotion refers to marketing activity other than advertising, personal selling, or publicity. It includes trade shows, trade fairs, demonstrations, and other non-recurrent selling efforts not in the ordinary routine (Asheghian and Ibrahimi, 1990). Trade shows are events at which firms display their products in exhibits at a central location and invite dealers or customers to visit the exhibits. They are a cost-effective way of reaching a large number of customers who might otherwise be difficult to reach. Adding to their benefit, from a cost and efficiency standpoint, is that trade shows help exporters to contact and evaluate potential agents and distributors. Trade fairs also provide an important opportunity for exporters to introduce, promote, and demonstrate new products, cultivate new contacts, collect market intelligence, as well as close deals with a number of attendees who often have direct responsibility for purchasing products and services.

Trade fairs can be organized by certain industries, trade associations, or chambers of commerce. For example, the Hanover trade fair in Germany organizes regional and national fairs and exhibitions in various product sectors targeted at specialized audiences as well as the general public. Every year it organizes around fifty trade fairs and exhibitions which attract over 28,000 exhibitors and 2.5 million visitors from over 100 countries around the world. The Seoul International Gift and Accessories show is one of the largest trade fairs for gift and fashion accessories in Asia. It attracts about 32,000 local and overseas visitors resulting in about $15 million in sales.

Trade shows are also supported or organized by governments in order to pro-mote exports. In the United States, the Department of Commerce (DOC) organizes various export promotion events such as exhibitions, seminars, trade missions, and other customized promotions for individual U.S. companies. Under the International Buyer Program, the DOC selects leading U.S. trade exhibitions each year in indus-tries with high export potential. The DOC offices abroad recruit foreign buyers and distributors to attend these shows, while program staff help exhibiting firms make con-tact with international visitors at the show to achieve direct export sales and/or inter-national representation. The DOC, through the certified trade fair program, supports private-sector organized shows. Exhibitors use U.S. pavilions to create enhanced visibility and also receive the support of commercial services from U.S. embassies and consulates. The DOC and state agencies also jointly organize U.S. company catalogs and product literature to present to potential customers abroad and send the trade leads directly to participating U.S. firms. Many developed countries have similar programs to promote the sale of their products abroad.

Trade missions are another export sales promotion tool. Under a trade mission, a group of businesspeople and/or government officials visits foreign markets in search of business opportunities. Missions typically target specific industries in selected countries. Events are also organized by private organizations or government agencies so that foreign buyer groups can come to the United States to meet individually with U.S. companies, exporters, or relevant trade associations. At these events, foreign businesses buy U.S. products, negotiate distributor agreements, find joint venture partners, or learn about current industry trends.

Publicity

Publicity is communicating with an audience by personal or non-personal media that are not explicitly paid for delivering the messages. This is done by planting commercially significant news about the exporter and/or products in a published medium or obtaining favorable presentation on the local media without sponsoring it. A carefully managed advertising and public relations program is essential to the long-term success of an export firm. The public relations (publicity) program could include charitable donations to schools, hospitals, and other social causes; sponsorship of youth athletic teams; participation in local parades; inviting the media to cover special events sponsored or supported by the export company.

INTERNATIONAL PERSPECTIVE 4.4

A Typical Export Transaction

Step 1: The exporter establishes initial contact by responding to an overseas buyer's advertisement for a product that she/he can supply. Such ads are available in various trade publications. The exporter's letter briefly introduces the company and requests more information on the product needed as well as bank and trade references.

Step 2: The prospective buyer responds to the exporter's email, letter or fax by specifying the type and quantity of product needed, with a sample where appropriate. The potential importer also sends his or her trade references.

Step 3: The exporter checks with the consulate of the importer's country to determine 1) whether the product can be legally imported and whether any restrictions apply, and 2) whether any requirements need to be met. The consulate may indicate that a certificate of origin is needed to clear shipment at the foreign port. The exporter also verifies the buyer's bank and trade references through its bank and other U.S. government agencies, such as the Department of Commerce.

Step 4: The exporter (if an agent) contacts the manufacturers of the product to 1) establish if the given product is available for export to the country in question, and 2) obtain and compare price lists, catalogs, and samples.

Step 5: The exporter selects the product from responses submitted by manufacturers based on quality, cost, and delivery time. The sample selected is sent by airmail to the overseas customer to determine if the product is acceptable. In the meantime, the exporter prepares and sends a price quotation, suggestions for the mode of transportation, and a letter of credit terms. The price quotation should include commission and markup.

Step 6: The exporter obtains a positive response from the overseas customer and is requested to send a pro forma invoice to enable the latter to obtain an import and foreign exchange permit. The exporter sends the pro forma invoice.

Step 7: The overseas customer receives the pro forma invoice, opens a confirmed irrevocable letter of credit for the benefit of the exporter, and sends an order to the latter to ship the merchandise.

Step 8: The exporter verifies with its bank the validity of the letter of credit and finds that it meets the agreed conditions in the export contract and that it will be honored by the bank if the exporter meets the terms. The exporter ships the merchandise and submits the required documents (such as a bill of lading, commercial invoice, consular invoice, certificate of origin, packing list, etc.) to the bank with a request for payment. The exporter is paid, the merchandise arrives at its destination, and the transaction is completed.

CHAPTER SUMMARY

Assessing and selecting the product	In order to establish market potential for a product/service, it is important to consider:
	Success of the product in the domestic market, participation in overseas trade shows, advertising in foreign media, market data.
	Approaches to selecting a product for exports: 1. *Systematic approach:* Product selection based on overall market demand. 2. *Reactive approach*: Selection of a product based on immediate (short-term) market need.
International Market Research (IMR)	IMR helps business organizations in making business decisions that lead to the proper allocation of resources in markets with the greatest potential for sales.
	It involves six steps: Preliminary screening (basic need and potential); secondary screening (financial and economic conditions); third screening (political and economic forces); fourth screening (socio-cultural forces); fifth screening (competitive forces); final selection (field trip).
Developing an export/import business plan	*Typical structure of a business plan*: Executive summary, general description of industry and company, target market, marketing plan and sales strategy, management and organization, long-term development plan, financial plan.
Sources of export counseling	*Public Sources*: The U.S. Department of Commerce, US Export Assistance Centers, and The Small Business Administration.
	Private sources: Commercial banks, trading companies, world trade clubs, chambers of commerce and trade associations, trade consultants.
Business travel and promotion abroad	*Planning and preparing for the trip*: Making prior arrangements, acquiring basic knowledge of host country, using the ATA carnet, preparing for business negotiations, documentation.
	Overseas Promotion: Advertising, personal selling, sales promotion, and publicity.

REVIEW QUESTIONS

1. Discuss the two major approaches to selecting a product for export. Why is it important to participate in overseas trade shows?
2. What are the disadvantages of the reactive approach to selecting a product for export?

3. Explain the importance of the following factors in the selection of products for export: shifting spending patterns, quality, and niche marketing.
4. Do a country's imports completely measure the market potential for a product? Discuss.
5. Why should an export firm consider financial and economic conditions in importing countries?
6. What is the importance of political and legal forces in international market assessment?
7. Identify the public sources of export counseling in the United States.
8. Discuss three private sources of export assistance. What is the Gold Key Service?
9. Explain the steps involved in a typical export transaction.
10. What is SCORE?

REFERENCES

Asheghian, P. and Ebrahimi, B. (1990). *International Business.* London: HarperCollins.

Beal, M. (2000). Competing effectively: environmental scanning, competitive strategy and organizational performance in small manufacturing firms. *Journal of Small Business Management*, 38(1): 27–47.

Cohen, W. (1995). *Model Business Plans for Product Business.* New York: John Wiley and Sons.

Czinkota, M., Ronkainen, I., and Buonafina, M. (2004). *The Export Marketing Imperative.* Mason, OH: Thomson.

Czinkota, M., Ronkainen, I., and Moffett, M. (2010). *International Business.* New York: Wiley.

Geringer, M., McNett, J., and Ball, D. (2020). *International Business.* New York: McGraw-Hill.

Hisrich, R., Peters, M., and Shepherd, D. (2012). *Entrepreneurship.* New York: McGraw-Hill.

Karimian, M. (2007). *Role of Culture in International Marketing Activities.* New Jersey: Papers of New Management Conference.

Schwartz, M. (2006). ABM research finds trade shows attract buyers; Despite success of Internet, traditional advertising still pushing sales needle. *B to B*, vol. 9 (July 10).

Silvester, J. (1995). *How to Start, Finance and Operate your Own Business.* New York: Birch Lane Press.

Subramanian, R., Fernandes, N., and Harper, E. (1993). Environmental scanning in U.S. companies: Their nature and their relationship to performance. *Management International Review*, 33: 271–275.

U.S. Department of Commerce (2015). *A Basic Guide to Exporting.* Washington, DC: ITA.

Weiss, K. (2007). *Building an Import–Export Business.* New York: John Wiley and Sons.

Williams, E. and Manzo, S. (1983). *Business Planning for the Entrepreneur.* New York: Van Nostrand Rienhold Co.

World Wide Web Resources

SBA

Information on starting, financing, and expanding a small business: www.sba.gov/

U.S. Export Inc.

Export assistance to small and medium-sized firms:

www.export.gov/

www.trade.gov/

www.usda.gov/wps/portal/usdahome

TABLE 4.3 Are You Ready for Export?

Dimensions (D)	Criteria	Yes (5)	To some extent (3)	No (0)
Firm competitiveness (D1)	• Is your domestic market for the product profitable? • Has your profitability and cash flow position been sustainable for the last three years? • Is your product line competitive in terms of price, quality, and other attributes? • Has your firm implemented a budget management system over the last three years?			
Desire for internationalization (D2)	• Do you intend to export as part of your long-term strategy? • Do you have a formal export business plan with goals and strategies? • Are your levels of commitment similar to those for the domestic market? • Have you undertaken international market research to identify markets for your products?			
Level of commitment from owners and managers (D3)	• Are your owners and managers ready to commit sufficient resources (people, time, money) to develop export markets? • Is there a person with primary responsibility for exports? • Are you willing to exercise some patience to reach your goals? • Does your current export staff have export/international marketing experience?			

TABLE 4.3 Cont.

Dimensions (D)	Criteria	Yes (5)	To some extent (3)	No (0)
Product readiness (D4)	• Can you fulfil large orders from foreign buyers?			
	• Have you taken the necessary measures to ensure that your product is compliant with your target market's trade and safety regulations?			
	• Are you able to adapt the product to meet foreign customer preferences?			
	• Are you able to provide the necessary technical support or training in the target market?			
Resources: knowledge/skills (D5)	• Are you knowledgeable in matters relating to shipping and freight costing?			
	• Are you knowledgeable about exchange rates and international payments such as letters of credit?			
	• Do you have knowledge of foreign competition, pricing, and marketing strategies?			
	• Do you have an online presence through a website or advertising?			

Assessment of your export readiness			
Dimensions	**Low**	**Medium**	**High**
D1	0–7	8–14	15–20
D2	0–7	8–14	15–20
D3	0–7	8–14	15–20
D4	0–7	8–14	15–20
D5	0–7	8–14	15–20

For each dimension calculate your score.
0–25: You need more time to organize yourself for exports.
26–40: You are on the right track. Some additional work is needed.
41–65: You have the potential to be a successful exporter. Tie up a few loose ends and you will make it.
66–85: You are almost there. You need a little more preparation.
86–100: You have all the elements to be a successful exporter. You are ready to export.

International Trade Closing Cases and Discussions

1. Developing Export Markets

A recent survey by Babson College and the London Business School on entrepreneurship noted that middle-income countries have a larger share of individuals engaged in business ventures with high growth potential than high-income countries. The study also notes that these middle-income countries have higher percentages of people starting businesses. This is partly attributed to the deployment of existing technologies to exploit their comparative advantages. High rates of early-stage entrepreneurship, however, do not necessarily translate into high rates of established business. Rich countries such as Japan, for example, have low levels of early-stage entrepreneurial activity but a large number of established businesses. This is because the start-ups are opportunity-driven companies with lower rates of business failures than those in middle-income or poor countries that are largely motivated by the necessity to earn a living. In rich countries, there is also a tendency for entrepreneurial activity to shift from the consumer such as retailing to business services.

Export of luxury tea from Argentina. During the worst financial crisis in Argentina (2001), three young entrepreneurs founded a luxury tea business with just $10,000. They focused on quality with a view to selling in high-value export markets. The bags are a hand-tied sack of muslin (which does not alter the flavor of the tea) containing one of five types of organic tea: cedron, black-leaf tea, peppermint, Patagonian rosehip, and mate, lightened for the overseas market. They traveled to different parts of Argentina to locate the best growers. After finding suitable suppliers, the partners agreed to create a premium product to be sold in up-market outlets and trendy stores. Over 75 percent of the output is sold in overseas markets: in the United States, United Kingdom, Continental Europe, the Middle East, and Asia. Over the last few years, the company has registered substantial increases in sales.

The partners note that 1) exporting maximizes the benefits of selling from countries with weak currencies, 2) it is necessary to focus on quality materials, production, and packaging to charge premium prices, 3) high quality products should be sold in high quality outlets, and 4) it is important to disprove national stereotypes such as lack of punctuality, honesty, etc. with buyers and distributors.

Exports by Rwanda's nascent entrepreneurs. Rwanda is a small land-locked country with a population of eight million and located in the Great Lakes Region of East-Central Africa. Despite the legacy of genocide and war, the country is showing signs of rapid development. J. Nkubana, one of a number of women entrepreneurs, sells over 5,000 Christmas ornaments and baskets to Macy's in New York. Another rising entrepreneur, Beatrice Gakuba, founder of Rwanda Floral, is the nation's largest exporter of roses. She sells over five tons of flowers a week at auctions in Amsterdam. Exporters, however, face a number of challenges in Rwanda: 1) regular electricity outages resulting in lost productivity, 2) Rwanda's landlocked status requires the use of ports in neighboring countries and this delays shipments and delivery of exports, 3) borrowing costs are high (17 percent interest on loans) and banks require 100 percent collateral. Public funding is almost non-existent to promote exports.

Questions

1. Comment on the statement that "exporting maximizes the benefits of selling from countries with weak currencies."
2. Based on the information provided, what is your advice to the government of Rwanda to increase exports?

2. Strategies for Entering New Markets

A. *Picking the right country*

- Select a country that understands the value of your product
- Target a country with growth potential
- Start with homogeneous markets or markets of strong trading partners
- Target a country where you can sell at a competitive price

B. *Understanding the overseas market*

- Be flexible and open minded in establishing the needs of overseas consumers, i.e., unmet needs that can be satisfied by your product
- Determine the skills you require to meet customer needs
- Position your company to deliver superior value to your consumers
- Design products tailored to each market

C. *Dealing with the competition*

- Pick the right market segment
- Invest in product attributes that will keep you ahead of the competition
- Build an effective global supply chain

D. *Enhancing capabilities*

- Identify core capabilities that enables you to compete overseas
- Partner to augment your capabilities

E. *Bridging the cultural gap*

- Establish rapport before getting down to business
- Learn about society's concept of value, time, punctuality, taste, dress code, etc.

Question

Think of any additional advice for the exporter who plans to venture into a new export market in Central America.

CHAPTER 5

Export Channels of Distribution

LEARNING OBJECTIVES:

5.1 Describe the theoretical motivations for channels of distribution

5.2 Understand how direct channels differ from indirect channels of distribution

5.3 Identify the factors that determine channel choice

5.4 Understand the different types of exporter under direct and indirect channels

5.5 Learn the different ways of locating, contacting, and evaluating agents and distributors

5.6 Understand pertinent clauses in representation agreements

International Trade in Practice

Extreme Luxury Fashion Distribution and Sales Model

In the fashion industry, globalization has been used as an important strategy to enter foreign markets. It has been accompanied by a shift from independent family-run stores to multinational firms (established through mergers and acquisitions) with unique brands and new distribution channels (Guercini and Milanesi, 2017). The overall luxury market (including luxury goods and experiences) was estimated at US$1.45 trillion globally in 2020 and poised to grow by US$83.06 billion during 2019–2023. Teece (2010) describes a business model in terms of how firms deliver value to the consumer and how they capture value from innovation and organization activities. A business model identifies customer needs and creates and delivers value to a segment of the market that is willing and able to pay, thus generating sales and profits for the firm (Richardson, 2008). Johanson and Vahlne (1977) suggest that internationalization of firms (exports, overseas investment) begins with foreign markets that exhibit a certain level of proximity to the home country in terms of language and culture. The revised model of 2006 also suggests that firms doing business abroad have to overcome the liability of foreignness.

In the personal luxury sector, efforts have been made over the years to increase sales by selling accessories and licensed products that are less expensive. This process of "luxury democratization" and promoting "less exclusive" forms of luxury has contributed to enlarging the market. However, the extreme luxury market is one that maintains "maximum exclusiveness" and caters for a small segment of the market that likes to possess status symbols that associate with personal and social identity. In this sector, the internationalization model that characterizes certain factors as liabilities may end up as assets for the firm.

Based on a case study of an Italian extreme luxury firm, Guercini and Milanesi (2017) show that the firm developed a collection of shirts, shoes, casual wear, and ties in the luxury market segment for the most affluent upper class. Average prices range from US$550 for ties to over US$170,000 for leather or fur coats. The firm's business model can be summarized as follows:

a. Home country production: The firm has a full range of entirely handmade products with valuable raw materials all located in Italy. Products also prominently display "made in Italy" labels on the product.
b. High average prices: Products are positioned (in terms of price and other attributes) to distinguish them from other accessible luxury items. It is based on the premise that the higher the price, the more attractive the product for the extreme luxury consumer.
c. Control of distribution and sales: The firm sells in multi-brand exclusive locations, firm-owned flagships and department stores. They have some licensed stores in Russia, Turkey, and other locations but the firm exercises tight controls on store designs, labels, and other matters.
d. Marketing communication: Marketing communication is done through fashion shows, events, art catalogs, and advertisements in specialized journals such as sailing or golf magazines.

The international model underscores the liability of foreignness arising from distances and differences but this business model shows that foreignness (with production of the item in Italy, a country highly regarded in the industry) is an asset rather than a liability.

Questions

1. What are the defining characteristics of the extreme luxury fashion business model?
2. What is the relationship between the extreme luxury business model and firm internationalization?

Global competition is motivating firms to seek innovative ways of entering new markets. Export managers have to decide which marketing functions are to be delegated to other intermediaries or partners and which are to be performed internally.

Selecting and managing the right distribution systems is the key to successful internationalization. They provide a competitive advantage in global markets by helping to identify market opportunities. Channels are difficult to change and thus require careful planning.

Williamson (1991) argues that contracting is determined by the governance mechanism that seeks to minimize transaction costs. He states that "assets specificity, uncertainty and frequency" determine the efficient transaction governance form. Specific assets are involved in investments made in market research, branding, product design, and human assets. "Uncertainty" refers to changes in market forces stemming from individuals' limited information or opportunistic motives of other actors. "Frequency" concerns the frequency and volume of transactions. Studies indicate that asset specificity, uncertainty, and frequency of transactions are associated with direct forms of market entry (vertical integration). There is an incentive to integrate distribution channels to minimize transaction costs (McNaughton, 1996; Tesfom, Lutz, and Ghauri, 2004). In many developing countries, direct entry may be needed, in spite of their limited market size, due to the problem of asset specificity, and a lack of contract-enforcing institutions. Ogunrin and Inegbenebar (2015) examining the distribution channels used by Nigerian apparel producers show that the small percentage of apparel that is exported is carried out through ethnic-commercial networks involving overseas-based family and friends. An insignificant number of producers supply overseas buyers through formal channels, filling orders placed by these buyers.

Export firms can be involved in two principal channels of distribution when marketing abroad: indirect and direct channels.

INDIRECT CHANNELS

With indirect channels, the firm exports through an independent local intermediary that assumes responsibility for moving the product overseas. Indirect exporting entails reliance on another firm to act as a sales intermediary and to assume responsibility for marketing and shipping the product overseas. The manufacturer incurs no start-up cost, and this method provides small firms with little experience in foreign trade access to overseas markets without their direct involvement. However, using indirect channels has certain disadvantages: 1) the manufacturer loses control over the marketing of its product overseas, and 2) the manufacturer's success totally depends on the initiative and efforts of the chosen intermediary. The latter could provide low priority to, or even discontinue marketing the firm's products when a competitor's product provides a better sales or profit potential (Figure 5.1).

DIRECT CHANNELS

With direct channels, the firm sells directly to foreign distributors, retailers, or trading companies. Direct sales can also be made through agents located in a foreign country. Direct exporting can be expensive and time consuming. However, it offers manufacturers opportunities to learn about their markets and customers in order to forge better relationships with their trading partners. It also allows firms greater control over various activities. He, Brouthers, and Filatotchev (2013), using a database of Chinese exporters, find that firms with strong market orientation capabilities use hierarchical export channels. This is because such firms want to control these

FIGURE 5.1 Direct and Indirect Channels

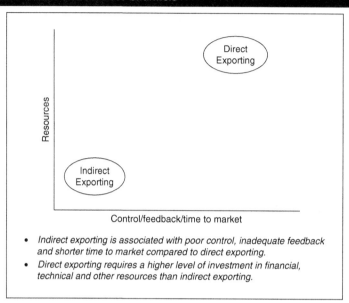

- *Indirect exporting is associated with poor control, inadequate feedback and shorter time to market compared to direct exporting.*
- *Direct exporting requires a higher level of investment in financial, technical and other resources than indirect exporting.*

capabilities to obtain reliable information about potential competitors, customers, and other parties.

The choice of a foreign distribution channel represents long-term commitment and, once selected, is often difficult to change if it is found to be inappropriate. This is partly attributed to laws in various countries that make it difficult and often costly to terminate existing arrangements with local partners. Distribution choices also have long-term implications for the firm's ability to exploit the given market.

The choice of a given channel has to be evaluated in terms of the benefits and costs of using various alternatives. For example, using the manufacturer's internal sales force to market products overseas may lead to higher levels of sales and degree of control but it will be expensive and may not provide the flexibility and immediate contact with the market that is needed to increase sales. Thus, such decisions have to be considered not only in terms of economic returns but also in terms of control and adaptive implications.

The decision to market products directly or use the services of an intermediary is based on the following important factors.

INTERNATIONAL MARKETING OBJECTIVES OF THE FIRM

The marketing objectives of the firm with respect to sales, market share, profitability, and level of financial commitment will often determine channel choice. Direct exporting is likely to provide opportunities for high profit margins even though it requires a high degree of financial commitment. A firm may want to limit or restrict its investment in one country to less than US$3 million or operate in markets that generate more than US$10 million a year. In some cases, the goal may be to gain a

TABLE 5.1 Pricing under domestic sales and indirect exporting

	Price/cost		Price/cost
Price to domestic distributor	*1000*	*Price to indirect exporter*	*800*
(Manufacturer's price to distributor)		*(20% discount)*	
Direct costs (material/labor)	*-400*	*Direct costs (material/labor)*	*-400*
Manufacturing overhead (15% direct costs)	*-60*	*Manufacturing overhead*	*-60*
Total manufacturing cost	*-460*	*Total manufacturing cost*	*-460*
Manufacturing gross profit	*540*	*Manufacturing gross profit*	*340*
Corporate overhead (20% direct costs)	*-80*	*Corporate overhead (20% direct costs)*	*-80*
Net profit	*460*	*Net profit*	*260*

*Profits under indirect exporting may be higher if manufacturing and corporate overheads are taken out.
Such expenses are borne by the indirect exporter. Indirect exporters also require a deeper discount.

certain market share that can only be achieved in countries with a particular competitive profile. A firm may also prefer to operate in markets with a stable political and economic environment. Each of these objectives has implications for channel choices (Figure 5.1 and Table 5.1).

Manufacturer's Resources and Experience

The resource aspects of distribution alternatives could be considered in several ways. First, firms with strong financial resources are likely to establish channels that they either own or control (direct channels). In some cases, indirect channels may require significant investment in terms of loans and subsidies in cases of competitive adversity such as poor exchange rates, demand for frequent deliveries, stocking costs, or training costs for post-sales service. Secondly, even though direct channels may result in high profit margins, it is important to realize that the additional sales generated by intermediaries may, in the long run, more than compensate for the difference. Thirdly, when intermediaries hold and pay for stock or undertake cooperative advertising (splitting the costs of promotion), they ease cash flow problems for the exporter (manufacturer).

A direct channel structure may be neither feasible nor desirable in light of the firm's limited resources and/or commitment. Small to medium-sized firms appear to use indirect channels due to their limited resources and small export volumes, whereas large firms use similar channels because of trade barriers in the host country that may restrict or prohibit direct forms of ownership. Firms in the early phases of their internationalization efforts tend to use independent intermediaries compared to those with greater experience (Anderson and Coughlin, 1987; Kim, Nugent, and Yhee, 1997).

Nature and Availability of Intermediary

Every country has certain distribution patterns that have evolved over the years and are complemented by supportive institutions. Firms that have used specific types of distribution channel in certain countries may find it difficult to use similar channels in other countries. This occurs in cases in which distributors have exclusive arrangements with other suppliers or competitors or when such channels do not exist. Timex, for example, had difficulty persuading jewelers to stock its watches during the early stages of its development and opted to use a different channel (supermarkets).

Customer Characteristics

Customer characteristics in term of age, gender, or education (demographics), interests, attitudes, and values (psychographics) are important in making channel design decisions. These factors along with questions relating to when, how, or why customers buy the product help the firm make appropriate channel choices that lead to a firm's relative positional advantage. Appropriate evaluation of customer needs may result in the introduction of two types of channel to serve different market needs.

If the number of consumers is large and concentrated in major population centers, the company may opt for direct or multiple channels of distribution. In Japan, for example, over half of the population lives in the Tokyo–Nagoya–Osaka market area (Cateora, Gilly, and Graham, 2010). Another factor is that customers may also have developed a habit of buying from a particular channel and so are reluctant to change in the short term.

Direct exporting is often preferable if customers are geographically homogeneous, have similar buying habits, and are limited in number, which allows for direct customer contact and greater control (Seifert and Ford, 1989).

Product Characteristics

The choice of channel structure is primarily dictated by market considerations. However, in certain situations, the nature of the product determines channel choice. Industrial equipment of considerable size and value that requires more after-sales service is usually exported to the user or through the use of other direct channels. Direct channels are also frequently used for products of a perishable nature or high unit value (since it will bring more profit) or for products that are custom-made or highly differentiated. Smaller equipment, industrial supplies, and consumer goods, on the other hand, tend to have longer channels. In Canada, for example, consumer goods are purchased by importing wholesalers, department stores, mail-order houses, chain stores, and single-line retailers.

Marketing Environment

Examination of the marketing environment requires a focus on the country's distribution culture as well as the characteristics of the market. Most countries have a distribution system that has evolved over years and that has established linkages and structures between channel members for specific products. In Japan, for example, there are links between producers, importers, distributors, and retailers based on ownership or other contractual relations. In Southern Europe, family ties are prominent in certain channels. The characteristics of the market have implications for channel choice. This includes but is not limited to the size of the market, levels of disposable income, potential market growth, and purchasing habits.

The use of direct channels is more likely in countries that are more similar in culture to the exporter's home country. For example, U.S. sales to Canada are characterized by short (direct) marketing channels compared to the indirect channels used in Japan and Southeast Asia. In certain cases, firms have limited options in the selection of appropriate channels for their products. In the lumber industry, the use of export intermediaries is the norm in many countries. In Finland, over 90 percent of distribution of nondurable consumer goods is handled by four wholesale chains. Exporters have to use these distribution channels to gain a significant penetration of the market (Czinkota, Ronkainen, and Moffett, 2008). Legislation in certain countries requires that foreign firms be represented by local firms that are wholly owned by nationals of the country. Exporters must market their goods indirectly by appointing a local agent or distributor. In Vietnam, for example, foreign firms that seek to open additional retail stores (beyond the first store) are subject to an economic needs test (impact assessment, contribution to socioeconomic development). Small and medium-sized stores are exempt. Similarly, Indonesia caps foreign ownership of distribution outlets to 67 percent. Large and well-established firms can easily find intermediaries because of their size and reputation.

Some studies support the use of direct/integrated channels when there is a high degree of environmental uncertainty. The establishment of integrated channels is intended to place the firm closer to the market so as to react and adapt to unforeseen circumstances (Klein, Frazier, and Roth, 1990).

Control

A direct or integrated channel affords the manufacturer more control over its distribution and its link to the end user. However, it is not a practical option for firms that do not have adequate foreign market knowledge or the necessary financial, operational, and strategic capabilities.

Firms that use indirect channels are still able to exercise control mechanisms to coordinate and influence foreign intermediary actions. Two types of control are available for the manufacturer/exporter: *process controls* and *output controls*. Under process controls, the manufacturer's intervention is intended to influence the means intermediaries use to achieve desirable ends (selling technique, servicing procedure, promotion, etc.). Output controls are used to influence indirectly the ends achieved by the distributor. The latter includes monitoring sales volume, profits, and other performance-based indicators (Bello and Gilliland, 1997). It is important to note the following salient points with respect to manufacturers' coordination and control of independent foreign intermediaries:

- Manufacturers must rely on both unilateral and bilateral (collaboration) control mechanisms in order to organize and manage their export relationships with independent foreign intermediaries.
- The use of output controls tends to have a positive impact on foreign intermediaries' overall performance. Process controls, however, do not appear to

account for performance benefits, largely due to manufacturers' inadequate knowledge of foreign marketing procedures.

- Firms that export highly technical and sophisticated products tend to exercise high levels of control (process and output controls) over foreign intermediaries in order to protect their proprietary rights (trade secrets/know-how) and address unique customer needs.

Coverage

An important measure of distribution coverage is the level of product availability. Such decisions are of most concern to firms producing consumer goods. How a company distributes its goods in order to reach a target market has implications for brand image, sales, and expenses.

There are three different levels of distribution coverage: Intensive (mass) coverage, exclusive coverage, and selective coverage. An intensive coverage strategy aims at selling products using multiple sales and distribution channels to reach the target market. They are commonly used for low-priced items that appeal to a large market (soft drinks, candy). Such a mass coverage strategy to distribute goods in most locations can increase costs but can be offset with high sales volume. Exclusive coverage strategy is often used for high-end products (high quality, expensive) with a relatively narrow customer base and that require a high level of customer service. They are sold through an exclusive group of retailers that agree to abide by certain contractual terms including placement (display of product) and price. Apple uses this strategy to sell its products. In some cases, this strategy is also used to sell products in exclusive locations such as company-owned stores. Selective coverage strategy appeals to smaller markets with fewer locations that provide greater sales opportunities. For example, certain products such as men's wristwatches are sold in about 40 percent of available outlets and yet account for about 80 percent of sales.

In terms of coverage, firms that use longer channels tend to use different intermediaries (intensive coverage). However, recent studies show a positive relationship between channel directness and intensive coverage. This means that firms employing direct methods to reach their overseas customers tend to use a large number of different types of channel intermediary.

TYPES OF INTERMEDIARY

One of the distinguishing features of direct and indirect channel alternatives is the location of the second channel. If the second channel is located in the producer's country, it is considered an indirect channel, whereas if it is located in the buyer's country, it is assumed to be a direct channel. This means that agents, distributors, or other middlemen could be in either category, depending on whether they are located in the buyer's or seller's country.

Channel alternatives are also defined on the basis of ownership of the distribution channel: a direct channel is one owned and managed by the company, as opposed to one in which distribution is handled by outside agents and middlemen. A firm's channel structure is also defined in terms of the percentage of equity held in the distribution organization: majority ownership (greater than 50 percent) is treated as a direct or integrated channel, while less than majority ownership is considered an indirect channel. The first definition of channel alternatives is used in this chapter.

Indirect Channels

Several intermediaries are associated with indirect channels and each type offers distinct advantages. Indirect channels are classified here on the basis of their functions.

Exporters that Sell on Behalf of the Manufacturer

Manufacturer's Export Agents (MEAs)

Manufacturer's export agents usually represent various manufacturers of related and noncompeting products. They may also operate on an exclusive basis. It is an ideal channel to use especially in cases involving a widespread or thin overseas market. They are also used when the product is new and demand conditions are uncertain. Examples of export agencies are numerous. Moriizo Shuzo, a major Japanese distillery of spirits recently appointed Jalux, Inc. (a Japanese company that sells aviation-related products and operates airport stores) as its sole export agent to sell its famous distilled spirits overseas. Najing Pharmaceutical Co. of China, which manufactures and distributes medicines in China and overseas markets, also provides export agency services for several domestic firms.

The usual roles of the MEA are as follows:

- Handle direct marketing, promotion, shipping, and sometimes financing of merchandise. The agent does not offer all services.
- Take possession but not title to the goods. The MEA works for commission; risk of loss remains with the manufacturer.
- Represent the manufacturer on a continuous or permanent basis as defined in the contract.

Export Management Companies (EMCs)

Export management companies act as the export department for one or several manufacturers of noncompetitive products. Over 2,000 EMCs in the United States provide manufacturers with extensive services that include, but are not limited to, market analyses, documentation, financial and legal services, purchase for resale, and agency services (locating and arranging sales). An EMC often does extensive research on foreign markets, conducts its own advertising and promotion, serves as a shipping/forwarding agent, and provides legal advice on intellectual property matters. It also collects and forwards credit information on overseas customers.

Most EMCs are small and usually specialize by product, foreign market, or both. Some are capable of performing only limited functions such as strategic planning or promotion. Export management companies solicit and carry on business in their own name or in the name of the manufacturer for a commission, salary, or retainer plus commission. Occasionally, they purchase products by direct payment or financing for resale to their own customers. Export management companies may operate as agents or distributors. Alliance Experts BV of the Netherlands is one example of an EMC that acts as an export department of various non-competing manufacturers and suppliers in over thirty countries. It selects the right country for the product by conducting international market research, engages suitable distributors or online channels, and manages the distribution channels as a local representative or resident director of a subsidiary. Similarly, ECI Global, a U.S. firm, provides a full range of services to assist U.S. manufacturers increase their exports. They provide turn-key export assistance (export compliance, export financing), freight forwarding and shipping, marketing, as well as logistics services (selecting qualified buyers, preparing quotes, invoices, insurance, letters of credit and customs documentation).

The following are some of the disadvantages of using EMCs:

- Manufacturers may lose control over foreign sales. To retain sufficient control, manufacturers should ask for regular reports on marketing efforts, promotion, sales, and so forth. This right to review marketing plans and efforts should be included in the agreement.
- Export management companies that work on commission may lose interest if sales do not come immediately. They may be less interested in new or unknown products and may not provide sufficient attention to small clients.
- Exporters may not learn international business since EMCs do most of the work related to exports.

Despite these disadvantages, EMCs have marketing and distribution contacts overseas and provide the benefit of economies of scale. Export management companies obtain low freight rates by consolidating shipments of several principals. By providing a range of services, they also help manufacturers to concentrate on other areas.

International Trading Companies (ITCs)

Trading companies are the most traditional and dominant intermediary in many countries. In Japan, they date back to the nineteenth century and in Western countries, their origins can be traced back to colonial times. They are also prevalent in many less developed countries. They are demand driven; that is, they identify the needs of overseas customers and often act as independent distributors linking buyers and sellers to arrange transactions. They buy and sell goods as merchants taking title to the merchandise. Some work on a commission. They may also handle goods on consignment.

In the United States, an ETC is a legally defined entity under the Export Trading Company Act, 1982. It is difficult to set up an ETC unless certain special certifications and requirements are met: The U.S. Export Trading Act (ETCA) allows bank participation in trading companies, thus facilitating better access to capital and more trading transactions. Antitrust provisions were also relaxed to allow firms to form joint ventures and share the cost of developing foreign markets. Joint venture partners can do market research and development, overseas bidding, transportation, and shipping. Since 2000, The U.S. Department of Commerce has certified about seventy-three associations or ventures. Trade associations often apply for certification for their members. To be effective, ETCs must find a balance between the demands of the markets and the supply of the members (trade associations; see International Perspective 5.1). Florida Citrus Growers (FCG) of Vero Beach, Florida was certified in 1995 as a joint venture of nine members that includes packing houses and grower-owned cooperatives. The certificate allows them to share transportation and market development costs, engage in joint promotional activities, negotiate with one voice with overseas buyers, and prepare joint bids without fear of antitrust actions by the government.

Trading companies offer services to manufacturers similar to those provided by EMCs. However, there are some differences between the two channels:

- Trading companies offer more services and have more diverse product lines than export management companies. Trading companies are also larger and better financed than EMCs.
- Trading companies are not exclusively restricted to export–import activities. Some are also engaged in production, resource development, and commercial banking. Korean trading companies, such as Daewoo and Hyundai, for example, are heavily involved in manufacturing. Some trading companies, such as Mitsubishi (Japan) and Cobec (Brazil) are affiliated with banks and engaged in extending traditional banking into commercial fields (Meloan and Graham, 1995).

The disadvantages of ITCs are similar to the ones mentioned for EMCs.

INTERNATIONAL PERSPECTIVE 5.1

International Trading Companies in Global Markets

Trading companies have been the most traditional channels for international commercial activity. Trading companies supported by governments, such as the English East India Company (1600), the Dutch East India Company (1602), and the French Compagnie des Indes Orientales (1664), enjoyed not only exclusive trading rights but also military protection in exchange for tax payments. Today, trading companies also perform the important function of exporting, importing, investing, and counter trading. In Japan, for example, the Sogo Shosha, which includes the top nine trading companies such as Mitsubishi and Mitsui conducts about two-thirds of the country's imports and a half of its exports. In Korea, trading companies similar in scope to the Sogo Shosha (Daewoo, Hyundai, Samsung) are responsible for a substantial part of the country's exports and imports. In addition to trade, trading companies in these countries are involved in mega projects, participate in joint ventures, and act as financial deal makers. The success of these conglomerates is due to: 1) extensive market information that allows for product or area diversification, 2) economies of scale that allow them to obtain preferential freight rates, etc., and 3) preferential access to capital markets that makes it easy to undertake large or risky transactions.

In view of the success of these trading companies, Brazil, Turkey, and the United States have enacted domestic legislation that allows the establishment of trading companies. The Brazilian Decree (No. 1298) of 1972, for example, sets up conditions for the registration of new enterprises with the government and allows local producers to export by selling to a trading company without losing their export incentives. In the United States, the Export Trading Company Act of 1982 allows businesses to join together to export goods and services or to assist unrelated companies to export their products without fear of violating antitrust legislation. Bank participation in trading companies was permitted to enable better access to capital. The legality of any action can be ascertained by precertification of planned activities with the U.S. Department of Commerce.

Exporters that Buy for Their Overseas Customers

Export commission agents (ECAs) represent foreign buyers such as import firms and large industrial users and seek to obtain products that match the buyer's preferences and requirements. They reside and conduct business in the exporter's country and are paid a commission by their foreign clients. In certain cases, ECAs may be foreign government agencies or quasi-government firms empowered to locate and purchase desired goods. They could operate from a permanent office location in supplier countries or undertake foreign government purchasing missions when the need arises. In some countries, the exporter may receive payment from a confirming house when the goods are shipped. The confirming house may also carry out some functions performed by the commission agent or resident buyer (making arrangements for the shipper and so on). For the exporter, this is an easy way to access a foreign market. There is little credit risk and the exporter has only to fill the order.

Another variation of the ECA is the resident buyer. The major factor that distinguishes the resident buyer from other ECAs is that in the case of the former, a long-term relationship is established in which the resident buyer not only undertakes the purchasing function for the overseas principal at the best possible price, but also ensures timely delivery of merchandise and facilitates principals' visits to suppliers and vendors. This allows foreign buyers to maintain a close and continuous contact with overseas sources of supply. One disadvantage of using such channels is that the exporter has little control over the marketing of products (Onkvisit and Shaw, 2008).

Exporters that Buy and Sell for Their Own Accounts

Export Merchants

Export merchants purchase products directly from manufacturers, pack and mark them according to their own specifications, and resell them to their overseas customers. They take title to the goods and sell under their own names, and, hence, assume all risks associated with ownership. Export merchants generally handle undifferentiated products or products for which brands are not important. In view of their vast organizational networks, they are a powerful commercial entity dominating trade in certain countries.

When export merchants, after receiving an order, place an order with the manufacturer to deliver the goods directly to the overseas customer, they are called export drop shippers. In this case, the manufacturer is paid by the drop shipper, who in turn, is paid by the overseas buyer. Such intermediaries are commonly used to export bulky (high-freight), low-unit value products such as construction materials, coal, lumber, and so forth.

Another variation of export merchant is the export distributor (located in the exporter's country). Export distributors have exclusive rights to sell manufacturers' products in overseas markets. They represent several manufacturers and act as EMCs.

The disadvantage of export merchants as export intermediaries relates to a lack of control over marketing, promotion, or pricing.

Cooperative Exporters (CEs)

These are manufacturers or service firms that sell the products of other companies in foreign markets along with their own (Ball et al., 2013). This generally occurs when a company has a contract with an overseas buyer to provide a wide range of products or services. Often, the company may not have all the products required under the contract and turns to other companies to provide the remaining products. The company (providing the remaining products) could sell its products without incurring export marketing or distribution costs. This helps small manufacturers that lack the ability or resources to export. This channel is often used to export products that are complementary to that of the exporting firm. A good example of this is the case of a heavy equipment manufacturer that wants to fill the demand of its overseas customers for water drilling equipment. The heavy equipment company exports the drilling equipment along with its product to its customers (Sletten, 1994). Companies engage in cooperative exporting in order to broaden the product lines they offer to foreign markets or to bolster decreasing export sales. In the 1980s, for example, the French chemical company Rhone-Poutenc sold products of several manufacturers through its extensive global sales network.

Export Cartels

These are organizations of firms in the same industry for the sole purpose of marketing their products overseas. They include the Webb–Pomerene Associations (WPAs) in the United States, as well as certain export cartels in Japan. The WPAs are exempted from antitrust laws under the U.S. Export Trade Act of 1918 and permitted to set prices, allocate orders, sell products, negotiate and consolidate freight, as well as arrange shipment. There are WPAs in various areas such as pulp, movies, sulphur, and so on. Webb–Pomerene Associations are not permitted for services and the arrangement is not suitable for differentiated products because a common association label often replaces individual product brands. In addition to member firms' loss of individual identity, WPAs are vulnerable to a lack of group cohesion, similar to other cartels, which undermines their effectiveness. Under the Export Trade Act, the only requirement to operate as a WPA is that the association must file with the Federal Trade Commission within thirty days after formation (see International Perspective 5.2).

INTERNATIONAL PERSPECTIVE 5.2

Indirect Channel Structures

Advantages

- Little or no investment or marketing experience needed. Suitable for firms with limited resources or experience.
- Helps increase overall sales and cash flow.
- Good way to test-market products, develop goodwill, and allow clients to be familiar with firm's trade name or trademark before making substantial commitment.

Disadvantages

- Firm's profit margin may be diminished due to commissions and other payments to foreign intermediaries.
- Limited contact with and feedback from end users.
- Loss of control over marketing and pricing. Firm totally dependent on the marketing initiative and effort of foreign intermediary. Product may be priced too high or too low.
- Foreign intermediary may not provide product support or may damage market potential.
- Limited opportunity to learn international business know-how and develop marketing contacts. Creates difficulty in taking over the business after the relationship has ended.

Direct Channels

A company could use different avenues to sell its product overseas, employing the direct channel structure. Direct exporting provides more control over the export process, potentially higher profits, and a closer relationship to the overseas buyer and the marketplace (Table 5.1). However, the firm needs to devote more time, personnel, and other corporate resources than are needed in the case of indirect exporting.

Direct Marketing From the Home Country

A firm may sell directly to a foreign retailer or end user, and this is often accomplished through catalog sales or traveling sales representatives who are domestic employees of the exporting firm. Such marketing channels are a viable alternative for many companies that sell books, magazines, housewares, cosmetics, travel, and financial services. Foreign end users include foreign governments and institutions, such as banks, schools, hospitals, or businesses. Buyers can be identified at trade shows, through international publications, and so on. If products are specifically designed for each customer, company representatives are more effective than agents or distributors. The growing use of the Internet is also likely to dramatically increase the sale of product and/or services directly to the retailer or end user. For example, Amazon.com has become one of the biggest bookstores in the United States with over 2.5 million titles. Its books are sold through the Internet. Direct sales can also be undertaken through foreign sales branches or subsidiaries. A foreign sales branch handles all aspects of the sales distribution and promotion, displays manufacturers' product lines and provides services. The foreign sales subsidiary, although similar to the branch, has broader responsibilities. All foreign orders are channeled through the subsidiary, which subsequently sells to foreign buyers. Sales subsidiaries are often used for lucrative markets with growth potential or products with a high intellectual property content as well as those that require sophisticated training and after-sales service. This approach may raise issues of transfer pricing.

Direct marketing is also used when the manufacturer or retailer desires to increase its revenues and profits while providing its products or services at a lower cost. The firm could also provide better product support services and further enhance its image and reputation.

A major problem with direct sales to consumers results from duty and clearance problems. A country's import regulations may prohibit or limit the direct purchase of merchandise from overseas. Thus it is important to evaluate a country's trade regulations before orders are processed and effected.

Marketing Through Overseas Agents and Distributors

Overseas Agents

Overseas agents are independent sales representatives of various noncompeting suppliers. They are residents of the country or region where the product is sold and usually work on a commission basis, pay their own expenses, and assume no financial risk or responsibility. Agents rarely take delivery of and never take title to goods and are authorized to solicit purchases within their marketing territory and to advise firms on orders placed by prospective purchasers. The prices to be charged are agreed upon between the exporters and the overseas customers. Overseas agents usually do not provide product support services to customers. Agency agreements must be drafted carefully so as to clearly indicate that agents are not employees of the exporting companies because of potential legal and financial implications, such as payment of benefits upon termination. In some countries, agents are required to register with the government as commercial agents.

Overseas agents are used when firms intend to 1) sell products to small markets that do not attract distributor interest, 2) market to distinct individual customers (custom-made for individuals or projects), 3) sell heavy equipment, machinery, or other big-ticket items that cannot be easily stocked, or 4) solicit public or private bids. Firms deal directly with the customers (after agents inform the firms of the orders) with respect to price, delivery, sales service, and warranty bonds. Given their limited role, agents are not required to have extensive training or to make a substantial financial commitment. They are valuable for their personal contacts and intelligence and help reach markets that would otherwise be inaccessible. The major disadvantages of using agents are: 1) legal and financial problems in the event of termination (local laws in many countries discriminate against alien firms (principals) in their contractual relationships with local agents), 2) firms assume the attendant risks and responsibilities, ranging from pricing and delivery to sales services including collections, and 3) agents have limited training and knowledge about the product and this may adversely impact product sales.

Overseas Distributors

These are independent merchants that import products for resale and are compensated by the markup they charge their customers. Overseas distributors take delivery of and title to the goods and have contractual arrangements with the exporters as well as the customers. No contractual relationships exist between the exporters and the customers and the distributors may not legally obligate exporters to third parties. Distributors may be given exclusive representation for a certain territory, often in return for agreeing not to handle competing merchandise. Certain countries require the registration and approval of distributors (and agents) as well as the representation agreement.

Distributors, unlike agents, take possession of goods and also provide the necessary pre- and post-sales services. They carry inventory and spare parts and maintain adequate facilities and personnel for normal service operations. They are responsible for advertising and promotion. Some of the disadvantages of using distributors are: 1) loss of control over marketing and pricing (they may price the product too high or too low), 2) limited access to or feedback from customers, 3) limited opportunities to learn international business know-how and about developments in foreign markets, and 4) dealer protection legislation in many countries that may make it difficult and expensive to terminate relationships with distributors (International Perspectives 5.3 and 5.4).

SELECTING THE RIGHT CHANNEL

No single distribution channel may be appropriate for a product in all markets. The choice is often based on a market-by-market analysis. Here are some relevant points to consider:

- A firm may use a direct channel for its lucrative markets, or markets where it has some internal strength and experience. It will use indirect channels for unfamiliar, small, or risky markets.
- A firm may use both channels if it has different product lines with different customer profiles. It can use direct channels for the product in which it has a good network of resources and customers and use indirect channels such as cooperative exporting for other product lines where certain advantages do not exist.
- Indirect channel options should not be ignored just because the firm has long-term plans to go direct. Early indirect entry could facilitate the product's success (when it eventually goes direct) if a good product image and customer support has been created by the indirect partner.

INTERNATIONAL PERSPECTIVE 5.3

The Japanese Distribution System

Distribution channels in Japan are very different from our own; they are as inefficient as they are complex. The system is characterized by multiple layers of wholesalers who have developed close, personal relationships with other wholesalers, manufacturers, importers, and retailers. Moreover, these intimate relationships often serve as an informal barrier to U.S. companies wishing to sell directly to end users or retailers.

Many American exporters find retailers and end users unwilling to disrupt their long-standing, personal relationships with Japanese suppliers even when the U.S. company can offer a product of superior or equal quality at a cheaper price. Many Japanese retailers and end users are unwilling to make the switch to an "unreliable" foreign supplier. They fear a lack of commitment on the part of the foreign supplier will lead to problems. This system, although inefficient, does offer some important advantages for the participants. First, these close business relationships make it far easier for retailers and distributors to suggest product modifications and improvements. Second, this system encourages the sharing of information on product trends, innovations, competition, and overall market opportunities. Third, it contributes to a more cooperative business relationship.

The number of retail outlets in Japan is nearly the same as in the United States, despite the fact that the population of Japan is roughly half that of the United States and Japan is slightly smaller in geographical size than California. Distribution channels vary considerably from industry to industry and product to product, with particular differences between consumer and industrial goods. A foreign firm must understand existing distribution channels in order to utilize them or develop an innovative approach.

LOCATING, CONTACTING, AND EVALUATING AGENTS AND DISTRIBUTORS

Once the firm has identified markets in which to use agents and distributors, it could locate these intermediaries by using various sources: government trade offices (The Department of Commerce in the United States), chambers of commerce, trade shows, international banks and other firms, trade and professional associations, and advertisements in foreign trade publications. After identifying potential agents and distributors in each desired market, the firm should write directly to each, indicating its interest in appointing a representative and including a brochure describing the firm's history, resources, product line, personnel, and other pertinent information (Table 5.2).

The evaluation and selection of potential representatives (agents or distributors) are often based on some of the following factors: local reputation and overall background, experience with a similar product or industry and adequate knowledge of the market, commitment not to represent competing brands, genuine interest, and ability to devote sufficient time and effort to the product line. In the case of distributors, it is also important to evaluate sales organization; financial, marketing, and promotion capability; installation and after-sales service; timely payments and similar characteristics. Once the firm has selected an agent or distributor based on the aforementioned criteria, the next step will be to negotiate a formal agreement. Foreign representatives are interested in firms that are committed to the market and willing to provide the necessary product support and training. They also want to protect their territory from sales by third parties or the firm itself.

CONTRACTS WITH FOREIGN AGENTS AND DISTRIBUTORS (REPRESENTATIVES)

It is estimated that about 50 percent of global trade is handled through overseas agents and distributors. Laws governing agents and distributors are complex and

TABLE 5.2 Sourcing and Evaluating Overseas Agents and Distributors (OADs)

Sources for locating OADs	Networking with industry groups and associations
	International Partner Search services of the U.S. Department of Commerce (USDOC)
	Customized Market Analysis Report (CMA) of USDOC
	Catalogs (displayed at trade shows) and trade missions organized by USDOC or state agencies
	Chambers of Commerce
	State offices in foreign countries
	Existing list of OADs
	Internet sources: dandb.com; kompass.com; usgtn.net; exportzone.com.
Evaluating and selecting OAD	***Background and experience***
(Evaluation criteria)	Years in business, sales volume, management structure, expertise, financial strength (ownership, debts, bank references), reputation, profile of customers, product line, territory, industry focus, or specialization
	Knowledge of market and ability
	Experience of particular market, contacts with the media
	Logistics capability
	Warehouse capability, shipping expertise, customer support
	Infrastructure
	Computer and other systems, resources to launch product, pricing ability, technical ability
	Motivation/attitude
	professionalism, attitude, long-term plans

vary from country to country. In certain countries, protective legislation favors local representatives with respect to such matters as market exclusivity, and duration or termination of contracts. In the event of termination without good cause, a Belgian distributor, for example, is entitled to an indemnity.

Similar laws exist in France, Germany, and other countries. In Germany, maximum compensation payable to agents usually equals one year's gross commissions based on an average over the previous five years or the period of existence of the agency, whichever is shorter. In countries such as Egypt, Indonesia, Japan, and South Korea, representation agreements must be formally registered with, and their contents must be approved by, the appropriate authority. In many Latin American countries, local law governs service contracts if the services are to be performed in local jurisdictions and any representative agreement that is not in conformity with local law will be invalid and unenforceable. Thus, it is important that in the negotiation and drafting of such agreements, sufficient attention is given to the impact of local laws and other pertinent issues.

INTERNATIONAL PERSPECTIVE 5.4

Parallel Versus Multiple Exporters

Parallel (gray) market goods are products that enter a country outside regular, authorized distribution channels. They differ from black market products since they often enter the market legally. Factors contributing to the rise of parallel exports include:

- Substantial differences in the prevailing prices of the same product between two national markets.
- Differences in marketing and administrative expenses between the authorized distributor and the parallel distributor.
- Sales of distressed merchandise at deep discount to overseas markets sometimes gives rise to re-exports to the home market.
- Price discounts to distributors in the home market but not to nearby foreign markets.
- The authorized foreign distributor may have restrictive credit terms or be unable (or unwilling) to carry sufficient inventory to service the market.

There is a flourishing market in parallel market goods in the United States in cars, watches, etc., estimated at over US$6 billion. The major problems created by parallel export channels is a) a reduction in sales and profits for the authorized distributor, b) disruption in manufacturer–distribution relations, and c) difficulty in maintaining a consistent image, quality, and reputation of a product.

Companies recognizing these problems should develop appropriate corporate policies such as creating product differentiation between the domestic and exported product and flexibility in the export price of the product sold to the foreign distributor.

Multiple channels are used by many firms in order to gain long-term sustainable advantages in global markets. A firm could supplement agents with their own salespeople to prevent lock-in and establish a credible alternative. A few strategic markets can be identified and developed by integration, while other markets are served by third parties, thus spreading the risk. Such channels are common in sectors where transaction costs and uncertainty are high (knowledge-intensive sectors like software development).

MAJOR CLAUSES IN REPRESENTATION AGREEMENTS

Definition of Territory

The contract should define the geographical scope of the territory to be represented by the agent or distributor and whether the representative has sole marketing rights. In exclusive contracts, the agreement has to clearly specify whether the firm reserves the right to sell certain product lines to a specific class of buyers such as governments or quasi-government agencies. If agreements do not explicitly state that they are exclusive, they will often be deemed exclusive if no other representatives have been appointed within a reasonable time. The contract should also state whether the representative could appoint subagents or subdistributors and the latter's status in relation to the firm. It is also important to explicitly state the intention of the parties not to create an employer–employee relationship due to financial and tax implications.

Definition of Product

The contract should identify those products or product lines covered by the agreement as well as the procedures for the addition of successive products. It should also provide for the alteration or deletion of certain product lines based on the exporter's continued production, representative's performance, or other events.

Representative's Rights and Obligations

The agreement should state that the representative will do its best to promote and market the product and cooperate to attain the objectives of the exporting firm. It should also include 1) the representative's commitment to periodically inform the exporter of all pertinent information related to market conditions and its activities; 2) the parties' agreement to provide due protection to each other's confidential information as defined in the contract, which often includes seller's patents, trade secrets and know-how, as well as the representative's marketing information including customer lists; 3) a provision as to whose responsibility it is to arrange for all the necessary approvals, licenses, and other requirements for the entry and sale of goods in the foreign country; and 4) the right of the representative to carry non-competitive and complementary products.

An agency agreement should state the nature and scope of an agent's authority to bind the exporter (which is often denied) as well as the agent's discretion with respect to pricing. All sales of products are to be in accordance with the price list and discount structure as established in the contract. The parties could also agree on mechanisms to implement changes in prices and terms. It is also important to stipulate the amount of compensation (commission) when it accrues to the account of the agent, and the time of payment. Most agreements state that all commissions do not become due and payable until full settlement has been received by the firm. The agent could also be given the responsibility for collection with respect to sales it initiated.

Distributor agreements should state clearly that the overseas distributor acts as a buyer and not as an agent of the seller. The agreement could require the distributor to maintain adequate inventories, facilities, and competent personnel. The exporter could stipulate that orders representing a minimum value or quantity must be placed within a fixed time. The agreement also defines the advertising and promotion responsibilities of the distributor, including an undertaking to advertise in certain magazines or journals a minimum number of times a year at its own expense, for example:

> The distributor agrees during the lifetime of this contract to provide and pay for not less than seven full-page advertisements per year, appearing at regular monthly intervals in the national journals or magazines of the industry circulating generally throughout the territory.

Exporter's Rights and Obligations

In agency contracts, the exporter is often required to provide the agent with its price schedules, catalogs, and brochures describing the company, its product, and other pertinent features. In distributor contracts, the exporter is required to provide the distributor and his/her personnel with training and technical assistance as is reasonably required in order to service, maintain, and repair products. In both agency and distributor agreements, the exporter should only warrant that the product complies with the specified standards of quality and also state the party that will be responsible for warranty service.

The exporter is also required to provide sufficient supplies of the product and new developments in products, as well as marketing and sales plans.

Definition of Price

In agency agreements, all sales of products are made in accordance with the price list and discount structure agreed upon between the parties. However, the seller reserves the right to change prices at any time, usually upon thirty or sixty days prior notice.

Distributor agreements also contain provisions relating to the price to be charged by the seller upon purchase of goods by the distributor. Any discounts available are also stated. In the case of products that are affected by inflation, the parties could set a definite price ruling on a specific date, such as the date of the sales contract or shipment. The parties could also agree that the exporter charge the distributor the best price it provides other customers at the time of sale (the most-favored-customer price) except for those products supplied to a holding company, subsidiary, or other associated companies of the supplier. The distributor agreement should also stipulate the terms of sale such as FOB (free on board) or CIF (cost, insurance, and freight), as well as the method of payment (open account, letter of credit, etc.). For example:

> The prices specified are in U.S. dollars, exclusive of taxes and governmental charges, freight, insurance, and other transportation charges. Payment shall be on consignment. The product will be shipped FOB (Miami) to the buyer's address in Colombia.

Renewal or Termination of Contract

In many countries, issues relating to appointment, renewal, or termination of representatives are largely determined by local law. Many foreign representation agreements provide for a short trial period followed by a longer-term appointment if the representative's performance proves satisfactory. It is important to state the duration of appointment and the basis for renewal or termination. Any renewal or termination requires an act of notification to the representative.

In certain countries, the longer the period the representative has been appointed, the more difficult and expensive it is to terminate the contract. Representative agreements are terminated in cases when one of the parties is guilty of nonperformance or of not performing to the satisfaction of the other party, for example:

> In the event that either party should breach any term or condition of this agreement or fail to perform any of its obligations or undertakings, the

other party may notify the defaulting party of such default, and if such default is not rectified within sixty days, the party giving notice shall have the right, at its election, to terminate the agreement.

The previous clause is often used to terminate nonperforming representatives. It is, however, important to set certain targets and objective performance criteria against which representative's performance will be measured: sales volume, inventory turnover rates, advertising, and market share. It is also advisable to include other causes of termination, such as the following:

Right to Terminate Without Cause: A significant number of contracts allow for termination of the contract by either party with no prerequisite of action or omission by the other party upon giving advance notice, for example:

Either party shall have the right to terminate the agreement at any time by giving not less than 180 days prior written notice of termination to the other party.

Force Majeure: Most contracts state the occurrence of specific events beyond the control of the parties as a basis for termination of the contract. The enumerated actions or events fall into four major categories: 1) acts of God, 2) wars and civil disorder, 3) acts of government such as exchange controls, host government regulations, and 4) other acts beyond the parties' control.

Other Causes of Termination: Some contracts provide for termination of the contract in cases such as bankruptcy or liquidation of either party, assignment of contractual rights or duties, change of ownership or management, nonexclusivity, or the firm's decision to establish its own sales office or assembly operations.

In most countries, the exporter can terminate a representative in accordance with the contractual terms and without payment of indemnity. In situations lacking reasonable grounds for termination, courts impose a liability for unjust termination that is often based on the volume of sales, goodwill developed by the representative, and duration of the contract. A typical formula is to award a one year's profit or commission to the distributor or agent based on an average over the previous five years or the duration of the contract, whichever is shorter. It may also include the cost of termination of the representative's personnel.

Applicable Law and Dispute Settlement

The parties are at liberty to agree between themselves as to what rules should govern their contract. Most contracts state the applicable law to be that of the manufacturer's home state. This indicates the strong bargaining position of exporters and the latter's clear preference to be governed by laws about which they are well informed, including how the contract will function and its repercussions on the whole commercial and legal situation of the parties. In cases with no express or implied choice of law, courts have to decide what law should govern the parties' contract based on the terms and nature of the contract. Many factors are used to settle this issue in the absence of an express choice of law, including the place of contract, the place of performance, the location of the subject matter of the contract, as well as the place of incorporation and place of business of the parties. The contract should also provide for a forum (court) to settle the dispute relating to the validity, interpretation, and performance of the agreement.

Many representative contracts also provide that any dispute between the parties shall be submitted to arbitration for final settlement in accordance with the rules of the International Chamber of Commerce.

MAINTAINING AND MOTIVATING OVERSEAS REPRESENTATIVES

Agents and distributors can be motivated in many ways to do the best possible job of marketing and promoting the firm's product. This could be accomplished by, for example, developing good communications through regular visits from the home office, the organization of conferences, or providing inexpensive free trips for representatives during a given period. It is also important to inform representatives of the company's goals and principles and to keep them abreast of new developments in the product line, supplies, and promotion strategies and to assist in training and market development. Firms could also motivate representatives through the provision of better credit terms or price adjustments based on sales volume or other performance-based criteria.

CHAPTER SUMMARY

Export channels of distribution	Channels of distribution used to market products abroad: 1. *Indirect channels:* Exports through independent parties acting as sales intermediary 2. *Direct channels:* Direct sales to foreign distributors, retailers, or trading companies
Determinants of channel selection to market products abroad	1. International marketing objectives of the firm 2. Manufacturer's resources and experience 3. Availability and capability of intermediary 4. Customer and product characteristics 5. Marketing environment 6. Control and coverage
Indirect channels	Types of indirect channels: 1. *Exporters that sell on behalf of the manufacturer:* Manufacturer's export agents, export management companies, international trading companies 2. *Exporters that buy for their overseas customers:* Export commission agents 3. *Exporters that buy and sell for their own account:* Export merchants, cooperative exporters, Webb–Pomerene Associations
Direct channels	Types of direct channel: 1. Direct marketing from the home country 2. Marketing through overseas agents and distributors
Major clauses in representation agreements	1. Definition of territory and product 2. Representative's rights and obligations 3. Exporter's rights and obligations 4. Definition of price 5. Renewal or termination of contract

REVIEW QUESTIONS

1. Distinguish between direct and indirect channels of distribution. What are the advantages and disadvantages of using indirect channels?
2. Discuss three major determinants of channel selection to market products abroad.
3. Do firms that export high-technology products exercise high levels of control?
4. Discuss the role and function of manufacturer's export agents.
5. Discuss the disadvantages of using export management companies.
6. What are the differences between export trading companies and export management companies?
7. Briefly describe Webb–Pomerene Associations.
8. What are some of the disadvantages of using overseas distributors?
9. State some of the clauses (provisions) in representation agreements.
10. Briefly describe force majeure.

REFERENCES

Anderson, E. and Coughlin, A. (1987). International market entry and expansion via independent or integrated channels of distribution. *Journal of Marketing*, 51(1): 80–85.

Ball, D., Geringer, J., Minor, M., and McNett, J. (2013). *International Business*. New York: McGraw Hill-Irwin.

Bello, D. and Gilliland, D. (1997). The effect of output controls, process controls and flexibility on export channel performance. *Journal of Marketing*, 61: 22–38.

Cateora, P., Gilly, M., and Graham, J. (2010). *International Marketing*. New York: McGraw Hill-Irwin.

Czinkota, M., Ronkainen, I., and Moffett, M. (2008). *International Business*. New York: Wessex Press.

Guercini, S. and Milanesi, M. (2017). Extreme luxury fashion: business model and internationalization process. *International Marketing Review*, 34(3): 403–424.

Johanson, J. and Vahlne, J. E. (1977). The internationalization process of the firm—a model of knowledge development and increasing foreign market commitments. *Journal of International Business Studies*, 8(1): 23–32.

Johanson, J. and Vahlne, J. E. (2006). Commitment and opportunity development in the internationalization process: A note on the Uppsala internationalization process model. *Management International Review*, 46(2): 165–178.

He, X., Brouthers, K. D., and Filatotchev, I. (2013). Resource-based and institutional perspectives on export channel selection and export performance. *Journal of Management*, 39(1), 27–47.

Kim, L., Nugent, J., and Yhee, S. (1997). Transaction costs and export channels of small and medium-sized enterprises. *Contemporary Economic Policy*, 15(1): 104–120

Klein, S., Frazier, G., and Roth, V. (1990). A transaction cost analysis model of channel integration in international markets. *Journal of Marketing Research*, 27: 196–208.

McNaughton, R. (1996). Foreign market channel integration decisions of Canadian computer software firms. *International Business Review*, 5(1): 23–52.

Meloan, T. and Graham, J. (1995). *International Global Marketing*. New York: Irwin.

Ogunrin, F. O. and Inegbenebor, A. U. (2015). Distribution channels and internationalization in a developing-country clothing industry. *Journal of Research in Marketing and Entrepreneurship*, 17(2): 130–148.

Onkvisit, S. and Shaw, J. (2008). *International Marketing*. New York: Routledge.

Richardson, J. (2008). The business model: an integrative framework for strategy execution. *Strategic Change*, 17(5–6): 133–144.

Seifert, B. and Ford, J. (1989). Export distribution channels. *Columbia Journal of World Business*, 24(2): 14–18.

Sletten, E. (1994). *How to Succeed in Exporting and Doing Business Internationally.* New York: Wiley.

Teece, D. J. (2010). Business models, business strategy and innovation. *Long Range Planning*, 43(2–3): 172–194.

Tesfom, G., Lutz, C., and Ghauri, P. (2004). Comparing export marketing channels: developed versus developing countries. *International Marketing Review*, 21(4/5): 409–422.

Williamson, O. (1991). Comparative economic organization: the analysis of discrete structural alternatives. *Administrative Science Quarterly*, 36(2): 269–274.

World Wide Web Resources

Information on overseas distributors and other channels: https://legacy.trade.gov/Guide_To_ Exporting.pdf

Assistance with international trade for U.S. exporters: https://ustr.gov/trade-topics/trade-toolbox/export-assistance

World Business Exchange: includes topics/assistance with exporting, channels of distribution, market research, service exports, pricing, documentation, and financing: www.wbe.net/ index.phtml

International Trade Closing Cases and Discussions

Distribution and Sales Channels: Japan versus Thailand

Japan: Distribution and sales channels have undergone substantial transformation over the last few decades. They vary by the type of goods sold. Even though the Keiretsu system whereby firms establish alliances with other firms, suppliers, distributors, and finance companies has weakened over the years, it still poses a challenge for new exporters to Japan. The scale of direct marketing in Japan (mail order, telemarketing, internet sales) is relatively modest although online sales via the computer or other mobile devices is estimated to reach over US$80 billion in the next few years. Indirect sales are typically conducted through agents and distributors. Importers are often appointed as sole agents for the entire country. Distributors cover a given industry or territory. Once the firm has established a foothold on the market, it is advisable to open a representative office in Japan in order to support marketing efforts as well as provide technical support to suppliers and customers (for technical goods such as industrial equipment). Here are important points about exporting to Japan:

a. The Japanese consumer puts more emphasis on quality than price

b. large Japanese wholesalers and retailers do not often deal with non-Japanese suppliers unless they have an office in Japan

c. most imported goods go through specialized distributors who purchase these products for resale. They represent several foreign firms and sell directly to wholesalers or retailers

d. one way to find distributors with a good track record is to contact Japanese companies that are already importing and distributing complementary foreign products.

Thailand: Even though the laws in Thailand do not require the use of agents and distributors, it is advisable to use them to successfully enter the Thai market since they know the local business practices and legal requirements. Direct marketing is used through a variety of channels such as radio, newspapers, mail order, catalogs, email, and other online channels. It is widely used for the sale of healthcare products, cosmetics, cleaning products, and appliances. Some of the problems with direct marketing relate to product quality, loss during delivery, and refund policies. TV home shopping is quite popular. Industrial goods are either distributed through a Thai importer who sells to the consumer or are directly exported to the consumer. A local agent or distributor would be used for goods that require after-sales service. Consumer goods tend to use a longer channel:

Exporter-----Thai importer-----Thai retailer-----Thai consumer (mostly for perishables)
Exporter-----Thai importer-----Thai wholesaler----Thai consumer (wholesalers provide better market coverage)
Exporter-----Thai retailer-------Thai consumer

Price, quality, and availability of service are important selling factors in Thailand.

Questions

1. Briefly describe the Japanese channel of distribution.
2. How does the Japanese channel differ from the Thailand channel of distribution?

CHAPTER 6

International Logistics, Risk, and Insurance

LEARNING OBJECTIVES:

6.1 Describe the two categories of business logistics

6.2 Understand the external forces that influence international logistics decisions

6.3 Identify and discuss risks in foreign trade

6.4 Learn the various types of marine insurance and marine insurance policy

6.5 Identify and discuss the various forms of marine cargo insurance

International Trade in Practice

One Belt One Road Initiative

One Belt One Road (OBOR) is a massive project initiated by the Chinese government in 2013 to enhance connectivity and cooperation across multiple countries in Africa, Asia, and Europe (fifty-four countries; see Figure 6.1 and Table 6.1). It attempts to re-establish the old Chinese Silk Road, which connected Asia to Europe, and expands its reach to more countries and territories. It extends the land route through Central Asia and Europe, and the southern maritime route through Southeast Asia on to South Asia, Africa, and Europe.

One Belt One Road will connect Asia and the Pacific, Europe, and Africa across the following five routes.

The silk road economic belt focuses on three economic corridors linking China to:

- Europe through Central Asia and Russia
- The Middle East through Central Asia

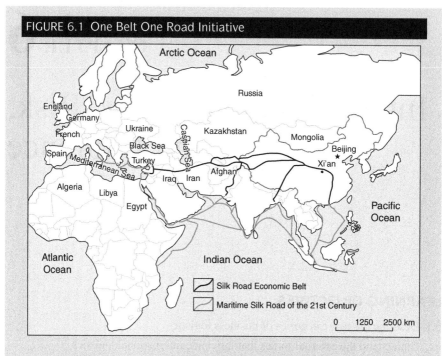

FIGURE 6.1 One Belt One Road Initiative

- Southeast Asia, South Asia, and ports in the Indian Ocean.

  The maritime silk road will link Chinese coastal ports to:

- Europe through the South China Sea and Indian Ocean
- The southern Pacific Ocean through the South China Sea.

The projects entail building a network of roads, railways, ports, power grids, oil and gas pipelines, and other similar infrastructure projects.

The OBOR project has several economic benefits for China: (i) it fosters a trade revival; (ii) it addresses overcapacity issues; (iii) it develops the less-connected provinces in China with other nations through trade and commerce; iv) it creates new markets for Chinese goods; v) it facilitates access to raw materials, critical for Chinese manufacturing; vi) it promotes free trade and investment and establishes free trade zones with countries along the belt. For countries that are part of OBOR, it provides access to China's overseas direct investment, helps them invest and upgrade their infrastructure, and promotes regional economic integration. In November 2014, China contributed US$40 billion to infrastructure projects and the exploitation of resources as well as for the promotion of financial and industrial cooperation.

One Belt One Road is expected to enhance trade and logistics activities within and between the various participants across the globe. Better logistics allow more market access and foster trade. However, many of the countries along the route show substantial gaps in trade and transport-related infrastructure (Afghanistan, Myanmar, Bhutan). Analysis of the logistics performance index (LPI) shows that many of these countries need to upgrade their logistics infrastructure such as rail, road, and maritime transportation. These gaps in

TABLE 6.1 Countries that Participate in the OBOR Initiative

Region	Participating countries
Central Asia	Kazakhstan, Kyrgyzstan, Tajikistan, Turkmenistan
Mongolia and Russia	Mongolia and the Russian Federation
Southeast Asia	Vietnam, Laos, Cambodia, Thailand, Malaysia, Singapore, Indonesia, Brunei, Philippines, Myanmar, East Timor
Middle East and Europe	Poland, the Czech Republic, Slovakia, Hungary, Slovenia, Croatia, Romania, Bulgaria, Serbia, Montenegro, Macedonia, Bosnia and Herzegovina, Albania, Estonia, Lithuania, Latvia, Ukraine, Belarus, Moldova
West Asia and the Middle East	Turkey, Iran, Syria, Iraq, UAE, Saudi Arabia, Qatar, Bahrain, Kuwait, Lebanon, Oman, Yemen, Jordan, Israel, Armenia, Georgia, Azerbaijan, Egypt

infrastructure will impede trade and inward investment into these countries. The LPI index is a quantitative assessment of a country's logistics infrastructure, divided into two major areas.

a. Policy regulations (inputs): Efficiency of customs administration, trade and transport-related infrastructure, competence and quality of logistics services
b. Service delivery performance (output): Timeliness of delivery, international shipments (ease of arranging competitively priced shipments), ability to track and trace shipments.

The countries that could benefit from the initiative will be those that develop their logistics infrastructure as well as countries that engage in developing their countries' comparative advantages to produce goods and services for the regional market. An opportunity exists for developing goods and services for the growing Chinese market by domestic firms or through links with global value chains.

INTERNATIONAL LOGISTICS

Logistics is a total systems approach to management of the distribution process that includes the cost-effective flow and storage of materials or products and related information from point of origin to point of use or consumption.

There are two categories of business logistics:

1. *Materials management*: In the context of export–import trade, logistics applies to the timely movement or flow of materials or products from the sources of supply to the point of manufacture, assembly, or distribution (inbound materials). This includes the acquisition of products, transportation, inventory management, storage, and the handling of materials for production, assembly, or distribution. For example, products can be assembled in Canada for distribution in Canada and the United States.

2. *Physical distribution*: The second phase relates to the movement of the firm's product to consumers (outbound materials). It includes outbound transportation, inventory management, and proper packaging to reduce damage during transit and storage.

Materials management primarily deals with inbound flow, whereas physical distribution is concerned with the outbound flow of materials or products (Guelzo, 1986; David and Stewart, 2010). Both inbound and outbound activities are interdependent and influence the company's objective of reducing costs while conforming to customer needs. The interdependence of such activities can be illustrated by the example of U.S. flower imports from Latin America. Atlantic Bouquet, a U.S. company, purchases most of its flowers from its sister company that has flower farms in Latin America. Continental Air freights the flowers from company-owned farms in Latin America to a warehouse in Miami before they are moved nationwide by air, or truck for distances of less than 300 miles. A proper management of the logistics system, that is, the unique combination of packaging, handling, storage, and transportation, will ensure that the product is imported and made available to the customer at the right time and place and in the right condition.

The interdependence of functional activities has been articulated through various new approaches or concepts:

1. *The systems approach*: The systems concept is based on the premise that the flow of materials within and outside the firm should be considered only in the context of their interaction (Czinkota, Ronkainen, and Moffett, 2014). This approach puts more emphasis on maximizing the benefits of the corporate system as a whole as opposed to that of individual units.
2. *The total cost approach*: This is a logistics concept based on evaluation of the total cost implications of various activities.
3. *The opportunity cost approach*: This approach considers the trade-off in undertaking certain logistic decisions. For example, the benefits and costs of sourcing components abroad versus buying from domestic sources. Additional costs associated with transportation, increases in safety stock inventory, warehousing costs, and so forth, are examined to ensure that the total opportunity cost of outsourcing abroad is not greater than other available options.

What is the importance of logistics to international trade? One of the major contributions of logistics to international trade is in the area of efficient allocation of resources. International logistics allows countries to export products in which they have a competitive advantage and import products that are either unavailable at home or produced at a lower cost overseas, thus allowing for efficient allocation of resources. For example, natural resource advantages and low-cost labor has enabled Colombia to export flowers to the United States and to import technology. Colombian flower exports have driven less efficient U.S. producers out of their own markets and forced the Dutch out of the U.S. rose and carnation markets (Thuermer, 1998). Such advantages from international trade cannot be realized without a well-managed logistics system. To the extent that logistics facilitates international trade, it contributes to the expansion of economic growth and employment. As import firms expand their ability to procure needed raw materials or components for their customers, international logistics management becomes a critical source of competitive advantage for both the firms and their customers. Such material procurement and sourcing decisions include the number and location of warehouses, levels of inventory to maintain, as well as selection of the appropriate transportation mode and carrier (Christopher, 1992). The development of advanced logistics systems and capabilities has also increased the efficient production, transportation, and distribution of products. For example, by outsourcing logistics to third-party operators, pharmaceutical and healthcare companies can reduce costs associated with inventory, overhead, labor, and warehousing. The use of various transportation modes facilitates rapid and consistent delivery service to consumers, which in turn reduces the need for safety stock inventory. Transportation cost is also reduced through shipment consolidation and special contracts with carriers for large shipments without adversely affecting delivery time. In short, a well-managed international logistics system can result in optimal inventory levels and optimal production capacity (in multi-plant operations), thereby maximizing the use of working capital. All this helps to strengthen the competitive position of domestic companies in global trade. (See International Perspective 6.1 for logistics and trade facilitation.)

EXTERNAL INFLUENCES ON LOGISTICS FUNCTIONS

A number of external factors influence international logistics decisions.

Regulations

Governments in many countries encourage their domestic carriers to handle their exports or imports since the provision of such transportation services contributes to the nation's balance of payments. This can be illustrated by U.S.–China trade, which is mostly transported by Chinese vessels. This occurs because the Chinese Foreign Trade Agency insists, whenever possible, on terms that allow it to control most of the transportation and thus use its state-run transport companies (Davies, 1987).

International logistics activity in the form of overseas transportation, handling of shipment, and distribution management also creates jobs. Besides the need to earn or save foreign currency and the creation of employment opportunities, governments support their national carriers to ensure national shipping capacity during wars or other emergencies. Governments also control or limit the export and import of certain commodities through a host of devices, such as export controls, import tariffs, and non-tariff barriers, for example, quotas or cumbersome import clearance procedures. There are also bilateral negotiations between countries on airline routes and the provision of various services such as insurance. All this has an influence on international logistics and transportation. The process of privatization and deregulation in transportation and communications has reduced shipping costs and increased productivity. This has also increased the possibilities for different prices and services, thus underscoring the need to integrate marketing and logistics functions.

Competition

The proliferation of new products and services and short product life cycles creates pressures on firms to reexamine their logistics systems. This often requires a reduction in inventory, lower overall costs, and the development of appropriate logistics networks and delivery systems to retain and enhance firms' customer base. Crucial to the success of any logistics system is a holistic examination of the relationship between transportation, warehousing, and inventory costs in order to adapt to the changing competitive environment. Such a re-examination of various logistics functions resulted in a substantial reduction in inventory costs and delivery time for Cisco Systems of San Jose, California, in 1997. The company ships routers to Europe and needed to let customers know when orders would arrive and to be able to reroute an order to fill urgent requests. It hired UPS Worldwide Logistics to handle the various logistics functions. Using its expertise, UPS can now track Cisco's routers from San Jose, California, to European customers in less than four days as opposed to three weeks. In cases in which UPS's planes or trucks cannot offer the quickest route, it subcontracts the job to other carriers such as KLM or Danzas, a European trucking firm. This results in more savings in inventories (Woolley, 1997).

Technology

Technology improvements, added to the deregulation of transportation and communications, have transformed the logistics industry. They have helped to increase logistics options, improve performance, and decrease costs. The use of communications technology has now integrated marketing and distribution activities with overseas customers, enabling the latter to know the date of shipment, the location of the cargo in transit, and the expected date of arrival. Importers have achieved total visibility of goods in transit and can make adjustments when a shipment is running late. Such tracking and tracing of cargo has the added advantage of synchronizing promotions and long-term inventory decisions for customers.

TYPICAL LOGISTICS PROBLEMS AND SOLUTIONS

Each export–import firm must use a logistics system that best fits its product line and chosen competitive strategy (see Table 6.2 for differences between domestic and international logistics).

TABLE 6.2 Differences Between Domestic and International Logistics

Domestic Logistics	International Logistics
• Domestic currency used • One national regulation on customs procedures, documentation, packaging, and labeling requirements • Most goods transported by truck or rail • Generally, short distances, short lead times, and small inventory levels	• Different currency and exchange rates • Different national regulations and many intermediaries participating in the distribution channel (customs brokers, forwarders, banks, etc.) • Most goods transported by air or sea • Long distances, longer lead times, and the need for higher inventory levels

Example 1

Arturo Imports Incorporated, a firm based in Boca Raton, Florida, specializes in the importation of gift articles from South America and the Caribbean. It sells its products through company-owned retail stores in thirty U.S. states. The company has distribution centers in twenty locations all over the country and spends over $650,000 a year in warehousing costs. Over the last few years, it has come under increasing attack from competitors and has lost about 20 percent of its market share. Its profits also declined by over 15 percent in 2010 alone. The firm hired a consultant to advise it on how to reverse the situation. Based on the advice it received, Arturo Imports consolidated its operations in six distribution centers; reduced dead, obsolete, and slow-moving stock; and decreased the likelihood of an item being out of stock for products customers want to buy. It centralized its purchasing functions and switched to an intermodal air and truck (from ocean and rail) combination to ensure rapid delivery. The company began to see its market share and profit margin grow six months after implementing its new logistics systems.

Example 2

A U.S.-owned export firm in Bangor, Maine, serves a narrow product line in eastern Canada from two distribution centers located in Montreal and Toronto. The company began to re-examine its logistical infrastructure in response to its loss of profits and market share to competitors. It increased the number of branch warehouses and level of fast-moving inventory while reducing the market area served by each warehouse. It also extended its product line. In spite of the additional expenses incurred, the company began to see a marked increase in its profits and sales volume.

INTERNATIONAL PERSPECTIVE 6.1

Trade Facilitation in the ASEAN

Trade facilitation refers to efforts by governments and organizations to simplify and standardize government regulations and procedures relating to the movement of goods across nations. Such measures deal with procedures for customs and trade documents, clearance of goods, computerization and automation, and increased communication between customs authorities with a view to reducing the costs of cross-border shipment and speeding up the movement of goods. Enhancing the efficiency of the logistics industry is an important aspect of trade facilitation.

Logistics supports trade and commerce across nations through its network of services beyond transportation. It includes warehousing, storage, terminal operations at ports and airports, customs brokerage, and information management. Scholars suggest that logistics costs have a greater effect on trade than tariffs. Coordinating various stages of the production process within and across nations requires the ability to move goods in a quick, reliable, and efficient manner.

This can be illustrated by the inability of the logistics industry in Vietnam to meet the growing demand for foreign and domestic business. During the China–United States trade war, there was a migration of firms from China to Vietnam to escape U.S. trade restrictions. However, many firms were disappointed to see congested ports and roads, increasing costs for land and labor, and burdensome regulations. The country's share of global container traffic is less than 3 percent compared to 40 percent for China. Vietnam needs to develop its ports and enhance shipping container capacity, third party logistics, and freight forwarding services. In view of limited skilled manpower, wages are rising for talented workers (especially those who can speak Chinese).

The barriers to logistics services in ASEAN can be summarized as follows.

A. Customs-related barriers
  • Time-consuming customs procedures
  • Different classifications of goods

B. Foreign investment-related barriers
  • Requirement for joint ventures (except for Singapore and Brunei)
  • Licensing requirements (except Singapore): Brand licenses, import licenses, distribution licenses

ASEAN countries need to address existing gaps in their logistics services by promoting investment in infrastructure, liberalizing the logistics sector to allow for greater competition, harmonizing logistics processes (customs procedures and formalities), and developing human resources.

THE INTERNATIONAL LOGISTICS PROCESS

In export–import transactions, the following steps represent the approximate order of physical movement and distribution of goods to a foreign buyer.

Step 1

As a result of previous correspondence between the prospective seller and buyer, the prospective customer (buyer) places an order to purchase the desired merchandise, including such essential items as terms of sale, payment method, and other conditions. The parties must ensure that there are no restrictions on the export or import of the merchandise in question. The prospective exporter confirms receipt of the order and commits to fill the order based on the given terms and conditions. The seller's acceptance without modification of the terms creates a binding contract. In the event of any modification by the prospective seller, a binding contract is created only upon acceptance of the proposed modification by the prospective customer. A pro forma invoice is then prepared by the exporter, stipulating the essential terms and conditions of sale, and when accepted by the overseas customer, it may also serve as a contract. The prospective exporter must meet packaging, labeling, and other documentary requirements. In cases in which the exporter has inventory in different locations or countries, a determination has to be made as to which goods should be supplied on the basis of proximity to customer, tariff benefits, and so on. The exporter prepares the order for transportation. The order is then picked, packed, and labeled.

Step 2

A freight forwarder arranges for goods to be picked up and delivered to a carrier. The freight forwarder selects the transportation mode (airline, ship, truck, etc.) and the carrier, and then books the necessary space for the cargo. Such decisions will influence packing and documentation requirements. The forwarder confirms booking with the supplier, who will in turn confirm with the overseas customer. If the consignee is different from the buyer, the forwarder notifies the consignee.

Step 3

The carrier loads the cargo and the merchandise is transported to the customer. Unless otherwise stipulated in the contract, the buyer is responsible for the cost of pre-shipment inspection. Many developing countries have adopted this practice primarily to conserve foreign currency earnings and to control illegal flights of currency through transfer pricing, that is, over-invoicing of imports and under-invoicing of exports. Pre-shipment inspection also ensures that the shipment conforms to the contract of sale. However, it is costly and time-consuming for exporters and delays the physical movement and distribution of merchandise. Appropriate precautions should be taken to detect and control possible diversion of merchandise into the gray market. Export products may be sold below domestic prices if domestic advertising or R&D is not allocated to the export price. Such export products, if diverted to the domestic market, could potentially undermine the exporter's market position. Some of the warning signs of potential diversion include offers of cash payment when the terms of sale would normally call for financing, little or no background in the particular business, vague delivery dates, or shipping instructions to domestic warehouses. After the merchandise is transported, the forwarder sends the necessary documentation, that is, the commercial invoice, customs invoice, packing list, bill of lading or air waybill, and certificate of origin, to the customs broker, who clears goods for the overseas customer at the port of destination.

Step 4

The customs broker submits documents to customs to obtain the release of the merchandise. In some countries, assessed taxes and duties have to be paid before release of the merchandise. Customs may also physically examine the merchandise. Penalties may be imposed if any serious errors or problems are found in the documentation or with the imported merchandise. The customs broker informs the forwarder of the release of the merchandise.

Step 5

If the terms of sale provide for the seller to obtain release of merchandise from customs and deliver to the consignee, the forwarder picks up the merchandise from customs and arranges for delivery to the consignee. This step depends on the terms of sale. The consignee signs the bill of lading or air waybill, noting any irregularities, and accepts the merchandise (see International Perspective 6.2).

INTERNATIONAL PERSPECTIVE 6.2

Attributes of a World Class Logistics System: Denmark

Denmark holds the world's top spot in logistics. Its excellence in logistics is attributed to a number of factors:

- *Investment in infrastructure*: Denmark has an international airport within about thirty minutes of ten international ports and free trade zones. It provides direct access to European rail and highway networks with direct connections to many European cities. It has international forwarders and integrators with bonded warehouse facilities. It provides substantial investment for infrastructure maintenance and development (bridges, airports, and seaports). It has an efficient air cargo handling facility. Customs clearance of goods is done before payment of duties, with minimum red tape. Information technology helps streamline procedures for exports or imports and links shippers and consumers.
- *Human resources*: It has a highly skilled and motivated labor force, twenty-four-hour, seven-day operations and good management–labor relations (walk-outs or strikes are virtually non-existent).
- *Business environment*: It has free trade zones and bonded warehouses, low trade restrictions and a stable economic/political environment.

LOGISTICS FUNCTIONS

Labeling

Importers are required to comply with domestic labeling laws. Even though an imported product may comply with the labeling requirements of the country where it was manufactured, it may not comply with the labeling laws of the importing country. Labeling requirements are imposed in many countries to ensure proper handling (e.g., "Do Not Roll"; "Keep Frozen") or to identify shipments (e.g., "Live Animals"). Exporters need to be aware of certain labeling requirements to avoid unnecessary delays in shipping. As standard practice, the cartons or containers to be shipped must be labeled with the following: shipper's mark, or purchase order number, country of origin, weight in both pounds and kilograms, the number of packages, handling instructions, final destination and port of entry, and whether the package contains hazardous material. Markings should appear on three faces of the container. It is also advisable to repeat the instructions in the language of the importing country.

Under the U.S. Clean Air Act (amended in 1990), all products containing ozone-depleting substances are required to be labeled. More detailed and specific regulations can be obtained from freight forwarders, since they keep track of changing labeling laws in various countries.

Packing

The rigors of long-distance transportation of goods require protection of merchandise from possible breakage, moisture, or pilferage. This means that goods in transit must be packed not only to allow the overseas customer to take delivery of the merchandise but also to ensure its arrival in a safe and sound condition. Consumers in many countries often prefer packaging with recyclable or biodegradable containers due to environmental concerns. For example, about 70 percent of packaging material used in any of the federal states in Germany must be recycled or reused. Packaging cost has an influence on product design. In certain cases, it is considered less costly to ship disassembled parts or dense cargo.

Merchandise should be packed in strong containers, adequately sealed, and filled with the weight evenly distributed. Goods should be packed on pallets if possible, to ensure greater ease of handling, and should be made of moisture-resistant material. Packing must be done in a manner that will ensure safe arrival of the merchandise and facilitate its handling in transit and at its destination. (See International Perspective 6.3 for an example of product packing tips.)

Insufficient packing not only results in delays in the delivery of goods but will also entitle the customer to reject the goods or claim damages. Export products must be packed to comply with the laws of the importing country. For example, Australia and New Zealand prohibit the use of straw or rice husk as packaging materials. The United Nations has adopted standards for packaging hazardous materials and provides training for personnel in the use of internationally accepted standards and certain other conditions. Freight forwarders and marine insurance companies can advise on packaging.

Traffic Management

Traffic management is the control and management of transportation services. Such functions include selection of mode of transportation and carrier, consolidation of small cargo, documentation, and filing of loss and damage claims. The international logistics manager's selection of a given mode of transportation depends on a number of factors. First, for products that are perishable, such as cut flowers, delivery speed is of the essence. Speed may also be required in cases involving important delivery dates or deadlines. In such cases, airfreight becomes the only viable mode of transport to successfully deliver the product to the overseas customer on time. Airfreight is also more reliable than other modes of transport that have more cumbersome unloading operations, which could expose the cargo to loss or damage. Second, the selection of transportation mode is influenced by cost considerations. Since airfreight is more expensive than other modes of transport, the international logistics manager has to determine whether such high costs are justified. Export firms tend to transport compact products or high-priced items by air because such products are more appropriate for airfreight or because the price justifies the cost. Third, government pressures could be imposed on exporters to transport by national carriers, even when other more economical alternatives exist. The choice of airport or port may be another important decision to be made. Such choices may be influenced by the desire to consolidate cargo or the presence of adjoining highways (to the port) on which weight limits are not rigorously enforced (Guelzo, 1986; David and Stewart, 2010).

Inventory and Storage

The proper management of an export–import firm's inventory is a critical logistics function. The costs associated with holding inventories can easily account for 25 percent or more of the value of the inventories themselves and could potentially create liquidity problems for many firms. In addition to this are the cost of storage, interest paid on borrowed money, and the risks of deterioration and obsolescence. It is important to establish certain guidelines with respect to such issues as maximum holding period, time of shipment of inventories to the supplier, and other related factors. Acceptable levels of inventory can still be maintained to serve overseas customers on time without unduly increasing costs and creating storage problems. To reduce warehousing costs, it may be necessary to store inventory in distribution centers based on customer needs. Inventories that are slow moving (no activity for six to twelve months) can be shipped from the exporter or manufacturer. Appropriate inventory planning and control will reduce the number of storage facilities as well as carrying and freight costs.

In certain situations, accumulating inventories may have its own benefits. In countries that have certain macroeconomic problems, inventory may be a good edge against inflation and devaluation of currency.

INTERNATIONAL PERSPECTIVE 6.3

Packing Handicraft Exports: Important Pointers

Prior to Packaging: Dusting, cleaning, removing fingerprints and drying items.

Major problems to consider in packaging: Tarnishing, corrosion, staining, decay, breakage, moisture.

Preventing Moisture: Use of a drying agent (silica gel) to reduce humidity, reducing surface area of package, drying items, and packaging materials in packages with a moisture-tight seal.

Preventing Damage: Cushioning fragile or high-cost handicrafts. Handicrafts exported in large quantities should be palletized when possible.

Heavy Items: For heavy handicrafts, wooden boxes are recommended.

Small Items: Bulk packaging with separators to protect individual items.

Outer Packaging: Corrugated fiber-board and wooden boxes are recommended.

RISKS IN FOREIGN TRADE

Businesses conducting export–import trade face a number of risks that may adversely impact their operations, such as the following:

- *Political risk*: Actions of legitimate government authorities to confiscate cargo, war, revolution, terrorism, and strikes that impede the conduct of international business.
- *Foreign credit risk*: Nonpayment or delays in payment for imports (foreign credit risk)
- *Foreign exchange/transfer risk*: Depreciation of overseas customer's currency against the exporter's currency before payment or the non-availability of foreign currency for payment in the buyer's country
- *Transportation risk*: Loss (partial/total) or damage to shipment during transit.

Political Risks

Many export–import businesses are potentially exposed to various types of political risk. Wars, revolution, or civil unrest can lead to destruction or confiscation of cargo. A government may impose severe restrictions on export–import trade, such as limitations or control of exports or imports, restrictions of licenses, currency controls, and so on. Even though such risks are less likely in Western countries, they occur quite frequently in certain developing nations. A study by Bilgin, Gozgor and Demir (2018) shows that government instability in importing countries has an adverse effect on the volume of Turkish exports. A one standard deviation increase in the political stability index in importing countries leads to a 15.3 percent rise in Turkish exports to Islamic Development Bank countries. In view of the deteriorating political relationship between China and Australia, Chinese importers are considering shifting orders for Australian beef, dairy, seafood, and other products to suppliers from Europe or New Zealand.

Such risks can be managed by taking the following steps.

Monitoring Political Developments

Private firms offer monitoring assistance to assess the likelihood of political instability in the short and medium term. Such information can be obtained from specialized sources for specific countries such as political risk services (e.g., Political Risk Services of Syracuse, a unit of International Business Communications, Incorporated), the Economic Intelligence Unit, and Euromoney. Public agencies such as the Export–Import Bank of the United States (EXIM Bank) and the Department of Commerce also provide country risk reports.

Insuring Against Political Risks

Most industrialized nations provide insurance programs for their export firms to cover losses due to political risks. In the United States, EXIM Bank offers a wide range of policies to accommodate many different insurance needs of exporters. Private insurers cover ordinary commercial risk, but EXIM Bank assumes all liability for political risks. (See Chapter 14 on government export financing.)

Foreign Credit Risks

A significant percentage of export trade is conducted on credit. It is estimated that about 60 percent of business-to-business sales in Western Europe and 51 percent in Asia Pacific are sold on open account (Atradius, 2019). This means that the risk of delays in payment or nonpayment could have a crucial effect on cash flow and profits. Payment terms vary across countries and even within countries that have close economic relations, such as the European Union, payment terms range from twenty-eight days in the Netherlands to forty-eight days in Spain. Thirty percent of the invoices in 2018 remained unpaid on the due date in Western Europe. Payments are, on average, twenty days overdue in Denmark, thirty-five days in the United Kingdom and Greece, thirty-two days in France, and twenty-four days in the Netherlands (Atradius, 2019).

Payment practices appear to be a function of the global/local economic conditions as well as the local business culture. In many developing countries, delays may be due to foreign exchange shortages, which in turn result in delays by central banks in converting local currencies into foreign exchange. The likelihood of bad debt from an overseas customer (0.5 percent of sales) is generally less than that from an American company. However, this does not provide comfort to an exporter whose cash flow and profit could be adversely affected by late payments and default. For most companies, their accounts receivables are among their largest assets. Just one big unpaid bill could spell doom. A default by an overseas customer is still costly even when the exporter has insurance to cover commercial credit risks. The exporter must follow strict procedures to obtain payment before insurance claims will be honored. The following measures will help export companies in dealing with problems of defaults and/or delays in payment.

Appropriate Credit Management

Appropriate credit management involves the review of credit decisions based on current and reliable credit reports on overseas customers. Credit reports on foreign companies can be obtained from international banks that have affiliates in various countries and private credit information sources such as Dunn and Bradstreet, Graydon America, Owens Online, TRW Credit Services, and the NACM (National Association of Credit Management Corporation). A number of foreign credit information firms also provide accurate and reliable information on overseas customers. Government agencies such as the U.S. Department of Commerce, the EXIM Bank, and the Foreign Credit Insurance Association (FCIA) also offer credit reporting services on foreign firms. Export firms need to have a formal credit policy that will help them recover overdue or bad debts and substantially reduce the occurrence of such risks in future.

Requiring Letters of Credit and Other Conditions

A confirmed, irrevocable letter-of-credit transaction avoids risks arising from late payments or bad debts because it ensures that payments are made before the goods are shipped to the importer. However, such requirements (including advanced payments before shipment) do not attract many customers, and exporters seeking to develop overseas markets often have to sell on open account or consignment to enable the foreign wholesaler or retailer to pay only after the goods have been sold. The exporter can also require the payment of interest when payment is not made within the time period agreed or, failing that, within a given number of days. The introduction of a similar measure in Sweden in the mid-1970s is believed to have substantially reduced late payments to fewer than seven days. Another safeguard would be to secure collateral to cover a transaction.

Insuring Against Credit Risks

Many export firms do not insure trade receivables, and yet, such cover is as necessary as fire or car insurance. It is estimated that in most developed countries, less than 20 percent of trade debts are insured. Credit insurers tend to have extensive databases that allow them to assess the credit worthiness of an insured's customer. This helps export companies to distinguish those buyers with the money to pay for their orders from those which are likely to delay payments or default. A credit insurance policy also provides confidence to the lender and may help exporters obtain a wide range of banking services and an improved rate of borrowing.

Few private insurance firms cover foreign credit risk: American Credit Indemnity, Continental Credit Insurance, Fidelity and Deposit Company, and American Insurance Underwriters are among those that provide such coverage. Such firms could be contacted directly or through brokers stationed in various parts of the country. Policies often cover commercial and political risks, although, in some cases, they are limited to insolvency and protracted default in eligible countries. Minimum premiums range from $1,250 per policy year to $10,000.

EXIM Bank provides various types of credit insurance policies: credit insurance for small businesses (umbrella policy, small business policy), single and multi-buyer policies; a letter-of-credit policy and so on. EXIM Bank's major features are U.S. content requirements and restrictions on sales destined for military use or to communist nations. (See Chapter 14, Government Export Financing Programs.)

Foreign Exchange Risks

Export–import firms are vulnerable to foreign exchange risks whenever they enter into an obligation to accept or deliver a specified amount of foreign currency at a future point in time. These firms could face a possibility that changes in foreign currency values could either reduce their future receipts or increase their payments in foreign currency. Different methods are used to protect against such risks, for example, shifting the risk to third parties or to the other party in an export contract (for details, see Chapter 10 on exchange rates and trade).

TRANSPORTATION RISKS: MARINE AND AVIATION INSURANCE

Export–import firms depend heavily upon the availability of insurance to cover against risks of transportation of goods. Risks in transportation are an integral part of foreign trade, partly due to our inability to adequately control the forces of nature or to prevent human failure as it affects the safe movement of goods. Insurance played an important part in stimulating early commerce. In Roman times, for example, money was borrowed to finance overseas commerce, whereby the lender would be paid a substantial interest on the loan only if the voyage was successful. The loan was canceled if the ship or cargo was lost as a result of ocean perils. Bottomry is the transaction under which the shipowner borrowed money to carry out the venture by pledging the vessel as security for the loan. Similarly, respondentia bonds were used for arrangements where cargo was pledged as security. The interest charged in the event of a successful voyage was essentially an insurance premium (Greene and Trieschmann, 1984; Mehr, Cammack, and Rose, 1985; Gürses, 2019).

The primary purpose of insurance in the context of foreign trade is to reduce the financial burden of losses arising from the movement of goods over long distances. In export trade, it is customary to arrange extended marine insurance to cover not only the ocean voyage but also other means of transport that are used to deliver the goods to the overseas buyer. There are five essential elements to an insurance contract (Vance, 1951; Reuvid and Sherlock, 2011):

1. The insured must have an insurable interest, that is, a financial interest based on some legal right in the preservation of the property. The insured must prove the extent of the insurable interest to collect and recovery is limited by the insured's interest at the time of loss. The purpose of requiring insurable interest is to prevent gambling and profiting from the willful destruction of vessels or cargo.
2. The insured is subjected to risk of loss of that interest by the occurrence of certain specified perils.
3. The insurer assumes the risk of loss.
4. This assumption is part of a general scheme to distribute the actual loss among a large group of persons bearing similar risks.
5. As a consideration, the insured pays a premium to a general insurance fund.

Since insurance is a contract of indemnity, a person may not collect more than the actual loss in the event of damage caused by an insured peril. An export firm, for example, is not permitted to receive payment from the carrier for damages for the loss of cargo and also recover for the same loss from the insurer. On paying the exporter's claim, the insurer stands in the position of the exporter (insured party) to claim from the carrier or other parties who are responsible for occasioning the loss or damage. This means that the insurer is subrogated to all the rights of the insured after having indemnified the latter for its loss. This is generally described as the principle of subrogation.

An important point to consider is whether an exporter, as an insured party, can assign the policy to the overseas customer. It appears that assignment is generally allowed insofar as there is an agreement to transfer the policy with the merchandise to the buyer and the seller has an insurable interest during the time when the assignment is made.

Another important principle of insurance is that of utmost good faith, that is, the insurer and insured are under an obligation to disclose important information that is likely to affect the judgement of the other. Information is considered material if a prudent insurer would have regarded the non-disclosure as increasing the risk.

Marine Insurance

A marine policy is the most important type of insurance in the field of international trade. This is because 1) ocean shipping remains the predominant form of transport for large cargo, and 2) marine insurance is the most traditional and highly developed branch of insurance. All other policies, such as aviation and inland carriage, are largely based on principles of marine insurance. Practices and policies are also more standardized across countries in the area of marine insurance than in insurance of goods carried by land or air (Day and Griffin, 1993).

The different types of marine insurance include the following:

- *Marine cargo insurance*: Cargo insurance caters specifically to the cargo of the ship and also pertains to the belongings of a ship's voyagers. This chapter will focus on cargo insurance.
- *Hull insurance*: Hull insurance mainly caters to the torso and hull of the vessel along with all the articles and pieces of furniture in the ship. This type of marine insurance is mainly taken out by the owner of the ship in order to avoid any loss to the ship in case of any mishaps occurring. It covers shipowners against risk or damage to the ship such as grounding or fire or complete loss such as the sinking of a vessel. It also covers damage due to collision with another ship as well as shipowners' general average contributions. Hull insurance depends on the seaworthiness of the vessel.
- *Liability insurance*: Liability insurance is that type of marine insurance where compensation is provided to any liability occurring on account of a ship crashing or colliding and on account of any other induced attacks. It includes liability for oil spills, injury, or death.
- *Freight Insurance*: Freight insurance provides protection to merchant vessels' corporations which stand to lose money in the form of freight when cargo is lost due to the ship being involved in an accident. This type of marine insurance solves the problem of companies losing money because of a few unprecedented events and accidents occurring.

Developments in the Marine Insurance Market

- *Overcapacity in the shipping industry*: Shipowners have ordered too many big ships to meet demand for container and bulk space over the last few years. This was accompanied by increasing outside investment into cargo and hull insurance that contributed to lower premiums for shippers. Oversupply has remained a structural feature in most shipping segments, causing downward pressure on freight rates. This is particularly the case in the container ship segment. Depressed market conditions and poor financial returns of recent years have been driving container shipping companies to adopt coping strategies, such as mergers and acquisitions, consolidation, vertical integration, and changes in deployment patterns (UNCTAD, 2019).

  The marine insurance market has low entry barriers and investors have entered the market hoping to get higher returns than the equity or bond markets.
- *Developments in technology and environmental regulations*: Maritime autonomous vessels are likely to be a reality in the near future. These are ships that are controlled remotely and have wireless monitoring and control functions. They could provide increased safety and cost savings by removing the human element from certain operations. Given the fact that human error is one major factor behind marine accidents and liability claims, it will have serious implications

for marine insurance premiums and costs. Furthermore, such technology will reduce crew costs and the risks of piracy and hostage taking.

Maritime shipping heavily relies on fossil fuels with high sulphur content. In January 2020 the International Maritime Organization began implementation of its regulation to reduce sulphur content in fuel oil from 3.5 percent in 2012 to 0.5 percent. Compliance with the new regulations in the form of adjustment costs (investing in new environmental equipment such as scrubbers, low sulphur fuels, and vessels powered by natural gas) has implications for freight costs and the insurance industry.

- *Decline in the cost of piracy insurance:* A dramatic fall in pirate attacks off the Somali coast is forcing down the cost of piracy insurance for commercial ships. The use of international navies to crack down on pirates, armed guards and defensive measures on vessels including barbed wire, as well as strikes on the pirates' coastal bases has dramatically reduced pirate attacks on ships. According to data from the International Maritime Bureau, there were thirty-eight pirate attacks during the first three months of 2020 compared to forty-seven during the same period in 2019. In 2019, there were 162 incidents of piracy and armed robbery against ships worldwide compared to 201 in 2018 (ICC, 2019). However, the Gulf of Guinea appears to be a major hotspot for pirates. In the first three months of 2020 alone, there were twenty-one attacks on ships in the Gulf of Guinea. The average ransom payment for each incident has gone up by about 400 percent, reaching one million USD. In response to these developments, the kidnap and ransom insurance market which has grown from scratch is estimated to be worth over $250 million in little more than five years (ICC, 2019). In April 2010 the US President issued an executive order prohibiting the payment of any ransom to certain persons listed in an Annex to the Executive Order. It prevents ransom payments only if a) it is made or facilitated by a person subject to U.S. jurisdiction, and b) to one of the persons listed on the Annex to the Executive Order, either directly or indirectly.
- *Popularity of trade disruption insurance (TDI):* There are two sides to the supply chain from the perspective of insurance cover. One deals with the protection of physical assets (goods) in transit while the other protects revenue from supply chain disruption. Trade disruption insurance covers, inter alia, losses from political, credit, and other supply chain risks. A fuel supply company, for example, purchases TDI to cover alternative delivery costs if weather interrupts shipments to remote Alaskan facilities. Multinational food companies that sell fresh produce often purchase TDI to cover losses for spoilage because of supply-chain delays or disruption. In the event of a natural disaster—even if there is no physical damage—TDI covers losses incurred from plant downtime, storage costs, contractual penalties, or lost revenue. Companies can be protected from lost market share or new facility construction costs. Trade disruption insurance is growing at about 14 percent a year.

Types of Marine Insurance Policy

Voyage Policies and Time Policies

Cargo policies may be written for a single trip or shipment (voyage policies), for instance, from New York (USA) to Istanbul (Turkey). They are commonly used in international sales transactions. A time policy insures the subject matter for a specified period, usually one year. For example, a ship is insured for one year commencing at noon on January 25, 2021. Hulls are often insured under time policies. It is also possible to insure under a mixed policy where the policy covers a particular voyage for a given period of time. For example, a vessel can be insured for a voyage from Dubai to Singapore and for sixty days commencing on June 21, 2021.

Open Policies and Floating Policies

Open policies are the most popular in the insurance market because of their flexibility. The majority of cargo policies are written on open contracts. They are used for several consignments of cargo sent over a specified period, usually one year. The premium rates are fixed and all shipments are automatically covered. The names of ships, dates, and value of shipments must be declared when the goods are shipped. Multiple shipments are automatically and successively insured until the policy is cancelled or the sum insured exhausted, whichever comes first. When full information is not available at the time a declaration is made, a provisional report may be submitted to the insurance agent (this is closed when the value is finally known). Declarations are prepared by the assured and forwarded daily, weekly or as shipments are made. The premium is billed monthly based on the schedule of rates provided in the policy. Similarly, floating policies provide the insurance cover in general terms and the names of the ship and other particulars are made in subsequent declarations. However, unlike open policies, floating policies only provide cover up to a certain amount and are exhausted once the aggregate value of the shipment reaches the agreed limit.

Insurance Certificates

Open policies are not legally enforceable and are binding in honor only. Furthermore, since they do not provide the insurance status of a specific shipment, they are not accepted as proof of insurance by banks to process letters of credit. In many cases, the exporter is required to provide a certificate of insurance to the buyer and the bank.

The insurer provides a pad of insurance certificates to the exporter and a copy of the completed certificate (with details of goods, destination, type and amount of insurance required, etc.) is mailed to the insurance company whenever a shipment is made. Certificates save time and facilitate a more efficient operation of international business transactions.

Besides what is often included in declarations, certificates include additional information such as the names of the beneficiary. Certificates can be made to other parties "to order" and are negotiable (bought and sold in the market).

Perils of the Sea

Perils of the sea refer to chance accidents, that is, the loss is not intentional or inevitable. This is because insurance is a contract of indemnity against accidents which may happen (not against accidents which must happen). Marine insurance claims are made due to perils of the sea and the latter does not cover every accident that occurs on the sea. It excludes the following:

- Ordinary wear and tear: Marine policies generally exclude ordinary actions of the wind and waves. A claim lies only if these actions are the immediate cause of the loss.
- Unseaworthiness of the vessel: In voyage policies, there is an implied warranty that the ship is seaworthy at the beginning of the voyage. Even in time policies, insurers will not be liable if the ship is sent to sea in a state in which it is not seaworthy. Thus, unseaworthiness of the ship is not considered a peril of the sea.
- Inherent vice: Risk of deterioration of the goods shipped due to their natural behavior in the ordinary course of the voyage (in the absence of external intervention) is not considered a peril of the sea. This includes the inherent inability of the goods to withstand the ordinary conditions of the voyage. For example, a cargo of soybeans arrives at the port of destination in a heated and deteriorated condition in the absence of any external condition (in spite of sufficient ventilation, proper handling of cargo on board). It is a case where the cargo damaged itself.
- Ordinary leakage: Ordinary loss in weight and volume of cargo due to moisture (agriculture products) or evaporation (petroleum).
- Inadequate packing: Goods must be properly packed for sea voyage to protect against water damage. They should be secured in a crate or container.

Coverage under Marine Cargo Insurance Policy

There are two general types of marine cargo insurance policy that can be purchased by shippers to protect their cargo. The first group of policies, "Institute of Marine Cargo Clauses (ICC)-A, B & C" are used by Lloyd's insurers and also insurers that are members of the Institute of London underwriters (most of the U.K. insurance market). The second group of policies (all-risks, with average and free of particular average) are written by U.S.-based underwriters. Their coverage is quite similar (ICC-A to all risks; ICC-B to with average and ICC-C to free of particular average). They cover pre- and post-shipment risks. They cover cargo from the moment it leaves the warehouse in a named place for commencement of transit until delivery at agreed place or port of destination (Table 6.3).

All-Risks Policy

The all-risks policy provides the broadest level of coverage except for those expressly excluded in the policy. It is appropriate for any type of goods and most U.S. policies require that the goods be shipped "under deck" i.e., stowed inside the ship to reduce damage.

A typical clause reads:

> To cover against all risks of physical loss or damage from any external cause irrespective of percentage, but excluding, nevertheless, the risk of war, strikes, riots, seizure, detention and other risks excluded by the F.C & S (free of capture and seizure) (losses due to war, civil strife or revolution) warranty and the S.R & C.C (strikes, riots and civil commotion) warranty, excepting to the extent that such risks are specifically covered by endorsement.

TABLE 6.3 Comparing Cargo Policy Coverage

Peril	All-Risks	WA	FPA	ICC-A	ICC-B	ICC-C
Collision	Y	Y	Y	Y	Y	Y
Discharge of cargo at port	Y	Y	Y	Y	Y	Y
Cost of general average and salvage	Y	Y	Y	Y	Y	Y
Jettison	Y	Y	Y	Y	Y	Y
Overturning or derailment of land conveyance	Y	Y	Y	Y	Y	Y
Vessel grounded, sunk, or stranded	Y	Y	Y	Y	Y	Y
Earthquake, volcano, lightening	Y	Y	N	Y	Y	N
Entry of sea, lake, or river water into vessel or place of storage	Y	Y	N	Y	Y	N
Total loss of cargo overboard during loading or unloading	Y	Y	N	Y	Y	N
Washing overboard	Y	Y	N	Y	Y	N
Breakage, loss, or damage from any external cause	Y	N	N	Y	N	N
Contact with other cargo	Y	N	N	Y	N	N
Deliberate damage or destruction	Y	N	N	Y	N	N
Fresh water	Y	N	N	Y	N	N
Hook damage, mud, grease	Y	N	N	Y	N	N
Improper stowage by shipowner	Y	N	N	Y	N	N
Non-delivery	Y	N	N	Y	Y	Y
Pilferage	Y	N	N	Y	N	N
Ship sweat, steam of hold	Y	N	N	Y	N	N
Theft	Y	N	N	Y	Y	Y

*WA: With average; FPA: Free of particular average; ICC-A: Institute of Cargo Clauses, clause A; ICC-B: Institute of Cargo Clauses, clause B; ICC-C: Institute of Cargo Clauses, clause C.

In the case of an all-risks policy, the burden to prove that the loss was due to an excluded clause rests with the underwriter. Additional coverage can be provided through an endorsement on the existing all-risks policy or through a separate war risks policy.

With Average Policy

A with average (WA) policy (a named-perils policy) covers total as well as partial losses. Most with average policies limit coverage to those losses that exceed 3 percent of the value of the goods. A standard with average coverage may read:

> Subject to particular average if amounting to 3%, unless general or the vessel and/or craft is stranded, sunk, burnt, on fire and/or in collision, each package separately insured or on the whole.

This policy provides protection against partial losses by sea perils if the damage amounts to 3 percent or more of the value of the shipment. If the vessel is stranded, sunk, burnt, on fire and/or in collision, the percentage requirement is waived and the losses are recovered in full. Such policy covers loss or damage to goods attributable to fire or explosion, stranding, collision, etc. (Table 6.3).

Free of Particular Average Policy

A free of particular average policy (FPA) (a named-perils policy) provides limited coverage. It provides that in addition to total losses, partial losses from certain specified risks such as stranding or fire are recoverable. Partial losses will be covered only if they result directly from the specified risks such as fire, stranding, and other losses. A standard FPA clause reads:

> Free of particular average (unless general) or unless the vessel or craft be stranded, sunk, burnt, on fire or in collision with another vessel.

An FPA is inadequate for international shipments of containerized or bulk cargo since it does not cover many of the risks associated with such shipments. It does not meet the minimum requirements of cost, insurance, and freight (CIF) or cost and insurance paid to (CIP) shipment. ICC clause C has slightly broader coverage than an FPA in areas such as non-delivery or theft (Table 6.3).

Exporters that sell on credit and use terms of sale where the buyer is responsible for insurance (Free Alongside Ship (FAS), Free On Board (FOB), and so on) should consider taking out contingency insurance for the benefits of the overseas buyer in case the latter's insurance becomes inadequate to cover the loss. By paying a small premium for such insurance, the exporter creates a favorable condition for the buyer to pay for the shipment. Contingency insurance is supplementary to the policy taken out by the overseas buyer and recovery is not made under the policy unless the buyer's policy is inadequate to cover the loss.

Marine cargo insurance covers only the period when the goods are on the ship. The marine extension (warehouse to warehouse clause) extends the standard marine coverage to the period before the loading of the goods and the period between off-loading and delivery to the consignee.

TABLE 6.4 Types of Loss

Total Loss	
1. Actual total loss	Goods are completely damaged or destroyed or so changed in their nature as to be unmarketable.
2. Constructive total loss	Actual loss is inevitable (such as frustration of voyage for an indefinite time), or damaged cargo can only be saved at considerable cost (i.e., cost greater than its value).
Partial Loss	
1. General average loss	These are goods sacrificed as part of a general average act or as a cargo owner's contribution for the general average loss of others.
2. Particular charges	These are expenses incurred to prevent loss or damage to insured cargo from risk that is insured against. Example: expenses for extra fodder for a cargo of horses while the ship is under repair for hurricane damage that was covered under the policy.
3. Particular average loss	This includes partial losses that are not covered by general average and particular charges.

General Average

During a sea voyage, two interests are at risk: the ship and cargo. Both face a common peril since they are exposed to the same risks. When they encounter a common peril, it may become necessary to make an extraordinary sacrifice or to incur an extraordinary expenditure to preserve the cargo/ship endangered in this common adventure.

Examples: The ship may encounter heavy weather and it may be necessary to jettison part of the cargo or ship equipment to lighten the cargo. An extraordinary expenditure may be incurred to secure the physical safety of the ship or cargo such as entering a port of refuge (to repair the ship or warehouse cargo).

Given the fact that the sacrifice is made for the benefit of all in the common adventure, the owners of all interests saved by this deliberate sacrifice of items onboard the ship contribute proportionately to this loss. The risks that may fall on the cargo owner under general average are covered under all cargo policies (ICC-A, B, and C as well as all-risks, WA, and FPA).

General Average: Illustration

A vessel carrying a cargo of copper was stranded and part of the cargo had to be sacrificed (thrown away) to lighten the vessel. The vessel had sustained certain damage and a salvage vessel was employed to refloat it. Adjustment of the general average will be as follows:

Value of the cargo (thrown away) less duty and handling charges		10,000
Cost of repairs for vessel (chargeable to general average)	40,000	
Services for salvaging vessel	35,000	
Disbursement at port and other charges	15,000	
Total *"vessel"* Sacrifice		*90,000*
Amount to be allowed in general average		100,000
Value of cargo (including sacrifice)		100,000
Value of vessel (including sacrifice)		300,000
Total Contributory Value		*400,000*

Rate of general average contribution $\dfrac{\underline{100,000}}{400,000}$

Cargo's contribution   25% (100,000) = 25,000
Vessel's contribution   25% (300,000) = 75,000
Cargo owner's liability = Assigned contribution − value of cargo sacrificed
  Thus, 25,000 − 10,000 = 15,000 (to be paid)
Vessel's liability = Assigned contribution − vessel's sacrifice
  Thus, 75,000 − 90,000 = 15,000 (to receive)

INTERNATIONAL PERSPECTIVE 6.4

Typical Clauses in Cargo Insurance Contracts

1. **Inchmaree clause:** This clause covers any loss or damage to cargo due to the bursting of boilers, breakage of shafts, or any latent defect in machinery, as well as from negligence of the captain or crew when it is the proximate cause of a loss.

2. **Free of particular average clause:** This relieves the insurer of liability for partial cargo losses, except for those caused by the stranding, sinking, burning, or collision of the vessel with another.

3. **The labels clause:** In the case of damage to labels, capsules, or wrappers, the insurer is not liable for more than the cost of the new items and the cost of reconditioning the goods.

4. **The delay clause:** This relieves the insurer of liability for loss of market due to delay in the delivery of the cargo.

5. **The general average clause:** A general average loss occurs when a sacrifice is voluntarily made or an expense is incurred in times of imminent peril to preserve the common interest from disaster. Payments of apportioned losses are secured by a general average deposit before goods are released by the carrier. When the actual shipper's share is established, appropriate adjustments are made and any excess is returned. A general average clause covers the amount of the insured shipper's contribution.

6. **Craft and lighter clause:** In this clause, the insurer agrees to provide lighters or other craft to deliver cargo within the harbor limits.

7. **Marine extension clause:** Under this clause, no time limit is to be imposed on the insurance coverage at the port of discharge while goods are delayed in transit to their final destination insofar as the delay is occasioned by circumstances beyond the control of the insured.

8. **Shore clause:** This covers certain risks to cargo, such as collision, hurricane, floods, and so on, while the goods are in docks, wharves, or elsewhere on shore.

9. **Warehouse to warehouse clause:** This covers cargo while on transit between the initial point of shipment and the point of destination, subject to terms of sale and insurable interest requirement. The policy is effective from the time the goods leave the warehouse or store named in the policy for the commencement of transit to the final warehouse at the point of destination stated in the policy.

Air Cargo Insurance

A modified form of marine insurance coverage is issued for air cargo insurance. Some airlines sell their own coverage. In general, airfreight policies are written as all-risks policies. They exclude inherent vice, improper packing, ordinary loss in weight and volume, and unairworthy aircraft. They also exclude strikes, riots, and civil commotion coverage, damage from cold, and changes in atmospheric pressure.

Reinsurance

An insurer may share the risk of loss on a cargo or ship with other insurers i.e., reinsure it with another insurer. This is a common practice in the insurance industry.

Example: Drilling equipment will be carried on a ship from the port of Miami to port Klang in Malaysia and insured by ABC under a voyage policy. ABC may insure the risk with a reinsurer, XYZ Co. Ltd. This is a case where a single risk is insured and then reinsured. Both parties share the risk and the premium proportionally. If the equipment is worth a million dollars, the insurer indemnifies the insured for that sum in the event of total loss and then claims half of the loss from XYZ (assuming that XYZ took 50 percent of the risk).

INSURANCE CLAIMS AND PROCEDURES

Claims

Shippers can claim from carriers or insurers with respect to loss or damage to their cargo. Shippers often attempt to recover from carriers when they have a reasonable basis to believe that the loss or damage was caused by the negligent act or omission of the carrier that was easily preventable through exercise of due diligence in the transportation and handling of the cargo. Another motivating factor for the insured to obtain a satisfactory settlement with carriers could be to maintain a healthy loss to premium and keep premiums low. It could also be that the loss or damage is not covered by the insurance policy. However, in most cases, shippers claim from their insurers partly because carriers reject claims received from the insured or because the shippers find that the adjustment for loss or damage is inadequate due to liability limitations. It may also be that some shippers find it more convenient and efficient to handle claims with insurance companies.

Settling losses under insurance contracts is the function of claims management. Claims management is often accomplished through employed (in-house) or independent adjusters who negotiate a settlement with the insured. The claims department is responsible for ascertaining the validity of the loss, investigating, estimating the extent and amount of the loss, and finally approving payment of the claim. It is important to note the following in relation to insurance claims:

- To recover, the loss or damage incurred by the insured must be covered by the insurance policy. The insurer will avoid liability if the particular risk is specifically excluded or is not reasonably attributable to the risk insured against.
- The burden of proof falls on the insured to show that the loss or damage to the cargo is covered by the policy.
- The insured must take prudent measures to protect the merchandise from further loss or damage. Under the sue and labor clause that is incorporated in most cargo insurance contracts (see International Perspective 6.4 for other typical clauses), the insured is required to take all necessary steps to safeguard the cargo and save it from further damage, without in any way prejudicing its rights under the policy. The underwriter agrees to pay any resulting expense (Tables 6.3 and 6.4 and International Perspective 6.4).
- Once the insurance company settles the insured's claim, it could exercise its subrogation right to claim from parties responsible for the loss or damage.

Under the principle of subrogation, the right to recover from carriers and other parties who are responsible for the loss or damage passes from the insured to the insurer on payment of the insurance money. Since the insurer stands in the shoes of the insured in claiming from third parties, the insurer does not have a better right than that of the insured. Any payments obtained by the insured shipper from the carrier or other parties must be transferred to the insurer (after settlement with the insurer) because under the principle of subrogation, the insured is not allowed to recover more than once for the same loss. (See International Perspective 6.5 for common perils of the air and sea.)

Claims are generally valid for two years from the date of arrival for air shipments and one year in the case of ocean shipments. Claims are invalid if not initiated within this period unless legal action is pursued.

Typical Steps in Claim Procedures

Step 1: Preliminary Notice of Claim

The export–import firm (the insured) must file a preliminary claim by notifying the carrier of a potential claim as soon as the loss is known or expected. A formal claim may follow when the nature and value of the loss or damage is ascertained.

Step 2: Formal Notice of Claim

The consignee must file a formal claim with the carrier and the insurance company once the damage or loss is ascertained. The claim should include freight and other transportation costs, documentation, and other items. If the insurance policy is 110 percent of the CIF value, the insured could add 10 percent of the value of the goods to the claim. Assuming that the insured intends to claim from the insurer (not the carrier), the insured should arrange for a survey with the claims agent of the insurance company. The formal claim form should be submitted with certain documents: a copy of the commercial invoice; a signed copy of the bill of lading/air waybill; the original certificate of insurance; a copy of the claim against the carrier, or reply thereto; any survey report; the packing list; and a copy of the receipt given to the carrier on delivery of the merchandise. It could also include photographs, a repair invoice, and an affidavit from the carrier, if possible.

Step 3: Settlement of Claim

If the claim is covered by the policy and claims procedures are appropriately followed, the insurance company will pay the insured. If the insurance company declines to approve payment, the insured could pursue arbitration or other dispute settlement procedures as provided in the insurance contract.

The claim is filed by the party that assumes the risk of loss on transit. For example, in CIF contracts, the exporter takes out an insurance policy for the benefit of the buyer and the risk of loss is transferred to the buyer once goods are put on board the vessel at the port of shipment. The exporter will send the necessary documents and detailed instructions to the overseas customer (consignee) to follow in the event of loss or damage. The consignee should be instructed to examine the goods upon delivery to determine any apparent or concealed loss or damage to cargo. Any loss or damage discovered upon such inspection should be noted on the carrier's delivery receipt or air waybill. Once the carrier obtains a clean receipt from the consignee, it becomes difficult for the latter to successfully make a claim.

The best way to deal with claims is to prevent the occurrence of loss or damage to cargo as much as is practically feasible. It is estimated that proper packing, handling, and stowage can prevent about 70 percent of cargo loss or damage. The frequent occurrence of damage or loss to cargo not only becomes a source of friction or suspicion on the part of insurance companies but also discourages the growth and expansion of trade. It could also have the effect of reducing sales abroad if overseas customers are discouraged by the frequency of such occurrences, since it could consume the parties' time and effort. If payment has already been made to the exporter, the buyer's capital is tied up with merchandise that cannot be sold.

INTERNATIONAL PERSPECTIVE 6.5

Common Perils of the Air and Sea

Perils of the Air

- *Cargo movement*: Inadequate packing and improper marking of cargo are the leading causes of air cargo losses. Rough or "bumpy" flight conditions, improper handling and storage of cargo before, during, and after the flight often give rise to damage to cargo.
- *Theft and pilferage:* High-value cargo is particularly susceptible to theft when not in the aircraft or terminal.
- *Exposure to the weather*: Inadequate coverage of cargo could lead to water damage.
- *Inadequate packing and handling:* Inadequate preparation for the toughest leg of the journey, trucking to air terminal, handling in terminals, stowing in aircraft, in-flight conditions, unloading aircraft, transfer to terminals, trucking to consignee. Special packing and handling are required for different types of goods such as large or liquid cargo.

Perils of the Sea

- *Cargo movement*: Damage to cargo during multiple handlings at various stages of the journey. Cargo is subject to the constant movement and stress of maritime transport. In heavy seas, the cargo is exposed to compressive forces due to pitching and rolling. Effective securing of the load throughout the entire transport process is important.
- *Theft and pilferage*: Theft and pilferage account for about 20 percent of cargo loss.
- *Damage from water or fire:* Improper packing. Cargo stowed over the deck could be subject to water damage in a stormy sea. Some cargo may also fall

overboard. Improper packing and handling of flammable products such as chemicals, fireworks, and compressed gases could also lead to fire damage to cargo.

- *Sinking or stranding of ship*: Bad weather and collision could cause the sinking of the ship. The vessel may accidentally run aground and suffer considerable damage.
- *Contamination*: Cargo contamination due to contact with other cargo. Food products could acquire the smell of the cargo hold of the vessel or could be tainted if stowed close to spices or gasoline.
- *Jettison*: Jettison refers to throwing a part of the cargo overboard with a view to lightening the ship in an emergency.
- *Barratry*: Barratry is a wrongful act willfully committed by the captain or crew in contravention of their duties, thereby causing prejudice to the owners, for example, intentionally setting fire to the ship or running the ship aground.
- *Abandonment*: Abandonment of the ship by the owners due to bankruptcy or other factors could create problems for the crew and delivery of the cargo.
- *Improper equipment*: Inadequate equipment for loading or unloading could damage cargo.

CHAPTER SUMMARY

Logistics	*Logistics:* The process of planning, implementing, and controlling the flow and storage of materials from the point of origin to the point of consumption.
Two categories of logistics	1. *Materials management:* The timely movement of materials from source of supply to point of manufacture, assembly, or distribution. 2. *Distribution:* Movement of a firm's products to consumers.
Logistics concepts	1. *The systems approach:* Emphasis on maximizing benefits of the corporate system as a whole as opposed to that of individual units. 2. *The total cost approach* 3. *The opportunity cost approach*
Importance of logistics to international trade	1. *Efficient allocation of resources* 2. *Expansion of economic growth and employment.*
External influences on logistics decisions	1. *Regulations:* Export controls, tariffs, non-tariff barriers, privatization and deregulation of transportation and communications. 2. *Competition:* Competitive pressures on firms to examine logistics systems to reduce costs, etc. 3. *Technology:* New technologies now enable importers to know the date of shipment, location of cargo on transit, and expected date of arrival. It also handles other logistics functions.

Logistics functions	*Labeling, packing, traffic management, inventory, and storage*

Risks in foreign trade	1. *Political risks:* Actions of government authorities, war, revolution, terrorism, strikes.
	    Managing political risk: Monitoring political developments, insuring against political risks.
	2. *Foreign credit risk:* Risks of buyer's default or delay in payment.
	    Managing foreign credit risk: Appropriate credit management, letters of credit and other conditions, insurance.
	3. *Foreign exchange risk:* Changes in currency values that could reduce future exporter's receipts or increase importer's payments in foreign currency.
	    Managing foreign exchange risk: Shifting the risk to the other party or to third parties.
	4. *Transportation risk:* Loss or damage to merchandise during transit.

Insurance	Two essential principles: 1. *The Principle of Insurable Interest:* A financial interest based on some legal right in the preservation of the insured property. 2. *The Principle of Subrogation:* On paying the insured's claim, the insurer stands in the position of the former (the insured) to claim from other parties who are responsible for the loss or damage.

Marine insurance	Types of policy:
	1. Perils only policy: Coverage for cargo loss/damage:
	    a. *Free of particular average:* Policy covers total loss and partial loss from certain specified risks insured against.
	    b. *With average policy:* Policy covers total loss and partial losses greater than a given percentage and insurer is liable for the total amount lost.
	2. All-risks policy: Covers the broadest level of coverage except for those expressly excluded in the policy.

Claims and procedures	Claims for loss or damage to shipment on transit can be claimed from carriers or insurers. Most cargo claims are settled with insurance companies. Typical claims procedure: *Preliminary notice of claim, formal notice, and settlement.*

REVIEW QUESTIONS

1. Discuss the importance of logistics to international trade.
2. What is the systems approach to logistics?
3. State the external factors that influence international logistics decisions.
4. What is materials management and how does it differ from physical distribution?
5. State some of the differences between domestic and international logistics.

6. What are political risks in foreign trade. How can they be managed?

7. What kinds of risk does marine insurance cover? How does an FPA policy differ from a WA policy?

8. A shipper obtains a marine policy covering the shipment of textiles from China to Poland. The declared value of the shipment was $15,000 although the real (market) value of the merchandise was $7,500. If the goods are lost at sea, is the insurance company liable for $15,000?

9. How does actual total loss differ from constructive total loss? What is general average loss? You receive compensation from a marine insurance company because your goods were jettisoned from a ship as a general average act. Does the insurance company have a claim for general average against the shipowner and the other cargo owners?

10. Discuss typical steps followed in claims from carriers or insurers with respect to loss or damage to cargo.

REFERENCES

Atradius (2019). Managing risk, enabling trade. Western Europe: Businesses' financial stability at risk. October 22, 2019. https://group.atradius.com/publications/payment-practices-barometer-western-europe-2019.

Bilgin, M. H., Gozgor, G., and Demir, E. (2018). The determinants of Turkey's exports to Islamic countries: The impact of political risks. *The Journal of International Trade & Economic Development*, 27(5), 486–503.

Christopher, M. E. (1992). *Logistics: The Strategic Issues*. London: Chapman and Hall.

Czinkota, M., Ronkainen, I., and Moffett, M. (2014). *Fundamentals of International Business*. New York: Wessex.

David, P. and Stewart, R. (2010). *International Logistics*. New York: Cengage.

Day, D. and Griffin, B. (1993). *The Law of International Trade*. London: Butterworths.

Davies, G. (1987). The international logistics concept. *International Journal of Physical Distribution and Material Management*, 17(2): 17–23.

Fabey, M. (1997). Software for shippers. *World Trade*, September, 54–56.

Green, M. and Trieschmann, J. (1984). *Risk and Insurance*. Cincinnati, OH: South-Western Publishing Co.

Guelzo, M. (1986). *Introduction to Logistics Management*. New Jersey: Prentice Hall.

Gürses, Ö. (2019). *Marine Insurance Law*. London: Taylor & Francis.

International Chamber of Commerce (ICC) (2019). *Commercial Crime Services*. www.icc-ccs.org/piracy-reporting-centre.

Malbon, J. and Bishop, B. (2006). *Australian Export: A Guide to Law and Practice*. Sydney: Cambridge University Press.

Mehr, R., Cammack, E., and Rose, T. (1985). Principles of Insurance. Homewood, IL: Irwin.

Reuvid, J. and Sherlock, J. (2011). *International Trade*. London: Kogan Page.

Thuermer, K. (1998). Move 'em or wilt. *World Trade*, 11(3), March: 61.

United Nations Conference on Trade and Development (UNCTAD) (2019). *Review of Maritime Transport*. Geneva: UN.

Vance, W. (1951). *Handbook of the Law of Insurance*. St. Paul, MN: West Publishing Co.

Woolley, S. (1997). Replacing inventory with information. *Forbes*, 159(6), March: 2–3.

Wu, P., Chen, M., and Tsau, C. (2017). The data-driven analytics for investigating cargo loss in logistics systems. *International Journal of Physical Distribution and Logistics Management*, 17(1): 68–83.

World Wide Web Sources

Logistics World
www.logisticsworld.com/http://209.51.193.25/logtalk.asp (International logistics)

Risks and insurance
www.industryweek.com/companies-amp-executives/7-steps-prevent-cargo-theft (cargo theft)
www.duke.edu/~charvey/Country_risk/pol/pol.htm (political, economic, and financial risk)
www.duke.edu/~charvey/Country_risk/pol/polappa.htm (country risk)

Case Study 6.1 Marine Insurance

Actual total loss versus constructive total loss: Goods are regarded as having become an *actual total loss* as soon as they cease to be goods of the kind insured from a commercial point of view. It occurs when a ship or goods have been actually lost and the freight can no longer be recovered. The three elements that constitute actual total loss include the following:

1. Destruction of subject matter: The cargo ship is destroyed by fire, sinking, or enemy attack.
2. The subject matter ceases to be of the kind insured: Example: A cargo of dates is damaged by water in the cargo hold that makes it unfit for human consumption. A cargo of tobacco is rendered worthless by the stench of rotten hides that are damaged by the entry of seawater into the cargo hold.
3. The insured is deprived of the subject matter: Example: Capture or seizure of a ship by an enemy could amount to irretrievable deprivation.

There is *constructive total loss* when the subject matter insured is reasonably abandoned on account of its actual total loss appearing to be unavoidable or because it could not be preserved from actual total loss without an expenditure which would exceed its value. Constructive total loss occurs under any of the following circumstances:

1. where the insured is deprived of the possession of the ship or goods by a peril insured against. Example: A cargo of goods is detained by the enemy and there is no likelihood of recovery within a reasonable time.
2. the cost of repair is in excess of the value of the property. In the case of damage to the ship, the cost of repairing the damage would exceed the value of the ship when repaired.

Case Study 6.2 Marine Insurance: The Inchmaree Clause

A forty-foot wooden hull fishing vessel sprang an unexpected leak a few days after leaving port. As more water entered the vessel, the engine was flooded and the vessel eventually sank. Inspection of the vessel during the leak showed that the water was coming from underneath a refrigerated space in the front part of the vessel. In view of its construction style, the bilge underneath the vessel was inaccessible. The underwriter refused to indemnify the insured for the loss of the vessel by claiming that the latter had not exercised diligence to make the vessel seaworthy prior to the developing of the leak (as provided under the Inchmaree Clause; see International Perspective 6.4). The owner/master of the ship had no knowledge of the leak before the ship started its voyage.

Questions

1. An old cargo vessel was being towed to a particular location to be dismantled and broken up. During the passage, the vessel ran aground on the Florida coast. The owner contends that it will be quite expensive to bring it to the shore. He intends to hire a company to rescue the cargo ship. The ship had no cargo on board when it ran aground.

   Is this actual or constructive total loss? Explain your answer.
2. In case 6.2, do you think the loss is covered under the policy? (See International Perspective 6.5.)

Historical evolution of marine insurance

Origins

Centuries before the introduction of marine insurance as we know it today, countries secured the benefits of insurance through "loans on bottomry" i.e., loans made on the security of ship and cargo on the condition that a loan (with high interest) was to be paid only in the event of safe arrival of the vessel (indemnity was paid in advance). Such bonds were popular among members of the Roman nobility because of their high returns. Historical documents show that in 533 AD the Roman Emperor Justinian fixed the rate of interest for such loans at 12 percent. This practice approximates today's insurance. Modern day insurance originated in Italy among the Lombard merchants at the beginning of the thirteenth century and then spread to the Netherlands, Portugal, and Spain. It was later brought to England by the Lombards in the sixteenth century and spread to the various commercial centers of Europe. Principles and precedents on marine insurance developed in England form the basis of U.S. decisions. The development of marine insurance in England is closely associated with Lloyd's (originally a coffee house owned by Edward Lloyd), which provided information on the purchase and sale of ships, cargo, lost or stolen goods etc. and later become a place for marine underwriting. Even today, Lloyd's provides shipping news to London and beyond, detailed information on local and foreign ships, a register of captains, and a record of losses.

Development of Marine Insurance in the United States

The development of marine insurance in the United States is quite different from that in England. The Lloyd's system of underwriting that was prevalent in the United Kingdom never obtained a prominent foothold in the United

States. Secondly, unlike the dominant role of Lloyd's in the United Kingdom, U.S. corporations often failed, or changed the character of their business. The development of marine insurance in the United States can be divided into four distinctive periods.

1774–1793: The only form of insurance upon goods and vessels was provided by British private underwriters based in London. Historical records show that there was no insurance office in the United States as late as 1721. In New York city, the first marine insurance office was established in 1778. Underwriting was done by wealthy individuals and partnerships.

1794–1840: This period is characterized by the establishment of corporate underwriting. The legal (problems of suing individual underwriters) and economic (stability and financial strength) factors induced Pennsylvania to provide a charter to the Insurance Company of North America in 1794 (Philadelphia was the commercial center of the country at the time). By 1811, there were eleven companies in Philadelphia alone, seven of which underwrote marine policies. New York had twelve marine stock companies by 1825 and Boston had about a dozen of such companies. This was followed by more marine companies being established in different parts of the country. This period was characterized by an increase in the ratio of losses partly due to growing competition, the Napoleonic wars, and limited knowledge about the business. For example, 600 U.S. vessels were seized or detained in British ports from November to March 1794.

1841–1860: This period is characterized as the golden period of American marine insurance. The U.S. clipper ship was developed and became the most efficient carrier in the world. Tonnage in foreign carrying trade increased and U.S. vessels carried about 80 percent of the country's exports and imports. In many cases, the merchants who owned the ships that carried their cargo insured with U.S. companies. Increasing commerce, risky and long voyages, and high rates revived the American marine insurance industry.

1861–present: Marine insurance companies began to fight against over whelming misfortunes. The growing competition from iron steamship companies in the United States and the civil war reduced profits and increased losses. Several companies went bankrupt and the remaining ones barely survived around 1867. The United Kingdom had captured most of the carrying trade of the world. Furthermore, U.S. shipping was affected by countries' preferences to use their own vessels. The U.S. insurance market came out strong after World War I, however, as German and Russian insurers withdrew from the market. The depression in the 1930s and World War II adversely affected international trade and the fortunes of the U.S. marine industry. Following the war, the expanding economy and burgeoning consumer-driven market provided fertile ground for the expansion of U.S. trade and this led to a vibrant and profitable marine insurance industry.

International Trade Closing Cases and Discussions

1. Cargo Loss and Insurance

According to the World Shipping Council, about 130 million freight containers with an estimated value of US$12 trillion were transported in 2017 and more than 10,000 containers fall into the ocean every year due to accidents or severe weather. These losses could run into millions of dollars if they involve high-priced items. Cargo loss includes cargo damage and cargo theft. Cargo theft by criminal syndicates is one of the major causes of cargo theft. Electronic products appear to be the product category that is often targeted by thieves. Burges (2012) states that a single cargo theft leads to a total supply chain cost that is six times the value of the cargo. Criminal syndicates use various means to steal cargo such as using fake transportation companies, or impersonating a real transport company.

Even though cargo owners that insure their cargo often obtain compensation for their losses, the process of filing claims, the cost of reproducing the products, the increased insurance costs all raise transaction costs. Furthermore, the firm has to contend with reputational damage and loss of potential market opportunity. Scholars observe that there are certain factors that determine cargo loss severity: transit type, product category, and shipping destinations.

A case study (Wu, Chen, and Tsau, 2017) of cargo loss in electronic products shows that the primary cargo loss in terms of monetary value occurs in sea transportation (77%), followed by air (13%), and truck (10%). The frequency of cargo loss cases in air transportation (59%) is about three times that of sea transportation (22%). In terms of product categories, the study shows that most of the losses relate to laptop computers (84%) and MB/VGA cards (7%). They dominate in terms of frequency of losses and monetary value.

International treaties and the Carmack Amendment (in U.S. law) limit the monetary liability of carriers. Given these restrictions and various exclusions, the reimbursement for cargo loss may be as low as US$100.

2. Types of Insurance

Some of the types of insurance for cargo include:

- Land cargo insurance (cargo carried by trucks, UPS, FedEx). It covers for cargo damage or theft. Given the low level of carrier liability, it is important to consider buying additional cargo insurance for items of high value.
- Ocean and air: Marine cargo insurance often covers transportation by sea or air and includes damage during loading or unloading, weather damage, piracy and disaster.
- General average loss: The captain of a ship may have to jettison some cargo containers in order to save the ship. Such losses are amortized over the entire load and all shippers with cargo onboard pay a calculated share. Cargo insurance should cover general average loss (even if cargo is not damaged) because a percentage of the loss needs to be paid before the goods are released from the port.

3. Cargo Loss Prevention Strategies

- A recent study (Wu, Chen and Tsau, 2017) shows that land transportation of high value items tends to provoke cargo theft. It is important to coordinate with freight forwarders to ensure that appropriate security precautions are taken to avoid such cargo loss. Given the fact that the frequency and level of financial loss is high in sea transportation, it is also important to take appropriate precautions.
- Educate the supply chain staff about ways to identify and avoid cargo loss.
- Remove identifying marks from products that are at high risk of theft.
- Use cargo tracking systems to track and trace cargo.
- Use appropriate packing and stage loads at secure facilities. Frequent audits and reviews of supply chain partners will help in alleviating the problem.
- Consider distributing high risk items across several loads, carriers, or modes of transport.

PART III

Executing the Transactions

CHAPTER 7

Pricing in International Trade

LEARNING OBJECTIVES:

7.1 Describe the various determinants of export prices

7.2 Understand the different approaches to export pricing

7.3 Learn the ways to calculate the export price

7.4 Learn the important changes in Incoterms 2020

7.5 Identify and discuss Incoterms (2020) for any mode of transport and sea and inland waterways

International Trade in Practice

China's Export of Solar Photovoltaic Products: A Case of Price or Quality Competition?

Solar photovoltaics (SPV) is an important technology that produces electricity from sunlight. We see solar panels on rooftops in homes and businesses in different parts of the world and SPV dominates the world solar market. Its advantage is that the technology is not constrained by material supply, land requirements, or security considerations. Furthermore, it generates electricity at a cost of a half to two-thirds of commercial or retail electricity. A recent SPV market report (Mints, 2019) forecasts that the world's total renewable-based energy capacity will grow by 50 percent during the period 2019–2024. This growth amounts to 1,200 gigawatts (equivalent to current total U.S. power capacity) and largely driven by cost reductions and government incentives. It is estimated that SPV will account for about 60 percent of this growth. As costs continue to fall, the use of solar panels on residences is likely to grow in the next decade. So far, the largest consumers are businesses and industries.

China has dramatically increased its manufacturing capacity of SPV products over the last few years. It exports most of its production at declining

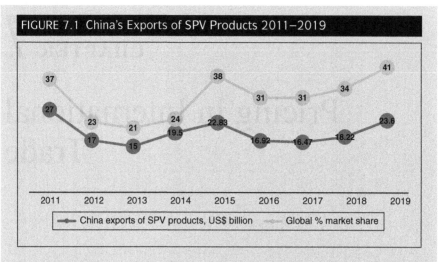

FIGURE 7.1 China's Exports of SPV Products 2011–2019

prices to Europe and the United States. From 2016–2019, its exports of SPV products increased from US$16.7 billion to US$23.6 billion, accounting for a global market share of 41 percent in 2019 (UN, 2020), as illustrated in Figure 7.1.

Source of Competitiveness: Harrigan, Ma, and Shlychkov (2015) suggest that export prices differ systematically across exporting firms and destinations. This is consistent with developments in the SPV industry. For example, the average price of U.S. SPV products imported from China is about 42 percent higher than those exported to Canada. Market positioning is based on price and quality. Melitz (2003) observes that only firms with productivity above a certain threshold can export. This is because firms with higher productivity have lower marginal costs, which in turn leads to lower prices and higher revenues. Other studies show that market competitiveness can be achieved through product differentiation i.e., better quality or more expensive inputs, which in turn lead to higher marginal costs and higher prices. Some scholars also observe the relationship between prices and distance arguing that trade costs increase with distance (Baldwin and Ito, 2008).

Price versus quality: A study by Wang et al. (2019) based on firm-level data from 2,600 Chinese firms exporting SPV products to about 140 destinations (2000–2013) found that more productive firms and firms exporting to larger markets tend to compete on quality, whereas firms with better financial conditions are more likely to engage in price competition.

Price is an important factor in determining a firm's ability to compete in world markets. For many companies, pricing policies and procedures are secret information and not easily available to outsiders. Export prices should be high enough to make a reasonable profit and yet low enough to be competitive in the market. Products rarely sell on one factor alone, and the exporter should be competitive on more than just price. Sources of nonprice competition include reliable delivery, short delivery time, product reliability, product quality, as well as any other feature considered unique by customers. This form of product differentiation based on specific characteristics of a product or service gives firms a competitive advantage (Dussauge, Hart, and Ramanantsoa, 1987; Harr, 2020). Apple increased its market share in Japan not only by slashing prices but also by broadening distribution outlets and through the addition of Japanese software packages.

The crucial element in determining price relates to the value consumers place on the product. Value results from consumers' perceptions of the total satisfaction provided by the product (Hiam and Schewe, 1992; Heda, Mewborn, and Caine, 2017). Companies can charge high prices and manage to remain competitive if the price charged is lower than, or in alignment with, the perceived value of the product or service. In competitive markets, high prices represent an indication of the social desirability of producing the product or service. They may also be justified in export markets if the sale also involves transfers of technology or training.

Pricing in world markets is often used as an instrument of accomplishing the firm's marketing objectives. The firm could use price to achieve certain levels of market share, profits, return on investments, or to reach some other specific goal. The following policies for pricing and markups generally apply to both domestic and export markets:

- High markups are common in industries with relatively few competitors. Markups are also higher in industries in which companies produce differentiated products rather than homogeneous ones. The high markups could be taken as rent arising from market power. For example, in the chemical industry, the biggest profits lie in specialty chemicals designed and produced for particular industrial uses (Reich, 1991; Yue and Wang, 2020). High markups may also be due to R&D expenditures and costs of increasing the skills of the workforce.
- Export prices tend to be relatively low in sectors in which there is increased competition. Changes in competitors' prices or the state of demand are more likely to trigger a reduction in export prices. Markups are relatively low for textiles, food, electric machinery, and motor vehicles; they remain high in industries such as medicines, computers, industrial chemicals, and television and communications equipment (Martens, Scarpetta, and Pilat, 1996; Zhang, 2014). The low markups for the former are due to the fragmented and nondifferentiated nature of these industries, which makes it difficult to exercise market power.

A company needs to develop a workable guideline with respect to pricing of its product or service in export markets. Its pricing policy should be firm enough to achieve the targeted level of profits or sales, while maintaining some flexibility to accommodate the overall marketing objectives of the firm. Flexibility is seen as an absolute necessity for optimizing profits, and a firm may use all pricing methods according to the type of product being sold, the class and type of customer, and the competitive situation in the marketplace. Mismanagement of export pricing could often lead to pressures for price reductions or the development of parallel markets. Parallel, or gray, markets are created when the product is purchased at a low price in one market and sold in other markets enjoying higher prices. For example, Eastman Kodak prices its films higher in Japan than in other countries. An importer in Japan can purchase the product at a discount in a foreign country and sell it in the Japanese market at a price lower than that charged by authorized dealers. Appropriate pricing and control systems of quality and distribution outlets are important in reducing such incidences of parallel markets.

DETERMINANTS OF EXPORT PRICES

A number of variables influence the level of export prices. Some of these are internal to the firm; others are factors that are external to the firm. A major internal variable is the cost that is to be included in the export price. The typical costs associated with exports include market research, credit checks, business travel, product modification, special packaging, consultants, freight forwarders, and commissions (Incoterms, 2020). An additional cost is the chosen system of distribution. The long distribution channels in many countries are often responsible for price escalation. The use of manufacturers' representatives offers greater price control to the exporter. Another internal variable is the degree of product differentiation, that is, the extent of a product's perceived uniqueness or continuance of service. Generally, the higher the product differentiation a firm enjoys, the more independent it can be in its price-setting activities.

The external forces that influence export pricing include the following:

- *Supply and demand:* The pricing decisions for exports are subject to the influence of the supply of raw materials, parts, and other inputs. In a competitive economy, any increase in demand is followed by a higher price, and the higher price should, in turn, moderate demand. It is often stated that exports of manufactured goods exhibit the same price characteristic as primary products, their prices varying with the state of world demand and supply (Silberston, 1970; Mankiw, 2018). The classical supply-and-demand approach—whereby price acts as an allocating device in the economy and supply equals demand at an equilibrium price—is largely based on certain assumptions: perfect buyer information, substitutability of competing goods, and marginal cost pricing. The classical assumption that reducing prices increases demand ignores the interpretation of price changes by buyers. Studies have shown that consumers perceive price as an indicator of quality and may interpret lower product prices as a sign of poor quality (Piercy, 1982; Ding, Ross, and Rao, 2010). If a product has a prestigious image, price can be increased without necessarily reducing demand.
- *Location and environment of the foreign market:* Climatic conditions often require product modification in different markets, and this is reflected in the price of the export product. Goods that deteriorate in high-humidity conditions require special, more expensive packaging. For example, engines that are to be exported to countries in the tropics require extra cooling capacity.
- *Economic policies such as exchange rates, price controls, and tariffs also influence export pricing:* Exchange rate depreciation (a drop in the value of a currency) improves price competitiveness, thus leading to increased export volumes and market shares. For example, the weakening of the euro's value against the dollar over the last few years has made it easier for German car companies to sell their small, European-built car models profitably in the United States. In export markets where buyers are used to negotiating prices, a flexible price is preferable over one that uniformly applies to all buyers.

- *Government regulations in the home country:* Different regulations in the home country have a bearing on export pricing. For example, U.S. government action to reduce the impact of its antitrust laws on competition abroad has enhanced the price competitiveness of American companies.

PRICING IN EXPORT MARKETS

The export price decision is distinct from the domestic price decision in the home market. The export decision has to consider variations in market conditions and the existence of cartels or trade associations, as well as the different channels of distribution. The presence of different environmental variables in export markets militates against the adoption of a single export-pricing policy (ethnocentric pricing) around the world. Another factor against uniform pricing is that different markets may be at different stages in the life cycle of a product at any given time.

It is customary to charge a high price during the introduction and growth stages of a product and to progressively reduce the price as the product matures. Other pricing alternatives include 1) polycentric pricing, which is pricing sensitive to local conditions, and 2) geocentric pricing, whereby a firm strikes an intermediate position. There are four approaches to export pricing.

Cost-based Pricing

The most common pricing approach used by exporters is one that is based on full-cost-oriented pricing. Under this procedure, a markup rate on full cost is determined and then added to the product's cost to establish the price. The markup rate could be based on the desired target rate of return on investment.

Marginal Pricing

Marginal pricing is more common in exporting than in domestic markets. It is often employed by businesses that have unused capacity or to gain market share. In this case, the price does not cover the product's total cost, but instead includes only the marginal (variable) cost of producing the product to be sold in the export market. This will result in the sale of a product at a lower price in the export market than at home and often leads to charges of dumping by competitors.

Skimming versus Penetration Pricing

Skimming, or charging a premium price for a product, is common in industries that have few competitors or in which the companies produce differentiated products. Such products are directed to the high-income, price-inelastic segment of the market.

A penetration-pricing policy is based on charging lower prices for exports to stimulate market growth. Increasing market share and maximizing revenues could generate high profits.

Demand-based Pricing

Under this method, export prices are based on what consumers or industrial buyers are willing to pay for the product or service. When prices are set by demand, market surveys will help supply the data to identify the level of demand. The level of demand generally establishes the range of prices that will be acceptable to customers. Companies often test-market a product at various prices and settle on a price that results in the greatest sales.

A firm does not have to sell a product at or below market price to be competitive in export markets. A superior or unique product can command a higher price. Cartier watches and Levi jeans are examples of products that, despite their high prices, generate enormous sales worldwide due to their reputation. These are products for which consumers feel a strong demand and for which there are few or no substitutes (products with inelastic demand). In cases in which demand for the product is elastic, consumers are sensitive to changes in price. For example, rebates and other discount schemes often revive lagging export sales in the auto industry (which is characterized by elastic demand). A few years ago, Toyota launched a special sales campaign in Tokyo to give away money (about one million yen) to 100 customers of the competitor car it sells in Japan on behalf of General Motors.

Competitive Pricing

Competitive pressures are important in setting prices in export markets. In this case, export prices are established by maintaining the same price level as the competition, reducing prices or increasing the price with some level of product improvement. However, price-cutting is generally a more effective strategy for small competitors than for dominant firms. An important factor in establishing a pricing strategy is also a projection of likely responses of existing and potential competitors (Oster, 1990; Coyne and Horn, 2009).

PRICING OBJECTIVES

An exporter's pricing objectives have an important influence on its pricing strategy. If a firm prefers an aggressive expansion strategy into foreign markets, it may opt for a lower profit margin than domestic sales. It will charge minimum prices in all markets to generate the highest volume of sales. This means that they will choose penetration pricing or cost-based pricing strategies to take high volume, low profit sales. Other export firms may prefer to achieve a high profit level by conveying an image of prestige and charge a high price in all markets. They could charge different prices based on what the market will bear. Such firms will opt for price skimming to take high profit, low volume sales. Between these two extremes, export firms use other pricing strategies such as marginal or competitive pricing (Figure 7.2).

CALCULATING THE EXPORT PRICE

Calculating Landed Cost and Distributor/Retail Price

There are two steps involved in calculating the export price:

- *Calculating the landed cost*: Landed cost is the total cost of a product once it has arrived at the buyer's door. It includes the original cost of the item, all

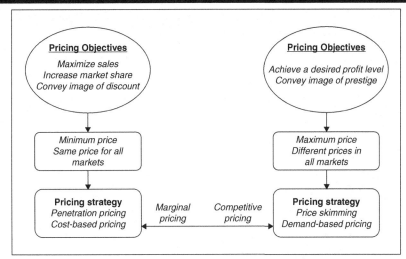

FIGURE 7.2 Pricing Objectives and Pricing Strategy

brokerage and logistics fees, complete shipping costs, customs duties, taxes, insurance, currency conversion, crating costs, and handling fees. Not all of these components are present in every shipment. It is advantageous to reduce the cost of each or any component of landed cost. This will allow the seller to lower the final selling price or increase the margin associated with that sale (Table 7.1).

• *Calculating the distributor's and retailer's price*: Every industry has a standard mark-up from cost to price. In the gifts and housewares industry, for example, the standard mark-up is 100 percent. In other industries, it ranges from 35 percent to 60 percent (Table 7.1).

Improving the odds: Achieving export competitiveness: There are a number of potential options for U.S. exporters who find themselves in an uncompetitive position in foreign markets (Table 7.2). With the assistance of their home government, they can devise strategies that will contribute to enhancing their competitiveness.

Long-term options:

• Free trade agreements will help reduce or eliminate tariffs and non-tariff barriers.
• Foreign direct investment will eliminate the additional cost of import duties. Locally produced components can be assembled into a final product in the export market.
• A manufacturer can license the use of its technology for production in the export market.

Short-term options:

• Long distribution channels contribute to price escalation. Firms can shorten the channel or export through an overseas representative.
• Product differentiation: Successful product differentiation creates a competitive advantage for the seller, as customers view these products as unique

TABLE 7.1 Export Price Calculation

Itemized cost	U.S. dollars
Ex works (EXW) price (Miami, Florida)	30,000
Freight to Port Manaus, Brazil	2,500
Insurance	750
CIF price	33,250
Landing charges	
Import duty (25% of CIF)	8,312.5
Marine tax (20% ocean freight)	500
Warehousing tax (0.65% of CIF)	216.13
Terminal handling charge (per container)	350
Custom broker's union fee	140
Custom brokerage fee	750
Bank costs (2% EXW price)	600
Total landing charges	*10,868.63*
Landed cost at Port Manaus (without local taxes)	**44,118.63**
Cost to Brazilian distributor	44,118.63
Distributor markup (50%)	22,059.32
Cost to retailer	66,177.95
Retailer markup (60%)	39,706.77
Price to Brazilian consumer before local taxes	105,884.72
Local taxes (manufactures tax and local state tax)	6,500.00
Price to Brazilian consumer after taxes	**112,384.72**

or superior. Product differentiation provides the firm some autonomy in its price-setting objectives.

- Offering discounts tied to promotions or quantity discounts

Calculating Export Prices : Another Approach

A Dutch company sells consumer products to the United States. It exports to a U.S. importer who sells it to a dealer.

Customer price in the United States: 500
Duty: 5%; Freight: 7%; Manufacturing cost: 120.
If the importer expects a 35% margin and the dealer expects a 40% margin, what is the export price?
Export price = X; duty= .05X; freight= .07X
Landed cost= X+0.05X+.07X=1.12X
Importer sales to dealer= 1.12X/0.65 = 1.72X
Dealer sales to customer= 1.72X/0.60= 2.86X

Calculating export price (X): 2.86 X= 500; export price (X)=174.83
If we know the manufacturing cost, we can also calculate the profit: 174.83 − 120=54.83

TRADE TERMS

Despite wide differences among national laws, there is a high degree of uniformity in contract practices for the export and import of goods. The universality of trade

TABLE 7.2 Export Price Comparisons

Itemized cost	U.S. product (US$)	Similar local product	Similar product from Uruguay
EXW price	30,000.00	30,000.00	30,000.00
Freight to Port Manaus, Brazil	2,500.00	None	150.00
Insurance	750.00	None	175.00
CIF price	33,250.00	30,000.00	30,325.00
Landing Charges			
Import duty (25% CIF)	8,312.50	None	FTA, duty free*
Marine tax (20% ocean freight)	500.00	None	500.00
Warehousing tax (0.65% of CIF)	216.13	None	216.13
Terminal handling charge (per container)	350.00	None	350.00
Custom broker's union fee	140.00	None	140.00
Custom brokerage fee	750.00	None	750.00
Bank costs (2% EXW price)	600.00	None	600.00
Total landing charges	*10,868.63*	*None*	*2,556.13*
Landed cost at Port Manaus (without local taxes)	**44,118.63**	**30,000.00**	**32,881.13**
Cost to Brazilian distributor	44,118.63	30,000.00	32,881.13
Distributor markup (50%)	22,059.32	15,000.00	16,440.57
Cost to retailer	66,177.95	45,000.00	49,321.70
Retailer markup (60%)	39,706.77	27,000.00	29,593.02
Price to Brazilian consumer before local taxes	105,884.72	72,000.00	78,914.72
Local taxes (manufactures tax and local state tax	6,500.00	6,500.00	6,500.00
Price to Brazilian consumer after taxes	**112,384.72**	**78,500.00**	**85,414.72**

* Exporters from Uruguay to Brazil do not pay import duty since Uruguay has a free trade agreement with Brazil.

practices, including terms of sale, is due to the development of the law merchant through international mercantile custom. The law merchant refers to the body of commercial law that developed in Europe during the medieval period for merchants and their merchandise (Brinton et al., 1984).

Trade terms are intended to define the method of delivery of the goods sold and the attendant responsibilities of the parties. Such terms also help the seller in the calculation of the purchase price. A seller quoting the terms of sale as FOB, for example, will evidently charge a lower price than if quoting CIF because the latter includes not only the cost of goods but also expenses incurred by the seller for insurance and freight to ship the goods to the port of destination.

The Purpose and Function of Incoterms

Incoterms (International Commercial Terms) is a body of predefined commercial terms that deal with the seller's delivery obligation under an international sales contract. The International Chamber of Commerce (ICC) has been responsible for the development of Incoterms. It is a non-governmental entity and has undertaken eight revisions since 1936 (1953, 1967, 1976, 1980, 1990, 2000, 2010, and 2020) to make it adaptable to changes in global trade, technology, and contemporary commercial practice. The 2010 changes, for example, were necessitated by 1) the need to adapt trade terms to domestic law in important trading nations such as the USA (Uniform Commercial Code, Sarbanes–Oxley Act of 2002); 2) the desire to increase participation and input from emerging nations that are significant players in global trade such as Brazil and China; and 3) the increased importance of multimodal transportation and the need for a broader scope of shipping terms to address land, ocean, and air movements.

The current revision of Incoterms (2020) was published and came into effect on January 1, 2020. Incoterms, 2020 does not introduce any significant changes to Incoterms, 2010. It retains many of the key 2010 elements, such as the classification of eleven terms based on the type of transport (multimodal and maritime). It also retains the obligations of buyer and seller except for minor changes pertaining to the inspection of goods. Incoterms, 2020 introduces some specific changes in areas such as:

- providing parties with an option of bill of lading notation for Free Carrier (FCA)
- requiring maximum insurance coverage for Carriage and Insurance Paid To (CIP) contracts
- replacing Delivered at Terminal (DAT) with Delivered at Place Unloaded (DPU) (the obligations remain the same)
- cost/risk issues relating to customs clearance
- inland transport by seller's or buyer's own means for FCA, Delivered at Place (DAP), Delivered Duty Paid (DDP), Delivered Duty Unpaid (DDU) contracts
- security-related requirements.

It also uses language that is non-technical and easy to understand by the trading community.

Incoterms is a set of rules and not laws. It is neither national legislation nor an international treaty. However, when parties to an international sales contract agree to be governed by Incoterms, the term takes on the force of law and questions pertaining to delivery of goods will be interpreted according to Incoterms. If the parties do not explicitly agree to be governed by Incoterms, it could be made an implicit term of the contract as part of international custom.

Businesses that understand the implications of Incoterms excel at facilitating the movement of goods, stabilize lead times, and often reduce the landed cost of merchandise. This could serve as a source of competitive advantage (International Perspectives 7.1 and 7.2). In short, Incoterms accomplishes the following objectives:

- It provides a set of international rules for the interpretation of the most commonly used terms of sale.
- It reduces uncertainty arising from different interpretations of such terms in different countries.
- It defines the rights and obligations of the parties to the contract of sale pertaining to the delivery of goods sold (who organizes carriage or insurance

of the goods or who will be responsible for export/import license or shipping documentation).

- It clearly delineates the tasks, costs, and risks associated with the transportation and delivery of goods (when risk transfers from seller to buyer, who bears the cost of transportation, packaging, loading, or unloading goods).

The national laws of each country often determine the rights and duties of parties with respect to terms of sale. In the United States, the Revised American Foreign Trade Definitions (1941) and The Uniform Commercial Code (UCC) govern terms of sale. Since 1980, the sponsors of the Revised American Foreign Trade Definitions recommend the use of Incoterms. In order to avoid any misunderstanding, parties to export contracts should always state the application of the current version of Incoterms. The UCC and Incoterms complement each other in many areas. Trade terms are not understood in the same manner in every country and it is important to explicitly state the law that governs the contract. For example, a contract should state "FOB New York (Incoterms, 2020)" or "CIF Liverpool (Uniform Commercial Code)."

All trade terms are classified into four groups based on the point of transfer of risk (delivery) from seller to buyer. They are displayed in order of increasing obligations for the seller. This means that a Group E term such as EXW signifies the least obligation to the seller compared to a Group D term that imposes the maximum amount of responsibility on the seller (Tables 7.3 and 7.4).

1. **Group E term (EXW):** This grouping has only one term and represents the seller's minimum obligation, i.e., to place the goods at the disposal of the buyer. There are no contractual arrangements between seller and buyer with regard to insurance, transportation, or export.
2. **Group F terms (FCA, FAS, FOB):** The seller is expected to bear the risk and expense of delivery to a nominated carrier. It is the buyer's responsibility to arrange and pay for the main carriage to the point of destination.
3. **Group C terms (Cost and freight [CFR], CIF, CPT, CIP):** C terms establish the point of delivery (transfer of risk) from seller to buyer at the point of shipment. However, they extend the seller's obligation with regard to the costs of carriage and insurance up to the point of destination. This means that the seller bears certain costs even after the critical point for the division of the risk or damage to the goods. They are often referred to as shipment terms.
4. **Group D terms (DPU, DAP, DDP):** The seller's delivery obligation extends to the country of destination. This means that the seller could be held liable for breach of contract if the goods are lost or damaged after shipment but before arrival at the agreed point of destination. The seller may be required to provide substitute goods or other forms of restitution to the buyer. They are often referred to as arrival terms. It is not ideal for letter of credit transactions since the bill of lading or air waybill does not show actual arrival.

Incoterms 2020 consists of eleven terms, divided into two major groups:

- *Group for any mode of transport*: This includes trade terms used for carriage by road, rail, air, and multimodal, i.e., EXW, FCA, CPT, CIP, DPU, DAP, and DDP.

TABLE 7.3 Groups of Incoterms, 2020

Group (based on Incoterms 2020)	Any Mode of Transport	Maritime Transport	Transfer of Risk
Group E: Departure *Seller makes goods available to buyer at seller's premises*	Ex Works (EXW) *Maximum obligation to buyer*		**EXW:** When goods are placed at the disposal of the buyer
Group F: Main Carriage Unpaid *Seller delivers goods to a carrier nominated by buyer* *Facilitates importer security filing (ISF) (10+2) reporting for U.S. importers to screen for dangerous cargo*	Free Carrier (FCA)	Free Alongside Ship (FAS) Free On Board (FOB)	**FCA:** Upon seller's delivery to the carrier at the named place **FAS:** When goods are placed alongside the ship **FOB:** When goods are placed on board the vessel at the port of departure
Group C: Main Carriage Paid *Seller contracts for carriage of goods but does not assume the risk of loss/damage after shipment. U.S. Importers rely on supplier's forwarder for ISF documentation*	Carriage Paid To (CPT) Carriage and Insurance Paid To (CIP)	Cost and Freight (CFR) Cost, Insurance and Freight (CIF)	**CPT:** Upon seller's delivery to the main carrier at the place of departure **CIP:** As CPT **CFR:** When goods are placed on board the vessel at the port of departure **CIF:** As CFR
Group D: Arrival *Seller responsible for all costs and risks required to deliver the goods to destination* *U.S. importers rely on supplier's forwarder for ISF documentation*	Delivered At Place Unloaded (DPU) Delivered At Place (DAP) Delivered Duty Paid (DDP) *Maximum obligation to seller*		**DPU:** When the goods are unloaded from the arriving vehicle (not cleared) at the buyer's disposal at the agreed place of destination **DAP:** When the goods are placed at the buyer's disposal at the agreed destination (not unloaded and not cleared) **DDP:** When goods cleared and duty paid (not unloaded) are placed at the buyer's disposal at the agreed destination

TABLE 7.4 Incoterms 2020: Division of Costs, Licenses, and Formalities

Term	Main Transport	Transport Insurance	Export Clearance	Import Taxes	Export License	Import License
EXW	Buyer	No party obligated to insure	Buyer	Buyer	Buyer	Buyer
FCA	Buyer	No party obligated to insure	Seller	Buyer	Seller	Buyer
FAS	Buyer	No party obligated to insure	Seller	Buyer	Seller	Buyer
FOB	Buyer	No party obligated to insure	Seller	Buyer	Seller	Buyer
CFR	Seller	No party obligated to insure	Seller	Buyer	Seller	Buyer
CIF	Seller	Seller	Seller	Buyer	Seller	Buyer
CPT	Seller	No party obligated to insure	Seller	Buyer	Seller	Buyer
CIP	Seller	Seller	Seller	Buyer	Seller	Buyer
DDU	Seller	No party obligated to insure	Seller	Buyer	Seller	Buyer
DAP	Seller	No party obligated to insure	Seller	Buyer	Seller	Buyer
DDP	Seller	No party obligated to insure	Seller	Seller	Seller	Seller

- *Group for maritime transport*: Trade terms under this group are used for carriage over water from port to port including inland waterways. They include FAS, FOB, CFR, and CIF.

Incoterms and Scope of Coverage

Incoterms only covers the delivery aspects of an international sales contract. Seller's delivery obligations include responsibility for risk of loss or damage to the goods, transportation and customs-related costs as well as other functional responsibilities (packaging, export clearance, contract of carriage, etc.). Incoterms, however, does not cover or address the following areas:

- *Transfer of title*: Incoterms does not deal with transfer of ownership of goods.
- *Payment terms or methods*: Incoterms does not address matters pertaining to payment terms such as cash in advance or letter of credit. Such issues must be covered with a separate clause in the contract of sale.

- *Remedies for breach of contract*: Incoterms does not cover consequences for breach of contract.
- *Any other non-delivery-related issues*: Incoterms is not a substitute for contracts of sale, carriage, or insurance. These questions must be addressed separately.

The Concept of Delivery under Incoterms

Sellers' delivery obligations under Incoterms do not always entail the physical transfer of possession of goods to the buyer (Chikwava, 2012). There are many cases where such delivery is completed well before the arrival of goods at their destination. Incoterms links delivery to the risk of loss or damage to the goods. This means that a seller's delivery obligation is completed at the point where risk of loss or damage to the merchandise is transferred from the seller to the buyer. In CIF contracts, for example, delivery takes place when the goods are placed on board the ship at the port of departure while in FCA contracts, such delivery (transfer of risk) takes place when the goods have been delivered to the carrier at the named place (Table 7.4).

Incoterms 2020: Trade Terms

All trade terms are classified into four groups based on the concept of progressive delivery responsibility of the seller. They provide a standardized, universal set of shipping terms that are consistent with contemporary business practices and modes of transportation for domestic and international shipments.

Group E (EXW): Delivery at Agreed Point of Collection

Under this term, the buyer or agent must collect the goods at the seller's works, warehouse, or store. The seller bears all risk and expenses until the goods are placed at the disposal of the buyer at the time and place agreed for delivery. The seller has neither the obligation to load the goods nor clear the goods for export.

Risk is not transferred to the buyer if damage or loss is attributed to the failure on the part of the seller to deliver the goods in conformity with the contract (e.g., damage due to inadequate packing of goods).

The buyer bears all risk and charges pertaining to pre-shipment inspection, export/import licenses, and customs duties/taxes needed for exportation. The buyer is also responsible for clearance of goods for export, transit, and imports since the seller makes the goods available to the buyer in the country of export. The seller must provide the goods and the commercial invoice as provided in the contract.

This term of sale is similar to a domestic sales transaction, even though the product is destined for export. This term may be out of line with international business practice since many countries require exporters to be responsible for export clearance or compliance with export regulations. There may be concern with diversion of goods since the buyer is the party that is responsible for export and documentation. Furthermore, there is no standard as to what documentation constitutes evidence of delivery.

Ex works terms are suitable for sellers with limited international experience. It is advisable to use FCA when sending full containers because the seller loads the goods on the carrier sent by the buyer. It may be used irrespective of the mode of transport.

Group F (FCA, FAS, and FOB): Delivery on Buyer's Side of Anticipated Carriage

Free Carrier (FCA) (Named Place of Delivery)

The seller bears the risk and costs relating to the goods until delivery to the carrier or any other person nominated by the buyer. The place of delivery could be the carrier's cargo terminal, port, or airport or a vehicle sent to pick up the goods at the seller's premises. In the latter case, the seller is responsible for loading the goods onto the buyer's collecting vehicle. If the place of delivery is the carrier's cargo terminal, port, or airport, the seller is only required to bring the goods to the terminal, port, or airport (and is not obligated to unload them). The carrier is more likely to have the necessary personnel and equipment to unload the goods at its own terminal or other location than the seller.

The carrier nominated by the buyer could be a trucker, a freight forwarder, a steamship line, or an airline. The seller must fulfill the export formalities. Free Carrier terms are suitable for carriage by road, rail, and air, or for multimodal transport, in particular when using containers. If the parties agree, the buyer can instruct the carrier to issue to the seller (at the buyer's cost and expense) a transport document stating that the goods have been loaded (bill of loading with onboard notation).

Upon delivery of the goods to the carrier, the seller receives (from the carrier) a receipt which serves as evidence of delivery and contract of carriage made on behalf of the buyer. Neither party is required to insure under FCA. However, the seller must provide the buyer (upon request) with the necessary information for procuring insurance. When using full container load (FCL), risk of loss shifts to the buyer once the goods are loaded, primarily in the factory or on the seller's premises. In the case of less than full container load (LCL), risk is transferred after the goods are delivered to the groupage warehouse named by the buyer. Similar to FAS and FOB terms, FCA only covers pre-transport (the main transport risk lies with buyer). If the seller arranges and pays for carriage and insurance, it turns into CIP shipment (or CPT without insurance) (Table 7.5).

Besides payment of the purchase price as provided in the contract, the buyer has the following obligations:

- Obtain at his/her own risk and expense any import license and other official authorization necessary for importation of the goods as well as for their transit through another country
- Contract at his/her own expense for carriage of the goods from the named place of delivery
- Pay the costs of any pre-shipment inspection except when such inspection is mandated by the exporting country.

Free Alongside Ship (FAS) (Named Port of Shipment)

This term requires the seller to deliver the goods to a named port alongside a vessel to be designated by the buyer (Incoterms, 2020). "Alongside the vessel" has been

TABLE 7.5 Price Determination Worksheet

Price (or cost) per unit _____ X _____ unites = total	+
Profit (or markup)	+
Commissions	+
Financing costs	+
EX FACTORY	=
Crating/containerization charges (if done at factory)	+
Labeling and marking costs (if done at factory)	+
Drayage charges (usually associated with movement of containers from railroad ramp to plant and back to ramp)	+
Loading charges, if applicable	+
Demurrage and detention charges, if applicable	+
Other charges (specify)	+
FREE CARRIER (FCA)	=
TRUCK OR RAILCAR AT POINT OF ORIGIN	
Inland freight charges (including fuel surcharges)	+
Unloading charges at port facilities	+
Drayage to packer (crater/containerized), if applicable	+
Containerization/crating charges (if done at port)	+
Labeling and marking (if done at port)	+
Freight forwarding and documentation charges (includes charges associated with consular fees, export license, postage, telex, and telephone/telegram use, etc.)	+
Drayage to warehouse and unloading, if applicable	+
Warehousing charges, if applicable	+
Loading and drayage to pier from packer or warehouse, if applicable	+
Wharfage charges	+
Terminal notification charges	+
Demurrage/detention at port	+
FREE ALONGSIDE SHIP AT PORT OF _____	=
Vessel loading charges	+
Heavy lift or extra-length charges, if applicable	+
Other charges (specify)	+
FREE ON BOARD VESSEL AT PORT OF _____	=
Ocean freight charges	+
Bunker or other surcharges, if applicable	+
COST AND FREIGHT TO _____	=
Insurance	+
COST, INSURANCE, AND FREIGHT TO _____	=

understood to mean that the goods be within reach of a ship's lifting tackle. The risks to the goods pass to the buyer upon the seller's delivery alongside the ship. This implies that all charges and risks for the goods are borne by the buyer from the time they have been effectively delivered alongside the vessel.

The seller must obtain at his own risk and expense any export license and other official authorizations including customs formalities that are necessary for the export of the goods. The seller's obligation to clear the goods for export is similar to that of FOB contracts. There is an implied duty on the part of the seller to cooperate in arranging a loading and shipping schedule and render at the buyer's request and expense every assistance in obtaining necessary documents for the import of the goods and their transit through another country. The seller must provide the buyer (at his/her own expense) with the usual proof of delivery.

The buyer must contract (at his/her own expense) for the carriage of goods from the port of shipment. Since the buyer has to nominate the ship, he/she has to pay any additional costs incurred if a) the named vessel fails to arrive on time, or b) the vessel is unable to take the goods. In such cases, a premature passing of risk will occur. Costs of any pre-shipment inspection are borne by the buyer except when such inspection is mandated by the exporting country.

The use of FAS was appropriate in cases where sellers took their shipments to the pier and deposited it close enough for loading. However, nowadays most of the outbound cargo is delivered to shipping lines days before placement alongside the vessel. Neither is it applicable in cases of rolling cargo (cars, trucks) that can be driven aboard vessel or ports with shallow harbors that do not allow for vessels to come alongside the pier. Free Alongside Ship terms are often used for oversized cargo such as heavy equipment in oil and gas or mining as well as bulk or break bulk shipments that require special handling during loading or transit. The seller does not wish to assume the risk of loss during the loading of the vessel.

Free on Board (FOB) (Named Port of Shipment)

The central feature of FOB contracts is the notion that the seller undertakes to place the goods on board the ship designated by the buyer. This includes responsibility for all charges incurred up to and including delivery of the goods over the ship's rail at the named port of shipment (Incoterms, 2020). The buyer has to nominate a suitable ship and inform the seller of its name, loading point, and delivery time. If the ship that was originally nominated is unable or unavailable to receive the cargo at the agreed time for loading, the buyer has to nominate a substitute ship and pay all additional charges. Once the seller delivers the goods on board the ship, the buyer is responsible for all subsequent charges such as freight, marine insurance, unloading charges, import duties, and other expenses due on arrival at the port of destination. Unless otherwise stated in the contract of sale, it is customary in FOB contracts for the seller to procure the export license and other formalities necessary for the export of the goods since the latter is more familiar with licensing practices and procedures in the exporting country than the buyer. Transfer of risk occurs upon the seller's delivery of the goods on board the vessel (uploaded, placed, and tied in the hold or on the ship's deck). The seller and buyer need to agree on what constitutes loading on board the vessel since different products are loaded differently. The seller is responsible for the performance of the carrier loading the ship even though the latter is chosen by the buyer (Incoterms, 2020).

The seller's responsibility for loss or damage to the goods terminates on delivery to the carrier.

Free on Board does not appear to be consistent with current practice except for shipments of non-containerized, bulk, or general cargo, or shipments by chartered vessel. It is ideal for bulk/break bulk shipments that are loaded directly on the ship. In many other cases, sellers are required to deliver their outbound cargo to shipping lines days before actual loading of the cargo. In cases where merchandise is transported in containers to ports of shipment, Incoterms 2020 recommends using FCA instead of FOB since containers are delivered in the port's container terminal (not loaded on the ship). It is a common term used with letter of credit transactions.

INTERNATIONAL PERSPECTIVE 7.1

Incoterms 2010 versus Incoterms 2020: Important differences

Incoterms

- *General changes*: Incoterms 2020 attempts to eliminate technicalities and legal terminologies to make it easier for people who do not have legal knowledge or expertise. It also provides detailed explanatory notes and a breakdown of cost allocations.
- *FCA (option of bill of lading with on-board notation)*: Prior to 2020, problems occurred when the seller was responsible for load goods on a truck or other means of transport hired by the buyer (not the international carrier). Banks required sellers to present a bill of lading with an on-board citation to get paid (letters of credit payments). This made it difficult for them to receive payment since international carriers issue such bill of lading only when goods are directly presented to them. Incoterms 2020 allows buyers, if the parties agree, to instruct international carriers to issue a bill of lading on behalf of the sellers with an on-board notation indicating that the goods have been loaded on the ship. This is intended to provide proof of delivery of goods and thereby facilitate payment to the seller. For example, the seller in Davie, Florida, where goods are picked up by the buyer's truck, may need a bill of lading (BL) (for letters of credit requirements) to state that the goods have been placed on board the ship in Port Everglades, Florida (even though carriers do not normally issue a BL since Davie is not a port and goods cannot be placed on board a vessel in Davie).
- *CIP and CIF*: Incoterms 2010 rules provide that for both CIP and CIF contracts, the seller is obligated to obtain at its own expense insurance complying at least with the minimum cover i.e., Institute of Cargo clause C or FPA. Incoterms 2020 retains the minimum cover for CIF contracts (CIF is commonly used for bulk transport such as raw materials or minerals whose prices are low per pound or kilo). However, it requires maximum cover (ICC-A) for CIP contracts, which are often used for manufactures and relatively expensive merchandise. The latter is mandatory for letter of credit transactions.
- *DAT to DPU*: A new term is introduced (DPU). This term replaces DAT, although the obligations remain the same.
- *Cost/risk for customs clearance*: Incoterms 2020 clarifies the cost/risks for customs clearance.
- *Inland transport with seller's or buyer's own means of transport*: Unlike Incoterms 2010, Incoterms 2020 recognizes that goods can be transported without the use of third-party carriers and that sellers or buyers may be using their own means of transportation to deliver or collect goods.. For example, a U.S. buyer in Miami who acquired the goods can transport the merchandise to Houston using its own means.

- *Security-related requirements:* Incoterms 2020 addresses security in terms of a) transportation from country of origin to country of destination and b) customs clearance formalities and procedures. In the case of transportation of goods, the security liability falls on the parties that are responsible for the carriage of goods i.e., seller (CPT, CFR, CIP, CIF, DAP, DDP, DPU) or buyer (EXW, FCA, FAS, FOB). The party responsible for customs clearance also assumes the liability for safety.

Group C (CIF, CFR, CPT, CIP): Delivery on Seller's Side of Anticipated Carriage

Cost, Insurance, and Freight (CIF) (Named Port of Destination)

The CIF contract places upon the seller the obligation to arrange for shipment of the goods. The seller has to ship goods described under the contract to be delivered at the destination and arrange for insurance to be available for the benefit of the buyer or any other person with insurable interest in the goods. In the absence of express agreement, the insurance shall be in accordance with the minimum cover provided by the Institute of Cargo Clauses (Clause C) or a similar set of guidelines. The cost of freight is borne by the seller (Incoterms 2020). The seller must notify the buyer that the goods have been delivered on board the vessel to enable the buyer to receive the goods.

The seller has to tender the necessary documents: commercial invoice, bill of lading, and policy of insurance to the buyer so that the latter can obtain delivery upon arrival of the goods or recover for their loss. The buyer must accept the documents when tendered by the seller when they are in conformity with the contract of sale and pay the purchase price. Import duties/licenses, consular fees, and charges to procure a certificate of origin are the responsibility of the buyer while export licenses and other customs formalities necessary for the export of the goods have to be obtained by the seller.

The CIF contract may provide certain advantages to the overseas customer because the seller often possesses expert knowledge and experience to make favorable arrangements with respect to freight, insurance, and other charges. This could be reflected in terms of reduced import prices for the overseas customer.

Under a CIF contract, risk passes to the buyer upon delivery, that is, when the goods are put on board the ship at the port of departure. However, risk is not transferred to the buyer unless the merchandise is uploaded, placed, and tied in the hold or on the ship's deck. All costs and risks of unloading the goods at the port of destination are borne by the buyer.

Rejection of documents versus rejection of goods: When proper shipping documents that are in conformity with the contract are tendered, the buyer must accept them and pay the purchase price. The right to reject the goods arises when they are landed and, after examination, they are found not to be in conformity with the contract. The buyer can claim damages for breach of contract relating to the goods. The buyer's acceptance of conforming documents does not impair subsequent rejection of the goods and recovery of the purchase price if upon arrival the goods are not in accordance with the terms of sale. It may also happen that while the goods conform to the contract, the documents are not in accordance with the contract of sale (discrepancies between documents such as bill of lading, commercial invoice, draft, and the letter of credit or contract of sale). In this case, the buyer may waive the discrepancies and agree to accept the goods. Thus, under a CIF contract, the right to reject the documents is separate and distinct from the right to reject the goods.

Payment is often made against documents. Tender of the goods cannot be an alternative to tender of the documents in CIF contracts.

Loss of goods: If the goods shipped under a CIF contract are destroyed or lost during transit, the seller is entitled to claim the purchase price against presentation of proper shipping documents to the buyer. Since insurance is taken for the benefit of the buyer, the buyer can claim against the insurer insofar as the risk is covered by the policy. If the loss is due to some misconduct on the part of the carrier, not covered by the policy, the buyer could recover from the carrier. Cost, insurance, and freight terms are better suited for bulk cargo and not for containerized shipments since the latter are delivered at the port terminal and not loaded onto the vessel by the seller. It is a common term used with letter of credit transactions (the seller keeps control of shipping terms specified in the letter of credit).

The only difference between CIF and CFR terms is that the latter does not require the seller to obtain and pay for cargo insurance.

Carriage Paid To (CPT) (Named Place of Destination)

These terms are similar to the CFR terms, except that it may be used for any other type of transportation. Even though the seller is obligated to arrange and pay for the transportation to a named place of destination, he/she completes delivery obligations and thus transfers risk of loss/damage to the buyer when the goods are delivered to the first carrier (named by the seller) at the place of shipment. The seller pays the main carriage to the destination but does not carry the transport risk. The buyer is required to collect the goods at the place and on the date agreed by the parties. All costs and risks of unloading at the destination are borne by the buyer.

The seller must notify the buyer that the goods have been delivered to the carrier (or first carrier in the case of multimodal transportation) and also give any other notice required to enable the buyer to take receipt of the goods. These terms are appropriate for multimodal transportation. When several carriers are involved (e.g., pre-carriage by road or rail from the seller's warehouse for further carriage by sea to the destination), the seller has fulfilled his/her delivery obligation under CPT terms when the goods have been handed over for carriage to the first carrier. In CFR and CIF contracts, delivery is not completed until the goods have reached a vessel at the port of shipment.

In the absence of an explicit agreement between the parties, there is no requirement to provide a negotiable bill of lading (to enable the buyer to sell the goods in transit). The buyer must pay the costs of any pre-shipment inspection unless such inspection is mandated by the exporting country. The CPT terms are similar to the CIP terms, except the seller is not required to arrange or pay for insurance coverage of the goods during transportation. Carriage Paid To and CIP are the non-maritime counterparts of CFR and CIF and better suited to container transport.

INTERNATIONAL PERSPECTIVE 7.2

Incoterms and Business Strategies

- *Which Incoterms are appropriate?* The choice is dependent on the type of cargo and whether the buyer's intention is to sell the goods in transit. It also depends on the ability of the parties to obtain the most favorable contract of carriage.
- *Appropriateness of C versus F terms*: In cases where the seller can procure marine insurance at a competitive price and where there are government regulations to use national shipping lines, it may be appropriate to use CFR and CIF. If the parties prefer the seller to procure carriage (CPT) and insurance, CIP may be appropriate. When the buyer can procure insurance at a competitive rate, the parties may prefer to use FAS or FOB.
- *Manufactured goods*: Exporters of manufactured goods often sell on extended terms using DDP (the seller makes goods available to the buyer at the destination) to remain competitive. Since such goods are normally containerized, the parties can also use FCA, CPT, or CIP.
- *Use of EXW, FCA*: Large buyers such as wholesalers or department stores may find it advantageous to arrange for transportation in order to ensure just-in-time deliveries.

Group D (DPU, DAP, DDP): Delivery at Destination (Arrival Terms)

All Group D terms can be used with all modes of transport. These terms share certain common features:

a. They are arrival/destination terms.
b. The seller is required to arrange for transportation, pay freight, and bear the risk of loss to a named point of destination.
c. The seller must place the goods at the disposal of the buyer (varied according to the chosen term).
d. There is no requirement for use of a negotiable bill of lading and delivery occurs only after arrival of the goods.
e. Incoterms do not require insurance during transportation. The seller may have to arrange and pay for insurance or act as self-insurer during transportation.
f. The buyer must pay the costs of any pre-shipment inspection except when such inspection is mandated by the exporting country. There are no provisions for post-shipment inspection.

Delivered at Place Unloaded (DPU) (Named Terminal at Port or Place at Destination)

DPU is a new addition to Incoterms 2020. It replaces DAT and applies to all modes of transport. This is the only term where goods are delivered unloaded at the destination. The seller must deliver goods to the buyer by unloading from the arriving means of transport and placing them at the disposal of the buyer. The DPU terms were introduced to replace DAT because of the diversity of delivery locations with facilities for unloading such as airports, ports, free zones, and transport terminals.

The seller is responsible for export clearance and transport costs up to the named place of destination. The customer is responsible for customs clearance, duties, and taxes. These terms are included in light of the recognition that air and ocean shipments are often off-loaded at agreed locations such as free zones instead of the named place of destination. It works well for LCL or consolidation shipments. It is suitable for bulk complex goods, containers that are delivered unloaded at the port or free trade zones (see International Perspective 7.3).

Delivered at Place (DAP) (Named Place of Destination)

These terms are similar to DPU except that in the case of DAP, the buyer is responsible for unloading the goods at the named place of destination. Delivered at Place is used when the buyer provides equipment such as forklifts for unloading. It is ideal for sales between countries with no customs formalities.

Delivery Duty Paid (DDP) (Named Place of Destination)

Delivery Duty Paid is similar to DAP except that the seller bears the costs, including duties and taxes, and risks involved in bringing the goods into the country of destination. It is also similar to DPU except that import clearance is done by the buyer in the case of DPU while this responsibility falls on the seller in the case of DDP. Delivery Duty Paid is suitable for courier shipments of low value. It is risky for exporters since they have to deal with foreign customs that are not familiar to them. These terms are recommended for firms with extensive experience in trade and logistics, sales within MNCs such as to branches and subsidiaries, and exports of high-value goods such as jewelry since the seller retains ownership and possession throughout the process.

The major differences between arrival contracts and a CIF contract are as follows:

- In arrival contracts, delivery takes place when the goods are placed at the disposal of the buyer. Under CIF terms, delivery is upon loading the goods on board the vessel at the port of departure.
- In arrival contracts, the buyer is under no obligation to pay the purchase price if the goods are lost on transit. In CIF contracts, the buyer is required to pay against documents. However, the loss of goods gives the buyer the right of claim from the carrier or the insurance company depending on the circumstances.

INTERNATIONAL PERSPECTIVE 7.3

Application of Incoterms

Parties to a business transaction that intend to use Incoterms should consider the following steps before they apply Incoterms to their transaction:

- **Select the appropriate rule**: It is important to consider carefully which of the rules is appropriate to the type of goods being delivered, the means of transport used, and the allocation of responsibilities, costs and risks desired by the parties.

- **Use a formal sales contract**: Incoterms cannot be a substitute for a sales contract as they do not provide a comprehensive set of terms. Consequently, Incoterms needs to be incorporated into a formal sales contract which deals with the areas on which Incoterms is silent, such as: specifications of the goods, price, payment, transfer of title to the goods, tax, warranties, consequences of breach, governing law, and dispute resolution.
- **Expressly incorporate the rule into the sales contract**: For Incoterms to apply to a transaction, it needs to be expressly incorporated into the sales contract by specific reference to the relevant rule chosen from Incoterms. Care should be taken to reference the appropriate version/year of Incoterms to be applied.
- **Specify the place or port for delivery as precisely as possible**: The more precisely the place or port for delivery is specified the less room there is for confusion or disputes between the parties.

CHAPTER SUMMARY

Sources of export competitiveness	Price and nonprice factors such as reliable delivery, short delivery time, product reliability, product quality, design flexibility, support services, financial services.
Export pricing objectives	Market share, profits, a targeted level of return on investment.
Pricing and markup policy	1. High markups are common in industries with relatively few competitors and which produce differentiated products. 2. Low markups are common in sectors of increased competition.
Determinants of export prices	*Internal Variables* Cost of production, cost of market research, business travel, product modification and packing, consultants, freight forwarders, and level of product differentiation. *External Variables* Supply and demand, location and environment of foreign market, and home country regulations.
Approaches to export pricing	1. Cost-based pricing: export price is based on full cost and markup or full cost plus a desired amount of return on investment. 2. Marginal pricing: export price is based on the variable cost of producing the product. 3. Skimming versus penetration pricing: price skimming is charging a premium price for a product; penetration pricing is based on charging lower prices for exports to increase market share. 4. Demand-based pricing: export price is based on what the market can bear. 5. Competitive pricing: export prices are based on competitive pressures in the market.

Incoterms 2020

Rules for any mode of transport

1. EXW, Ex Works (named place of delivery): Buyer or agent must collect the goods at the seller's works or warehouse.
2. FCA, Free Carrier (named place of delivery): Place of delivery could be the carrier's cargo terminal (seller not obligated to unload) or a vehicle sent to pick up the goods at the seller's premises (seller required to load the goods on the vehicle).
3. CPT, Carriage Paid To (named place of destination): Seller delivers goods to the carrier nominated by him/her and also pays the cost of carriage necessary to deliver the goods to the named destination.
4. CIP, Carriage and Insurance Paid To (named place of destination): Similar to CPT, except that the seller is required to arrange and pay for insurance.
5. DPU, Delivered at Place Unloaded (named terminal, port or other place of destination): Seller delivers and unloads the goods at agreed destination.
6. DAP, Delivered at Place (named place of destination): Seller delivers still loaded but ready for unloading at an agreed place of destination in buyer's country.
7. DDP, Delivery Duty Paid (named place of destination): Seller delivers still loaded but ready for unloading at an agreed place of destination. Seller bears all costs and risks to bring the goods to country of destination, including duties and taxes.

Rules for sea and inland waterway transport

1. FAS, Free Alongside Ship (named port of shipment): Requires the seller to deliver goods to a named port alongside a vessel to be designated by the buyer. Seller's responsibilities end upon delivery alongside the vessel.
2. FOB, Free On Board (named port of shipment): Seller is obliged to deliver the goods on board a vessel to be designated by the buyer.
3. CIF, Cost, Insurance, Freight: This term requires the seller to arrange for carriage by sea and pay freight and insurance to a port of destination. Seller's obligations are complete (transfer of risk) when the goods are put onboard the ship at the port of departure.
4. CFR, Cost And Freight: Similar to CIF, except that the seller is not obligated to arrange and pay for insurance.

TABLE 7.6 Reference Guide to Incoterms 2020

Services	Rules for Any Mode of Transport							Sea/Inland Waterway			
	EXW	FCA	CPT	CIP	DPU	DAP	DDP	FAS	FOB	CFR	CIF
	Party Responsible for Payment of Services										
Export packing	Seller	Seller	Seller	Seller	Seller	Seller	Seller	Seller	Seller	Seller	Seller
Marking & Labeling	Seller	Seller	Seller	Seller	Seller	Seller	Seller	Seller	Seller	Seller	Seller
Block & brace	A	A	A	A	A	A	A	A	A	A	A
Export clearance (license/EEI/AES)	Buyer	Seller	Seller	Seller	Seller	Seller	Seller	Seller	Seller	Seller	Seller
FF documentation fees*	Buyer	Buyer	Seller	Seller	Seller	Seller	Seller	Buyer	Seller	Seller	Seller
Inland freight to main carrier	Buyer	B	Seller	Seller	Seller	Seller	Seller	Seller	Seller	Seller	Seller
Original terminal charges	Buyer	Buyer	Seller	Seller	Seller	Seller	Seller	Buyer	Seller	Seller	Seller
Vessel loading charges	Buyer	Buyer	Seller	Seller	Seller	Seller	Seller	Buyer	Seller	Seller	Seller
Ocean/air freight	Buyer	Buyer	Seller	Seller	Seller	Seller	Seller	Buyer	Buyer	Seller	Seller
Nominate export forwarder	Buyer	Buyer	Seller	Seller	Seller	Seller	Seller	Buyer	Buyer	Seller	Seller
Marine insurance	C	C	C	Seller	C	C	C	C	C	C	Seller
Unload main carrier charges	Buyer	Buyer	D	D	Seller	Seller	Seller	Buyer	Buyer	D	D
Destination terminal charges	Buyer	Buyer	D	D	D	Seller	Seller	Buyer	Buyer	D	D
Nominate on-carrier	Buyer	Buyer	E	E	E	E	E	Buyer	Buyer	Buyer	Buyer
Security info requirements	Buyer	Buyer	Buyer	Buyer	Buyer	Buyer	Buyer	Buyer	Buyer	Buyer	Buyer
Customs broker clearance fees	Buyer	Buyer	Buyer	Buyer	Buyer	Buyer	Seller	Buyer	Buyer	Buyer	Buyer
Duty/customs/taxes	Buyer	Buyer	Buyer	Buyer	Buyer	Buyer	Seller	Buyer	Buyer	Buyer	Buyer
Delivery to buyer at destination	Buyer	Buyer	E	E	E	E	E	Buyer	Buyer	Buyer	Buyer
Delivery carrier unloading	Buyer	Buyer	Buyer	Buyer	Seller	Buyer	Buyer	Buyer	Buyer	Buyer	Buyer

A: Stowage within containers not covered in Incoterms. It is subject to sales contract between parties.

B: FCA seller's facility; other FCA qualifiers. Seller arranges and loads pre-carriage carrier and pays inland freight to the "F" delivery place.

C: Insurance of goods not addressed.

D: Charges paid by buyer or seller depending on the contract.

E: Charges paid by seller if through bill of lading or door-to-door rate to buyer's destination.

* Freight forwarder documentation fees.

REVIEW QUESTIONS

1. High markups are common in industries with relatively few competitors. Discuss and provide examples.
2. The large influx of shrimp imports into the United States from Asia and Latin America depressed wholesale prices by over 40 percent between 1997 and 2002. Despite such lower prices, shrimp entrées at some U. S. seafood restaurants rose by about 28 percent during the same period. Discuss why prices (e.g., shrimp prices at seafood restaurants) are not aligned with costs.
3. What is the difference between marginal and cost-based pricing?
4. A seller agreed to deliver 300 tons of coffee to a buyer, FOB port of Montreal, Canada. The goods were transported and unloaded at the port and kept at a customs shed for inspection and payment of duties. The buyer was notified of the arrival of the merchandise and its location. Before the buyer picked up the goods, the customs shed (including the merchandise in it) was destroyed by fire. The buyer claims refund of the purchase price stating that she did not receive the goods. Is the seller responsible?
5. With reference to Q. 4, would the outcome be different if the contract had been DPU port of Montreal?
6. A seller in New York agreed to ship goods to a buyer in Lima, Peru under a CIF contract. The goods were loaded on the ship and the seller tendered the necessary documents to the buyer for payment (in New York). The buyer refused payment, claiming that it will only pay after inspection upon arrival of the goods at the port of destination. Is the seller entitled to payment before arrival of the goods?
7. Discuss the major differences between CIF and arrival contracts such as DDP.
8. State the major differences between Incoterms 2010 and Incoterms 2020.
9. What are the limitations of Incoterms?
10. In what cases would export–import managers prefer to use FAS (shipment) terms?

REFERENCES

Baldwin, R. E. and Ito, T. (2008). *Quality Competition Versus Price Competition Goods: An Empirical Classification* (No. w14305). National Bureau of Economic Research.

Brinton, C., Christopher, J., Wolff, R., and Winks, R. (1984). *A History of Civilization* (Volume I). Upper Saddle River, NJ: Prentice-Hall.

Burges, D. (2012). *Cargo Theft, Loss Prevention and Supply Chain Security*. London: Butterworths-Heinemann.

Chikwava, K. (2012). *Sustaining Contractual Business: An Exploration of the New Revised International Commercial Terms*. New York: Xlibris.

Coyne, K. P. and Horn, J. (2009). Predicting your competitor's reaction. *Harvard Business Review*, 87(4): 90–97.

Ding, M., Ross Jr., W. T., and Rao, V. R. (2010). Price as an indicator of quality: implications for utility and demand functions. *Journal of Retailing*, 86(1): 69–84.

Dussauge, P., Hart, S., and Ramanantsoa, B. (1987). *Strategic Technology Management*. New York: John Wiley and Sons.

Harr, E. (2020). *Competitive Differentiation: A Playbook for Winning in a Congested Market-place*. NY: Hinge. https://hingemarketing.com/blog/story/competitive-differentiation-a-playbook-for-winning-in-a-congested-marketplace.

Harrigan, J., Ma, X., and Shlychkov, V. (2015). Export prices of US firms. *Journal of International Economics*, 97(1): 100–111.

Heda, S., Mewborn, S., and Caine, S. (2017). How customers perceive a price is as important as the price itself. *Harvard Business Review*, 3: 2–5.

Hiam, A. and Schewe, C. (1992). *The Portable MBA in Marketing*. New York: John Wiley and Sons.

International Chamber of Commerce (2010; 2020). Incoterms. New York: ICC Publishing.

Mankiw, G. (2018). *Principles of Microeconomics*. New York: Cengage.

Martens, J., Scarpetta, S., and Pilat, D. (1996). Mark-up ratios in manufacturing industries. OECD Working Paper, No. 162 (April): 10–12.

Melitz, M. J. (2003). The impact of trade on intra-industry reallocations and aggregate industry productivity. *econometrica*, 71(6), 1695–1725.

Mints, P. (2019). SPV market research. www.spvmarketresearch.com/.

Oster, S. (1990). *Modern Competitive Analysis*. London: Oxford University Press.

Piercy, N. (1982). *Export Strategy: Markets and Competition.* London: Unwin Hyman.

Reich, R. (1991). *The Work of Nations*. New York: Knopf.

Silberston, A. (1970). Price behavior of firms. *Economic Journal*, 80(319): 511–570.

UN (2020). Trademap. New York: UN. www.trademap.org/.

Wang, L., Zhuang, R., Huang, S., and Zhao, Y. (2019). quality competition versus price competition: why does China dominate the global solar photo-voltaic market? *Emerging Markets Finance and Trade*, 55(6): 1326–1342.

Yue, W. and Wang, J. (2020). Government subsidies and firm-level markups: impact and mechanism. *Sustainability*, 12(7): 2726.

Zhang, M. (2014). 37 products with crazy-high markups. *Personal Finance.* www.businessinsider.com/personal-finance/products-high-markups-2014-7.

World Wide Web Resources

Export pricing
www.trade.gov/pricing-strategy

Pricing for profits
www.smartbiz.com/sbs/arts/ieb6.htm (information on pricing for an export–import business)

www.austrade.gov.au/Australian/Export/Guide-to-exporting/Export-pricing (Guide to exporting and export pricing)

Incoterms 2020
https://iccwbo.org/resources-for-business/incoterms-rules/

International Trade Closing Cases and Discussions

1. Incoterms (CIF)

A contract of sale was entered into between a U.S. company BAT Inc. of Calumet city, Illinois (buyer) and a German scientific equipment manufacturing firm Tola (seller), for the sale of a mobile MRI scanner. Tola sent the requested MRI machine to the buyer aboard the ship *Superior Carrier* in good working condition. However, when it reached its final destination, it had been damaged and was in need of extensive repair. The buyer and its insurance company believe that the MRI scanner was damaged in transit. BAT's insurance company, St. Guardian Insurance, covered the cost of the damage, which was $350,000. In turn, the insurance company intends to recover from Tola. However, Tola claims that, since the goods were shipped under CIF (New York) terms, they were under no obligation for the loss, that is, its contractual obligation with regard to risk of loss ended when it delivered the machine to the vessel at the port of shipment. The buyer's insurance company contends that Incoterms was inapplicable since they were not specifically incorporated into the contract. They also argue that the seller's explicit retention of title modified the risk of loss.

Question

Do you agree with BAT and Guardian Insurance? Why/why not?

2. Incoterms (C&F)

In August 2006, International Commodities Export Corporation (ICEC) entered into an agreement for the sale of 230 tons of Chinese white beans to North Pacific Lumber company (NPL). According to the agreement, the beans were to conform to sample pc-16 and the shipment was to be made on the basis of C&F. Thirteen separate containers of beans were loaded on board two vessels at the port of Hong Kong to Portland, Oregon. An independent surveyor found the bean quality to be in conformity with the description of the goods in the shipper's invoice.

The U.S. Food and Drug Administration (FDA) detained the shipment on arrival in Portland, Oregon on the ground that the goods contained dirt and were unfit for human consumption. The beans were stored in a warehouse under federal government detention. After efforts to obtain release of the cargo, the buyer rejected the shipments for failure to conform to the contract (sample pc-16).

Questions

1. Did title pass from seller to buyer? If so, when?
2. Is the seller responsible for the goods under C&F when the goods are onboard the vessel? How about after delivery to the buyer?

CHAPTER 8

Export Sales Contracts

LEARNING OBJECTIVES:

8.1 Describe the essential elements of CISG

8.2 Understand the importance of harmonization of international contract law

8.3 Learn the major differences between CISG and the Uniform Commercial Code

8.4 Identify and discuss the major clauses in export contracts

8.5 Understand the importance of guarantees and bonds in export contracts

International Trade in Practice

The Role of Export Contracts for Non-traditional Exports from Developing Countries

Several studies show that besides the level of exports, the degree of diversification of such exports is important for sustained economic growth. Many developing countries depend on a few commodities for a major part of their export revenues. Such a narrow basket of goods often leads to instability arising from fluctuating global demand. Export diversification is one way to alleviate these constraints. In view of this, there is an effort to diversify exports into new commodities.

The Case of Chayote Exports from Costa Rica

Chayote is a pear-shaped fruit grown in areas of high humidity. Its quality is determined by its freshness, ripeness, size, appearance, color, and absence of residue. It is an important part of traditional diets across Central America. It is also consumed in many parts of Europe, North America, and Asia. In Costa Rica, the government provides targeted incentives for the development and export of non-traditional products. Private traders and processors are encouraged to guarantee inputs and access to foreign markets. Chayote is one of the non-traditional exports targeted by the government and accounts for an increasing share of the country's non-traditional export. Specialization in chayote production is largely based not only on prices, terms of payment, and extension of credits for inputs, but also on delivery contracts that provide sufficient certainty. Contracts reduce uncertainty to the farmer and increase loyalty towards the export processor.

The vast majority of Costa Rica's chayote exports go to North America. Cultivation is labor intensive and accounts for about 70 percent of total production cost. Exporters are required to deliver high quality produce at an established delivery frequency. They tend to use more material inputs and demand credit facilities to access registered varieties and processing equipment. Since storage can damage the fruit, farmers prefer to deliver their produce to the export processor with high frequency. Producers with contractual arrangements receive about 25 percent higher prices but also face higher risks of rejections. Contractual arrangements (between farmers and processors who export the produce) have many positive benefits for farmers:

- They generate economies of scope and reduce marketing risks.
- They reduce price uncertainty.
- They provide access to marketing information, technical assistance, specialized inputs, and financial resources. These facilities also help farmers produce better quality produce for the export market.
- They help improve quality due to better land use, crop management, and handling
- They enhance a sense of loyalty as farmers are assured of high delivery frequency since this helps in maintaining post-harvest quality and reducing rejection rates.

The Case of Horticultural Exports from Zimbabwe

Zimbabwe's economy suffers from ongoing economic weakness, high inflation, and shortages of foreign currency. It has begun, however, to show some signs of improvement. One of these areas is the promotion of non-traditional horticultural exports. This is mainly carried out through contract farming whereby horticultural exporters make contractual arrangements to buy produce from over 4,000 small scale producers for the export market. The horticultural firm (that processes the products for export) established seventeen collection centers distributed across the country. From then on, the firm takes ownership and undertakes preliminary screening for quality prior to export. It has formal and informal agreements with producers, which includes the provision of inputs (seeds etc.) for the crops on credit, minimum prices for the crops, and strict quality criteria which are enforced at collection. Important factors motivating small and medium-sized producers to enter into contractual arrangements with the firm are as follows:

- A reduction in market uncertainty through guaranteed minimum prices, a guaranteed market for crops, a reliable supply of inputs, and no need to transport crop to market
- Indirect benefits—acquisition of knowledge for use on traditional and new crops, stepping stone to other projects
- Earning extra income, in the absence of alternative sources of income
- Intangible benefits—promoting the benefits to other farmers, satisfaction from growing export products

HARMONIZATION OF CONTRACT LAW

Export sales contracts are central to international commercial transactions and around them revolves a series of connected, but distinct, relationships, including, cargo insurance, transportation, and payment arrangements. The rules and practices governing such contracts vary from one export transaction to another, based on the agreement of the parties as well as the legal system. National legal systems on contracts may differ, but the basic principles of contracts, such as good faith and consideration, are generally recognized and accepted in many countries. There is also a movement towards convergence among the world's different legal systems in the area of international commercial law (Lubman, 1988; DiMatteo, 1997; DiMatteo and Dhooge, 2006). Today, it is almost difficult to identify any examples of substantial divergence that produce important and predictable differences in the outcome of commercial disputes (Rosett, 1982). Certain differences in theory or approach are often offset by the countervailing force of international usage or custom, which brings about a predictable and harmonious outcome in commercial dispute resolution. It is pertinent to identify the motives behind the move towards harmonization of international contract law:

- *Increase in trade and other economic relations between nations*
- *The growth of international customary law:* Commercial custom and usage have often been used in the drafting and interpretation of commercial law. Today, certain customs and practices, derived from merchants in Europe, regarding documentary drafts, letters of credit, and so forth, are universally accepted and form the basis for domestic and international commercial law.
- *The adoption of international conventions and rules:* There have been several attempts at unification of international contract law. The most recent attempt at progressive harmonization of the law of international trade is one undertaken by the United Nations Commission on International Trade Law (UNCITRAL). UNCITRAL produced a set of uniform rules (Convention on International Sale of Goods or CISG) on international trade that are a product of different national legal systems. The CISG, which entered into force on January 1, 1988, governs the formation of international sales contracts and the rights and obligations of parties under these contracts. Many important trading nations, such as France, Germany, Italy, The Netherlands, Singapore, and the United States, have signed or ratified the convention. As of September 2019, ninety-three countries accounting for over two-thirds of world trade have adopted the convention. The CISG is largely identical to the provisions

of the U.S. Uniform Commercial Code. However, there are several important distinctions (see Table 8.1). The CISG applies to contracts for the commercial sale of goods between parties whose "place of business" are in different nations that have agreed to abide by the convention. "Place of business" is often interpreted to mean the country that has the closest relationship to the contract and is closest to where it will be performed, for example, the place where the contract is to be signed or the goods delivered. Parties to a sales contract are at liberty to specify the application of a law of some third country that recognizes the convention in the event of a dispute. The CISG does not apply to certain types of contract, such as sales of consumer goods, securities, labor services, electricity, ships, vessels, aircraft, or to the supply of goods for manufacture if the buyer provides a substantial part of the material needed for such manufacture or production. The CISG is intended to supersede the two Hague conventions (UNIDROIT rules) on international sales.

CISG: ESSENTIAL ELEMENTS

Validity of International Contracts

The CISG primarily deals with issues relating to the formation of the contract and the remedies available to the buyer and seller. It specifically excludes matters about the legality of the contract, the competency of the parties, the rights of third parties, and liability for death or personal injury. Some of these are sensitive issues that are best dealt with by domestic laws. For example, the legality of a contract (gambling contracts or contracts that restrain business) or competency (agreements with minors, or insane or intoxicated persons) are diverse since they are based on the social and religious values of society. To avoid any disagreement, the convention excludes these issues, to be decided by domestic laws.

Oral Contracts/Statements

A contract need not be concluded in or evidenced in writing. Import companies that negotiate contracts by phone may be under the impression that the agreement will not be enforceable since it is not made in writing. However, they could be held liable under CISG if they either verbally accept an offer or their verbal offer is accepted by the other party. The CISG, however, allows members to opt out of this provision (in favor of domestic law that requires a contract in writing).

> *Example.* ABC Inc., a cellular phone manufacturer in Florida contacts various suppliers of semiconductors. The import manager negotiated an oral contract with suppliers in Italy and Germany. Both suppliers orally accepted the offer made by ABC Inc. (covering type, quality, quantity, and price of the semiconductors). A few days later, the import manager was advised that a Russian company makes similar goods at lower prices and that the price includes transportation costs to ABC Inc. in Florida. The import manager of ABC Inc. called the suppliers in Italy and Germany to cancel the contract. He thought that oral contracts would not be valid

TABLE 8.1 CISG versus Uniform Commercial Code

	CISG Convention	**Uniform Commercial Code**
Oral testimony	The provisions of a written contract can be modified by a prior or contemporaneous oral agreement.	A written sales contract between the parties cannot be modified by prior or contemporaneous written or oral agreement.
Enforceability of oral contracts	CISG does not require that contracts for sale of goods be in writing to be enforceable. i.e., agreements made on the phone or in a meeting are enforceable.	Oral contracts for the sale of goods worth $500 or more are not enforceable unless the existence of a contract is admitted or that there has been payment or delivery and acceptance.
Perfect tender rule	A buyer may not reject the goods or cancel the contract unless the non-conformity constitutes a fundamental breach of the contract. Buyer can demand substitute goods in the event of a fundamental breach of contract by seller.	A buyer may reject the goods and cancel the contract even if the defects are not serious and the buyer would have received substantial performance.
Specification of quantity/price	A contract is not sufficiently definite if it fails to indicate the goods and does not expressly or implicitly fix or make provisions for determining the quantity and price.	A contract is valid despite missing terms on provisions pertaining to performance and price insofar as the parties intend to be bound by the contract.
Revocability of an offer/terms of acceptance	An offer to sell goods becomes irrevocable if it indicates a fixed time for acceptance or states that it is irrevocable or someone acts by relying on the statement. Acceptance of sale offer by buyer/seller occurs upon receipt by seller/buyer, respectively.	A firm offer to buy or sale goods made in writing, promising to keep the offer open for a period (no longer than 3 months) is valid and enforceable. Acceptance of sales offer by buyer/seller occurs when it is mailed or transmitted by seller/buyer, respectively.
Additional terms	Expression of acceptance of the contract by buyer or seller that has additions, limitations, or other modifications is considered to be a rejection and a counteroffer.	Expression of acceptance by buyer or seller of contract terms is valid even if it contains additional terms to that expressed in the offer. In the absence of any objections, the additional terms that do not materially alter the offer (other than quantity, price, and warranty) become part of the contract.

and thus unenforceable. Since each party is located in a different CISG country, CISG applies. The oral contracts with the German and Italian suppliers are enforceable. This means that ABC Inc. is obligated to buy the semiconductors or pay damages.

Offer and Acceptance

An offer is a proposal by one party to another indicating their intention to enter into a contract under specified terms. The pro forma invoice is an example of an offer commonly used in international trade. An offer must be sufficiently definite so that a court can determine the actual intent of the parties (stating quantity, price, and other particulars) and must be communicated to the other party. As a general rule, offers may be withdrawn at any time before acceptance. However, firm offers have to be kept open for a fixed period of time (the exception to the rule). They are valid even if they are not in writing. Furthermore, an offer may not be revoked if the offeree reasonably relies on the offer as being irrevocable and acts in reliance on the offer.

> *Example.* John makes a firm offer to sell his car to Victoria for $5,000 and promises to keep the offer open for one week. John has to keep the offer open for one week and cannot sell it to another buyer. If John sells to another buyer before the stated time, Victoria can sue for breach of contract.

A contract is not formed unless the offer is accepted by the offeree (the person to whom the offer is made). Acceptance under the CISG may take the form of a statement or conduct by the offeree that indicates the offeree's intention to be bound to the contract. An offeree may accept by dispatching the goods or payment of the price without notice to the offeror (insofar as the parties have an established practice or it is routinely accepted in the trade and done within the time fixed for acceptance by the offeror). The general rule is that the acceptance must be identical to the offeror's terms (mirror image rule). The CISG states that a reply to an offer that purports to be an acceptance but contains additions, limitations, or modifications is a rejection of the offer and constitutes a counteroffer.

> *Example 1.* Harold completes a mail order form for a $650 camera depicted on p. 200 of a catalog. He signs the form, encloses a money order and sends it to the seller. Upon receipt, Harold's order is an offer. If the company ships the camera, it is an act of acceptance.

> *Example 2.* A seller offers to sell a car for $20,000 and provides the details: brand, year, color, condition, etc. A buyer accepts the exact terms of the offer. Under the mirror image rule, a contract has been created. However, if the potential buyer demands additional terms such as satellite radio, specialty leather seats, the mirror image rule has not been met and there is no contract.

> *Example 3.* Joanne sends a note to Shirley stating "I will assume that you have agreed to purchase my lawnmower for $250 unless I otherwise hear from you before the end of this month." Silence does not constitute acceptance unless the offeree indicates that his/her silence means assent.

Parol Evidence Rule

Prior oral statements (including witness testimony) are potentially enforceable and can be used to challenge the provisions of a written contract. Thus, exporters–importers have to be cautious about representations made during the negotiations which are not intended to be part of the written contract since oral statements could be construed as part of the written contract (if used to prove intent). One solution is to include an integration clause which states that the written contract was the entire agreement and that no other agreements or evidence that is contradictory would be admissible.

> *Example.* An Australian supplier of dairy products orally agreed to pay the cost of insurance during transportation of the goods to the buyer's warehouse in Portland, Oregon. However, the written terms of the contract drawn up subsequently explicitly provided for payment by the U.S. buyer.

The prior oral statement by the supplier is admissible and can be used to modify the terms of the written contract. The supplier would be obligated to pay the cost of insurance.

Battle of the Forms

A reply to a sales offer which purports to be an acceptance but contains additions or modifications is a rejection of the offer and constitutes a counteroffer. However, if the counteroffer does not materially alter the terms of the offer, it constitutes an acceptance unless objected and notified by the offeror. Material terms include price, payment, quantity and quality of goods, place and time of delivery, and liability.

> *Example.* A manufacturer of leather shoes in Italy sends a purchase order for 500 pounds of polished leather from New Zealand at $10 per pound with a three-year warranty. The supplier in New Zealand accepted the order but modified the terms: "$12 per pound and a two-year warranty." The terms added by the supplier are material to the contract, and hence constitute rejections of the offer or considered a counteroffer.

General Standards of Performance

The parties are generally required to perform as promised. The seller is required to deliver the goods, handover any documents relating to the goods, and ensure that the goods conform to the contract. The buyer is required to pay the purchase price and take delivery of the goods.

Duty to Inspect and Proper Notice

In the event that the buyer receives nonconforming goods, he/she must give timely (within as short a period as is practicable) and effective notice of nonconformity (specifying the nature of nonconformity). The buyer's notice such as "the goods are rancid" or "poor workmanship and improper fitting of the goods" were considered by courts as being insufficiently specific and regarded as no notice (International Perspective 8.2).

Right to Remedy Deficiencies

A buyer may breach a sales contract by refusing to pay for the goods or wrongfully returning the goods. Remedies include specific performance (compel the buyer to take delivery of goods and pay the price), avoiding the contract for a fundamental breach, and damages.

A seller may breach the contract by failing to deliver the goods as agreed in the contract or delivering goods that are not in conformity with the contract. Buyer's remedies include specific performance, avoiding the contract for a fundamental breach or non-delivery, reduction of the purchase price, and damages

The CISG permits the seller to remedy the delivery of defective goods after the time of performance has expired unless such delivery would cause the buyer "unreasonable inconvenience and uncertainty." The buyer reserves the right to sue for damages caused by the delay or buy the initial delivery of nonconforming goods.

Exemptions from Liability

The CISG exempts a party from liability for failure to perform any of his/her obligations due to reasons beyond his/her control and not foreseeable at the time of the contract formation. Prompt notice of the impediment is required to avoid damages. The following circumstances do not give rise to exemptions from liability: Financial difficulties of the seller's supplier, the buyer's inability to obtain foreign currency, increases in the cost of goods, and delivery problems due to production stoppages.

Limitation Period

There are no provisions in the CISG on the limitation period (the time within which a buyer must bring a court action or seek arbitration). Another United Nations (UN) convention, "Convention on the limitation period in the International Sale of Goods" provides rules on the limitation period and has been ratified by eighteen countries, including the United States in 1994. The convention provides a four-year limitation period for most claims.

The International Chamber of Commerce (ICC) has also published several valuable documents on international trade. The Uniform Rules for Contract Guarantees (1978) deals with the issue of performance and bank guarantees supporting obligations arising in international contracts. The ICC also has rules on the adaptation of long-term contracts to changing economic and political circumstances.

Standard contract forms are often used in certain types of international commercial transactions, such as trade in commodities or in capital goods. These contracts are prepared by trade associations, such as The Cocoa Association of London, The Refined Sugar Association, or certain agencies of the United Nations (model contracts for supply of plant, equipment, and machinery for export or for the export of durable consumer goods and engineering articles).

PERTINENT CLAUSES IN EXPORT CONTRACTS

An export contract is an agreement between a seller and an overseas customer for the performance, financing, and other aspects of an export transaction. An export transaction is not just limited to the sale of final products in overseas markets but extends to supply contracts for manufacture or production of the product within a given time period. Parties should have a well-drafted and clear contract that properly defines their responsibilities and provides for any possible contingencies. This is critical in minimizing potential conflicts and allowing for a successful conclusion of the transaction (International Perspective 8.1).

Although many export contracts are concluded between the seller and an overseas buyer (the main contract), the buyer may also enter into a contract with an independent consultant for technical assistance and with a lender for financing in the case of complex projects. The exporter as prime contractor may enter into joint venture agreements with other firms, such as subcontractors or suppliers, to bid on and perform on a project. Parties could also establish a partnership, corporation, or a consortium in order to bid on and undertake different aspects of the transaction while assuming joint responsibility for the overall project. Such collaboration is common when one firm lacks the financial or technical resources to perform the contract.

INTERNATIONAL PERSPECTIVE 8.1

Tendering for Export Contracts

In many countries, government purchases over a certain size are required to be awarded under tender. Purchase of goods under tender is common in cases involving goods and services purchased in large volumes and the likelihood of price competition. Tenders are also offered in the case of contracts for purchase or installation of complex projects that involve the purchase of goods and services. Tenders provide the purchaser the unique advantage of selecting the best supplier from among a large pool of bidders in terms of quality, price, and other factors, allowing the purchaser to avoid charges of patronage and favoritism.

The tendering process begins with a purchaser of goods and services inviting potential suppliers for submission of tenders (bids). However, with important projects, bidders are pre-qualified before submitting tenders to ensure that they satisfy the basic criteria that are critical for awarding the contract: necessary technical qualifications and compliance with local laws in submitting the bid. The invitation to submit bids (for prequalification or final selection) is usually announced in newspapers and this guarantees a fair, competitive, and transparent tendering process and affords some protection against corruption and nepotism among civil servants and members of the government.

The invitation to submit tenders is announced in the newspapers to the public or to selected bidders who are prequalified. This stage in the tendering process is often called a request for proposal (RFP). At this stage, potential bidders are invited to submit tenders with certain conditions (e.g., technical specifications, commercial terms, etc.) that are to be included in the proposal. Suppliers may be requested to submit bid bonds to ensure that a supplier will not decline to sign the contract when the bid is accepted.

Once a proposal is accepted, the successful supplier is awarded the contract. In most cases, however, the award is just a first step prior to negotiation of the contract. In the event of failure to conclude the final contract, the customer would have to negotiate with the second bidder on the list.

It is relevant to state briefly how these joint venture arrangements differ from one another. Members may form a partnership for the purpose of undertaking the export contract. Each of the members remains responsible for the entire transaction even though the parties may be carrying out different portions of the export transaction. Parties could also establish a new corporation to act as exporters or prime contractors. In the case of a consortium, each partner of the venture has a separate contract with the customer for performance of a portion of the work and, hence, is not responsible to the other members.

Scope of Work Including Services

The goods to be sold should be clearly spelled out in the contract. There is also a need to include the scope of work to be performed by the exporter, such as installation, training, and other services. The scope of work to be performed is usually contained in the technical specification, which should be incorporated into the main contract (by listing it with the other documents intended to form the contract). It is also important to specify whether the agreed price covers certain services, such as packaging, special handling, or insurance. Any contribution by the overseas customer should be explicitly stated as to the consequences of the failure to perform those services to enable the exporter to complete the transaction on time. Such contributions could include provision of office space and other support services, such as secretarial and translation, government licenses, permits, and personnel necessary for the performance of the contract.

INTERNATIONAL PERSPECTIVE 8.2

Chicago Prime Packers v. Northern Trading Co.

Chicago Prime, a Colorado Corporation (seller) and Northam Trading, a partnership under the laws of Ontario, Canada (buyer) entered into an agreement for the sale of pork back ribs. In March 2001, Chicago Prime contracted to sell 40,500 pounds of pork back ribs to Northam for $178,200 with payment due within seven days of the shipment. Chicago Prime purchased the ribs specified in the contract from Brookfield Farms (Brookfield) and Northam's carrier (Brown Trucking was hired by Northam) picked up the ribs from Brookfield and signed a bill of lading acknowledging that the goods were in apparent good order. The bill of lading also indicated that the "contents and condition of contents of packages were unknown." Brown Trucking delivered the goods to Northam's customer, Beacon Premium Meats, which also signed a second bill of lading indicating that they had received the shipment in "apparent good order."

As Beacon Premium Meats noticed some unusual conditions with the quality of the meat, it requested inspectors at the U.S. Department of Agriculture (USDA) to examine the product. The inspectors concluded that the inspected product had arrived at Beacon in rotten condition and condemned the entire shipment. Even after Northam informed Chicago Prime of the results of the USDA's inspection, Chicago Prime continued to demand payment and later filed suit. At trial, Northam submitted that it was relieved of its payment obligation because the product was spoiled when Brown Trucking received it for delivery to Beacon Prime Meats. The district court awarded Chicago Prime the contract price on grounds that the damage to the goods occurred after the risk had passed to the buyer. It also held that the contract was governed by CISG. Northam appealed stating that: a) the court erred in placing the burden of proof on Northam to show that the ribs were spoilt at the time of transfer, and b) the evidence did not support the court's finding.

The court of appeal affirmed the ruling of the district court. It agreed that the contract at issue was governed by CISG. Second, it stated that the CISG did not clearly provide as to which party bore the burden of proving that the product conformed to the contract. Given the similarity of the CISG with the provisions of the UCC, the court interpreted the CISG by comparing it with the general principles of the UCC. It stated that, as the buyer bears the burden of proving breach of implied warranty of fitness under the UCC, the buyer needs to prove nonconformity at the time of transfer to Brown Trucking. Also, Northam did not provide credible evidence to show that the ribs were spoiled at the time of delivery to the trucking company. (408 F. 3rd 894. 2005 U.S.App.)

Price and Delivery Terms

The total price could be stated at the time of the contract, with a price escalation clause that provides for increases in the price if certain events occur. Such provisions are commonly used with goods that are to be manufactured by the exporter over a certain period of time and when inflation is expected to affect material and labor costs. Such a clause also extends to increases in costs arising from delays caused by the overseas customer. It is important to draft the contract with a clear understanding between the parties as to whether such a clause applies when there is an excusable delay. In many contracts, the price escalation clause is in force in cases of excusable delay in performance by the exporter.

The contract should also specify the currency in which payment is to be made. Foreign exchange fluctuations could adversely affect a firm's profit. In addition, government exchange controls in the buyer's country may totally or partially prevent the exporter from receiving payment for goods and services. Hence, it is important to provide the necessary protection against such contingencies. The following contract provisions would be helpful to the exporter.

Shifting the Risk to the Overseas Customer

An exporter may shift the risk by providing in the contract that payment is to be made in the exporter's country and currency. This ensures protection against currency fluctuations and exchange controls.

Payment in Importer's Currency

Even though the seller will generally prefer payment in U.S. dollars, such a requirement may be difficult to comply with if U.S. dollars are not readily available in the buyer's country. The exporter may have to accept payment in the importer's currency. In such a situation, the exporter could fix the exchange rate in the invoice and would thus be compensated in the event of devaluation. Suppose Smith, Incorporated, of California exports computers to Colombia; the price could be stated as follows: "300 million Colombian pesos at the exchange rate of $1=1,000 pesos. The importer will compensate the exporter for any devaluations in the peso from the rate designated in the contract."

Another method of protection against fluctuations in the importer's currency is to add a risk premium on the price at the time of the contract. Yet another method is to establish an escrow account in a third country in an acceptable (more stable) currency from which payments would be made under the contract.

The contract should clearly indicate the delivery term (e.g., FOB, New York, or CIF, London) since there are different implications in terms of risk of loss, insurance, ownership, and tax liability. The seller would ideally prefer to be paid cash in advance (before delivery of goods or transfer of title) in its own currency or by using a confirmed irrevocable letter of credit. The buyer would often desire payment in its own currency on open account or consignment. Hence, the provision to be included in the contract has to accommodate the competing interests of both parties.

Delivery, Delay, and Penalties

The most common type of clause included in export contracts is one that provides for a fixed or approximate delivery date and that stipulates the circumstances under which the seller will be excused for delay in performance and even for complete inability to perform. Most contracts state that either party has the right to cancel the contract for any delay or default in performance if it is caused by conditions beyond its control, including, but not limited to, acts of God and government restrictions, and that neither of the parties shall be liable for damages (force majeure clause). The force majeure clause may also cover a number of specified events, including the inability of the exporter to obtain the necessary labor, material, information, or other support from the buyer to effect delivery. It should also include certain warranty obligations, such as delays in manufacture of replacement components. It is important to state that the force majeure (excusable delay) clause will apply even if any of the causes existed at the time of bidding, were present prior to signing the contract, or occurred after the seller's performance of its obligations had been delayed for other reasons. Some force majeure clauses provide for the temporary suspension of the contract until the causes for the nonperformance are removed; others state that the agreement will be terminated at the option of either of the parties if performance remains impossible for some stated period.

Contracts often provide for damages if the delay is caused by one of the parties. In the event that the delay is caused by the exporter (i.e., unexcused delay), some contracts specify that the importer will be entitled to recover liquidated damages (even in the absence of actual damages), whereas others provide that payment would be limited to damages actually incurred by the buyer (see International Perspective 8.3).

The converse of the seller's obligation to deliver is the buyer's obligation to accept delivery as stipulated in the contract. If delay in delivery is caused by the buyer, most contracts provide that the seller will be entitled to direct damages incurred during the delay, such as warehousing costs, salaries and wages for personnel kept

idle, or loss of profit. Some contracts even provide for payment of indirect (consequential) damages, such as loss of productivity or loss of future profits due to delays
caused by the buyer. Both parties can possibly eliminate or reduce potential risks of
excusable delay by inserting 1) a best-efforts clause, without expressly providing
for consequences in the event of delay, or 2) an overall limitation of liability clause.
In cases in which the contract does not expressly impose the previous obligation on
the customer, the customer remains responsible for delays caused personally or by
someone for whom the customer is responsible. In most legal systems a party has an
implied duty to cooperate in the performance of the work by the other party or to not
interfere with the performance of the other party.

Quality, Performance, and Liability Limitations

Most contracts state that the seller warrants to the buyer that the goods manufactured
by the seller will be free from defects in material, workmanship, and title and will be
of the kind and quality described in the contract. It is not uncommon to find deficiencies in performance, even when the exporter provides a product with state-of-the-art
design, material, and workmanship. Hence, it is advisable to use certain approaches
to limit risk exposure:

- Specify in the contract the performance standards that are to be met, and provide warranties for those that can be objectively tested, such as machine efficiency, for a specified period, usually a year.
- Stipulate the kinds of damage that may be suffered by the buyer for which the
  seller is not responsible, such as loss of profit for machine downtime, or extra
  costs of acquiring substitute services, as well as other damages that are incidental or consequential.
- Limit the liability, especially in exports of machinery and equipment, to a specific amount expressed either with reference to the total contract price or as a
  certain sum of money. This limit should cover all liability or liabilities arising
  from product quality or performance.
- Carefully evaluate the cost implications of an extended warranty or an ever-
  green warranty provision before agreeing to include it in the contract. An ever-
  green warranty is automatically renewed each time a failure protected under the
  warranty provision is corrected. (See International Perspectives 8.2 and 8.3.)

Taxes and Duties

In the United States, Canada, and other developed countries, an exporter will not be
subject to any taxes (i.e., when products are exported to these countries) if business
is not performed through an agent, a branch, or a subsidiary. However, when the
price includes a breakdown for installation and other services to be performed in the
importing country, such income could be taxable as earnings from services. In some
cases, it may be advisable to reserve the right to perform these services through a
local affiliate to restrict exposure to foreign taxes. It is thus important to consider
the tax and customs duty implications of one's pricing and other export decisions
relating to shipment of components or assembly of (final) products. It is also helpful
to evaluate the impact of tax treaties with importing countries.

Guarantees and Bonds

It is quite common for overseas importers to require some form of guarantee or bond against the exporter's default. Public agencies in many countries are often prohibited from entering into major contracts without some form of bank guarantee or bond. Guarantees are more commonly used than bonds in most international contracts. These are separate contracts and independent of the export agreement.

Bid guarantees or bonds are often provided at the first stage of the contract from all bidders (potential exporters) to provide security to the overseas customer. Then, performance guarantees or bonds are provided by the successful bidder(s) to protect the overseas customer against damages resulting from failure of the seller to comply with the export contract. Last, payment guarantees or bonds are provided so the importer can secure a refund of the advance payment in case of the exporter's default.

In the case of a bank guarantee, a standby letter of credit is issued by a bank, under which payment is made to the importer on demand upon failure of the exporter to perform its obligation under the export contract. Most importers favor a contract provision that allows them to obtain payment from the bank by simply submitting a letter that the exporter has defaulted and demanding payment. However, it may be advisable to stipulate in the standby credit that the amount of the credit becomes payable to the importer only upon the finding by a court or arbitration tribunal that the supplier of goods or services is in default of the contract.

A bank guarantee (standby credit) and a bond are similar in that both instruments are a form of security provided by a third party (a bank in the case of a guarantee; a surety company in the case of a bond) to the importer against the exporter's default. Both instruments are only issued if the exporter has a good credit standing, and they both specify the amount payable in the event of default, the period within which such claims can be made, as well as the fee charged for such services.

In export trade, there is a tendency to make standby credits payable on the submission of a letter by the importer that simply alleges default by the exporter and demands payment. This is not usually the case with bonds, which are payable only when the importer has shown that the exporter is in default under the export contract. Bonds also usually require that the importer has met its obligations under the contract before realizing any benefits from the bond. In short, the surety company will conduct an investigation on the conduct of the parties before making a decision about payment. Second, the bank in the case of a standby letter of credit does not have the option of performing the contract (e.g., completing delivery of goods not made by the exporter, paying losses incurred by the exporter, etc.), as in the case of a surety company. The bank guarantor is required to pay the full amount of the standby credit without regard to the actual damages suffered. Under a bond, the surety is obliged to make good on only the actual damages suffered by the overseas buyer. In both cases, the exporter has to reimburse the bank or the surety company for any payments made under the guarantee or bond, respectively. In view of the widespread use of guarantees (standby credits) in international trade and the possibility of abuse, many countries provide their exporters with an insurance program that protects them against wrongful drawing on the credit. In 1978, the International Chamber of Commerce adopted the "Uniform Rules for Contract Guarantees," which deals with guarantees, bonds, and other undertakings given on behalf of the seller and applies only if the guarantee or bond explicitly states the intentions of the parties to be governed by these rules. In view of the limited acceptance of the Uniform Rules for Contract Guarantees, the ICC adopted, in 1992, the "Uniform Rules for Demand Guarantees," which attempts to standardize existing guarantee practice. As in the case of contract guarantees, the parties have to state their intention to be subject to these rules.

Applicable Law and Dispute Settlement

The fundamental principle of international contract law is that of freedom of contract. This means that the parties are at liberty to agree between themselves as to what rules should govern their contract. Most contracts state the applicable law to be that of the exporter's country. This indicates the strong bargaining position of exporters and their clear preference to be governed by laws about which they are well informed. It may be possible to arrange a split jurisdiction, whereby the portion of the contract to be performed in the customer's country will be interpreted under the importer's laws and the portion to be performed in the exporter's country will be governed by the laws of that country.

In cases where there is no express or implied choice of law, it may be the role of the courts to decide what law should govern the contract based on the terms and nature of the contract. The factors to be considered often include the place of negotiation of the contract, the place of performance, location of the subject matter, place of business, and other pertinent matters.

For several reasons, a large and growing number of parties to export contracts provide for arbitration to settle disputes arising under their contracts. Despite the wide use of arbitration clauses, the superiority of arbitration over judicial dispute resolution is not quite clear-cut, and parties considering arbitration should also be aware of the disadvantages in this choice, such as lack of mandatory enforcement mechanisms and difficulty obtaining recognition and enforcement of the award, which requires a separate action of law. It is also stated in some contracts that the parties agree to abide by the award and that the award is binding and final and enforceable in a court of competent jurisdiction.

INTERNATIONAL PERSPECTIVE 8.3

Contracts for Export Joint Ventures

There is a link between trade, growth, and poverty alleviation. However, many developing countries that are predominantly dependent on primary commodity exports do not participate in the benefits of economic integration. Export joint ventures (EJV) offer firms the opportunity to reduce export costs and spread risks. Success in export markets requires the requisite knowledge and financing which is often unavailable to small and medium-sized enterprises in developing countries. One effective way of addressing this problem is through the development of EJVs. Their benefits include market research and development, transportation and shipping, services, and promotion. Export joint ventures take many forms. Some are set up to obtain technical knowledge while others are intended to procure access to foreign marketing networks. Contracts are needed to define the nature of the relationship, delineate the rights and obligations of the parties, and enable third parties such as banks and government agencies to recognize its existence.

It is important to examine the legal framework within which the EJV operates, local laws on foreign investment, joint ventures, corporate, tax, and banking laws, to assess their implications for the EJV and importance during the course of its operations. Initial discussions between the local partner and foreign firm are often followed with a letter of intent (prepared by either party or both) which states the parties' objectives, time frame and implementation modalities, and their intention to enter into a contract. This encourages continued discussions and the future course of action. The parties may also enter into other similar agreements such as memoranda of understanding or similar preliminary arrangements prior to a formal EJV agreement. Here are some of the provisions that are generally included in EJV agreements between a local partner and a foreign firm.

Parties: It is important to clearly specify the parties to the EJV agreement. They must have the requisite authority to enter into the contract.

Preamble: The preamble broadly states the purpose, general intentions, business goals, strategies, and other relevant information.

Objectives and scope: Scope of operations, legal form of the organization, manufacturing, exports, products, services, implementation schedule.

Contributions of each partner: Foreign partner's contribution such as capital, product know-how, design, other specialized expertise. Local partner may provide land, knowledge of the local situation, relations with government, capital etc.

Responsibility of partners: This may be related to responsibility with regard to implementation of the agreement, start-up operations, loan negotiations, procurement and installation of machinery, preparation of site and construction, recruitment, training, marketing, distribution, suppliers, quality control etc.

Equity ownership: Distribution of ownership, share of profits, and management of the firm.

Direction and management: Board of directors and composition, appointment of company's officers, and division of responsibility.

Technology agreements: Technology transfer agreements providing for territorial coverage, duration, fees, or royalties.

Procurement and marketing: Procurement of raw materials and supplies, export marketing and distribution, use of trademarks.

Financial aspects: Sources of finance, retained earnings, declaration of dividends, selection of an external auditor acceptable to both parties.

Applicable law and dispute settlement: Specify the applicable law in the event of a dispute between the parties and ways of dispute settlement such as mediation, arbitration, or litigation.

Commencement and termination: This provision indicates the commencement of the EJV and duration. It can have an indefinite life span.

CHAPTER SUMMARY

Export contract	An export contract is an agreement between a seller and an overseas customer for the performance, financing, and other aspects of an export transaction. It also includes supply contracts for the manufacture of a product within a given period.

Factors behind the move toward harmonization of international contract/ commercial law	1. Increases in global trade and economic relations between nations
	2. The growth of international customary law
	3. The adoption of international conventions and rules
	   • The Vienna Convention on international sale of goods
	   • The ICC rules on contract agreements
	   • Standard contracts developed by trade associations.
	CISG Essential elements: a) oral contracts, b) parol evidence, c) battle of the forms, d) duty to inspect and proper notice, e) right to remedy deficiencies and f) limitation period.

Major clauses in export contracts	• Scope of work • Price and delivery terms • Quality, performance, and liability • Taxes and duties • Guarantees and bonds • Applicable law and dispute settlement

REVIEW QUESTIONS

1. What are some of the factors that militate in favor of harmonization of international contract law?
2. Discuss the major differences between the CISG and the Uniform Commercial Code.
3. In certain transactions involving transfer of technology, the contract provides for the sale of goods and services. Does the CISG apply to such contracts?
4. The CISG does not apply to certain types of contract. Discuss.
5. An Italian seller agreed to produce and supply 250 pieces of leather furniture to a buyer in the United States. The contract included certain specifications and was signed by the parties. It also stated that any changes may only be modified in writing signed by both parties. A few days after the contract was signed, both parties agreed by phone to change the specifications. A couple of months later, when the seller delivered the furniture with the modified specifications, the buyer refused to accept them stating that the latest agreement was not binding since it was not part of the written (original) contract. Does the CISG apply? If it does, is the buyer obligated to accept the furniture?
6. A manufacturer in California, United States and a distributor in British Columbia, Canada agreed for the delivery of routers. The contract choice of law clause adopted "California Law." In the event of a dispute, does it mean that the CISG will not apply?
7. What is the battle of the forms under the CISG?

8. Discuss a typical tendering process for export contracts.
9. Discuss three provisions in a typical export contract.
10. How does an exporter protect against foreign exchange fluctuations? What contract clauses can be included to limit such risk that could adversely affect its future receipts?

REFERENCES

DiMatteo, L. (1997). An international contract formula: The informality of international business transactions plus the internationalization of contract law equals unexpected contractual liability. *Syracuse Journal of International Law and Commerce* 23: 67–111.

DiMatteo, L. and Dhooge, L. (2006). *International Business Law: A Transactional Approach.* Mason, OH: Thomson-West.

Lubman, S. (1988). Investment and exports in the People's Republic of China: Perspectives on the evolving patterns. *Brigham Young University Law Review* 3: 543–565.

Rosett, A. (1982). Unification, harmonization, restatement, codification and reform of international commercial law. *North Carolina Journal of International and Commercial Regulation* 7(1): 683–698.

United Nations (1984). United Nationals Conference on Contracts for the International Sale of Goods. (Official Records, United Nations A/CONF/97/18.)

World Wide Web Resources

Information on electronic commerce: www.uncitral.org/uncitral/en/uncitral_texts/electronic_commerce.html

Information on international commercial law, electronic commerce, treaties, rules, and other laws pertaining to international business: www.jus.uio.no/lm/

Information on international trade law: www.law.cornell.edu/wex/index.php/International_trade

Guide to international economic law: www.asil.org/resource/iel1.htm

International Trade Closing Cases and Discussions

1. The Case of Wombat: CISG

Wombat Inc. is a Florida Corporation engaged in the rental and sale of tiles, while Pinochet Inc. is an Italian corporation engaged in the manufacture of ceramic tiles. Representatives of Wombat negotiated an agreement with Pinochet to purchase tiles based on samples examined at a trade show in Bologna, Italy. After finalizing an oral agreement on important terms of the contract such as price, quality, delivery, and payment, the parties recorded these terms on one of Pinochet's pre-printed order forms and the president of Wombat signed the contract. The agreement provided for the sale of high-grade ceramic tiles at specific discounts as long as Wombat purchased sufficient quantities.

Wombat delayed payments for some of the shipments since it was not satisfied with the quality of the tiles. Pinochet stopped shipments and cancelled the contract with Wombat claiming that the provisions on the printed form gave him the right to cancel or suspend the contract in the event that the buyer defaulted or delayed payment. Pinochet was not informed of the defects in writing. The contract provided for notification of any defects in writing by means of certified letter within or no later than ten days after receipt of the merchandise. Wombat argues that the parties never intended the terms printed on the reverse of the order form to apply to the agreement. It also submitted affidavits from translators and Pinochet's representatives that the parties subjectively intended not to be bound by the terms on the reverse of the order form.

Questions

1. Is the contract governed by CISG?
2. Are the parties bound by the terms on the reverse side of the printed form?

2. The Case of *China National Products v. Apex Digital Inc.*

China National is a Beijing-based corporation organized under the laws of China with specific foreign trading rights. It facilitates the import and export of goods between Chinese and foreign companies. Apex is a company incorporated in Ontario, California and engaged in the import and distribution of consumer electronic goods. In 2000, China National entered into a purchase agreement with Apex for the export of DVD players. The purchase agreement was formalized with the conclusion of several but substantially identical written contracts for the different types of player. Each contract contained two significant provisions:

a. in the event of nonconformity of the goods with the contract, Apex should claim for quality discrepancy within thirty days after arrival of the goods at the port of destination,
b. all disputes arising from the contract shall be submitted to a certain arbitration tribunal specified in the contract and the award is final and binding on both parties.

Apex imported and sold the products to major retailers such as Circuit City, Best Buy, and K-Mart. Soon after distribution of the imported goods, Apex began receiving reports from its retailers that consumers were dissatisfied with the quality of the DVD players: disk loaders did not open; they did not load after a DVD was inserted; they did not recognize certain music files; the front panel of the loader fell off, etc. Some were returned. In spite of these problems, Apex continued to place more orders with China National. It did, however, express its concerns to China National. Apex declined to pay China National claiming "financial troubles" as well as China National's refusal to correct the defects. In an effort to obtain payment, China National wrote several letters to Apex threatening legal action. It eventually filed suit in California.

The central issue to be decided by the court was whether Apex had rejected the goods or, if it had not, whether it would later be relieved of liability. The court stated that if buyers accept nonconforming goods and do nothing, the law deems them to have accepted those goods. Apex's actions in continuing to order and sell known defective goods constituted an acceptance of those goods.

Such conduct of ordering and selling defective goods was inconsistent with the seller's ownership and acceptance. It ordered Apex to pay for all unpaid invoices. (Source: 141 F. Supp. 2nd 1013. 2001 U.S. Dist.)

Questions

1. Is the contract governed by the CISG?
2. Do you agree with the decision of the court. Why/why not?

CHAPTER 9

Trade Documents and Transportation

LEARNING OBJECTIVES:

9.1 Describe the various documents used in export–import trade
9.2 Understand the factors that influence the growth in airfreight
9.3 Learn the Conventions that govern the carriage of goods by air, sea, and road/rail
9.4 Learn the important developments in international maritime trade
9.5 Identify and discuss the various forms of ocean cargo and ocean vessels

International Trade in Practice

Air Cargo Competitiveness of Airports

Airports are gateways between nations and play an important role in facilitating the movement of passengers and cargo. According to Boeing (2019/2020) air cargo traffic is expected to grow 4.2 percent per year in the next twenty years. Growth in international transportation and air cargo volumes is largely driven by industrial development and expansion of foreign trade. Studies find that airports in close physical proximity to shippers, and shorter delivery time tend to attract regional cargo traffic (Zhang, 2003). They underscore the importance of certain factors that give airports a competitive edge: Infrastructure, customs, intermodal transportation, and international aviation policy. Other factors include opening hours, total costs, reputation in cargo transport, demands for local origin/destination cargo, influence of freight forwarders, transportation from the airport, and financial incentives.

Chao et al. (2013) identify eleven indicators relevant for assessing airport competitiveness in terms of air cargo. They are classified into three major categories: Airline transport capacity, airport facilities, and operations and economic development (Table 9.1).

TABLE 9.1 Measures of air cargo competitiveness

A. Airline transport capacity	A.1 Number of airlines
	A.2 Number of flights
	A.3 Number of fleets
	A.4 Number of source and destination cities
B. Airport facilities and operations	B.1 Airport charges
	B.2 Airport opening hours
	B.3 Cargo clearance times
	B.4 Quotas for runway use
C. Economic development	C.1 Annual cargo volumes
	C.2 National income
	C.3 GDP

Source: Chao and Yu (2013)

DOCUMENTATION IN EXPORT–IMPORT TRADE

The completion and submission of required documents is critical to the successful shipment, transportation, and discharge of cargo at the port of destination. The accuracy and conformity of these documents often determines whether the goods clear for export, get through customs on arrival, or whether the exporter gets paid. They require careful attention to detail. The documents used depend on the requirements of both the exporting and importing countries. Much of the documentation is routine for freight forwarders or customs brokers acting on the firm's behalf, but the exporter is ultimately responsible for the accuracy of the documentation. Information on documentation requirements in importing countries can be obtained from overseas customers, foreign government embassies and consulates, as well as various export reference books, such as the *Export Shipping Manual* and *Air Cargo Tariff Guide*. In the United States and other developed countries, government departments have specialists on individual foreign countries and can advise on country conditions and documentation requirements.

Transportation Documents

Air Waybill

The air waybill is a contract of carriage between the shipper and air carrier. It is issued by the air carrier and serves as a receipt for the shipper. When the shipper gives the cargo to a freight consolidator or forwarder for transportation, the air waybill is obtained from the consolidator or forwarder. Air waybills are nonnegotiable and cannot be issued as a collection instrument. Air waybills are not particular to a given airline and can be from any airline that participates in the carriage (Wood et al., 1995; U.S. ITA, 2015).

Bill of Lading (B/L)

A bill of lading is a contract of carriage between the shipper and the steamship company (carrier). It certifies ownership and receipt of goods by the carrier for shipment. It is issued by the carrier to the shipper. A straight bill of lading is issued when the consignment is made directly to the overseas customer. Such a bill of lading is not negotiable. An order bill of lading is negotiable, that is, it can be bought, sold, or traded. In cases in which the exporter is not certain about payment, the exporter can consign the bill of lading to the order of the shipper and endorse it to the buyer on payment of the purchase price. When payment is not a problem, the bill of lading can be endorsed to the consignee (Zodl, 1995; Wells and Dulat, 1996; U.S. ITA, 2015).

Clean/Claused Bill of Lading

The bill of lading form is normally filled out in advance by the shipper. The carrier will check the goods loaded on the ship to ensure that they comply with the goods listed (quantity, condition etc.) on the bill of lading. If all appears proper, the carrier will issue a clean bill of lading certifying that the goods have been properly loaded on board the ship. However, if there is a discrepancy between the goods loaded and the goods listed on the bill, the carrier will issue a claused bill of lading to the shipper. Such bill of lading is normally unacceptable to third parties including the buyer under a CIF contract or bank that is expected to pay under documentary credit on receipt of the bill of lading and other documents (Bade, 2015).

Inland Bill of Lading

An inland bill of lading is a bill of lading issued by the railway carrier or trucking firm certifying carriage of goods from the place where the exporter is located to the point of exit for shipment overseas. This document is issued by exporters to consign goods to a freight forwarder who will transport the goods by rail to an airport, seaport, or truck for shipment.

Through Bill of Lading

A through bill of lading is used for intermodal transportation, that is, when different modes of transportation are used. The first carrier will issue a through bill of lading and is generally responsible for the delivery of the cargo to the final destination. (Bade, 2015).

Dock Receipt

This receipt is used to transfer accountability when the export item is moved by the domestic carrier to the port of embarkation and left with the international carrier for export. The international carrier or agent issues it after delivery of the goods at the carrier's dock or warehouse. A similar document, when issued upon receipt of cargo by a chartered vessel, is called a mate's receipt.

Manifest

A manifest is a detailed summary of the total cargo of a vessel (by each loading port) for customs purposes. It covers condition of the cargo, and summarizes heavy lifts and their location.

Compliance Documents

Consular Invoice

Certain nations require a consular invoice for customs, statistical, and other purposes. It must be obtained from the consulate of the country to which the goods are being shipped and usually must be prepared in the language of that country (U.S. ITA, 2015).

Certificate of Origin

A certificate of origin is required by certain countries to enable them to determine whether the product is eligible for preferential duty treatment. It is a statement as to the origin of the export product and is usually obtained from local chambers of commerce (U.S. ITA, 2015).

Destination Control Statement (DCS)

This statement appears on the commercial invoice, bill of lading, air waybill, and shipper's export declaration. It is intended to notify the carrier and other parties that the item may only be exported to certain destinations (U.S. ITA, 2015).

Shipper's Export Declaration (SED)

A shipper's export declaration (SED) is issued to control certain exports and to compile trade data. It is required for shipments valued at more than $2,500. Carriers and exporters are also required to declare dangerous cargo (U.S. ITA, 2015).

Other Export Documents

Inspection Certificate

Some purchasers and countries may require a certificate attesting to the specifications of the goods shipped, usually performed by a third party. Such requirements are usually stated in the contract and quotation. Inspection certificates are generally requested for certain commodities with grade designations, machinery, equipment, and so forth (Foley, 2017).

Insurance Certificate

When the exporter provides insurance, it is necessary to furnish an insurance certificate that states the type, terms, and amount of insurance coverage. The certificates are negotiable and must be endorsed before presentation to the bank. In most cases, the seller arranges for insurance and add the costs to the invoice. The certificate may be issued by the insurance company, seller or freight forwarder. It is often 110 percent of CIF value covering all specified risks (U.S. ITA, 2015; Foley, 2017).

Bill of Exchange (Draft)

A bill of exchange is an unconditional written order by one party (the drawer) that orders a second party (the debtor or drawee) to pay a certain sum of money to the drawer (creditor) or designated third party. For example, Hernandez Export, Incorporated, of Lawton, Oklahoma, sends an importer in Uzbekistan a draft for $30,000 after having shipped a truckload of autoparts. The company's draft orders the overseas buyer in Uzbekistan to pay $30,000 to its agent, Expotech, in Uzbekistan. In this scenario, Hernandez, Incorporated, is the drawer, the importer is the drawee, and Expotech is the payee. In many cases, the drawee is the overseas buyer and the drawer/payee is the exporter. When a draft is payable at a designated future date, it is a time draft. If it is payable on sight, it is a demand or sight draft (Carr and Stone, 2017).

Commercial Invoice

A commercial invoice is a bill for the merchandise from the seller to the buyer. It should include basic information about the transaction: description of the goods, delivery and payment terms, order date, and number. The overseas buyer needs the commercial invoice to clear goods from customs, prove ownership, and arrange payment. Governments in importing countries also use commercial invoices to determine the value of the merchandise for assessment of customs duties.

Pro Forma Invoice

A pro forma invoice is a provisional invoice sent to the prospective buyer, usually in response to the latter's request for a price quotation. A quotation usually describes the product, states the price at a specific delivery point, time of shipment, and the terms of payment. A pro forma invoice is also needed by the buyer to obtain a foreign exchange or import permit. Quotations on such invoices are subject to change without notice partly because there is a lag between the time when the quotation is prepared and when the shipment is made to the overseas customer.

Export Packing List

An export packing list itemizes the material in each individual package and indicates the type of package (e.g., box, carton). It shows weights and measurements for each package. It is used by customs in the exporting and importing countries to check the cargo and by the exporter to ascertain the total cargo weight, the volume, and shipment of the correct merchandise. The packing list should be either included in the package or attached to the outside of a package in a waterproof envelope marked "packing list enclosed" (Bade, 2015; U.S. ITA, 2015).

TRANSPORTATION

Three modes of transportation are available for exporting products overseas: air, water (ocean and inland), and land (rail and truck). Whereas inland water, rail, and truck are suitable for domestic transportation and movement of goods between neighboring countries (the United States to Canada, France to Germany, etc.), air and ocean transport are appropriate for long-distance transportation between countries that do not share a common boundary.

Export–import firms may use a combination of these methods to deliver merchandise in a timely and cost-efficient manner. The exporter should consider market location (geographical proximity), speed (e.g., airfreight for perishables or products in urgent demand, etc.), and cost when determining the mode of transportation. Even though air carriers are more expensive, their cost may be offset by reduced packing, documentation, and inventory requirements. It is important to establish with the importer the destination of the goods, since the latter may wish the goods to be shipped into a free-trade zone that allows for exemption of import duties while the goods are in the zone.

AIR TRANSPORTATION

Airfreight accounts for less than 3 percent of world trade by weight and approximately 40 percent of world trade by value. Demand for airfreight is correlated with world economic growth, fuel prices, and the availability/competitiveness of surface transport options. (see Table 9.2 for advantages and disadvantages of this transportation type).

Air cargo traffic has shown slower growth since 2004 (3.7 percent over the period 2004–2011) compared to its historic growth trend of 6.7 percent between 1981 and 2004. It fully recovered in 2017 and grew by about 10 percent compared to its long-term average growth rate of 4.2 percent partly due to synchronized global economic expansion, increasing industrial production, and growth in world trade (Boeing, 2019/2020). In 2020, air cargo traffic faced significant challenges due to the trade tension between the United States and China and the EU, the corona virus pandemic, and weakening consumer confidence. Overall, the airline industry experienced a loss of about US$84 billion, and US$37.54 per passenger due to the virus. Concerns for safety essentially shut down the airline industry. In spite of low fuel prices, overall costs did not fall as fast as demand. Non-fuel unit costs rose as fixed costs are spread over fewer passengers (IATA, 2020).

Airfreight (air cargo) declined by over 10 million tons during 2020 to about 50 million tons. However, the severe shortage in cargo capacity due to the grounding of passenger aircraft pushed rates to an all-time high, thus boosting air cargo revenues.

TABLE 9.2 Advantages and Disadvantages of Air Transportation

Advantages	Disadvantages
• Faster delivery of perishable commodities, production parts, etc. Well suited for commodities that have a high value-to-weight ratio, required on short notice or can be quickly obsolete. • Ideal for products when demand is unpredictable, infrequent, or seasonal. • Shipments do not require heavy packing (standard domestic packing is sufficient). • Reduces inventory and storage costs. • Reduces insurance cost and documentation. • Achieves savings in total transportation cost and provides reliability of service.	• Generally expensive for high-bulk freight. Value must be high enough to justify higher freight cost. • Inefficient for shorter distances, which are handled faster by trucks. Only the express air services, such as UPS or DIIL, have equally competitive services. • Shipping containers must be small enough to fit into an air carrier. • Not suitable for products that are sensitive to low pressures and variations in temperature.

TABLE 9.3 Air Cargo Growth Rates and Forecast to 2037 (percent)

Markets	2007–2017	2018–2037
World	2.60	4.20
Intra North America (NA)	2.3	2.3
East Asia–North America	1.2	4.7
Latin America–NA	-0.3	4.1
Latin America–Europe	3.0	4.0
Intra Europe	3.1	2.3
Europe–North America	0.0	2.5
Europe–East Asia	4.2	4.7
Middle East–Europe	3.3	3.2
Africa–Europe	-1.0	3.7
Intra East Asia	3.8	5.8
South Asia–Europe	2.4	4.2
Domestic China	5.0	6.3

Source: Boeing (2019/2020)

Cargo revenues contributed to over a quarter of industry revenues compared to 12 percent in 2019. Boeing (2019/2020) forecasts world air cargo traffic to grow in the next twenty years from 256 billion revenue ton kilometers (RTKs) to 584 RTKs in 2037 (Table 9.3) (Boeing, 2019/2020).

There are a number of factors that are likely to contribute to such growth in airfreight:

1. *The world economy*: Global economic growth is expected to return to its long-term historic growth trend. Long-term growth rates are favorable for both advanced and developing nations. For example, GDP growth rates for African, Latin American, and Asian countries is expected to be over 3–4 percent for 2018 through 2037, while GDP growth in Europe and the United States is expected to reach 1.7 percent and 2 percent, respectively. The rising success of air cargo is also due to the changing composition of global trade. Goods that are likely to be transported by air (computers, electronics) have registered higher growth rates than heavy or bulky commodities such as fuel or grains. The growing proportion of high value, time sensitive products in world trade has created increased opportunities for air cargo business. This trend is likely to continue positioning air cargo to outgrow overall trade (Boeing, 2019/2020; Abeyratne, 2018).

2. *Infrastructure investment in developing countries*: In view of the heavy infrastructure investment being made in many developing countries, the potential need exists for imports of heavy equipment and services. Certain types of equipment exports to these countries, such as bulldozers, buses, or oil-drilling equipment, often do not fit in a standard ocean container (Reyes and Gilles, 1998).

3. *Just-in-time deliveries*: Since many of these projects are built from supplies shipped to the sites on a just-in-time basis, delays in delivering cargo can lead to heavy financial losses or penalties for the suppliers. Such needs cannot be accommodated by using the traditional modes of carriage for heavy freight. Airfreight becomes the only viable means of moving such cargo to ensure timely delivery. This also helps reduce working capital by reducing stocks (Abeyratne, 2018).

4. *Changes in technology*: Technological changes over the last few decades have significantly altered the size and design of aircraft to handle heavy cargo. For example, the recent version of the Boeing 747 (747-8 freighter) has more cargo volume than the 747-400 and can carry more freight (even with passengers) than all-cargo versions of the previous generation of jets. The all-cargo plane has a payload capacity of about 148 tons and offers an additional 4,225 cubic feet of volume accommodating four additional main-deck pallets and three additional lower-hold pallets. Furthermore, improvements in terminal facilities in many countries have also contributed to increased speed and better handling and storage of shipments at airports, thus minimizing loss or damage to merchandise (International Perspective 9.1) (David, 2017).

5. *The role of integrators and forwarders*: The development of air carriers that provide integrated services (e.g., DHL, UPS) has increased the amount of air cargo. For example, UPS Sonic Air Service offers a guaranteed door-to-door service to most international destinations, regardless of size or weight limitations, within twenty-four hours. In addition, the role of forwarders as consolidators of small shipments makes it easier for shippers to send their merchandise by air without being subject to the minimum charge for small shipments. The forwarder consolidates various small shipments and tenders them to the airline in volume in exchange for a bill of lading furnished as the shipper of the cargo. The role of a forwarder is similar to that of a non-vessel-operating carrier in ocean freight (Abeyratne, 2018).

Airfreight Calculations

Airfreight rates are based on a "chargeable weight" because the volume or weight that can be loaded on an aircraft is limited. The chargeable weight (CW) will be either the "actual weight" or the "volumetric weight," whichever is highest. It is calculated as follows.

> *Actual weight*: Take cargo weight in pounds, divided by 2.2046 to convert the weight into kilos = actual kilos
> *Volumetric weight*: multiply cargo measurements in inches divided by 366 = volume kilos

Sample shipment:

> Medical equipment, with dimensions of 45 x 45 x 60 inches / Weight: 1500 lbs.
> Actual weight: 1500 lbs. / 2.2046 = 680 kilos
> Volumetric weight: 45 x 45 x 60 inches / 366 = 322 kilos
> Freight charges would be assessed on the actual weight

The International Air Transport Association (IATA) standard dimensional weight is based on 6000 cubic centimeters per one physical kilogram (length in cm x width in cm x height in cm) / 6000= Volume kilos.

Air Cargo Rates

Determinants of Air Cargo Rates

Distance to the point of destination as well as weight and size of the shipment are important determinants of air cargo rates. The identity of the product (commodity description) and the provision of any special services also influence freight rates. If a product is classified under a general cargo category (products shipped frequently), a lower rate applies.

Products can also be classified under a special unit load (for shipments in approved containers) or a commodity rate (negotiated rates for merchandise not classified as general cargo). Special services such as charter flight or immediate transportation could substantially increase the freight rate.

Rate Setting

The IATA is the forum in which fares and rates are negotiated among member airlines. Over the last few years, such fares and rates have been set by the marketplace, and tariff conference proposals have tended to become reference points. The IATA's cargo service conferences also promote among members the negotiation of certain standards and procedures for cargo handling, documentation and procedures, and shipment of dangerous goods, and so on.

International Air Express Services (the Integrators)

The big carriers are under increasing competitive pressure from the integrated air service providers such as Federal Express or UPS. While the traditional carriers provide airport-to-airport service, the integrators have the added advantage of furnishing direct delivery services to customers, including customs clearance and payment of import duties at foreign destinations. Even though the strength of integrators had been in the transportation of smaller packages, they are now offering services geared to heavyweight cargo (Bridges, 2000). (See International Perspective 9.1.)

INTERNATIONAL PERSPECTIVE 9.1

Types of Aircraft and Air Services

Types of Aircraft

- *Passenger aircraft*: Passenger operators offer freight capacity in the bellyhold of their aircrafts. Freight services are usually secondary and represent a source of additional income. Low-cost carriers do not provide cargo freight services.
- *Combination carriers:* These are designed to carry both passengers and cargo on the main deck of the aircraft. Examples include the Boeing 737, 747, and 757 and the Airbus 330 and 340.
- *Air freighters:* Air freighters are entirely dedicated to the transportation of cargo. For example, the Airbus A-330-200F's large main deck cargo door allows the aircraft to accept all pallets and containers, and ensures loading and unloading using roller decks. Other examples include the Belugas produced by Airbus used for transportation of military and satellite launch vehicles.

- *Quick change aircraft:* Aircraft canbe quickly converted between passenger and freight operations. The Airbus 330-200 and 300 versions are eligible for passenger-to-freight conversions when they have completed their useful operational service as passenger aircraft.

Types of Air Service

- *Airmail services*: Air mail services now accounts for a small share (less than 4 percent) of airline revenue.
- *Express freight services*: Express cargo has a guaranteed pre-determined delivery date and time. Such services account for over 13 percent of airline cargo traffic. Major players in this market include FedEx, UPS, DHL, and TNT.
- *Scheduled freight services*: Services are delivered on a published schedule (specific dates and times). Passenger airlines, freighters, and integrators provide such services. The majority of air cargo traffic is handled through such services.
- *Charters and leased cargo services*: Charter companies provide individual private aircraft for specific itineraries, urgent or time-sensitive cargo, air ambulance, and any other form of ad hoc air transportation. Aircraft can also be leased with or without crew and insurance. Freight carriers are increasingly attracted to leasing because they do not have to pay cash for purchasing the plane and the lease terms are subject to negotiation.
- *Airfreight forwarder services*: Forwarders provide a number of services such as consolidating shipments, buying space, etc. Many of the integrators such as UPS also provide such services.

Carriage of Goods by Air

Soon after World War I, governments not only recognized the need for faster and safer air transportation but also the importance of international cooperation in regulating air transportation. This included, inter alia, the establishment of uniform rules on the use of air space and navigation as well as on liability limits of air carriers for damages. The most important international regime pertaining to liability of air carriers for loss or damage to cargo (as well as death and bodily injury to passengers) during air travel was the Warsaw Convention of 1929 (amended in 1955). Despite various efforts invested to modernize the Warsaw regime, it was still unable to accommodate the dynamic requirements of the airline industry and that of shippers.

For example, some of its provisions were out of date, liability limits were too low and the Convention was not adapted to electronic commerce. In view of this, member countries adopted a new treaty in 1999 (The Montreal Convention) to govern international carriage of goods by air. The treaty became effective in 2003 and as of September 2018, 132 countries had ratified the Montreal Convention of 1999 including the United States, all members of the European Union (EU), Australia, Canada, China, India, Japan, Korea, and Mexico.

The Convention re-establishes urgently needed uniformity and predictability of rules relating to the international carriage of passengers, baggage, and cargo. Whilst maintaining the core provisions of the Warsaw System, which have successfully served the international air transport community for several decades, the new convention achieves the required modernization in a number of key areas:

- Increased air carrier liability limits for all damages from death or bodily injury (for proven damages) of up to US$152,384 as of 2017 and such liability can be increased if negligence is proved.
- Advanced liability limits in the event of delay in transporting cargo, baggage, or passengers
- Modernization of transport documents (electronic airway bills and tickets).

Scope of the Montreal Convention

The Convention governs the liability of the carrier while the goods are in its charge, whether at or outside an airport. It applies when the departure and destination points set out in the contract of carriage are in two countries that subscribe to the Convention. The Convention applies only to passengers ticketed for international travel. Claims for cargo loss or damage can be brought at the country where the air waybill for cargo was issued, the country of final destination, or the country where the carrier is incorporated or has its principal place of business.

Air Consignment Note (Air Waybill)

A consignment note (air waybill) is a document issued by the air carrier to a shipper that serves as a receipt for goods and evidence of the contract of carriage. However, it is not a document of title to the goods, as in the case of a bill of lading. The carrier requires the consignor to make out and hand over the air waybill with the goods.

The Montreal Convention encourages carriers to use electronic records and requires only three things to appear on the waybill that accompanies a consignment of goods: a) the place of departure and destination, b) an intermediate stopping place in a different state (if the places of departure and destination are in the same state), and c) the weight of the consignment.

Liability of Carrier

The carrier is liable for damages sustained to cargo under its control up to 19 Special Drawing Rights (SDRs) per kilo (i.e., foreign exchange reserve assets defined and maintained by the International Monetary Fund) unless the shipper has declared a higher value on the waybill and paid the additional fee. The carrier is not responsible in cases where the damage resulted from inherent vice, defective packaging, or armed conflict. Liability for baggage loss is limited to 1,131 SDRs for each passenger unless a higher value was declared. Airlines may be liable for delays up to 4,694 SDRs per passenger. However, carriers will not be held responsible if they took reasonable measures to avoid the damage or that it was impossible to take such measures (Schaffer et al., 2018).

Limitation of Liability

The liability of the carrier with respect to loss or damage to the goods, or delay in delivery, is limited to the sum specified under the Convention unless the consignor has declared a higher value and paid a supplementary charge.

Limitation of Action

The right to damages will be extinguished if an action is not brought within two years after the actual or supposed delivery of cargo. Notice of complaint (of the damage) must be made within fourteen days from the date of receipt of cargo (no later than seven days in the case of checked baggage). In the case of damage for delayed cargo, claims must be made in writing and within twenty-one days from the actual date of delivery of cargo or baggage (Schaffer et al., 2018).

International Air Cargo Security

Potential risks associated with air cargo security include introduction of explosive and incendiary devices in cargo placed aboard aircraft; shipment of undeclared or undetected hazardous materials aboard aircraft; cargo crime including theft and smuggling; and aircraft hijackings and sabotage by individuals with access to aircraft. Current aviation security regulations require that each passenger aircraft operator and indirect air carrier develop a security program for acceptance and screening of cargo to prevent or deter the carriage of unauthorized explosives. However, the volume of air cargo handled and the distributed nature of the air cargo system presents significant challenges for screening and inspecting air cargo.

Presently, in the United States, about fifty air carriers transport air cargo on passenger aircraft handling cargo from nearly 2 million shippers per day (Elias, 2007). About 80 percent of these shippers use freight forwarders who operate about 10,000 facilities across the country. Analysts warn that the cost of screening every piece of air cargo that enters the shipping system in a bid to prevent terror gangs from downing airliners might bankrupt international shipping companies, hobble the already weakened airlines, and still would not provide comprehensive protection. However, efforts are being made to increase airline security without putting undue financial burden on the private sector.

Security guidelines are constantly changing in view of technological developments as well as the unpredictable nature of terrorism. Furthermore, security requirements are different for cargo shipped on freighters and for cargo shipped on passenger aircraft.

The U.S. Transportation Security Administration (TSA) (part of Homeland Security) secures the nation's airports and screens all commercial airline passengers and baggage. The air cargo division of the TSA is responsible for the security of the air cargo supply chain. The TSA uses a multi-layered approach that includes vetting companies that ship and transport cargo on passenger planes to ensure they meet TSA security standards, establishing a system to enable Certified Cargo Screening Facilities (CCSFs) to physically screen cargo using approved screening methods and technologies, employing random and risk-based assessment to identify high-risk cargo that requires increased scrutiny, and inspecting industry compliance with security regulations through the deployment of TSA inspectors (U.S. Customs and Border Protection, 2020a).

A number of programs have been introduced to enhance air cargo security.

- *Customs-Trade Partnership Against Terrorism (C-TPAT)*: C-TPAT is a partnership of over 10,000 importers, freight forwarders, carriers, and other entities. It establishes clear supply chain security criteria for members to meet and in return provides incentives and benefits such as expedited processing. When they join the anti-terror partnership, companies sign an agreement to work with Customs and Border Protection (CBP) to protect the supply chain, identify security gaps, and implement specific security measures and best practices. Additionally, partners provide CBP with a security profile outlining the specific security measures the company has in place. Members of C-TPAT are considered low-risk and are therefore less likely to be examined. This designation is based on a company's past compliance history, security profile, and the validation of a sample international supply chain (U.S. Customs and Border Protection, 2020d).

- *Air Cargo Advanced Screening (ACAS)*: Airlines send manifest data of inbound cargo to CBP several hours before departure. By analyzing this data in advance, the TSA and CBP have a fast and efficient way to screen vast amounts of cargo and zero in more quickly on the precise items requiring further scrutiny. Air Cargo Advanced Screening may request additional information, or require the air carrier or its authorized representative to screen or hold identified shipments. Screening requests from ACAS require the air carrier or its authorized representative to screen identified shipments according to current TSA Standard Security Programs. It targets high risk shipments for enhanced screening (U.S. Customs and Border Protection, 2020a, 2020e).

- *Certified Cargo Screening Program (CCSP)*: This program requires air carriers to screen 100 percent of all cargo aboard international inbound passenger flights. The law requires the Department of Homeland Security to establish a system that would screen all cargo transported on passenger aircraft to be "commensurate" with the level of security used for checked baggage. The program was designed to enable TSA vetted, validated, and certified facilities to screen air cargo prior to delivering the cargo to the air carrier. Facilities that successfully complete the TSA certification process (including an on-site assessment of the facility), will be designated a CCSF. A Certified Cargo Screening Facility must adhere to TSA-mandated security standards, including the employment of a secure chain of custody methods to establish and maintain the security of screened cargo throughout the supply chain. The TSA will only certify those facilities that demonstrate adherence to these requirements through the TSA certification process (U.S. Customs and Border Protection, 2020a, 2020c).

- *Indirect Air Carrier Program:* An Indirect Air Carrier (IAC) is any person or entity within the United States not in possession of a Federal Aviation Administration air carrier operating certificate, that undertakes to engage indirectly in air transportation of property and uses for all or any part of such transportation the services of a passenger air carrier. Each Indirect Air Carrier must adopt and carry out a security program that meets current TSA requirements.

The Indirect Air Carrier Regional Compliance Coordinators are responsible for the application process for freight forwarders working to become classified as Indirect Air Carriers. These coordinators complete annual renewals for current Indirect Air Carriers and provide assistance with program compliance (U.S. Customs and Border Protection, 2020b, 2020f).

- *International Collaboration*: The TSA's efforts to harmonize activities with foreign partners will increase global air cargo security and reduce burdens on trade. The TSA's agreements with the European Commission as well as Canada, Australia, and European Union member states (signed in 2008), will facilitate common and practical solutions to air cargo screening. This harmonization will contribute greatly to achieving the 100 percent screening requirement of the 9/11 Commission Act, 2007.

OCEAN FREIGHT

Ocean shipping is the least expensive and the dominant mode of transportation in foreign trade. It is especially suitable for moving bulk freight such as commodities and other raw materials. Today, an increasing part of ocean freight travels by containers, which results in minimal handling at ports. In terms of value, containerized cargo accounts for the largest share of global trade (over 50 percent), followed by the tanker trade (25 percent) and general and dry cargo (20 percent). In terms of volume, container trade (minor bulk and residual cargo) accounts for about 42 percent of world trade followed by main bulk (iron ore, grain) and tanker trade (UNCTAD, 2019) (Tables 9.4 and 9.5).

Important Developments in International Maritime Trade

- *Slow growth in world seaborne trade*: International seaborne trade lost momentum in 2020 due to the coronavirus and trade tensions between the United States and China. Factory shutdowns and other restrictions to control the virus reduced global cargo volumes. Bookings for container ships, tankers, and dry bulk vessels fell rapidly since the beginning of the pandemic in January 2020. This has had ripple effects on supply chains across countries.

TABLE 9.4 World Fleet by Vessel Type 2018–2019 (thousands of deadweight (dwt), % share)

Vessel Type	2018	2019	% Change
Oil tankers	562,035 (29%)	567,533 (28.7%)	0.98
Bulk carriers	818,921 (42.5%)	842,438 (40.6%)	2.87
General cargo ships	73,951 (3.8%)	74,000 (6.9%)	0.07
Containerships	253,275 (13.1%)	265,668 (12.9%)	4.89
Other vessel types	218,002 (11.3%)	226,854 (6.5%)	4.06
World total	**1,926,183**	**1,976,491**	**2.61**

Source: UNCTAD, 2019

TABLE 9.5 World Seaborne Trade (in Million Tons Loaded)

Vessel Type	2015	2016	2017	2018
Tanker trade*	2932	3,058	3,146	3,194
Main bulk**	2930	3009	3151	3210
Other dry cargo***	4161	4228	4419	4601

Source: UNCTAD, 2019

*Crude oil, refined petroleum products, gas, and chemicals
**Iron ore, grain, coal, bauxite, and phosphate
***Minor bulks, containerized trade, and residual general cargo

This, added to the trade tensions, Brexit, and other supply-side disruptions is likely to slow down global seaborne trade below the historic average of 3.0 percent in 2020. The UN forecasts international seaborne trade to grow by 3.5 percent during the 2019–2024 period (UNCTAD, 2019).

- *Growth in world shipping fleet*: The world fleet continued to expand reaching more than 1.9 billion deadweight tons (dwt) in 2019, an increase of over 31 percent since 2012. However, new orders for ships are much lower than previous years due to uncertainty in the global economy. The reduction is significant for dry bulk carriers and oil tankers. Orders in the container ship segment now cover large vessels. The gas tanker segment is likely to register an increase in orders due to the growing demand for trade in liquefied natural gas. China, Japan, and South Korea built more than 90 percent of the tonnage delivered in 2018 (UNCTAD, 2019). Oversupply of ships poses a serious challenge to the profitability of shipping companies, while benefitting importers and exporters.

- *Developing nations in the maritime sector*: One third of the world fleet is owned by shipowners in developing nations and twelve of the top twenty container operators are from developing nations. The top twenty container ports accounted for about 44 percent of world container throughput in 2018. The leading role of Asian countries shows the importance of the region as a center of international trade and the subsequent demand and growth for container ports (Tables 9.6 and 9.7).

- *Freight rates and transportation costs*: Oversupply of ships and weak trade growth resulted in low freight rates in general in 2018–2019. However, a temporary surge in trade triggered by increased shipments from China to the United States (before the imposition of tariffs in 2019) led to a temporary rise in freight rates. During the pandemic, carriers attempted to control capacity to keep rates stable. For many developing nations of Asia and the Americas, shipping costs (as a percentage of the value of goods imported) continue to drop. Rates for African countries have not declined due to port congestion, low productivity, and high charges.

- *Environmental initiatives*: A set of measures to increase energy efficiency and reduce greenhouse gas emissions from international shipping was adopted in 2011 and entered into force in 2013. A new International Maritime Organization

TABLE 9.6 Top Ten Ship-owning Countries by Selected Vessel Type (as at January 1, 2019) (US$ million)*

Countries	Tankers	Bulk carriers	General cargo	Containerships
Greece	30569	37218	197	7463
Japan	8634	35492	3577	9489
United States	5562	4102	984	1112
China	9666	27833	5341	14385
Norway	5423	3942	1021	2108
Singapore	10481	12674	980	5715
Germany	2416	6694	3957	17685
United Kingdom	3375	4164	995	3446
Hong Kong, China	6244	12461	774	9073
Bermuda	5507	5200	0	1328
All others	19064	15,836	8746	3808

* Value estimated for all commercial ships of 1000 gross tons and above.

TABLE 9.7 Top Twenty Container Ports and Their Throughput (TEUs)

Port Name	2018	% change
Shanghai (China)	42,010,000	4.4
Singapore	36,600,000	8.7
Ningbo (China)	26350,000	6.9
Shenzhen (China)	25,740,000	2.1
Guangzhou (China)	21,920,000	7.6
Busan (South Korea)	21,660,000	5.5
Hong Kong (China)	19,600,000	-5.6
Qingdao (China)	19,320,000	5.5
Tianjin (China)	16,000,000	6.2
Dubai (UAE)	14,950,000	-2.9
Rotterdam (The Netherlands)	14,510,000	5.7
Port Klang (Malaysia)	12,030,000	0.4
Antwerp (The Netherlands)	11,100,000	6.2
Xiamen (China)	10,700,000	3.1
Kaohsiung (Taiwan)	10,450,000	1.8
Dalian (China)	9,770,000	0.6
Los Angeles (USA)	9,460,000	1.3
Tanjung Pelepas (Malaysia)	8,790,000	6.4
Hamburg (Germany)	8,780,000	-0.2
Long Beach (USA)	8,070,000	3.7

^Data shows the number of twenty-footer equivalent units (TEU) moved within a given time.

Source: UNCTAD (2019).

regulation, which entered into force in 2020 (IMO 2020), reduces the sulphur cap in fuel oil for ships from 3.5 percent to 0.5 percent. Other international environmental instruments and voluntary standards were adopted on ship-building, shipyards, standards of design, and construction of ships.

Types of Ocean Carrier

The following are the three major types of ocean carriers. (See also International Perspective 9.2.)

Private Fleets

These are large fleets of specialized ships owned and managed by merchants and manufacturers to carry their own goods. Apart from its cost advantages, ownership of a private fleet ensures the availability of carriage that meets the firm's specific needs. Such ships can occasionally be leased to other firms at times of limited activity. Some firms in certain industries, such as oil, sugar, or lumber, own their own fleets.

Tramps (Chartered or Leased Vessels)

Tramps are vessels leased to transport, usually, large quantities of bulk cargo (oil, coal, grain, sugar, etc.) that fill the entire ship (vessel). Chartered vessels do not operate on a regular route or schedule. Charter arrangements can be made on the basis of a trip or voyage between origin and destination or for an agreed time period, usually several months to a year. The vessel could be leased with or without a crew (a bare-boat charter). The major factors for the continued existence of tramp shipping are that 1) it provides indispensable ocean transportation at the lowest possible cost, and 2) it is adaptable to the changing and/or unanticipated requirements for transportation. When charter rates are low, commodity traders tend to move materials in advance of actual delivery time to take advantage of low transportation costs (Wood et al., 1995; Breskin, 2018). The just-in-time system that delivers products when they are needed is not often feasible in cases in which transport and distribution could be impeded by severe winter weather. A commodity trader's decision to purchase and export a product is influenced by the spread between the export and purchase price, the charter rate, and any warehousing or storage cost. This means that an exporter can purchase and export a product even before delivery time if the charter rate and storage cost are substantially less than the spread to allow for a reasonable profit margin.

Conference Lines

A shipping conference line is a voluntary association of ocean carriers operating on a particular trade route between two or more countries. Shipping conferences date back to the nineteenth century when such associations were established for trade between England and its colonies. One of the distinguishing features of a liner service is that sailings are regular and repeated from and to designated ports on a trade route, at intervals established in response to the quantity of cargo generated along that route. Even though the sailing schedule is related to the amount of business available, it is general practice to dispatch at least one ship each month (Kendall, 1983). The purpose of a shipping conference is the self-regulation of price competition, primarily through the establishment of uniform freight rates and terms and conditions of service among the member shipping lines. In spite of its cartel-like structure, it is considered to be a necessary evil to ensure the stability and growth of international trade by setting rate levels that are more stable and predictable and by reducing predatory price competition (Breskin, 2018).

Conference agreements become effective between carriers, unless rejected, on the forty-fifth day after filing with the Federal Maritime Commission (FMC), or the thirtieth day after publication of notice of filing in the Federal Register, whichever day was later.

Conferences serving U.S. ports must be "open," that is, they must admit any common carrier willing to serve the particular trade or route under reasonable and equal terms and conditions. This is generally intended to preclude conferences from using membership limitations as a means of discriminating against other U.S. carriers. Conferences are also allowed to form an exclusive patronage contract with a shipper, allowing the latter to obtain lower rates by committing all or a fixed portion of its cargo to conference members. Vessels engaged in liner service may be owned or leased. Conferences compete with independent lines, chartered vessels, and each other, although the same carrier could belong to several conferences.

Example: An exporter in Taiwan intends to arrange for shipment of its textiles by a conference carrier to New York. A case for a lower (tariff) rate for large shipments can be made to a conference rate-making committee that consists of member lines. If the conference elects to reject the application for a lower rate, several options are available to the exporter: 1) the exporter may request a member of the conference to establish the rate independently of the conference, 2) the product could be shipped through nonconference carriers (independent or other conference lines) that offer a reasonably low tariff, 3) the product could be shipped through other ports using other conference carriers, or 4) the shipper could consider non-vessel-operating common carriers (NVOCC) or tramp vessels, depending on the amount of cargo. Non-vessel-operating common carriers take possession of smaller shipments from several shippers and consolidate them into full container loads for shipment by an ocean carrier. They charge their own tariff rates and obtain a bill of lading as the shipper of the consolidated merchandise.

INTERNATIONAL PERSPECTIVE 9.2

Types of Ocean Cargo/Vessels

Types of Ocean Cargo

Containerized: Cargo loaded at a facility away from the pier, or at a warehouse into a metal container usually 20 to 40 feet long, 8 feet high and 8 feet wide. The container is then delivered to a pier and loaded on to a "containership" for transportation. Some cargo cannot be containerized, e.g., automobiles, live animals, bulk products.

Bulk: Cargo that is loaded and carried in bulk, without mark or count, in a loose unpackaged form, having homogenous characteristics. To be loaded on a containership, bulk cargo would be put in containers first. It could also be stowed in bulk instead of being loaded into containers. Examples: coal, iron ore, raw sugar, etc.

Break-Bulk: Packaged cargo that is loaded and unloaded on a piece-by-piece basis, i.e., by number or count. This can be containerized or prepared in groups of packages covered by shrink wrap for shipment. Examples: coffee, rubber, steel, etc.

Neo-Bulk: Certain types of cargo that are often moved by specialized vessels. Examples: autos, logs.

Types of Ocean Vessel

Tankers: Vessels designed to carry liquid cargo such as oil in large tanks. They can be modified to carry other types of cargo such as grain or coffee.

Bulk Carriers: Vessels that carry a variety of bulk cargo.

Neo-Bulk Carriers: Vessels designed to carry specific types of cargo such as autos, logs, etc.

General Cargo Vessels: These include:

1. containerships: vessels that carry only containerized cargo;
2. roll-on and roll-off (RO/RO) vessels: vessels that allow rolling cargo such as tractors or cars to be driven aboard the vessel; and
3. LASH (lighter aboard ship) vessels: vessels that can carry very large containers such as barges. It enables cargo to be loaded on barges in shallow waters and then loaded on board a vessel.

Barges: Unmanned vessels generally used for oversized cargo and towed by a tugboat.

Combination Carriers: Vessels that carry passengers and cargo, oil, and dry bulk, or containers and bulk cargo. Other combinations are also possible.

Carriage of Goods by Sea

International transportation of cargo by sea is governed by various conventions. The Hague Rules of 1924 have won a certain measure of global support. The U.S. law on the carriage of goods by sea is based on the Hague Rules. Subsequent modifications have been made to the Hague Rules (the Hague–Visby Rules, 1968), which are now in force in most of Western Europe, Japan, Singapore, Australia, and Canada. In 1978, the United Nations Commission on International Trade Law (UNCITRAL) was given the task of drafting a new convention to balance the interests of carriers and shippers. Although the Hague–Visby Rules were intended to rectify the pro-carrier inclination of the Hague Rules, many developing countries felt that the Hague–Visby rules did not go far enough in addressing the legitimate concerns of cargo owners or shippers. The commission's deliberations led to an agreement in 1978 (the Hamburg Rules). They came into effect in 1991, and their impact remains to be seen. Unlike the Hague and Hague–Visby Rules, which have been ratified by many developed and developing nations, the Hamburg Rules are mostly followed by developing nations, except Austria (Flint and O'Keefe, 1997). In view of the widespread acceptance of the Hague Rules, it is important to briefly examine some of their central features (see International Perspective 9.3).

Scope of Application

The application of the rules depends on the place of issuance of the bill of lading; that is, the rules apply to all bills of lading issued in any of the contracting states. The Carriage of Goods by Sea Act (COGSA) applies to all bills of lading issued between a U.S. port and a foreign port. Shipments between U.S. ports are governed by the Harter Act (1893) and not by COGSA (Schaffer et al., 2018).

Carrier's Duties Under a B/L

A carrier transporting goods under a B/L is required to exercise "due diligence" in 1) making the ship seaworthy; 2) properly manning, equipping, and supplying the ship; 3) making the ship (holds, refrigerating chambers, etc.) fit and safe for reception, carriage, and preservation of the goods; and 4) properly and carefully loading, handling, stowing, carrying, and discharging the goods. Whenever loss or damage occurs due to unseaworthiness of the ship, the burden of proving the exercise of due diligence falls on the carrier. When different modes of transportation are used, the issuer of the bill of lading undertakes to deliver the cargo to the final destination. In the event of loss or damage to merchandise, liability is determined according to the law relative to the mode of transportation at fault for the loss. If the means of loss is not determinable, it will be assumed to have occurred during the sea voyage (Schaffer et al., 2018).

Carrier's Liability and Exemptions

The carrier's liability applies to loss or damage to the goods. It does not extend to delays in the delivery of the merchandise. The rules exempt carriers from liability that arises from actions of the servants of the carrier (master, pilot, etc.) in the management of the shipment, fire and accidents, acts of God, acts of war, civil war, insufficient packing, inherent defects in the goods, and other causes that are not the actual fault of the carrier. The fact that loss or damage to the goods falls within one of these exemptions does not automatically absolve the carrier from liability if the damage/ loss could have been prevented by the carrier's exercise of due diligence in carrying out its duties (Yancey, 1983; Carr and Stone, 2017).

Period of Responsibility

The period of responsibility begins from the time the goods are loaded to the time they are discharged from the ship.

Limitations of Action

All claims against the carrier must be brought within one year after the actual or supposed date of delivery of the goods. This means that lapse of time discharges the carrier and the ship from all liability in respect to loss or damage. The Hague Rules also stipulate that notice of claim be made in writing before or at the time of removal of the goods.

Limits of Liability

The maximum limitation of liability is $500 per package. Under the Hague–Visby rules, it is $1,000 per package. In some cases, a container is considered as one package, and the carrier's liability is limited to $500. To ensure the application of liability limits to their agents and employees, carriers add the "Himalaya Clause" to their bills of lading. The clause entitles such agents and employees the protection of the Hague Rules. Exporters can, however, obtain full protection against loss or damage by paying an excess value charge or by taking out an insurance policy from an independent source (Force, 1996; Schaffer et al., 2018).

Proposed Rotterdam Rules

In 2008, a new treaty was adopted (the Rotterdam Rules) that replaces the Hague Rules and currently awaits ratification. As of 2018, it had been ratified by only five countries. Twenty countries have to ratify the treaty before it enters into force. The Rotterdam Rules build upon the previous conventions and establish a modern and uniform legal regime governing the rights and obligations of shippers, carriers, and consignees under a contract for door-to door carriage (which includes international maritime transportation). The rules provide a legal framework that takes into account commercial and technological developments such as containerization and electronic transport documents as well as door-to-door carriage under a single contract and carriage that involves other modes of transport (Carr and Stone, 2017).

INTERNATIONAL PERSPECTIVE 9.3

The Hague, Hague–Visby, and Hamburg Rules: An Overview

All three rules define the rights and duties of parties in a contract of carriage of goods by sea, insurance for goods, and transfer of title. The Hague and Hague–Visby Rules are generally identical except for provisions dealing with limitations of liability, third parties, and a few minor areas. The Visby amendments to the Hague Rules increase the limits of carrier's liability, change the method of expressing the limitation amount (by weight), and protect third parties acting in good faith.

The Hamburg Rules have been criticized by carriers and their insurers as favoring shippers (cargo interests). The prominent differences between the Hamburg and Hague/Hague–Visby Rules are as follows: 1) The Hamburg Rules have higher limits of liability and set higher damages against carriers, 2) under the Hamburg Rules, the carrier is liable for delays in delivery, in addition to loss or damage to goods; 3) under the Hamburg Rules, any loss or damage to goods in transit imposes a burden of proof on the carrier to show that the latter was not at fault, whereas such burden is only triggered when the loss or damage resulted from an unseaworthy condition of the ship under the Hague and Hague–Visby Rules; and 4) the limits of carrier's liability may not extend to acts of independent contractors, unlike under the other two Rules.

Container Security

As part of its efforts to target high-risk cargo containers for inspection, the CBP uses various sources of information to screen containers in advance of their arrival in the United States (Figure 9.1). It works on the basis of:

- *The 24-hour rule*: CBP's 24-hour rule requires that vessel carriers submit cargo manifest information to CBP twenty-four hours before cargo bound for the United States is loaded onto a vessel.
- *Automated Targeting System* (ATS): The ATS is a mathematical model that uses weighted rules to assign a risk score to arriving cargo shipments based on shipping information. The CBP uses the ATS as a decision support tool in targeting cargo containers for inspection (U.S. Customs and Border Protection, 2020a).
- *The 10+2 rule*: The cargo information required by the 10+2 rule comprises ten data elements from importers, such as country of origin, and two data elements from vessel carriers, such as the position of each container transported on a vessel, all of which are to be provided to the CBP in advance of arrival at a U.S. port (U.S. Customs and Border Protection, 2020f).
- *Cargo Security Initiative* (CSI): The CBP temporarily assigns inspectors at foreign ports to inspect containers bound for the United States. Currently, there are over fifty operational CSI ports in Europe, Asia, Africa and the Middle

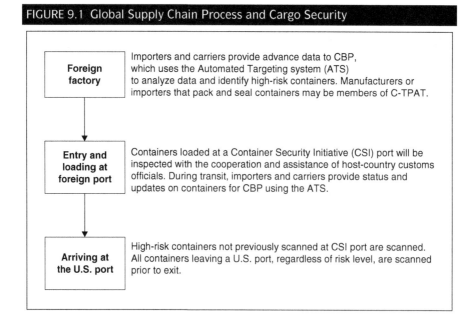

FIGURE 9.1 Global Supply Chain Process and Cargo Security

| **Foreign factory** | Importers and carriers provide advance data to CBP, which uses the Automated Targeting system (ATS) to analyze data and identify high-risk containers. Manufacturers or importers that pack and seal containers may be members of C-TPAT. |

| **Entry and loading at foreign port** | Containers loaded at a Container Security Initiative (CSI) port will be inspected with the cooperation and assistance of host-country customs officials. During transit, importers and carriers provide status and updates on containers for CBP using the ATS. |

| **Arriving at the U.S. port** | High-risk containers not previously scanned at CSI port are scanned. All containers leaving a U.S. port, regardless of risk level, are scanned prior to exit. |

East, and North and South America. These ports collectively accounted for over 90 percent of the cargo containers shipped to the United States (U.S. Customs and Border Protection, 2020c).

- *Customs-Trade Partnership against Terrorism* (C-TPAT): The C-TPAT program is a government-to-business partnership program that provides benefits to supply chain companies that comply with predetermined security measures. Under C-TPAT, CBP officials work with private companies to review their supply chain security plans and improve members' security measures. In return, C-TPAT members may receive benefits, such as reduced scrutiny or expedited processing of their shipments (U.S. Customs and Border Protection, 2020d).
- *International Collaboration*: CBP also partners with international trade and security groups to develop supply chain security standards that can be implemented by the international community. In 2005, the World Customs Organization (WCO) developed the Framework of Standards to Secure and Facilitate Global Trade for which the core concepts are based on components of the CBP's CSI and C-TPAT programs.

INTERNATIONAL PERSPECTIVE 9.4

NVOCCs and Other OTIs Face Intense Scrutiny

Non-vessel-operating common carriers and ocean freight forwarders (FFs) together constitute the category of ocean transportation intermediary (OTI). They are regulated and licensed by the Federal Maritime Commission. An entity can operate as FF and NVOCC but cannot serve in both roles on the same transaction. This means that if you perform as FF on one shipment, you cannot also issue your own bill of lading or collect ocean freight at your published rate for the shipment. Non-vessel-operating common carriers consolidate small shipments from multiple points of origin bound for the same port in a single container for overseas shipment. Their functions include purchasing transportation services from common carriers for resale, payment of transportation charges, issuing bills of lading, paying lawful compensation to FFs, leasing containers, and making arrangements with agents at origin and destination. They offer competitive pricing for small cargo.

Many trademark and copyright owners have experienced a growing incidence of counterfeit/pirated shipments being imported into the United States and other countries with the assistance of NVOCCs and other OTIs. There is increasing evidence to show that these transport intermediaries are willfully or negligently involved in the distribution of counterfeit goods. For example, U.S. Homeland Security reported about 26,503 seizures of counterfeits with a retail price of over US$1.3 billion in 2020. It includes brand name watches, jewelry, handbags, wallets, consumer electronics, clothing, and pharmaceuticals.

The International Anti-Counterfeiting Coalition (IACC) and concerned shippers have filed complaints with the Federal Trade Commission alleging that many of the counterfeits being imported into the United States originate with the assistance of OTIs. The typical scheme deployed by counterfeiters is described as follows:

*   Foreign criminals secure shipping and commercial documentation from a legitimate foreign supplier that exports merchandise to a U.S. buyer.
*   Having secured such documentation, they then provide the requisite information to NVOCCs in order to book the illicit cargo. They also provide this information to relevant authorities in their home country and the country to which the product is being exported. This false information is entered into the automated Manifest System of U.S. Customs (as reported by NVOCCs).
*   Goods are shipped based on the false shipping and commercial documentation. Goods are described to appear legitimate. Consignees are not those described in the bill of lading issued by the NVOCC.
*   The foreign-based NVOCC or its U.S. agent uses a customs broker who is directed to provide the merchandise to a designated party (partner in crime) and not to the importer on record. The consignee on the bill of lading is not aware of the shipment, that the shipment is being made in its name, or that its corporate identity has been stolen.

OTIs need to i) take more aggressive and proactive steps such as a "know your customer" approach, and ii) pay more attention to cargo originating from China and Hong Kong (since most counterfeits come from there). Brand owners should also take certain measures to prevent or minimize such practices: review supply chains, identify players and the nature of schemes deployed, and consider investigation and litigation options.

Freight Calculation

Ocean freight is calculated as follows:

Volume: Multiply cargo measurements in *centimeters*, divide by 35.32 = cubic meters
or multiply cargo measurements in *inches*, divide by 1728, divide by 35.32 = cubic meters
Weight: Divide the cargo weight, in pounds, by 2.2046 = kilos

Sample shipment:

Medical equipment with dimensions of 45 x 45 x 60 inches / Weight: 1500 lb.
Actual weight: 1500 lbs. / 2.2046 = 680 kilos
Volume: 45 x 45 x 60 inches− 121,500 cu.in. / 1728 − 70.3 cu.ft / 35.32 = 1.99 m³.
1,000 kilos is equivalent to one cubic meter
Freight charges would be assessed on the volume (measurement)

LAND TRANSPORTATION

Land transportation carriers (trucks, trains) are mainly used to transport goods to neighboring countries as well as to move goods to and from an airport or seaport.

A substantial volume of U.S. exports to Canada and Mexico is moved by rail and/ or trucks. Compared to rail transport, trucking has the advantage of flexibility, faster service, lower transportation costs, and less likelihood of damage to merchandise in transit. Rail transport has its own unique advantages. It is reliable and cost-effective and capable of handling bulk cargo.

With the proliferation of free-trade agreements in various regions, there is likely to be a marked growth in the role of land carriers in transporting goods between countries that are in the same geographical area. For example, in eastern and southern Africa, an agreement that allows movement of land carriers across countries would make trucks and trains the dominant mode of transportation for exports. This is because land transport already accounts for over 80 percent of the region's freight movements and with a regional trade agreement, these transportation services could easily be extended to neighboring countries with limited capital investment.

Road Transportation

Trucks transport about 65 percent of the value of trade between the United States, Canada, and Mexico each year. This represents $300 billion and $256 billion annually, respectively, in U.S. truck-transported trade with Canada and Mexico.

The truck industry subsector provides road transportation of cargo using motor vehicles, such as trucks and tractor trailers. The subsector is subdivided into general freight trucking and specialized freight trucking. This distinction reflects differences in equipment used, type of load carried, scheduling, terminal, and other networking services. General freight transportation establishments handle a wide variety of general commodities, generally palletized, and transported in a container or van trailer. Specialized freight transportation is the transportation of cargo that, because of size, weight, shape, or other inherent characteristics, require specialized equipment for transportation (David, 2017).

In the United States, economic slowdowns tend to affect the trucking industry far more than the railroad sector. This is due to the fact that unlike trucking, the railroad sector is more inclined toward transportation of non-cyclical commodities such as coal and agricultural products that are largely subject to stable demand despite economic conditions. The trucking industry, which is more dependent on manufacturing and retail demand, experiences comparatively steep decreases in volume during economic slowdowns.

Deregulation of the trucking industry has given rise to volatile market conditions for commercial fleets, where intense competition, particularly price based, threatens the existence of several independent carriers. Other factors affecting the performance of the industry include:

- A set of different domestic rules on weight, temperature, height, and width of merchandise. Switzerland, for example, prohibits trucks weighing more than 28 metric tons from going further than 6 miles into its territory, forcing truckers to piggyback on railroad cars. Poland does not allow trucking when temperatures reach 30 degrees celsius.
- The state of infrastructure such as road conditions and speed limits affect the smooth transportation of goods within and across countries.
- Government taxes on diesel fuels, pollution standards, and highway tolls affect the performance and profitability of trucking.

Rail Transportation

The U.S. freight rail network is widely considered one of the most dynamic freight systems in the world consisting of 140,000 rail miles (operated by seven Class I railroads, 21 regional railroads and 510 local railroads). The U.S. freight railroads are private organizations that are responsible for their own maintenance and improvement projects. Compared with other major industries, they invest a high percentage of their revenues to maintain and add capacity to their system.

The rail network accounts for approximately 40 percent of U.S. freight moves by ton-miles (the length freight travels) and 16 percent by tons (the weight of freight moved). It is estimated that about 90 percent of rail freight consists of bulk commodities, such as agriculture and energy products, automobiles and components, construction materials, chemicals, coal, equipment, food, metals, minerals, and paper and pulp. The rest is intermodal traffic, which generally consists of consumer goods and other miscellaneous products (David, 2017).

Freight tends to move from ports, manufacturing hubs and other areas of specific economic activity (such as rural areas for agriculture and energy products) to population centers or outlying regions where power plants and large manufacturing facilities are located. Internationally, the U.S. freight rail network connects with Canada and Mexico through several key gateways along the borders. These gateways allow freight railroads to participate in achieving national export goals and facilitating the safe and efficient importation of goods.

Rules Governing Inland Carriage

Transportation of merchandise almost always involves the use of an inland carrier (a trucking or rail company) to move merchandise from the exporter's warehouse to the seaport or airport. Inland transportation is governed by domestic legislation unless goods are shipped to a different country or such movement of cargo from warehouse to port is the first part of intermodal transportation to a foreign country. In the United States, different laws, including the Carmack Amendment, govern domestic transportation. Under the Carmack Amendment, rail and motor common carriers are liable for the full value of the goods lost, damaged, or delayed in transit. However, there are certain exceptions to this strict liability: act of God, act of shipper, inherent vice (defects in the goods), act of a public enemy, and intervention of law. Even though there are no universal agreements, a few regional treaties regulate transportation of goods by road and rail (Murray, 2006). Prominent among these is the Convention on the Contract for the International Carriage of Goods by Road (Convention relative au Contract de Transport International de Merchandises par Route, or CMR, 1956) and the Convention Concerning International Carriage by Rail (Convention relative au Transports Internationaux Ferroviaires, or COTIF, 1980). Members include most European countries, and a few Middle Eastern nations in the case of COTIF. The respective conventions cover areas such as scope of application, liability of the carrier, the use of multiple carriers, and time limits:

- The conventions generally apply to contracts for the carriage of goods by road or rail between two countries, of which at least one is a contracting party. The convention also applies to carriage by states or public institutions.

- A carrier is required to issue a (nonnegotiable) consignment note as evidence of contract of carriage and condition of the goods. The consignee has a right to demand delivery of the goods in exchange for a receipt and to sue the carrier in its own name for any loss, damage, or delay for which the carrier is responsible. The shipper can change the place of delivery or order delivery to another consignee at any time before the delivery of the consignment note or cargo to the first consignee.
- In cases involving multiple carriers, each carrier is responsible for the entire transaction.
- Carriers are liable for loss, damage, or delays up to a liability limit insofar as the contract is governed by the CMR or COTIF. There are, however, certain exceptions to liability in cases such as inherent vice in the goods, circumstances that the carrier could not avoid, and the consequences of which he was unable to prevent, or negligence on the part of the shipper.
- There is a limitation period for bringing action (one year) and for notice of reservations (i.e., notice of damage or loss).

MULTIMODAL TRANSPORTATION

Intermodal transport is not just limited to moving goods between rail and truck; it is also used for any service that requires more than one means of transportation (e.g., rail and ocean, truck and ocean) under one bill of lading. Such arrangements, ideally, must seek the fastest and least costly transportation for the shipper.

The essence of intermodal contract is an agreement between different types of carrier (steamship lines, railroads, trucking firms, airlines, etc.) to achieve certain well-defined and carefully described functions. The advantages of such a mode of transport is simplicity for the shipper and consignee (one bill of lading and no other arrangements necessary), reduced damage because of less handling, and reduced pilferage due to limited exposure of cargo. Such services are already offered by the integrators in the airline industry.

Examples of Intermodal Service

A truck will move merchandise from the exporter's warehouse outside New York City to a railroad yard some 50 miles away. The railroad will take the container to a New York port where it will be placed aboard a ship to Rotterdam, Holland. The whole movement would be covered by a single contract of carriage issued by the trucker as the initiating carrier.

Fresh oranges that arrive by sea from Chile to Miami, Florida, are then distributed to a network of inland points by air and then delivered door to door to customers by truck.

The UN Convention on International Multimodal Transportation of 1980 (MTC) defines international multimodal transport as the carriage of goods by at least two different modes of transport on the basis of a multimodal transport contract from a place in one country at which the goods are taken in charge by the multimodal transport operator to a place designated for delivery situated in a different country. The term "multimodal transport operator" includes any person who on his own behalf (or through another person acting on his behalf) concludes a multimodal transport contract and who acts as a principal, assuming responsibility for the performance of the contract.

Thus, the main features of a multimodal transport are: the carriage of goods by two or more modes of transport, under one contract, one document, and one responsible party (MTO) for the entire carriage. The MTO might subcontract the performance of some, or all, modes of the carriage to other carriers. The terms "combined transport" and "intermodal transport" are often used interchangeably to describe the carriage of goods by two or more modes of transport.

The development of new transportation techniques, such as containerization and other means of unitization of goods introduced a significant need for modification of commercial and traditional approaches to transport. Goods stowed in a container could be moved by different means of transport, such as ships, railway wagons, road vehicles, or aircrafts, from the point of origin to the final place of destination, without being unpacked for sorting or verification when being transferred from one means of transport to another. Gradually, more and more operators took responsibility for the whole transport chain under one single transport contract. Shippers or consignees needed to pursue one single operator, in the event of loss or damage to the goods involved in multimodal transport and this single operator would be responsible for the overall transport, rather than several unimodal carriers.

The MTC failed to attract the thirty ratifications needed for entry into force. A number of reasons are attributed for its lack of popularity:

- It is seen as overly consignor-friendly by the transport industry. Its close association with the Hamburg Rules failed to gain support among major maritime nations.
- Higher limitation of liability and a uniform liability system: The monetary limitation of liability was modeled on the Hamburg Rules. Under the uniform liability scheme, the MTO is responsible for loss, delay, or damage while the goods are in his/her control. To escape liability, the MTO must show that he/she took all necessary measures to avoid the occurrence and its consequences.

In view of the absence of a uniform international convention regulating multimodal transport, there has been a proliferation of diverse regional, sub-regional, and national laws to fill the gap. Significant differences remain among these sets of rules, thus creating further disunity at the international level (Faghfouri, 2006).

FREIGHT FORWARDERS IN TRANSPORTATION

A freight forwarder is the party that facilitates the movement of cargo to the overseas destination on behalf of shippers and processes the documentation or performs activities related to those shipments. Freight-forwarding activity dates back to the thirteenth century when traders employed middlemen, or "frachtors," to cart and forward merchandise throughout Europe. The frachtor's responsibility later extended to the provision of long-distance overseas transportation and storage services, issuance of bills of lading, and collection of freight, duties, and payment from consignees (Murr, 1979).

In the United States, the forwarding industry developed in the latter part of the nineteenth century. It started in New York, where the bulk of U.S. export trade was handled, to provide various transportation services to shippers. Ullman succinctly points out the changing role of the ocean freight forwarder in the United States:

> Many forwarding concerns originally started as freight brokers, but with the continuing increase in manufactured shipments, the forwarding work took precedence over the broker activity. Today, some forwarders handle ship loads of large parcels either on a common carrier or tramp vessels as brokers, but for the most part, forwarders deal with individual shipments varying in size or containers.
>
> (Ullman, 1995, p. 130)

Role and Function of Freight Forwarders

The freight forwarder 1) advises the exporter on the most economical choice of transportation and the best way to pack and ship the cargo to minimize cost and prevent damage, and 2) books for air, ocean, or land transportation (or intermodal movement of cargo) and arranges for pickup, transportation, and delivery of the goods. The forwarder also ensures that the goods are properly packed and labeled and documentation requirements are met so the cargo is cleared at the port of destination. When a letter of credit is used, the forwarder ensures that it is strictly complied with to enable the exporter to receive payment. Thus, the advantage of a forwarder goes far beyond moving freight. Forwarders help shippers and consignees by tracking and tracing cargo. They can also negotiate better rates with carriers because they can purchase space on airlines or ships at wholesale prices. The wide array of services they provide also helps shippers save time and money.

Freight forwarders are a significant part of U.S. commerce and facilitate the growth and expansion of international trade. A U.S. Senate report on the industry describes freight forwarding as follows:

> a highly important segment of the economy of the United States in that its functioning makes possible participation in the nation's foreign commerce by many industries and businesses whose lack of familiarity with the complexities and formalities of exporting procedures might hinder or even preclude such participation if forwarding services were not freely available.
>
> (Ullman, 1995, p. 133)

Today, it is generally estimated that over 90 percent of export firms use the services of an international freight forwarder. Most of the forwarding activity is still concentrated in ocean shipping, although some diversification into air and land transportation has occurred.

A forwarder is distinguishable from an NVOCC. An NVOCC is an international ocean carrier that does not operate its own vessels. It fulfills the role of the shipper with respect to carriers and that of a carrier with respect to shippers. A typical NVOCC will guarantee a steamship line a certain amount of freight per week or month and purchase the necessary space on a wholesale basis for the shipment of cargo to and from a given port. They publish their own tariffs and receive and consolidate cargo of different shippers for transportation to the same port. They issue bills of lading to acknowledge receipt of cargoes for shipment. Unlike NVOCCs, freight forwarders do not publish their own tariff and consolidate small shipments. Forwarders use the services of NVOCCs and facilitate the movement of cargo without operating as carriers. Non-vessel-operating common carriers are often owned by freight forwarders or large transportation companies.

A forwarder also differs from a customs broker in that the latter deals with the clearing of imports through customs, whereas a forwarder facilitates the transportation of exports. The broker is licensed by the Treasury Department, whereas the forwarder is licensed by the Federal Maritime Commission (FMC).

Licensing Requirements

To be eligible for an ocean freight forwarder's license, the applicant must demonstrate to the FMC that 1) he or she has a minimum of three years' experience in ocean freight forwarding duties in the United States and the necessary character to render such services, and 2) the individual has obtained and filed a valid surety bond with the FMC. A shipper whose primary business is the sale of merchandise can perform forwarding services without a license to move its own shipments. In such a case, the shipper is not entitled to receive compensation from the carrier for its services. A license is not required for an individual employee or unincorporated branch office of a licensed ocean freight forwarder. A common carrier or agent thereof may also perform forwarding services without a license with respect to cargo carried under such carrier's own bill of lading (U.S. Department of Commerce, 2019; FMC, 1984).

Other Obligations and Responsibilities

- A description of the freight forwarder as consignee on an inland (i.e., truck or rail) transport bill of lading may subject the forwarder to liability for freight charges to the airport or seaport. This can be avoided by clearly indicating on the forwarder's delivery instructions that the forwarder is acting merely as an agent and does not have any ownership interest in the merchandise (see International Perspectives 9.4 and 9.5).
- The forwarder is liable to the shipper for its own negligence in selecting the carrier, handling documentation, directing cargo, and classifying shipments. The forwarder, for example, must not totally rely on the shipper's instructions with respect to the classification of a shipment. The forwarder must take reasonable measures to ensure that the classification is proper and consistent with the description on the commercial invoice, bill of lading, and other documents.
- In cases in which the forwarder acts as an NVOCC, liability is that of a common carrier for loss or damage to cargo.
- The forwarder's liability is limited to the lesser of $50.00 per shipment or the fee charged for its services. Any claims by the exporter against the forwarder must be presented within ninety days from the date of exportation.
- Each freight forwarder is required to maintain current and accurate records for five years. The records should include general financial data, types of services, receipts, and expenses.

• Forwarders are prohibited from providing any rebates to shippers or sharing any compensation or forwarding fees with shippers, consignees, or sellers. Non-vessel-operating common carriers can receive compensation from carriers only when they act as mere forwarders, that is, when they do not issue bills of lading or otherwise undertake carriers' responsibilities.

INTERNATIONAL PERSPECTIVE 9.5
Generally Accepted Principles and Practices in Ocean Transportation

a. **Freight Forwarders:** The freight forwarder acts as an agent for the shipper in selecting a common carrier and booking cargo space. It does not issue a bill of lading and is not liable for damage to the goods while in possession of the carrier. Liability may, however, arise in cases where the freight forwarder was negligent in selecting the carrier or customs broker.

b. **Removal of Limitation to Carrier's Liability:** The carrier shall become liable for any loss or damage in connection with the transportation of goods in an amount not exceeding $500 per package or in cases of goods not shipped in packages, per customary freight unit or the equivalent of that sum in other currency unless the nature and value of such goods have been declared by the shipper on the bill of lading. The carrier can be held fully responsible for all damages (without the benefit of the liability limitation) in the following cases: 1) material deviation (carrier's geographical departures from course, unauthorized on-deck storage); 2) failure to give the shipper fair opportunity to declare a higher value; 3) misdelivery—the carrier that issued the bill of lading is responsible for releasing the cargo only to the party who presents the original bill of lading, unless otherwise agreed with the shipper.

c. **Burden of Proof for Shipper and Carrier:** The initial burden of proof falls on the shipper to prove that the goods delivered to the carrier were in sound condition. This burden can be met by providing a "clean" bill of lading. The provision of a clean bill of lading shifts the burden to the carrier to prove that the damage or loss to the merchandise was not caused by its negligence.

d. **Four Parameters to Establish Seaworthiness of Ship:**
   1. Is the ship appropriate for the type of cargo?
   2. Is the ship properly equipped for the goods (for reception, carriage, and preservation of the goods)?
   3. Is the ship staffed with a competent crew?
   4. Did the carrier properly load, handle, stow, and discharge the goods carried? Proper storage varies according to the type of goods transported.

CHAPTER SUMMARY

Documents frequently used in export–import transactions	1. Air waybill 2. Bill of exchange 3. Bill of lading 4. Through bill of lading 5. Consular invoice 6. Certificate of origin 7. Inspection certificate 8. Insurance certificate 9. Commercial invoice 10. Dock's receipt 11. Destination control statement 12. Shipper's export declaration 13. Pro forma invoice 14. Export packing list 15. Manifest
Air transportation	*Reasons for the Growth of Airfreight* Growing demand for imports of heavy equipment and services in many developing countries; the need for timely delivery of imports; technological changes; the role of integrators and forwarders *Determinants of Air Cargo Rates* Distance, weight and size of cargo, commodity description, special services *Carriage of Goods by Air* Major international rules: 1. The Warsaw Convention (1929) 2. The Warsaw Convention—Amended (1955) 3. The Montreal Convention (1999)
Ocean freight	Types of ocean carriers: private fleet, tramps, conference lines
Carriage of Goods by Sea	Major international rules: 1. The Hague Rules (1924) 2. The Hague–Visby Rules (1968) 3. The Hamburg Rules (1978) 4. The proposed Rotterdam Rules (2008) The rules cover rights and duties of parties to a contract of carriage by sea: Duty of carrier, carrier's liability, period of responsibility, limitation of action, and limits of carrier's liability
Land transport	1. Rail transport: handles bulk cargo; absorbs loading, unloading, and other charges 2. Trucking: compared to rail transport, trucking has the advantage of flexibility, faster service, and lower transportation costs

Inland carriage	Inland carriage is the use of an inland carrier to move merchandise from the exporter's warehouse to the sea or airport. Major international rules governing inland carriage:
	1. Convention on the Contract for the International Carriage of Goods by Road
	2. Convention Concerning International Carriage by Rail
	Both conventions cover areas such as liability for loss or damage to shipment, delays in delivery, and time limits for bringing action
Freight forwarders	A freight forwarder facilitates the movement of cargo to the overseas destination on behalf of shippers and processes the documentation or performs activities related to those developments
	Role and function of a freight forwarder:
	1. Advises shipper on the most economical choice of transportation
	2. Books space and arranges for pickup, transportation, and delivery of goods
	Licensing requirements: To be eligible for a license as a freight forwarder, the applicant must demonstrate to the FMC that he or she has:
	1. a minimum of three years' experience in ocean freight forwarding duties in the United States
	2. the necessary character to render such services
	3. a valid surety bond filed with the FMC

REVIEW QUESTIONS

1. What is the difference between a bill of exchange and a bill of lading? Are straight bills of lading negotiable?
2. What is the significance of these documents for importers: certificate of origin, destination control statement, pro forma invoice?
3. What factors are likely to contribute to the growth in air freight in future? Is it a major mode of transportation for cargo?
4. What are the three major types of ocean carrier?
5. What is the carrier's duty under a bill of lading? Discuss the "Himalaya clause."
6. State the major differences between the Hamburg Rules and the Hague/Hague–Visby rules on carriage of goods by sea.
7. Discuss the difference between a freight forwarder and an NVOCC.
8. BG, a stevedore company in the employment of Tatek shipping, negligently dropped several containers of soft drinks as it was loading them on a ship from Port Everglades, Florida. Is the container a package under COGSA? The contents of the container were described in the bill of lading as 2,300 cases of soft drinks, with each case containing four six-packs. Can the shippers claim from Tatek and/or BG?

REFERENCES

Abeyratne, R. I. R. (2018). *Law and Regulation of Air Cargo*. New York: Springer.

Bade, D. (2015). *Export/Import Procedures and Documentation*. New York: Amacom.

Boeing (2019/2020). *World Air Cargo Forecast*. Seattle, WA: Boeing. www.boeing.com/commercial/market/cargo-forecast/.

Breskin, L. (2018). *The Business of Shipping*. Centerville, MD: Cornell Maritime Press.

Bridges, G. (2000). Air cargo in the 21st century. *International Airport Review*, 4(4): 14–19.

Carr, I. and Stone, P. (2017). *International Trade Law*. London: Routledge.

Chao, C. and Yu, P. (2013). Quantitative evaluation model of air cargo competitiveness and comparative analysis of major Asia-Pacific airports. Transport Policy, 30: 318–326.

David, P. (2017). *International Logistics*. Berea, OH: Cicero Books.

Elias, B. (2007). Air cargo security. Congressional Research Service. Prepared for members and committees of Congress (RL32022).

Faghfouri, M. (2006). International regulation of liability for multimodal transport. *WMU Journal of Maritime Affairs*, 5(1): 95–114.

Federal Maritime Commission Regulations of Ocean Freight Forwarders. Part 510, 49 Federal Regulations 36297, September 14, 1984; 46 U.S. Code app. 1702–1708.

Flint, D. and O'Keefe, P. (1997). Admiralty and maritime law. *The International Lawyer*, 31: 234–243.

Foley, J. F. (2017). *Global Entrepreneur* (4th ed.). New York: Jamric Press International.

Force, R. (1996). A Comparison of the Hague, Hague–Visby and Hamburg Rules: Much Ado About Nothing. *Tulane Law Review*, 70: 2051–2089.

IATA (June, 2020). *Industry Losses to Top 84 Billion USD in 2020*. Geneva: IATA.

International Maritime Organization (IMO) (2020). IMO and the sustainable development goals. www.imo.org.

Kendall, L. (1983). *The Business of Shipping*. Centerville, MD: Cornell Maritime Press.

Murr, A. (1979). *Export/Import Traffic Management and Forwarding*. Centerville, MD: Cornell Maritime Press.

Murray, C. (2006). *Schmitthoff's Export Trade*. London: Sweet & Maxwell.

Reyes, B. and Gilles, C. (1998). Lufthansa fights back. *American Shipper*, April: 94–98.

Schaffer, R., Augusti, F., Dhoogie, L., and Earle, B. (2018). *International Business Law and its Environment*. New York: South Western.

Ullman, G. (1995). *U.S. Regulation of Ocean Transportation, Under the Shipping Act of 1984*. Centerville, MD: Cornell Maritime Press.

UNCTAD (2019). *Review of Maritime Transport*. Geneva: United Nations.

U.S. Customs and Border Protection (2020a). Air cargo advance screening program goes into effect. www.cbp.gov/newsroom/national-media-release/air-cargo-advance-screening-program-goes-effect.

U.S. Customs and Border Protection (2020b). Cargo programs. www.tsa.gov/for-industry/cargo-screening-program.

U.S. Customs and Border Protection (2020c). Cargo security initiative www.cbp.gov/border-security/ports-entry/cargo-security/csi/csi-brief#.

U.S. Customs and Border Protection (2020d). Customs–Trade Partnership Against Terrorism. www.cbp.gov/border-security/ports-entry/cargo-security/ctpat.

U.S. Customs and Border Protection (2020e). Indirect Air Carrier Program. www.tsa.gov/for-industry/cargo-screening-program.

U.S. Customs and Border Protection (2020f). Importer security filing "10+2." www.cbp.gov/border-security/ports-entry/cargo-security/importer-security-filing-102.

U.S. Department of Commerce (2019). *A Basic Guide to Exporting*. Chicago, IL: NTC.

U.S. International Trade Administration (ITA) (2015). U.S. Commercial Service. http://export.gov.

Wells, F. and Dulat, K. (1996). *Exporting from Start to Finance*. New York: McGraw-Hill Publishing.

Wood, D., Barone, A., Murphy, P., and Wardlow, D. (1995). *International Logistics*. New York: Chapman and Hall.

Yancey, B. (1983). The Carriage of Goods: Hague, COGSA, Visby and Hamburg, *Tulane Law Review*, 57: 1238–1259.

Zhang, A. (2003). Analysis of an international air-cargo hub: The case of Hong Kong. *Journal of Air Transportation Management*, 9(2): 123–138.

Zodl, J. (1995). *Export-Import*. Cincinnati, OH: Betterway Books.

World Wide Web Resources

www.shippingsolutions.com/export-documentation-procedure

www.trade.gov/common-export-documents

www.iata.org/en/iata-repository/publications/economic-reports/airline-industry-economic-performance-june-2020-presentation/

www.icc-ccs.org/reports/2019_Annual_Piracy_Report.pdf

International Trade Closing Cases and Discussions

1. What Constitutes a Package Under COGSA?

In 1936, Congress enacted the Carriage of Goods by Sea Act (COGSA) in order to implement the Hague Rules, which the United States had signed in 1924. The language in COGSA is almost identical to the Hague Rules except in regard to the carrier's limitation of liability. The Hague Rules limit a carrier's liability to £100 per package or unit whereas COGSA limits such liability to $500 per package or in the case of goods not shipped in packages, per customary freight unit. They both indicate that the limitation of carrier's liability applies unless the nature and value of such goods have been declared by the shipper before shipment and inserted in the bill of lading.

Given the absence of a definition for the term "package," courts and scholars in the field have provided different interpretations. It has become a major source of litigation in cargo damage claims. Carriers often argued that pallets and containers, not their contents, were COGSA packages for the application of the statutory maximum. However, shippers contended that the individual product unit qualified as a package. Each choice has implications for the amount that would be recovered for cargo damage.

Judicial efforts at defining a "package" have largely focused on two approaches: the manner in which the shipper bundled the goods for shipment and the intention of the parties as reflected in the shipping contract (declaration in the bill of lading and sales contract). With regard to the first criterion, an article is considered a package if it was completely enclosed in a wooden box. This definition expanded to include a class of cargo to which some packaging preparation has been made to facilitate handling (regardless of size or shape and not necessarily enclosed). Other definitions of "package" also relate to a unit in which goods are packed (the functional test), that is, a set of goods bundled by the shipper so it can be shipped break-bulk.

In a case where a company sought damages from a carrier for the loss of 1,680 television tuners shipped from New York to Rio de Janeiro, the court rejected the claim that each cardboard carton was a package and held that each pallet constituted a package. The complete shipment consisted of nine pallets, each loaded with six cardboard cartons holding forty tuners. The dock receipt, the bill of lading, and other documents all indicated that the shipment consisted of nine packages.

2. The Case of a Container Load of Perfumes and Cosmetics

The case involves a container load of perfumes and cosmetics shipped from France to Florida that mysteriously disappeared while in a marine terminal at Port Everglades, Florida. The perfumes and cosmetics in the missing container were packaged in a total of 2,270 shoebox-sized corrugated cardboard cartons, which were then consolidated into 42 larger units. They were bound together with plastic wrap and packed onto 42 pallets with two cartons remaining. The insurance company paid the shipper for the loss under a cargo insurance policy and brought a subrogation action against the carrier. The onboard bill of lading described the cargo as 4 container units. The pro forma invoice and the revised bill of lading stated 42 packages plus two cartons. The carrier issued a clean bill of lading with these particulars (44 packages). If the bill of lading does not show how many separate packages there are, then each container is generally considered a package.

3. The Container Revolution

Until the 1960s, nearly all international cargo was delivered to the dockside in small packages and shipped on break-bulk ships. They came in boxes, crates, barrels, and drums and were loaded on board ship, stowed, and, at the end of the voyage, unloaded individually. This process was complicated, time consuming, and exposed cargo to damage and theft.

The container revolution involved the introduction of truck-trailer-sized boxes as cargo containers. These standardized containers can be filled with cargo at the farm, factory, or loading depot, sealed, and taken by truck, train, or barge to a port where it is put on board a ship. It greatly reduces cargo handling time (it costs much less to load and unload containers by crane than it does to load and unload individual packages). Containers also eliminate costs associated with shore-side warehouses to protect conventional cargo from the weather. Export costs relating to crating, packaging, etc. as well as potential loss or damage to cargo is substantially reduced.

In typical container transportation a) the shipper puts individual packages or cartons in a container, usually at an inland facility; b) the container is moved by rail or truck to a container yard close to a seaport. Once the ship arrives, the container is pulled by a tractor alongside the ship and placed on board the containership by cranes. Containerships have specially built vertical cells that are designed to firmly hold the containers in place during the voyage. Today over 90 percent of world trade is moved in containers. Only a handful of commodities are shipped in break-bulk: steel, paper, and plywood. Even rubber and cocoa beans, which were largely shipped in break-bulk, are now moved in containers. The container revolution necessitated the development of port infrastructure such as dockside cranes, standardized containers, including connections to railways and highways, as well as the designation and building of specific areas for containers.

Questions

1. In case 9.1, what is the correct number of COGSA packages?
2. Discuss the major benefits of cargo containers.

4. Inland Damage of Ocean Cargo: Carrier Liability Under Multimodal Transport

In today's globalized economy, merchandise is carried over long distances before it reaches the consumer. Cargo is often carried from an inland location such as a warehouse or manufacturing plant in one location (e.g., Bordeaux, France) to an inland location such as a warehouse in Fort Beach, Florida. This may typically require two or three modes of transport under different contracts of carriage. The cargo would travel by land (under an inland bill of lading), then by sea (under an ocean bill of lading) and then again by truck or rail (under another inland bill of lading). Each of these bills of lading (contracts) are governed by separate legal regimes. The inland part of the carriage from Europe is governed by a regional convention relating to road or rail transport whereas the inland legs in the United States are subject to the Carmack Amendment (The Carmack Amendment now applies to rail and road carriage). Shipments to and from U.S. ports are subject to the Carriage of Goods by Sea Act (COGSA). Under COGSA, a carrier's liability begins from the time when goods are loaded on board a vessel to the time when goods are unloaded at the port of discharge (tackle-to-tackle).

- Does COGSA apply in cases where cargo is damaged during the inland leg of carriage (rail or road)?
- Would COGSA apply in cases where separate bills of lading (contracts) are made for the different types of carriage and damage occurs during the inland leg?
- Would COGSA apply when the cargo is covered by a multimodal contract of carriage that includes the inland and ocean legs of the carriage and where cargo is damaged during the inland leg?

It seems that US courts have moved in the direction of applying COGSA for multimodal carriage, that is, as long as a multimodal bill of lading requires a substantial carriage of goods by sea, it is considered a maritime contract (even though the contract includes maritime and non-maritime elements). However, in cases where separate bills of lading are issued for inland carriage, the inland portion of the multimodal shipment is subject to laws pertaining to inland carriage such as the Carmack Amendment in the United States.

The Rotterdam Rules (UN Convention on Contracts for the Carriage of Goods Wholly or Partly by Sea) creates a liability regime intended to supersede the Hague, Hague–Visby and Hamburg Rules. The Rotterdam Rules are often called "maritime plus" because even though the rules deal primarily with maritime carriage, they add elements of other modes of transport. They apply to cases where domestic transport forms part of the same maritime contract. Ratification of the Rotterdam Rules has been difficult in the United States because railroad and motor carriers do not want the extension of the Rules to the land portion of any cargo transportation. They prefer to be governed by the Carmack Amendment because they extend the ocean carrier's defenses and limitations inland. Furthermore, ports and terminals believe that the rules would impose risks of potential cargo damage liability (COGSA does not have a liability provision for cargo damage on ports and terminals). It remains to be seen whether the United States will ratify the Rotterdam Rules. The Rotterdam Rules will enter into effect a year after twenty countries have ratified that treaty. So far, only five countries have ratified the convention.

PART IV

Payment Terms and Procedures

CHAPTER 10

Exchange Rates and International Trade

LEARNING OBJECTIVES:

10.1 Describe the reasons why firms and governments enter into foreign exchange markets
10.2 Understand the types of transaction that contribute to foreign exchange risk
10.3 Learn the ways to protect against exchange rate risks
10.4 Learn about cryptocurrencies
10.5 Identify and discuss the implications of cryptocurrencies for international trade

International Trade in Practice

Exchange Rates and Global Imbalances

Trade theory predicted that comparative advantage would lead to specialization and trade. This began to change in the 1960s when transnational companies substituted trade in final goods with the movement of entire production facilities into foreign markets. For example, U.S. corporations' investment in Canada, Latin America, and Europe was to produce inside tariff barriers to serve domestic markets. Today, we still have movement of final goods and foreign direct investment but the goods and investments are not within a single country. Trade is dominated by the export and import of intermediate goods in global value chains in a world of multinational corporations. The globalization of production chains has been accompanied by the internationalization of finance and financial institutions. Trade in intermediate goods is financed by banks and other financial institutions located in the home markets of exporting firms as well those in host countries. With the proliferation of global value chains, every product traded may be a byproduct of three or four cross-border trades in semi-finished goods before final assembly and export to foreign markets. This explains the reason why some countries trade more goods than they produce.

Global imbalances: Global imbalances are usually measured by current account balances, that is, net changes in exports and imports of goods and services and other unilateral transfers such as gifts and migrant worker earnings. Some countries such as Germany and the Netherlands enjoy large current account surpluses (they export more than they import) while countries such as the United States have persistent deficits. China has a large but declining current account surplus with the United States but a deficit in its trade with Asia. Bilateral trade imbalances and necessary adjustment mechanisms appear to be illogical in a global economy that is characterized by global supply chains (a reduction in export prices may be more than compensated by an increase in import costs).

The role of tariffs and exchange rates in the adjustment process: Some countries would like to resolve trade imbalances by tariff adjustment. The latter may have worked during times when trade was largely limited to finished goods produced in individual countries. However, it would be quite ineffective in this era when goods are international composites and components come from different countries. Imports generate a need for foreign borrowing and generate debt service payments, which will require payment in foreign currency. Large trade deficits are likely to lead to a weaker currency as the country adjusts to create surpluses to pay foreign investors. In the short run, the relationship is weak, especially if investors prefer to hold on to foreign currency such as the dollar. In the case of the United States, for example, given the confidence foreigners have in the U.S. dollar (compared to other currencies), they finance the export of goods to the U.S. market, increasing domestic consumption financed by foreign borrowing.

FOREIGN EXCHANGE TRANSACTIONS

An exchange rate is the number of units of a given currency that can be purchased for one unit of another currency. It is a common practice in world currency markets to use the indirect quotation, which quotes all exchange rates (except for the British Pound) per U.S. dollar. *The Financial Times* foreign exchange data for August 8, 2020, for example, shows the quotation for the Canadian dollar as being 1.34 per one U.S. dollar. Direct quotation is the expression of the number of U.S. dollars required to buy one unit of foreign currency (Table 10.1). The direct U.S. dollar quotation on August 8, 2020, for the Canadian dollar was US$0.75. Although it is common for foreign currency markets around the world to quote rates in U.S. dollars, some traders state the price of other currencies in terms of the dealer's home currency (cross rates), for example, Swiss francs against Japanese yen, Hong Kong dollar against Colombian peso, and so on.

Strictly speaking, it is reasonable to state that the rate of the foreign currency against the dollar is a cross rate to dealers in third countries.

The foreign exchange market is a place where foreign currency is purchased and sold. In the same way that the relationship between goods and money in ordinary business transactions is expressed by the price, so the relationship of one currency to another is expressed by the exchange rate. A large proportion of the foreign exchange transactions undertaken each day is between banks in different countries. These

TABLE 10.1 Currency Trading, Saturday, August 8, 2020

Selected Countries	Indirect Quotation	Cross Rates
	Currency per US$	(per euro/per yen)
Canada	1.34	0.0126/1.58
France	0.85	0.008/--------
Germany	0.85	0.008/--------
United Kingdom	0.77	0.0072/0.903
Japan	105.93	------ /124.87
U.S.	--------	0.0094/ 1.18

Source: money.cnn.com/data/currencies, August 8, 2020

transactions are often a result of the wishes of the banks' customers to consummate commercial transactions, that is, payments for imports or receipts for exports. Other reasons for individual companies or governments to enter into the foreign exchange market as buyers or sellers of foreign currencies include the following:

- Foreign travel and purchase of foreign stocks and bonds; foreign investment; receipt of income such as interest, dividends, royalties, and so on, from abroad; or payment of such income in foreign currency
- Central banks enter the foreign exchange market and buy or sell foreign currency (in exchange for domestic currency) to stabilize the national currency, that is, to reduce violent fluctuations in exchange rates without destroying the viability and freedom of the foreign exchange market
- Speculation, that is, purchase of foreign currency at a low rate with the hope to sell it at a profit.

Foreign exchange trading is not limited to one specific location. It takes place wherever such deals are made, for example, in a private office or even at home, far away from the dealing rooms or facilities of companies. Most of these transactions are carried out between commercial banks and their customers as well as among commercial banks themselves, which buy and sell foreign currencies in response to the needs of their clients. For example, a Canadian bank sells Canadian dollars to a French bank in exchange for euros. This transaction, in effect, allows the Canadian bank the right to draw a check on the French bank for the amount of the deposit denominated in euros. Similarly, it will enable the French bank to draw a check in Canadian dollars for the amount of the deposit.

Foreign exchange rates are based on the supply and demand for various currencies, which, in turn, are derivatives of the fundamental economic factors and technical conditions in the market (Salvatore, 2019). In the United States, for example, the continuous deterioration in the trade deficit in the 1970s, mainly due to increased consumption expenditures on foreign goods, led to an oversupply of dollars in foreign central banks. This in turn resulted in a lower dollar in foreign exchange markets. Besides a country's balance of payments position, factors such as interest rates, growth in the money supply, inflation, and confidence in the government are important determinants of supply and demand for foreign currencies and, hence, the exchange rate. The following are some examples:

- The U.S. dollar exchange rate has been at its all-time high relative to other currencies due to the economic uncertainty engendered by the coronavirus and high unemployment that left over 20 million people unemployed in 2020.
- The Turkish lira has been in decline since 2013 partly due to poor economic management, high levels of foreign debt, and limited foreign currency reserves. The central bank has been using its foreign reserves to prop up the lira.
- The Japanese yen, which is traditionally considered a safe-haven currency was hit hard by the spread of the coronavirus, the cancellation of the Tokyo Summer Olympics, and an overall drop in business sentiment.
- The Chinese Renminbi has appreciated against major currencies partly because of the country's faster recovery from the coronavirus, increasing exports and favorable trade balance.

Exchange rate fluctuations can have a profound effect on international trade. Export–import firms are vulnerable to foreign exchange risks whenever they enter into an obligation to accept or deliver a specified amount of foreign currency at a future point in time. These firms are then faced with a prospect that future changes in foreign currency values could either reduce the amount of their receipts or increase their payments in foreign currency. United States importers of Japanese goods, for example, are likely to incur significant losses when the dollar takes a fall against the yen, often wiping out a significant portion of their profits. Conversely, it may also be that changes in exchange rates will bring about financial benefits.

The most important types of transaction that contribute to foreign exchange risks in international trade include the following:

- purchase of goods and services whose prices are stated in foreign currency, that is, payables in foreign currency
- sales of goods and services whose prices are stated in foreign currency, that is, receivables in foreign currency
- debt payments to be made or accepted in foreign currency.

Most export–import companies do not have the expertise to handle such unanticipated changes in exchange rates. Banks with international trade capabilities and consultants can help assess currency risks and advise companies to take appropriate measures. (See International Perspective 10.1.)

The impact of exchange rate fluctuations on export trade can be illustrated by the following example. Since the dollar began to decline against major currencies, many European and Asian exporters to the U.S. market have been faced with the difficult task of balancing the need to increase prices to preserve profit margins and the importance of keeping prices stable to maintain market shares. Many exporters have been reluctant to increase the prices of their exports to fully offset the decline in the dollar. Some have responded by shifting factories to North America in order to cushion them from currency fluctuations. Prominent examples include the establishment of production facilities by DaimlerChrysler in Alabama, BMW in South Carolina, and so on.

The impact of exchange rate risks is felt more by export–import companies than domestic firms. To the extent that an exporter's inputs are domestic, a strong domestic currency could lead to a loss of domestic and foreign markets. Importers also face a loss of domestic markets due to the rise in the price of imports if the domestic currency weakens. In addition, such firms are vulnerable to exchange risks arising from receivables or payables in foreign currency.

INTERNATIONAL PERSPECTIVE 10.1

Exchange Restrictions

There are only a few countries that impose no restrictions on the use of the foreign exchange market. This means that their currency is fully convertible into foreign currency for all uses: both trade in goods and services as well as international financial activities. Western economies such as Canada, the United States, Japan, the United Kingdom, and Germany have convertible currencies.

Currencies of most developing and former communist nations, however, are either not convertible or legally convertible only at artificial, government-established rates. Such exchange restrictions may be imposed for competitive reasons (keeping a lower value), to promote foreign investment, or to discharge debt payments (maintaining a high value). The most extreme form of exchange restrictions (control) is limitation of the availability of foreign currency to purchase imports. Limits could also be placed on the use of foreign currency for certain transactions, such as imports of luxury goods, to conserve foreign currency. In terms of exports, exchange control rules could require that exports are properly paid for and payment is forthcoming within a reasonable time, that is, proceeds from exports are to be repatriated to the country's bank within a given period of time after shipment.

PROTECTION AGAINST EXCHANGE RATE RISKS

There are several ways in which export–import companies can protect themselves against unanticipated changes in exchange rates. The risk associated with such transactions is that the exchange rate might change between the date when the export contract was made and the date of payment (the settlement date), which is often sixty to ninety days after contract or shipment of the merchandise.

Shifting the Risk to Third Parties

Hedging in Financial Markets

Through various hedging instruments, firms could reduce the adverse impact of foreign currency fluctuations. This allows firms to lock in the exchange rate today for receipts or payments in foreign currency that will happen at some time in the future. Current foreign exchange rates are called spot prices; those occurring at some time in the future are referred to as forward prices. If the currency in question is more expensive for forward delivery (for delivery at some future date) than for ordinary spot delivery (i.e., for delivery two business days following the agreed-upon exchange date), it is said to be at a premium. If it is less expensive for forward delivery than spot delivery, it is said to be at a discount.

TABLE 10.2 Hypothetical Exchange Rates, Currency per U.S. Dollar

	Danish Krone	Canadian Dollar
Spot rate	1.8037	1.4257
Thirty-day forward	1.7948	1.4296
Ninety-day forward	1.7887	1.4273

In Table 10.2, the forward Danish Krone is at a premium since the forward Krone is more expensive than the spot. The forward Canadian dollar is at a discount because its forward price is cheaper than spot. When viewed from the point of view of the U.S. dollar, it can also be stated that the forward dollar is at a discount in relation to the Krone or that the forward U.S. dollar is at a premium in relation to the Canadian dollar.

It is pertinent to underscore some salient points about hedging in foreign exchange markets:

- *Hedging is not always the most appropriate technique to limit foreign exchange risks:* There are fees associated with hedging, and such costs reduce the expected value from a given transaction. Export–import firms should seriously consider hedging when a high proportion of their cash flow is vulnerable to exchange rate fluctuations. This means that firms should determine the acceptable level of risk that they are willing to take. In contrast, firms with a small portion of their total cash exposed to foreign exchange rate movements may be better off playing the law of averages—shortfalls could be eventually offset by windfall gains.
- *Hedging does not protect long-term cash flows:* Hedging does not insulate firms from long-term adjustments in currency values. (O'Connor and Bueso, 1990). Thus, it should not be used to cover anticipated changes in currency values. A U.S. importer of German goods would have found it difficult to adequately hedge against the predictable fall of the dollar during the 2007–2009 period. The impact of such action is felt in terms of higher dollar prices paid for imports.
- *Forward market hedges are available in a very limited number of currencies:* Most currencies are not traded in the forward market. However, many countries peg their currency to that of a major industrial country whose currency is traded in the forward market. Many Latin American countries, for example, peg their currencies to the U.S. dollar. This insulates U.S. firms from foreign exchange risk in these countries unless the country changes from the designated (pegged) official rate. Foreign firms, that is, non-U.S. firms, in these countries can reduce potential risks by buying or selling dollars forward (in the event of purchases or sales to these countries), as the case may be.
- *Example:* Suppose the Colombian peso is pegged to the U.S. dollar at $1 = 1,000 pesos. A British firm that is to make payment in pesos for its imports from Colombia could hedge its position by buying U.S. dollars forward. On the settlement date, pounds will be converted into dollars, which, in turn, could be converted into pesos. This assumes that Colombia does not change the pegged rate during the period.

- *Hedging should not be used for individual transactions:* Since most export–import firms engage in transactions that result in inflows and outflows of foreign currencies, the most appropriate strategy to reduce transaction costs is to hedge the exported net receivable or payable in foreign currency.
- *Example:* Suppose a Canadian firm has receivables from two Japanese buyers amounting to 5 million yen and payables to four Japanese suppliers worth 9 million yen. Instead of hedging all six transactions, the Canadian firm should cover only the net short position (i.e., 4 million yen) in yen. This reduces the transaction cost of exchanging currencies for the firm.

Spot and Forward Market Hedge

As previously noted, a spot transaction is one in which foreign currencies are purchased and sold for immediate delivery, that is, within two business days following the agreed exchange date. The two-day period is intended to allow the respective commercial banks to make the necessary transfer. A forward transaction is a contract that provides for two parties to exchange currencies on a future date at an agreed-upon exchange rate. The forward rate is usually quoted for one month, three months, four months, six months, or one year. Unlike hedging in the spot market, forward market hedging does not require borrowing or tying up a certain amount of money for a period of time. This is because the firm agrees to buy or sell the agreed amount of currency at a determinable future date, and actual delivery does not take place before the stipulated date.

Example 1: Spot market hedge. On September 1, a U.S. importer contracts to buy German machines for a total cost of 600,000 euros. The payment date is December 1. When the contract is signed on September 1, the spot exchange rate is $0.5000 per euro and the December forward rate is $0.5085 per euro. The U.S. importer believes that the euro is going to appreciate in value in relation to the dollar.

The import firm could buy 600,000 euros on the spot market on September 1 for $300,000 and deposit the euros in an interest-bearing account until the payment date. If the firm does not hedge, and the spot exchange rate rises to $0.5128 euro on December 1, the importer will suffer a loss of $7,680, or (0.5128–0.5000) x 600,000.

The import firm could also borrow $300,000 and convert at the spot rate for 600,000 euros. The euros could be lent out, put in certificates of deposit, and so forth, until December 1, when payment is to be made to the exporter. The U.S. dollar loan will be paid from the proceeds of resale etc., without any foreign exchange exposure. This is often referred to as a credit hedge.

Example 2: Forward market hedge. On September 1, a U.S. exporter contracts to sell U.S. goods to Switzerland for SF250,000. The goods are to be delivered and payment received on December 1. When the contract is signed, the spot exchange rate is $0.6098/SF and the December forward rate is $0.6212/SF. The Swiss franc is expected to depreciate and the December 1 spot exchange rate is likely to fall to $0.5696/SF.

The U.S. exporter has two options: First, it can sell its franc receivable forward now and receive $0.6212 per franc on the settlement date (December). Second, it can wait until December and then sell francs on spot. Clearly, the forward market hedge is preferable, and the U.S. exporter would gain: (0.6212–0.6098) x 250,000 = $2,850. The decision to use the forward market is to be made upon an assessment of what the future spot rate is likely to be. It is also important to bear in mind the impact of transaction costs before a firm makes a decision on what action to take. A credit hedge could have been feasible if the spot rate in the United States had been higher than the forward rate.

Swaps

A swap transaction is a simultaneous purchase and sale of a certain amount of foreign currency for two different value dates. The central feature of this transaction is that the bank arranges the swap as a single transaction, usually between two partners. Swaps are used to move out of one currency and into another for a limited period of time without the exchange risk of an open position.

Example: A U.S. firm sells semiconductor chips to Nippon, a Japanese firm for 60 million yen, and payment was made upon receipt of shipment on October 1. The U.S. firm has payables to Nippon and other Japanese firms of about 60 million yen for the purchase of merchandise, with payment due on January 1. The spot exchange rate on October 1 is 120 yen per dollar and the January sixty-day forward rate is 125 yen per dollar.

The U.S. firm sells its 60 million yen receipts on the spot market for $500,000 at the price of $1=120 yen. Simultaneously, the firm contracts with the same or a different bank to purchase 60 million yen in sixty days at the forward price of 125 yen per dollar. In addition to its normal profits on its exports, the U.S. firm has made a profit of 2.5 million yen from its swap transaction. In cases in which the delivery date to the Japanese firms is not certain, the U.S. firm could use a time option that leaves the delivery date open, while locking the exchange rate at a specified rate.

Other Hedging Techniques

Export–import companies can use other techniques in order to avoid foreign exchange risk:

- *Hedging receipts against payables:* An export firm that has receivables in foreign currency (30 million British pounds) could hedge its receipts against a payable of 30 million pounds to the same or another firm at about the same time. This is achieved with no additional cost and without going through the foreign exchange market. The same method could be used between export–import firms and their branches or other affiliate companies abroad.
- *Acceleration or delay of payments:* If an importer reasonably believes that its domestic currency is likely to depreciate in terms of the currency of its foreign supplier, it would be motivated to accelerate its payments. This could be achieved by buying the requisite foreign currency before it appreciates in value. However, payments could be delayed if the buyer believes that the foreign currency in which payment is to be made is likely to depreciate in value in terms of the domestic currency.

Guarantees and Insurance Coverage

In certain cases, exporters require a guarantee by the importer, a bank, or another agency against the risk of devaluation or exchange controls. Certain types of insurance coverage are also available against exchange controls. In view of its high cost, hedging is a better alternative than insurance.

Shifting the Risk to the Other Party

Invoicing in One's Own Currency

Risks accompany all transactions involving a future remittance or payment in foreign currency. If the payment or receipt for a transaction is in one's own currency, the risk arising from currency fluctuations is shifted to the other party. Suppose a Korean firm negotiated to make payments (ninety days after the contract date) in its domestic currency (won) for its imports of equipment from a Canadian manufacturer. This shifts the foreign currency risk to the exporter, which will have to convert its won receipts into Canadian dollars. Payment in one's own currency not only shifts the risk of devaluation to the other party but also the risk of imposition of exchange controls by the importing country against convertibility and repatriation of foreign currency.

Invoicing in Foreign Currency

In the event that the agreement stipulates that payment is to be made in foreign currency, it is important for the exporter to require inclusion of a provision that protects the value of its receipts from currency devaluation. In the previous example, the contract could provide for an increase in payment to compensate the Canadian manufacturer/exporter for losses arising from currency fluctuations. (See International Perspective 10.2.)

Another method would be to make certain assumptions about possible adverse changes in the exchange rate and add it to the price. If currency changes are likely to result in a 10 percent loss, the price change could be increased by that percentage. An export contract could also provide for the establishment of an escrow account in a third country's currency (stable currency) from which payments will be made. This protects the exporter from losses due to depreciation of the importer's currency.

INTERNATIONAL PERSPECTIVE 10.2

The US Dollar Versus the Euro as Reserve Currency

In the aftermath of World War II, the U.S. dollar emerged as the undisputed leader among international currencies. It was the only currency that was convertible into gold at a fixed exchange rate well into the 1920s. The U.K. pound retained its key currency status in the interwar years due to historical reasons despite the fact that the United Kingdom was a net debtor, and had lost its economic leadership and other trappings of international hegemony. However, by 1945 the dollar had unseated the U.K. pound as the sole global currency and still remains an important reserve currency (Chinn and Frankel, 2008).

The euro is a common currency that replaced all the separate currencies of some of the individual countries of the European Union (EU). On January 1, 1999 the euro became the legal currency of eleven EU member states. In 2002, the euro paper currency and coins became the sole legal tender in the nineteen participating members of the EU. In order to participate in the single European currency, countries were required to meet certain conditions: inflation rates below 2 to 3 percent, public debt to be no more than 60 percent of GDP, and the budget deficit had to be less than or equal to 3 percent of GDP.

Both the U.S. dollar and the euro are important reserve currencies that are used for international business transactions. The role of the U.S. dollar has been dominant. There are important factors that determine reserve currency status and we attempt to establish how well each currency fares in relation to these factors.

- Medium of exchange: Both currencies are used as vehicle currency for international trade and investment. In 2019, the average daily turnover of the U.S. dollar in global foreign exchange markets was estimated at about 88 percent compared to 32 percent for the euro. The U.S. dollar is the world's premier currency for trade and investment.
- Unit of account: The U.S. dollar serves as a leading reserve currency for invoicing goods and services in international business transactions. In 2019, the share of the U.S. dollar as an invoicing currency was 3.1 times its share in world exports compared to 1.2 times for the euro. Many non-U.S. exporters invoice their exports in U.S. dollars. For example, while only 15 percent of India's exports go to the United States (5 percent of its imports come from the United States), 86 percent of its total trade (export and imports) are invoiced in U.S. dollars.
- Store of value: Investors and market participants hold their assets in currencies in which they have confidence that their value will not erode over time. The U.S. dollar share of equity and debt securities is higher than the euro. For example, the international stock of debt securities issued in U.S. dollars is 48 percent compared to 36 percent for the euro (2019). Foreign central banks hold reserve currencies to back liabilities and influence monetary policy. In 2018, foreign central banks held 3.1 times as many U.S. dollars as euros in their foreign reserves.

CHAPTER SUMMARY

Exchange rates	An exchange rate is the number of units of a given currency that can be purchased for one unit of another currency.
Reasons for the existence of the foreign exchange market	1. Foreign travel 2. Purchase of foreign stocks and bonds 3. Foreign investment and other receipts and payments in foreign currency 4. Reduction of currency fluctuations 5. Speculation

REVIEW QUESTIONS

1. Differentiate between spot and forward exchange rates. How can a U.S. import firm use the forward market to protect itself from the adverse effect of exchange rate fluctuations?
2. What does it mean when a currency is trading at a discount to the U.S. dollar in the spot market?
3. Why do export–import firms enter the foreign exchange market?
4. Hedging is not always the most appropriate technique to limit foreign exchange risks. Discuss.
5. If a Canadian exporter accepts payments in foreign currency from buyers in the United States, which party bears the currency fluctuation risk? Explain.
6. The euro has now replaced nineteen national currencies. What are the implications of this development to companies exporting to the European Union?
7. Suppose that the spot rate of the U.K. pound today is $2.00 while the six-month forward rate is $2.05. a) how can a U.S. importer who has to pay 30,000 U.K. pounds in six months hedge his/her foreign exchange risk?
8. In reference to Q. 7, what happens if the U.S. importer does not hedge and the spot rate of the pound goes up to $2.10?
9. Suppose the spot rate of the yen today is $0.0084 while the three-month forward rate is $0.0076. a) how can a U.S. exporter who is to receive 350,000 yen in three months hedge his/her foreign exchange risk? b) what happens if the exporter does not hedge and the spot rate of the yen in three months is $0.0078?
10. Do you think the U.S. dollar will continue to maintain its key currency status? Explain.

REFERENCES

Boz, E., Casas, C., Georgiadis, G., Gopinath, G., Le Mezo, H., Mehl, A., and Nguyen, T. (2020). *Patterns in Invoicing Currency in Global Trade*. IMF Working Paper (wp/20/126). Washington, DC: IMF.

Chinn, M. and Frankel, J. (2008). Why the Euro will rival the dollar. *International Finance*, 11(1): 49–73.

Maggiori, M., Neiman, B., and Schreger, J. (2019, May). The rise of the dollar and fall of the Euro as international currencies. *AEA Papers and Proceedings*, 109: 521–26).

Norrlof, C. (2009). Key currency competition: The Euro versus the dollar. *Cooperation and Conflict*, 44(4): 420–442.

O'Connor, D. and Bueso, A. (1990). *International Dimensions of Financial Management*. London: MacMillan.

Salvatore, D. (2019). *Introduction to International Economics*. New York: Wiley.

World Wide Web Resources

Exchange Rates
Information on Federal Reserve data on exchange rates, balance of payments, and trade: http://research.stlouisfed.org/fred2/categories/13

Exchange Rates and Trade

Information from the Federal Reserve on inflation and exchange rates: www.house.gov/jec/fed.htm

Risk Management

Guide to risk management and information related to this subject:
www.contingencyanalysis.com/

International Trade Closing Cases and Discussions

1. Will the U.S. Dollar Maintain its Key Currency Status?

What is Key Currency?

A key currency is an important currency that is stable and one that is predominantly used for international trade and investment. It is also used to set the values of other currencies. Key currencies are domestic currencies of countries that are economically stable, strong, developed, and well-connected with the global economy. Presently, the key currencies include the U.S. dollar, the euro, the U.K. pound, the Japanese yen, the Canadian dollar, and the swiss franc. Other contenders such as the Chinese yuan and Mexican peso also exist.

National central banks hold key currencies as reserve currencies to pay international debt obligations, support investments, and conduct international business transactions. Key currencies are also used as intervention currency by national central banks to intervene in the foreign exchange markets to stabilize the currency, that is, they use key currency to buy the domestic currency to reduce its supply in the market and thereby strengthen it or vice versa). A large percentage of commodities such as oil and gold is priced in key currencies requiring countries to hold these currencies to pay for these goods.

The Role of the U.S. Dollar

The U.S. dollar has been the leading key currency since 1944 and has played a role in setting the rate for the value of other currencies. Under the Bretton Woods agreement (fixed exchange rate system), IMF member nations' currency par values were based on gold and the dollar. The U.S. dollar was convertible into gold and other countries accumulated reserves of U.S. dollars as they considered it to be a safe store of money (Norrlof, 2009; Maggiori, Neiman, and Schreger, 2019). With growing concerns about the stability of the dollar and the increasing demand for gold, the U.S. government was forced to de-link the dollar from gold, leading to flexible exchange rates. Today, the U.S. dollar still remains the dominant currency in the world. In 2020, more than 61 percent of all foreign bank reserves are held in U.S. dollars compared with 20 percent for the euro, 6 percent for the Japanese yen, and 2 percent for the Chinese yuan. It is also the leading vehicle currency for conducting international trade and investment (Boz et al., 2020).

The United States has maintained a strong dollar policy because this keeps U.S. inflation low (due to the low price of imports) and makes U.S. assets expensive for foreign investors. Countries exchange their exports for dollars, which are often invested in U.S. treasuries to shore up the value of their domestic currencies.

A number of factors lead one to believe that the U. S. dollar will continue to maintain its key currency status.

- U.S. economic growth has been and will remain significantly stronger than Japan and other major euro-zone countries. Inflation has been tamed due to low-cost imports.
- The United States. has a large, open credit market, diversified financial institutions, and an independent central bank. Japanese and European financial institutions lack the breadth and depth of their U.S. counterparts. Many are beginning to recover after scandals.
- Incentives for investments (rates of return, yields) in the United States are higher than in Japan and Europe.

Questions

1. Why does the U.S. government maintain a strong dollar policy?
2. Do you think the euro will replace the U.S. dollar as a key global currency in the coming decade? Discuss.

2. Currency Wars

Many countries (particularly advanced economies such as the United States and Europe) are finding economic growth difficult to achieve because of a lack of domestic demand: consumers and businesses are not spending. One way in which governments can try to drive economic growth is by adopting policies that increase their country's exports.

There are various options for doing this, but a favored choice has been to depreciate the local currency, so that a country's goods and services become relatively cheaper on the global stage. A weak currency also increases the cost of imports, thus making domestic producers more competitive in the national economy, again driving growth.

Since mid-2008, a number of the large exporting countries have adopted policies that have resulted in their currencies remaining weak. The Chinese government is following such policies, and the renminbi remains undervalued (although it has been appreciating against major currencies over the last few years). The United States has been very critical of the Chinese government, but its own bursts of quantitative easing (QE), which were undertaken in an effort to underpin the economy, have impacted the U.S. currency, and the Chinese administration in turn argues that the United States is also employing policies to ensure its own currency remains weak (despite its strong dollar policy). Similarly, the United Kingdom has implemented QE to support the economy. Meanwhile, the sovereign debt crisis in Europe and politicians' failure to agree to a long-term solution to the problems of certain member countries has weakened the euro. Japan also recently decided in favor of deliberately weakening the yen.

Currency wars can seriously affect the risks associated with doing cross-border business. Three key risks exist:

- *Policy uncertainty*: As countries attempt to offset weak currencies, governments can implement policies that affect cross-border business. One example is the pegging of the Swiss franc to the euro, which effectively devalued the Swiss franc overnight by 6 percent, leaving traders with an unexpected potential loss.
- *Currency uncertainty*: Although currency volatility can be offset through hedging, this adds further costs to businesses, undermining profits amid already-shrinking margins.
- *Supply chain disruption*: Countries with stronger currencies implement policies to protect their domestic sector. Barriers to trade such as tariffs and import quotas threaten the smooth running of supply chains.

What Usually Happens When Currency Wars Break Out?

The most famous currency wars example is from the 1930s, when countries got into a vicious spiral of currency devaluations in order to try to maintain the competitiveness of their exporters. All that was achieved was that these countries' trading partners sank deeper into the mire of recession, further curtailing trade and leading to more depreciations. Thus, the global economy shrank and global trade and investment was devastated, a situation that only ended after the outbreak of the Second World War. Although we are not predicting that the current situation will lead to such a severe outcome, there are some parallels between the significant problems in each historical case.

As countries rush to protect the competitiveness of their exports, currency wars will prompt a number of problems, such as asset-price volatility (particularly in the currency markets), increased adoption of trade protection policies, and a rise in anti-dumping and countervailing duty disputes. These all raise risks for cross-border trade and investment.

Questions

1. Do you think the policy of keeping currencies weak will continue in the long run?
2. What other alternatives are available for countries?

CHAPTER 11

Methods of Payment

LEARNING OBJECTIVES:

11.1 Describe the various payment terms in foreign trade

11.2 Understand the importance of open account sales

11.3 Learn the differences between documentary collection and documentary letter of credit

11.4 Learn the liability of banks in documentary collection and documentary letter of credit

11.5 Identify and discuss the three common types of discrepancy in letters of credit

11.6 Describe the new digital and financing alternatives in foreign trade

11.7 Learn about some of the protective measures against documentary fraud

International Trade in Practice

Digitization of Trade Finance

Existing traditional finance such as open account sales or documentary letters of credit is associated with high costs and burdensome procedures involving multiple parties in a trade transaction. They can also be risky and parties are often faced with issues of trust and fraud. For example, in open account transactions, buyers can profit by defaulting on their obligations. In cases where the seller has received advance payments, buyers run the risk that the seller will disappear instead of delivering the goods. Even in cases of letters of credit which represent a guarantee by a bank to pay the exporter (on behalf of the buyer), there are many cases of fraud (falsified documents, inferior cargo, or double bills of lading issued for the same cargo) resulting in huge losses to banks and related parties.

The use of letters of credit has declined over the years from about 50 percent in the 1970s to a mere 15 percent today. Much of the trade has now moved

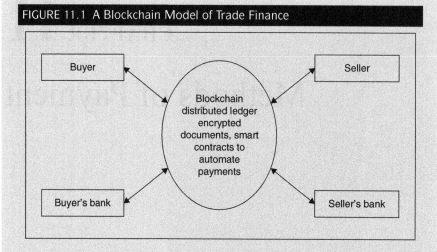

FIGURE 11.1 A Blockchain Model of Trade Finance

to open account sales whereby goods are shipped and delivered before payment (often due in 30 to 90 days). This shift is due to considerations of cost (letters of credit fees range from 0.125 percent to 1.00 percent of total cost), established relationships based on trust between the parties, and the inconvenience of submitting multiple documents and the potential occurrence of errors (two-thirds of letter of credit transactions require revision due to errors in documentation).

These challenges have led banks and IT companies to explore the potential of blockchain technology to facilitate trade finance (Figure 11.1). It is intended to provide easier, faster, and more efficient digital trade transactions. A documentary collection transaction using blockchain technology would proceed as follows:

Step 1: A sales contract between buyer and seller is shared with the buyer's bank using a smart contract on blockchain.

Step 2: In real time, the buyer's bank reviews the sales contract and draft credit terms and submits payment terms to the seller's bank.

Step 3: The seller's bank reviews the contract and payment terms and, upon approval, generates a smart contract on blockchain.

Step 4: The seller will receive the smart contract, which it signs, and prepares the shipment of goods. Goods will be inspected by third parties, approved by customs on blockchain's smart contract.

Step 5: Goods are shipped to the buyer.

Step 6: Goods are delivered to buyer. As the buyer acknowledges receipt of the goods, payment is triggered from importer to exporter via the smart contract.

In May, 2018, HSBC completed the first trade transaction using blockchain for a shipment of soybeans (by Cargill group) from Argentina to Malaysia. It was conducted on the Voltron blockchain platform for letters of credit built by a group of eleven banks. The transaction, which was based on a single shared platform, took less than 24 hours to complete compared to five to ten days using the traditional letter of credit process. This reduces the time to complete the trans-action and minimizes the risk of fraud. Other benefits include lower processing costs for banks and participants, transparency and visibility of all the steps from purchase to payment and accurate representations of each record.

There are certain limitations in implementing such technology on a wide scale:

- Widespread adoption will require a certain level of standardization of existing technology platforms. Presently, there is an increasing number of distributive ledger technology platforms whose systems are not compatible across networks.
- The flow of information across participants (which can identify parties) may raise data protection and privacy concerns.
- There is no global regulatory regime that governs such technology. Some countries, for example, do not recognize digital signatures. Since smart contracts do not identify certain particulars, they may be difficult to enforce in certain countries.

The rapid growth and expansion in global trade cannot be sustained without effi-cient and timely payment arrangements. Nonpayment or delays in payment for imports could tie up limited credit facilities and create liquidity problems for many exporting companies. Advance payments by overseas customers would similarly tie up a buyer's limited resources and do not necessarily guarantee delivery of the agreed merchandise. The ideal payment method is one that protects the contending interests of both sellers and buyers.

Exporters often seek to develop foreign markets by using payment arrangements that are less costly to the buyer, such as consignment sales, open accounts, and docu-mentary drafts, whereby the seller is paid by the foreign wholesaler or retailer only after the goods have been received or sold. It is estimated that about 35 to 50 percent of exports from the United States and the United Kingdom are sold on open account and/or consignment (Cheeseright, 1994; Madura, 2011). This means that the risk of delay in payment or nonpayment could have a crucial effect on cash flow and profits (see Figure 11.2).

FIGURE 11.2 Export Payment Terms Risk/Cost Tradeoff

Risk to Exporter

Least Risk<--->Highest Risk

Cash in Advance	Confirmed Irrevocable Letter of Credit	Irrevocable Letter of Credit	Bank Collection (Sight Draft)	Bank Collection (Time Draft)	Consignment Sales, Open Account

Highest Cost<--->Least Cost

Cost to Buyer

Export companies need access to credit reports on a global basis. There is a need to increase the existing database on companies in different parts of the world to ensure that formal reviews on credit decisions are based on current and reliable information. It is also important to consider credit insurance and other safeguards.

CONSIGNMENT SALES

This is a method in which the exporter sends the product to an importer on a deferred payment basis; that is, the importer does not pay for the merchandise until it is sold to a third party. Title to the merchandise passes to the importer only when payment is made to the exporter (Shapiro, 2006). Consignment is rarely used between unrelated parties, for example, independent exporters and importers (Goldsmith, 1989). It is best used in cases involving an increasing demand for a product for which a proportioned stock is required to meet such need (Tuller, 1994; U.S. ITA, 2021). It is also used when a seller wants to test-market new products or test the market in a new country.

For the exporter, consignment is the least desirable form of selling and receiving payment. The problems associated with this method include the following:

- *Delays in payment:* Consignee bears little or no risk, and payment to seller is delayed until the goods are sold to a third party. This ties up limited credit facilities and often creates liquidity problems for many exporting firms.
- *Risk of nonpayment:* Even though title to the goods does not pass until payment is made, the seller has to acquire possession of merchandise (to sell in the importer's country or ship back to home country) in the event of non-payment. This involves litigation in the importer's country, which is often time-consuming and expensive.
- *Cost of returning merchandise:* If there is limited success in selling the product, there is a need to ship it back to the exporter. It is costly to arrange for the return of merchandise that is unsold.
- *Limited sales effort by importers:* Consignees or importers may not be highly motivated to sell merchandise on consignment because their money is not tied up in inventory. They are likely to give priority to products in which they have some financial involvement.

In view of these risks, consignment sales should be used with overseas customers that have extremely good credit ratings and are well known to the exporter. They would also be satisfactory when the sale involves an affiliated firm or the seller's own sales representative or dealer (Onkvisit and Shaw, 2008). This method is frequently used by multinational companies to sell goods to their subsidiaries.

A number of issues should be considered before goods are sold on consignment between independent exporters and importers. First, it is important to verify the creditworthiness of foreign importers, including data on how long particular companies take to settle bills. Exporters can have instant access to information on overseas customers from credit agencies. No exporting company should consider itself too small to take advice on credit matters. Bad and overdue debts erode profit margins and can jeopardize the viability of an otherwise successful company.

Information on credit worthiness should also include analysis of commercial or country risk factors such as economic and political stability as well as availability of foreign currency to purchase imports. United States banks and their overseas correspondents and some government agencies have credit information on foreign customers.

It is also advisable to consider some form of credit insurance to protect against default by overseas customers. Outstanding debt often makes up about 30 percent of an export company's assets, and it is important to take credit insurance to protect these assets. Credit insurance also helps exporters obtain access to a wide range of banking services and an improved rate of borrowing (Kelly, 1995; Powell, 2010). Financial institutions tend to look more favorably on businesses that are covered and are often prepared to lend more money at better terms. The parties should also agree on who will be responsible for risk insurance on merchandise until it is sold and payment received by the seller, and who pays for freight charges for returned merchandise.

OPEN ACCOUNT

An open account is a contractual relationship between an exporter and importer in which a trade credit is extended by the former to the latter whereby payment is to be made to the exporter within an agreed period of time. The seller ships the merchandise to the buyer and separately mails the relevant shipping documents. Terms of payment range from 30 days to 120 days after date of shipping invoice or receipt of merchandise, depending on the country (Reynolds, 2003).

As in the case of consignment sales, open account is rarely used in international trade between independent exporters and importers. Exporters are often apprehensive of potential defaults by overseas customers. They lack accurate information or may doubt the reliability of available data on foreign buyers to evaluate and determine their credit worthiness to purchase on open account. Unlike consignment sales, importers are expected to remit payment within a certain agreed-upon period regardless of whether they resold the product to third parties.

Open account is often used to increase sales by assisting foreign distributors to start new, or expand existing, product lines. It could also be used when a seller wants to test-market a new product or try a new market in a different country.

This arrangement gives the buyer/distributor enough time to resell the product to domestic customers and then pay the exporter, while generating business goodwill for future dealings. Many developing nations prohibit purchases on open account and consignment sales because of currency restrictions and lack of control over their balance of payments (Shapiro, 2006).

A major weakness of this method is that the importer could delay payment until merchandise is received, even when the importer is expected to pay within a specified period after shipment. There is also a greater risk of default or nonpayment by the buyer. This makes it difficult to sell the account receivable.

Open account financing is often used for trade between parent and subsidiary companies. It is also used for sales to well-established customers with good credit ratings. When open-account sales to third parties are contemplated, it is important to verify the integrity of the buyers through a credit investigation. This should also take into account the importing country's political and economic conditions. Sources range from commercial credit agencies, such as Equifax, or Dunn & Bradstreet, to chambers of commerce, trade associations, commercial banks, and public agencies, such as the Department of Commerce. It is advisable for the exporter to insure trade debts to protect their business against default by the importing company. Another safeguard would be to secure collateral to cover a transaction.

DOCUMENTARY COLLECTION (DOCUMENTARY DRAFT)

The documentary collection or documentary draft is one of the most customary methods of making payments in international trade. To facilitate the transaction, two banks are usually involved, one in the exporter's country and one in the buyer's country. The banks may be independent banks or branches of the same bank.

A draft can be drawn (documents payable) in the currency of the country of payment or in a foreign currency. This method of payment falls between the open account, which favors the buyer, and letter of credit, which protects the exporter. Bank fees are less expensive, usually a specific sum for each service, as opposed to a percentage of the transaction amount, which is used for letters of credit.

A typical documentary collection procedure includes the following steps (see also Figure 11.3):

- After the exporter (drawer) and overseas customer (drawee) agree on the terms of sale, the exporter arranges for shipment and prepares the necessary documents such as the invoice, bill of lading, certificate of origin, and draft.
- The exporter forwards the documents to its bank (remitting bank) with instructions.
- The remitting bank then forwards the documents to its overseas correspondent bank (collecting bank) in the importer's country, with the exporter's instruction letter that authorizes release of documents against payment (D/P) or acceptance (D/A) or other terms.

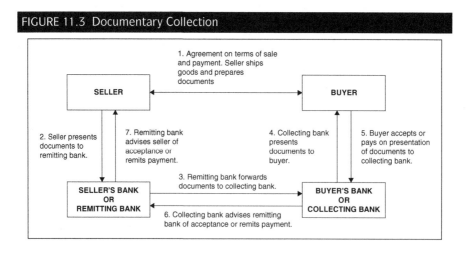

FIGURE 11.3 Documentary Collection

- The collecting bank contacts the importer to effect or accept payment. If the instruction is D/P, the importer pays the collecting bank in exchange for the documents. The collecting bank will then send proceeds to the remitting bank for payment to the seller. If the instructions are D/A, the collecting bank will release documents to the overseas customer only upon formal acceptance of the draft. Once accepted, the collecting bank will release the documents to the buyer. On or before maturity, the collecting bank will present the accepted draft for payment. When the buyer pays, the collecting bank will remit the funds in accordance with instructions.

The basic instructions for collection of shipping documents (in addition to those pertaining to release of documents and remittance of funds) include the following:

- Procedures as to how nonpayment or non-acceptance is to be communicated to the remitting bank.
- Instructions as to who pays the bank's collection charges.
- Listing of documents enclosed.
- Name of a party to be contacted in case a problem arises.

The banking practice relating to documentary draft is standardized by the Uniform Rules for Collections (International Chamber of Commerce, [ICC], 1995). The uniform rules apply only when the parties to the contract agree to be governed by those standards. The rules set out the rights and duties of banks and users of documentary collections (Reynolds, 2003).

Documents Against Payment

In a typical D/P transaction, the exporter draws a draft on the foreign buyer (drawee) through a foreign bank (collecting bank) that receives the collection documents from the exporter's remitting bank (Wells and Dulat, 1991; Bade, 2015). In this instance, a sight draft is presented with other documents specified by the buyer or the buyer's country and the collecting bank will provide these documents to the buyer upon payment. This means that the buyer does not receive the documents and thus will not obtain possession of the goods until payment is made to the collecting bank. This method is widely used in foreign trade and often designated as "sight draft, documents against payment" (S/D, D/P).

The original order bill of lading giving title to the goods is made out to the order of the shipper and is endorsed by the latter either in blank or the order of the collecting bank (Maggiori, 1992). This ensures that the seller retains title and control of the shipment until it reaches its destination and payment is made to the collecting bank. When the collecting bank is paid, it endorses the bill of lading and other documents to the buyer. The original bill of lading must be properly endorsed by the buyer and surrendered to the carrier before the buyer procures possession of the shipment.

Order bills of lading are not available with air shipments. If the importer's name is on the airway bill (not a negotiable document) as consignee, often nothing more is needed to hand over the merchandise to the buyer (importer) than the latter's identification, and the importer could obtain the goods without payment. This problem can be resolved by designating a third party, such as a custom broker or, with prior permission, a collecting bank as consignee on the airway bill. The importer's name should be mentioned as the party to be notified for identification of shipment.

In using S/D, D/P, there remains the potential risk of nonpayment by the importer. The buyer's ability or willingness to pay may change between the time the goods are shipped and the time the draft is presented for payment (McMahon et al., 1994; Bade, 2015). It could also be that the policy of the importing country may change (e.g., exchange controls), making it difficult for the importer to make payments. In the event of nonpayment by the buyer, the exporter has the choice of having the merchandise shipped back or selling it to another buyer in the importing country.

Documents Against Acceptance

In this method, the exporter allows the overseas customer a certain period of time to effect payment for the shipment. The buyer receives the documents, and thus the title, to the goods in exchange for acceptance of the draft to pay at some determinable future date. A time draft is used to establish the time of payment; that is, the payment is due within a certain time after the buyer accepts the draft. A date draft, which specifies the date of payment, is sometimes used. When a time draft is used, the customer can potentially delay payment by delaying acceptance of the draft. An exporter can prevent such delays by either using a date draft or tying the payment date to the date on the bill of lading (e.g., thirty days from the date of the bill of lading) or draft. The collecting bank holds the draft to present for payment on the maturity date.

This method offers less security than an S/D, D/P because documents that certify ownership of merchandise are transferred to an overseas customer prior to payment. Even when the customer is willing and able to pay, payment can be prolonged by delaying acceptance of the time draft. This method is quite similar to open-account sales in which the exporter extends a trade credit to an overseas customer in exchange for payment at some determinable future date. One major difference between the two methods is that in the case of documents against acceptance (for which a time or date draft is used), the draft is a negotiable instrument (unlike an account receivable in an open account) that can be sold and easily converted into cash by the exporter before maturity.

A draft drawn on and accepted by a bank is called a banker's acceptance. Once accepted, the draft becomes a primary obligation of the accepting bank to pay at maturity. If the draft is accepted by nonbank entities such as importers, it is known as a trade acceptance. The greater the credit worthiness of the party accepting the draft, the greater the marketability of the banker's or trade acceptance. They are important tools which can be negotiated or discounted to companies engaged in trade finance and which can serve the financing needs of exporters.

Example: A U.S. Company (ABC) agreed to sell a ton of oranges to a food company in Singapore (XYZ) for $100,000. A draft drawn by ABC is accepted by XYZ's bank to pay on an agreed-upon future date. ABC has two options:

A. It may hold the acceptance until maturity and then collect. The exporter would receive the face amount less the bank's acceptance commission of 1.2 percent per annum ($ acceptance of $100,000.00 for three months)

Face amount of the acceptance:	$100,000.00
Less 1.2% per annum commission	
for 3 months:	- 300.00 {0.012 x 3/12 x 100,000}
Amount received by exporter in 3 months:	$99,700.00

B. ABC may decide to discount i.e., sell at a reduced price and receive the money at once. In this case, ABC will receive the face amount of the acceptance less the acceptance fee and discount rate.

Face amount of the acceptance:	$100,000.00
Less 1.2% per annum commission	
for 3 months:	− 300.00 {0.012 x 3/12 x 100,000}
Less 1.15% per annum discount rate	
for 3 months:	−287.50 {0.0115 x 3/12 x 100,000}
Amount received by exporter in 3 months:	$99,412.50

Direct Collection

Exporters can bypass the remitting bank and send documents directly to the foreign collecting bank for payment or acceptance. This reduces bank charges and speeds the collection process. In this case, the collecting bank acts as the exporter's agent for follow-up and collection without the involvement of the remitting bank.

Liability and Responsibility of the Banks

The Uniform Rules for Collections (ICC, 1995) distinguish two types of collection arrangement: clean collections and documentary collections. In the case of clean collections, a draft is presented to the overseas buyer for the purpose of obtaining payment or acceptance without being accompanied by shipping documents. Documentary collections, which is the subject of this chapter, however, involve the presentation of shipping (commercial) and financial documents (draft or promissory note) by the collecting bank to the buyer. In certain cases in which a collection is payable against shipping documents without a draft (the invoice being used in lieu of a draft), it is termed cash against documents.

In documentary collections, banks act as agents for collection and assume no responsibility for the consequences arising out of delay or for loss in transit of any messages, letters, or documents (ICC, 1995). They do not question documents submitted for collection and are not responsible for their form and/or content or for the authenticity of any signatures for acceptance. However, they have to act in good faith and exercise reasonable care in execution of the collection order. The bank's major responsibilities include the following:

- *Verification of documents received*: The banks check whether the documents appear to be as listed in the collection order and advise the party in the event of missing documents.

- *Compliance with instructions in the collection order:* The exporter instructs the remitting bank on payment whether the documents shall be handed to a representative in case of need and what to do in the event of nonpayment or non-acceptance of the draft. These instructions are then sent along with other documents by the remitting bank to the collecting bank. The latter is only permitted to act upon these instructions.

In the event that the buyer refuses to pay, accept the draft, or pay the accepted draft at maturity, exporters often instruct the collecting bank to 1) protest (i.e., to present the dishonored draft again), 2) warehouse the merchandise, or 3) send the merchandise back to the exporter. The collecting bank may be requested to contact the exporter's agent for clearance of the merchandise. All charges for carrying out these instructions are borne by the exporter. If the collecting bank releases the documents to the overseas customer contrary to instructions, the bank is liable to the seller; it has to pay the seller and collect from the buyer (International Perspective 11.1).

The use of documentary collections offers certain advantages. It reduces transaction costs for both parties, helps maintain suitable levels of control for exporters, and speeds up the flow of transactions. The major risk with this method, however, is the buyer being unable or unwilling to pay or accept the draft on presentation. It is thus important to check credit references, consider taking out credit insurance, or secure collateral to cover the transaction.

INTERNATIONAL PERSPECTIVE 11.1

Protesting with Delinquent Overseas Customers

When a foreign buyer refuses to pay a sight collection or to accept a term draft, the collecting bank will advise the exporter and either proceed according to the collection instruction or new instruction from the exporter or its bank.

There are a number of reasons why buyers are unwilling to pay or accept a term draft.

- If the price of goods falls after order, buyers often try to find excuses to refuse the goods.
- The amount invoiced is higher than what was agreed in the contract or the shipment was made earlier or later than the agreed date.
- The description of the goods is not consistent with what was agreed between the parties.
- Certain documents are missing to clear goods through customs or an import license was not obtained for the goods.

One course of action available to the exporter is to protest (through its bank) the customer's refusal to honor the sales contract (other available options include negotiating the terms, finding a new buyer, or shipping the goods back to the exporter). Protest entails contacting a notary public or attorney (in the buyer's country) for the purpose of legally presenting a draft to the importer. It enables the exporter to maintain his/her right of recourse against the overseas buyer. There are a number of limitations to protest actions:

- Protests are not allowed in certain countries. In some countries such as Peru, a supplier must protest within seven days after the maturity date of the draft. This does not provide sufficient time to the exporter to assess the situation.
- Protests can be quite costly in some countries.
- Such actions may damage future business dealings with customers, especially if the exporter was partly responsible for the problem.

DOCUMENTARY LETTER OF CREDIT

A letter of credit (L/C) is a document in which a bank or other financial institution assumes liability for payment of the purchase price to the seller on behalf of the buyer. The bank could deal directly or through the intervention of a bank in the seller's country. In all types of letters of credit, the buyer arranges with a bank to provide finance for the exporter in exchange for certain documents. The bank makes its credit available to its client, the buyer, in consideration of a security that often includes a pledge of the documents of title to the goods, or placement of funds in advance, or of a pledge to reimburse with a commission (Reynolds, 2003). The essential feature of this method, and its value to an exporter of goods, is that it superimposes upon the credit of the buyer the credit of a bank, often one carrying on business in the seller's country. The letter of credit is a legally enforceable commitment by a bank to pay money upon the performance of certain conditions, stipulated therein, to the seller (exporter or beneficiary) for the account of the buyer (importer or applicant).

A letter of credit is considered an export or import L/C depending on the party. The same letter of credit is considered an export L/C by the seller and an import L/C by the buyer. The steps involved in Figure 11.4 are as follows:

1. The Canadian buyer in Montreal contracts with the U.S. seller in New York. The agreement provides for the payment to be financed by means of confirmed, irrevocable documentary credit for goods delivered CIF, port of Montreal.
2. The Canadian buyer applies to its bank (issuing bank), which issues the letter of credit with the U.S. seller as beneficiary.
3. The issuing bank sends the letter of credit to an advising bank in the United States, which also confirms the letter of credit.
4. The advising bank notifies the U.S. seller that a letter of credit has been issued on its behalf (confirmed by the advising bank) and is available on presentation of documents.
5. The U.S. seller scrutinizes the credit. When satisfied that the stipulations in the credit can be met, the U.S. seller will arrange for shipment and prepare the necessary documents, that is, commercial invoice, bill of lading, draft, insurance policy, and certificate of origin. Amendments may be necessary in cases in which the credit improperly describes the merchandise.
6. After shipment of merchandise, the U.S. seller submits relevant documents to the advising/confirming bank for payment. If the documents comply, the advising/confirming bank will pay the seller. (If the L/C provides for

FIGURE 11.4 Documentary Letter of Credit

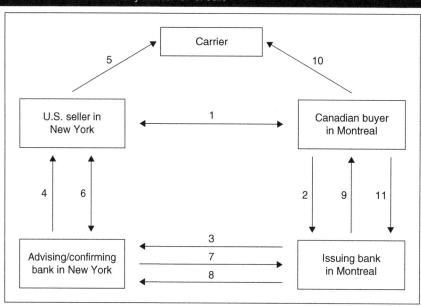

acceptance, the bank accepts the draft, signifying its commitment to pay the face value at maturity to the seller or bona fide holder of the draft. This is called an acceptance L/C. It is a straight L/C if payment is made by the issuing bank or the bank designated in the credit at a determinable future date. If the credit provides for negotiation at any bank, it is a negotiable L/C.)

7. The advising/confirming bank sends documents plus settlement instructions to the issuing bank.

8. After inspecting the documents for compliance with instructions, the issuing bank reimburses/remits proceeds to the advising/confirming bank.

9. The issuing bank gives documents to the buyer and presents the term draft for acceptance. With a sight draft, the issuing bank will be paid by the buyer on presentation of documents.

10. The buyer arranges for clearance of the merchandise, that is, gives up the bill of lading and takes receipt of the goods.

11. The buyer pays the issuing bank on or before the draft maturity date.

Issuing banks often verify receipt of full details of the L/C by the advising bank. This is done by using a private test code arrangement between banks. Credits are opened and forwarded to the advising/confirming bank by mail, telex, or cable. Issuing banks can also open credits by using the SWIFT system (Society for Worldwide Interbank Financial Telecommunications), which allows for faster transmission time. It also allows member banks to use automatic authentication (verification) of messages (Ruggiero, 1991).

The letter of credit consists of four separate and distinct bilateral contracts: 1) a sales contract between the buyer and seller; 2) a credit and reimbursement contract between the buyer and issuing bank, providing for the issuing bank to establish a letter of credit in favor of the seller and for reimbursement by the buyer; 3) a letter of credit contract between the issuing bank and the beneficiary (exporter), attesting that the bank will pay the seller on presentation of specified documents; and 4) the confirmed advice, which also signifies a contract between the advising/confirming bank and the seller, in which the bank will pay the seller on presentation of specified documents.

When the letter of credit is revocable, the issuing bank could amend or cancel the credit at any time after issue without consent from, or notice to, the seller. Revocable L/Cs are seldom used in international trade except in cases of trade between parent and subsidiary companies because they do not provide sufficient protection to the seller. Under the Uniform Customs and Practice for Documentary Credits (UCP), letters of credit are deemed irrevocable even if there is no indication to that effect (ICC, 2007). Irrevocable credits cannot be amended or cancelled before their expiry date without express consent of all parties to the credit. The terms revocable and irrevocable refer only to the issuing bank.

In cases in which sellers do not know of, or have little confidence in, the financial strength of the buyer's country or the issuing bank, they often require a bank in their country to guarantee payment (i.e., confirm the L/C).

There are several advantages of using letters of credit. They accommodate the competing desires of the seller and overseas customer. The seller receives payment on presentation of documents to the bank after shipment of goods, unlike open-account sales or documentary collection. In cases in which the advising bank accepts the L/C for payment at a determinable future date, the seller can discount the L/C before maturity. Buyers also avoid the need to make prepayment or to establish an escrow account. Letters of credit also ensure that payment is not made until the goods are placed in possession of a carrier and that specified documents are presented to that effect (Shapiro, 2006).

One major disadvantage with an L/C for the buyer is that issuing banks often require cash or other collateral before they open an L/C, unless the buyer has a satisfactory credit rating. This could tie up the available credit line. In certain countries, buyers are also required to make a prior deposit before establishing an L/C. Letters of credit are complex transactions between different parties, and the smallest discrepancy between documents could require an amendment of the terms or lead to the invalidation of the credit. This may expose the seller to a risk of delay in payment or nonpayment in certain cases.

A letter of credit is a documentary payment obligation, and banks are required to pay or agree to pay on presentation of appropriate documents as specified in the credit. This payment obligation applies even if a seller ships defective or nonexistent goods (empty crates/boxes). The buyer then has to sue for breach of contract. The interests of the buyer can be protected by structuring the L/C to require, as a condition of payment, the following:

- The presentation of a certificate of inspection executed by a third party certifying that the goods shipped conform to the terms of the contract of sale. If the goods are defective or nonconforming to the terms of the contract, the third party will refuse to sign the certificate and the seller will not receive payment. In such cases, it is preferable to use a revocable L/C.
- The presentation of a certificate of inspection executed or countersigned by the buyer. It is preferable to use a revocable L/C to allow the bank to cancel the credit.

- A reciprocal standby L/C issued in favor of the buyer in which the latter could draw on this credit and obtain a return of the purchase price if the seller shipped nonconforming goods (McLaughlin, 1989).

Governing Law

The rights and duties of parties to a letter of credit issued or confirmed in the United States are determined by reference to three different sources:

- *The Uniform Commercial Code (UCC):* The basic law on letters of credit is codified in article 5-101 to 5-117 of the UCC. This article has been adopted in all states of the Union. However, some states (New York, Missouri, Alabama) have introduced an amendment providing that article 5 will not apply if the letter of credit is subject, in whole or in part, to the Uniform Customs and Practice for Documentary Credits.
- *The Uniform Customs and Practice for Documentary Credits (UCP):* Parties to the letter of credit frequently agree to be governed by the rules of the UCP, which is a result of collaboration between the International Chamber of Commerce, the United Nations, and many international trade banks. The UCP is periodically revised to take into account new developments in international trade and credit (the latest revision was in 2007) (see International Perspective 11.2). The UCC and UCP provisions on letters of credit complement each other in many areas. Under both the UCC and UCP, the terms of the credit can be altered by agreement of the parties.
- *General principles of law*: In cases in which the UCC or UCP provisions are not sufficient to resolve a dispute, courts apply general principles of law insofar as they do not conflict with the governing law (UCC or UCP) or agreement of the parties.

INTERNATIONAL PERSPECTIVE 11.2

Understanding the UCP 600

The UCP 600 is a revision of the rules of practice for letters of credit prepared under the auspices of the International Chamber of Commerce. It replaces UCP 500 which was released in 1993. It became effective on July 1, 2007. The revision was largely triggered by a high frequency of technical rejections of documents under UCP 500. In spite of several comments and suggestions from national committees all over the world, very few substantive changes were made to UCP 500.

The major changes were:

- *Time to examine documents*: UCP 500 gave banks a "reasonable time" to examine the documents and identify discrepancies. UCP 600 replaces "reasonable time" with five banking days.
- *Addresses of applicant and beneficiary*: UCP 500 required that addresses of applicants and beneficiaries in letters of credit match the addresses stated in

commercial documents. This was amended to state that the addresses need not match insofar as they are in the same countries.

- *Discrepant documents, waiver, and notice*: This relates to cases where the buyer decides to pay against discrepant documents that have been refused by the bank. There is no provision in UCP 500 that allows banks to rescind its refusal. UCP 600 states that a bank that has refused documents is permitted to later rescind its refusal unless the seller provides contrary instructions i.e., the issuing bank delivers the documents to the buyer without obtaining the acceptance of the seller or the presenting bank (if the seller and presenting bank have not objected).
- *Nomination of a bank obligates it to honor deferred payments*: UCP 500 does not impose an obligation on nominated banks to honor deferred payments (unlike acceptance of time drafts). UCP 600 now states that a letter of credit that is available by deferred payment implicitly authorizes the bank (with which it is available) to discount (i.e., to pay immediately with interest deducted from payment, if required to do so by the beneficiary).
- *Banks must follow strict rules for refusing payment*: If documents do not strictly comply (this was modified to state that data in the documents must not conflict), banks may refuse payment but must themselves follow strict rules for refusing payment.

Role of Banks under Letters of Credit

The buyer's bank issues the letter of credit at the request of the buyer. The details of the credit are normally specified by the buyer. Since the seller wants a local bank available at which the seller can present the letter of credit for payment, an additional bank often becomes involved in the transaction. The second bank usually either "advises" or "confirms" the letter of credit. A bank that advises on the L/C gives notification of the terms and conditions of the credit issued by another bank to the seller. It assumes no liability for paying the letter of credit. Its only obligation is to ensure that the beneficiary (seller) is advised and the credit delivered, and to ensure the apparent authenticity of the credit.

An issuing bank may also request a bank to confirm the letter of credit. A confirming bank promises to honor a letter of credit already issued by another bank and becomes directly obligated to the beneficiary (seller), as though it had issued the letter of credit itself. It will pay, accept, or negotiate a letter of credit upon presentation of specific documents that comply with the terms and conditions of the credit. A confirming bank is entitled to reimbursement by the issuing bank, assuming that the latter's instructions have been properly executed. However, it faces the risk of non-payment if the issuing bank or the buyer is unable or unwilling to pay the confirming bank, in which case it will be left with title to the goods and obliged to liquidate them to offset its losses.

Both the confirming and issuing banks have an obligation toward the exporter (beneficiary) and the buyer to act in good faith and with reasonable care in examining the documents. The basic rule pertaining to a bank's liability to a beneficiary is that the bank should honor the L/C if the documents presented comply with the terms of the credit. The following circumstances cannot be used by banks as a basis to dishonor (refuse to pay or accept a draft) letters of credit:

- *Dishonor to serve the buyer's interests:* In this case, claims are made by a bank's customer (the buyer) that the beneficiary has breached the sales contract or that the underlying agreement has been modified or amended in some way in the face of complying documents. This includes cases of dishonor based on the bank's knowledge or reasonable belief that the goods do not conform to the underlying contract of sale.
- *Dishonor to serve the bank's own interests:* This occurs when the sole reason for dishonor is the bank's belief that it would not obtain reimbursement from its insolvent customer. This involves situations in which the buyer becomes insolvent after the L/C is issued and before the beneficiary's draft is honored.
- *Dishonor after express waiver of a particular discrepancy:* A bank dishonors an L/C after it has expressly agreed to disregard a particular discrepancy.
- *Dishonor without giving the beneficiary an opportunity to correct the discrepancy:* If the issuing bank decides to refuse the documents, it must give notice to that effect, stating the discrepancy without delay, and must also state whether it is holding the documents at the disposal of and returning them to the remitting bank or beneficiary, as the case may be (Artz, 1991; Rosenblith, 1991).

Banks may properly dishonor a letter of credit in cases of fraud or forgery, even if the documents presented to the beneficiary appear to comply with the terms of credit. This assumes that there are no innocent parties involved in the presentation of the letter of credit to the bank. Banks are subject to two principles in the conduct of their letter-of-credit transactions: the independent principle and the rule of strict compliance.

The Independent Principle

The letter of credit is separate from, and independent of, other contracts relating to the transaction. Each of the four contracts in a letter-of-credit transaction is entirely independent. It is irrelevant to the bank whether the seller/buyer has fully carried out its part of the contract with the buyer/seller. The bank's duty is to establish whether the stipulated documents have been presented in order to pay (accept to pay) the exporter. It is not the bank's duty to ascertain whether the goods mentioned in the documents have been shipped or whether they conform to the terms of the contract. Article 4 of the UCP states:

> Credits by their nature are separate transactions from the sales or other contract(s) on which they may be based and banks are in no way concerned with or bound by such contract(s), even if any reference whatsoever to such contract(s) is included in the credit.
>
> (ICC, 2007, p.5)

The independent principle is subject to a fraud exception. A bank can refuse payment if it has been informed that there has been fraud or forgery in connection with the letter-of-credit transaction and the person presenting the documents is not a holder in due course (a third party who took the draft for value, in good faith, and without knowledge of the fraud). In one case, for example, a buyer notified the issuing bank not to pay the seller under the letter of credit, alleging that the seller had intentionally shipped fifty crates of rubbish in place of fifty crates of bristles. The bank's refusal of payment was accepted by the court as a justifiable reason in view of fraud in the underlying transaction (Ryan, 1990). United States courts have held in several cases that banks are justified in dishonoring L/Cs when the documents are forged or fraudulent. Banks assume no liability or responsibility for the form, sufficiency, accuracy, genuineness, or legal effect of any documents. The obligation to honor an irrevocable L/C exists provided the stipulated documents are presented. In credit operations, all parties concerned deal in documents and not in the goods to which the documents relate. Thus, when the L/C is governed by the UCP, it appears that the bank must pay, regardless of any underlying fraud. A bank would, however, be liable for the money paid out if it participated in the fraud.

The Rule of Strict Compliance

The general rule is that an exporter cannot compel payment unless it strictly complies with the conditions specified in the credit (Rosenblith, 1991). When conforming documents are presented, the advising bank must pay, the issuing bank must reimburse, and the buyer is obliged to pay the issuing bank. In certain cases, courts have refused to recognize the substantial-compliance argument by banks to recover their payments from buyers (unless it involves minor spelling errors or insignificant additions or abbreviations in drafts) (Rubenstein, 1994). The reason behind the doctrine of strict compliance is that the advising bank is an agent of the issuing bank and the latter is a special agent of the buyer. This means that banks have limited authority and have to bear the commercial risk of the transaction if they act outside the scope of their mandate (Macintosh, 1992; Barnes, 1994). In addition, in times of falling demand, the buyer may be tempted to reject documents that the bank accepted, alleging that they are not in strict compliance with the terms of the credit.

Two assumptions underlie the doctrine of strict compliance:

1. *Linkage of documents*: The documents (bill of lading, draft, invoice, insurance certificate) are linked by an unambiguous reference to the same merchandise.
2. *Description of goods*: The goods must be fully described in the invoice, but the same details are not necessary in all the other documents. What is important is that the documents, when taken together, contain the particulars required under the L/C. This means that the invoice could include more details than the bill of lading as long as the enlarged descriptions are essentially consistent with those contained in the bill of lading (Murray, 2007).

Discrepancies

Discrepancies occur when documents submitted contain language or terms different from the L/C or some other apparent irregularity (International Perspectives 11.3 and 11.4). Most discrepancies occur because the exporter does not present all the documents required under the L/C or because the documents do not strictly conform to the L/C requirements (Reynolds, 2003).

Example: Dushkin Bank issued an irrevocable L/C on behalf of its customer (the buyer), John Textiles, Incorporated. It promised to honor a draft of KG

Company (the exporter) for $250,000, covering shipment of "100% Acrylic Yarn." KG Company presented its draft with a commercial invoice describing the merchandise as "Imported Acrylic Yarns."

Discrepancy: The description of the goods in the invoice does not match that stated in the L/C. Dushkin Bank could refuse to honor the draft and return the documents to the exporter.

To receive payment under the credit, the exporter must present documents that are in strict accord with the terms of the L/C. It is estimated that over 80 percent of documents presented under L/Cs contain some discrepancy.

There are three types of discrepancy:

- *Accidental discrepancies*: These are discrepancies that can easily be corrected by the exporter (beneficiary) or the issuing bank. Such discrepancies include typographical errors, omission to state the L/C number, errors in arithmetic, and improper endorsement or signature on the draft. Once these discrepancies are corrected (within a reasonable period of time), the bank will accept the documents and pay the exporter.
- *Minor discrepancies*: These are minor errors in documents that contain the essential particulars required in the L/C and can be corrected by obtaining a written waiver from the buyer. Such errors include failure to legalize documents, non-presentation of all documents required under the L/C, and discrepancy between the wording on the invoice and the L/C. Once these discrepancies are waived by the buyer, the transaction will proceed as anticipated.
- *Major discrepancies*: These are discrepancies that fundamentally affect the essential nature of the L/C. Certain discrepancies cannot be corrected under any circumstances: presentation of documents after the expiry date of the L/C, shipment of merchandise later than the specified date under the L/C, or expiration of the L/C. However, other major discrepancies can be corrected by an amendment of the L/C. Amendments require the approval of the issuing bank, the confirming bank (in the case of a confirmed L/C), and the exporter. Examples of discrepancies that can be amended include presentation of an incorrect bill of lading, a draft in excess of the amount specified in the credit, and making partial shipments not allowed under the credit.

Discrepancies that can be corrected (accidental, minor, and certain major discrepancies) must be rectified within a reasonable period of time after shipment and before the expiry of the L/C. Most L/Cs require that the documents be submitted within a reasonable period of time after the date of the bill of lading. If no time is specified, the UCP requires submission of shipping documents by the beneficiary to banks no later than twenty-one days after the date of shipment and in any event no later than the expiry date of the credit.

In cases in which the buyer is looking for an excuse to reject the documents (when the price of the product is falling, the product is destroyed on shipment, etc.), the buyer may not accede to a waiver or amendment of the discrepancy or may do so in consideration of a huge discount off the contract price. The buyer could also delay correction, in which case the exporter loses the use of the proceeds for a certain period of time. Besides incurring further bank charges to correct the discrepancy, the seller also faces the risk that the credit will expire before the discrepancies are corrected.

When the discrepancy stands (the discrepancy cannot be corrected or the buyer refuses to waive or amend the terms of the credit), the seller can still attempt to obtain payment by requesting the bank to obtain authority to pay or send the documents for collection (documentary collection) outside the terms of the L/C. If the buyer refuses to accept the documents, the bank will not pay the seller (exporter) and the exporter has to either find a buyer abroad or have the merchandise returned. If the confirming/issuing bank accepts documents that contain a discrepancy, then it cannot seek reimbursement from its respective customers (issuing bank/buyer, respectively) (International Perspective 11.4).

When the issuing bank decides to refuse the document, it must notify the party from which it obtained the document (the remitting bank or the exporter) without delay, stating the reasons for the rejection and whether it holds the documents at the disposal of, or is returning them to, the presenter.

INTERNATIONAL PERSPECTIVE 11.3

Common Discrepancies in Letters of Credit

Over 80 percent of L/C documents are rejected by the bank upon presentation. It is thus important to ensure that errors are avoided or detected, and appropriate corrections made to avoid nonpayment or delays in payments. Here are some of the common discrepancies:

* Draft is not signed, or it is not consistent with the L/C (in terms of the amount, maturity date, etc.) and shows evidence of forgery or alteration.
* Insurance policy is not consistent with the invoice or L/C, it is dated after the date of the bill of lading or is not endorsed.
* Commercial invoice does not conform to description of goods (including quantity and measurements) in the draft or IL/Ct and fails to show terms of shipment.
* Bill of lading/air waybill differs from the L/C, shows evidence of forgery or alteration, or is not endorsed. It may also be that onboard notations are not dated or signed and that the bill of lading is incomplete (missing originals).
* Incomplete documentation, description of merchandise is not consistent in all documents, the L/C is overdrawn/expired or the draft and documents are presented after the time called for in the L/C.

INTERNATIONAL PERSPECTIVE 11.4

Unworkable Terms in Letters of Credit

* *Compliance with certain national policies*: Some Middle Eastern countries require a document certifying that the ship carrying the merchandise destined to them will not make stops at Israeli ports. Complying with

such requirements, for example, will violate the antiboycott provisions of U.S. law.

- *Contradictory/different terms*: The requirement of the use of the term FOB (free on board) with an additional statement that freight be prepaid to destination or a requirement that the beneficiary submit a certificate providing the origin of each component in an assembled product (Chambers of Commerce will only certify local (not foreign) components). Requiring a carrier's insurance policy (as opposed to certificate of insurance) will also make it difficult for buyers to comply.
- *Setting unrealistic performance conditions*: Different motivations often lead to the setting of shipping dates, expiration dates or presentation dates for payments that are not realistic and often difficult to fulfill.

CASH IN ADVANCE

This method of payment requires the buyer to pay before shipment is effected. The seller assumes no risk of bad debt and/or delays in payment because advance payment is a precondition to shipment.

Sellers often require advance payment in cases in which the creditworthiness of the overseas customer is poor or unknown and/or the political/economic conditions of the buyer's country are unstable. Cash in advance is sometimes used between related companies. It is also common to require money in advance for samples.

NEW PAYMENT AND FINANCING ALTERNATIVES

Since the 1990s, there has been a rapid expansion of online business-to-business transactions. One of the most significant challenges to this continued growth has been the lack of a payment mechanism for large cross-border transactions. Existing trade payment processes have not evolved and continue to be labor and document intensive. Any discrepancy in L/C documents, for example, can delay or even hinder the entire delivery and payment process. Open account sales also pose a risk of non-payment by the buyer (Yuan, 2007).

Innovative online payment and financing platforms are beginning to revolutionize the way international trade is conducted. Companies such as GT Nexus, TradeBeam, and Bolero now offer a business-to-business e-commerce infrastructure that enables buyers and sellers to initiate, conduct, and settle international trade transactions securely over the Internet.

These online platforms have several advantages over traditional payment methods such as L/Cs:

- *Less paperwork and enhanced visibility*: Export–import companies are often faced with complex financing and extensive documentation that can increase the cost of goods shipped by 4 to 6 percent. It is estimated that over 70 percent of documents are found discrepant, thus leading to delays in payment or nonpayment. The online platform stores the documents electronically and allows parties to view them and correct any discrepancy online. There is also the benefit of enhanced visibility into the movement of products and payments throughout the transaction lifecycle.

- *Cost savings*: Online platforms require less investment in hardware (they use the Internet) and less costly than L/Cs. They handle documentation, payments, and other services.
- *Value-added services*: They provide access to a community of service providers that offer logistics, inspection, export financing, and credit checks of customers.

MS Mode, a Netherlands-based women's clothing retailer with over 400 stores throughout Europe, deployed TradeCard's (now GT Nexus) online platform to increase sourcing from Bangladesh without using L/Cs (Anonymous, 2012). Several other retailers such as Levi Strauss, Columbia Sportswear, Guess, and Rite Aid are also using these platforms to streamline transaction flows, ranging from purchase orders to shipment and payments.

Banks are competitors as well as logistic partners to these online platforms, which offer L/C and open account services. They also partner with banks for financing services to their customers (see International Perspective 11.5).

In spite of the benefits that the new payment platforms provide, they have yet to achieve universal acceptance within the business community. The benefits of such platforms can only be efficiently exploited when all partners and service providers subscribe to the same platform (David, 2017).

INTERNATIONAL PERSPECTIVE 11.5

Trade card: A Typical Transaction Process

1. Buyer logs into the GT Nexus e-commerce site by entering username and password.
2. Buyer creates and approves the procurement documents such as purchase order and cargo insurance, which are stored in its secure proprietary database.
3. Seller is notified by email of the pending order to be reviewed. Seller then logs into the GT Nexus e-commerce site.
4. Buyer and seller negotiate purchase order terms online and digitally sign the procurement documents. Once the purchase order is complete, seller begins fulfillment.
5. Seller creates and approves commercial invoice and packing list as goods are ready to be shipped. Service providers are notified and facilitate the process including the creation and submission of the requisite documents into the platform: proof of delivery, inspection certificate.
6. Once all documents are submitted, the patented compliance engine is activated. Buyer approves the payment authorization document, reviews, negotiates, and approves any discrepancies online.
7. Once all compliance requirements are met, GT Nexus sends instructions to a bank to debit the buyer's account and credit the seller's account.

> The platform allows parties to track the status of their transaction, view document status, contract details, receive email reminders, and other pertinent matters.

FRAUD IN DOCUMENTARY CREDITS

International trade fraud is not a new phenomenon. Ever since trade began, merchants have been victims of fraud and other criminal activity. As early as the first century BC, there were pirate states along the Anatolian coast, threatening the commerce of the Roman Empire in the eastern Mediterranean. Roman ships were attacked by pirates who seized their cargoes of grain and olive oil. The Vikings (which means sea-raider) were renowned for attacking shipping and coastal settlements.

There are different types of trade fraud ranging from piracy and theft to marine insurance fraud. This section will focus on documentary (L/C) fraud.

Common Features of Documentary Fraud

Fraud by Seller

- *Fraudulent seller ships worthless goods or goods of lower quality*: The seller ships worthless goods or goods of lower quality, pays for freight costs, and obtains a genuine bill of lading that enables it to receive payment from the advising or issuing bank for the shipment.
- *Fraudulent seller does not ship any merchandise*: The seller will forge an entire set of documents required under the L/C and presents them to the bank for payment. Such sellers even furnish the buyer with a performance bond (for 10 percent of the value of the cargo) and obtain full value of the purchase price without sending any merchandise to the buyer.

Fraud by Buyer

- *Fraudulent buyer forges original documents for payment*: The seller sends cargo (under documents against payment arrangement) to buyer and submits the original documents to the collecting bank in the buyer's country for presentation against payment. Meanwhile, a copy of the original documents is sent directly to the buyer. The buyer will forge the original documents and present them to the carrier to clear the cargo. The authentic documents are still with the collecting bank.
- *Fraudulent buyer receives merchandise from carrier on the strength of letter of indemnity*: Indemnities are issued to enable the discharge of cargo (or induce the carrier to discharge at a different destination if sold to another party while on transit) without presentation of the bill of lading. The letter of indemnity substitutes for the bill of lading, thus allowing the buyer to receive the goods. This occurs when the cargo arrives before the bill of lading. The buyer obtains delivery of the goods and sells the bill of lading to an innocent buyer.

Fraud by Buyer, Seller, and Other Parties

- *Buyer and seller conspire to defraud paying bank*: The seller and buyer conspire to defraud the paying bank by using forged documentary credits. The seller may also induce the buyer into sending goods on a fraudulent L/C.
- *Seller and carrier falsify the actual order and condition of the goods*: The seller and carrier falsify to the buyer the order and condition of the goods by issuing a clean bill of lading. A letter of indemnity taken out by the seller covers the carrier against any liability in connection with the release of the goods. This is fraud on the buyer who receives a clean bill of lading and assumes the cargo to be in good condition.

Protective Measures Against Documentary Fraud

Proactive Measures by Sellers

- Verify the background and credibility of your partner through your government agency, bank, or professional associations.
- Stipulate the required documents and other pertinent conditions in the sales contract.
- Check the validity of the L/C as well as the credibility of the issuing bank. It is also important to verify that the terms in the letter of credit comply with the sales contract.

Proactive Measures by Buyers

- Verify the background and credibility of your partner through your government agency, bank, or professional associations.
- Choose the FOB trade term rather CIF in a sales contract so that you have more control over the shipment. It is also important to verify the availability of the ship, its capacity to carry the agreed merchandise, and its physical location.
- Use independent inspectors to verify the quality and quantity of goods and whether they have been loaded on the vessel.
- Choose time drafts (instead of sight drafts) to allow you to make payment some days after acceptance of the draft. This allows the buyer to discover fraud after the goods have arrived but before the date of payment. It is also possible to condition the passage of title upon a buyer's inspection and approval of the goods.
- Verify the authenticity of the documents, especially the bill of lading, before they are presented to the bank for payment. To reduce possible forgery, the buyer can require that original bills of lading be sent directly to banks and not to the seller (shipper) in CIF contracts.
- Sellers can provide a performance guarantee to a buyer to carry out its obligations. In the event of fraud by the seller, the issuing bank will be obligated to compensate the buyer, solely upon demand by the buyer. Buyers can also take export credit insurance.

Proactive Measures by Banks

- The paying bank should offer an additional service for a fee. Banks can undertake an investigation into the validity, genuineness, or accuracy of the documents before payment. The Bank of China, for example, provides a commercial credibility investigation service for its customers. The service includes a report on the foreign partner's background, credit status, solvency, name of loading ship, port, and condition of the goods, as well as information on the carrier.
- Make further investigations in cases where fraud is suspected to avoid future occurrences.

OTHER LETTERS OF CREDIT

Transferable Letter of Credit

Exporters often use a transferable L/C to pay a supplier, while keeping the identity of the supplier and the foreign customer from each other, lest they conduct the next transaction without the exporter. This method is often used when the exporter acts as an agent or intermediary. Under a transferable L/C, the exporter (beneficiary) transfers the rights and certain duties, such as shipment, under the credit to another person, usually its supplier (transferee), who receives payment, provided that the conditions of the original credit are met. The bank requested by the beneficiary to effect the transfer is under no obligation to do so, unless it has expressly consented to it.

It is important to note the following with respect to such L/Cs:

- A credit is transferred only if it is expressly designated as "transferable" by the issuing bank.
- It can be transferred only once. The credit is automatically divisible and can be transferred in fractions, provided that partial shipments are not excluded.
- The name and address of the first beneficiary may be substituted for that of the buyer. This masks the identity of the true suppliers of the merchandise from the buyer.
- The transferee receives rights under this type of L/C. Such a transfer requires the consent of the buyer and of the issuing bank.
- The supplier might demand that the exporter actually transfers the L/C in its entirety, without substitution of invoices. The beneficiary (exporter) will receive a commission independent of the L/C transaction.

Example: A Canadian bank opens a transferable credit in the amount of $90,000 in favor of a U.S. exporter in Florida for a shipment of tomatoes. The exporter had located a supplier in Texas and had decided to use $85,000 of the credit to pay the supplier. The exporter asks the advising bank in Florida to effect a transfer in favor of the supplier. The supplier is advised of the transfer by the advising bank. The new credit does not mention the amount of the original credit or the name of the foreign buyer but substitutes the name of the exporter (original beneficiary) as the buyer. When the supplier presents conforming documents to the advising bank in Florida, the bank substitutes the exporter's invoice for that of the supplier, pays $85,000 to the supplier, and pays the difference to the exporter. The advising bank forwards the documents to the Canadian bank, which has no knowledge of the transfer for reimbursement.

A transferable L/C is different from assignment of proceeds under the credit. In assignment, the exporter asks the bank holding the L/C to pay either the entire amount or a percentage of the proceeds to a specified third party, usually a supplier. This allows the exporter to make domestic purchases with limited capital by using the overseas buyer's credit. This is done by assigning the proceeds from the buyer's L/C. The beneficiary (exporter) of an L/C may assign its rights to the proceeds of the L/C, even if the L/C expressly states that it is nontransferable. Only the beneficiary (not assignee) has rights under the credit, and the overseas buyer as well as the issuing bank often have no knowledge of the assignment.

Example: A U.S. exporter has an L/C for $40,000 from a buyer in Brazil. The exporter had located a supplier within the United States that will sell the product for $25,000. However, the supplier would not release the product for shipment without some down payment or collateral. The exporter (assignor) could assign part of the proceeds ($25,000) from the L/C to the supplier (assignee). The assignee will then provide the merchandise to the exporter, who will arrange shipment. The exporter (assignor) must submit documents that comply with the credit in order for the advising bank to pay the assignee (supplier). The remainder ($15,000) will be paid to the exporter.

Back-to-Back Letter of Credit

This is a letter of credit that is issued on the strength of another letter of credit. Such credits are issued when suppliers or subcontractors demand payment from the exporter before collections are received from the customer. The back-to-back L/C is separate from the original L/C, and the bank that issued the former is obligated to make payment to suppliers regardless of the outcome of the latter. If there is a default on the original L/C, the bank is left with worthless collateral.

Example: A Japanese manufacturer (exporter) of cars has an L/C issued for 1,000 cars by a buyer in New York. Payment is to be made ninety days after shipment. However, subcontractors require payment to be made for spare parts purchased in ten days (earlier than the date of payment provided under the L/C). The Japanese exporter presents the buyer's L/C to the advising bank in Tokyo and asks the bank to issue a new L/C to the subcontractor, payable in ten days. The first L/C is used as collateral to issue the second L/C in favor of the subcontractor.

Revolving Letter of Credit

Banks make available letters of credit with a set limit for their customers that allow for a free flow of merchandise until the expiry date of the credit. This avoids the need to open credits for each shipment. The value of the credit allowed can be reinstated automatically or by amendment. If credits designated for use during one period can be carried over to the next period, they are termed "cumulative." They are noncumulative if any unused amount is no longer available.

Example 1: Queen's Bank in Fort Lauderdale opens a revolving line of credit for up to $150,000 in favor of Kegan Enterprises, Incorporated, for the importation of handicrafts. Kegan Enterprises agrees to purchase toys (for $50,000) from Korea and requests Queen's Bank to open an L/C for $50,000 in favor of the seller in that country. If the credit provides for automatic reinstatement, $100,000 will be readily available for other purchases. In other cases, Kegan Enterprises will have to wait for approval from the bank, reinstating the credit ($100,000) to use for another shipment.

Example 2: Suppose Queen's Bank opens a letter of credit of up to $15,000 a month for six months in favor of Kegan Enterprises. If the credit states that it is cumulative, $30,000 credit not used during the first two months could still be used during the next four months. If it is noncumulative, the credit not used during the two-month period cannot be carried over for use in the next four months.

Red-Clause Credit

Such credits provide for advance payment to an exporter before presentation of shipping documents. It is intended to provide pre-export financing to an agent or distributor for purchase of the merchandise from a supplier. When financing is conditional on presentation of negotiable warehouse receipts issued in favor of the advising bank, it is termed green-clause credit.

Deferred-Payment Credit

This is a letter of credit whereby the bank undertakes an obligation to pay at a future date stipulated on the credit, provided that the terms and conditions of the credit are met.

Example: Suppose a U.S. buyer agrees to buy lumber valued at $40 million from a Canadian seller. The parties agree to use a deferred-payment credit. In this case, the U.S. buyer asks its bank to open (issue) a letter of credit obligating itself to pay the seller sixty days after the date of the bill of lading. If the documents are as stipulated in the credit, the bank undertakes an obligation to pay the Canadian seller sixty days after the date of the bill of lading. No draft, however, need accompany the documents.

What are the major differences between an acceptance letter of credit and a deferred-payment credit?

In the case of acceptance credits, the bank undertakes an obligation to accept drafts drawn on itself provided that stipulated documents are presented. Assume that a Canadian seller and a U.S. buyer agreed to use an acceptance credit payable sixty days after presentation of shipping documents. Once the Canadian seller presents the requisite shipping documents and draft of the advising bank, the bank will stamp the draft "accepted," if it is in strict compliance with the credit. This represents the bank's obligation to pay on the maturity date of the draft. Once accepted by the bank, the draft becomes a negotiable instrument that can be discounted by the accepting bank, enabling the seller to receive payment for the goods in advance of the maturity date of the acceptance. In the case of deferred-payment credits, no draft accompanies the documents. The agreement providing for the Canadian bank to pay the seller sixty days after the date of the bill of lading represents the bank's undertaking of a deferred-payment obligation. In this case, no negotiable draft is generated and there is no way to discount the bank's deferred payment obligation. Any advance payment by the bank to the seller often requires a collateral or security interest in the proceeds of the deferred credit.

Such credits developed primarily as a way of avoiding charges and fees associated with acceptance credits.

Standby Letter of Credit

The standby L/C is generally used to guarantee that a party will fulfill its obligation under a contract. Such credits are opened to cover the account party's business obligations to the beneficiary. A standby L/C is thus a bank's guarantee to the beneficiary that a specific sum of the money will be received by the beneficiary in the event of default or nonperformance by the account party under a sales or service contract (Reynolds, 2003). Similar to the documentary L/C, a standby credit is payable against presentation of documents that comply with the terms of the standby credit. The documents required to be presented by the beneficiary often include a sight draft and the beneficiary's written statement of default by the account party.

A major problem with such credits is that payments are often required to be made upon the issuing bank's receipt of a signed statement by the beneficiary that the account party did not perform under the contract and that the credit is currently due and payable. There is a possibility of unfair and capricious calling in of the credit, despite the absence of default or nonperformance by the account party. To protect account parties under a standby credit from such unjustified demand by beneficiaries, the following steps are often recommended:

- Include a clause under the credit requiring that the beneficiary present certification by a third party or court that default has occurred.
- Take out an insurance policy that covers commercial and political risk. This would cover exporters against, inter alia, contract repudiation as well as unfair callings by private entities or governments.
- Take out a surety bond issued by an insurance company (instead of a performance bond issued by a bank) to guarantee performance under the contract. Whereas banks honor a drawing under a standby L/C based on the face

value of the beneficiary's statement of default, insurance companies verify the validity of the claim before payment. If the claim is unfounded, the insurance company will deny payment. However, if the insured's default is proven, payment is made under the credit and thereafter the company will recover from the insured (Kozolchyk, 1996).

The standby L/C is commonly used in the case of contractor bids and performance bonds, advance payments, open account sales, and loan guarantees.

Contractor Bids and Performance Bonds

Bid bonds are issued to a customer to show the seller's real interest and ability to undertake the resulting contract. This is intended to protect buyers from losses incurred in accepting invalid bids. The bid would be legitimately called in if a successful bidder failed to accept the contract.

Example: The Ministry of Defense of the state of Urbania want to buy 400,000 pairs of winter boots for the military. They invite domestic and foreign manufacturers to submit bids. All bidders are also required to submit a bid bond issued by a reputable surety company or a bank. Nunez Shoes, Limited, a U.S. footwear company, is awarded the contract. A few days later, Nunez Shoes writes a letter to the Ministry of Urbania, stating that it cannot carry out the contract because the company does not have enough supplies and an adequate labor force. Based on the contract, the ministry will be entitled to draw under the credit.

Standby credits are also issued to guarantee performance under a sales and service contract. Using the pervious example, suppose Nunez Shoes signs the contract to deliver 400,000 winter boots to Urbania. The ministry could require Nunez Shoes to post a performance bond issued by a reputable bank as guarantee that it will live up to the terms of the sales contract. Performance bond credits are issued for a percentage of the total contract value. Suppose Nunez Shoes manages to deliver only 50 percent of the shoes before the expiry of the sales contract. The ministry will then be entitled to draw under the credit on presentation of the necessary documents.

Performance Guarantees Against Advance Payments

These are bonds issued to guarantee the return of cash advanced by the customer if the seller does not comply with the terms of the contract.

Example: Using the previous example, suppose Nunez Shoes signs the contract with the Ministry of Urbania to supply the winter boots but requires an advance payment of $40,000. The ministry, in turn, could require Nunez Shoes to post an advance payment bond (a standby L/C with a bank to guarantee the return of money advanced by the ministry in the event of default by the seller). In the event that Nunez Shoes does not deliver the product as agreed under the contract, the ministry would be entitled to call in the credit, that is, to recover its advance payment on presentation of complying documents.

Guarantee Against Payments on Open Account

This type of credit protects the seller in the event that the buyer fails to pay or delays payment. The seller asks the buyer to have a standby L/C issued in its favor. Suppose payment is to be made within ninety days to the seller under an open account trans-action and the buyer fails to pay. The seller could then request payment under the credit against presentation of stipulated documents, such as a sight draft, commercial invoice, and the seller's signed written statement.

Loan Guarantees

Standby credits are often issued by banks when an applicant guarantees repay-ment of a loan taken by another party. Suppose a subsidiary of Nunez Shoes, in England, borrows 200,000 British pounds from a bank in London. If the applicant's financial position is not well-known to the bank, the bank could agree to extend the loan, provided the parent company (Nunez Shoes in the United States) guaran-tees payment. Under this arrangement, Nunez Shoes, United States, would have a standby L/C issued in favor of the bank in London. Upon receiving the credit, the London bank will grant the loan to the subsidiary. If Nunez Shoes, England, defaults in repaying the loan, the bank will draw on the credit. In addition to this situation, standby credits are employed to cover rental payments, customs duties, royalties, and tax shelter transactions.

CHAPTER SUMMARY

Consignment sales	Exporter sends product to importer on a deferred-payment basis. Importer pays seller upon sale of product to a third party. Exporter retains title to goods until payment.
Open-account sales	Exporter ships merchandise to overseas customer on credit. Payment is to be made within an agreed time after receipt of merchandise.
Documentary draft	This is a service offered by banks to sellers to facilitate payment of a sale of merchandise on an international basis. Under this method, the exporter draws a draft on a buyer after shipment of the merchandise, requesting payment on presentation of documents (documents against payment) or acceptance of the draft to pay at some future determinable date (documents against acceptance).

Banker's (trade) acceptance	If a draft is drawn on and accepted by a bank, it is called a banker's acceptance. If a draft is accepted by non-bank entities, such as importers, it is trade acceptance.
Role of banks	1. Verification of documents: This is to determine whether the documents appear as listed in the collection order and to advise the party in the event of missing documents. 2. Compliance with instructions in the collection order. 3. Act as agents for collection and assume no responsibility for damages arising out of delay or for the substance and form of documents. However, they have to act in good faith.
Clean collections	This is a documentary draft presented to a buyer for payment of acceptance without being accompanied by shipping documents.
Documentary collections	This is a documentary draft accompanied by shipping documents.
International rules governing documentary collections	Uniform Rules for Collections, 1995, International Chamber of Commerce Publication No. 522.
Documentary letter of credit (L/C)	A document in which a bank or other financial institution assumes liability for payment of the purchase price to the exporter on behalf of an overseas customer.
Parties to the contract	1. Sales contract: Exporter (beneficiary) and importer (account party). 2. Credit reimbursement contract: Importer and issuing bank. 3. L/C contract: Opening bank and beneficiary. 4. Confirmation agreement: Confirming bank and beneficiary.
International rules on L/Cs	The Uniform Customs Practices for Documentary Credits (UCP) 600.
Role of banks in documentary L/Cs	1. Banks should act equitably and in good faith. 2. Independent principle: Credits are separate transactions from sales or other contracts, and banks are in no way concerned with, or bound by, such contracts. The independent principle is subject to a fraud exception. 3. Rule of strict compliance: Exporter cannot compel payment by banks unless the documents presented strictly comply with the terms specified in the credit.

Discrepancies	*Accidental Discrepancies* Discrepancies that can easily be corrected by the beneficiary or the issuing bank. *Minor Discrepancies* Discrepancies that can be corrected by a written waiver from the buyer. *Major Discrepancies* Discrepancies that either cannot be corrected or can only be corrected by an amendment to the L/C.
Cash in advance	A method of payment requiring the buyer to pay before shipment is effected.
Online payment platforms	These platforms enable buyers and sellers to initiate, conduct, and settle international trade transactions over the Internet. They have several advantages over traditional payment methods: less paperwork and enhanced visibility, cost savings, and provision of value-added services.
Fraud in documentary credits	Fraud can be perpetrated by sellers, buyers, or other parties. It can be prevented by taking proactive measures such as verifying the background and credibility of the parties, choosing certain trade terms, and verifying the authenticity of documents.

LETTERS OF CREDIT: SUMMARY

1. *Irrevocable.* L/Cs that cannot be amended or canceled without the agreement of all parties to the credit, i.e., the beneficiary, the buyer, and the issuing bank.
2. *Revocable.* L/Cs that may be amended or canceled by the issuing bank without prior notice to the exporter (beneficiary). However, issuing banks must honor drafts duly negotiated by other banks prior to revocation.
3. *Confirmed.* A credit in which another bank, usually the advising bank, confirms its obligation to honor drafts and documents presented by the beneficiary, in accordance with the terms of the credit. This applies only to an irrevocable L/C, as the revocable L/C would become irrevocable if another bank added its confirmation.
4. *Transferable.* L/Cs that permit a beneficiary to transfer the credit to a second beneficiary. Similar to back-to-back L/Cs, but only one credit is issued.
5. *Back-to-back.* A letter of credit that is issued on the strength of another L/C.
6. *Revolving.* An agreement in which the buyer is allowed to replenish the credit after it is drawn down by a seller.
7. *Red-clause credit.* Advances or pre-export financing provided to an agent or distributor for the purchase of merchandise from a supplier. Such advances are made without presentation of documents.
8. *Green-clause credit.* When advances are made on presentation of warehouse receipts.
9. *Deferred-payment credit.* The seller agrees not to present a sight draft until after a specified period following presentation of documents. No draft need accompany

the documents. When it is accompanied by a draft, it becomes an acceptance L/C.

10. *Standby.* Credit used to guarantee that a party will fulfill its obligation under a sales or service contract. Types of standby L/Cs: contractor bids and performance bonds, performance guarantees against advance payments, guarantees against payments on open account, and loan guarantees.

11. *Straight.* An L/C that is payable at the issuing bank or at a designated bank nominated in the L/C.

12. *Negotiable.* An L/C that can be negotiated at any bank. This means that the issuing bank will reimburse any bank that pays against the documents stipulated in the credit.

REVIEW QUESTIONS

1. Discuss the distribution of risk in the following export payment terms: consignment; time draft.

2. What are the advantages and disadvantages of these payment terms: documentary collections, open account sales, revocable letters of credit?

3. State the different steps involved in a confirmed documentary letter of credit, with payment terms of ninety days sight.

4. Compare and contrast documentary collections and documentary letters of credit.

5. The manager of the letter of credit division of Citibank in Chicago learns that the ship on which a local exporter shipped goods to Yokahama, Japan was destroyed by fire. He knows that the buyer in Yokahama will never receive the goods. The manager, however, received all the documents required under the letter of credit. Should the manager pay the exporter or withhold payment and notify the overseas customer in Japan?

6. Compare the role and responsibility of banks in documentary collections and letters of credit.

7. What is the independent principle?

8. Discuss the rule of strict compliance.

9. Provide an example of a major discrepancy in letters of credit.

10. Briefly describe the following: transferable L/C, back-to-back L/C, deferred L/C, standby L/C.

REFERENCES

Anonymous (2012). Ms Mode deploys TradeCard's trade platform. Trade Finance (March).

Artz, R. (1991). Punitive damages for wrongful dishonor or repudiation of a letter of credit. *Uniform Commercial Code Law Journal*, 24(3):3–48.

Bade, D. (2015). *Export/Import Procedures and Documentation*. New York: Amacom.

Barnes, J. (1994). Defining good faith letter of credit practices. *Loyola of Los Angeles Law Review*, 28: 103–107.

Cheeseright, P. (1994). Market of Reliant in receivership. *Financial Times* (November 5): 7.

David, P. (2017). *International Logistics. The Management of International Trade Operations*. Berea, OH: Cicero Books.

Goldsmith, H. (1989). *Import/Export: A Guide to Growth, Profits and Market Share.* Upper Saddle River, NJ: Prentice-Hall.

International Chamber of Commerce (ICC) (1995). *Uniform Rules for Collections*, no. 522. New York: ICC Publishing Co.

International Chamber of Commerce (ICC) (2007). *Uniform Customs and Practice for Documentary Credits*, no. 600. New York: ICC Publishing Co.

Kelly, J. (1995). Credit management. *Financial Times* (March): i–v.

Kozolchyk, B. (1996). The financial standby: A summary description of practice and related problems. *Uniform Commercial Code Law Journal*, 28(4): 327–374.

Macintosh, K. (1992). Letters of credit: Curbing bad faith dishonor. *Uniform Commercial Code Law Journal*, 25(3): 3–48.

Madura, J. (2011). *International Financial Management.* Mason, OH: South-Western.

Maggiori, H. (1992). *How to Make the World Your Market.* New York: Burning Gate Press.

McLaughlin, G. (1989). Structuring commercial letters of credit transactions to safeguard the interests of the buyer. *Uniform Commercial Code Law Journal*, 21(3): 318–325.

McMahon, A., Marsh, A., Klitzke, P., and Issenman, J. (1994). *The Basics of Exporting.* Austin, TX: Southern United Trade Association.

Murray, C. (2007). *Schmitthoff's Export Trade.* London: Sweet and Maxwell.

Onkvisit, S. and Shaw, J. (2008). *International Marketing: Strategy and Theory.* New York: Routledge.

Powell, G. (2010). Export credit insurance. In Bullivant, G. ed. *Credit Management.* London: Gower.

Reynolds, F. (2003). *Managing Exports: Navigating the Complex Rules, Controls, Barriers and Laws.* New York: Wiley.

Rosenblith, R. (1991). Letter of credit law. *Uniform Commercial Code Law Journal*, 21(3): 171–175.

Rubenstein, N. (1994). The issuer's rights and obligations under a letter of credit. *Uniform Commercial Code Law Journal*, 17(2): 129–174.

Ruggiero, A. (1991). *Financing International Trade.* New York: UNZ and Co.

Ryan, R. (1990). Who should be immune from the fraud in the defense in a letter of credit transaction. *Brooklyn Law Review*, 56: 119–152.

Shapiro, A. (2006). *Multinational Financial Management.* New York: Wiley.

Tuller, L. (1994). *Exporting, Importing and Beyond.* Holbrooke, MA: Bob Adams.

UNCTAD (2009). *Documentary Risk in Commodity Trade.* Geneva: UN.

U.S. ITA (2021). *Basic Guide to Exporting.* New York: Skyhorse Publishing.

Wells, F. and Dulat, K. (1991). *Exporting from Start to Finance.* New York: McGraw-Hill.

Yuan, S. (2007). The TradeCard financial supply chain solution. *International Journal of Cases and Electronic Commerce*, 3(1): 48–70.

World Wide Web Sources

Exports/trade payments

www.shippingsolutions.com/blog/10-terms-you-need-to-know-to-help-you-get-paid-for-exports

Institute of International Banking Law and Practice on financing exports and related topics: www.iiblp.org/

International Trade Closing Cases and Discussions

1. Dishonoring Letters of Credit

In June 2005, JFTC, a Chinese company, agreed to purchase 1,000 metric tons of fertilizers from VA Trading Corporation (VATC) located in Houston, Texas. JFTC obtained a letter of credit from the Bank of China for the purchase price of $1.2 million. Payment was to be made to VATC after delivery of the merchandise and presentation of requisite documents to the Bank of China in accordance with UCP 500.

The market price of fertilizers had declined significantly and the buyer requested a concession. VATC refused to reduce the price. VATC presented the documents specified under the L/C (after shipping the goods to JFTC) to Texas Commerce Bank (TCB), which would forward the documents to the Bank of China. Although TCB pointed out certain discrepancies between the documents and L/C, it did not believe that they would lead to any problems.

The Bank of China notified TCB of the discrepancies and indicated its willingness to contact the buyer (JFTC) about acceptance. JFTC refused to waive the discrepancies and the Bank of China returned the documents to TCB. VATC was not paid for the shipment.

Questions

1. Discuss the various options available to VATC.
2. Do you think the alleged discrepancies between the documents and L/C could be adequate grounds for dishonoring the L/C?
3. Do you think JFTC or its bank provided adequate notice to VATC according to UCP 500?

2. The Independent Principle in Letters of Credit

A bank in New York issued an L/C to a beneficiary (seller) in Spain at the request of the buyer covering the shipment of building products. When the seller presented the documents to the bank for payment, the bank declined to pay on the ground that it had no opportunity to test the quality of the products. The letter of credit did not require that a testing certificate from an independent laboratory accompany the documents.

Questions

1. Was the bank justified in withholding payment?
2. Does the buyer or the bank have the right to demand inspection of the quality of the merchandise?
3. What is the importance of the independent principle for this case?

3. Deferred Payment in Letters of Credit

Bank A issued a deferred-payment L/C in favor of Martin Co. with a promise to pay sixty days from the bill of lading (BL). It also undertook to cover the confirming bank at maturity. Martin Co. presented complying documents to the confirming bank after which the latter made a discounted payment. The beneficiary (Martin Co) then assigned the L/C to the confirming bank. Bank A was not notified of the assignment.

Bank A gave notice to the confirming bank that the L/C was forged and refused payment. It also stated in its response that the confirming bank should have delayed payment till the maturity date before which the fraud would have been discovered. Bank A claims that it did not ask the confirming bank to discount or give value to the documents before the maturity date. The L/C was subject to UCP 600.

Questions

1. Should Bank A pay the confirming bank? Why/why not?
2. Would the outcome be different if Bank A issued an acceptance L/C?

4. Cases of Fraud Using Letters of Credit

Letters of credit are widely used as a means of payment in international trade transactions. They shift the payment risk from the applicant buyer to the bank that guarantees payment to the exporter. According to the independent principle, the letter of credit is separate from and independent of other contracts relating to the transaction. This means that the beneficiary (exporter) does not need to prove fulfilment of his/her obligation in an underlying contract and that the mere presentation of complying documents will entitle the exporter to receive payment from the bank. The increasing number of cases of fraud in L/C transactions has resulted in the recognition of fraud as an exception to the independence principle. A United Nations Report (UNCTAD, 2009) identifies four types of fraud in L/C transactions:

- Falsification of documents by exporters to receive payment from the issuing bank for non-existent cargo.
- Cargo delivered by exporter does not comply with the contract of sale in terms of quality and quantity.
- The same cargo is sold to two or more parties.
- A bill of lading is issued twice for the same cargo.

Case A

The arrangement: A business firm (GSP Ltd) in Indonesia opens an L/C with the Bank of Indonesia (BOI) for the purchase of plastic machinery equipment from a Korean manufacturer (LEK Ltd.). Given the company's credit history with the bank, the BOI opened the L/C for US$74 million in favor of LEK Ltd and required the submission of the contract of sale and a deposit amounting to 1 percent of the value of the L/C as cash collateral. A deferred L/C (the bank pays the exporter on the stipulated date in the L/C provided the terms and conditions are met) was sent to the exporter (LEK Ltd) via the Korean correspondent bank (KB) as advising bank that covered the first phase of the payment (US$40 million).

The two requirements were not met by the buyer: Sales contract was not submitted and no collateral was deposited by the importer. Furthermore, the importer convinced the issuing bank (BOI) to change the L/C from a deferred to a red-clause L/C, which allows the bank to disburse payments to the exporter before delivery of the goods or without delivery of documents. Red-clause credits are rarely provided by banks because of the risks they pose to banks and buyers. The exporter received the payments and never sent the goods. In the meantime, the buyer declared bankruptcy and disappeared. The BOI was left holding the bag.

Lessons: a) Lack of due diligence by the bank, b) there may have been collusion between the buyer and seller, c) the bank should not have agreed to the red-clause credit arrangement.

Case B

The arrangement: A company in Taiwan (ABC Ltd.) enters into a sales contract to purchase scrap metal from a U.S. company (Joe Metals: JM). The contract provided for 100,000 tons to be loaded from the Port of Miami (CIF, to Taipei, Taiwan). For logistics and import duty purposes, it was agreed that the cargo be discharged in South Korea and then loaded (to be arranged by the carrier) on a boat to Taipei. Two L/Cs were opened. The first L/C was payable upon presentation of the bill of lading and other documents and covered 65 percent of the contract price. The second L/C represented the balance upon discharge of the merchandise (freight collect clause).

Only 35,000 tons of scrap metal were loaded but documents showed that 100,000 tons were loaded. The carrier issued documents indicating the loading of 35,000 but these documents were altered by the seller which then allowed the latter to cash the first L/C. The buyer in Taiwan did not receive the merchandise for a while and enquired about the fate of the cargo. The seller responded, stating that the cargo had arrived in Korea and was waiting to be discharged. A few days later, the seller informed the buyer that they were unable to send the cargo because they did not have the money and asked the buyer to release the second L/C. They buyer did as requested.

The seller tells the carrier that the buyer declined to pay the balance and that he/she is putting up the cargo for sale. The carrier was given a letter of indemnity from the seller against any claim and released the goods. The seller sold the goods for the second time and disappeared.

Lessons: a) The bank should not have opened two L/Cs, that is, one for merchandise and one for freight. It should have insisted on one payment "freight prepaid"; b) the buyer should have used a reputable company to inspect and report on the status of the loading operations. The L/C could also include a provision that payment is conditional on the inspection certificate provided by the buyer's inspector; c) due diligence by the buyer, checking on the status of the cargo, could have prevented the fraud.

Case C

Background: In warehouse finance, banks provide finance against collateral of physical stocks of commodities in a warehouse. It is commonly used by farmers in rural areas to access finance against their commodities deposited in warehouses while managing the sale of their crops. It is an ideal means of securing financing because they often do not have sufficient conventional loan collateral.

The bank (finance company) agrees with an independent warehouse operator who is charged with the responsibility of warehousing and controlling the goods on behalf of the bank. Goods are released only upon explicit authorization of the bank. Credit is provided to the owner of the goods up to a certain percentage of the value of the merchandise. Under this arrangement, the warehouse manager issues receipts for each deposit of merchandise and financing is against these warehouse receipts.

The arrangement: A warehousing firm (WF) in Dallas, Texas became involved with Franco Oil (FO) of Houston, Texas, which held a substantial share of the export market for vegetable oils. It was storing FO's merchandise (vegetable oils) in its warehouse in Dallas and issued warehouse receipts against which FO was able to borrow money. In practice, WF used FO to manage the warehouse. There was no effort on the part of WF to investigate information on discrepancies in FO's records. One time, FO reported stocks equal to twice the entire production of the United States. WF's auditors saw water in the samples and they simply accepted the explanation that it was due to broken steam pipes. Neither of these incidents raised any suspicion on the part of WF. A good number of the tanks were filled with salt water and yet WF auditors were told which tanks to check. Subsequent government investigations showed that the merchandise in the warehouse was mostly worthless and FO had received financing estimated at US$200 million.

Lessons: a) borrowers may overstate the value of their merchandise or remove inventory that has already been pledged as collateral from the bank's control. The buyer may also collude with the seller providing invoices with inflated prices; b) banks should use due diligence in making sure that they finance against the fair value of the goods. Warehouse managers should be independent agents who cannot be manipulated by the bank or borrower and their warehouse receipts must correctly reflect the actual volume and quality of merchandise.

CHAPTER 12

Countertrade

LEARNING OBJECTIVES:

12.1 Describe the origins of countertrade

12.2 Understand how countertrade benefits exporters

12.3 Identify the mechanics of a countertrade transaction

12.4 Understand the different theories on countertrade

12.5 Learn the various types of countertrade

12.6 Understand the position of the U.S. government and other multilateral institutions such as the WTO and IMF on countertrade

---

International Trade in Practice

Countertrade Cases

Malaysia expands its countertrade deals with other countries: In 2018, Rostec, a Russian firm, agreed to buy Malaysian palm oil in substantial quantities partly to improve the bilateral trade balance in exchange for arms and other defense products.

Bombardier, a Canadian multinational manufacturer of business jets and rail, signed a contract to deliver rolling stock to Malaysia. The rolling stock will be used on the Kelana Jaya Light Rail transit project. It will work with its local partner to deliver local content estimated at US$600 million for the delivery of twenty-seven new trains. Fourteen local firms are expected to bring another US$100 million of components and services, thus increasing the use of local content to 35 percent.

The Industrial Cooperation Agreement requires vendors to transfer technology, provide industrial training, open access to global markets, develop the local supply chain, and maximize local content.

India's countertrade and offset deals: Russia's firms are opening a helicopter service center in India (and also in Brazil, Peru, and Mexico) under offset deals related to the sale of helicopters. India approved an additional US$1.9 billion for the procurement of 464 Russian-made battle tanks, which will be assembled locally. The Russian firm is expected to increase local production from 40 to 80 percent.

Thales Australia and India's Kalyani Group agreed the design, development, and manufacture of next-generation weapons systems for the defense and law enforcement sectors in India. It supports Thales' bid for the procurement of 350,000 battle carbines. The Australian firm will offer a variant of the F90/EF-88 rifle used by the Australian Defense Force. The Kalyani Group will manufacture the weapon in India combining Thales' technology, know-how, and experience with its own development and manufacturing capabilities. They are produced for Indian and international markets.

India awarded a $2.13 billion contract to Boeing for the production of eight Poseidon anti-submarine warfare aircraft in 2009. The agreement included an offset worth $614 billion with Indian firms to be completed within seven years. Overseas defense companies are required to offset a minimum of 30 percent of the total value of the contract through the transfer of technology, direct purchase of parts or components from Indian defense companies, the creation of manufacturing facilities, and development and training. Boeing has made substantial investment hiring over 12,000 people and working with about 160 local suppliers. However, by 2019, only 20 percent of the US$11 billion offset commitments had materialized. Boeing could be subject to penalties. Overseas defense firms often complain that they find it difficult to find the right local partners to execute offset contracts.

Bilateral barters between Myanmar and China: Myanmar and China agreed to exchange Myanmar's agricultural products such as rice and livestock for China's construction materials, farm implements, and fertilizer. China has appointed a firm to prepare a list of acceptable goods while Myanmar also prepares a list of export products.

ORIGINS OF COUNTERTRADE

Countertrade is any commercial arrangement in which sellers or exporters are required to accept in partial or total settlement of their deliveries, a supply of products from the importing country. In essence, it is a nation's (or firm's) use of its purchasing power as a leverage to force a private firm to purchase or market its marginally undesirable goods or exact other concessions in order to finance its imports, obtain needed hard currency or technology. Although the manner in which the transaction is structured may vary, the distinctive feature of such arrangements is the mandatory performance element that is either required by the importer or importer's government, or made necessary by competitive considerations (Verzariu, 1985; 1992).

The origins of countertrade can be traced to ancient times when international trade was based on the free exchange of goods. Barter flourished in Northern

Mesopotamia as early as 3000 BC when inhabitants traded in textiles and metals. The Greeks also profited by the exchange of olive oil and wine for grain and metals sometime before 2000 BC (Brinton et al., 1984; Anyane-Ntow and Harvey, 1995). Even with the flourishing of a money economy, barter still continued as a medium of exchange. Present-day countertrade involves more than the use of simple barter. It is a complex transaction that includes the exchange of some currency as well as goods between two or more nations. A countertrade transaction may, for example, specify that the seller be paid in foreign currency on the condition that the seller agrees to find markets for specified products from the buyer's country.

The resurgence of countertrade has often been associated with East–West trade. At the start of the 1950s the former communist countries of Eastern Europe faced a chronic shortage of hard (convertible) currency to purchase needed imports. In their dealings with Western countries, they insisted that their products be taken in exchange for imports from the latter countries. This practice also proved quite attractive to many developing nations, which also suffer from a shortage of convertible currency. The use of countertrade has steadily increased and is presently estimated to account for about 20 to 30 percent of world trade (Hennart and Anderson, 1993; Howse, 2010; IRTA, 2021). Although there may be disagreements concerning the current volume of countertrade, the broad consensus is that countertrade constitutes a significant and rapidly growing portion of world commerce (McVey, 1984; Bost and Yeakel, 1992; IRTA, 2021).

A large number of U.S. corporations find it difficult to conduct business with many countries without relying on countertrade. For example, about two-thirds of foreign purchases of American commercial and military jets are paid for with local products instead of cash (Bragg, 1998; Angelidis, Parsa, and Ibrahim, 2004). Businesses are resorting to countertrade in response to increasing costs and declining availability of trade finance. In response to this growing interest, some U.S. banks have established their own countertrade departments (Welt, 1990).

In the 1980s countertrade was mainly used as a vehicle for trade finance. It is now used to meet a broad range of business objectives: capital project financing, production sharing, repatriation of profits from countries with hard currency shortages, and competitive bidding on major government procurements (Caves and Marin, 1992; Egan and Shipley, 1996).

Examples of Countertrade

- Malaysia signed a deal swapping palm oil for fertilizer and machinery with North Korea, Cuba, and Russia. Thailand and Iran agreed to barter rice for oil.
- Indonesia negotiated for a power station project with Asea Brown Boveri and for an air traffic control system with Hughes Aircraft. Counter-purchase obligations were to be 100 percent of the FOB values. The firms export, through a trading company, a range of Indonesian products: cocoa to the United States, coal to Japan, fertilizer to Vietnam and Burma.
- Lockheed Martin agreed to sell F-16 military aircraft to Hungary in exchange for large investment and counter-purchase commitments. The firm agreed to buy US$250 million-worth of Hungarian goods. It established an office in Budapest to participate in tendering and to procure the country's industrial goods for export.

- Taiwan purchased sixty Mirage 2000-5 from a French aviation company, Dussault. In return, Dussault undertook a joint venture with Taiwan's aerospace company, Chenfeng, for the production of key aircraft parts and components for local aircraft and export.

BENEFITS OF COUNTERTRADE

Benefits for Buyers

Transfer of Technology

In exchange for a guaranteed supply of raw materials or other scarce resources, a developed nation will provide the capital, equipment, and technology needed to develop such resources. Western firms, for example, assisted Saudi Arabia in the development of its refinery and petrochemical industry in exchange for the right to purchase a certain amount of oil over a given period of time.

Alleviating Balance of Payments Difficulties

The financial crisis, coupled with adverse movements in the price of key export commodities, such as coffee or sugar, left many developing countries with severe balance-of-payments difficulties. Countertrade has been used as a way of financing needed imports without depleting limited foreign currency reserves. Some countries have even used it as a way of earning hard currency by promoting the export of their domestic output. Countertrade has thus helped these nations avoid the burden of additional borrowing to finance imports as well as the need to restrict domestic economic activity. Countertrade is also used as a method of entering a new market, particularly in product areas that invite strong competition.

Maintaining Stable Prices for Exports

Countertrade allows commodity exporters to maintain nominal prices for their products even in the face of limited or declining demand. The price of the product that is purchased in exchange could be increased to take into account the inflated price of exports. In this way, an exporter can dispose of its commodities without conceding the real price of the product in a competitive market. In the case of cartels, such as OPEC (Organization of Petroleum Exporting Countries), a member could attract customers through countertrade opportunities without violating price guidelines.

Benefits for Exporters

Increased Sales Opportunities

Countertrade generates additional sales that would not otherwise be possible. It also enables entry into difficult markets.

Access to Sources of Supply

Countertrade provides exporters access to a continuous supply of production components, precious raw materials, or other natural resources in return for sales of manufactured goods or technology.

Flexibility in Prices

Countertrade enables the exporter to adjust the price of a product in exchange for overpriced commodities (International Perspective 12.1).

THEORIES ON COUNTERTRADE

A limited number of empirical studies on countertrade has been conducted. The following findings characterize some of the theoretical studies on countertrade practices:

- Countertrade is positively correlated with a country's level of exports. This means that a higher level of international commercial activity is associated with a high level of countertrade (Caves and Marin, 1992; Hennart and Anderson, 1993).
- Countertrade is often used as a substitute for foreign direct investment (FDI). Even though foreign direct investment reduces market transaction costs (i.e., by internalizing sources of raw materials and components through vertical integration), multinational companies resort to countertrade as a second-best solution when host countries impose restrictions on inward FDI. Countries engaged in heavy countertrade tend to be those that severely restrict inward FDI. Foreign direct investment may be less attracted to politically risky countries, in spite of their positive attitudes toward foreign investment. Such countries are likely to have a high level of countertrade activity (Hennart, 1990).
- The stricter the level of exchange controls, the higher the level of countertrade activity. This appears to be a response to the restrictions imposed on the acquisition of foreign currency. Some studies also show that a significant percentage of countertrade has little to do with foreign exchange shortages, but rather was intended to reduce high transaction costs that affect the purchase of technology or intermediate products.
- Countertrade is positively correlated with a country's level of indebtedness. Casson and Chukujama (1990) show that countries with higher debt ratios are more strongly engaged in barter. A country's creditworthiness, as measured by a composite of ratings of international banks, is positively correlated with its barter activities (Hennart and Anderson, 1993).

INTERNATIONAL PERSPECTIVE 12.1

The Mechanics of a Barter Transaction

Suppose a private firm is selling drilling equipment to country A in exchange for ten tons of basmati rice. One method is to use reciprocal performance guarantees such as performance bonds or standby letters of credit (L/Cs). Each party posts a guarantee, and this provides payment to the aggrieved party in the event of failure by the other party to perform its part of the contract (i.e., failure to deliver the goods or delivery of nonconforming goods). However, the fees charged by banks for such guarantees are quite high. Another method is to use an escrow account to secure performance of an obligation by each party. The steps used are as follows:

- The firm opens a documentary L/C in favor of country A. In cases where the product is passed to a trading company, the L/C is opened by the trading company in favor of the nation.
- Country A delivers the rice to the firm or trading company and title is transferred.
- When the title passes to the firm, funds equal to the value of the rice shipped is transferred by the firm under the L/C into an escrow account.
- The firm makes delivery of the drilling equipment simultaneously, or at a later date, to country A and title is transferred to the nation.
- Funds in the escrow account are released to the firm.
- In the event the firm delivers nonconforming goods or fails to deliver the goods, the funds in the escrow account are paid to the nation.

FORMS OF COUNTERTRADE

Countertrade takes a variety of forms (see Figure 12.1). Such transactions can be divided into two broad categories:

- Transactions in which products and/or services are traded in exchange for other products and/or services: these include barter, switch trading, and clearing arrangements.
- Transactions that feature two parallel money-for-goods transactions: these include buy-back, counter-purchase and offset arrangements.

Exchange of Goods (Services) for Goods (Services)

Barter

A classic barter arrangement involves the direct exchange of goods/services between two trading parties (see International Perspective 12.1). An exporter from country A to country B is paid by a reciprocal export from country B to country A and no money changes hands. The transaction is governed by a single contract. In view of its limited flexibility, barter accounts for about 4 percent of countertrade contracts (Fletcher, 2009). The major problems with barter relate to the determination of the relative value of the goods traded and the reluctance of banks to finance or guarantee such transactions.

Examples: In 2009, India agreed to barter its machinery and equipment used for gemstone cutting and polishing for precious and semi-precious stones from the Philippines. Thailand agreed to barter its fruits for Chinese locomotives, passenger buses, and armored cars.

FIGURE 12.1 Classification of Forms of Countertrade

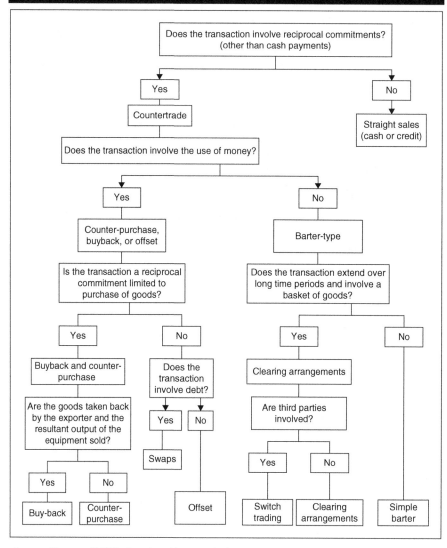

Source: Hennart (1990). Reprinted by permission

Switch Trading

This is an arrangement in which a switch trader will buy or market countertraded products for hard currency (Figure 12.2). The switch trader will often demand a sizable fee in the form of a discount on the goods delivered.

> ***Example:*** A U.S. company exports fertilizer to Pakistan. However, the goods to be counter delivered by Pakistan are of little interest to the U.S. seller. A Romanian company (a switch trader) converts the Pakistani goods into cash, pays the U.S. exporter and retains a commission.

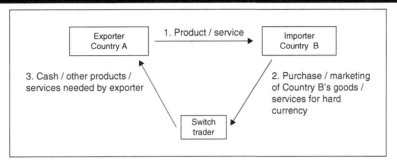

FIGURE 12.2 Switch Trading

FIGURE 12.3 Clearing Arrangement

Clearing Arrangements

Under these arrangements, two governments agree to purchase a certain volume of each other's goods and/or services over a certain period of time, usually a year. Each country sets up an account in one currency, for example, clearing dollar, pound, or local currency. When a trade imbalance exists, settlement of accounts can be in the form of hard-currency payments for the shortfall, a transfer of goods, issuance of a credit against the following year's clearing arrangement, or by switch trading. In switch trading, the creditor country can sell its credit to a switch trader for a discount and receive a cash payment. The switch trader will subsequently sell the corresponding goods to third parties (see Figure 12.3).

> *Example:* A Swedish company, Sukab, accumulated a large surplus in its clearing account with Pakistan. Sukab sold its credit to Marubeni, a Japanese company, at a discount and Marubeni in turn liquidated this imbalance by purchasing Pakistani cotton and exporting it to a third county for hard currency.

Parallel Transactions

Buyback (Compensation Agreement)

In a buyback or compensation transaction, a private firm will sell or license technology or build a plant (with payment in hard currency) and agree to purchase, over a given number of years, a certain proportion of the output produced from the use of the technology or plant. The output is to be purchased in hard currency. However, since the products are closely related, a codependency exists between the trading

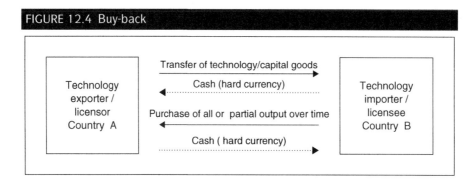

FIGURE 12.4 Buy-back

parties (see Figure 12.4). The duration of a compensation arrangement could range from a few years to thirty years or longer in cases in which the technology supplier (seller) is dependent upon the buyer's output for itself and its subsidiaries. The arrangement involves two contracts, each paid in hard currency, that is, one for the delivery of technology and equipment and another for the buyback of the resulting output. The two contracts are linked by a protocol that, inter alia, stipulates that the output to be purchased by the technology supplier is to be produced with the technology delivered. Since the agreement entails a transfer of proprietary technology, it is important to pay special attention to the protection of patents, trademarks, and know-how, as well as to the rights of the technology recipient (importer/buyer) with respect to these industrial property rights. Buybacks are estimated to account for 21 percent of countertrade transactions (International Perspective 12.2).

> *Examples:* A Japanese company exports computer chip processing and design technology to Korea, Singapore, and Taiwan, with a promise to purchase a certain percentage of the output over a given period of time. Levi Strauss transfers its know-how and trademark to a Hungarian firm for the production and sale of its products, with an agreement to purchase and market the output in Western Europe.

Counter-purchase

As in a compensation arrangement, counter-purchase consists of two parallel hard currency-for-goods transactions (see Figure 12.5). However, in counter-purchase, a firm sells goods and/or services to an importer, promising to purchase from the latter or other entities in the importing nation goods that are unrelated to the items sold. The duration of such transactions is often short (three to five years), and the commitment usually requires a reciprocal purchase of less than the full value of the original sale. In cases in which the reciprocal purchase involves goods that are of low quality or in excess supply, the firm usually resells them to trading companies at a discount. Since the arrangement is often governed by two separate contracts, financing can be organized in a way that is similar to any other export transaction. In addition to flexibility in financing, the contractual separation also provides for separate provisions with regard to guarantee coverage, maturity of payments, and deliveries. As in compensation agreements, the two contracts are linked by a third contract that ties the purchase and sales contracts together and includes terms such as the ratio

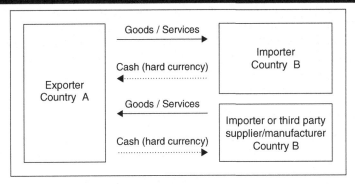

FIGURE 12.5 Counter-purchase

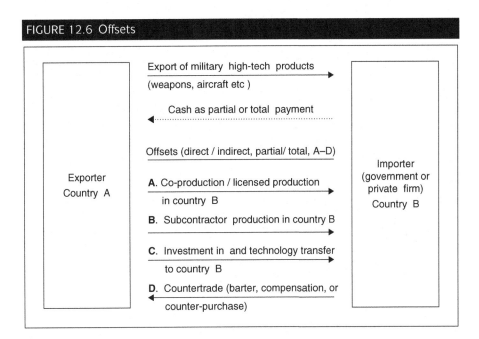

FIGURE 12.6 Offsets

between purchases and sales, starting time of both contracts, the import–export verification system, and so forth (Welt, 1990). Counter-purchase accounts for 54 percent of countertrade transactions (Fletcher, 2009) (International Perspective 12.3).

Examples: Rockwell and the Government of Zimbabwe signed a contract in which Rockwell offered to purchase Zimbabwe's ferro chrome and nickel in exchange for its sale of a printing press to Zimbabwe.

Offsets

An offset is a transaction in which an exporter allows the purchaser, generally a foreign government, to "offset" the cost of purchasing its (the exporter's) product (Cole, 1987) (see Figure 12.6). Such arrangements are mainly used for defense-related sales,

sales of commercial aircraft, or sales of other high-technology products. Offsets are used by many countries as a way to compensate for the huge hard-currency payments resulting from the purchase as well as to create investment opportunities and employment. Such arrangements became widespread after 1973 when OPEC sharply increased the price of oil and countries were left with limited hard currency to pay for major expenditures (Schaffer, 1989; Egan and Shipley, 1996).

Direct Offsets

These are contractual arrangements often involving goods or services related to the products exported. Direct offsets include co-production, sub-contractor production, investments, and technology transfer.

Coproduction: This is an overseas production arrangement, usually based on a government-to-government agreement that permits a foreign government or producer to acquire the technical information to manufacture all or part of equipment or a component originating in the exporting country. It may include a government-to-government production under license. The essential difference between coproduction and licensed production is that the former is normally a joint venture, while the latter does not entail ownership and/or management of the overseas production by the technology supplier. In coproduction, there is usually a government-to-government negotiation, whereas licensed production is based on direct commercial arrangements between the foreign manufacturer and host government or producer. In most cases, coproduction and licensed production are direct offsets because the resulting output directly fulfills part of the sales obligation.

> *Example:* France purchased AWACS (airborne warning and control system) aircraft from Boeing, based on a co-production arrangement between the U.S. and French governments. According to the agreement, 80 percent of the contract value was to be offset by the purchase of engines produced through a joint venture between General Electric and a French firm.

Subcontractor production: This is usually a direct commercial arrangement between a manufacturer and an overseas producer (in the host country) for the production of a part or component of the manufacturer's export article. Such an arrangement does not often involve licensing of technological information.

> *Example:* Lockheed Martin and the government of Poland reached a $3.8 billion deal for the latter's purchase of F-16s that included subcontracts with Polish firms to produce "the Pratt & Whitney engine for the F-16" as well as "commercial jet parts for business aircraft," which would then be exported by Poland back to the United States (Peterson, 2011).

Overseas investments: These are investments arising from the offset agreement that usually take the form of capital investment to establish or expand a company in the purchasing country.

Example: Company A, a U.S. firm, makes an investment in Company B, a foreign firm located in country C, so that Company B can create a new production line to produce a component of a defense article that is subject to an offset agreement between Company A and country C. The transaction would be categorized as investment and would be a direct offset because the investment involves an item covered by the offset agreement.

Technology transfer: Even though technology transfer provisions could be included in coproduction or licensed production arrangements, they are often distinct from both categories. A technology transfer arrangement usually involves the provision of technical assistance and R&D capabilities to the joint venture partner or other firms as part of the offset agreement.

Example: Spain purchases F–18 aircraft from the United States under an offset arrangement that requires the transfer of aerospace and other related technology to Spain.

Indirect Offsets

Indirect offsets are contractual arrangements in which goods and services unrelated to the exports are acquired from or produced in, the host (purchasing) country. These include, but are not limited to, certain forms of foreign investment, technology transfer, and countertrade.

Example: As part of the cooperative defense agreement, the Netherlands purchased patriot fire units from Raytheon Corporation of the United States for $305 million. Raytheon agreed to provide $115 million in direct offsets and $120 million in indirect offsets. The latter obligation was to be discharged through the purchase of goods and services in the Netherlands.

Arms sales account for a substantial part of offset transactions, which, in turn makes up for the largest percentage of countertrade deals.

Examples: Company A, a U.S firm, makes arrangements for a line of credit at a financial institution for Company B, a foreign firm located in country C, so that Company B can produce an item that is not subject to the offset agreement between Company A and country C. The transaction would be categorized as credit assistance and would be indirect because the credit assistance is unrelated to an item covered by the offset agreement.

Company A, a U.S. firm, purchases various off-the-shelf items from Company B, a foreign firm located in country C, but none of these items will be used by Company A to produce the defense article subject to the offset agreement between Company A and country C. The transaction would be categorized as purchases and would, like all purchase transactions, be indirect.

INTERNATIONAL PERSPECTIVE 12.2

Organizing for Countertrade

Once a firm has made a decision to countertrade, it has two organizational options: to use third parties such as consultants and trading houses, or establish a countertrade department within the company. The latter approach has the following benefits and disadvantages.

Advantages	Disadvantages
Direct contact with the customer	Costly and mostly suitable for multinational companies with broad-based product lines
Opportunity for learning and flexibility	Complex and involves corporate planning and coordination of staff
Confidentiality and control over the operation	Limited expertise; problems with disposing of countertraded goods

COUNTERTRADE AND THE WTO

The prevalence of countertrade practices has directed the attention of policymakers to its potentially disruptive effects on international trade. Trade experts claim that countertrade represents a significant departure from the principles of free trade and could possibly undermine the delicate multilateral trading system that was carefully crafted after World War II. This movement towards bilateral trading arrangements deprives countries of the benefits of multilateral trade that GATT/WTO negotiated to confer upon members. Private countertrade transactions, however, fall outside the purview of the GATT, which regulates only governmental actions.

In addition, countertrade tends to undermine trade based on comparative advantage and prolongs inefficiency and misallocation of resources. A country, for example, may have to purchase from a high-cost/low-quality overseas supplier to fulfill its obligation under the export arrangement. Countertrade also slows down the exchange process and results in higher transaction costs in the form of converting goods into money, warehousing, and discounting to a trader when it cannot use the goods received.

Countertrade is also inconsistent with the national treatment standard, which is embodied in most international and regional trade agreements. The national treatment standard of the GATT/WTO, for example, requires that imported goods be taxed and regulated in the same manner as domestically produced goods. Any commercial transaction that requires the overseas supplier (exporter) to purchase a specified portion of the value of the exports from the purchaser would violate the national treatment standard (Roessler, 1985).

Countertrade constitutes a restriction on imports. The GATT/WTO prohibits restrictions other than duties, taxes, or other charges applied to imports. This means that if import licenses are granted on the condition that the imports are linked to exports, such countertrade practices would constitute a trade restriction prohibited under the general agreement. Without this government restriction, the producer would be able to import any amount of product that efficiency and consumer demand dictated. Such restrictions would be in conformity with the agreement if they are imposed to safeguard a country's balance of payments (external financial position), as well as to protect against a sudden surge in imports of particular products (emergency actions).

COUNTERTRADE AND THE INTERNATIONAL MONETARY FUND

The International Monetary Fund (IMF) imposes a dual regime: on the one hand, it attempts to deter members from restricting international payments and transfers for current international transactions, while, on the other hand, it permits its members to regulate international capital movements as they see fit. Payments for current transactions involve an immediate quid pro quo (i.e., payments in connection with foreign trade, interest, profit, dividend payments, etc.), while capital payments are unilateral (loans, investments, etc.). A governmental measure requiring or stimulating countertrade would constitute an exchange restriction on current transactions if it involved a direct limitation on the availability or use of foreign currency.

GOVERNMENTS' ATTITUDES TOWARD COUNTERTRADE

Consistent with their commitment to a nondiscriminatory trading system, many countries are opposed to government-mandated countertrade because it distorts the free flow of trade and investment. Yet, they do not publicly discourage firms from engaging in countertrade (U.S. ITC, 1985; Office of Management and Budget, 1986).

The U.S. policy on countertrade was developed in 1983 by an interagency working group. The policy:

- prohibits federal agencies from promoting countertrade in their business or official contracts
- adopts a hands-off approach toward those arrangements which do not involve the U.S. government or are pursued by private parties. This means that the U.S. government will not oppose participation of U.S. companies in countertrade deals unless such activity has negative implications on national security
- provides no special accommodation for cases involving such transactions. The Export–Import Bank (EXIM Bank) will not provide financing support for the countertrade component of a transaction or accept countertrade as security, but the U.S. export component is eligible for all types of EXIM Bank support. Any repayment to EXIM Bank must be in hard currency and not conditional on the fulfillment of a side contract associated with countertrade.

In view of congressional concern with respect to such practices, the 1998 Trade Act mandated the establishment of an office of barter within the Department of Commerce's International Trade Administration and of an interagency group on countertrade. The Barter and Countertrade Unit established in 2005 within the Department of Commerce provides advisory services to firms interested in such transactions, while the interagency group on countertrade reviews and evaluates U.S. policy on countertrade and makes recommendations to the president and Congress.

Some countries have officially instituted mandatory countertrade requirements for any transaction over a certain value. Australia, for example, mandates local content and other investment requirements for all defense purchases valued at US$5 million and above (Liesch, 1991). Certain countries have passed laws providing for counter-purchase operations and the extension of bank guarantees in the form of perform-ance bonds. Indonesia, for example, established a countertrade division within the Ministry of Trade and has mandated countertrade requirements for any transaction exceeding $500,000 (Verdun, 1985; Liesch, 1991). Other countries may not have an official policy on countertrade or may even be opposed to it due to their position on free trade. However, this opposition often yields to the realities of international trade and competition, and a number of these countries are seen providing tacit approval to such transactions (International Perspective 12.4).

INTERNATIONAL PERSPECTIVE 12.3

Negotiating Countertrade Contracts: Pointers

Costs

All costs are included in one price. The price also includes the commission pay-able to dispose of the countertraded goods.

Contract(s)

One or separate contracts can be used. Separate contracts are signified by three legal documents: the original sales contract, which is similar to any standard export contract; the subsequent agreement to purchase from the original buyer a certain amount of goods over a given time period, and some type of protocol that ties the two contracts together.

Barter Contracts

Barter usually requires one contract. Key provisions include:

1. description of goods to be sold and countertraded;
2. guarantee of quality;
3. penalty or other arrangements in the event of late delivery, failure to deliver, or delivery of nonconforming goods. This includes a bank guar-antee or other guarantee in the form of standby L/C in the event of default and providing for full payment; and
4. provisions for settlement of disputes.

Buy-backs, Counter-purchase, and Offset Contracts

Such contracts require the use of one or separate contracts. Key provisions include:

1. The compensation ratio: This establishes the counter-purchase commitment by the original exporter.
2. The range of products to be countertraded: Parties must agree on the list of products to be purchased.
3. Assignment clause: This enables the original seller to transfer its counter-purchase or buyback obligation to a trading house or a barter business club.
4. Penalty clause: This provides for penalties in the event that the original seller fails to fulfill its obligations (i.e., quality specifications and delivery schedules).
5. Marketing restrictions: It may be important to secure the right to dispose of the countertraded goods in any market.
6. Provisions on force majeure (delay or default in performance caused by conditions beyond the parties' control), applicable law (i.e., the law governing the contract), and dispute settlement.

INTERNATIONAL PERSPECTIVE 12.4

Countertrade with Latin American Countries

A study on countertrade with Latin American countries (Angelidis et al., 2004) reported the results of a survey of firms engaged in countertrade transactions. The survey revealed that the following industries account for over 75 percent of transactions: defense (33.3 percent), manufacturing (30.3 percent) and chemicals (27.3 percent). The participants largely employed counter-purchases and offsets.

The survey also provided a detailed analysis of the major reasons for and challenges of countertrading with these countries.

Reasons for countertrade

- Inadequate foreign currency reserves
- A way to gain competitive advantage
- The only way to do business, demanded by customers
- Increases production capacity and helps achieve growth
- Supply of reliable and low-cost inputs
- Circumvents protectionist regulations; reduces adverse impact of foreign currency fluctuations
- Releases blocked funds
- Increased difficulty of obtaining credit for the buyer
- Availability of expertise in countertrade for buyer or seller

Challenges of Countertrade

- Often involves complicated and time-consuming negotiations
- May result in increased transaction costs, product mismatch, and the purchase of low-quality goods

- Problems with disposition of acquired (lack of ready) merchandise, price-setting, and loss of purchasing flexibility
- Involvement of third parties and the possibility of customers becoming competitors.

CHAPTER SUMMARY

What is countertrade?	Countertrade is any commercial arrangement in which the exporter is required to accept in partial or total settlement of his/her deliveries, a supply of products from the importing country. Barter can be traced to ancient times. Presently, countertrade is estimated to account for 15–20 percent of world trade.
Benefits of countertrade	Benefits for buyers: *1. Transfer of technology* *2. Alleviation of balance of payments difficulties* *3. Market access and maintenance of stable prices* Benefits for exporters: *1. Increased sales opportunities* *2. Access to sources of supply* *3. Flexibility in prices*
Theories on countertrade	*1. Countertrade is positively correlated with a country's level of exports.* *2. Countertrade is partly motivated in order to substitute for foreign direct investment.* *3. The stricter the level of exchange controls, the higher the level of countertrade activity.*
Forms of countertrade	Exchange of goods/services for goods/services 1. *Barter:* Direct exchange of goods and services between two trading parties. 2. *Switch trading:* An arrangement in which the switch trader will buy or market countertraded goods for hard currency. 3. *Clearing arrangement:* A method in which two governments agree to purchase a certain volume of each other's goods/services over a given period of time. In the event of trade imbalance, settlement could be in hard currency payments, transfer of goods, issuance of credit, or use of switch trading. Parallel transactions 1. *Buy-back:* An arrangement in which a private firm will sell or license technology to an overseas customer with an agreement to purchase part of the output produced from the use of such technology. The agreement involves two contracts, both of which are discharged by payment of hard currency.

2. *Counter-purchase:* Two parallel transactions in which a firm exports a product to an overseas buyer with a promise to purchase from the latter or other parties in the country goods not related to the items exported.
3. *Offsets:* A transaction in which an exporter allows the purchaser, usually a foreign government, to reduce the cost of purchasing the exporter's product by co-production, sub-contracting, investments, and transfers of technology.

Offsets

Direct offsets
1. *Co-production:* Joint venture or licensing arrangements with overseas customer.
2. *Sub-contractor production:* Arrangement for production in the importing country of parts or components of the export product destined to the latter.
3. *Investments and transfer of technology:* Certain offset agreements provide for investments and technology transfer to the importing country.
Indirect offsets: Offset arrangements in which goods and services unrelated to the exports are acquired from or produced in the importing country.

Countertrade and the GATT/WTO

Concerns of the GATT/WTO with countertrade:
1. *Countertrade represents a significant departure from the principles of free trade based on comparative advantage.*
2. *Countertrade results in higher transaction costs.*
3. *Countertrade is inconsistent with the national treatment standard which is embodied in most trade agreements.*

Governments' attitude towards countertrade

U.S. government policy towards countertrade:
1. *U.S. government prohibits federal agencies from promoting countertrade in their business.*
2. *Adopts a hands-off approach in relation to private transactions.*
Some countries have a countertrade requirement for certain purchases exceeding a given amount. Such transactions are quite common in defense purchases.

REVIEW QUESTIONS

1. What are the major factors accounting for the resurgence of countertrade?
2. What is the benefit of countertrade for exporters?
3. "Countertrade is used as a substitute for foreign direct investment." Discuss.
4. What is the difference between switch trading and a clearing arrangement?
5. Describe the steps involved in a typical barter transaction.
6. Compare and contrast buy-back with a counter-purchase arrangement.
7. Discuss direct offsets and its components.

8. What are the challenges of countertrade with Latin American countries?
9. What is the U.S. government's attitude toward countertrade?
10. Discuss the concerns of WTO with countertrade.

REFERENCES

Angelidis, J., Parsa, F., and Ibrahim, N. (2004). Countertrading with Latin American countries: A compare analysis of attitudes of United States firms. *International Journal of Management*, 21(4): 435–444.

Anyane-Ntow K. and Harvey, C. (1995). A countertrade primer. *Management Accounting*, 76(10): 47–50.

Bost, P. and Yeakel, J. (1992). Are we ignoring countertrade? *Management Accounting*, 76(6): 43–47.

Bragg, A. (1998). Bartering comes of age. *Sales and Marketing Management*, January: 61–63.

Brinton, C., Christopher, J., Wolff, R., and Winks, R. (1984). *A History of Civilization* (vol. I). Upper Saddle River, NJ: Prentice-Hall.

Casson, M. and Chukujama, F. (1990). Countertrade theory and evidence. In Buckley, P. and Clegg, J., eds. *Multinational Enterprises in Less Developed Countries*. London: Macmillan.

Caves, R. and Marin, D. (1992). Countertrade transactions: Theory and evidence. *Economic Journal*, 102(414): 1171–1183.

Cole, J. (1987). Evaluating offset agreements: Achieving a balance of advantages. *Law and Policy in International Business*, 19: 765–811.

Egan, C. and Shipley, D. (1996). Strategic orientations toward countertrade opportunities in emerging markets. *International Marketing Review*, 13: 102–120.

Fletcher, R. (2009). Countertrade and international outsourcing: A relationship and network perspective. *Journal of International University in Geneva (IUG) Business Review*, 2(1): 25–43.

Hennart, J. F. (1990). Some empirical dimensions of countertrade. *Journal of International Business Studies*, 21: 243–270.

Hennart, J. and Anderson, E. (1993). Countertrade and the minimization of transaction costs: An empirical examination. *Journal of Law, Economics and Organization*, 9: 290–314.

Howse, R. (2010). International trade: Beyond the countertrade taboo: Why the WTO should take another look at barter and countertrade. *University of Toronto Law Journal*, 60: 289–303.

International Reciprocal Trade Association (IRTA) (2021). The Barter and Trade Industry. www.commPRO.biz

Liesch, P. (1991). *Government Mandated Countertrade: Deals of Arm Twisting*. Brookfield, VT: Gower Press.

McVey, T. (1984). Commercial practices, legal issues and policy dilemmas. *Law and Policy in International Business*, 16: 23–26.

Office of Management and Budget (OMB) (1986). *Second Annual Report on the Impact of Offsets in Defense–Related Exports*. Washington, DC: U.S. Government Printing Office.

Peterson, C. (2011). Defense and commercial trade offsets: Impacts on the US industrial base raise economic and national security concerns. *Journal of Economic Issues*, XLV(2): 485–491.

Roessler, F. (1985). Countertrade and the GATT legal system. *Journal of World Trade Law*, 19(6): 604–614.

Schaffer, M. (1989). *Winning the Countertrade War: New Export Strategies for America*. New York: Wiley.

U.S. Department of Commerce, Bureau of Industry and Security (2020). *Offsets in Defense Trade.* Washington, DC: U.S. Government Printing Office. www.bis.doc.gov/osies.

U.S. International Trade Commission (ITC) (1985). *Assessment of the Effects of Barter and Countertrade Transactions on U.S. Industries.* Washington, DC: U.S. Government Printing Office.

Verdun, V. (1985). Are governmentally imposed countertrade requirements violations of the GATT? *Yale Journal of International Law*, 11:191–215.

Verzariu, P. (1985). *Countertrade, Barter and Offsets: New Strategies for Profit in International Trade*. New York: McGraw–Hill.

Verzariu, P. (1992). Trends and developments in international countertrade. *Business America*, 113: 2–6.

Welt, L. (1990). Unconventional forms of financing: Buyback/compensation/barter. *Journal of International Law and Politics*, 22: 461–473.

World Wide Web Resources

Information on global countertrade, legal and regulatory environment and conferences pertaining to countertrade and information on the American Countertrade Association: www.globaloffset.org/

Articles on countertrade: www.investopedia.com/terms/c/countertrade.asp

News and publications on countertrade: www.barternews.com/countertrade.htm

International Trade Closing Cases and Discussions

1. The Bofors–India Countertrade Deal

Bofors AB is a Swedish company that specializes in the manufacturing and sales of weapon systems such as anti-aircraft/anti-tank guns, artillery, and other ammunition. The Indian government concluded an agreement with Bofors AB for the purchase of 410 FH77B howitzers ($1.3 billion) in 1986. The FH77B howitzer is a powerful, highly mobile artillery system. It has a gun with a range of 30 km and the capability to fire three rounds in 13 seconds. It can be integrated with a 6x6 all-terrain vehicle.

The agreement provided for the purchase of goods from India amounting to not less than 50 percent of the value of the contract. Given its lack of experience in countertrade, Bofor AB signed a contract with other Swedish and U.S. trading companies to fulfill its countertrade agreement with India. Among these companies, Sukab took the leading role due to its vast experience in international trade and expertise in countertrade. Sukab is owned by over eighty Swedish companies and was set up after World War II to promote Swedish exports.

Pursuant to the agreement, Sukab promoted the sale of Indian goods in Sweden through various channels including seminars held by Swedish trade councils and chambers of commerce. It also set up offices in India to provide training on the best ways to export Indian goods to Sweden.

The Indian government had to approve all the products being exported. Bofors AB was provided with a list of approved products. Certain products were specifically excluded from exports.

The major factor that motivated India to enter into the countertrade arrangement was its lack of sufficient hard currency to pay for the purchase of the howitzers. The countertrade arrangement provided an opportunity to India to generate enough hard currency to fulfill a portion of its commitments. Furthermore, the arrangement allowed India to expand its distribution channels and gain new markets. The countertrade arrangement also allowed Bofors AB to win the contract over other competing firms.

Questions

1. Do you think this to be an ideal trading arrangement for Bofors AB?
2. Would this form of trade arrangement be more beneficial to India than Bofors? Explain.

2. Offsets in U.S. Defense Trade

Offsets in defense trade encompass a range of industrial compensation arrangements required by foreign governments as a condition of the purchase of defense articles and services from a non-domestic source. This mandatory compensation can be directly related to the purchased defense article or service or it can involve activities or goods unrelated to the defense sale. The U.S. government policy on offsets in defense trade states that the government considers offsets to be "economically inefficient and trade distorting," and prohibits any agency of the U.S. Government from encouraging, entering directly into, or committing U.S. firms to any offset arrangement in connection with the sale of defense articles or services to foreign governments. Defense contractors in the United States generally see offsets as a reality of the marketplace for companies competing for international defense sales. Several U.S. defense contractors acknowledge that offsets are usually necessary in order to make defense sales—sales which can help support the U.S. industrial base. United States firms are required to report annually on contracts for the sale of defense articles or defense services to foreign governments or foreign firms that are subject to offset agreements exceeding $5 million in value, and offset transactions completed in the performance of existing offset commitments for which offset credit of $250,000 or more has been claimed from the foreign representative (U.S. Department of Commerce, 2020).

During 1993–2018, sixty-four U.S. firms reported entering into 1,179 offset-related defense export sales contracts worth $203.6 billion with fifty-one countries. The associated offset agreements were valued at $120 billion. During that period, direct offsets accounted for 39.25 percent of the actual value of the reported offset transactions, with indirect offsets accounting for 59.12 percent. In 2018, direct offsets (transactions directly related to the defense export sale with an associated offset agreement) accounted for 53.85 percent of the actual value of reported offset transactions. Indirect offsets (transactions not directly related to the defense export sale with an associated offset agreement) accounted for 46.31 percent of the actual value of reported offset transactions. The top three

TABLE 12.1 U.S. Merchandise Exports and Reported Offset Activity, 2003–2018 (U.S $ million)

Year	Total merchandise exports	DR merchandise* exports	Value of DR exports with offset contracts	Value of offset agreements
2003	724,771	11,565	7293	9110
2004	814,875	11,884	4934	4331
2005	901,082	12,835	2260	1464
2006	1,025,968	16,629	5265	3655
2007	1,148,199	16,894	6932	5469
2008	1,287,442	16,594	6442	3835
2009	1,056,043	14,796	11,065	6,847
2010	1,278,495	15,304	4019	2451
2011	1,482,508	14,911	10,989	5,665
2012	1,545,821	17,231	25,717	10,425
2013	1,578,517	17,617	10,015	5,182
2014	1,621,874	20,555	13,075	7,709
2015	1,503,328	19,933	8,180	3,183
2016	1,451,460	21,270	4,352	1,491
2017	1,547,195	18,965	3,201	2,091
2018	1,665,688	18,357	1,462	5,147

*DR: Defense-related merchandise exports.

Source: U.S. Department of Commerce, 2020

TABLE 12.2 Summary of U.S. Offset Transactions, 2003–2018

Year	Actual offset transaction value (US$ million)	Credit offset transaction value (US$ million)	Number of U.S. firms	Number of transactions	Number of countries
2003	3563	4008	17	689	31
2004	4935	5366	16	710	33
2005	4722	5439	13	624	30
2006	4706	4906	16	661	28
2007	3805	4742	19	633	28
2008	3291	4768	22	671	30
2009	3495	4129	23	702	28
2010	3608	4477	25	707	28
2011	3880	5062	21	740	31
2012	3438	3843	22	690	30
2013	3189	3563	21	546	32
2014	3864	4289	17	672	29
2015	5049	5323	19	651	26
2016	2634	3064	20	508	26
2017	4577	5349	21	543	29
2018	4314	4387	12	422	25

Source: U.S. Department of Commerce, 2020

TABLE 12.3 Number of U.S. Offset Transactions by Category and Type with Multipliers, 1993–2018

Transaction category	Total	Direct	Indirect	Unspecified	MGT1
Purchasing	7,455	313	7134	8	531
Subcontracting	3,740	3,176	559	5	326
Technology transfer	1,811	836	953	22	400
Co-production	599	583	12	4	33
Training	481	219	253	9	165
Investment	403	50	347	6	114
Licensed production	329	201	126	2	27
Credit assistance	183	18	165	0	33
Other	1,172	308	778	86	287
Total	16,173	5704	10,327	142	1,916

Source: U.S. Department of Commerce, 2020

offset transaction categories reported by industry for 2018 were purchases, subcontracting, and technology transfer (U.S. Department of Commerce, 2020). These three categories represented 66 percent of all offset transactions reported for 2018 (by value) (Figures 12.1 to 12.3). United States prime contractors develop long-term supplier relationships with foreign subcontractors based on short-term offset requirements. These new relationships, combined with the mandatory offset requirements related to offset agreements, can limit future business opportunities for U.S. subcontractors and suppliers, with negative consequences for the domestic industrial base.

PART V

Financing Techniques and Vehicles

CHAPTER 13

Capital Requirements and Private Sources of Financing

LEARNING OBJECTIVES:

13.1 Describe the external sources of export financing

13.2 Learn about the several funding facilities provided by the SBA for exporters

13.3 Identify the sources of equity funding for potential exporters

13.4 Learn about export factoring

13.5 Understand intermediate and long-term methods of export financing such as buyer credit, forfaiting, and export leasing

International Trade in Practice

Private Sources of Export Financing: The Case of Myanmar

Myanmar is a country located in Southeast Asia and occupies a strategic location near major Indian Ocean shipping lanes. In 2016, it emerged out of economic isolation that had lasted for five decades. With the introduction of democracy and other political reforms, Western countries have lifted most of the economic sanctions and the country has been actively engaged in international business. It attracts interest from the international business community due to its rich natural resources, a growing market of over 53 million people, a young labor force, and prime geographical location close to major Asian countries such as China and India. It exports a range of commodities such as natural gas, wood products, fish, rice, textiles, and minerals to countries such as China, Thailand, Japan, Singapore, and India. The country has a growing trade imbalance with imports exceeding exports by over US$4 billion a year since 2014. Its major imports include vehicles, fuel, vegetable oil, pharmaceuticals, industrial machinery, and construction equipment. Presently, it puts major emphasis on the creation of private sector opportunities and attraction of investment by welcoming foreign companies to speed up and sustain economic growth.

Myanmar has a small but growing financial industry. It has nineteen small-scale closely held banks, four state-owned banks, several insurance companies, and a handful of microfinance institutions. The financial system makes a modest contribution to economic growth. The ratio of financial sector credit to GDP is relatively small (14 percent of GDP) compared to 97 percent for Vietnam and 154 percent for Thailand. Less than 10 percent of private sector firms borrow from the banking sector. Most commercial transactions are settled by cash.

The trade finance sector needs major improvements in order to facilitate international trade transactions.

- Only a small number of banks provide documentary-based credits for importers or exporters. The prohibition of trade credit insurance also limits the expansion of open account sales, critical for industries with a short payment cycle such as textiles and clothing.
- The use of letters of credit (L/Cs) is limited by the banks' requirements for collateral anywhere between 30 and 100 percent of the value of the credit. The rules allow for collateral in the form of cash or land but exclude movable assets.
- Receivables financing such as factoring is at an initial stage of development and most banks are not familiar with such facilities.
- In order to protect the local banking industry, foreign banks are confined to offering trade finance to foreign firms, joint ventures, and domestic banks only and not directly to local firms.
- Myanmar exporters and importers use parent companies registered in Singapore or Hong Kong to act as an intermediary with trading or banking counter-parties. They can send money to the parent company to guarantee the issuance of L/Cs by banks in Singapore or Hong Kong to guarantee payments to foreign suppliers.

Many small and medium-sized businesses (SMEs) suffer from undercapitalization and/or poor management of financial resources, often during the first few years of operation. The entrepreneur typically either overestimates demand for the product or severely underestimates the need for capital resources and organizational skills. Undercapitalization may also be a result of the entrepreneur's aversion to equity financing (fear of loss of control over the business) or the lender's resistance to provide capital due to the entrepreneur's lack of credit history and a comprehensive business plan (Gardner, 1994; Hutchinson, 1995; Hanks et al., 2011).

Large corporations have an advantage in raising capital compared with small businesses. They have greater bargaining strength with lenders, they can issue securities, and they have greater access to capital markets around the world. However, major changes are taking place in SME financing due to three important factors: technology, globalization, and deregulation. Information technology enables the financial world to operate efficiently, to decentralize while improving control. It also provides businesses seeking capital to choose from a vast range of financial instruments (Grimaud, 1995; Farkhanda, 2007). Globalization allows businesses to turn increasingly to international markets to raise capital. With a touch of a button, businesses have access to individual or corporate sources of finance around the world. With deregulation, in many countries, competition in financial products is allowed across all depository institutions. The distinction between investment and commercial banking is quite blurred, and both sectors now compete in the small business financing market. In spite of this, many SMEs still face hurdles in accessing affordable trade financing.

It is important to properly evaluate how much capital is needed, in what increments, and over what time period. First are the initial capital needs to start the export–import business. Start-up costs are not large if the exporter–importer begins as an agent (without buying for resale) and uses his or her own home as an office. Initial capital needs are for office supplies and equipment—telephone, fax, computer—and perhaps a part-time assistant. The business could also be started on a part-time basis until it provides sufficient revenues to cover expenses, including the owner's salary. However, when the business is commenced with the intention of establishing an independent company with products purchased for resale (as a merchant, distributor, etc.), a lot more capital is needed to prepare a business plan, travel, purchase and distribute the product, and exhibit in major trade shows. Second, capital is needed to finance growth and expansion of the business. It is thus critical to anticipate capital needs during the time of growth and expansion as well as during abnormal increases in accounts receivable, inventory levels, and changes in the business cycle.

The capital needs and financing alternatives of an export–import business are determined by its stage of evolution, ownership structure, distribution channel choice, and other pertinent factors. A very small sum of money is often needed to start the business as an agent because no payments are made for merchandise, transportation, or distribution of the product. However, initial capital needs are substantial if a person starts the business as a merchant, distributor, or trading company with products available for resale. This entails payments for transportation, distribution, advertising and promotion, travel, and other expenses.

Capital needs at the start-up stage may be smaller compared to those needed during the growth and expansion period. However, this depends on the degree of expansion and the capital needed to support additional marketing efforts, inventories, and accounts receivable. The ownership structure of an export–import firm tends to have an important influence on financing alternatives and little or no influence on capital needs. Studies on small business financing indicate the following salient features:

- Incorporated companies are more likely to receive equity (and other non-debt) financing than debt financing because lenders perceive the incorporated entity as having a greater incentive to take on risky ventures due to its limited liability (Brewer et al., 1996).
- Younger firms are more likely to obtain equity (non-debt) than debt financing. The probability of receiving debt financing increases with age. This is consistent with standard theories of capital structure, which state that such businesses have little or no track record on which to base financing decisions and are often perceived as risky by lenders (Coleman, Cotei, and Farhat, 2016).
- Firms with high growth opportunities, a volatile cash flow, and low liquidation value are more likely to finance their business with equity than debt. In

firms with high growth opportunities, conflicts are likely between management and shareholders over the direction and pace of growth options, and this reduces the chances of debt financing. However, businesses with a good track record and high liquidation value (with assets that can be easily liquidated) have a greater chance of financing their business with debt rather than equity (Williamson, 1988; Stulz, 1990; Schleifer and Vishny, 1992; Cheng, 2009).

CAPITAL SOURCES FOR EXPORT–IMPORT BUSINESSES

Capital needs to start the business or to finance current operations or expansion can be obtained from different sources. Internal financing should be explored before resorting to external funding sources. This includes using one's own resources for initial capital needs and then retaining more profits in the business or reducing accounts receivables and inventories to meet current obligations and finance growth and expansion. Such reductions in receivables or inventories should be applied carefully so as not to lead to a loss of customers or goodwill, both of which are critical to the viability of the business.

External financing takes different forms and businesses use one or a combination of the following:

- *Debt or equity financing:* Debt financing occurs when an export–import firm borrows money from a lender with a promise to repay (principal and interest) at some predetermined future date. Equity financing involves raising money from private investors in exchange for a percentage of ownership (and sometimes participation in management) of the business. The major disadvantage with equity financing is the owner's potential loss of control over the business (Cheng, 2009; Colwell, 2019).
- *Short-term, intermediate, or long-term financing:* Short-term financing involves a credit period of less than one year, while intermediate financing is credit extended for a period of one to five years. In long-term financing, the credit period ranges between five and twenty years.
- *Investment, inventory, or working capital financing:* Investment financing is money used to start the business (to buy a computer, fax machine, telephone, etc.). Inventory capital is money raised to purchase products for resale. Working capital supports current operations such as rent, advertising, supplies, wages, and so on. All three could be financed by debt or equity.

Several sources of funding are available to existing export–import businesses that have established track records. However, financing is quite limited for initial capital needs, and the entrepreneur has to use his/her own resources or borrow from family or friends (Colwell, 2019). It is also important to evaluate funding sources not just in terms of availability (willingness to provide funding) but also in regard to the capital's cost and its effect on business profits, as well as any restrictions imposed by lenders on the operations of the business. Certain loan agreements, for example, prevent the sale of accounts receivable or equipment or require the representation of lenders in the firm's management. The following is an overview of possible sources of capital for export–import businesses.

Internal Sources

This is the best source of financing for initial capital needs or expansion because there is no interest to be paid back or equity in the business to be surrendered and start-up businesses have limited chances of obtaining loans. Internal sources include money:

- in saving accounts, certificates of deposit, and other personal accounts;
- in stocks, bonds, and money market funds.

External Sources

Family and Friends

This is the second-best option for raising capital for an export–import business. The money should be borrowed with a promissory note indicating the date of payment and the amount of principal and interest to be paid. As long as the business pays a market interest rate, it is entitled to a tax deduction and the lender gets the interest income. In the event of failure by the business to repay the loan, the lender may be able to deduct the amount as a short-term capital loss. Such an arrangement protects the lender and also prevents the latter from acquiring equity in the business.

Banks and Other Commercial Lenders

The largest challenge to successful lending is the turnover rate of small businesses. In general, fewer than half of all small businesses survive beyond the third-year mark. However, the survival rate for export–import businesses is generally higher than that of other businesses. Due to the level of risk, banks and other commercial lenders tend to avoid start-up financing without collateral. A 2017 small business credit survey shows that firms sought financing most frequently at large banks (48 percent), small banks (47 percent), online lenders (24 percent) as well as auto/equipment dealers, farm lending institutions, family, friends, nonprofits, private investors, and government entities (18 percent). Online lenders have attracted more interest in recent years because of their faster credit decisions, high approval rates, and lack of collateral requirements. However, they tend to charge high interest rates and have unfavorable payment terms (Small Business Credit Survey, 2017).

Banks remain the cheapest source of borrowed capital for export–import firms as well as other small businesses. To persuade a bank to provide a loan, it is essential to prepare a business plan that sets clear financial goals, including how the loan will be repaid. Banks always review the ability of the borrower to service the debt, and whether sufficient cash is invested in the business, as well as the nature of the collateral that is to be provided as a guarantee for the loan. Bankers always investigate the five Cs in making lending decisions: character (trustworthiness, reliability), capacity (ability and track record in meeting financial obligations), capital (significant equity in the business), collateral (security for the loan), and condition (the effect of overall economic conditions) (Lorenz-Fife, 1997; Hisrich, Peters, and Shepherd, 2019). Even though it is often difficult to obtain a commercial loan for start-up capital, a good business plan and a strong, experienced management team may entice lenders to make a decision in favor of providing the loan. The following are different types of financing offered by banks and other commercial lenders.

- *Asset-based financing.* Banks and other commercial lenders provide loans secured by fixed assets, such as land, buildings, and machinery. For example, they will lend up to 80 percent of the value of one's home minus the first mortgage. These are often long-term loans payable over a ten-year period. Business assets, such as accounts receivable, inventories, and personal assets (e.g., savings accounts, cars, jewelry), can be used as collateral for business loans. Commercial lenders usually lend up to 50 percent and 80 percent of the value of accounts receivable and inventories, respectively. Use of saving accounts as collateral could reduce interest payments on a loan. Suppose the interest on the savings account is 4 percent and the business loan is financed at 12 percent. The actual interest rate that is to be paid is reduced to 8 percent.
- *Lines of credit.* These are short-term loans (for a period of one year) intended for purchases of inventory and payment of operating costs. They may some-times be secured by collateral such as accounts receivable based on the credit-worthiness and reputation of the borrower. A certain amount of money (line of credit) is made available, and interest is often charged on the amount used. Certain lenders do not allow use of such lines of credit until the business's checking account is depleted.
- *Personal and commercial loans.* Owners with good credit standing could obtain personal loans that are backed by the mere signature and guarantee of the borrower. They are short-term loans and subject to relatively high interest rates. Commercial loans are also short-term loans that are often backed by stocks, bonds, and life insurance policies as collateral. The cash value of a life insurance policy can also be borrowed and repaid over a certain period of time (Hisrich, Peters, and Shepherd, 2019).
- *Credit cards.* Credit cards are generally not recommended for capital needs for new or existing export–import businesses because they are one of the costliest forms of business financing. They charge extremely high interest rates and there is no limit on how much credit card issuers can charge for late fees and other penalties (Fraser, 1996). If financing options are limited, credit cards could be used if the probability of the business succeeding is very high (if you have made definite arrangements with foreign buyers, for example). One should shop for the lowest available rates and plan for bank or credit union financing at a later date, if the debt cannot be retired within a short time period, possibly with an account receivable or inventory as collateral.

Small Business Administration (SBA)

The SBA has several facilities for lending that can be used by export–import businesses for capital needs at different stages of their growth cycle (see Table 13.1), including the following.

- *Small business investment companies (SBICs).* These are private companies funded by the SBA that were established to provide loan (sometimes equity) capital to small businesses. Even though they prefer to finance existing small

TABLE 13.1 SBA Funding for Export–Import and Other Small Businesses

Program	Brief Overview
1. The 7(A) Loan Guaranty: Start-up/expansion/ up/ expansion/working capital	SBA can guarantee as much as 85 percent on loans of up to $150,000 and 75 percent on loans of more than $150,000. SBA's maximum exposure is $1.5 million. 7(a) loans have a maximum loan amount of $5 million. Funds could be used to buy land and buildings, to expand facilities, to purchase equipment, or for working capital.
2. Certified Development Company (CDC)/504 Loan	CDCs are nonprofit economic development agencies, certified by the SBA. They work with participating lenders to provide financing. Applicants must have a tangible net worth less than $7.5 million and an average net income less than $2.5 million after taxes for the preceding two years. Loans cannot be made to businesses engaged in speculation or investment in rental real estate. The maximum SBA debenture is $5 million when meeting a public policy goal such as expansion of exports. Loans can be used to purchase land, for improvement or renovation of facilities, and to purchase machinery or equipment. Project assets are often used as collateral. It cannot be used for working capital.
3. Small Business Investment Companies (SBICs)	These are licensed by SBA and lend their own capital as well as funds borrowed through the federal government to small businesses, both new and already established. SBICs make either equity investments or long-term loans to companies with growth potential. Investment is not to exceed 20 percent of its private capital in securities or guarantees in any one concern. (Loans for start-up or expansion.)
4. International Trade Loan	Used for businesses preparing to engage in, or are already engaged in, international trade or for those adversely affected by competition from imports. Used to develop and expand export market or for working capital. Loans are guaranteed up to $5 million. (Loan guarantees to expand market/working capital.)
5. Export Express	May be used for revolving lines of credit. Loan enables businesses to enter new or expand existing export market. Maximum loan amount is $500,000. 90 percent guarantee for loans of $350,000 or less. To qualify, the borrower must have been in business for at least a year.
6. Export Working Capital (EWC)	EWC loan provides short-term working capital to exporters. May be asset or transaction based. Can also support standby L/Cs. Maximum loan amount is $5 million. 90 percent loan guarantee up to $4.5 million.
7. Microloans	The program provides loans up to $50,000. Average loan is about $13,000. Funds available to nonprofit intermediaries, who in turn make loans to small business borrowers. Collateral and personal guarantee are required. Loan maturity may be as long as six years. (Loan for start-up/expansion/working capital.)

(*continued*)

TABLE 13.1 Cont.

Program	Brief Overview
8. Cap lines: Working capital; contract; seasonal and builders' cap lines	Finance seasonal and/or short-term working capital needs; advance against existing inventory and receivables; consolidate short-term debt. Maximum loan is $5 million. Maturity is up to 10 years except for builders' cap line which is 5 years.
9. STEP: State Trade Expansion Program	Provides financial awards to state and territory governments to help small businesses export their products. STEP helps small businesses learn how to export, participate in foreign trade missions and trade shows, obtain services to support foreign market entry, develop websites to attract foreign buyers, and design international marketing products or campaigns.

businesses with a track record, they also consider loans for start-up capital. Members of a minority group could also consider a similar lending agency funded by the SBA that is intended to finance minority start-up or existing businesses.

• *The SBA guaranteed loan (7(a) Loan Guaranty Program).* The guarantee by the SBA permits a lending institution to provide long-term loans to start-up or existing small businesses. Export–import businesses can use the money for their working capital needs, for example, to purchase inventory and help carry a receivable until it is paid, to purchase real estate to house the business, and for the acquisition of furniture and fixtures. The SBA guarantee is available only after the business has failed to obtain financing on reasonable terms from other private sources. It is considered to be a lender of last resort.

• *The Certified Development Company.* The Certified Development Company (CDC 504) program assists in the development and expansion of small firms and the creation of jobs. This program is designed to provide fixed-asset financing and cannot be used for working capital or inventory, consolidating, or repaying debt. (For an overview of SBA loans, see International Perspective 13.1)

INTERNATIONAL PERSPECTIVE 13.1

SBA Loans and their Features

1. **Guaranty Loans:** The loans are made and disbursed by private lenders and guaranteed by the SBA up to a certain amount. This means that if the borrower defaults on the loan, the SBA will purchase an agreed-upon percentage of the unpaid balance. Direct and participation loans (loans made jointly by the SBA and other lenders) are quite rare and have even decreased over the years.

2. **Interest Rates:** Maximum allowed interest rates range from highs of prime plus 6.5 percentage points to prime plus 2.75 percentage points, though

lenders can and often do charge less. These rates may be higher or lower than rates on nonguaranteed loans. Banks making SBA loans cannot charge "commitment fees" for agreeing to make a loan, or prepayment fees on loans under fifteen years (a prepayment penalty kicks in for longer loans), which means the effective rates for SBA loans may be, in some instances, superior to those for conventional loans.

3. **Guarantee Fee**: Payment of a guarantee fee is required for all guaranteed loans. Loans are to be secured by a collateral and personal guarantee.

4. **Guarantees of Last Resort**: SBA loans are provided as a matter of last resort i.e., when borrowers cannot obtain credit without an SBA guarantee. The borrower is expected to have some personal equity to operate the business on a sound financial basis.

Finance Companies

The following are different ways of raising capital from finance companies to start or expand an export–import business.

- *Loans from insurance companies and pension funds:* Life insurance policies can be used as collateral to borrow money for capital needs. Pension funds also provide loans to businesses with attractive growth prospects. Pension funds and insurance company loans are intermediate and long-term credits (five to fifteen years). Banks often introduce such lending agencies to their clients when the funds are needed for longer than the banks' maximum maturity period.

- *Commercial finance companies:* These companies grant short-term loans using accounts receivable, inventories, or equipment as collateral. They can also factor (buy) accounts receivable at a discount and provide the export–import firm with the necessary capital for growth and expansion. Factoring is a way of turning a firm's accounts receivable into immediate cash without creating new debt. The factoring company will collect the accounts receivable, assume credit risks associated with the accounts receivable, conduct investigations into the firm's existing and prospective accounts, as well as do the bookkeeping with respect to the credit. In most cases, a factoring company will advance 50 to 90 percent of the face value of the receivables and later pay the balance less the factor's discount (4 to 7 percent of face value of receivables) once the receivables are collected. An export–import firm could easily factor its receivables so long as it sells to government clients or to major companies that have good credit. The disadvantage with this method is that it is expensive and could absorb a good part of the firm's profits.

Equity Sources

For many export–import businesses, the ability to raise equity finance is quite limited. Although such funding provides the owner with initial capital needs, money for expansion, or working capital, it means some dilution of ownership and control. Finding compatible business partners and shareholders is always difficult. There are three sources for equity funding:

- Family and friends
- *Business angels (invisible venture capitalists):* Business angels provide start-up or expansion capital and are the biggest providers of equity capital for small businesses. They can be found through networking advertisements or newspapers or the World Wide Web. This segment is estimated to represent about 2,000 individuals or businesses investing between $10 billion to $20 billion each year in over 30,000 businesses (Lorenz-Fife, 1997).
- *Venture capitalists:* Venture capitalists provide equity capital to businesses that are already established and need working or expansion capital. The SBA estimates that 500 venture capital firms are currently investing about $4 billion a year in some 3,000 ventures. They may not be suitable for small export–import firms because

1. Their minimum investment is about $50,000 to 100,000;
2. They seldom provide funding for start-up capital because they are interested in companies with a proven track record and market position; and
3. They expect high returns (10 to 15 percent) on their investments over a relatively short period of time.

PRIVATE SOURCES OF EXPORT FINANCING

In many export transactions, the buyer is unable or unwilling to pay for the goods at the time of delivery. This means that the seller has to agree to payment at some future date or that the buyer should seek financing from third parties. The seller may seek financing from the buyer or third parties for purchasing goods from suppliers, to pay for labor, or to arrange for transportation and insurance (pre-shipment financing). The exporter may also need post-shipment financing of the resulting account or accounts receivable or both (Silvester, 1995; Hisrich, Peters, and Shepherd, 2019).

Competitive finance is a crucial element in export strategies, especially for SMEs. Exporters should carefully consider the type of financing required, the length of time for repayment, the loan's effect on price and profit, as well as the various risks that may be associated with such financing.

In extending credit to overseas customers, it is important to recognize the following:

1. Normal commercial terms range from 30 to 180 days for sales of consumer goods, industrial materials, and agricultural commodities. Custom-made or high-value capital equipment may warrant longer repayment periods.
2. An allowance may have to be made for longer shipment periods than are found in domestic trade because foreign buyers are often unwilling to have the credit period start before they receive the goods.
3. Customers are usually charged interest on credit periods of a year or longer and seldom on short-term credit of up to 180 days. Even though the provision of favorable financing terms makes a product more competitive, the exporter should carefully assess such financing against considerations of cost and risk of default.

Financing by the Exporter

Open Account

Under this arrangement, an exporter will transfer possession or ownership of the merchandise on a deferred-payment basis (payment deferred for an agreed period of time). This can be done in the case of creditworthy customers who have proven track records. In the case of customers who are not well-known to the exporter, such arrangements should not be undertaken without taking out export credit insurance.

Consignment Sales

Importers do not pay for the merchandise until it is sold to a third party. Exporters could take out an insurance policy to cover them against risk of nonpayment.

Financing by the Overseas Customer

Advance Payment

The buyer is required to pay before shipment is effected. The advance payment may comprise of the entire price or an agreed percentage of the purchase price. An importer may secure the advance payment through a performance guarantee provided by a third party. Export trading or export management companies, for example, often purchase goods on an advance-payment or cash-on-delivery basis, thus eliminating the need for financing. They can also use their vast international networks to help the exporter obtain credit and credit insurance.

Progress Payment

Payments are tied to partial performance of the contract, such as production, partial shipment, and so on. This means that a mix of advance and progress payments meets the financing needs of the exporter.

Financing by Third Parties

Short-Term Methods

Loan secured by a foreign account receivable: An exporter can borrow money from a bank or finance company to meet its short-term working capital needs by using its foreign account receivable as collateral. In most cases, the overseas customer is not notified of the loan. As the customer makes payment to the exporter, the exporter, in turn, repays the loan to the lender. It is also possible to notify the overseas customer about the collateral and instruct the latter to pay bills directly to the lender. This may, however, put into question the financial standing of the exporter in the eyes of the overseas buyer.

An exporter can usually borrow 80 to 85 percent of the face value of its accounts receivable if the receivables are insured and the exporter and overseas customer have good credit ratings.

Most banks are reluctant to lend against receivables that are not insured. The bank's security is effected through assignment of the exporter's foreign accounts receivable. Documentary collections are easier and less expensive to finance than sales on open accounts because the draft in documentary collections is a negotiable instrument (unlike open account sales, which are accompanied by an invoice and transport documents) that can easily be sold or discounted before maturity. Although most lenders are interested in providing a loan against foreign receivables, it is not uncommon to find some that would purchase them with full or limited recourse. In both cases, most banks require insurance. (Once the receivables are sold, the exporter will be able to remove the receivables and the loan from its balance sheet.)

Trade/banker's acceptance: This arises when a draft drawn by the seller is accepted by the overseas customer to pay a certain sum of money on an agreed date. The exporter could obtain a loan using the acceptance as collateral or discount the acceptance to a financial institution for payment. In cases in which the debt is not acknowledged in the form of a draft, the exporter could sell or discount the invoice (invoice acceptance) before maturity. In both cases, the acceptances are usually sold without recourse to the exporter and the latter is relieved of the responsibility of collection.

A draft drawn on, and accepted by, a bank is called a banker's acceptance. Once accepted, the draft becomes a primary obligation of the accepting bank to pay at maturity. This occurs in the case of documents against acceptance (documentary collection or acceptance credit), whereby payment is to be made at a specified date in the future. The bank returns the draft to the seller with an endorsement of its acceptance, guaranteeing payment to the seller (exporter) on the due date. The exporter may then sell the accepted draft at a discount to the bank or any other financial institution. The exporter could also secure a loan using the draft as collateral. The marketability of a banker's or trade acceptance is dependent on the creditworthiness of the party accepting the draft.

Letter of credit: In addition to the acceptance credit discussed previously, the L/C could be an important instrument of financing exports:

1. *Transferable L/C:* Using this method, the exporter transfers its rights under the credit to another party, usually a supplier, who receives payment. When the supplier presents the necessary documents to the advising bank, the supplier's invoice is replaced with the exporter's invoice for the full value of the original credit. The advising bank pays the supplier the value of the invoice and will pay the difference to the exporter.
2. *Assignment of proceeds under the L/C:* The beneficiary (exporter) may assign either the entire amount or a percentage of the proceeds of the L/C to a specified third party, usually a supplier. This allows the exporter to make purchases with limited capital by using the overseas buyer's credit. It does not require the assent of the buyer or the buyer's bank.
3. *Back-to-back L/Cs:* An L/C is issued on the strength of another L/C. Such credits are issued when a supplier or subcontractor demands payment from the exporter before collections are received from the customer. The exporter remains obligated to perform under the original credit, and if default occurs, the bank is left holding a worthless collateral.

Factoring: Factoring is a continuous arrangement between a factoring concern and the exporter, whereby the factor purchases export receivables for a somewhat discounted price (usually 2 to 4 percent less than the full value). The amount of the discount depends on a number of factors, including the kind of products involved, the customer, the factoring entity, and the importing country. Factoring enables exporters to offer terms of sale on open account without assuming the credit risk. Importers also prefer factoring because by buying on open account, they forgo costly payment arrangements such as L/Cs. It also frees up their working capital. In the case of importers that have not yet established a track record, banks often will not issue L/Cs and open account sales may be the only available option.

In export factoring, the exporter receives immediate payment and the burden of collection is eliminated. Factors have ties to banks and financial institutions in other countries through networks such as Factors Chain International, which enables them to check the creditworthiness of an overseas customer, to authorize credit, and to assume the financial risk.

Increases in global trade and competition have resulted in the search for alternative forms of financing to accommodate the diverse needs of customers. In highly competitive markets, concluding a successful export deal often depends on the seller's ability to obtain trade finance at the most favorable terms for the overseas customer (Brewer et al., 1996; Klapper, 2007).

A typical export factoring procedure begins with the following steps: Upon receipt of an order from an overseas customer, the exporter verifies with the factor, through its overseas affiliate, the customer's credit standing and determines whether the factor is willing to authorize credit and to assume the financial risk. If the factor's decision is in favor of authorizing credit to the overseas customer, then the parties follow the procedure described in Figure 13.1.

Arrangements with factors are made either with recourse (exporter is liable in the event of default by the buyer or other problems) or without recourse, in which case a larger discount may be required since the exporter is free of liability (for advantages and disadvantages of this financing method, see Table 13.2).

Intermediate and Long-Term Methods

Buyer credit. Some export sales, such as those involving capital equipment, often require financing terms that extend over several years. The importer may obtain credit from a bank or other financial institution to pay the exporter. The seller often cooperates in structuring the financing arrangements to make them suitable to the needs of the buyer.

Forfaiting: Forfaiting is the practice of purchasing deferred debts arising from international sales contracts without recourse to the exporter. The exporter surrenders possession of export receivables (deferred-debt obligation from the importer), which are usually guaranteed by a bank in the importing country, by selling to a forfaiter at a discount in exchange for cash. The deferred debt may be in the form of a promissory note, bill of exchange, trade acceptance, or documentary credit, which are unconditional and easily transferable debt instruments that can be sold on the secondary market.

The origins of forfaiting date back to the 1940s, when Swiss financiers developed new ways of financing sales of West German capital equipment to Eastern

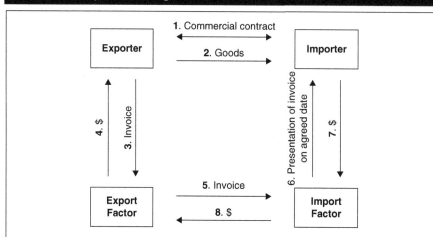

FIGURE 13.1 Export Factoring

1. The exporter and importer enter into a commercial contract and agree on the terms of sale (i.e., open account).
2. The exporter ships the goods to the importer.
3. The exporter submits the invoice to the export factor.
4. The export factor provides (cash in advance) funds to the exporter against receivables until money is collected from the importer. The exporter often receives up to 30 percent of the value of the receivables ahead of time and pays the factor interest on the money received, or the factor pays the exporter, less a commission charge, when receivables are due (or shortly thereafter). The commission often ranges between 1 and 3 percent.
5. The export factor passes the invoice to the import factor for assumption of credit risk, administration, and collection of the receivables.
6. The import factor presents the invoice to the importer for payment on the agreed date.
7. The importer pays the import factor.
8. The import factor pays the export factor. In cases where the export factor advanced funds up to a certain percentage (e.g., 30 percent) of the exporter's receivables, the remaining portion (70 percent of receivables less interest or other charges) is paid by the export factor to the exporter.

Europe. Since Eastern European countries did not have enough hard currency to finance imports, they sought intermediate-term financing from their suppliers. The leading forfait houses are still located in Europe.

In a typical forfaiting transaction, the overseas customer does not have hard currency to finance the sale and requests to purchase on credit, usually payable within one to ten years. The exporter (or exporter's bank) contacts a forfaiter and provides the latter with the details of the proposed transaction with the overseas customer. The forfaiter evaluates the transaction and agrees to finance the deal based on a certain discount rate and other conditions. The exporter then incorporates the discount into the selling price. Discount rates are fixed and based on the London Interbank Offered Rate (LIBOR), on which floating interest rates are based. The forfaiter usually requires a guarantee or aval (letter of assurance) from a bank in the importer's country and often provides the exporter with a list of local banks that are acceptable as guarantors. The guarantee becomes quite important, especially in cases of receivables from developing countries. Once an acceptable guarantor is found, the exporter ships the goods to the buyer and endorses the negotiable instruments in favor

TABLE 13.2 Advantages and Disadvantages of Export Factoring

Advantages	Disadvantages
• Factoring allows immediate payment against receivables and increases working capital.	• Factoring is not available for shipments with values of less than $100,000. It is appropriate for continuous or repetitive transactions (not one-shot deals). Factors often require access to a certain volume of the exporter's yearly sales..
• Factors conduct credit investigations, collect accounts receivable from importer, and provide other bookkeeping services.	• Factors do not work for receivables with maturity of over 180 days.
• Factors assume credit risk in the event of buyer's default or refusal to pay (non- recourse).	• Factors generally do not work with most developing countries because of their inadequate legal and financial frameworks.
• Factoring is a good substitute for bank credit when the latter is too restrictive or uneconomical.	• Exporter could be liable for disputes concerning merchandise (quality, condition of goods, etc.) and contract of sale.

of the forfaiter, without recourse. The forfaiter then pays the exporter the discounted proceeds.

Although export factoring and forfaiting appear quite similar, there are certain differences in terms of payment terms, products involved, continuity of transaction, and overall use:

1. Factors are often used to finance consumer goods, whereas forfaiters usually work with capital goods, commodities, and projects.
2. Factors are used for continuous transactions, but forfeiters finance one-time deals.
3. Forfeiters work with receivables from developing countries whenever they obtain an acceptable bank guarantor; factors do not finance trade with most developing countries because of unavailability of credit information, poor credit ratings, or inadequate legal and financial frameworks.
4. Factors generally work with short-term receivables, whereas forfaiters finance receivables with a maturity of over 180 days (see Table 13.3 for advantages and disadvantages of this financing method).

The following are some examples of forfaiting transactions:

- The Bankers Association for Foreign Trade (BAFT) arranged with a cotton machinery company to sell over $500,000 worth of cotton lint removal machinery payable eleven months from the date on the bill of lading. A Greek commercial bank issued the L/C, which called for acceptance drafts. Bankers Trust of New York confirmed the letter of credit, and Midland Bank undertook the forfaiting transaction.
- Morgan Grenfell Trade Finance Limited purchased receivables from U.S. exporters to Peru. The finance company required the guarantee of one of the large Peruvian banks and accepted a repayment period of up to five years.

TABLE 13.3 Advantages and Disadvantages of Forfaiting

Advantages
1. Forfaiters purchase receivables as a one-shot deal without requiring an ongoing volume of business, as in the case of factoring.
2. Financing can cover 100 percent of the sale. Improves cash flow and reduces transaction cost for the exporter since responsibility for collection is assumed by the forfaiter. Forfaiter also assumes all of the payment risk (i.e., credit risk of the guarantor bank, the interest rate risk, as well as the buyer's country risk).

Disadvantages
1. It is not available for short-term financing (less than 180 days). Terms range from one to ten years.
2. Transaction size is usually limited to $250,000 or more.
3. Interest and commitment fees (if advance payment is required by exporter) may be high.
4. Exporter is responsible for quality, condition of goods, delivery, over-shipment, and other areas of contract dispute.
5. Exporter is responsible for obtaining a bank guarantee for the buyer.

- Morgan Grenfell financed the down payment in cash (forfaiting) of the sale of electric turbines to Mexico, which was financed by EXIM Bank. EXIM Bank required a 15 percent down payment.
- The Export Development Corporation (EDC) of Canada purchases accounts receivable from Canadian exporters provided the promissory notes issued by the overseas customer are guaranteed by a bank acceptable to the EDC, the transaction complies with the Canadian content requirement, and the promissory note does not exceed 85 percent of the contract price.

Export leasing. This is a financing scheme in which a third party, be it an international leasing entity or a finance firm, purchases and exports capital equipment with a view to leasing it to the importer in another country on an intermediate- to long-term basis. This arrangement is suitable for the export of capital goods. The lessor could be located in the exporting or importing country. Whether it is an operating or finance lease, the legal ownership of the asset remains with the lessor and only possession passes to the lessee. Under the operating lease, the lease rentals are not intended to amortize the capital outlay incurred by the lessor when the equipment was purchased. Instead, the capital outlay and profit are intended to be recovered through the re-leasing of the equipment and/or through its residual value on its eventual sale. It is not a method of financing the acquisition of the equipment, but a lease for a specified period. The lease is reflected in the balance sheet of the lessor and not the lessee. Under the finance lease, the lease rentals are intended to amortize the capital costs of acquisition as well as to provide profit. Usually, the lessee chooses the equipment to be leased and bears the cost of maintenance and insurance. The lease is reflected in the balance sheet of the lessee and not the lessor.

For businesses that need new equipment but lack the necessary resources or hard currency to purchase, leasing becomes an attractive option. It requires little or no down payment, and the equipment can be bought at the end of the lease agreement for a nominal price. Lease payments are tax deductible in many countries. Since such payments do not appear as liabilities in the financial statements, they preserve the lessee's financial position and do not reduce its ability to borrow for other reasons. Other advantages of leasing are that 1) one can lease up-to-date equipment that may be too expensive to purchase, and 2) the lessee can always trade in the old equipment in the event of obsolescence and obtain new, even before the end of the lease. There are, however, certain disadvantages: 1) it may attract adverse tax consequences in certain countries, and 2) the cost of leasing is often higher than other financing methods.

CHAPTER SUMMARY

Major changes in small business financing	Technology, globalization, and deregulation
Determinants of capital needs and financing alternatives	Stage of evolution, ownership structure, and distribution channels.
Internal financing	Using one's own resources, retaining more profits in the business, and reducing accounts receivable and inventories.
External financing	*Forms of external financing* Debt or equity financing; short-term/intermediate/long-term financing; investment, inventory, or working capital financing.
	Sources of external financing Family and friends, banks (asset-based financing, lines of credit, personal and commercial loans, credit cards), Small Business Administration, finance companies, and equity sources.
Financing by the exporter	1. Open account: Payment is deferred for a specified period of time. 2. Consignment contract: Importer pays after merchandise is sold to a third party.
Financing by the importer	1. Advance payment: Payment is before shipment. 2. Progress payment: Payment is related to performance.
Financing by third parties	*Short-term methods* 1. Loan secured by a foreign accounts receivable: Account receivable used as collateral to meet short-term financing needs. 2. Trade/banker's acceptance: A draft accepted by the importer is used as collateral to obtain financing. 3. Letter of credit: Transferable L/C, assignment of proceeds under an L/C, or a back-to-back L/C used to secure financing.

4. Factoring: An arrangement between a factoring concern and exporter whereby the factor purchases export receivables for a discount.

Intermediate and long-term methods
1. Buyer credit: Importer obtains credit from a bank or financial institution to pay the exporter.
2. Forfaiting: Purchase of deferred debts arising from international sales contracts without recourse to the exporter.
3. Export leasing: A firm purchases and exports capital equipment with a view to leasing.

REVIEW QUESTIONS

1. What are the major changes taking place in small and medium-sized business financing?
2. What factors determine capital needs and financing alternatives in export–import trade?
3. State the common external sources of financing for export–import businesses.
4. Describe the following: SBICs, Certified Development Company, CDC/504 loan program, international trade loan.
5. Discuss the various methods in which a letter of credit can be used to finance exports.
6. What is export factoring? How does it differ from forfaiting?
7. State the typical steps involved in export factoring.
8. What are the disadvantages of factoring?
9. Is venture capital generally suitable for export firms?
10. What are the various loan facilities provided by the SBA to export businesses?

REFERENCES

Asia Development Bank (ADB) (2014). *ADB Trade Finance Gaps, Growth, and Jobs Survey.* Manila: Asian Development Bank.

BIS (2016). *Correspondent Banking,* Basel: BIS.

Brewer II, E., Genay, G., Jackson III, W., and Worthington, P. (1996). How are small firms financed? Evidence from small business investment companies. *Federal Reserve Bank of Chicago,* 20: 1–18.

Cheng, M. (2009). Relative effects of debt and equity on corporate operating performance: A quantile regression study. *International Journal of Management,* 26(1): 142–145.

Coleman, S., Cotei, C., and Farhat, J. (2016). The debt-equity financing decisions of US startup firms. *Journal of Economics and Finance,* 40(1), 105–126.

Colwell, C. (2019). *Starting a Business.* New York: ClydeBankMedia.

Farkhanda, S. (2007). The ICT environment, financial sector and economic growth: A cross country analysis. *Journal of Economic Studies,* 34(4): 352–370.

Fraser, J. (1996). Control those credit cards. *INC,* 18 (December): 128.

Gardner, L. (1994). Opportunities and pitfalls in financing during business growth. *Secured Lender,* 50: 39–42.

Grimaud, A. (1995). The evolution of small-business financing. *Canadian Banker*, 102(3) (June): 36–37.

Hanks, G., Barnett, S., Durden, L., and Woodrum, W. (2011). Isolating relevant policy issues: Exploration of small business bankruptcies in Georgia. *Journal of Management Policy and Practice*, 12(2): 11–26.

Hisrich, R., Peters, M., and Shepherd, D. (2019). *Entrepreneurship*. New York: McGraw-Hill.

Hutchinson, R. (1995). The capital structure and investment decisions of the small owner-managed firm: Some exploratory issues. *Small Business Economics*, 7: 231–239.

International Chamber of Commerce (ICC) (2013). *Global Risks. Trade Finance Report*. Paris: ICC Banking Commission.

International Chamber of Commerce (ICC) (2015). *Trade Register Report*. Paris: ICC Banking Commission.

Klapper, L. (2007). *The Role of Factoring for Financing Small and Medium-sized Enterprises*. World Bank Working Paper. Washington, DC: World Bank.

Lorenz-Fife, I. (1997). *Financing Your Business*. Englewood Cliffs, NJ: Prentice-Hall.

Schleifer, A. and Vishny, R. (1992). Liquidation values and debt capacity: A market equilibrium approach. *Journal of Finance*, 47: 1343–1366.

Silvester, J. (1995). *How to Start, Finance and Operate Your Own Business*. Seacaucus, NJ: Carol Publishing Group.

Small Business Credit Survey (2017). www.fedsmallbusiness.org/survey/2018/report-on-employer-firms.

Stulz, R. (1990). Managerial discretion and optimal financing policies. *Journal of Financial Economics*, 26: 3–15.

Williamson, O. (1988). Corporate finance and corporate governance. *Journal of Finance*, 43: 567–591.

World Bank (2015). *Global Financial Development Database*. Washington, DC: World Bank.

World Wide Web Resources

Small business trends: https://smallbiztrends.com/2016/01/small-business-finance-basics.html

Financial education: www.sba.gov/sites/default/files/files/PARTICIPANT_GUIDE_FINANCIAL_MANAGEMENT.pdf

Financing options: www.businessnewsdaily.com/1733-small-business-financing-options-html

Foundation for Enterprise Development: www.fed.org

Trade finance programs: www.sbaonline.sba.gov/oit/loans.html

Factoring: http://ucfunding.com

International Trade Closing Cases and Discussions

1. Tadoo's Sales to Belgium

Tadoo Inc. is a chemical company incorporated in the state of Tennessee and engaged in the production and sale of various chemical products used to kill harmful insects or strip leaves from trees. Since the company was established in 1980, it has generated gross sales of over $60 million largely from sales in the United States and West European countries. Its sales agents and distributors are located in over a dozen countries.

In September 2000, the Belgian government advertised for a purchase of $20 million of chemical products. The winner of the bid was required to provide financing for a period of two years. Given Tadoo's inability to secure private or public financing for the sale, it decided to contact a forfaiter to explore the possibility of financing the deal. Tadoo provided the forfaiter with important details to establish the viability of the transaction including its delivery date, repayment terms (four semi-annual repayments over a two-year period), interest rate (payable by buyer) and an L/C instrument to be opened in favor of Tadoo through a Belgian bank.

The forfaiter calculated the expected costs (discount rate, commitment fees, etc.) necessary to sell the receivable and added it to the commercial contract so that Tadoo would be able to receive 100 percent of the required cash value. This helped Tadoo to submit a contract price that would include financing expenses. The forfaiter also examined the structure of the transaction to ensure that it had maximum liquidity. This includes the financing period, country risk, and credit risk. The forfaiter is expected to resell the transaction in the market.

Prior to the submission of the bid, Tadoo entered into a detailed contract with the forfaiter. The contract required Tadoo to sell the receivable to the forfaiter and stated the terms and conditions of the contract. It also provided Tadoo with the option to cancel the contract with no liability in the event that Tadoo fails to win the bid. A month after the submission of the bid, the Belgian government informed Tadoo that it has been awarded the contract.

Tadoo began to manufacture the product and supplied the product to the buyer in special shipping containers in accordance with the terms of the contract. Four bills of exchange were accepted by the Belgian Bank and later endorsed by Tadoo to the forfaiter without recourse and provided to the latter with supporting documentation. The forfaiter received and verified the documents and paid $20 million to Tadoo. Tadoo is required to honor all its contractual commitments pertaining to product support and warranty but the financial risk associated with the bill of exchange maturing over a two-year period had been sold to the forfaiter without recourse.

Questions

1. Would Tadoo encounter problems if it was exporting to a developing country?
2. Is this method more beneficial to Tadoo than other forms of financing?

2. Constraints on Trade Finance

Trade finance bridges the gap between the time when exporters wish to be paid and the time when importers are ready to pay. It provides the credit, insurance, or payment guarantee that is needed to facilitate payment of export transactions. Trade finance is considered an important lubricant of trade as it shapes export opportunities. It is estimated that about 80 percent of global exports are supported by some form of trade finance. This includes inter-company trade credit (supplier's credit) or bank-intermediated trade finance such as documentary credits. Global surveys by the IMF and Bankers' Association of Finance and Trade show that about 42–48 percent

TABLE 13.4 Risk Characteristics of Short-term Trade Finance Products (Global, 2008–2011)

Category	Transaction default rate	Maturity (days)	Recovery rate*	Defaulted transaction loss rate**	Specific transaction level loss rate
Import LCs	0.020%	80	71	42	0.008%
Export confirmed LCs	0.016%	70	40%	68%	0.011%
Loans for import	0.016%	110	45%	64%	0.010%
Loans for export: Bank risk	0.029%	140	32%	73%	0.021%
Loans for export: Corporate risk	0.021%	70	51%	57%	0.012%
Performance guarantees	0.034%	110	18%	85%	0.029%
Total	**0.021%**	**90**	**52%**	**57%**	**0.012%**

*Recovery rate: Recoveries as a percentage of defaulted exposure across products.
** Estimated economic loss rate as a percentage of defaulting exposure after discounting and costs.

Source: ICC (2013)

of international trade transactions are based on open account, 19–22 percent on cash-in-advance, while 33–36 percent use bank-intermediated finance. The market for trade finance is estimated at US$12–18 trillion a year. The Bank for International Settlements (BIS) estimates bank-intermediated trade finance at US$6–8 trillion of which about US$3 trillion was letters of credit (BIS, 2016).

Trade finance is considered to be a safe form of finance credit since it is often backed by strong collateral and documented trade operations. Trade data indicates that the average default rate on short-term trade credit is 0.021 percent, of which 57 percent is recovered by the sale of the underlying asset. Such low risk holds across regions. For example, the transaction default rate for Africa is 0.39 percent compared to the European average of 0.38 percent. In spite of this, rejection rates on trade finance transactions are 19 percent for Africa compared to 12 percent for Europe (Tables 13.4 and 13.5). Furthermore, financing gaps are the greatest in the poorest countries, notably Africa and developing Asia. Even in advanced countries, finance gaps are a serious problem for SMEs. For example, about 32 percent of U.S. manufacturing SMEs (45 percent of

TABLE 13.5 Actual Risk of Trade Finance and Rejection Rates

Region	Transaction default rate (%, 2007–2014)	Rejection rate on trade finance transactions (%, 2014)	Financial depth (%, 2014)
Africa	0.39	19	46
Middle East	2.43	19	48
APAC	0.29	29	130
Central & S. America	0.50	8	51
USA	0.0	8	195
CIS	1.28	17	55
Europe	0.38	12	100

Source: ICC (2015), ADB (2014), World Bank (2015).

service firms) identify trade finance as a leading impediment to engaging in global trade.

Country surveys show similar results for France and Japan. Major constraints to the additional supply of trade finance include constraints on banks' capital, insufficient collateral from the firm, lack of dollar liquidity, previous dispute or unsatisfactory performance of issuing banks, low country ratings, issuing bank's low credit ratings, and Basel regulatory requirements. The dependence on certain types of trade finance varies by region. For example, Asia and the Pacific accounted for about 70 percent of global L/Cs, compared to North America (13 percent), Africa (2 percent), and Latin America (1 percent) in 2016.

CHAPTER 14

Government Export Financing Programs

LEARNING OBJECTIVES:

14.1 Describe the role of export credit agencies in promoting national exports

14.2 Learn about the difference between buyer and supplier credits

14.3 Identify and explain the OECD guidelines on export credits

14.4 Learn the importance of the U.S. EXIM Bank in assisting the financing of U.S. exports

14.5 Describe the four major export financing programs provided by EXIM Bank

International Trade in Practice

A Tale of Two Official Export Credit Agencies (ECAs): U.S. EXIM and China's Exim and Sinosure

The Export–Import (EXIM) Bank of the United States provides financing and insurance to facilitate the export of U.S. goods and services. EXIM was reauthorized in December 2019 with the mandate to offer loans that rival rates and terms offered by China. The agency intends to direct about $27 billion of its total financing toward this purpose. It has recently provided record loans for the production of liquefied natural gas to Mozambique ($4.7 billion) and a rural electrification project in Senegal. It plans to compete more aggressively in Africa.

The Export–Import Bank of China was founded in 1994 and is entirely owned by the Chinese government. The bank facilitates the export and import of products and assists Chinese firms in their offshore contract projects and outbound investment. In addition to financing exports, it supports imports. In 2019, for example, it set up a credit line of US$42 billion to help firms finance imports in areas such as advanced equipment, smart manufacturing, energy, and other high technology products (Table 14.1). Sinosure also provides insurance and guarantees to support Chinese overseas investment and trade.

TABLE 14.1 Comparing Export–Import Banks in the United States and China

United States	China
EXIM Bank is the only official U.S. ECA that provides financing and insurance to facilitate the export of U.S. goods and services.	China has two official ECAs: The Export–Import Bank of China (China EXIM) and China Export and Credit Insurance Corporation (Sinosure). There are also other state-owned enterprises that provide export financing to support China exports.
Objectives: Support U.S. jobs and provide credits and guarantees for exports when the private sector is unwilling or unable to finance alone as well as to counter foreign ECA financing.	*Objectives:* Support China's economic and trade goals. Its mandate is not limited to exports but also supports imports and overseas investments.
Size of financing: EXIM Bank provided US$5 billion in export credits in 2019.	*Size of financing*: China's ECAs provided about US$34 billion in official export credits in 2019. Its medium- and long-term (MLT) credit and trade financing by state-owned banks approaches US$76 billion in 2019.
Products: Direct loans, loan guarantees, insurance, and working capital loans and guarantees.	*Products:* China EXIM: Export credits, loans for investment, and foreign exchange tools. Sinosure: Insurance and guarantee products to support investment and trade. A range of entities can fund export credits under Sinosure's cover including state-owned banks and international commercial and policy banks.
Authorization: EXIM Bank is subject to authorization by Congress every few years. Its current authorization lasts for seven years until 2026.	*Authorization:* China's ECAs are permanent state agencies and not subject to frequent authorizations.
OECD Guidelines: EXIM Bank abides by the OECD arrangement on officially supported credits.	*OECD Guidelines: China is not a member of the OECD and its ECAs are not regulated by OECD guidelines. A large part of its official financing operates without common principles, rules, or transparency.*

Export credits are financing arrangements designed to mitigate the risks to buyers and sellers associated with international transactions. With globalization and increased efforts to win export markets, many nations are providing export finance to their exporters.

Government financing could be in the form of supplier credit or buyer credit. Supplier credits are credits extended to the buyer by the exporter, that is, the exporter arranges for government financing. Such credits also include a direct extension of credit by the exporter, as well as the latter's arrangement of financing from other private sources. Buyer's credits are extended to the buyer by parties other than the exporter. Banks, government agencies, or other private parties (domestic or foreign) could provide buyer credits.

Programs are usually categorized as short-term (usually under two years), intermediate-term (usually two to five years), and long-term (usually over five years) financing. This chapter is primarily devoted to supplier or buyer credits that are extended by government agencies.

Such government-supported financing is provided when exporters are not able to secure financing from the private sector due to political or other risks as well as to level the playing field by matching credit support that other nations provide their exporters. Over the last decade, China and other emerging economies have adopted creative financing mechanisms that provide government support while skirting guidelines from the Organization for Economic Cooperation and Development (OECD). In recent years, for example, Chinese firms with the backing of the government's export credit agencies have managed to outcompete Western firms by offering more favorable credit terms than are set by OECD guidelines. In 2017, Chinese firms won several contracts in Eastern Europe such as the high-speed rail link between Belgrade and Budapest (US$3.54 billion) and construction of several power plants (US$500–750 million). They charge a mere 2.2–2.5 percent interest for these loans with a repayment period of twenty to thirty years (Karnitschnig, 2017). The U.S. EXIM Bank has also begun to provide competitive financing. In 2019, it authorized a significant increase in its support for services export (from US$79 million to US$665 million). The bank provided a direct loan of $5 billion to Mozambique to support the export of U.S. goods and services from multiple states for the development and construction of an integrated liquefied natural gas project.

EXPORT CREDIT AGENCIES (ECAs) IN VARIOUS COUNTRIES

Export credit agencies differ in their goals, magnitude, and types of services. All offer medium- and long-term credits. They also provide other products and services such as short-term export credits; L/C guarantees, and bond unfair calling (see Table 14.2).

One area in which ECAs differ is in their mission and organizational structure. Some emphasize the need to support domestic jobs through exports (U.S. EXIM Bank) while others underline the importance of promoting exports and other business opportunities (ECAs of Canada, France, Germany, Italy, and the United Kingdom). The mission of Japan's ECA is primarily to secure natural resources, ensure competitiveness, and respond to disruptions in the global economy. Most are directed to supplement the private sector by playing a role as a lender or insurer of last resort, that is, supporting transactions that are too risky or undesirable for commercial support. Canada's Export Development Corporation, in contrast, has a commercial market

TABLE 14.2 Export Credit Agencies (ECAs) of Selected Countries: Range of Services

Agency/Country	Short-term insurance	Medium-/long-term export credit	Fixed rate financing	Foreign exchange risk cover	Direct loans	Investment insurance	Bond support	Unfair calling insurance	L/C cover	Working capital cover
EFIC Australia	×	✓	✓	×	✓	✓	✓	✓	✓	✓
EDC Canada	✓	✓	✓	×	✓	✓	✓	✓	✓	✓
Sinosure& EXIM China	✓	✓	×	×	✓	✓	✓	✓	✓	✓
Coface France	✓	✓	✓	✓	×	✓	✓	✓	✓	✓
Hermes Germany	✓	✓	✓	×	✓	✓	✓	✓	✓	✓
ECGC India	✓	✓	✓	✓	✓	✓	✓	✓	✓	✓
SACE Italy	✓	✓	✓	×	✓	✓	✓	✓	✓	✓
Nexi Japan	✓	✓	✓	×	✓	✓	✓	✓	✓	✓
Keic South Korea	✓	✓	✓	✓	✓	✓	✓	✓	×	✓
ECGD United Kingdom	✓	✓	✓	×	✓	✓	✓	✓	✓	✓
EXIM United States	✓	✓	✓	✓	✓	✓	✓	✓	✓	✓

All the above countries except China and India are members of the OECD.
L/C Cover: letter of credit: guarantee scheme.

Source: British Exporters Association, October, 2019 (www.bexa.co.uk)

TABLE 14.3 Domestic Content Policies of Selected ECAs

Country	Domestic content policy
USA	85% domestic content requirement to receive full financing. If less than 85%, EXIM Bank will finance the domestic content portion
Canada	No minimum domestic content requirement. National benefits policy first considers the GDP and employment impacts of the transaction and then takes into account other factors such as increased access to global markets
France	20% domestic content requirement
Germany	Three-tier policy: 70% and 51% minimum domestic content requirement for the first two tiers, respectively. For the third tier, transactions with less than 51% domestic content can be supported if there is a justification from the exporter and an interministerial committee.
Japan	30% domestic content requirement. It can be reduced if the project has strategic benefit.
United Kingdom	20% domestic content requirement. If less than 20%, the ECA will support the domestic content portion of the transaction.

Source: EXIM Bank (2012)

orientation and is not prevented from competing with the private sector. In terms of organization, ECAs range from government agencies such as EXIM Bank (USA), EDC (Canada), and ECGD (UK) to private companies contracted by the government (Coface in France; Hermes in Germany).

Export credit agencies receive specific mandates from government and put in place certain policy guidelines (Table 14.3). Certain governments emphasize the need to increase financing for small business exporters (USA, France, Italy, United Kingdom) while others have developed initiatives to support environmentally beneficial exports (USA, Italy).

The U.S. EXIM Bank has additional mandates:

- Promotion of exports to Sub-Saharan Africa
- Requirement to ship certain exports (financed through its direct loan and loan guarantee programs) on U.S.-flagged carriers
- Long term certainty: The law extends EXIM Bank to December 2026 to provide long-term certainty for U.S. businesses.
- Small business financing: The bank is expected to increase its small business financing by 30 percent. It also highlights the importance of engaging businesses that are owned by women, minorities, veterans, and persons with disabilities, and small businesses in rural areas.
- Increased focus on the financing of renewable energy, energy efficiency, and storage technology exports.
- Competitive financing with China: The bank reserves about 20 percent of its financing authority of over US$130 billion to compete with China by providing competitive financing, financing exports in transformative industries such as artificial intelligence, biotechnology, biomedical sciences, wireless

communications, renewable energy, financial technology, water treatment, and other associated services.

The OECD has developed guidelines on export credits for its members. These are intended to provide the institutional framework for an orderly export credit market, thus preventing an export credit race in which exporting countries compete on the basis of who provides the most favorable financing terms rather than on the basis of who provides the best-quality product at the lowest price. The arrangement applies to officially supported export credits with repayment terms of two years or more, relating to the export of goods and/or services. It does not apply to exports of military equipment and agricultural commodities. The guidelines provide for the following:

- *Cash payments*: A minimum of 15 percent of the contract price is to be paid in cash.
- *Maximum repayment term*: The maximum repayment term is eight and a half years for high-income countries and ten years for all others.
- *Minimum interest rates*: These rates are adjusted on a monthly basis to reflect commercial lending rates and to reduce the interest rate subsidy component in ECA support.
- *Minimum premium rates*: Minimum premium rates to reflect country credit risk including risk pertaining to that of the overseas buyer.
- *Tied aid*: Aid conditioned on the purchase of goods and services from donor countries is limited in two ways: the minimum grant (concessional) portion of such aid has been raised to 35 percent and such aid is prohibited to richer developing countries.
- *Special sector understandings:* Special sector arrangements have been reached for civil aircraft, nuclear power plants, renewable energy, and water projects.

While the scope of the OECD arrangement has expanded to cover additional areas, the increasing activities of nonmembers, particularly China, threaten the future ability of the agreement to provide a level playing field for exporters. There is a need to include these countries in future arrangements. Other areas of concern include market windows (ECA loans on market terms) as well as non-export credit financing activities such as untied lending and investment finance that fall outside the arrangement. Such arrangements can have an indirect linkage to exports.

EXPORT–IMPORT BANK OF THE UNITED STATES (EXIM BANK)

EXIM Bank was created in 1934 and established under its present law in 1945, with the aim of assisting in the financing of U.S. export trade. It was originally established to finance exports to Europe after World War II. EXIM Bank's role in promoting U.S. exports is likely to be more significant now than in the past few decades because 1) the U.S. economy is more internationalized and exports constitute a growing share of the GNP, and 2) there has been a substantial increase in the volume of international trade and competition for export markets is intense.

EXIM Bank is intended to supplement, but not compete with, private capital. It has historically been active in areas in which the private sector has been reluctant to provide export financing. EXIM Bank has three main functions: 1) provide guarantees and export credit insurance so that exporters and their bankers give credit to foreign buyers, 2) provide competitive financing to foreign buyers, and 3) negotiate with other countries to reduce the level of subsidy in export credits (EXIM Bank, 2019).

Since 2018, EXIM Bank has focused on a broad range of critical areas, such as provision of greater support to small businesses, export promotion to developing nations, and promoting exports of environmentally beneficial goods and services. It has also been engaged in expanding project finance capabilities as well as in reducing trade subsidies of other governments through bilateral or multilateral negotiations.

In its more than seventy years of operations, as at 2019 the bank had supported more than $450 billion of U.S. exports. It has assisted U.S. exporters to win export sales in many countries and undertakes risks the private sector is unwilling or unable to take. EXIM Bank also attempts to neutralize financing provided by foreign governments to their exporters when they are in competition for export sales with U.S. exporters. However, the bank does require reasonable assurance of repayment for the transactions it authorizes and closely monitors credit and other risks in its portfolio.

In 2019, EXIM Bank authorized US$8.2 billion in loans and loan guarantees (see Tables 14.4 and 14.5). The largest share of the Bank portfolio involves financing infrastructure projects such as transportation, power generation, and oil and gas. The highest geographic exposure is in Asia, with almost 23 percent of the total. EXIM Bank also has enhanced financing available for certain categories of exports: environmentally beneficial goods and services, medical equipment, and transportation security equipment.

The bank provides assistance to U.S. exporters of goods and/or services insofar as the exports include a minimum of 50 percent U.S. (local) content and are not military related. For all medium- and long-term transactions, the bank limits its support to the lesser of: i) 85 percent of the value of all goods and services contained within a U.S. supply contract or ii) 100 percent of the U.S. content of an export contract. In effect, it requires a minimum of 85 percent of U.S. content and a maximum of 15 percent foreign content for an export contract to receive the full extent of financing. In cases where the foreign content exceeds 15 percent, the bank's support is lowered proportionally. Its financing decision is determined, inter alia, upon an assessment of the borrower's capability to repay the loan. There are four major export

TABLE 14.4 EXIM Bank Authorizations and Top Beneficiaries by Region and by Industry, 2019 (US$ million)

Region	2019	% Total	Industry	2019	% Total
Asia	12,402	22.70	Air transportation	22,428	41.00
Latin America and Caribbean	8781	16.10	Oil and gas	13,084	23.90
Europe	7,012	10.60	Manufacturing	9,951	18.20
North America	2858	5.20	Power projects	3,064	5.60
Oceania	5050	9.20	All others	6,199	11.30
Africa	8363	15.3			
All others	1941.30	3.5			

TABLE 14.5 EXIM Bank's Geographic and Industry Exposure, 2019 (US$ million)

Loan term	Loan amount	Country	Authorizations	% total
Long term		Saudi Arabia	5093.50	9.30
Loans	5,000.00	Mozambique	5000.00	9.10
Subtotal	*5,000.00*	Mexico	4450.10	8.10
Medium term		China	3434.10	6.30
Loans	8.80	Australia	2975.4	5.40
Guarantees	239.80	others	33,778.80	61.80
Insurance	86.00			
Subtotal	*334.60*			
Short term				
Working capital	687.90			
Insurance	2191.70			
Subtotal	*2876.00*			
Total authorization	**8,214.20**		**54,725.90**	**100**

Source: EXIM Bank (2019)

financing programs provided by EXIM Bank (EXIM Bank, 2019) (see International Perspective 14.1):

- Working capital loan guarantees for U.S. exporters
- Credit insurance
- Guarantees of commercial loans to foreign buyers
- Direct loans to foreign purchasers.

Government support for EXIM Bank has been the subject of criticism from various groups:

- The environmental community contends that the bank provides loans and loan guarantees for projects that harm the environment. These groups raise concerns about the harmful effects of EXIM Bank-assisted oil drilling and pipeline projects in Chad and Cameroon, a coal-fired power plant in Indonesia, and loan guarantees for the sale of nuclear fuel to the Czech Republic.
- It is often stated that the bank's assistance is largely provided to a small number of large U.S. firms such as Boeing, Bechtel, GE, and Halliburton, as well as countries that do not need financial support in the form of loans, loan guarantees, or insurance. In view of the fact that EXIM Bank supports about 1 percent of U.S. exports, critics suggest that it has a marginal impact on overall U.S. exports or its trade balance. The bank has recently increased its loans and guarantees to small and medium-sized businesses.
- Some of EXIM Bank's loans to foreign companies have contributed to harm domestic industries. It is alleged that the foreign firms that receive such financing engage in exporting their output to the U.S. market, thus competing with local industries.

Working Capital Guarantee Program

The availability of adequate working capital is critical for the maintenance and expansion of a viable export–import business. Banks are often reluctant to make

FIGURE 14.1 Working Capital Guarantee Program

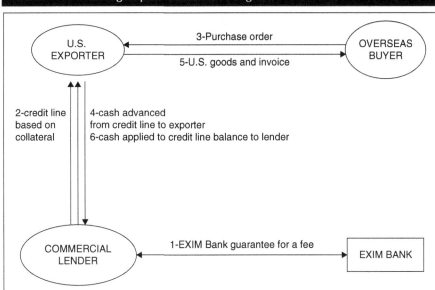

financing available because the businesses either have reached the borrowing limits set by their banks or do not have the necessary collateral. The working capital guarantee program is intended to encourage commercial lenders to make loans for various exports-related activities (see Figure 14.1). Such loans may be used for the purchase of raw materials and finished products for export and to pay for overheads, as well as to cover standbyL/Cs, such as bid bonds, performance bonds, or payment guarantees (EXIM Bank, 2020a).

Exporters may apply to EXIM Bank for a preliminary commitment for a guarantee. The lender also may apply directly for a final authorization. In the case of preliminary commitment, EXIM Bank will outline the general terms and conditions under which it will provide the guarantee to the exporter, and this can be used to approach various lenders to secure the most attractive loan package.

INTERNATIONAL PERSPECTIVE 14.1

General EXIM Bank Criteria for Loans and Loan Guarantees

Foreign content policy: To be eligible for support, items must be shipped from the United States and the foreign content (cost of foreign components incorporated in the item in the United States) must be less than 50 percent of the total cost to produce the item. In the case of U.S. items supplied to a foreign project under long-term program support, EXIM Bank support is available even though the U.S. items aggregate less than 50 percent of the total project cost (intermediate-term loans and guarantees).

Repayment terms: Repayment usually begins about six months after shipment or project completion, and payments of principal and interest must be made semi-annually. Applicable payment terms for a transaction can be determined by a) identifying the country group (I or II) in the list where the product is exported, b) finding the standard term that applies to the country group and the contract price of your transaction, and c) reviewing the terms in chart II and shorter/longer than standard terms.

Scope of coverage: EXIM Bank's loans, guarantees, and intermediate-term insurance cover 85 percent of the contract price. The foreign buyer is required to make a 15 percent cash payment. Fees charged are based on the risk assessment of the foreign buyer or guarantor, the buyer's country, and the term of the credit.

Interest rates and shipping: Interest rates and maximum maturity terms are subject to OECD guidelines. The lender sets the rate in guarantee programs while loans are often negotiated at fixed rates. EXIM Bank -supported sales of more than $20 million in loans or loan guarantee (and with repayment periods of over seven years) must be shipped in a vessel of U.S registry unless a waiver has been obtained by the foreign buyer from the U.S. Maritime Administration. This applies in the case of long-term financing programs.

The lender must apply for the final commitment. An exporter may also apply through a lender that has been granted a guarantee by EXIM Bank. Such lenders have been granted pre-approved credit authority (delegated authority) to process working capital loans under established criteria without pre-approval from EXIM Bank. For small business exporters, the small Business Administration (SBA) can guarantee a working capital loan up to $5 million under a co-guaranty agreement with EXIM Bank. Guarantees may be approved for a single loan or a revolving line of credit.

The major features of the working capital guarantee program are as follows.

Qualified Exports

Eligible exports must be shipped from the United States and have at least 50 percent U.S. content. If the export has less than 50 percent U.S. content, the bank will only support up to the percentage of the U.S. content. Military items as well as sales to military buyers are generally not eligible.

Guarantee Coverage and Term of the Loan

In the event of default by the exporter, EXIM Bank will cover 90 percent of the principal of the loan and interest, up to the date of claim for payment, insofar as the lender has met all the terms and conditions of the guarantee agreement. Guaranteed loans generally have maturities of twelve months and are renewable.

Collateral and Borrowing Capacity

Guaranteed loans are to be secured by a collateral. Acceptable collateral may include export-related inventory, export-related accounts receivable, or other assets. Inventory and accounts receivable include goods purchased or sales generated by use of the guaranteed loan. For service companies, costs such as engineering, design, or allocable overheads may be treated as collateral. In the case of L/Cs issued under the guaranteed loan, collateral is required only for 25 percent of the value of the L/C.

Exporters can borrow up to 75 percent of their inventory including work-in-process and up to 90 percent of their foreign accounts receivable, thus increasing their borrowing capacity. Table 14.6 illustrates borrowing capacity with and without the working capital facility.

Qualified Exporters and Lenders

Exporters must be domiciled in the United States (regardless of domestic/foreign ownership requirements), show a successful track record of past performance, including an operating history of at least one year, and have a positive net worth. Financial statements must show sufficient strength to accommodate the requested debt. There are lower collateral requirements for bid bonds, performance bonds, or advance payment guarantees.

Any public or private lender may apply under the program. Eligibility is determined on many factors, including the lender's financial condition, knowledge of trade finance, and ability to manage asset-based loans. Lenders may be approved as priority lenders or delegated authority lenders. Approved lenders under the priority lender program submit final commitment applications to EXIM Bank and receive a decision within ten business days. The lender, prior to submission to EXIM Bank, must approve the loan application. However, approved delegated authority lenders are allowed to approve loans and receive a guarantee from EXIM Bank without having to submit individual applications for approval.

> *Example*: Thrustmaster, a Houston-based small business that designs and manufactures marine thrusters (propulsion devices for the spacecraft and water-craft industries) obtained approval for a US$30 million EXIM Bank working capital loan guarantee through Amegy Bank of Texas. The firm exports about 80 percent of its output to customers all over the world, especially South Korea, Singapore, Brazil, India, and China.

Export Credit Insurance Program (ECIP)

The purpose of the ECIP is to promote U.S. sales abroad by protecting exporters against loss in the event of default by a foreign buyer or debt arising from commercial or political risks. The policy also enables exporters to obtain financing more easily because, with prior EXIM Bank approval, the proceeds of the policy can be readily assigned to a financial institution as collateral. EXIM Bank offers a wide range of policies to accommodate many different insurance needs of exporters and financial institutions. For example, insurance policies may apply to shipments to one buyer or many buyers, cover short-term (180 days or less) or intermediate-term (generally one to five years) credit, and provide comprehensive coverage for commercial as well as specific or all political risks. There is also a policy specifically geared to small businesses that are beginning to export their goods or services (the Small Business Policy). Some export credit insurance policies include the following:

TABLE 14.6 Increased Borrowing Capacity under the EXIM Bank Working Capital Guarantee Program

Collateral	Amount	Working capital without EXIM Bank		Working capital with EXIM Bank Guarantee	
		Advance Rate	Borrowing Base	Advance Rate	Borrowing Base
Export inventory supported by an export order					
Raw materials	*300,000*	*20%*	*60,000*	*75%*	*225,000*
Work in process	*300,000*	*0%*	*0*	*75%*	*225,000*
Finished goods	*600,000*	*50%*	*300,000*	*75%*	*450,000*
Foreign Account receivable (FAC)					
FAC	*500,000*	*0%*	*0*	*90%*	*450,000*
L/C backed account receivable	*600,000*	*70%*	*420,000*	*90%*	*540,000*
Total borrowing base			*780,000*		*1,890,000*

Source: EXIM Bank (2020b)

1. **Exporter policies (short-term)**: single-buyer/multi-buyer policy, small business policy;
2. **Lender policies (short-term):** L/C policy, financial institution buyer/supplier credit policy;
3. **Policies for exporters and lenders**: documentary and non-documentary policies;
4. **Other policies:** These include a leasing policy for operating and finance leases. The policies insure both the stream of lease payments and the fair market value of the leased product (Table 14.7 and Figure 14.2).

Example: Blockwise Engineering, a medical equipment manufacturer in Tempe, Arizona, exports about 50 percent of its total sales to China, Japan, Ireland, South Korea, Germany, and Italy. A Blockwise machine costs about US$50,000–100,000 each and the seller prefers advance payment before delivery. This is not customary in the export market and requirement could potentially decrease sales to competitors that accept open account terms. The firm now uses EXIM Bank's trade credit insurance as this covers 95 percent of its sales invoice if the customer defaults. The firm allows customers to pay thirty to ninety days after delivery. This arrangement enables it to enter new markets without a sense of apprehension about potential defaults by overseas customers.

Loan Guarantees (Medium- and Long-term)

EXIM Bank guarantees provide repayment protection for private-sector loans to creditworthy buyers of U.S. exports (see Figure 14.3). The program covers 100 percent of the commercial and political risks (guarantees 85 percent of U.S. contract amount). The foreign buyer is required to make at least a 15 percent cash payment. Exports supported under this program are capital equipment, services, and projects, and the loan guarantees are offered for intermediate- and long-term sales. Guarantees of up to $20 million with a repayment period of seven years or less do not require

TABLE 14.7 Export Credit Insurance Policies

Policy	Features
Exporter policies (short term)	
Multi-buyer policy	• Provides 90–95% commercial, 95–100% coverage against buyer default • Exporter's receivables can be assigned to a lender for immediate funding • Premium rates based on tenor, type of buyer, and country of buyer • Available for small business exporters
Single-buyer policy	• Supports single or multiple shipments to a single foreign buyer • Provides 90% coverage against buyer default with no first loss deductible • Exporter's receivables can be assigned to lender
Lender policies (short-term)	
Bank letter of credit policy	• Protects U.S. banks against losses on irrevocable L/Cs opened to finance U.S. exports (failure of a foreign issuing bank to make payments), i.e., confirmations and negotiations of irrevocable L/Cs by foreign banks. • Covers 95% for private sector; 100% for sovereign banks
Financial institution buyer credit policy	• Protects lenders that finance purchases by overseas buyers of U.S. exports • Used for one or several shipments from one or several exporters to same buyer • No first loss deductible • Covers 90% for private sector; 100% for sovereign banks
Exporters/lenders policy (medium term)	• Used for financing of capital equipment or services (one or more shipments); no first loss deductible • Insured financial institution disburses funds to exporter once insurance is approved • Insured portion is the lesser of 85% of the net U.S. contract value or the U.S. content of the exporter's supply contract

shipment on U.S.-registered vessels. The credit may be for any amount. The guarantee is unconditional and transferable.

Example: EXIM Bank of the United States approved a guarantee of a $350 million loan facility to provide the funds to assist Textron Inc. in financing the exports by two of its companies, Cessna Aircraft Company and Bell Helicopter Textron. The guaranteed lender is PNC Bank in Pittsburgh, PA.

The EXIM Bank-guaranteed loan facility will enable Textron's finance segment to provide financing to international customers that take delivery of new Cessna aircraft and Bell commercial helicopters. The repayment term is twelve years.

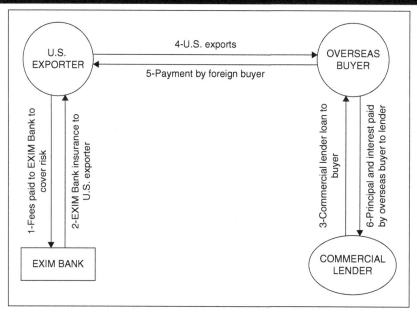

FIGURE 14.2 Export Credit Insurance

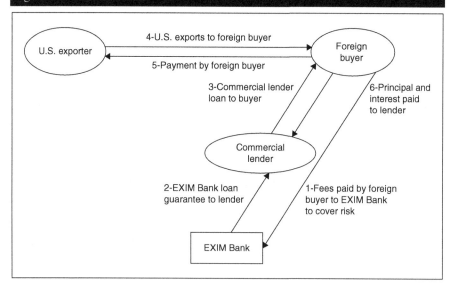

Figure 14.3 Loan Guarantee

Direct Loans Program (Intermediate/Long-term)

Under this program, EXIM Bank provides a fixed-rate loan directly to creditworthy foreign buyers for the purchase of U.S. capital equipment, projects, and related services. The loan covers the lesser of 85 percent of the U.S. export value or 100 percent of the U.S. content in all eligible exports. The buyer is, however, required to make a cash payment for the difference, that is, 15 percent of the value. The loan is often used by buyers when the financed portion exceeds $10 million. A loan agreement as well as shipment on U.S.-registered vessels is required. The program supports intermediate- and long-term sales. Transactions normally range from five to twelve years (eighteen years for renewable energy products), depending on the export value, the product, the importing country, and terms offered by the competition. All direct loans are subject to U.S. flag shipping requirements. There is no limit on transaction size. Direct loans cover 100 percent of commercial and political risks and finance up to 30 percent of local costs in addition to U.S. exports.

> ***Example***: EXIM Bank approved a $1.03 billion loan to Globalfoundries of Germany to finance the export of American-made semiconductor manufacturing equipment to Germany. EXIM Bank's credit will support the expansion of the Globalfoundries silicon-wafer fabrication facility in Dresden, Germany.

SMALL BUSINESS ADMINISTRATION

The Small Business Administration (SBA) also provides a few programs for U.S. exporters. To qualify for the programs, applicants must meet the definition of a small business under the SBA's size standards and other eligibility requirements. The SBA Act defines an eligible small business as one that is independently owned and operated and not dominant in its field of operation. It has established size standards that define the maximum size of an eligible small business. Table 14.8 represents general guidelines to determine a small business.

Some of the SBA programs that are intended to promote exports are as follows.

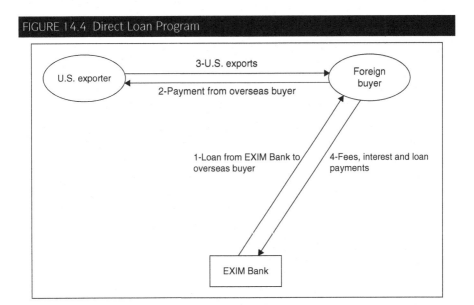

FIGURE 14.4 Direct Loan Program

TABLE 14.8 SBA Guidelines for Determining a Small Business

Industry	Maximum size (US$)
Retail and Service	7.5 million in average annual receipts
Construction	36.5 million in average annual receipts
Agriculture	750,000 in average annual receipts
Wholesale	100–250 employees
Manufacturing	500–1,500 employees

Export Working Capital Program Loans (EWCP)

The EWCP is a combined effort of the SBA and EXIM Bank to provide short-term working capital to U.S. exporters. To be processed by the SBA, loan guarantee requests must be equal to or less than $5 million. Loan requests greater than $5 million are processed by the EXIM Bank. The applicant must be in business for one year (not necessarily exporting) at the time of application. The agency can guarantee up to 90 percent of loans and accrued interest up to 120 days. The proceeds can be used for the payment of manufacturing costs of goods for export and the purchase of goods and services for export, to support standby L/Cs (to act as bid or performance bonds), and to finance foreign accounts receivable.

International Trade Loan Program

This program assists small businesses that are already engaged or preparing to engage in international trade and those which are adversely affected by import competition. The SBA can guarantee up to 90 percent of the loan to a maximum of $4.5 million (the maximum guarantee for the working capital component is $4 million). Maturity on the working capital loan is ten years. Collateral is required and must be located in the United States. Maximum loan amount is $5 million and SBA 7(a) loan program requirements apply. Proceeds can be used to acquire or modernize equipment in the United States to produce goods for export, for working capital, or for refinancing debt structured with unreasonable terms.

SBA Export Express Loan

The SBA Export Express Loan is a flexible financing tool available to assist small businesses in developing and expanding export markets. Export Express offers financing up to $500,000. It can take the form of a term loan or a revolving line of credit. For example, you can use funds to participate in a foreign trade show, support standby L/Cs and translate product literature for use in foreign markets. You may also use funds to finance specific export orders, expand production facilities, and purchase equipment inventory or real estate.

INTERNATIONAL DEVELOPMENT FINANCE CORPORATION (IDFC)

The International Development Finance Corporation (IDFC) is a wholly owned U.S. government corporation that supports U.S. exports and American private investment in developing nations and emerging market economies. Its programs are presently available for new and expanding businesses in some 150 countries worldwide. It is a consolidated agency that brings together the Overseas Private Investment Corporation (OPIC) and USAID's Development Credit Authority and came into effect in 2018. Its mandate is to enhance U.S. competitiveness abroad while advancing U.S. foreign policy.

> *Example*: In 2019, IDFC extended financing to Joshi technologies of Oklahoma to increase oil production in Colombia. The country's oil output had declined from 1 million barrels per day in 2013 to 858,000 barrels per day in 2018 partly due to aging oil fields that require investment to extend their production life. The firm is a pioneer in horizontal well technology and will help augment production.

Ownership

Projects wholly owned by governments are not eligible. The IDFC finances overseas ventures wholly owned by U.S. companies or joint ventures in which the U.S. investor has at least 25 percent equity. As a rule, at least 51 percent of the voting shares of the overseas venture must be held by the private sector. Financing is provided in cases in which the government holds majority ownership, insofar as management remains in private hands.

Eligibility

The IDFC puts emphasis on low- and lower-middle-income countries. Projects are evaluated on the basis of their contribution to economic growth, technology transfer, and inclusion (people in rural areas, women, underdeveloped areas). Evaluation also includes environmental and social impact analysis.

The IDFC assists U.S. firms through various activities designed to promote exports and overseas investment and reduce associated risks.

Financing of Business Through Loans and Loan Guarantees

The IDFC provides intermediate- and long-term project financing through loans and loan guarantees in countries where conventional financial institutions are often reluctant or unable to provide financing. All projects considered for financing must be commercially and financially sound and managed by people with a proven track record of success in the same or a related business. The IDFC, for example, carefully reviews whether the project will generate adequate cash flow to pay all operational costs, to service all debt, and provide owners with an adequate return on their investments. It provides limited-recourse long-term financing for private sector commercial projects and lending platforms. Direct loans and guarantees up to US$1 billion per project and up to twenty-year terms are provided under this program (for critical infrastructure, power generation, housing, financial services, and projects that have a positive impact in the host country). There are also specific programs tailored to small and medium-sized businesses.

Equity Financing

The IDFC provides equity financing either directly into specific projects or by supporting emerging market investment funds. These projects must have a developmental impact or advance U.S. foreign policy in developing countries. Such financing is also intended to provide beneficiary countries not only with access to long-term capital but also access to management and financial skills that help create new economic opportunities. The IDFC provides finance to a number of privately owned and managed investment funds so that these funds extend equity capital to facilitate business formation and expansion. Some funds invest primarily in small companies, whereas others invest in larger projects.

Debt Financing

The IDFC provides financing of over US$50 million to projects in critical infrastructure, energy, and other large investments. It also provides development credit on projects requiring less than US$50 million in financing.

Insuring Investments Against a Broad Range of Political Risks

The IDFC offers many programs to insure investments in developing nations against political risk. The following risks are covered:

1. *Currency inconvertibility:* This is the inability to convert profits, debt services, and other remittances from local currency into U.S. dollars.
2. *Expropriation:* This involves loss of investment due to expropriation, nationalization, or confiscation by the host government.
3. *Political violence:* This relates to loss of assets or income due to war, revolution, civil war, terrorism, and so forth. An investor may purchase a separate policy for loss of business, loss of assets, or both. Coverage is available for new or existing investments. Special insurance programs are available for the following sectors: financial institutions, leases, oil and gas projects, natural resource projects, contractors, and exporters.

An IDFC insurance policy is available to citizens of the United States, businesses created under U.S. law with majority ownership by U.S. citizens, and foreign companies with a minimum ownership of 95 percent equity by U.S citizens.

PRIVATE EXPORT FUNDING CORPORATION

The Private Export Funding Corporation (PEFCO) is a major source of capital for intermediate- and long-term fixed-rate loans for U.S. exports. It acts as a supplemental lender to traditional sources by making loans available for foreign purchasers of U.S. goods and services.

The Private Export Funding Corporation is a private corporation owned by banks and industrial and financial companies. It works closely with EXIM Bank. EXIM Bank, for example, unconditionally guarantees all PEFCO loans. It assists the financing of U.S. exports by providing a direct loan or buying export loans originated by lenders. PEFCO has a program for small business exporters to provide short-term working capital through private lenders or directly to small business exporters as a lender of last resort.

U.S. DEPARTMENT OF AGRICULTURE

The U.S. Department of Agriculture (USDA) provides financial support for U.S. agricultural exports through various programs, such as:

- The GSM–102 program provides credit guarantees for up to eighteen months and will cover 98 percent of the export value.
- Public Law 480 authorizes U.S. government financing of sales of U.S. agricultural products to friendly countries on concessional terms.

In addition to government programs, more than a dozen state governments have introduced export financing programs. Some of the programs implemented in California and Illinois have the following essential features: 1) state-funded loan guarantee programs, 2) pre-shipment and postshipment assistance in the form of loans to lenders and loan guarantees to exporters and their banks, and 3) state agency acting as a delivery agent for EXIM Bank programs.

CHAPTER SUMMARY

EXIM Bank	EXIM Bank is an independent agency of the U.S. government, the purpose of which is to aid in financing and to facilitate trade between the United States and other countries. The bank, which is expected to be self-sustaining (except for the initial capital of $1 billion to start operations), makes loans and guarantees with reasonable assurance of repayment. It complements private sources of finance.
Working Capital Guarantee Program	This enables exporters to meet critical pre-export financing needs, such as inventory build-up or marketing. EXIM Bank will guarantee 90 percent of the loan provided by a qualified lender. The guarantee has a maturity of twelve months and is renewable.
Export Credit Insurance Program	A wide range of policies to accommodate different insurance needs. Its major features are: U.S. content requirements, restrictions on sales destined for military use and to communist nations. The program covers exporter policies (short-term): 1) single-buyer/multi-buyer policies, small business policies, 2) lender policies (short-term): L/C policies, financial institution buyer/supplier credit policies, 3) policies for exporters and lenders: documentary and non-documentary policies, 4) other policies: leasing and foreign dealer policies.
Guarantees	The program provides repayment protection for private-sector loans to creditworthy buyers of U.S. goods and services. There is also special coverage for U.S. or foreign lenders on lines of credit extended to foreign banks or foreign buyers.

Direct Loan Program	This is an intermediate/long-term loan provided to creditworthy foreign buyers for the purchase of U.S. capital goods and services.
Small Business Administration (SBA)	The SBA provides certain programs for small business exporters.
	Export Working Capital This guarantees short-term working capital loans to U.S. small business exporters.
	International Trade Loan Program Guarantees loans to small businesses that are already engaged or plan to engage in international trade as well as those that are adversely affected by import competition.
International Development Finance Corporation (IDFC)	This self-supporting agency of the U.S. government insures U.S. investors against political and commercial risks and provides financing through loans and loan guarantees.
Private Export Funding Corporation (PEFCO)	This private corporation works in conjunction with EXIM Bank in the financing of foreign purchases of U.S. goods and services. PEFCO loans are guaranteed by EXIM Bank.
Department of Agriculture	The USDA provides financial support for the export of U.S. agricultural products through GSM–102 and Public Law 480.
State and local export financing programs	States provide different programs to expand exports: loans, loan guarantees. They also act as delivery agents for EXIM Bank programs.

REVIEW QUESTIONS

1. What is the difference between buyer and supplier credit?
2. State the OECD guidelines on export credits.
3. Describe the origins and activities of EXIM Bank.
4. What are some of the criticisms of EXIM Bank?
5. What is the difference between the Working Capital Guarantee Program and the Direct Loans Program?
6. What kinds of export are eligible under the Working Capital Program?
7. Compare and contrast the single-buyer and multiple-buyer policy.
8. Discuss the role of the IDFC in promoting U.S. exports.
9. How does PEFCO promote U.S. exports?
10. State some of the programs available to promote U.S. agricultural exports.

REFERENCES

EXIM Bank (2012). *Actions Needed to Promote Competitiveness and International Cooperation*. Washington, DC: U.S. Government Printing Office.

EXIM Bank (2019). *Small Business Information*. Washington, DC: U.S. Government Printing Office.

EXIM Bank (2020a). *General Information*. Washington, DC: U.S. Government Printing Office.

EXIM Bank (2020b). *Working Capital Loan Guarantees*. Washington, DC: EXIM Bank.

Karnischnig, M. (2017). Beijing's Balkan backdoor. *Politico*, July 13/17.

United States Agency for International Development (USAID) (2000). *Analysis of Microfinance Supply and Demand on Russia's Market*. Moscow: USAID.

World Wide Web Sources

British Exporters Association: www.bexa.co.uk

EXIM Bank (programs, projects fees etc.): www.exim.gov

Exporting Finance Program Guide: www. export.gov/finance/

IDFC: www.dfc.gov/

PEFCO: www.pefco.com

SBA: www.sbaonline.sba.gov

U.S. Department of Agriculture: www.usda.gov

International Trade Closing Cases and Discussions

1. Trade Finance for Small and Medium-sized Enterprises in the Commonwealth of Independent States (CIS)

Primary and intermediate commodities continue to dominate the composition of exports from the Commonwealth of Independent States (CIS): Armenia, Azerbaijan, Belarus, Georgia, Kazakhstan, Kyrgyzstan, Russia, Moldova, Tajikistan, Turkmenistan, Ukraine, and Uzbekistan. Such exports may not need elaborate long-term financial arrangements unlike the high value-added exports from countries of Central and Eastern Europe.

According to the OECD Consensus Risk Classification of June 2020, country risks for export credit are subdivided into seven levels with one signifying minimal risk and category seven indicating the highest risk. All CIS economies were categorized as very high-risk countries at Levels 5–7. Payment terms are largely based on L/Cs and cash in advance. In Russia, for example, three out of five import shipments require advance payments. For small and medium-sized imports in these countries, the use of L/Cs and cash in advance represents a significant cost, with an adverse effect on their competitiveness.

In many of these countries, the banking system is not sufficiently developed to handle foreign trade transactions. In 2020, for example, the sum of loans to the private sector was estimated at about 35–40 percent of GDP compared to that of over 100 percent for Eurozone countries (World Bank, 2020). Among CIS countries, it ranges from 12 percent for Tajikistan, 29 percent for Belarus, and 25 percent for Kazakhstan, to 52 percent for Russia.

Adequate trade finance facilities for small and medium-sized enterprises are limited in view of the banks' reluctance to service small companies due to the perception of high risk associated with such financing and the costs of evaluating the creditworthiness of small clients. Trade is often hampered by the limited availability of pre-shipment working capital financing as well as burdensome collateral requirements. In most of these countries, banks do not provide medium- and long-term trade financing. The average length of commercial credits granted in most countries varies from three to six months. The role of leasing in capital investment and trade financing remains quite limited.

Over the last few decades, some CIS economies have introduced export credit insurance and guarantee schemes, established ECAs and state-sponsored export–import banks. For many of these countries, both remain undercapitalized, lack reliable credit information, and face difficulties collecting "problem" loans.

Aggregate GDP for the region declined in 2019 due to a marked deceleration in the Russian economy due to economic sanctions. Global exports to Russia secured by L/Cs have substantially declined since the imposition of the sanctions. Meanwhile, there has been moderate growth in guarantees and growth with respect to supply chain finance products. Factoring has also shown modest growth in many of these countries. However, an International Chamber of Commerce report indicates that a majority of SMEs experience significant barriers in accessing trade credit. In 2015, SMEs in these countries submitted 44 percent of all trade finance proposals and accounted for about 60 percent of rejections by banks and other financial institutions.

Questions

1. Do many CIS economies use L/Cs as an important means of payment for international trade? Discuss.
2. Briefly discuss the role of trade financing in CIS economies.

2. Omni Helicopters International (OHI) of Brazil (Credit Guarantee)

The U.S. EXIM Bank guaranteed the export finance of U.S.-made helicopters to Brazil. The bank approved a final commitment to guarantee support for 85 percent of the U.S. content of the export, a portion amounting to $23.2 million. Omni Helicopters International S.A. (OHI) would buy the aircraft and assign them to its operating subsidiary, OTA. Philadelphia manufacturer AgustaWestland Philadelphia Corporation would supply its twin-engine helicopters in order for OHI to service its transportation contracts with Petrobras, which operates deep-water drilling rigs off the Brazilian coast. Brazil's state-owned Petrobras off-shore drilling industry increasingly demands new technology, including medium-lift helicopters to carry passengers to remote off-shore operations. The helicopter can carry fifteen passengers. It features a range of 575 miles and can fly at a cruising speed of 190 miles per hour. The bank's financing is estimated to support at least 500 American jobs in all phases of aircraft production and delivery, based on the number employed by the company.

3. BG Energy Holding of Trinidad and Tobago (Direct Loan)

EXIM Bank approved a $37.6 million direct loan to support exports by McDermott International Inc. and five American suppliers of natural gas compression equipment and technology for a United Kingdom energy project off the coast of Trinidad and Tobago. Under the terms of the direct loan, EXIM Bank will support exports of U.S.-only goods and services to a $150-million project to construct and install a gas compression system on the existing Hibiscus Platform situated off the northern coast of Trinidad. The borrower is BG Energy Holding Limited, and the buyer is BG Trinidad and Tobago (BGTT), which is responsible for 46 percent of the larger project.

McDermott International Inc. was hired to provide the detail engineering, equipment procurement, unit fabrication, transportation, heavy lift, and installation. The company is responsible also for start-up and commissioning. Houston-based McDermott International Inc. is an engineering, procurement, construction, and installation company that executes complex offshore oil and gas projects worldwide. Five U.S. suppliers will manufacture or provide components for the project.

4. Export of Cotton to Turkey (Credit Insurance)

EXIM Bank renewed a twelve-month export credit insurance policy for Wells Fargo to enable the export of American cotton to a large textile firm in Turkey, Menderes Tekstil. Farm workers in at least fifteen U.S. farms will produce the cotton for export. Depending upon agricultural factors, and the precise qualities of cotton needed for various textiles, the cotton will be exported from a combination of farms in North Carolina, South Carolina, Tennessee, Virginia, and other states. EXIM Bank's support is expected to facilitate $15 million in sales of what these farms produce.

The instrument renewed in this transaction was a Financial Institution Buyer Credit (FIBC), allowing Wells Fargo Bank to extend revolving credit to the Turkish textile manufacturer so it can import American cotton. The Menderes Tekstil firm is the largest home textiles producer in Turkey, and one of the largest in the world. The primary exporters benefiting from this FIBC policy are Cargill cotton and Carolinas cotton.

5. Ethiopian Airlines (Backing Bond Issued by Ethiopian Airlines)

EXIM Bank agreed to back bonds issued by Ethiopian Airlines to finance the export of four of ten Boeing 787 Dreamliner aircraft to Ethiopia. Ethiopian Airlines obtained competitive interest rates on its bonds.

EXIM Bank authorized the final commitment for the purchase of the Dreamliners, and Boeing delivered the first aircraft to Ethiopian Airlines a few months later. Nippon Export and Investment Insurance co-financed the transaction. The Boeing 787 aircraft delivered to Ethiopian Airlines is the first of its kind to be delivered to any airline outside Japan, and it is the first one to be financed by EXIM Bank.

Question

Describe how the above-mentioned financing programs differ in terms of their product and risk coverage.

PART VI

Export Regulations and Tax Incentives

CHAPTER 15

Regulations and Policies Affecting Exports

LEARNING OBJECTIVES:

15.1 Describe the objectives and scope of export administration regulations

15.2 Learn about the important steps in establishing whether a given export item is subject to a license

15.3 Identify and discuss the scope of coverage and objectives of U.S. antiboycott regulations

15.4 Learn about the anti-bribery and accounting provisions of the Foreign Corrupt Practices Act (FCPA)

15.5 Understand the various U.S. export cartels that are exempted from antitrust laws

15.6 Learn about the various incentives to promote U.S. exports

International Trade in Practice

U.S. Export Controls and Competitiveness in the Satellite Industry

Export controls are applied in the United States to products and technologies that have both military and commercial applications. Such products range from biological agents, lasers and sensors, and electronics to nuclear technology and designs. They are differentiated and high value-added industries that are critical for the country's competitiveness. The commercial satellite industry consists of manufacturing, launching, and other related services pertaining to commercial spacecraft (microwave, digital technology, and so on), employs about 250,000 people and has R&D spending estimated at over $2.2 billion a year.

Existing export licensing regulations have an adverse effect on the industry's export competitiveness. First, it is often characterized by long delays in obtaining export licenses and increasing incidences of denials. Even in cases where licenses are given, separate licenses are required for different activities, thus increasing compliance costs. This also leads to delays that may lead to losing potential bids while waiting for the license. A U.S. satellite manufacturer may need up to six licenses for marketing, manufacturing, design, and launch of a single communications spacecraft. Congressional notification is also required for export transactions exceeding a certain monetary threshold. Second, most dual-use goods or technology are not multilaterally controlled and are often available in global markets from different sources. For example, when the United States imposed unilateral controls, countries such as China were buying similar products from the EU and other advanced countries. Importers in China are required to obtain end-user statements from the Ministry of Commerce in China, thus imposing burdensome requirements on one of the fastest growing markets for U.S. exports. Presently, China is the third-largest destination for U.S. exports.

Third, such controls require the implementation of internal controls to comply with such regulations. Non-compliance can result in severe monetary and criminal penalties. Exporters have to screen potential customers, collect end-user information to prevent sales to denied persons, and determine product and country licenses. This leads to high transaction costs. A survey of over 200 aerospace firms indicates that compliance costs associated with export controls average US$49 million a year. Lost sales attributed to licensing were estimated at over $500 million in 2006 (Table 15.1).

TABLE 15.1 Compliance Costs Attributed to Licensing in the U.S. Aerospace Industry (US$ million, 2003–2006)

Compliance cost	Average (2003–2006)	% total cost
Compliance training cost	8.33	17
Salaries/outside legal costs	31.36	64
Monitoring/consulting/insurance cost	9.31	19
Total compliance cost	49	100

Source: U.S. Department of Commerce (2007)

EXPORT LICENSING AND ADMINISTRATION

Governments use export controls for a variety of reasons. Such controls are often intended to achieve certain desired political and economic objectives. The first U.S. export control was introduced in 1775 when Continental Congress outlawed the export of goods to Great Britain. Since then, the United States has restricted exports to certain countries through legislation such as the Embargo Act, Trading with the Enemy Act, The Neutrality Act, and the Export Control Act.

The Export Control Act of 1949 represents the first comprehensive export control program enacted in peacetime. Export controls prior to this time were almost exclusively devoted to the prohibition or curtailment of arms exports (arms embargoes). The 1949 legislation was primarily intended to curtail the export of certain commodities to communist nations during the cold war era. Export controls were thus allowed for reasons of national security, foreign policy, and short supply. Given

America's dominant economic position in the post-war era, it provided leadership in international economic relations and pursued an active foreign policy (Stenger, 1984; Moskowitz, 1996).

In 1969, the often stringent and far-reaching restrictions were curtailed and the new law (Export Administration Act, 1969) attempted to balance the need for export controls with the recognition of the adverse effects of an overly comprehensive export control system on the country's economy. This came at a time when the United States was losing ground to other nations in economic performance, such as balance of trade, exports, and so on. The overvalued dollar and inflation, for example, had adversely affected its competitiveness in foreign markets and shrank its trade surplus from $6.8 billion in 1964 to a mere $400 million in 1969. The promotion of exports was considered essential to improve the country's declining trade surplus and overall competitiveness as well as to reduce growing unemployment. The general trend in 1969 and thereafter has been to ease and/or strengthen the position of exporters and increase the role of Congress in implementing export control policy. Some examples are as follows:

1. The Equal Export Opportunity Act of 1972 curtailed the use of export controls if the product (subject to such restrictions) was available from sources outside the United States in comparable quality and quantity. This was because export controls would be ineffective if certain commodities were available from foreign sources. The 1977 amendment prohibited the president from imposing export controls without providing adequate evidence with regard to its importance to U.S. national security interests. In the event that the president decided to prohibit or control exports, the law required him to negotiate with other countries to eliminate foreign availability.

   The scope of presidential authority to regulate U.S. foreign transactions, including the imposition of export controls, was restricted to wartime only. A statute (the International Emergency Economic Powers Act, 50 U.S. Code 1701 4 seq.) was also passed to regulate presidential powers in the area of export controls during national emergencies. As of 2020, restrictions based on national emergencies have been imposed against Libya, North Korea, Iran, Myanmar, and Syria. In short, the president can impose export controls outside emergency and wartime periods only upon extensive review and consultation with Congress.

2. In 1977, Congress introduced limitations on the power of the executive branch to prohibit or curtail agricultural exports. Any prohibition of such exports was considered ineffective without the approval of Congress by concurrent resolution.

3. The 1979 Export Administration Act (EAA) also emphasized the important contribution of exports to the U.S. economy and acknowledged the necessity of balancing the need for trade and exports and national security interests. The law gave legal effect to the agreement of the Coordinating Committee for Multilateral Export Controls (COCOM), established in 1949 to coordinate export controls of technology to communist countries. It was dissolved in 1994, but was primarily intended to control three categories of goods: conventional arms, nuclear-related items, and dual-use items. Control of the latter was the most controversial since it restricted normal commerce and limited trade in goods and technologies that have both civilian and military applications (Hunt, 1983).

4. The 1985 amendments to the Export Administration Act further restricted the power of the president to impose foreign policy controls that interfere with contracts entered into before the decision to restrict exports, except under very specific circumstances. Congress also established validated licenses for multiple exports, allowing exporters to make successive shipments of the same goods under a single license, waived licensing requirements for certain low-tech goods exports to COCOM nations, and shortened by one-third the time period for issuing licenses for exports to non-COCOM members. In view of certain international incidents, such as the downing of a Korean aircraft by the former Soviet Union, the law tightened export controls on the acquisition of critical military goods and technology by the former Soviet Union and its allies.

Export controls were originally intended to be used against former communist countries. However, with the end of the Cold War, there was no longer a clearly defined, single adversary, and it became necessary to adjust the system of export controls to take into account the new reality in international relations. An increasingly global economy also presented new challenges for managing export controls. The growing number of global suppliers of high technology and defense-related items, increased levels of global R&D, and dissemination of dual use technologies, as well as divergent views among Western countries militated in favor of liberalization of export controls. Prior to September 11, 2001, substantial liberalization of controls had taken place in many areas, such as high performance computers, telecommunication, and so on. Export controls were aimed at, inter alia, restricting a narrow range of transactions that could assist in the development of weapons of mass destruction by certain countries. The control system essentially focused on a small group of critical goods and technology, on specific end uses and end users, in addition to certain "reckless" nations that must be stopped from acquiring weapons of mass destruction. The new multilateral arrangement that was developed after COCOM, the Wassenaar arrangement (1990) also focused on transfers of conventional arms and dual-use goods and technology. However, it is not binding and member countries implement the controls solely at their own discretion. Unlike COCOM, Wassenaar members do not have veto power over one another's exports and do not have an agreed list of restricted countries. Furthermore, the agreement does not require notification of exports prior to shipment. Even though Wassenaar member countries agree on the need to avoid destabilizing accumulations of weapons and dual-use items to countries of concern, they disagree about which countries are states of concern (particularly China) and what constitutes a destabilizing transfer (Corr, 2003).

Since the events of September 11, 2001, the U.S. government has introduced certain restrictions on exports. First, it prohibits the conduct of business with any group whose named members appear on the lists of denied persons maintained by the Office of Foreign Assets Control. The list includes terrorists and individuals and/or companies associated with terrorists or terrorist organizations. Second, a deemed export license is required before foreign nationals engaged in research on a U.S. university campus receive technology or technical data on the use of export-controlled equipment or materials. For a deemed license to be required, the information being conveyed would have to both involve controlled equipment (and other materials) and be publicly unavailable. The fundamental research exclusion applies to information in the United States that is broadly shared with the scientific community and not restricted for proprietary reasons or specific national security concerns. Thirdly, the Commerce Department bureau responsible for export controls on dual-use goods and technologies changed its name from the Bureau of Export Administration (BXA) to one that reflected trade and security: the Bureau of Industry and Security (BIS). A focus has also been placed on controlling the export of weapons of mass destruction to hostile countries. Since the terrorist attacks of September 11, 2001, many Western governments deny risky exports, while approving legitimate ones more efficiently (Walsh, 2002) (see International Perspective 15.3 for multilateral export controls). In 2019, BIS reviewed a total of 34,207 export license applications valued at US$487 billion and approved 85.7 percent, returned 13.3 percent, and denied less than 1 percent of the applications. In 2019 its average processing time for the review of license applications is about twenty-three days. The largest category of applications are for export of military aircraft, followed by chemical manufacturing and equipment, military gas turbine engines, human pathogens, and optimal sighting devices.

U.S. Export Administration Regulations

The Export Control Reform Act (ECRA) of 2018 provides a detailed legislative authority for the president to implement dual-use export controls. The new law repeals the Export Administration Act (EAA) of 1979 which was the underlying authority for dual-use export controls till it expired in 2001. However, when it expired, EAA was extended by a presidential declaration of a national emergency under the International Emergency Economic Powers Act. The ECRA, 2018 has no expiration date and requires the President to control the export, re-export and in-country transfer of items (within U.S. jurisdiction) whether by U.S. or foreign persons. It also includes the activities of U.S. persons (regardless of location) relating to nuclear devices, missiles, chemical/biological weapons, and foreign military services. The ECRA requires the Secretary of Commerce to:

- establish and maintain a list of controlled items as well as foreign persons and end uses that could endanger national security
- require export licenses
- prohibit unauthorized exports, re-exports, and in-country transfers of controlled items
- monitor shipments and other means of transport of controlled items.

The ECRA is implemented by the Export Administration Regulations (EAR). The EAR is administered by the U.S. Department of Commerce, Bureau of Industry and Security (BIS). The regulations also implement antiboycott law provisions.

Export controls in the United States are primarily imposed for the following reasons (EAR, part 742):

1. *Protect national security*: To restrict the export/re-export of items that would make a significant contribution to the military potential of any other country and that would prove detrimental to the national security of the United States. This includes the exports of high performance computers, software, and technology to particular destinations, certain end users and end uses. The list of controlled countries (Country Group D-1) includes Armenia, China, Laos, Russia, and Vietnam. The list of countries and products are periodically reviewed and

revised to take into account current developments. The national-security-based control list is consistent with the control list of the Wassenaar agreement. National security controls are subject to foreign availability determination, i.e., items must be decontrolled if they are available to controlled countries from sources outside the United States in sufficient quantity and comparable quality. In 2009, for example, export controls were lifted on night vision cameras but tightened on higher-end thermal imaging cameras (Fergusson, 2009; 2020).

2. *Further foreign policy goals*: To restrict the export/re-export of goods and technology to further the foreign policy objectives of the United States, that is, human rights, regional stability, and antiterrorism policies. They are also used to implement unilateral or international sanctions such as those imposed by the United Nations or the Organization of American States. This includes adherence to multilateral non-proliferation agreements in the areas of chemical and biological weapons, nuclear weaponry, and missile technology. Foreign policy controls must be renewed on an annual basis and not authorized for certain items such as sales of medical supplies or donated food and water resource equipment intended to meet basic human needs. The foreign availability of items is supposed to be removed through negotiations with other countries.

3. *Preserve scarce natural resources*: To restrict the export of goods, wherever necessary, to protect the domestic economy from the excessive drain of scarce resources (crude petroleum, certain inorganic chemicals) and to reduce the serious inflationary impact of foreign demand. Domestically produced crude oil and certain unprocessed timber harvested from federal and state lands are controlled for short supply reasons (EAR, part 754).

4. *Control proliferation*: To prevent the proliferation of weapons of mass destruction, such as nuclear, chemical, and biological weapons, which are often maintained as part of multilateral control arrangements (EAR, part 742.2).

The core of the export control provisions of the EAR concerns exports from the United States. However, the term 'exports' has been given broad meaning to include activities other than exports or to apply to transactions outside the United States.

The scope of the EAR covers the following:

- Exports from the United States. This includes the release of technology to a foreign national in the United States through such means as demonstration or oral briefing (deemed export). The return of foreign equipment to its country of origin after repair in the United States, shipments from a U.S. foreign trade zone, and the electronic transmission of nonpublic data that will be received abroad also constitute U.S. exports.
- Re-exports by any party of commodities, software, or technology exported from the United States.
- Foreign products that are direct products of technology exported from the United States.
- U.S. persons' activities. The EAR restricts the involvement of "U.S. persons" that is, U.S. firms or individuals, in the exportation of foreign-origin items or in the provision of services that may contribute to the proliferation of weapons of mass destruction. The regulations also restrict technical assistance by U.S. persons with respect to encryption commodities or software (EAR, part 732).

INTERNATIONAL PERSPECTIVE 15.1

Do You Need a Commerce Export License?

Even though the majority of U.S. export/re-exports do not require a license (EAR99), it is important to establish whether a license is required for your exports from the United States.

How do you establish whether you need an export license for your product?

a. *Nature of the product intended for export*: It is important to know whether the item you intend to export has a specific Export Control Classification Number (ECCN). You may require a license if your item is listed on the Commerce Control List (CCL) and the country chart in the Regulations states that a license is required for that country.

If your item falls under the jurisdiction of the Department of Commerce and not listed on the CCL, it is designated as EAR99 (low-tech items that do not require a license unless they are destined to an embargoed country, to an end user of concern in support of a prohibited end use).

b. *Ultimate destination, end user, and end use of the product intended for export*: A license is required for virtually all exports to embargoed destinations (e.g., Cuba, North Korea). You need to consult the list of embargoed countries by three agencies: the Departments of Commerce, State and the Treasury. Certain individuals and organizations are prohibited from receiving U.S. exports, while others may only receive such goods if they have been licensed (including EAR99 goods). It is important to consult the list of individuals and organizations engaging in activities related to the proliferation of weapons of mass destruction, terrorism, and narcotics trafficking, and the list of persons whose export privileges have been derived by BIS. A license requirement may be based on the end use in a transaction, primarily to control proliferation of weapons.

The BIS is the primary licensing agency for dual-use exports. The term 'dual use' distinguishes items (i.e., commercial items with military applications) covered by EAR from those covered by the regulations of certain other export licensing agencies, such as the Departments of State and Defense. Although dual use is often employed to refer to the entire scope of the EAR, the EAR also applies to some items that have solely civilian uses. It is important to note that the export of certain goods is subject to the jurisdiction of other agencies, such as the Food and Drug Administration (drugs and medical devices), the Department of State (defense articles), and the Nuclear Regulatory Commission (nuclear materials).

Commerce Export License

Exports and other activities that are subject to the EAR are under the regulatory jurisdiction of the BIS. They may also be controlled under export-related programs of other agencies. Before proceeding to complete any export transaction, it is important to determine whether a license is required. The modalities of transportation are immaterial in the determination of export licenses, that is, an item can be sent by regular mail, hand carried on an airplane, or transmitted via email or during a telephone conversation. (See International Perspectives 15.1 and 15.2.)

The following steps are important in establishing whether a given export item is subject to a license (Figure 15.1).

Step 1: Is the item (intended for export) subject to EAR? Items subject to the EAR regulations include all items in the United States or abroad (including those in a U.S. free trade zone), foreign-made items that are direct products of U.S.-origin technology or software (or that incorporate U.S.-origin materials exceeding

FIGURE 15.1 Steps to Determine Whether a Commerce Export Control License is Required.

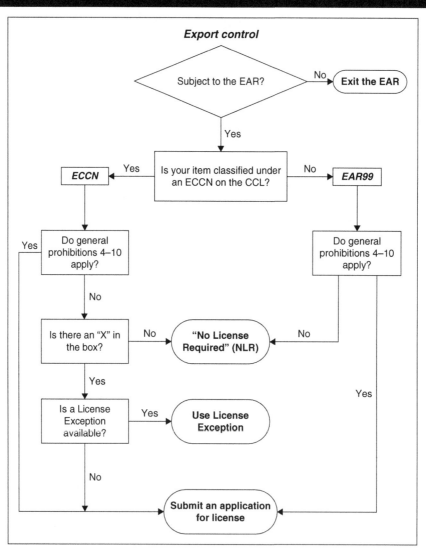

certain minimum levels) or certain activities of U.S. persons related to the prolif-eration of weapons of mass destruction and technical assistance (with regard to encryption commodities or software). It also covers activities of U.S. or foreign persons prohibited by any order (denied parties). Publicly available technology and software, phonograph records, magazines, and so on, are excluded from the scope of EAR.

If the item is subject to the EAR, it is necessary to classify it under an ECCN (Export Control Classification Number) on the CCL (Commerce Control List). If it is not subject to EAR, there is no need to comply with the EAR. It may be necessary to comply with the regulations of another agency.

Step 2: Is the item classified under the ECCN on the CCL? Any item con-trolled by the Department of Commerce has an ECCN. Exporters should classify their product against the CCL. They can also send an export classification request to the Department of Commerce. A request can also be made if an item has been incorrectly classified and/or should be transferred to another agency. Given cer-tain changes that are made with regard to product classifications and the EAR, it is important to monitor the CCL for any modifications to your product including eligi-bility for a license exception to certain destinations. Some companies may opt to use a computerized product/country license determination matrix. The CCL is composed of ten categories of items ranging from nuclear materials to propulsion systems, space vehicles, and equipment. Each of these categories is further divided into five functional groups. Each controlled item has an export classification number (ECCN) based on its category and group.

Step 3: Do the general prohibitions (4–10) apply? Whether a product is listed under an ECCN on the CCL or not (EAR99), it is important to determine if gen-eral prohibitions apply, that is, export/re-export to prohibited end uses, users or to embargoed destinations. The general prohibitions also include engaging in activities prohibited by a denial order or supportive of proliferation activities as well as routing in-transit shipments through certain destinations. If an item is not listed under the ECCN on the commerce control list (EAR99), and general prohibitions do not apply, no license is required. However, if the prohibitions apply (for items listed/not listed on ECCN), an application for a license should be submitted.

Step 4: Are there any controls on the country chart? The commerce country chart allows you to determine the export/re-export requirements for most items listed on the CCL. If an 'X' appears in a particular cell, transactions subject to that par-ticular reason for control (e.g., national security, antiterrorism)/destination combin-ation require a license unless a license exception applies. No license is required if the license exception is available provided that general prohibitions 4–10 do not apply to the proposed transaction. No license is required if there is no 'X' indicated in the CCL and the country chart (see sample analysis using the CCL and Country Chart in the Example below).

Step 5: Applying for an export license: The BIS provides formal classifica-tion for a product or service, and issues an advisory opinion or licensing decision upon review of a completed application submitted in writing or electronically. Even though it is the applicant's responsibility to classify the export, the BIS could be requested to provide information on whether the item is subject to the EAR and if so, its correct ECCN. In addition to classification requests, potential applicants could also seek advisory opinions on whether a license is required or is likely to be granted for a particular transaction. Such opinions, however, do not bind the BIS from issuing a license in the future.

Step 6: Destination Control Statement, shipper's export declaration, and record keeping: A Destination Control Statement (DCS) is intended to prevent items licensed for export from being diverted while in transit or thereafter. A typical DCS reads as follows:

> These commodities, technology or software were exported from the United States in accordance with the Export Administration Regulations for ultimate destination (name of country). Diversion contrary to U.S. law is prohibited.

A DCS must be entered on all documents covering exports from the United States of items on the CCL, but is not required for items classified as EAR99 (unless it is made under license exception BAG or GFT—see International Perspective 15.6). Destination Control Statement requirements do not often apply to re-exports. For holders of a Special Comprehensive License (SCL), use of a DCS does not preclude the consignee from re-exporting to any of the SCL holder's other approved consignees or to other countries for which prior BIS approval has been received. An SCL allows experienced, high-volume exporters to export a broad range of items. It was introduced in lieu of special license and allows exportation of all commodities to all destinations (with some exceptions). Another DCS may be required on a case-by-case basis. The DCS must be shown on all copies of a bill of lading, airway bill, and commercial invoice (EAR, part 748).

INTERNATIONAL PERSPECTIVE 15.2

Automated Services

AES (Automated Export System): A computerized method for filing shipper's export declarations, which streamlines the export reporting process by reducing the paperwork burden on the trade community.

SNAP-R (Simplified Network Application Process Redesign): A method for submitting applications over the Internet with a web browser. To use SNAP-R, one must first apply to BIS for issuance of a company identification number (CIN).

STELA (System for Tracking Export License Applications): An automated voice response system that provides applicants with the status of their license and product classification applications. When the application is approved without conditions, STELA allows exporters to ship their goods without the need to wait for a formal letter from BIS.

Even though there are a few exceptions, submission of a Shipper's Export Declaration (SED) to the U.S. government is generally required under the EAR. Information on the SED, such as value of shipment, quantity, and so on, is also used by the Census Bureau for statistical purposes. The exporter or the authorized forwarding agent submits the SED, which includes information such as the criterion under which the item is exported (i.e., license exception, no license required, license number and expiration date), the ECCN, and other relevant information.

The exporter is required to keep records for every export transaction for a period of five years from the date of export. The records to be retained include contracts, invitation to bid, books of account, financial records, restrictive trade practices, and boycott documents or reports (EAR, part 762).

The example below is an analysis using the CCL and Country Chart. In order to determine whether a license is required to export/re-export a particular item to a specific destination, it is essential to use the CCL in conjunction with the Country Chart (EAR, part 774). This analysis is provided to demonstrate the thought process needed to complete this procedure:

> *Example:* The item destined for export to India is valued at approximately $10,000 and classified under ECCN 2A000.a. Based on the item classification, we know that it is controlled for national security and antiterrorism reasons. The item appears in the Country Chart column and the applicable restrictions are NS Column 2 and AT Column 1. An "X" appears in the NS Column 2 cell for India, but not in the AT Column 1 cell. This means that a license is required unless it qualifies for a license exception or SCL. It may qualify under a license exception (GBS) (see International Perspective 15.6).

INTERNATIONAL PERSPECTIVE 15.3
Multilateral Export Regimes

- **The Australian Group (AG):** The AG was formed in 1985 to harmonize export controls on chemical and biological weapons. It has thirty-four member countries. Its activities serve to support the objectives of the Biological Weapons Convention (BWC) and Chemical Weapons Convention (CWC) by enhancing the effectiveness of national export licensing measures. The Group considers export licensing as a vital means of ensuring that legitimate trade in chemicals, biological agents, and related equipment is not adversely affected while facilitating transparency to discourage the sale of such products to parties that could develop a biological and chemical weapons program.
- **Nuclear Suppliers Group (NSG):** The NSG was established in 1992 by a group of nuclear supplier countries (forty member countries). It seeks to contribute to the non-proliferation of nuclear weapons through the implementation of guidelines for nuclear and nuclear-related exports.
- **Missile Technology Control Regime (MTCR):** The MTCR was established in 1987 to coordinate national export controls in order to prevent missile proliferation. It has thirty-three member countries. Through a system of export licenses, member countries attempt to control transfers that contribute to delivery systems for weapons of mass destruction.
- **Wassenaar Arrangement (WA):** The WA was founded in 1996 to replace the East–West technology control program under the Coordinating

Committee for Multilateral Export Controls (COCOM), which was disbanded in 1994. It is intended to review export controls on conventional arms and sensitive dual goods and technologies. It has thirty-three member countries. The agreement provides for enhanced cooperation between members through information exchange on a regular basis.

Current Developments in Export Controls

In 2009, the U.S. government announced the launch of a comprehensive review of the U.S. export control system. The reform process is driven by the following important principles:

- Export controls should focus on a small core set of key items that pose a serious threat to U.S. national security (see International Perspective 15.4 on U.S. export controls and China).
- Unilateral controls must address an existing legal or foreign policy objective.
- Export controls must be coordinated with other exporting nations in order to be effective.
- Export control lists must be revised on a regular basis (based on technological developments and foreign availability). Licensing processes must be predictable and timely with enhanced enforcement capabilities to address noncompliance.

The administration proposed a number of changes to streamline the export control system which have not yet been fully implemented:

- A single licensing agency: The present multiagency structure contributes to institutional squabbling among different agencies and having one agency could end jurisdictional disputes. Under the present regime, dual-use exports are subject to referral to four departments.
- A single control list that distinguishes in tiers the sensitivity of items.
- A single enforcement structure: The center coordinates export control enforcement efforts among various departments and serves as a liaison between law enforcement agencies, the intelligence community, and export licensing agency.
- A single information technology system to share information among the relevant agencies (Fergusson and Kerr, 2012).

INTERNATIONAL PERSPECTIVE 15.4

U.S. Export Controls and the Case of China

Exports from the United States to controlled countries total over US$120 billion, which represents about 8 percent of total U.S. exports. China is the largest single export market among the controlled country group with 86 percent of the total, followed by Russia (6 percent) and Vietnam (3 percent).

A significant number of U.S. license applications to China involve exports of manufacturing equipment for semi-conductors, chemicals, and electronics. United States export controls to China arise out of the conflicting interests and mutual suspicions on security issues including on the U.S. side: i) China's assertive foreign policy toward its neighbors such as Japan, Taiwan, and other U.S. allies, ii) China's increasing military capability and growing ability to conduct information warfare, including computer network attacks and cyber espionage, and iii) the growing integration between China's civilian and military industrial base which could mean that exports to Chinese civilian firms may benefit the Chinese military. United States exports of technical assistance, equipment, and management know-how to the Chinese shipbuilding industry, for example, have assisted in the building of China's own aircraft carriers (Cheng, 2010).

Few U.S. allies agree on the need to impose export controls on China. Furthermore, many European and Asian countries have acquired technological capabilities in various fields such as semi-conductors and satellites, such that unilateral U.S. controls will only hurt U.S. exports without curtailing China's access to these technologies. Effective reform of the U.S. export control regime should include identifying key areas of U.S. advantage (i.e., technologies in which the United States is dominant and which, if exported, could enhance China's military industry). Control lists must be revised regularly to take account of new and emerging developments.

Sanctions and Violations

The enforcement of the EAR is the responsibility of the BIS's, Office of Export Enforcement (OEE) (Department of Commerce). The OEE works with various government agencies to deter violations and impose appropriate sanctions. Its major areas of responsibility include preventive enforcement, export enforcement, and prosecution of violators.

Preventive enforcement is intended to stop violations before they occur by conducting pre-license checks to determine diversion risks, reliability of overseas recipients/end users of U.S. commodities/technology, as well as post-shipment verifications. In 2019, BIS's investigations resulted in the criminal convictions of thirty-six individuals and businesses, with $1.2 billion in criminal fines, $1.06 million in forfeitures, and 1,038 months of imprisonment (www.bis.doc.gov). The OEE also conducts investigations of potential export control violations. When preventive measures fail, it pursues criminal and administrative sanctions (Table 15.2). Violations of the EAR are subject to both criminal and administrative penalties. In addition, violators may be subject to prison time and denial of export privileges by placing them on the denied persons list, and/or seizure or forfeiture of goods (see International Perspectives 15.2, 15.5, and 15.6 for BIS automated services, control agencies, and general prohibitions).

The EAR also provides certain indicators to help exporters recognize and report a possible violation. It reminds exporters to look for the following in export transactions:

TABLE 15.2 BIS Enforcement of Export Control Regulations: Selected Cases

Sentencing date	Defendant	Criminal charges	Case detail
09/30/19	Rasheed Al Jijakli	Underlying criminal conviction for violating the International Emergency Economic Powers Act by conspiring with others to export tactical gear from the United States to Syria without having obtained the required license from BIS. The tactical gear included U.S.-origin laser boresighters and day- and night-vision rifle scopes.	Export privileges denied until December 20, 2028
9/30/19	Arash Sepehri, a.k.a. William Anderson, a.k.a. Aresh Sepheri Eshtajran	Underlying criminal conviction for knowingly and willfully conspiring to export U.S.-origin items, including high-resolution sonar equipment, data input boards, acoustic transducers, and rugged laptops, from the United States to Iran without the required licenses from the U.S. Government.	Export privileges denied until February 26, 2026
09/30/19	Kenneth S. Chait	Knowingly and willfully agreeing to attempt to export without the required Department of Commerce license ceramic metal triggered spark gaps, which are also known as nuclear triggered spark gaps and are listed on the CCL.	Export privileges denied until November 13, 2023
09/30/19	Barbara Jo Luque	Underlying criminal conviction for violating Section 38 of the Arms Export Control Act by intentionally attempting to willfully and knowingly export and cause to be exported from the United States to Mexico items designated as defense articles on the U.S. Munitions List, namely, 5,000 rounds of FMJ Russian 7.62x39 mm ammunition and 125 AK47 KCI thirty-round magazines, without the required U.S. Department of State licenses.	Export privileges denied until April 25, 2025

- Whether any of the parties to the transaction has a name or address that is similar to an entity on the U.S. Department of Commerce's list of denied persons.
- Whether the transaction has "red flags," such as a) the customer or purchasing agent is reluctant to offer information about the end use of the product; b) the customer is willing to pay cash for a very expensive item (when the terms

provide for financing), has little or no business background, is unfamiliar with the product and declines routine training, installation, or other services; c) the product ordered is incompatible with the technical level of the country and its packaging is inconsistent with the stated method of shipment or destination; and d) the shipping routes are abnormal for the producer and destination, delivery dates are vague, and a freight forwarding firm is listed as the product's final destination.

INTERNATIONAL PERSPECTIVE 15.5

U.S. Export Control Agencies

- *Bureau of Industry and Security (BIS)*: BIS is part of the U.S. Department of Commerce and administers the EAR. It controls dual-use technologies.
- *Office of Defense Trade Controls (DTC)*: The State Department's DTC is responsible for the implementation of the International Traffic in Arms Regulations (ITAR). It controls exports of munitions-related merchandise and technology. It consults with the Department of Defense in setting licensing policy and making decisions on license applications. In cases of jurisdictional claims (interdepartmental disputes) it has authority to decide which agency has jurisdiction.
- *Office of Foreign Assets Control (OFAC)*: The U.S. Treasury's Department of Foreign Assets Control administers country-specific, politically oriented sanctions programs. Transactions with an embargoed destination that is not covered by OFAC may be covered by BIS or vice versa.
- *Other agencies*: Nuclear-related export controls are administered by the Energy Department and the Nuclear Regulatory Commission. Even in cases where one agency exerts control over a particular type of technology, it will consult with other agencies before making a licensing decision.

INTERNATIONAL PERSPECTIVE 15.6

General Prohibitions and License Exceptions

General Prohibitions: Export/re-export and conduct subject to EAR which are prohibited without a license or a license exception from BIS:

- Export/re-export of controlled items to listed countries.
- Re-exports and export from abroad of foreign-made items incorporating more than a de minimis amount of controlled U.S. content. For certain countries and commodities, de minimis is defined as re-exports of a foreign-made commodity incorporating controlled U.S.-origin commodities valued at 10 percent or less of the total value of the foreign-made commodity.
- Re-export and export from abroad of the foreign-produced direct product of U.S. technology and software.

- Engaging in actions prohibited by a denial order, violation of any order, and proceeding with transactions with knowledge that a violation has occurred or is about to occur.
- Export or re-export to prohibited end uses or end users, to embargoed destinations.
- Engaging in actions that support proliferation activities and export/re-export through or transit through specific countries (Albania, North Korea, Russia, etc.) without a license or license exception (EAR, part 736).

License Exceptions: Items that can be exported without a license include the following:

- GBS: Authorizes export/re-exports to Group B countries (Western countries).
- LVS: Authorizes a single, limited-value shipment to a country Group B country.
- TSR: Technology/software export/re-exports destined to a Group B country.
- GFT: Allows export/re-exports of gift parcels to an individual or religious or charitable organization located in any country.
- BAG: Authorizes individuals leaving the United States to take to any destination personal baggage, effects, vehicles, and tools of trade.
- TMP: Authorizes various temporary exports/re-exports (EAR, part 740).

ANTIBOYCOTT REGULATIONS

The U.S. antiboycott provisions of the EARprohibited U.S. firms from participating in foreign boycotts or embargoes not authorized by the U.S. government. Even though this law was primarily aimed at the Arab boycott against Israel, it prevents U.S. firms from being used to implement foreign policies of other nations that are inconsistent or contrary to U.S. policy. The law requires companies to report boycott-related requests by other nations and imposes a range of sanctions in the event of violations. In May 2019, for example, Mirasco Inc. of Georgia agreed to pay a $15,500 civil penalty to settle charges that it violated the antiboycott provisions of the EAR. The BIS alleged that during the period 2014–2016, the firm violated the EAR by a) furnishing information about business relationships with boycotted countries or blacklisted persons; and b) failing to report the receipt of a request to engage in a restrictive trade practice or foreign boycott against a country friendly to the United States (BIS Annual Report, 2019).

Who Is Covered by the Laws?

The sources of U.S. antiboycott regulations can be found in the EAR and the Internal Revenue Code. The EAR applies to all "US persons" (individuals and companies located in the United States). It also covers foreign subsidiaries that are controlled by a U.S. company in terms of ownership or management. In such cases, the foreign affiliate will be subject to the antiboycott laws and the U.S. parent company will be held responsible for any noncompliance. The regulations cover the activities of individuals or companies relating to the sale, purchase, or transfer of goods or services within the United States or between the United States and a foreign country. This includes U.S. exports, imports, financing, forwarding and shipping, and certain other transactions that may take place outside the United States. To trigger the application of the antiboycott laws, the activity must involve U.S. Commerce with foreign countries (EAR, part 760).

What Do the Laws Prohibit?

Refusals to do business: The law prohibits any U.S. person from refusing to do business (expressly or implicitly) with any person pursuant to a request, agreement, or requirement from a boycotting country. The use of a designated list of persons also constitutes a refusal to do business prohibited under the act.

Discriminatory actions: The statute prohibits any U.S. person from discriminating against an individual (who is a U.S. person) on the basis of race, religion, gender, or national origin. It also prohibits similar action against a U.S. corporation based on the race, religion of the owner, officer, director, or employee. Such prohibitions apply when the action is taken in order to comply with or support an unsanctioned foreign boycott.

Furnishing information to a boycotting country: The statute prohibits furnishing information about any business relationship with or in a boycotted country or with blacklisted firms or persons. It also prohibits actual furnishing of, or agreements to furnish, information about the race, religion, sex, or national origin of another U.S. person or any U.S. person's association with any charitable organization that supports the boycotted country.

Implementing L/Cs with prohibited conditions or requirements: The statute also prohibits any U.S. person from implementing an L/C that contains a condition or requirement from a boycotting country. This includes issuing, honoring, paying, or confirming an L/C. The prohibition applies when a beneficiary is a U.S. person and the transaction involves the export of U.S. goods (i.e., shipment of U.S.-origin goods or goods from the United States).

Some exceptions to the prohibitions include the following:

- compliance with import requirements of a boycotting country
- compliance with unilateral and specific selections by buyers in a boycotting country
- compliance with a boycotting country's requirements regarding shipment and transshipment of exports
- compliance with immigration, passport, visa, employment, and local requirements of a boycotting country.

Reporting Requirements

The regulations require U.S. persons to report quarterly to the U.S. Department of Commerce any requests they have received to take any action to comply with, further, or support an unsanctioned foreign boycott. The U.S. Treasury also requires taxpayers to report activities in or with a boycotting country and any requests to participate in a foreign boycott (see International Perspective 15.7).

INTERNATIONAL PERSPECTIVE 15.7

Requests That Are Not Reportable

- To refrain from shipping on a carrier owned or leased by a particular country or its nationals or a request to certify to that effect.
- To ship goods via a prescribed route or refrain from shipping via a prescribed route or to certify to that effect.
- To supply information regarding the country of origin of goods, the name of the supplier, provider of services, or the destination of exports.
- To comply with the laws of another country other than one that requires compliance with the country's boycott laws.
- To supply information about the exporter or exporter's family for immigration, passport, or employment purposes.
- To supply a certificate by the owner or master that the vessel, aircraft, etc. is eligible to enter a particular port, airport, etc. pursuant to its laws.
- To supply a certificate from an insurance company stating that the company has an agent or representative in the boycotting country including the name and address of such agent.

Penalties for Non-compliance

The law provides both criminal and civil penalties for violations of the antiboycott statute. On the criminal side, a person who knowingly violates the regulations is subject to a fine of up to $50,000 or five times the value of the exports involved, whichever is greater. It may also include imprisonment of up to five years. In cases in which the violator has knowledge that the items will be used for the benefit of countries or persons to which exports are restricted for national security or foreign policy purposes, the criminal penalty varies. For individuals, a fine may be imposed up to $250,000 and/or imprisonment of up to ten years. For firms, the penalty for each violation can be $1 million or up to five times the value of the exports involved, whichever is greater. Administrative or civil penalties may include any or all of the following: revocation of export licenses, denial of export privileges, exclusion from practice, and imposition of fines of up to $11,000 per violation, or $100,000 if the violation involves items controlled for national security reasons. The Treasury may also deny all or part of the foreign tax benefits (Table 15.3).

FOREIGN CORRUPT PRACTICES

The Foreign Corrupt Practices Act (FCPA) of 1977 was enacted as a public response to the Watergate Scandal and to revelations of widespread bribery of foreign officials by U.S. companies. In the 1970s, the Security Exchange Commission (SEC) investigations revealed that more than 400 U.S. companies admitted making illegal payments in excess of $300 million to foreign government officials. More recent FCPA enforcement and compliance actions also show that substantial payments were made by companies such as Siemens AG ($1.6 billion), Halliburton ($579 million), and Wilbros Group ($32 million) to foreign officials to obtain government contracts

TABLE 15.3 BIS Enforcement of Anti-boycott Regulations: Selected Cases

Company Name and Location	Date Order Signed	Alleged Violations	Settlement Amount
Mitsubishi International Corporation (New York)	06/13/19	Furnishing information about business relationships with boycotted countries or blacklisted persons. Failure to report receipt of a boycott request.	$5,000
Mitsubishi International Polymer Trade Corporation (Newark, NJ)	06/13/19	Furnishing information about business relationships with boycotted countries or blacklisted persons. Failure to report receipt of a boycott request.	$15,000
Zurn Industries, LLC (Erie, PA)	05/20/19	Failure to report receipt of a boycott request.	$54,000

(Bixby, 2011). The overriding public concern was that this practice could tarnish the reputation of the United States in the world and was not in the best interest of U.S. corporations.

The legislation represents an attempt to enforce morality and ethics in the conduct of international business transactions. It was intended to halt corrupt business practices in order to create a level playing field for honest businesses and restore public confidence in the integrity of the marketplace. The FCPA was enacted as an amendment to the Securities and Exchange Act of 1934. It was later amended in 1988, as part of the Omnibus Trade and Competitiveness Act. In 1998, the FCPA was again amended to conform to the requirements of the OECD convention on combating bribery of foreign public officials in international business transactions. The OECD Anti-bribery Convention came into force in February 1999 with the United States as a founding member.

The principal objectives of the legislation are to:

- prohibit the bribery of foreign officials by U.S. individuals and corporations to obtain or retain a business; and
- establish standards for maintaining corporate records and internal accounting control objectives.

The anti-bribery provision applies to all publicly held corporations registered with SEC and all domestic concerns. The 1998 amendments expanded the application of the anti-bribery provisions to cover "any person" who commits bribery on U.S. territory regardless of whether the accused is a resident or does business in the United States. In addition, individual corporate employees can be prosecuted even if the corporation is found not guilty of violating the FCPA (Gleich and Woodward, 2005). The accounting standards and objectives apply only to SEC registrants or those that are required to file reports with the SEC.

The accounting provisions of the FCPA are intended to prevent companies from escaping detection by maintaining dubious accounts or slush funds. It requires any corporation that has certain classes of shares with the SEC to 1) make and keep accurate books and accounts that fairly reflect the transactions and 2) maintain a system of internal accounting controls in order to prevent the unauthorized use of corporate assets and transactions and to ensure the accuracy of corporate records.

Scope of Coverage

Who Is Subject to the FCPA?

Anti-bribery provisions: The anti-bribery provisions apply to all publicly held corporations registered with the SEC (issuers of stock in controlling corporations) and other domestic concerns. Domestic concerns are broadly defined to include all U.S. citizens and residents as well as any entity whose principal place of business is in the United States or incorporated under the laws of the United States (Atkinson and Tillen, 2005).

A U.S. parent company may be liable for corrupt payments by its foreign subsidiary if the U.S. parent company knew or participated in the subsidiary's corrupt action or took no measures to discourage such payments. DPC-Diagnostics Ltd. of Tianjin, China, a wholly-owned subsidiary of a California company that produces medical equipment, agreed to pay $4.8 million for violation of the FCPA in 2005. The firm admitted to paying $1.6 million in bribes to physicians and lab personnel in China to obtain business there. The guilty plea is based on the theory that the firm was an agent of the American company (Bixby, 2011).

The FCPA also applies to certain foreign nationals or entities (not issuers or domestic concerns) if they engage directly or through an agent in making or facilitating corrupt payments while in the United States.

The 1998 amendments to the FCPA established jurisdiction on the basis of the nationality principle (U.S. persons are liable even if the actions take place outside U.S. territory) and removed the requirement that there be a use of interstate commerce for acts in furtherance of a corrupt payment to a foreign official by U.S. companies or persons that took place wholly outside the United States.

Accounting provisions: In addition to the anti-bribery provisions, the FCPA contains accounting provisions applicable to public companies. They prohibits off-the-books accounting and generally attempt to strengthen the accuracy of corporate books and records as well as the reliability of the audit process.

The FCPA accounting provisions apply to any issuer whose securities trade on the national securities exchange in the United States, including foreign issuers with exchange-traded American depository receipts. They also apply to companies whose stock trades in the over-the-counter market in the United States and which file periodic reports with the SEC. A California company paid over $2 million in civil and criminal penalties when its two joint venture partners paid more than $400,000 in bribes to obtain business in China. The illicit payments were recorded on the books as "business fees" or "travel and entertainment expenses." The California company failed to provide adequate internal controls. Companies (including subsidiaries of issuers) and individuals may face civil liability for aiding and abetting an issuer's violation of the accounting provisions. This includes managers of subsidiaries who approve certain payments and should have known that they were improperly recorded or who otherwise circumvent internal controls.

Criminal liability can be imposed on companies and individuals for knowingly failing to comply with the FCPA's internal control provisions. As with the FCPA's ant-bribery provisions, individuals are only subject to the FCPA's criminal penalties for violations of the accounting provisions if they acted "willfully." For example, a French company was criminally charged with failure to implement internal controls and failure to keep accurate books and records.

What Is Covered by the FCPA?

The anti-bribery provision prohibits American businesses from using interstate commerce to pay off foreign officials to obtain or retain a business. The term "interstate commerce" also includes the intrastate use of any interstate means of communication or any other interstate instrumentality. Placing a telephone call or sending email or fax from, to, or through the United States involves interstate commerce, as does sending a wire transfer from or to a U.S. bank or otherwise using U.S. banks or travelling across state borders (or internationally to or from the United States) (US Department of Justice and SEC, 2012).

Payments to any foreign official to obtain the performance of routine governmental action is explicitly exempted. The 1988 amendments to the FCPA changed the knowledge requirement and the definition of grease payments, added certain defenses to charges of bribery under the statute, increased penalties, and authorized the president to negotiate an international agreement prohibiting bribery.

The knowledge requirement: The 1977 act prohibited any payments while knowing or having reason to know that they would be used to bribe foreign officials. It was believed that a broad application of the "reason to know" standard would put many multinational companies under the risk of liability for the actions of their sales agents who engage in bribery without their approval. Such a standard would also invite unwarranted scrutiny of distributors or sales agents in countries that are considered to be corrupt. Given such legitimate business concerns, the "reason to know" standard was removed from the act and objective criteria established with respect to such conduct. This standard is narrower and holds businesses liable only if they are substantially certain that the illicit payments are to occur or that such a circumstance exists (Hall, 1994). A person has the requisite knowledge when he is aware of a high probability of the existence of such circumstance (unless the person believes that such circumstance does not exist). The FCPA imposes liability not only on those with actual knowledge of wrongdoing but also on those who purposely avoid actual knowledge, that is, willful blindness or deliberate ignorance to avoid responsibility.

Affirmative defenses against charges of bribery: The FCPA anti-bribery provisions contain two affirmative defenses (the defendant bears the burden of proving them). Payments are not considered corrupt if:

a. They are lawful under the laws of the foreign country. To avoid prosecution, the conduct prohibited under the FCPA must be lawful under written, local law. An exception under the law of Azerbaijan, for example, relieving bribe payors who voluntarily disclose bribe payments to the authorities of criminal liability, does not make the bribes legal, that is, the host country's law did not actually legalize the bribe payment.

b. The money was spent as part of demonstrating a product or performing a contractual obligation. The FCPA allows companies reasonable and bona fide travel and lodging expenses to foreign officials for training, visits to company facilities, as well as for product demonstration and promotional activities.

Exemption of facilitating or expediting payments: A narrow exception is made for "facilitating or expediting payments" made in furtherance of routine governmental action. This includes processing visas or work orders, providing police protection or mail service, and supplying utilities like power or water. Paying a local official a small amount to have the power turned on at a factory may be considered a facilitating payment while paying an inspector to ignore the necessary permits to operate the factory would be considered a bribe. For example, an Oklahoma-based firm violated the FCPA when its subsidiary paid Argentine customs officials $166,000 to secure clearance for equipment that lacked requisite certifications or could not be imported under local law and to pay a lower than applicable duty rate.

Penalties: For individuals, the maximum fine was increased from $10,000 to $250,000. Individuals and corporate employees were made criminally liable even when the corporation is not in contravention of the FCPA.

Authorization to negotiate an international agreement: The act authorizes the president to negotiate an international agreement with countries that are members of the OECD to prohibit bribery.

Enforcement and Penalties

Enforcement of the FCPA is the joint responsibility of the SEC and the Department of Justice. The Department of Justice has authority for civil enforcement of violations by domestic concerns with respect to the anti-bribery provisions. It also has exclusive jurisdiction over criminal prosecution in relation to the accounting as well as anti-bribery provisions of the statute. The SEC has similar authority for civil enforcement of violations of the anti-bribery and accounting provisions.

Criminal penalties may reach up to $2 million for public corporations and domestic concerns and $250,000 and/or a maximum of five years imprisonment for officers, directors, or employees who commit willful violations of the anti-bribery provisions. With regard to civil penalties, a maximum of $21,400 may be levied against any company, employee, officer, or director. Injunctive relief is also available to forestall a violation. Enforcement agencies are also increasingly seeking disgorgement of company profits on "tainted contracts" secured through improper payments to foreign officials.

Violations of the accounting provisions can result in a fine of $25 million for companies. Culpable individuals can be subject to a criminal fine up to $5 million as well as imprisonment for up to twenty years. Such penalties may also include termination of government licenses and debarment from government contracting programs.

Since the introduction of the FCPA, several U.S. companies have been investigated for bribing foreign officials to obtain contracts. Over the last few years, some companies were indicted and fined for bribing foreign officials in order to use their influence to secure government contracts. Here are some examples:

- In August 2020, Herbalife Nutrition Ltd agreed to pay total penalties of over $122 million over its scheme to falsify books and records and provide corrupt payments and benefits to Chinese government officials with the aim of obtaining, retaining, and increasing its business in China. It had engaged in a decade-long scheme to falsify its books and records to conceal corrupt and improper payments to Chinese officials and China's state-owned entities (U.S. Department of Justice, 2020).
- In 2012, Smith & Nephew acknowledged responsibility for the actions of its affiliates, employees, and agents who made various improper payments to publicly employed healthcare providers in Greece from 1998 until 2008 to secure lucrative business. Smith & Nephew, a Delaware corporation, is headquartered in Memphis, Tennessee, and is a wholly owned subsidiary of Smith & Nephew plc, an English company traded on the New York Stock Exchange. The company manufactures and sells medical devices worldwide. In total, from 1998 to 2008, Smith & Nephew, its affiliates, and employees authorized the payment of approximately $9.4 million to the distributor's shell companies, some or all of which was passed on to physicians to corruptly induce them to purchase medical devices manufactured by Smith & Nephew. As part of the agreement, Smith & Nephew had to pay a $16.8 million penalty and was required to implement rigorous internal controls, cooperate fully with the department, and retain a compliance monitor for eighteen months.

FCPA enforcement against foreign firms with no operations or personnel in the United States has raised concerns about the extraterritorial application of U.S. laws and its infringement upon the sovereignty of other nations (McDonald, Yoshino, and Carr, 2010).

United States companies could seek an advisory opinion from the Department of Justice on whether a particular transaction would violate the FCPA. Any opinion by the Department that sanctions a proposed transaction would create a presumption of legality.

Measures for Compliance with the FCPA

Implementing due diligence procedures: Internal procedures should be developed to evaluate and select foreign partners and agents. Once an appointment has been made consistent with the internal procedures, a written agreement is needed to govern the relationship between the parties. Such an agreement should generally state that the agent/partner has no authority to bind the exporter and that the agreement is valid insofar as the foreign agent/partner complies with the FCPA and the foreign country's laws. It should also stipulate that the agent/partner is not an employee, officer, or representative of any government agency. The exporter should be promptly notified of any changes in representation (see International Perspective 15.8).

Seeking an advisory opinion from the government: The U.S. Department of Justice provides advisory opinions on the legitimacy of a proposed transaction. Other federal agencies also provide an advisory opinion.

Adopting internal measures and controls: Internal procedures should also be established to guide employees. Such programs include procedures for reporting and investigations, seeking the opinion of counsel, policies for employees, agents, or joint venture partners, and training programs for officers and employees.

Efforts to Control Corruption

The OECD Anti-bribery Recommendation, 1994
The OECD Convention on Combating Bribery, 1997
The ICC Rules of Conduct to Combat Extortion and Bribery, 1977 (revised 1996)
The United Nations Convention Against Corruption, 2003
The Inter-American Convention Against Corruption, 1996
Transparency International (TI), which has as its mission to enhance public transparency and accountability in international business transactions and in the administration of public procurement

INTERNATIONAL PERSPECTIVE 15.8

FCPA Compliance Challenges: The Case of SOEs in China

The number of state-owned enterprises (SOEs) in China is estimated at over 12,000 and this poses unique FCPA challenges for U.S. firms who do business with such firms in China. Even though these enterprises are majority-owned or controlled by the Chinese government, they have several attributes of a private enterprise, such as being publicly traded on a stock exchange. Certain activities of U.S. firms doing business in China can lead to FCPA exposure if:

- They do business or interact with employees of SOEs (employees are considered "foreign officials").
- They use "design institutes" in China to serve as an engineering or consulting firm in connection with certain contracts and projects. Many design institutes in China are state owned and employees of such firms are likely to be considered as "foreign officials" under the FCPA's ant-bribery provisions.
- Their employees or agents in China provide customers with company-funded gifts, travel, and entertainment to obtain business. Many executives, sales agents, and distributors in China do not view such gifts as improper or illegal. If the U.S. company provides the foreign official's travel, lodging, and other expenses, it has to represent a reasonable and bona fide expenditure that is directly related to the promotion, demonstration. etc. of products or services or the execution or performance of a contract with a foreign government or agency.
- It is important to note that a parent corporation remains indirectly liable for FCPA violations by its foreign subsidiary insofar as it has actual or constructive knowledge that the subsidiary is engaging in improper activity. United States companies must also ensure compliance by all other third parties engaged in China including agents, distributors, or other channel partners, because improper actions by such third parties can also be attributed to a parent corporation.

ANTITRUST LAWS AND TRADE REGULATION

Antitrust laws are intended to enhance efficiency and consumer welfare by proscribing practices that lessen competition or create a monopoly. Such laws also meet the sociopolitical objective of dispersing economic power. Historically, monopolies were often sanctioned in the area of trade and commerce. During the colonial period, for example, private companies such as the East India Company (1600), The Dutch West India Company (1621), and The Hudson Bay Company (1670) received charters from governments that granted them a monopoly of trade. In North America, British merchants were given monopolies over the export and import of goods.

The idea of monopoly rights was soon found unacceptable, as it restricted the rights of individuals from competing freely. In many European countries, it was viewed as incompatible with the competitive integrity of markets and free trade. By 1860, Britain had unilaterally abrogated the rights of commercial monopolies given to particular companies (Johns, 1988). In the United States, there was a call for legislation to control "dangerous conspiracies against the public good" (Shenefield and Stelzer, 1993). The Sherman Act was passed in 1890.

Antitrust laws are often referred to as the Magna Carta of free enterprise because they preserve free competition in domestic and foreign trade as well as minimize government intervention in business affairs.

U.S. Antitrust Regulations

Antitrust laws in the United States can be grouped into three categories:

1. *General prohibitions:* The Sherman Act, the Federal Trade Commission (FTC)
2. *Specific prohibitions:* The Clayton Act and amendments
3. *Exemptions*

General Prohibitions

The Sherman Act outlaws certain concerted activity in restraint of trade between two or more parties. The U.S. Supreme Court has developed certain criteria to determine the lawfulness of a given restraint: the per se rule and the rule of reason. The per se rule applies to those restraints of trade which are prohibited regardless of their effect on competition or economic welfare.

Per se violations include price-fixing, division of markets (market sharing) between competitors, and certain boycotts by sellers or buyers (i.e., an agreement between competitors not to deal with a customer or supplier). Restraints that are not categorized as per se violations are subject to the rule of reason; that is, practices are restricted only if they have an adverse effect on competition. This often requires analysis of the competitive structure of the firm, the firm's market share and/or power, and other relevant factors. The Sherman Act also prohibits monopoly abuse and attempts or conspiracies to monopolize trade or commerce with foreign nations. If a firm has a high market share as a result of improved productivity, it is not considered objectionable unless it is obtained through systematic conduct designed to harm competitors.

The Federal Trade Commission proscribes unfair competitive practices even if they do not violate specific provisions of either the Sherman Act or the Clayton

Act. It also prohibits unfair or deceptive practices in or affecting foreign commerce. The commission has authority to issue interpretative rules and general statements of policy, rules, and guidelines that define unfair or deceptive business practices.

Specific Prohibitions

The Clayton Act proscribes any acquisition of the stocks or assets of another entity affecting commerce in any part of the United States that results in the creation of a monopoly or a substantial lessening of competition. The Clayton Act is not limited to the acquisition of a competitor. It also prohibits price discrimination between two purchasers without just cause or exclusive dealing in foreign commerce that tends to create a monopoly or lessen competition in the United States. Exclusive dealing (tying) occurs when the seller sells a product only on the condition that the purchaser will not deal in the goods of the seller's competitor.

Exemptions for Export Cartels

There has been a long-standing practice in many countries to allow export cartel exemptions to antitrust laws. Export cartels exemptions (composed of exporters from a single country) allow firms to fix prices and coordinate conduct that, if pursued, would lead to antitrust scrutiny. There are three categories of exemptions for export cartels:

1. *Explicit exemptions*: The country's statute explicitly excludes export cartels from the scope of its national competition law. Some countries with explicit exemptions require notification or authorization (United States) while others do not have such a requirement (Canada).
2. *Implicit exemption*: domestic competition law covers only the conduct of firms operating on the national market (most EU member countries). National antitrust statutes are applied to export cartels only in cases of anticompetitive conduct affecting the domestic market. Ireland's Competition Act of 2002, for example, prohibits export cartels that restrict or distort competition within its domestic market.
3. *No statutory exemption:* there is neither an explicit nor an implicit exemption that allows fixing or similar conduct for export oriented activity (Levenstein and Suslow, 2004). Such a system exists in Luxembourg, Russia, Thailand, and Uruguay.

The rationale behind this exemption is that such activity that is conducted for foreign markets does not necessarily harm competition in the domestic market. It rests on a mercantilist paradigm under which national firms benefit at the expense of other countries' consumers and producers. Advocates of export cartels also believe that such cartels generate efficiency gains by reducing the costs related to selling in foreign markets i.e., centralization of sales activities avoids costly duplication of services and allows members to enjoy lower rates related to export services, such as insurance and freight. Export cartels are also intended to promote and facilitate small and medium-sized firms' exports by reducing overhead costs of exports and thus overcome the barriers to foreign trade (Desmarais, 2009).

The OECD study (OECD, 2004), however, acknowledges the adverse and anticompetitive effects of export cartels. The study indicates that export cartels distort international trade by restricting the volume of exports and forcing consumers to pay high prices. Export cartels may affect domestic markets indirectly through spillover effects of tacit collusion (Schultz, 2002; Marsden, 2003). Larsen (1970, p.497) states:

> it is naïve to expect association members to ignore the domestic market while they freely discuss prices and quotas for exports. . . the creation of an export association provides an excellent chance for large oligopolists to peacefully coexist both at home and abroad . . .

Even though some countries have taken steps to eliminate or limit antitrust exemptions, others are unwilling to relinquish their export cartel exemptions because of the presumed benefits that they may generate at the detriment of other countries.

U.S. Export Cartels

- *The Webb–Pomerene Act (WP Act), 1918*: Congress passed the WP Act as an export exemption to its antitrust laws in 1918 (exemption from section 1 of the Sherman Act which prohibits cartels) with a view to encouraging U.S. firms to work together in representing their own interests vis-à-vis powerful foreign cartels. It was also intended to overcome the high fixed costs of exporting that could be particularly burdensome to small firms. The exemption allows competing firms to set prices, allocate orders, consolidate freight, or arrange shipments. Export associations under the WP Act are provided the exemptions insofar as they do not reduce competition within the United States, that is, they do not restrain trade, enhance or depress prices within the United States, or adversely affect the export trade of other U.S. firms that are not members of the association. Webb–Pomerene Associations (WPAs) are required to register with the Federal Trade Commission (FTC) within thirty days of their creation and also to file annual reports with the FTC. As of 2016, the three WPAs registered with the FTC accounted for less than 1 percent of U.S. exports. They include export cartels or associations in the areas of cotton, soda ash, and specialty crops (US Federal Trade Commission, 2020).
- *The Export Trading Company Act (ETC) of 1982*: In view of the failure of WPAs to increase U.S. exports, Congress enacted the ETC to encourage U.S. exports and create more certainty in the application of antitrust laws to export activities. Under the ETC, export associations must apply for an issuance of a certificate exempting them from antitrust liability. Under this procedure, applicants disclose their plans for overseas trade with the government and obtain preclearance, that is, obtain the government's approval for their future export activity. The Commerce and Justice Departments issue the certificate to potential exporters after establishing that their conduct or activity does not substantially lessen competition or unreasonably affect prices in the United States. Applicants are exempt from antitrust laws so long as the minimum standards are met under the act. The ETC also provides protection to certificate holders against frivolous lawsuits by competitors that are intended

to forestall their export activities. In 2018, there were seventy-three certificate holders accounting for less than 1 percent of U.S. merchandise exports. The limited success of this effort may be attributable to the fear of disclosure of confidential business information to the U.S. government to receive certification, as well as the lack of precedent interpreting the scope of protection provided under the ETC (ITA, 2020) (see International Perspective 15.9).

• *The Foreign Trade Antitrust Improvements Act (FTAIA), 2000*: The FTAIA limits the application of the Sherman Act to trade with foreign nations unless such conduct has a direct, substantial, and reasonably foreseeable effect on domestic trade or commerce. Anticompetitive acts directed at exports without effect on domestic commerce of a U.S. person are treated as foreign transactions and out of reach of U.S. antitrust laws. In the absence of this legislation, the antitrust laws would otherwise have extended to any anticompetitive conduct (agreements, conspiracy, etc.), regardless of its effect on U.S. import, export, or domestic commerce. Although this exemption could be used as an alternative to export certification or preclearance, it does not provide the immunity from prosecution that is available under the latter arrangement (Desmarais, 2009).

The following are generally considered to be a checklist of practices that businesses should avoid:

1. Discussing prices with competitors
2. Pricing below cost to drive out a competitor or discourage a new entrant
3. Dividing markets with other competitors
4. Compelling dealers to charge a given price
5. Tying the sale of one product to another
6. Charging customers different prices without reasonable justification
7. Terminating a customer without reasonable justification
8. Abusing market power to the disadvantage of consumers and competitors
9. Joining with a competitor to the disadvantage of other competitors
10. Suggesting that a supplier purchase from another division of the subsidiary

It is important for companies to establish an antitrust compliance program.

Extraterritorial Application of U.S. Antitrust Laws

The U.S. antitrust laws are not limited to transactions that take place within U.S. borders. Overseas transactions with a substantial and foreseeable effect on U.S. commerce are subject to U.S. antitrust laws. Efforts by the United States to exercise its jurisdiction outside its borders have often been frustrated by foreign governments that did not want any infringements of their sovereignty. Some countries have enacted legislation to block the enforcement of U.S. laws within their countries, including any cooperation with respect to submission of evidence and documents. In view of such opposition, the U.S. government has resorted to bilateral antitrust agreements with various countries concerning the extraterritorial application of national antitrust laws. The agreements generally provide for the exchange of information, prior notification of enforcement actions, and consultation on policy matters.

Enforcement and Penalties

The Department of Justice and the Federal Trade Commission both enforce U.S. anti-trust laws. Whereas the Department of Justice can initiate civil or criminal suits against alleged violators, the Federal Trade Commission or states, through the attorney general, are empowered to bring only civil cases. Private parties that have been adversely affected by a violation of antitrust laws can also sue in the federal court for an injunction or damages.

Violations of U.S. antitrust laws lead to severe penalties. For example, violations of the Sherman Act—price fixing, bid rigging, or market allocation—are punishable by a fine of up to $100 million for corporate entities and a fine of up to $1 million or ten years' imprisonment (or both) for individuals. There are also civil penalties.

INTERNATIONAL PERSPECTIVE 15.9

Webb–Pomerene Act versus Export Trading Company Act

Both the WPA and the ETC were intended to increase U.S. exports by exempting export cartels from U.S. antitrust liability. Both are similar in the criteria they set for assessing the validity of the application. In both, export cartels are not liable for ancillary restraints on domestic trade. However, there are major differences between the two Acts.

- Unlike the WPA, where the FTC does not perform any approving function, the ETC empowers the Secretary of Commerce with such a function.
- WPA is limited to the export of goods whereas the ETCcovers both goods and services.
- WPA is limited to associations of firms while the ETC expands the exemption to individual firms.
- The WPA does not require antitrust preclearance while the ETC does require written preclearance.

INCENTIVES TO PROMOTE EXPORTS

From the 1870s until 1971, U.S. exports typically exceeded U.S. imports, except during World War II. Even during this period, U.S. exports fell below imports because a substantial percentage of the exports was not sold but provided to allies under the Marshall Plan. All this began to change in the 1970s. In 1971 the U.S. merchandise trade balance showed a $2.27 billion deficit in contrast to previous decades when exports exceeded imports. Some of the contributing factors to this state of affairs included the overvalued dollar and increased government expenditure at home and abroad that often resulted in purchases of foreign products and services. This situation was further exacerbated in 1973 when oil prices sharply increased and worsened the U.S. trade deficit due to large increases in expenditure for imports of petroleum products (Stein and Foss, 1992) (see International Perspective 15.10).

Domestic International Sales Corporations and the GATT

In an effort to remedy the worsening trade imbalance, the government enacted the Revenue Act of 1972. The act created the Domestic International Sales Corporation (DISC) to promote U.S. exports by providing tax incentives that would lower the cost of exporting goods in foreign markets. The legislation was also intended to remove the disadvantage of U.S. companies engaged in export activities through domestic corporations (Chou, 2005).

The DISC statute was also intended to offset the competitive disadvantage faced by U.S. firms in view of the various incentives provided by major trading nations to their export firms. Under the DISC scheme, a U.S. corporation could export its products through a subsidiary (known as a DISC) organized in the United States (a shell corporation) with minimum capital of $2,500. The DISC was required to engage almost exclusively in export sales. The tax implications of a corporation that elected to be treated as a DISC were as follows:

- Approximately half of a DISC's earnings were taxed at the shareholder level regardless of whether they were distributed to shareholders (constructive dividends).
- The remainder of a DISC's earnings was not taxable to the shareholder until actually distributed. This allowed for an indefinite deferral of tax. In effect, this amounted to a de facto tax exemption on about half of a DISC's earnings because deferred taxes may never become due.
- Deferred taxes became due when distributed to shareholders, when a shareholder disposed of its DISC stock, or the corporation ceased to qualify as a DISC.

The DISC came under increasing attack by U.S. trading partners as an unfair and illegal subsidy to U.S. exporters. In a complaint by the EEC and Canada against the United States, the GATT panel issued a report stating that the DISC scheme conferred a tax benefit to exports and resulted in the price of exports being lower than similar goods for domestic consumption. The panel concluded that the scheme was in violation of the GATT treaty (GATT, 1977). Even though the United States never conceded to the inconsistency of the DISC with the GATT agreement, it nevertheless proceeded to replace the DISC with an alternative scheme that was acceptable to the GATT (a vestige of the old DISC, the Interest Charge-DISC remains to date).

The Tax Reform Act of 1984 created the Foreign Sales Corporation (FSC) to promote U.S. exports. Once an FSC is incorporated outside the United States and satisfies other requirements in the statute, its earnings are exempt from U.S. taxation. Although FSC status provides a benefit to U.S. exporters comparable to the DISC, it is permitted under the GATT because the GATT treaty does not require member countries to tax "economic processes" that take place outside their territory (Levin, 2004).

The European Union filed a complaint in 1998 with the WTO asserting that the FSC regime was an illegal subsidy inconsistent with the GATT treaty. In 1999, the WTO ruled in favor of the EU and called for the elimination of the FSC regime by 2000. In response to the WTO ruling, the U.S. repealed the FSC and enacted the Extraterritorial Income Exclusion Act (ETI) (2000), which provides U.S. exporters with the same tax benefit as the FSC. The ETI allows U.S. exporters to exclude from federal income tax 15 percent of their net income from the export sale of qualified U.S.-origin goods. Alternatively, exporters of low profit items could exclude 1.2 percent of their gross receipts (not to exceed 30 percent of the net) from the export sale of qualified U.S.-origin goods (not more than 50 percent of the value is attributable to foreign content). The EU again challenged the ETI as an unfair subsidy to U.S. corporations and the WTO dispute settlement body found that it violated the treaty (2001). The ETI was phased out in 2004. The Interest-Charge Domestic International Sales Corporation (IC-DISC) appears to be one of the few remaining tax incentives for U.S. exporters (Clausing, 2005; Gravelle, 2005).

Interest-Charge Domestic International Sales Corporations (IC-DISCs)

The IC-DISC is a tax deferral vehicle (on the first US$10 million of export sales) that can be used by small and medium-sized exporting companies. It provides tax savings for qualifying U.S. exporters in view of the favorable dividend tax rules under the Jobs and Growth Tax Relief Reconciliation Act of 2003 (Loizeau, 2004).

To be eligible for IC-DISC status, a corporation must satisfy certain requirements:

1. It must be a U.S. corporation.
2. At least 95 percent of its foreign trading gross receipts for the tax year must be "qualified export receipts." Qualified export receipts include receipts from sales, leases, or rental of export property (Section 993(a)). It also includes gross receipts for services related to warranty, repair, transportation of export property, engineering or architectural services from overseas projects, and interest on qualified export assets.
3. The adjusted basis of its qualified export assets must be at least 95 percent of its total assets at the end of the tax year. Qualified export assets include accounts receivable, temporary investments, export property, assets used primarily in connection with the production of qualified export receipts, and loans to producers.
4. It has one class of stock with a minimum value (capital) of $2,500.
5. A timely election to be treated as an IC-DISC for the current tax year.
6. Certain personal holding companies, financial, insurance institutions as well as companies that are members of any controlled group of which an FSC is a member are ineligible to be treated as an IC-DISC.

How Does an IC-DISC Work?

Step 1: A U.S. exporter (or shareholder) forms a tax-exempt IC-DISC corporation.

Step 2: The U.S. exporter pays the IC-DISC commission. The allowable commission rate is the greater of either 50 percent export net income or 4 percent of gross export income.

Step 3: The U.S. exporter deducts the commission paid to the IC-DISC from its income taxed at 21 percent (The IC-DISC pays no U.S. income tax on the commission income).

Step 4: When the IC-DISC pays dividends to its shareholders, the shareholders pay dividend income tax of 15 percent.

Tax Benefits of IC-DISC

1. *Reduced taxable income*: The U.S. exporter pays an annual tax deductible commission on its export sales to the IC-DISC. This reduces its taxable base at the corporate level by the commission paid to the IC-DISC.
2. *Increased dividend income to shareholders*: The entire commission paid to the IC-DISC can then be distributed as a dividend at the end of the taxable year. This payment could be subject to only a 15 percent individual dividend tax rate rather than the corporate tax rate of 21 percent.
3. *Deferral of IC-DISC income from taxation*: The IC-DISC is not subject to tax. However, its U.S. shareholders are subject to tax on deemed dividend distributions from the IC-DISC which does not include income derived from the first $10 million of the IC-DISC's qualified export receipts each year. Thus, the IC-DISC allows a U.S. shareholder to defer paying tax on income attributable to export sales. The U.S. shareholder must, however, pay an interest charge on its IC-DISC earnings (deferred tax liability) until it is distributed (see Table 15.4).

Foreign-derived Intangible Income (FDII) Deduction

The Tax Cuts and Job Act (TCJA) of 2017 introduced new tax incentives for U.S. exporters. The section 250 deduction for foreign-derived intangible income (FDII) is available only for domestic corporations. The tax incentive is for U.S. corporations that export goods and services but locate their intangible assets (patents, trademarks, trade secrets, copyrights) in the United States. The corporation's FDII deduction is 37.5 percent of its FDII. The deduction yields a 13.13 percent effective corporation

TABLE 15.4 An Example to Illustrate IC-DISC Tax Savings

	Without IC-DISC	With IC-DISC		
		Combined	Exporter	IC-DISC
Foreign Trading				
Gross Receipts	5,000,000	5,000,000		
Cost of Goods Sold	3,000,000	3,000,000		
Selling, administrative expenses	1,000,000	1,000,000		
Export Net Income	1,000,000	1,000,000	1,000,000	
Tax Rate	21%			
Tax Paid	210,000			
IC-DISC Greater of:				
a) 4% Export gross receipts			200,000	
b) 50% Export net income			500,000	
IC-DISC Commission			500,000	
IC-DISC Commission deduction			500,000	500,000
Tax base after IC-DISC commission			500,000	500,000
Tax Rate			21%	15%
Tax Paid		180,000	105,000	75,000
Tax Saving (net)	210,000–180,000= 30,000			

tax rate on this income. After 2025, the deduction will be 22 percent, thus yielding an effective tax rate of 16 percent on that income. This incentive eliminates the need for U.S. companies to locate intangible assets in low-tax subsidiaries when selling into foreign markets. Since it applies to profits on foreign sales, it may be subject to challenge by U.S. trading partners at the WTO.

INTERNATIONAL PERSPECTIVE 15.10

U.S. National Export Initiative

In his State of the Union address in January 2010, President Obama said, "We will double our exports over the next five years." In real terms, that meant doubling our exports from $1.5 trillion at the end of 2009 to $3.1 trillion by the end of 2014 and boosting employment by over 2 million. The National Export Initiative (NEI) was a strategy intended to accomplish this objective by 2015. Its proposals included:

- Increase export assistance to small and medium-sized enterprises (SMEs).
- Promote federal resources and commercial advocacy to assist U.S. companies.
- In consultation with state and local government officials, as well as the private sector, lead trade missions to promote American exports.
- In partnership with the Export–Import Bank, increase access to financing for SMEs who are looking to export.
- Macroeconomic rebalancing, by promoting balanced and strong growth in the world economy through international partnerships.
- Reduce barriers to trade and improve market access for domestic producers, by opening new markets and enforcing trade agreements.
- Create a framework to promote services trade.

In 2015, U.S. exports went up to $2.279 trillion, showing a growth rate of 43 percent. In 2019, U.S. exports of goods and services increased to $2.528 trillion, thus pushing its growth rate to 59 percent since 2009. However, the objective of doubling exports has not yet been realized and additional measures of increasing U.S. exports are needed.

CHAPTER SUMMARY

Objectives of export controls	These include national security, foreign policy, nonproliferation of weapons of mass destruction, and prevention of excessive draining of scarce natural resources.
Export controls and major developments	With the end of the Cold War, controls have been substantially liberalized and simplified. Present controls focus on a small group of critical goods, technology, and countries. However, after the events of September 2001, certain restrictions were imposed on exports.

Scope of Export Administration Regulations (EAR)	The EAR covers exports, re-exports, foreign products that are made using U.S. technology, and U.S. persons' activities.
	Determining License Requirements
	Step 1: Is the transaction subject to Export Administration Regulations (EAR)?
	Step 2: If so, is an export license required based on product characteristics, destination, and use/user and the general prohibitions?
	Step 3: If yes, is there a license exception?
	Step 4: If no, apply for a license. If yes, no license required.
	Step 5: Whether export is made under a license or not, exporters have to comply with SED/DCS and record-keeping requirements.
	Indicators that Help Identify and Report Possible Violations
	Any of the parties to the transaction is on the list of denied persons or the transaction has red flags.
The U.S. antiboycott law	The law prohibits U.S. firms from participating in foreign boycotts not authorized by the U.S. government.
	Who Is Covered by the Laws?
	Individuals and companies located in the United States, foreign subsidiaries controlled by a U.S. company, and all activities involving U.S. commerce with foreign nations.
	What Do the Laws Prohibit?
	Prohibitions include refusals to do business, discriminatory actions against a U.S. individual or company in order to support an unsanctioned foreign boycott, furnishing information to a boycotting country, implementing L/Cs with prohibited conditions.
	Exceptions to the Prohibitions
	These include compliance with import/shipping and documentary requirements of boycotting country, compliance with shipment/transshipment/specific carrier or route selection requirements of boycotting country, compliance with immigration/passport/employment and other local law requirements of boycotting country.
	Enforcement and Penalties
	Penalties for noncompliance:
	1. Criminal penalties: Fines and/or imprisonment.
	2. Civil penalties: Revocation of export license, denial of export privileges, imposition of a fine, denial of tax benefits.
The Foreign Corrupt Practices Act (FCPA)	Principal objectives behind FCPA: To prohibit bribery of foreign officials by U.S. individuals and corporations to obtain or retain a business; to establish standards for maintaining corporate records and internal accounting control objectives.

Who Is Subject to the FCPA?

<u>Anti-bribery provisions</u>

A U.S. issuer, domestic concern, or any person including officers, directors, employees, agents, or shareholders acting on behalf of the issuer, domestic concern, or person.

Issuers and domestic concerns may also be held liable for any act in furtherance of a corrupt payment taken outside the United States. A foreign company or person is now subject to the FCPA if it causes, directly or through agents, any act in furtherance of a corrupt payment to take place within the United States.

U.S. parent corporations may be held liable for the acts of foreign subsidiaries.

<u>Accounting provisions</u>

Publicly-held entities (issuers) that either have securities registered with the SEC or are required to file reports with the SEC.

Enforcement and Penalties

FCPA is enforced by the Securities Exchange Commission and the U.S. Department of Justice.

Measures for Compliance with the FCPA

These include implementing due diligence procedures, seeking an advisory opinion from the government, and adopting internal measures and controls.

Antitrust regulation and U.S. trade

There are three categories of antitrust laws:

1. General prohibitions: The Sherman Act, The Federal Trade Commission.
2. Specific prohibitions: The Clayton Act. The latter covers restraints to commerce through mergers, acquisitions, exclusive dealing, and similar arrangements that lessen competition.
3. Exemptions: Exemptions from antitrust laws in the area of export trade include the Webb–Pomerene Act, Export Trade Certificate of Review, Title IV of the ETC Act.

Extraterritorial Application of U.S. Antitrust Laws

Overseas transactions with a substantial and foreseeable effect on U.S. commerce are subject to U.S. antitrust laws.

Enforcement and Penalties

Institutions that enforce U.S. antitrust laws:

1. The Department of Justice initiates civil or criminal suits against alleged violators.
2. The Federal Trade Commission initiates only civil cases.

Incentives to promote exports

IC-DISCs: Under this arrangement, taxes on export sales can be deferred. However, shareholders must pay interest on their proportionate share of the accumulated taxes deferred. Operational rules are similar to pre-1985 DISCs.

REVIEW QUESTIONS

1. State the U.S. regulations that have a major impact on exports.
2. Discuss current developments in U.S. export controls.
3. What are the major objectives of U.S. export regulations? How do you establish whether a product needs an export license?
4. What types of action does the U.S. antiboycott law prohibit? What kinds of request are not reportable?
5. Discuss the knowledge requirement under the FCPA. Provide examples of U.S. companies indicted for bribing foreign officials.
6. Describe some of the international efforts to control corruption.
7. Discuss the major antitrust exemptions in the area of export trade.
8. Discuss the major incentives to promote exporters since 1972.
9. How does the IC-DISC work?
10. Do you think the IC-DISC will be attacked by U.S. trading partners as an unfair subsidy to U.S. exporters? Why/why not?

REFERENCES

Atkinson, K. and Tillen, J. (2005). The Foreign Corrupt Practices Act: Compliance issues in the tax and customs area. *The Tax Executive*, September–October: 446–454.

Bixby, M. (2010–2011). The lion awakes: The Foreign Corrupt Practices Act 1977–2010. *San Diego International Law Journal*, 12: 89–146.

Bureau of Industry and Security (BIS) (2019). *Annual Report to Congress*. Washington, DC: USGPO.

Cheng, D. (2010). Export controls and the hard case of China. *The Heritage Foundation* (December 13, No. 2501): 1–14.

Chou, W. (2005). The $4 billion question: An analysis of congressional responses to the FSC/ET. *Northwestern Journal of International Law*, 25(2): 415–451.

Clausing, K. (2005). Tax holidays (and other escapes) in the American Jobs Creation Act. *National Tax Journal*, 58(3): 331–346.

Corr, C. (2003). The wall still stands: Complying with export controls on technology transfers in the post-cold war, post-9/11 era. *Houston Journal of International Law*, 25: 442–490.

Desmarais, F. (2009). Export cartels in the Americas and the OAS: Is the harmonization of national competition laws the solution? *Manitoba Law Journal*, 33(1): 41–88.

Federal Trade Commission (FTC) (2020). Protecting America's consumers. www.ftc.gov/about-ftc/bureaus-offices/bureau-competition

Fergusson, I. (2009). The Export Administration Act: Evolution, provisions and debate. *Congressional Research Service*, July 15 (7-5700/RL 31832): 1–27.

Fergusson, I. (2020). The US export control system and the export control reform initiative. *Congressional Research Service*, January 28 (R41916): 1–27.

Fergusson, I. and Kerr, P. (2012). The US export control system and the president's reform initiative. *Congressional Research Service*, February 16 (7-5700/R41916): 1–32.

GATT (1977). *Basic Instruments and Selected Documents.* Geneva: GATT (DOC L/4422).

Gleich, O. and Woodward, R. (2005). Foreign Corrupt Practices Act. *American Criminal Law Review*, 42: 545–571.

Gravelle, J. (2005). The 2004 corporate tax revisions as a spaghetti western: Good, bad and ugly. *National Tax Journal*, 58(3): 347–365.

Hall, C. (1994). Foreign Corrupt Practices Act: A competitive disadvantage, but for how long? *Tulane Journal of International and Comparative Law*, 2: 300–315.

Hunt, C. (1983). Multilateral cooperation in export controls: The role of COCOM. *University of Tulane Law Review*, 14: 1285–1287.

Johns, R. (1988). *Colonial Trade and International Exchange*. London: Pinter Publishers.

Larsen, D. (1970). An economic analysis of the Webb-Pomerene Act. *The Journal of Law and Economics*, 13(2): 461–500.

Levenstein, M. and Suslow, V. (2004). The changing international status of export cartel exemptions. Ross School of Business Working Paper Series, # 897: 1–36.

Levin, M. (2004). Tax changes in the American Jobs Creation Act of 2004. *The CPA Journal*, 54–55.

Loizeau, J. (2004). IC-DISCs may benefit S corporation and LLC exporters. *Business Entities*, July–August: 18–27.

Marsden, P. (2003). *Competition Policy for the WTO*. London: Cameron May.

McDonald, K., Yoshino, T., and Carr, A. (2010). Class action litigation. Bureau of National Affairs: 1–4.

Moskowitz, D. (1996). Lingering Cold War legacies. *International Business*, 9(7): 40–41.

OECD (2004). *Hard Core Cartels*. Paris: OECD.

Schultz, G. (2002). Export controls and domestic markets. *Journal of Industry, Competition and Trade*, 2: 200–233.

Shenefield, J. and Stelzer, I. (1993). *The Antitrust Laws*. Washington, DC: The American Enterprise Institute.

Stein, H. and Foss, M. (1992). *An Illustrated Guide to the US Economy*. Washington, DC: The America Enterprise Institute.

Stenger, G. (1984). The development of American export control legislation. *Wisconsin International Law Journal*, 6(1): 1–5.

U.S. Department of Commerce (2007). Defense Industrial Base Assessment: US Space Industry. Washington, DC: Office of Strategic Industries and Economic Security.

U.S. Department of Justice (2020). *FCPA Resource Guide*. Washington, DC: US GPO.

U.S. Department of Justice and the Securities Exchange Commission (SEC) (2012). *FCPA: A Resource Guide to the US Foreign Corrupt Practices Act*. Washington, DC: US GPO.

Walsh, K. (2002). *US Export Controls and Commercial Technology transfers to China. US-China Security Review Commission: Hearing on export controls and China*. Washington, DC: USGPO.

World Wide Web Resources

Bureau of Export Administration: www.bis.doc.gov

Export Administration Regulations: www.access.gpo.gov/bis/

The Foreign Corrupt Practices Act (FCPA): www.justice.gov/criminal-fraud/foreign-corrupt-practices-act

Convention on Combating Bribery of Foreign Officials: www.oecd.org/dataoecd/7/35/35109576.pdf

US Antitrust Law/Policy: www.usdoj.gov/

Antitrust Enforcement: www.justice.gov/atr

US Tax reform and opportunities for exporters: www.taxpolicycenter.org

Wassenaar Arrangement (1990): www.wassenaar.org/

Federal Trade Commission (Webb–Pomerene filings): www.ftc.gov/os/statutes/webbpomerene/index.shtm

ITA Trade Certificate of Review (2010): https://legacy.trade.godv/mas/ian/etca/tg_ian_002153.asp

International Trade Closing Cases and Discussions

1. Export Trade Certificate of Review

Joint Export Activities to Reduce Costs and Risks

Export Trade Certificates of Review (CORs) are issued by the Department of Commerce (with the concurrence of the Department of Justice) and provide antitrust protection for certain specified export activities. Companies holding certificates can work together in the appointment of exclusive agents or distributors, limitation of pricing, or the handling of competitive products. The benefits of COR include the reduction of transportation, warehousing, and marketing costs. It also allows firms to establish joint facilities, set common prices, divide markets and sales territories, and bid on large contracts, as well as share space in overseas trade shows. Small and medium-sized companies are able to spread costs and minimize risks in exporting without violating U.S. antitrust legislation. Congress viewed the uncertain application of U.S. laws to export activities as impediments to the growth and expansion of U.S. exports. The certificate provides antitrust preclearance for the specified export activities.

United States residents, partnerships, or corporations as well as state and local government entities can apply for COR. Over the last few years, a large number of trade associations have taken advantage of the program for their member firms. If the application meets certification standards, the Commerce Department is required to issue the COR within ninety days of submission. With COR, companies are immune from federal and state antitrust actions. In private antitrust actions, it alters the burden of proof to the advantage of the certificate holder (CH), shortens the statute of limitations covering the CH's conduct, provides for recovery of legal expenses (in cases where the CH prevails), and reduces liability. Since the introduction of the legislation in 1982, COR has only been challenged once in court (in 1998), by Horizon International over a certificate issued to another firm. The U.S. appeals court unanimously upheld the validity of the certificate (COR).

It is important to note that COR will not be granted if the export activity:

a. reduces competition in the United States or results in the substantial restraint of export trade of any U.S. competitor;
b. unreasonably affects prices of the covered product or services in the United States; and
c. is carried out with the expectation that the products or services will be re-exported to the United States.

Selected Holders of COR

* *The Association of Manufacturing Technology (AMT) of McLean, Virginia* represents the interests of American providers of manufacturing machinery and equipment. Founded in 1902, its goal is to promote technological advancements in the design, manufacture, and sale of members' products as well as act as industry advocate on trade matters to governments and

trade organizations throughout the world. The AMT received its COR in 1987 with a view to enhancing the trade competitiveness of its members. Recently, its members were able to cooperate in order to win the contract to supply a large Chinese aircraft plant with the requisite machinery to modernize and win Western aircraft parts contracts. Such cooperation would have been difficult without the COR.

- *The American Film Export Association (AFEA) of Los Angeles, California* is a trade association that provides members with marketing support services, government relations, and statistical data. It received its COR in 1987 and has used this opportunity to expand export opportunities for its members. The AFEA fosters the exchange of information among its exporting members on foreign market conditions including vital credit data on more than 500 film and television buyers in over fifty countries. It also assists members in reducing delays in product delivery to overseas distributors, provides international model licensing agreements, and administers its arbitration tribunal, which resolves disputes regarding distribution.
- *Florida Citrus Exports (FCE)* operates as an export joint venture of nine members including grower-owned cooperatives and packing houses. It received its COR in 1995 and has been able to assist members to cut export costs and increase export effectiveness. The COR allows members to share transportation and market development costs, engage in joint promotional activities, speak with one voice in negotiations with export service providers and foreign buyers, prepare joint bids, assist each other in maintaining quality standards and spread risks. The coordination of transportation is particularly important in exporting perishable commodities.

Questions

1. What are the benefits of certificates of review to U.S. exporters?
2. A certificate of review is not granted in certain cases. Discuss.

2. Selected Cases in Enforcement of FCPA

Ericsson: Ericsson, a Swedish telecommunications company was charged with conspiracies to violate the anti-bribery, books and records, and internal control provisions of the FCPA. It used slush funds, gifts, and bribes to pay high-ranking officials in China, Djibouti, Indonesia, Kuwait, and Vietnam to obtain a contract with state-owned telecommunications companies. The firm used third-party agents and consultants to bribe government officials and often used off-the-books slush funds. The firm agreed to pay over US$1 billion to resolve the case in December 2019.

Samsung Heavy Industries (SHI): SHI, a South Korean-based engineering company, paid over $20 million in commissions to a Brazilian intermediary (part of which was for bribe payments to government officials) in order to secure improper business advantage and cause the Brazilian company Petrobras to charter its ship that was being sold to a Houston-based oil drilling company. The bribe payments were intended to facilitate the sale of the ship to the Houston-based company. The firm agreed to pay $75 million in penalties in November 2019.

Edward Thiessen (ET): ET, President of Alstom, Indonesia, a firm that specializes in the design, construction, and services relating to power generation, power grids, and transportation systems conspired (along with others) to make payments to Indonesian officials in order to obtain and retain contracts to perform power-related services. The arrangement was partly accomplished in the United States. Edward Thiessen accepted responsibility and entered a plea to pay penalties.

Société General (SG): SG, a global financial service, paid bribes (2004–2009) of over US$90 million (through a broker) to high-ranking officials in Libya in order to secure investments from various state institutions. SG managed to secure about thirteen investments estimated at about US$4 billion and earned profits of over US$500 million. The firm agreed to pay US$860 million in criminal penalties in June 2018.

Source: U.S. Department of Justice (2020).

PART VII

Import Procedures and Techniques

CHAPTER 16

Import Regulations, Trade Intermediaries, and Services

LEARNING OBJECTIVES:

16.1 Describe the types of import restriction in the United States

16.2 Learn about the differences between tariff and non-tariff barriers

16.3 Identify product categories with no import restrictions and product categories that are generally prohibited

16.4 Learn about the various U.S. free trade agreements

16.5 Understand the role of customs brokers in facilitating the entry of imports

16.6 Learn about the importance of foreign trade zones and bonded warehouses in trade services

International Trade in Practice

U.S. Customs and Import Restrictions

Federal law prohibits the importation of merchandise mined, manufactured, or produced, wholly or in part, by forced labor, including convict labor, forced child labor, and indentured labor. Suspected products are detained at all U.S. ports of entry and importers of detained shipments are provided an opportunity to export their shipments or submit proof to Customs and Border Protection (CBP) that the merchandise was not produced with forced labor. The use of forced labor is not just a serious human rights issue, but it also brings about unfair competition.

In August 2020 a Withhold Release Order (WRO) was issued against the garments exported by the Hero Vast Group of China based on information that reasonably indicated the use of prison labor in the production of those garments. A similar order was issued against palm oil and palm oil products made by FGV of Malaysia based on investigation that raised concerns about the use of forced child labor in the production of palm oil.

On average, the U.S. CBP processes more than 420,000 parcels of mail and 180,000 express consignment shipments from China each day. Through Operation Mega Flex, CBP found that approximately 12.5 percent of targeted parcels contain counterfeit goods or contraband. Every day, hundreds of thousands of parcels arrive from China and other countries through international mail, many of which contain illegitimate goods that threaten the health and safety of consumers. For example, during the period 2019–2020, CBP detained more than 4,200 shipments of illicit goods and stopped about 2,400 agriculture violations. The seizures included counterfeit goods, illegal narcotics, fake identity documents, prohibited plant and animal products, and other items that threaten the health and safety of consumers.

The explosive growth of e-commerce has generated a substantial increase in international mail and express consignment shipments. Foreign sellers are exploiting this trend to ship counterfeit and other illicit goods into the United States and to commit other trade violations.

IMPORT RESTRICTIONS IN THE UNITED STATES

Tariffs

All goods imported into the United States are subject to duty or duty-free entry, depending on their classification under the applicable tariff schedule and their country of origin. For dutiable products, three different methods are used to levy tariffs:

1 *Ad valorem duty*: The duty levied is a percentage of the value of the imported product. It is the type of duty most often applied. An example would be a 2 percent ad valorem duty on imports of leather shoes. The duty obligation is proportional to the value of the dutiable cargo and bears no relation to the quantity imported. Example: The United States imposes a 10 percent tariff on whey cheese and curd. It also imposes a 2.5 percent tariff on imported vehicles.
2 *Specific duty*: This duty rate is based on the physical unit or weight or other quantity. Such duty applies equally to low- and high-priced goods. To the extent that the same duty rate is applied to similar goods with different import prices, specific duties tend to be more restrictive of low-priced goods. When the price of imports rises, the rate remains unchanged and the effect of the specific duty declines. Example: The United States imposes 0.9 cents specific duty on every live chicken weighing up to 185 g.
3 *Compound duty*: Compound duty combines both ad valorem and specific duty. An example would be $2.00 per pound and 4 percent ad valorem (chicken imports). Example: The United States imposes the following compound duty on wristwatches: 51 cents each + 6.25 percent on the case and strap + 5.3 percent on the battery.

Most merchandise imported into the United States is dutiable under the most-favored-nation (MFN) rate. The MFN principle is expressed in Article I of the GATT and in a number of bilateral and other treaties. Under this principle, any advantage or favor granted by the United States (a member of the GATT) to any import originating from any other country shall be accorded, unconditionally, to the like product originating from all other GATT/WTO members. If the MFN treatment is provided as a result of a bilateral treaty (MFN treatment for goods from a country that is not a member of the GATT/WTO), an obligation arises to treat imports from that country as favorably as imports from any other member of the GATT/WTO. Certain communist countries, such as Cuba and North Korea, are not accorded MFN status and thus denied the benefit of the low rates of duty resulting from trade agreements entered into by the United States.

Non-tariff Barriers

Even though most goods freely enter the United States, there are some restrictions on the importation of certain articles (see International Perspectives 16.1 and 16.2 and Table 16.1). The rules prohibit or limit the entry of some imports; limit entry to certain ports; restrict routing, storage, or use; or require treatment, labeling, or processing as a condition of release from customs. Non-tariff barriers used in the United States fall into the following categories (U.S. Department of Commerce, 2006).

Prohibited Imports

These imports include certain narcotics and drug paraphernalia (materials used to make or produce drugs); counterfeit articles; products sold in violation of intellectual property rights; obscene, immoral, and seditious matter, and merchandise produced by convicts or forced labor. For example, in September 2020 U.S. Customs intercepted a shipment of 20,000 counterfeit N95 respirator masks in Boston from Hong Kong with an appraised value of US$163,000. During the same month, CBP officers in Louisville seized five shipments containing counterfeit designer apparel that was worth more than $1.1 million.

Imports Prohibited Without a License

These include arms and ammunition, and products from certain countries such as Cuba, Iran, and North Korea. For example, the importation of biological materials and vectors (for prevention or cure of human diseases) is prohibited without a license by the Secretary of Health and Human Services.

Imports Requiring a Permit

Such imports include alcoholic beverages, animal and animal products, plant products, and trademarked articles. For example, all commercial shipments of meat and meat food products offered for entry into the United States are subject to the regulations of the Department of Agriculture and must be inspected by the USDA Inspection Service before release by customs. Similarly, the importation of milk and cream is subject to the requirements of the U.S. Food and Drug Administration (FDA). These products may be imported only by holders of permits issued by the FDA.

Imports with Labeling, Marking, and Other Requirements

Certain imports require special labeling. For example, wool and fur products must be tagged, labeled, or otherwise clearly marked to show the importer's name and other required information. All goods imported must be marked individually with the name of the country of origin in English.

Imports Limited by Absolute Quotas

These imports include dairy products, animal feed, chocolate, some beers and wines, textiles and clothing, cotton, peanuts, sugars, syrups, molasses, cheese, and wheat. In April 2018 absolute quotas were imposed on imports of steel mill products from South Korea, prohibiting the entry of any imports in excess of 30 percent of the total aggregate quantity provided in a calendar year for such country.

Imports Limited by Tariff Quotas

The tariff rates on these imports are raised after a certain quantity has been imported. This applies to cattle, whole milk, motorcycles, certain kinds of fish, and potatoes. Tariff quotas permit a specified quantity of merchandise to be entered or withdrawn for consumption at a reduced rate during a specified period. When imported merchandise exceeds a tariff quota, the importer is not allowed to commingle the merchandise with non-quota class goods. In March 2020 the government announced a country-specific, first-come, first served regime for additional allocations on imported raw cane sugar (from October 2019 to September 2020). Any imports beyond this quantity would be subject to higher tariffs.

The Buy-American Act 1933

The Buy-American Act provides for the purchase of goods by the U.S. government (for use within the country) from domestic sources unless they are not of satisfactory quality or too expensive, or not available in sufficient quantity. The procurement regulations allow for the purchase of domestic goods even though they are more expensive than competing foreign merchandise, insofar as the price differential does not exceed 6 percent (12 percent in high-unemployment areas) in favor of domestic goods.

INTERNATIONAL PERSPECTIVE 16.1

Consumer Products and Import Restrictions in the United States

Products or Product Categories with No Import Restrictions

Ceramic tableware, artwork, crafts, gems and gemstones, glass and glass products, household appliances, jewelry and pearls, leather goods that are not from endangered species, metals, musical instruments, optics and optical instruments, paper and paper products, plastics and plastic products, rubber and rubber products, sporting goods, tools, and other utensils.

Products or Product Categories Subject to Certain Restrictions or Requirements

Aerospace products, live animals and animal products, beverages, chemicals, combustibles, cosmetics, drugs and explosives, foods, radioactive and radio frequency devices, used merchandise, vehicles.

Products or Product Categories that Are Generally Prohibited

Food products grown or produced in disease-ridden regions, products derived from endangered species, products that infringe intellectual property rights, obscene or pornographic materials, as well as national treasures.

Source: U.S. Department of Commerce (2019).

INTERNATIONAL PERSPECTIVE 16.2

Import Restrictions in China

Since joining the World Trade Organization (WTO) in 2001, China has become a fearsome competitor on the field of global trade, increasing exports and growing at annual rates averaging 10 percent. China has achieved these gains by leveraging its tremendous productive capacity, low labor and capital costs, and strong state support for export-driven growth. They have also deployed an increasingly complex set of trade policies and strategies, both fair and unfair, to advance their economic interests—often at the expense of foreign competitors.

It's America's third-largest and fastest-growing export market, accounting for over $100 billion in U.S. exports of goods and services annually and growing by an average of over 10–15 percent each year. China is expected to be the largest source of global demand, as it adds over 260 million new middle class consumers to the world economy. An increase in U.S. exports by an additional 10 percent would add some $10 billion of new American exports and some 60,000 U.S. jobs. It is important to ensure that China opens its import market and thus complies with its WTO commitments. Here is a list of some trade barriers employed by China.

- *Tariffs and other import charges*: China still maintains high duties on some products that compete with sensitive domestic industries. Its average tariff rate is 10 percent. Its highest WTO-bound tariff rate is 65 percent for agricultural products. In 2018–2019, China imposed tariffs ranging from 15 to 25 percent on a range of agricultural and industrial goods exported from the United States, partly in retaliation to tariffs on its exports to the United States.
- *Customs valuation*: Many Chinese customs officials are still improperly using "reference pricing," which usually results in a higher dutiable value (not the transaction value the importer actually paid).

> • *Increasing use of antidumping, countervailing, and safeguard measures*: China has emerged as a significant user of antidumping measures. As of 2010, China had over 113 antidumping measures in place, affecting imports from seventeen countries and regions, with ten antidumping investigations in progress. During the same period, China also initiated countervailing duty investigations. There are issues in areas of transparency and procedural fairness.
> • Non-tariff barriers: These barriers include, for example, restrictions on market access in service sectors such as banking, insurance, and telecommunications, selective and unwarranted inspection requirements for agricultural imports, and the use of questionable sanitary and phytosanitary (SPS) measures to control import volumes.

TABLE 16.1 Import Permits, Other Requirements, and Respective Government Agencies

Agricultural commodities	U.S. Department of Agriculture (USDA) and The Food and Drug Administration (FDA)
• Cheese, milk, and dairy products, fruits and vegetables, meat and meat products (from sources other than cattle, sheep, swine goats, and horses), plant and plant products	
• Insects, livestock, and animals, meat and meat products (from cattle, sheep, etc.), plant and plant products, poultry and poultry products, seeds	USDA
Arms, ammunition, and radioactive materials	
• Arms, ammunition, explosives, and implements of war	Department of State and Department of the Treasury
Consumer and electronic products	
• Household appliances such as washers, dryers, air conditioners, refrigerators, heaters, etc.	U.S. Department of Energy
• Flammable fabrics	U.S. Consumer Safety Commission
• Electronic products such as microwave ovens, X-ray equipment, TV receivers	FDA
Foods, drugs, cosmetics, and medical devices	
• Foods and cosmetics	FDA
• Biological drugs	FDA
• Biological drugs for animals	USDA
• Narcotic drugs and derivatives	U.S. Department of Justice
• Pesticides and toxic substances	U.S. Customs
Textile, wool, and fur products	Federal Trade Commission
Wildlife and pets	U.S. Department of the Interior
Motor vehicles and boats	U.S. Department of Transportation
Alcoholic beverages	FDA
All bottle jackets made of plant materials	USDA
Administering agency for quotas, tariff quotas on imports	U.S. Customs

Source: U.S. Department of Commerce (2017)

U.S. FREE TRADE AGREEMENTS (FTAs)

The United States has 14 FTAs in force with 20 countries. It also renegotiated the North American Free Trade Agreement (NAFTA). Merchandise trade with the 20 FTA partners was estimated at $1.6 trillion in 2019, accounting for about 40 percent of U.S. merchandise trade. A substantial part of this trade is with Canada and Mexico, estimated at $1.2 trillion (accounting for 75 percent of U.S. trade with FTA partners). Imports from Jordan, Bahrain, and South Korea have shown substantial growth over the last few years (USITC, 2019). The United States and Japan signed two separate trade agreements in 2019. In pursuance of this agreement, Japan agreed to abolish tariffs on $4.3 billion of U.S. agricultural exports while the United States acceded to reduce or eliminate tariffs on certain agricultural imports from Japan (estimated at $40 million in 2019) and certain industrial goods such as bicycles and fasteners (USITC, 2019). They also agreed to liberalize digital trade. Formal trade negotiations are under way with the EU, Japan, and the United Kingdom.

One of the prominent exceptions to the MFN principle of nondiscrimination in the treatment of imports is that of free-trade areas and other preferential arrangements. This means that imports from countries with which the United States has free trade or similar arrangements are accorded low- or duty- free status. It also enables U.S. firms to bid on certain government procurements in the FTA partner country; obtain prompt, adequate, and effective compensation if its investment is taken over by the government (expropriated); and supply their services in the FTA partner country and participate in the development of product standards. These agreements also provide for the protection and enforcement of intellectual property rights in the FTA partner country (see International Perspective 16.3).

The United States/Israel Free Trade Agreement (FTA, 1985)

The agreement provides for free or low rates of duty for merchandise imports from Israel insofar as the imports meet the rules of origin requirements. For the preferential tariff rate, the product must be grown, produced, or manufactured in Israel, and imported directly into the United States, and the cost or value of the materials produced in Israel plus the direct costs of processing operations in Israel must be no less than 35 percent of the import value.

The US–Mexico–Canada Trade Agreement (USMCA, 2020)

The North American Free Trade Agreement (NAFTA) 1994 eliminated tariffs on most goods originating in Canada, Mexico, and the United States over a maximum transition period of fifteen years (i.e., until 2008). For most Canada–Mexico–U.S. trade, NAFTA eliminated existing duties immediately and/or phased them out over a period of five to ten years. On a few sensitive items, the agreement phased out tariffs over fifteen years. NAFTA duty treatment is applicable only to goods wholly produced or obtained in the NAFTA region, that is, goods produced in the NAFTA region wholly from originating materials. Goods processed or assembled from imported merchandise must contain 60 percent regional value content (transaction value method) or 50 percent value content using the net cost method.

The US–Mexico–Canada free trade agreement (USMCA), which entered into force in July 2020, replaces NAFTA. It updates NAFTA 1) with modern provisions on digital trade, intellectual property, cybersecurity, good regulatory practices, and treatment of state-owned enterprises, and 2) to rebalance NAFTA in a way that makes it easier to reduce the U.S. trade deficit with Canada and Mexico. The new agreement focuses on the following areas:

- Intellectual property rights: The amended agreement removes the obligation to have a ten-year period of data exclusivity for biologics, the period under which a "biosimilar" cannot use clinical trials generated by the branded biologic drug to obtain marketing approval.
- Motor vehicle trade: The agreement requires that all steel manufacturing processes must occur within North America for steel to be considered originating, beginning at year seven of the agreement.
- Labor: A new "rapid response" mechanism was introduced, which provides for an independent three-person panel to request on-site verification at "covered facilities" if denial of freedom of association and collective bargaining rights is suspected.
- Dispute settlement: The revisions prevent parties from blocking the establishment of a dispute settlement panel by ensuring the formation of a panel in cases where a party refuses to participate in the selection of panelists.

The U.S./Australia Free Trade Agreement (USAFTA, 2004)

The USAFTA, 2004, (implemented on January 11, 2005) provides for the elimination of tariffs on over 97 percent of Australia's non-agricultural exports (as well as two-thirds of U.S. tariffs on agricultural products) on the day the agreement took effect. Remaining U.S. tariffs on Australian exports are to be phased out over periods of ten and eighteen years. The agreement also provides for annual increases in quotas for Australian exports of beef, and dairy products. It outlines rules for determining the origin of goods being traded in order to establish eligibility. The agreement determines "an originating good" as one that is a) wholly obtained or produced entirely in the country, b) wholly produced from originating materials, or c) produced in the country partly from non-originating materials.

The agreement covers other areas such as cross-border trade in services, electronic commerce, investment, protection of intellectual property rights, competition policy, government procurement, labor and environmental standards, as well as provisions for dispute settlement.

Free Trade with Central America and the Dominican Republic (CAFTA-DR), 2004

The United States signed the CAFTA-DR with five Central American countries (Costa Rica, El Salvador, Guatemala, Honduras, and Nicaragua) and the Dominican Republic in August 2004. These countries make up the second-largest U.S. export market in Latin America, behind Mexico. The agreement provides for the elimination of customs duties on originating goods traded between the parties. Duties on most tariff lines covering industrial and consumer goods were eliminated as the agreement entered into force. Duties on other goods were to be phased out during a ten-year period. Clothing made in these countries is duty and quota free if they use U.S. or regional fabric and yarn. Additional access is also provided for their sugar exports to the United States through modest increases in quotas.

U.S. TRADE PREFERENCES

Generalized System of Preferences (GSP)

The GSP is a special arrangement by developed nations, agreed under the United Nations, to provide special treatment for imports from developing nations to encourage their economic growth. Under the GSP, tariff exemptions and reductions are provided by industrialized countries on a specified range of commodities exported from developing nations. The GSP scheme was first implemented in the United States in 1976 when the government specified some 2,700 articles that were to receive duty-free treatment if imported from 140 designated developing nations. The scheme has been extended since, with certain modifications and limitations.

Imports from eligible countries are subject to tariff exemptions or reductions if:

1. The merchandise is destined to the United States without contingency for diversion at the time of exportation;
2. The cost or value of materials produced in the beneficiary country and/or the direct cost of processing performed is no less than 35 percent of the appraised value of the goods; and
3. The United Nations Conference on Trade and Development certificate of origin is prepared and signed by the exporter and filed with the entry of the goods.

There are two important limitations to the application of the GSP. First, the president is required to suspend GSP eligibility on imports of specific articles from a particular country when the latter supplied more than $155 million in value of the article during the previous calendar year or over 50 percent of the value of U.S. imports. Since the $155 million limitation was based on the GDP of 2012, appropriate adjustments are made in light of the GDP for the current year. Such limitations do not apply to an eligible least-developed country. Second, the provision of GSP is restricted for the more advanced developing nations. For example, many products from countries such as Israel, Korea, Singapore, and Taiwan were graduated from GSP duty-free treatment.

Certain articles are prohibited by law from receiving GSP treatment. These include most textiles and clothing, watches, footwear, handbags, luggage, flat goods, work gloves, and leather apparel. In addition, the GSP statute precludes eligibility for import-sensitive steel, glass, and electronic articles. The GSP scheme saved beneficiary countries (128 countries in 2011) import duties of over US$1 billion in 2019 on total GSP imports estimated at US$19 billion. Top GSP beneficiaries of U.S. GSP include India, Thailand, Brazil, Indonesia, South Africa, Philippines, Turkey, and Russia.

The Caribbean Basin Initiative (CBI)

The CBI is a program intended to provide duty-free entry of goods from designated Caribbean and Central American nations to the United States. The program was implemented in 1984. For CBI duty-free treatment, the merchandise must be wholly produced or substantially transformed in the beneficiary country, be destined to the United States without contingency for diversion at the time of exportation, and meet the 35 percent value-added requirement similar to the GSP scheme. Value attributable to Puerto Rico, the U.S. Virgin Islands, and the U.S. customs territory may be counted toward the 35 percent value-added requirement. In the latter case, the attributable value is counted only up to a maximum of 15 percent of the appraised value of the imported article.

The United States–Caribbean Basin Trade Partnership Act (CBTPA, 2000) expands the trade benefits currently available to Caribbean and Central American countries under the CBI. Except for textiles and clothing, the CBTPA allows tariff treatment similar to NAFTA for goods excluded from the CBI program (watches, footwear, petroleum products, and so on). Clothing assembled in one or more CBTPA beneficiary countries made from U.S. or regional fabric or yarn are eligible for duty/quota free treatment when they enter the United States.

The trade benefits under CBTPA are expected to continue in effect until September 30, 2030.

The Andean Trade Preference (ATP)

This program was enacted in 1991 in order to provide duty-free treatment for imports of merchandise from designated beneficiary countries (Bolivia, Colombia, Ecuador, and Peru) to the United States. The eligibility requirements were similar to the CBI. It expired in 2001 and was renewed as part of the Trade Act of 2002. The new program, "The Andean Trade Promotion and Drug Eradication Act," provides the same benefits as the ATP. It extends the program, however, by 700 additional products.

A similar arrangement was also made with the Marshall Islands and the Federated States of Micronesia in 1989 and has no expiration date.

The African Growth and Opportunity Act (AGOA, 2000)

This Act was signed into law in May 2000. It is intended to offer beneficiary countries from Sub-Saharan Africa duty-free treatment on more than 1,800 items that are exported to the United States. This is in addition to the standard GSP list of approximately 4,600 items. The program also provides duty and quota exemptions on their exports of textiles and clothing to the U.S. market.

The benefits of the AGOA are extended to countries that are GSP eligible under the existing criteria. Beneficiary countries are also exempted from competitive need limitations, that is, preferential treatment is not suspended if a country is competitive in the production of the item.

As of June 2019, thirty-nine of the forty-eight Sub-Saharan countries were designated as AGOA beneficiaries. The Act was amended in 2002, 2004, and 2015. The latest revision (AGOA IV of 2015) extends preferential treatment for beneficiary countries until 2025. Over 90 percent of U.S. imports from AGOA-eligible countries enter duty free (either under AGOA, GSP, or zero duty MFN rates).

INTERNATIONAL PERSPECTIVE 16.3

U.S. Free Trade Agreements (USFTAs)

Global	Regional	Bilateral
WTO	APEC	Australia FTA
	CAFTA-DR	Bahrain FTA
	USMCA	Chile FTA
		Colombia FTA
		Israel FTA
		Jordan FTA
		Korea FTA
		Morocco FTA
		Oman FTA
		Panama FTA
		Peru FTA
		Singapore FTA

TRADE INTERMEDIARIES AND SERVICES

Customs Brokers

Customs brokers are persons who act as agents for importers for activities involving transactions with the customs service concerning 1) the entry and admissibility of merchandise, 2) its classification and valuation, and 3) the payment of duties and other charges assessed by customs or the refund or drawback thereof. A customs broker could be an individual, partnership, or corporation licensed by the U.S. Department of the Treasury. Finding an honest and knowledgeable broker is crucial to the success of an import firm (see International Perspective 16.4). Dishonest brokers have, for example, been known to make incorrect entries at higher rates of duty and to bill the importer and later seek and pocket the refund. Brokers' failure to make timely filing can be costly to the importer (Serko, 1985).

Duties and Responsibilities of Customs Brokers

Record of transactions: Customs brokers are required to keep a correct and itemized record of all financial transactions and supporting papers for at least five years after the date of entry. Such books and papers must be available for inspection by officials of the Treasury Department. Brokers are required to make a status report of their continuing activity with customs. A triennial status report and fee must be addressed to the director of the port through which the license was delivered to the licensee.

Responsible supervision: Licensed brokers must exercise responsible supervision and control over the transaction of the customs business. A broker must provide written notification to customs within thirty days after terminating any employee hired for more than thirty consecutive days.

Diligence in correspondence and paying monies: Each licensed broker is required to exercise due diligence in making financial statements, in answering correspondence, and in preparing and filing records of all customs transactions. Payments of duties and other charges to the government are to be made on or before the date that payments are due. Any payment received by a broker from a client after the due date is to be transmitted to the government within five working days from receipt by the broker. A written statement should be made by the broker (to the client) accounting for funds received for the client from the government, as well as those received from the client when no payment has been made or received from a client in excess of charges properly payable within sixty days after receipt.

Improper conduct. The regulations prohibit the filing of false information, the procurement of information from government records to which access is not granted, the acceptance of excessive fees from attorneys, or the misuse of a license or permit. The licensee of a broker that is a corporation or association can be revoked if it fails for 120 continuous days to have at least one officer who holds a valid broker license.

License Requirements

To obtain a customs broker license, an individual must be 1) a citizen of the United States (but not an officer or employee of the United States), 2) at least 21 years of age, 3) of good moral character, and 4) able to pass an examination to determine that he or she has sufficient knowledge of customs and related laws.

To obtain a broker's license, a partnership or corporation must have one member who is a licensed broker and must establish that the customs transactions are performed by a licensed member or a qualified employee under the supervision and control of the licensed member. Disciplinary action for infractions, such as making false or misleading statements in an application for a license, conviction after filing of a license application, violation of any law enforced by the customs service, and so on, could result in a monetary penalty as well as the revocation or suspension of a license or permit.

A license is not required to transact customs business by the exporter or importer on his or her own account. This also extends to authorized employees or officers of the exporter/importer or customs broker. Neither is a license required by a person transacting business in connection with the entry or clearance of vessels or by any carriers bringing merchandise to port. A broker who intends to conduct customs business at a port within another district for which he/she does not have a permit must submit an application for a permit to the director of the relevant port.

INTERNATIONAL PERSPECTIVE 16.4

Criteria for Selecting the Right Customs Broker or Freight Forwarder

- *Competitive rate*
- *Knowledge of the product*
- *Reputation/integrity*
- *Service and flexibility*
- *IT capability*
- *Account management, financial stability*
- *Networking capability*

Free-trade Zones

Free-trade or foreign-trade zones (FTZ) are areas usually located in or near customs ports of entry and legally outside the customs territory of the United States. Foreign goods brought into these zones may be stored, broken up, sorted, or otherwise manipulated or manufactured. While conducting these operations, duty payments are delayed until products officially enter into the customs territory.

Merchandise may be admitted into an FTZ upon issuance of a permit by the district director, unless the merchandise is brought in solely for manipulation after entry, is transiting the FTZ (for which a permit is granted), or is domestic merchandise.

Operation

Free- or foreign-trade zones are operated as public utilities under the supervision of the Foreign Trade Zones Board, which is authorized to grant the privilege of establishing a zone. Regulations are issued by the board covering the establishment and operation of FTZs. The Board, which is composed of the Secretary of Commerce (chairperson), the Secretary of the Treasury, and the Secretary of the Army, evaluates applications by public and private corporations for a zone based on the following criteria: the need for zone services in the area, suitability of the site and facilities, justification in support of a zone, extent of state and local government support, and the views of persons or firms to be affected, as well as regulatory policy and other applicable economic criteria. The board also accepts applications for subzones, that is, special-purpose zones established as adjuncts to a zone for a limited purpose. Such zones are single-user facilities, usually accommodating the manufacturing operations of an individual firm at its plant. Every port of entry is entitled to at least one FTZ (Rossides, 1986; U.S. Department of Commerce, 2003).

Economic Advantages

- Merchandise admitted into the zone is not subject to customs duty until it is admitted into the customs territory. There is no time limit as to the storage or handling of the merchandise within the zone.
- Businesses can import a product subject to a high rate of duty and manipulate and manufacture it into a final product that is classified under a lower rate of duty when imported into the customs territory. Importers can also bring in products for display to wholesalers or items restricted under a quota until the next quota period. A quota item may also be transformed in an FTZ into an item that can be freely imported without quota restrictions.
- The importer can establish the duty of foreign merchandise when entered into a zone by applying for a "privileged status." Under this scheme, only the duty previously fixed is payable upon entry of the merchandise into the customs territory at a later date even though its conditions may have changed or resulted in an article subject to a higher rate of duty.
- Duties are paid only on the actual quantity of such foreign goods incorporated in merchandise transferred from a zone of entry into the customs territory. This means that allowances are made for any unrecoverable waste resulting from manufacture or manipulation, thereby limiting the duty to articles actually

entered. Savings in duties and taxes may thus result from moisture taken out or dirt removed, and so on. Savings in shipping and taxes may also be possible from shipping unassembled parts into a zone for assembly.

- Merchandise may be remarked or reconditioned to conform to certain requirements for entry into the customs territory.

The popularity of FTZs has grown not only in the United States but also in different parts of the world. By 1998, the number of such zones in the Unites States exceeded 200. Similar growth in the number of FTZs is observed in Africa, Asia, and Eastern Europe. A substantial part of the merchandise (over 80 percent) entered under FTZs in the United States is imported into the United States for domestic consumption, while the rest is exported to foreign markets.

Bonded Warehouses

Bonded warehouses are secured, U.S. Customs-approved warehouse facilities in which imported goods are stored or manipulated without paying duty until the goods are removed and entered for consumption. Duty is not payable when goods under bond are exported, destroyed under customs supervision, or withdrawn as supplies for vessel or aircraft. Merchandise may be kept in the warehouse for up to five years from the date of importation. The advantages of a bonded warehouse are quite similar to those of FTZs.

Any person desiring to establish a bonded warehouse must submit an application to the district director where such facility is located. On approval of the application, a bond is executed to protect the duty liability. Customs regulations provide for different types of bonded warehouses.

The major differences between a bonded warehouse and an FTZ are as follows: 1) costs for the use of bonded warehouses are generally less than for FTZs, 2) bonded warehouses may be established on a user's facilities and with a limited degree of difficulty as compared to FTZs, and 3) the permitted types of manipulation are more limited in the case of a bonded warehouse than for an FTZ. For example, goods may be stored or otherwise manipulated in a bonded warehouse as long as the process does not involve manufacturing. The assembly of watch heads by combined domestic and foreign components is a manufacture (not a manipulation) prohibited under customs regulations. However, the repackaging of spare watch parts is a manipulation that is allowable.

CHAPTER SUMMARY

Tariffs and non-tariff barriers	*Methods of Levying Tariffs* 1. Ad valorem: Duty based on value of the imported product 2. Specific: Duty based on quantity or volume 3. Compound: Duty that combines both ad valorem and specific. *Non-tariff Barriers* Non-tariff barriers include quotas, tariff quotas, labeling requirements, licensing requirements, prohibiting the entry of certain imports, and requirements to purchase domestically produced goods.

Preferential trading arrangements	NAFTA, U.S./Israel FTA, U.S./Australia FTA, the Caribbean Basin Initiative, Andean Trade Preference, the Generalized System of Preferences, AGOA, USMCA.
Trade intermediaries and services	*Customs Brokers* Customs brokers act as agents for importers with regard to 1) the entry and admissibility of merchandise, 2) its classification and valuation, and 3) the payment of duties and other charges assessed by customs or the refund or drawback thereof. *Free-Trade Zones* Free-trade zones are designated areas, usually located in or near a customs port of duty, where merchandise admitted is not subject to a tariff until it is entered into the customs territory. Foreign goods brought into an FTZ may be stored, or otherwise manipulated or manufactured. FTZs are legally considered to be outside the customs territory of a country. *Bonded Warehouses* Bonded warehouses are secured, government-approved warehouse facilities in which imported goods are stored or manipulated without payment of duty until they are removed and entered for consumption.

REVIEW QUESTIONS

1. What are the different ways in which tariffs are levied in the United States?
2. Discuss the various types of non-tariff barriers imposed in the United States.
3. What is the difference between "imports requiring a permit" and "imports prohibited without a license"? Provide examples.
4. Does the U.S.–Israeli agreement eliminate all trade barriers between the two countries?
5. Discuss the U.S. GSP and conditions for eligibility.
6. Does AGOA allow free trade in textiles and clothing?
7. What is the difference between a customs broker and freight forwarder?
8. Discuss the duties and responsibilities of a customs broker.
9. What is a free-trade zone? How does it differ from a bonded warehouse?
10. Discuss some of the economic advantages of free trade zones.

REFERENCES

Rossides, E. (1986). *US Import Trade Regulation*. Washington, DC: The Bureau of National Affairs.

Serko, D. (1985). *Import Practice*. New York: Practicing Law Institute.

UN Comtrade (2020) *International Trade Statistics Database*. New York: UN.

U.S. Department of Commerce (2006). *Importing into the United States*. Rocklin, CA: Prima Publishing.

U.S. Department of Commerce (2017). *A Basic Guide to Exporting*. Lincolnwood, IL: NTC Books.

U.S. ITC (2019). *The Year in Trade 2019: Operations of the Trade Agreements Program*. Washington, DC: USGPO.

World Wide Web Resources

Information on Foreign Trade Zones: www.cbp.gov/xp/cgov/import/cargo_control/ftz/about_ ftz.xml

Information on U.S. Customs and Border Protection—importing, exporting, and NAFTA: www. cbp.gov/

Information on the U.S. Generalized System of Preferences: https://crsreports.congress.gov/ product/pdf/IF/IF11232

Importing into EU countries: www.cbp.gov/sites/default/files/documents/Importing%20 into%20the%20U.S.pdf

---

International Trade Closing Cases and Discussions

1. Tax Deduction for Processing in Maquilas: Mere Assembly or Fabrication?

Customs regulations in the United States provide for deduction of the costs of U.S. components or materials assembled abroad upon importation into the United States. In order to qualify for this exemption from duty assessment, the components must be exported in a condition ready for assembly without fabrication, having not lost their physical identity by change in form or shape. United States Customs also requires that the components are not advanced in value abroad except by mere assembly or operations incidental to the assembly process such as cleaning, lubricating, and painting. This has largely facilitated the establishment of maquilas (in-bond plants) along the U.S.–Mexico border in order to assemble U.S. components for re-export to the United States.

ABC Corporation of Phoenix, Arizona attempted to take advantage of this opportunity by shipping U.S. components to Mexico for assembly and re-export. The company shipped straight steel strips from Tuscon, Arizona to neighboring Nogales, Mexico for use in luggage, which was later imported into the United States. However, U.S. Customs denied a deduction from the value of the luggage for the cost of the steel strips, stating that shaping the steel strips before placing them within the luggage constituted a further fabrication and not mere assembly. In other words, the bending process was not incidental to the assembly of a component exported from the United States. ABC Corporation does not believe that the denial by U.S. Customs was justified.

Questions

1. Do you agree with U.S. Customs?
2. What is your advice to ABC Corporation?

2. Import Penetration in U.S. High-value Industries: Focus on China

The U.S. trade deficit in goods and services increased from $560 billion in 2011 to $577 billion in 2019. This reflects a $17 billion deterioration in the overall trade deficit. While the U.S. trade deficit in petroleum products has declined, the deficit in non-petroleum goods has increased. The growing deficit in non-petroleum products, especially manufactured products, represents a substantial threat to the recovery of U.S. manufacturing employment.

Much of the deficit on manufactured goods is with China, Japan, and South Korea. China alone is responsible for over 70 percent of the U.S. trade deficit in manufactured goods. In spite of increasing wages and transportation costs, Chinese-made, high-value products are taking an increasing share of the U.S. market. In 2016, for example, products made in China captured about 6 percent of total U.S. purchases of capital-intensive products. In many advanced manufacturing sectors, China's import penetration rates have substantially increased over the last ten to fifteen years.

Many factors have contributed to the growing U.S. market share of Chinese high technology industries:

- Rising productivity in China's export sector. This enables producers to absorb higher labor costs without passing them to consumers.
- Export subsidies to producers: The Chinese government provides support to its industries through lower costs for land, energy, water, and other inputs.
- Intervention in the foreign exchange markets to reduce renminbi appreciation. China's recent intervention is estimated at $250 million a day to either halt or limit currency appreciation (see Table 16.2).

TABLE 16.2 Most Traded Goods Between China and the United States (2020)

U.S. Imports from China (US$)	China's Imports from the United States (US$)
Telephones for cellular networks and other wireless networks (44 billion)	Airplanes and other aircraft (13.1 billion)
Automatic data processing machines (37 billion)	Soya beans (12.5 billion)
Tricycles, scooters, and similar wheeled toys (12 billion)	Vehicles (7.9 billion)
Communications apparatus (11 billion)	Electronic integrated circuits (8 billion)
Games (5 billion)	Oils and gold (6 billion)
Other monitors (4.7 billion)	Machines for the manufacture of semiconductor devices or other circuits (2 billion)
Units of automatic data processing machines (4.4 billion)	Private motor vehicles (2 billion)
Electronic static converters (4.6 billion)	Petroleum gases, copper (3 billion)

Source: UN Comtrade (2020)

Question

Compare U.S. trade with Germany and Japan using currently available data and examine whether it involves high-value goods or commodities.

CHAPTER 17

Selecting Import Products and Suppliers

LEARNING OBJECTIVES:

17.1 Describe the ways in which products are selected for importation
17.2 Learn about the differences between the reactive and proactive approaches to product selection
17.3 Learn about determinants of imports
17.4 Learn about the major factors in international supplier selection
17.5 Understand the common provisions in international purchase contracts
17.6 Learn about the way landed costs are calculated

International Trade in Practice

The ATA Carnet: Unlocking Customs for Temporary Entry of Goods

The ATA Carnet is an international customs document used by travelers to temporarily import certain goods without paying tariffs or going through customs formalities. The term "ATA" stands for the French words "Admission Temporaire." It is created by an international convention to promote world trade and can be used in over ninety countries. Major trading nations such as EU member countries, Australia, Bulgaria, Canada, China, Czech Republic, Hong Kong, Hungary, India, Israel, Japan, Malaysia, New Zealand, South Africa, Thailand, and the United States all accept ATA carnets. The United States acceded to the ATA carnet convention in 1986.

In the United States, carnets are issued and guaranteed by the U.S. Council for International Business (USCIB). The USCIB is liable for the payment of liquidated damages to customs in the event that the carnet holder fails to comply with customs regulations. The carnet is valid for one year from the date of issuance.

There are a number of benefits that can be derived by importers from using the ATA carnet: 1) avoidance of complicated customs procedures. The ATA carnet allows the importer to use a single document for clearing goods through customs in several different countrie; 2) it also allows for unlimited exits from and entries into the United States and participating foreign countries during the one-year period of validity; and 3) the importer will not be required to pay customs duty or post a temporary import bond.

ATA carnets cover virtually all goods except food and agricultural products (consumables), and disposable and hazardous items. Merchandise intended for sale or resale must be entered as a regular customs entry. The ATA guaranteeing association (USCIB in the case of the United States) requires a security deposit (about 40 percent of the value of goods) to cover any customs claim that might arise from a misused carnet. The deposit is returned upon the cancellation of the carnet. Application for a carnet is made online at www.merchandisepassport.org.

In the case of certain countries that do not accept ATA carnets, companies can apply for a temporary import bond (TIB), a document that can be purchased from a customs broker at the time of entry. Temporary import bond deposits and payments are made in the importing country each time a product is imported.

Harley-Davidson moved its classic bikes, motorcycle parts, and artifacts to ten cities around the world including Barcelona, Hamburg, Toronto, Sydney, and Tokyo and back to its headquarters in Milwaukee, Wisconsin in 2002–2003 using the ATA carnet. The tour, intended to celebrate the 100th anniversary of the company, was made easier by the carnet, which eliminated the need to pay duties and taxes as well as reduced the delays and costs of physically crossing international borders.

SELECTING PRODUCTS FOR IMPORTATION

One of the most important import decisions is the selection of the proper product that serves the market need. In the absence of the latter, one is left with a warehouse full of merchandise with no one interested in buying it. Nevertheless, importing can become a successful and profitable venture so long as sufficient effort and time is invested in selecting the right product for the target market.

How does one find the right product to import? There are two ways to select a product for importation: The reactive and proactive approach.

The Reactive Approach

This is a way of selecting a product without a proper assessment of market needs. Some people, for example, travel to an exotic location, stumble on a fascinating product and decide to import it for resale. The decision may be based on the uniqueness of the product, its quality, availability, or cost. It is also common to select a product based on government import data, identifying what is hot and trendy or exploiting trade leads that are often posted on the Internet.

Products that are unique and different can be appealing to customers because they are a welcome change from the standardized and identical products sold in the domestic market. The fact that a product is imported and different is, in itself, sufficient for many people to purchase the item. The provision of quality products at lower prices also provides importing firms a competitive advantage (Shippen, 1999). In the apparel sector, for example, imports presently account for over a half of total U.S. market share, mainly due to their cost advantage.

In cases where there is a continuous increase in demand for the product, imports become a major source of domestic supply because the product is either not produced in the country or not produced in sufficient quantities to satisfy the growing demand. The major reason for global sourcing in the chemical industry, for example, is the unavailability of needed products in the U.S. market. Many products manufactured abroad are of better quality than those produced domestically. German machine tools, Japanese cars, and French perfumes have proven market demand because of high quality. In some cases, certain designs could best be manufactured overseas. Identifying a quality product has the potential to increase profits. Any one or a combination of the following can be used in order to find, assess, and select the right product for importation.

Domestic Market Research

Primary market research can be conducted by a consulting firm to identify the best line of products for the domestic market. A variety of statistical sources provide data on projected total demand for certain products. Trade flows can also be examined to gather information on domestic demand and growth trends for various products. Some secondary sources also provide important market information, such as domestic market overviews, market share data, and opinions of industry experts. Such secondary market research studies and surveys can be purchased for a fraction of the cost of primary research. Online data can also provide industry and product information.

Trade Publications

Trade publications such as *Trade Channel, Asian Sources*, and *General Merchandise* provide business and trade opportunities in various countries. They include various advertisements of products and services available for import from all parts of the world (Weiss, 2007; Nelson, 2008). Certain banks with international departments often publish newsletters with offers to buy and sell. The prospective importer can also use electronic bulletin boards of the World Trade Centers to find out what products are available for import.

Foreign Travel

Whenever one visits a foreign country, it is important to look for products that may have a market at home. If a good product is obtained, it would create a profitable business opportunity. One could fine new and exciting products that are not currently imported in the public markets, bazaars, or gift stores. Once a good product is identified, a few samples can be purchased. The manufacturer's address can be obtained from the country's trade department or from local vendors, usually for a small referral fee. If one does not travel overseas, it is always possible to ask friends or agents abroad for product information.

Trade Fairs and Shows

One way of finding a product is to attend trade fairs and trade shows. Many exporters find such shows to be an effective means of promoting their products. It is estimated that almost 2,000 trade shows take place in over seventy countries every year. Trade shows represent an entry point into export markets worldwide. Importers will have an opportunity to consider a variety of potential products to buy, to establish personal contacts, identify new prospects or gather competitive information. Many exporters introduce their products to the foreign market with the hope of writing orders at the show or of finding suitable distributors or manufacturers' agents who will handle their products in overseas markets. Major shows in the United States are published in the *Exhibits Guide*. The Department of Commerce publishes information on upcoming trade fairs and trade shows in the United States and abroad. There are also online sources on various shows and exhibitions in certain product areas to be held in various parts of the world. A recent online announcement, for example, invites buyers and sellers of furniture to the international furniture fair in Copenhagen, Denmark, where major dealers from around the globe are expected to exhibit their furniture.

Foreign Countries' Trade Offices

Most countries have export promotion offices abroad. A trade promotion office provides important information on a country's major export products or services, suppliers, and other helpful contacts. In the absence of a trade promotion office for a nearby country, the embassy could be a good source of information on potential products to import.

The Proactive Approach

The proactive approach to selecting import products involves developing a product that solves problems encountered by consumers. Financial success largely reflects the value that is provided in the marketplace. It grows out of one's passion to improve a product's quality or functionality: Haagen Daz ice cream (to put seasonal fruits in the ice cream), Marcel Schurman greetings cards (to allow buyers to write their own sentiments) or edible supermarket labels (provide harmless labels in case they are inadvertently consumed by adults or children).The ability to provide such value is often influenced by one's experience, education, and enthusiasm for the product.

When selecting the product, one is guided by the following considerations:

- *Products with entry barriers*: Products with high entry barriers tend to earn above-average rates of profit. Entry barriers could be created by product differentiation (designing the product for the market) which gives the owner an exclusive right to make or trade the product. Entry barriers also include high capital requirements (for example, large industrial equipment that is expensive and subject to special shipping and handling requirements), and special access to channels of distribution (Grant, 2010).

- *Absence of close substitutes*: The absence of close substitutes for a product makes it difficult for consumers to choose another product in response to price increases (demand is inelastic with respect to price). For example, switching from Apple to Intel equipment involves new software and hardware. If an importer redesigns a product for a given market along with other complementary assets, the cost of switching by users to another product can be quite expensive.
- *Limited bargaining power of buyers*: The less differentiated the product, the more likely it is for the buyer to switch suppliers on the basis of price. It may not be profitable to start with big buyers such as Walmart since they use their strong bargaining power to pressure suppliers to lower prices.

Even though some imported products can be sold without any modification, most products imported into the United States are designed for the U.S. market. For example, all cars, watches, clothing, and furniture produced and sold in Asian countries are different from those imported and sold in the United States and Europe. They are redesigned to suit the market in terms of functionality, pattern, color etc. Baskets used in Asian countries for collecting clams on the seashore are redesigned as a single-serving bread basket for U.S. homes and restaurants. Clothing made in Central American countries has to redesigned or tailored for American sizes. The popular Mazda Miata was designed in California for the U.S. market (Spiers, 2001). Designers can be located at universities (engineering schools) or technical institutes and are often remunerated on a royalty basis.

The process of assessing the viability of your product with potential buyers or retailers begins with the first stage of product identification and continues throughout the process of redesigning and test marketing the new product. It may be necessary to redesign the product if test sales (product samples) indicate the need for further improvements.

Regardless of the method used to find the potential product to import, it is advisable to buy a sample or a small order to determine whether there are any prohibitions or restrictions to entry and whether the product can be sold at a competitive price. The sample can be inspected by a customs broker to establish whether the product can be freely entered and, if allowed entry, the applicable duty rate. The sample could also be shown to a freight forwarder to obtain an estimate of the shipping and insurance cost in order to calculate the price at which the merchandise will be sold. It is important to realistically evaluate the price in terms of competing products in the market. When calculating the total cost plus a decent profit margin, if the price is much higher than a competing product in the market, it may be necessary to go back to the drawing board.

Suppose the product is not subject to prohibitions or restrictions and can be sold at a competitive price, the next step is to pre-sell the product to likely buyers. This will determine whether people will buy the product and how much they are willing to pay for it. This can be done by the potential importer or salespeople. The process of supplier selection and negotiation to purchase the first shipment should be done only after making an assessment of how much one can realistically sell.

TABLE 17.1 Comparing Two Approaches to Selecting Products for Importation

	Reactive Approach	Proactive Approach
Where/how do you find the right product?	Trade publications, trade leads, market research, foreign travel, trade fairs, foreign embassies, or consulates.	Identify and solve problems faced by customers with regard to a given product.
How do you select the right product?	Product uniqueness, quality, price, shortages, popularity in home market.	Selection of the product is largely based on one's education, experience, and enthusiasm.
Major steps	Once the product is selected, a sample or small order is purchased to receive feedback from buyers or retailers and determine any import restrictions. If there are no restrictions and the feedback from retailers is positive, test market the product. You can then select the best supplier and negotiate a purchase agreement for your first shipment.	Identify a problem faced by customers based on your background and experience. Develop a product to solve the problem and contact suppliers for developing or designing the product. Check for any import restrictions, test market the product (samples) and make further improvements based on the feedback from test marketing. You can then select the best supplier and negotiate a purchase agreement for your first shipment.

Reactive versus Proactive Approach to Product Importation

The reactive approach to product importation is largely based on short-term market needs. Financial success is a product of long-term relationships and repeat sales. Importing umbrellas one year and moving on to furniture the next year is similar to building a business and abandoning it before it could pay off (Spiers, 2001). The proactive approach has several advantages.

- It seeks to identify and solve customer problems by selecting and designing the right product for the market (on the basis of your background and experience). Importing unfamiliar products solely driven by trade leads or market trends can be risky. Numerous products made overseas are unsafe for consumption. Choosing the right product based on your knowledge and experience is thus critical to long term success.
- Importing the appropriate product for the market requires the development of requisite infrastructure (product design, registration of patents, selection of the best suppliers, and access to distribution channels). Such investment of financial resources, time, and effort is inconceivable using the reactive approach because efforts invested to start one product are wasted when one begins to quickly replace it with another product (Table 17.1).

Factors to Consider When Importing

- *Long lead times*: Once you place an order and pay a small down payment, overseas suppliers will begin to manufacture your product. It may take the supplier one to four months to make the product.
- *A hefty minimum order*: It is not unusual for suppliers to request large minimum orders.
- *Payment terms*: Most suppliers expect to be paid by wire transfer until they establish a certain level of trust.
- *Quality control*: It takes a few shipments to get the product that meets all your specifications (International Perspective 17.1).
- *Language barriers*: Most vendors are able to read English much better than they can understand the spoken language.

INTERNATIONAL PERSPECTIVE 17.1

Quality Control for Imports

Ensuring quality is the best means of winning consumer confidence and sales. Many manufacturing firms find that they must meet new and different standards criteria (national, corporate, regional, or international) to compete in the global marketplace. Even though the majority of industrial standards are voluntary, there are mandatory government-imposed standards in the fields of health and safety, food and drugs, and the environment. In many European countries, consumers often base their purchasing decision on proof of certification for the product or service. European community directives also mandate that companies meet certain product certification standards in order to sell in the European Union.

In the area of imports, quality standards provide a basis for assessing the quality of products and services. Suppliers are provided with a guide as to the quality of the product to be manufactured, while buyers are provided with the confidence that the goods are safe and meet high quality standards. It is important to establish quality testing and inspection procedures, and in the case of large orders, the importer could appoint a quality inspector at the supplier's location to assess and advise the supplier on quality. Acceptance and payment on a letter of credit (L/C) can be made conditional on receipt of a satisfactory inspection certificate.

An example of a quality control program for imports is the one jointly created by the International Automotive Task Force for the auto-industry (ISO/TS 16949). TS16949 is based on ISO-9001 and aims at developing a quality management system that emphasizes continual improvement, defect prevention, and a reduction of variation and waste in the supply chain. The requirements are to be applied throughout the supply chain. It also encourages firms to be responsible stewards of the environment (ISO-14001).This is intended to ensure that products or services satisfy the customer's quality requirements and comply with any regulations applicable to those products or services.

DETERMINING IMPORT VOLUME

Much of the literature on imports underlines the importance of high per capita incomes and population size in determining import levels. All other things being equal, countries with higher per capita incomes will be able to import more per person than countries with lower levels (Lutz, 1994). Larger countries (in terms of population) import fewer manufactured goods on a per capita basis because they tend to have a diversified industrial base, as investment will be attracted to these countries to take advantage of their big markets. This view can be exemplified by the case of the United States and Japan, both of which have low import propensities compared to countries such as Belgium or the Netherlands. Economic theory also suggests that import levels are affected by other factors, such as the price of imports denominated in foreign currency, the exchange rate, as well as the price of domestic goods relative to imports (Warner and Kreinin, 1983; Deyak, Sawyer, and Sprinkle, 1993). While relative prices have a predictable and systematic impact on imports, price elasticities tend to be low, in most instances well below unity. This suggests that large relative price swings are required to have an appreciable impact on trade patterns (Reinhart, 1995). For developing countries, however, determinants of import demand include government restrictions on imports and the availability of foreign exchange (Sarmad, 1989). The study by Sarmad (1989) examining the factors influencing import demand in Pakistan from 1959 to 1986 found that the policy of devaluation or raising tariffs was not significant in reducing imports except in the case of imports of machinery and transport equipment. In countries with successful import-substitution strategies, the impact of relative prices and tariffs tends to decline in terms of their influence on import demand. Import substitution is a policy that taxes and restricts imports to protect and subsidize domestic industries. This policy, which paradoxically led to more import dependence (e.g., for purchases of raw materials, components) was a popular economic strategy among some developing nations (Lindert and Pugel, 1999).

INTERNATIONAL PERSPECTIVE 17.2

Major Factors in International Supplier Selection

- *Quality assurance*: Certification of potential suppliers for strict quality assurance, technical capability to prevent quality failures, and overall commitment to quality assurance.
- *Financial conditions*: Low-cost supplier (purchase price, transportation cost, documentation, etc.), provision of favorable payment terms (open account sales), freight terms such as FOB, CIF.
- *Service performance*: Supplier's commitment and capability for timely delivery of services, and technical assistance.
- *Perceived risks*: Political and economic risks such as political instability, currency inconvertibility, and unstable exchange rates.
- *Buyer–supplier relationships*: Financial stability, negotiation flexibility of supplier.

- *Trade restrictions*: Tariff and non-tariff barriers, countertrade requirements by supplier or country.
- *Cultural and communication barriers*: Language, business customs, ethical standards, communication barriers, electronic data exchange capability.

SELECTING THE SUPPLIER

The product selected for importation may be manufactured by several firms in different countries or within the same country. The next important step is to assess and select the right supplier based on a number of critical factors, such as quality, delivery time and supplier reliability, transportation cost, import duty implications, protection of intellectual property rights, and ability to meet standard requirements.

A study conducted in 1983 on the decision process of U.S. purchasing agents suggests timely delivery, product brand name, and style as important factors that determine purchasing decisions (Ghymn, 1983). A major concern in the minds of many U.S. importers is the quality of the imported product. In today's marketplace, where many firms are competing for the buyer's attention, it is the customer who defines quality in terms of his or her needs. To be successful, an importer should select a supplier who can deliver a product that satisfies consumer needs, has minimum defects, and is priced competitively. Also adding to the importance of quality and the local market appeal of the product is the availability of core supplier benefits, such as warranties, timely delivery, and favorable transportation terms, as well as after-sales service and reliability. Low-cost suppliers can also be identified based on their proximity to raw materials, labor costs, current exchange rates, or transportation costs.

Import duties could be eliminated or substantially reduced by selecting suppliers located in countries that participate in a preferential trade arrangement. In the United States, for example, most products imported from Canada or Mexico (USMCA), Caribbean countries (CBI), Israel (FTA), and countries eligible for GSP benefits are subject to duty-free treatment. For example, ceramic tiles imported from Italy are subject to a 13.5 percent duty, whereas an identical tile coming from Israel would cost the importer only 4.3 percent duty. To qualify for such favorable treatment, it is necessary to mark the country of origin of the import.

Selection of the supplier should also be based on the integrity of the product. Integrity of the product includes the assumption that the import does not violate any intellectual property rights registered in the country, such as patent, trademark, design, or copyright, and that it meets certain regulatory requirements, such as product compliance with the various import laws relating to marking, labeling, inspections, and safety. There has been a rise in the production and sale of counterfeit and pirated goods in many parts of the world. Industry experts, for example, estimate lost sales from unauthorized use of U.S. intellectual property rights at $60 billion annually. It is also important to select suppliers that use certain product safety standards. For example, food service ceramics must be tested for lead, and toys must meet labeling and safety standards (International Perspective 17.2).

A potential importer should be aware of any foreign laws that might affect the purchase, such as export restrictions or quotas. The importer also needs to ascertain whether the supplier has already appointed other distributors or sales agents in the territory and whether the distribution channels available are acceptable in terms of overall profitability and risk. For example, an agent is likely to realize limited profits if the supplier has a distributor in the market (see International Perspective 17.3 for a typical import transaction).

Once a small number of potential suppliers are identified, a personal visit can be made to perform the necessary evaluation and selection of the right supplier. Final selection will be made based on factors such as 1) international knowledge and experience of supplier, 2) supplier's willingness to devote sufficient time to develop the market, 3) supplier's willingness to provide necessary training, and 4) provision of market exclusivity and acceptable payment arrangements. It is also important to obtain a credit report of the supplier. Such evaluation is critical regardless of the marketing channels adopted by the importer.

Helpful Tips to Limit Choice of Countries/Suppliers

Once you have selected the product for importation, your next step is to link up with overseas suppliers. It is important to limit your choice of countries or suppliers from which you will import the selected product. Here are some helpful steps.

Step 1: Let us assume that you have chosen to import fertilizers in view of your background and previous work experience as an organic chemist in a fertilizer company.

Step 2: You can access a trade database (Comtrade.org or tradedataweb.gov) to get the Harmonized Tariff Schedule (HTS) number as well as establish the volume of imports and supplying countries during the past few years (Table 17.2).

Step 3: You see that U.S. imports in fertilizers are growing by about 4 percent a year. Note that imports do not always determine market potential. A product can always be adapted to suit the market. The data shows that Indonesia, Oman, and Israel have been gaining market share over suppliers from other countries.

Step 4: You can contact the embassies or commercial attaché,s of Indonesia, Oman and Israel (in the United States) to obtain a list of suitable manufacturers or suppliers. You can also consult the following trade publications on the Internet: Asianproducts.com; tradechannel.com; eximinfo.org; compass.com; made-in.com; alibaba.com; sourcing.tdc.trade.com; wand.com; worldchambers.com; Foreign-trade.com/exhibit.htm.

Step 5: Contact potential suppliers and request client references and licensing information (license to do business), as well as information on their manufacturing: Experience, cost, quality, production capacity delivery schedule, and intellectual property protection.

Step 6: Request product samples (prototypes) and evaluate whether they have sufficiently incorporated your design specifications and their overall quality. This will lead to a purchase agreement if everything is satisfactory (Table 17.3).

TABLE 17.2 U.S. Imports of Fertilizers 2016–2020 (hypothetical data, US$ thousands)

Exporters	Imported value in 2016	Imported value in 2017	Imported value in 2018	Imported value in 2019	Imported value in 2020	% Increase since 2016	% World Total 2020
World	8925503	4385484	7070067	9621736	9286668	4.05	100.00
Canada	4445271	2900024	3917550	4829403	4492821	1.07	48.38
Oman	15000	18947	167788	161485	517579	3350.53	5.57
Trinidad &Tobago	233001	118246	252184	449134	418558	79.64	4.51
Egypt	226998	52464	219490	279086	306089	34.84	3.30
Kuwait	393311	67753	159416	176167	225230	-42.73	2.43
Qatar	233210	141090	142071	169189	216724	-7.07	2.33
Saudi Arabia	249056	158399	186961	284440	205398	-17.53	2.21
China	394842	105373	279102	204580	195060	-50.60	2.10
Israel	68544	34908	98327	257895	190819	178.39	2.05
Bahrain	128140	87691	90475	161314	175238	36.76	1.89
Morocco	67977	6974	74150	118395	157877	132.25	1.70
Indonesia	337	260	13642	31251	144476	42771.22	1.56
Lithuania	140012	19222	35250	169602	143115	2.22	1.54
Romania	94709	15848	104551	202202	135742	43.33	1.46
Norway	104017	48449	98015	112098	135624	30.39	1.46
Netherlands	59009	33521	44788	90395	124823	111.53	1.34

** Data is hypothetical and used as an illustrative example. Data does not include all exporting countries and thus does not add up to 100.

TABLE 17.3 Imports: Purchase Documentation and Agreement

Common forms for purchase agreements	1. Price lists: Can be sent by seller as a result of buyer's request for quotation or recent communication with buyer. (Price lists are not considered offers.) 2. Quotation: Seller forwards price quotation (pro forma invoice) in response to buyer's offer to purchase a specific quantity. It contains all the terms and conditions. Buyer should review before placing any orders (offer to buyer). 3. Purchase order (PO): Buyer issues purchase order. If buyer wants to further negotiate certain terms such as price, he/she makes a counteroffer before sending the PO. 4. Acknowledgement and acceptance of PO: Once seller communicates acceptance of PO, it is considered confirmation of sales contract. Seller proceeds with manufacture and shipment of the product. 5. Seller prepares commercial invoice when product is ready for shipment to facilitate payment.
Important provisions in international purchase contracts	1. Quantity and price including rebates or discounts, issues relating to parallel imports. 2. Currency: Denomination of currency and responsibility in the event of currency fluctuations. 3. Payment method: open account, documentary collection, letter of credit, etc. 4. Import financing: Terms of financing and duration. 5. Security interest in the event of open account sales. 6. Passage of title, delivery, and risk of loss. 7. Warranties and product defects 8. Pre-shipment inspections. 9. Export licenses. 10. Governing law.

INTERNATIONAL PERSPECTIVE 17.3

A Typical Import Transaction

Step 1: Once a product is selected (see section on selecting products), the importer writes to overseas suppliers to send price lists and product catalogs.

Step 2: Upon receipt of the price lists and catalogs, the importer shows the catalogs to potential customers without disclosing the supplier's name and address.

Step 3: If there is a favorable response from potential customers, the importer contacts the overseas supplier to request product samples and pays for their shipment by air. In the meantime, importer checks with customs for the applicable duty and other import requirements for the product.

Step 4: Provided the importer finds the product samples acceptable, the importer orders a trial shipment and makes an advance payment to the supplier. The importer should communicate domestic marking, labeling, and other requirements to overseas supplier. Supplier's credit references can be obtained from the supplier, banks, and the U.S. Department of Commerce. Potential customers are approached to place orders for the product.

Step 5: As the goods arrive at the airport, the importer arranges with a customs broker to clear customs. The importer sets the selling price.

Step 6: If the trial shipment sells easily, the importer orders large shipments by sea freight and prepares a formal price list and product catalog.

PRICING THE IMPORTED PRODUCT

Knowledge of the price structure for imported goods makes it possible to determine the appropriate price to be charged for the merchandise. The example price structure in Table 17.4 could be used as a general guide.

TABLE 17.4 Landed-Cost Survey, Donga Michael Import Company, Davie, Florida (US$)

Supplier: V. Maundo, Nairobi, Kenya	
Quantity: 150 Makonde carvings	
Gross sales price	3500.00
Less cash discount (15%)	525.00
Net sales price	2975.00
Landed cost	
Purchase price	2975.00
Packing	-----
Inland freight	-----
Duty (2975 – insurance (50) + freight (800)) = 7% (2125.00)	148.75
Brokerage and banking charges	160.00
Custom bond fee	50.00
Merchandise processing fee	8.00
Harbor maintenance fee	2.00
Total landed cost (CIF, Miami)	**3343.75**
Expenses	
Advertising	-----
Repacking	15.00
Interest	10.00
Automatic broker interface fee	10.00
Total landed costs and expenses	**3378.75**
Unit cost	22.52
Suggested selling price	45.00
Net profit	6750 (45 x 150) – 3378.75 (22.52 x 150) = 3371.25

Note: Mark-up is generally 60–100 percent for consumer items; 20–30percent for industrial goods; 250–300 percent for mail order items.

IMPORT MARKETING CHANNELS

One of the fundamental decisions for foreign suppliers is whether to sell their products directly or through intermediaries. Relying on an intermediary relieves the producer of international marketing activities. However, the producer forgoes part of the export profit and does not obtain firsthand information on the market, and this in turn, may reduce the firm's product adaptation capacity (International Perspective 17.4).

Two of the important developments in marketing channels have been the involvement of large retail groups in direct importation, and subcontracting of production abroad by major manufacturing companies. In this age of intense competition, firms that manufacture standardized products can no longer rely on firm-specific advantages arising solely from technology. They should focus on ways of minimizing costs by manufacturing certain components (or subcontracting such production) in low-cost countries.

There are three major markets for imported goods in the United States:

a. Mass markets: Mass market retailers such as Walmart or ToysRUs account for about 55 percent of the U.S. retail market. There are a number of limitations to accessing these markets for new importers. First, they focus on popular and proven items for sale at the lowest possible price. Secondly, their orders contain a number of conditions that are quite difficult to meet for new importers. These conditions, if unmet lead to penalties and fees. Such conditions include but are not limited to requiring sellers to put the purchase order on all bills of lading, short delivery windows, or other shipping and delivery instructions.

b. The fashion market: Fashion markets represent less than 10 percent of the U.S. retail market. They focus on exclusive, expensive products for a narrow segment of the market. In view of the unpredictable nature of the market as well as small orders, there is limited competition.

c. The Regular Retailers: These include mainline retail stores (department stores), neighborhood stores, and stores in shopping malls and account for about 35 percent of the market. They are ideal markets for new importers.

Independent sales representatives (ISRs) are crucial in helping importers navigate through the uncharted territory of import marketing. They help with pricing, distribution, buyer credit checks, packaging, and other pertinent issues. It is important to sign a formal contract with an ISR covering pertinent issues such as sales territory, commissions, and incentives.

FINANCING IMPORTS

Imports can be financed by using methods such as documentary collection, L/Cs, transferable L/Cs, or back-to-back L/Cs. Read about the various L/Cs in Chapter 11.

INTERNATIONAL PERSPECTIVE 17.4

The Ten Most Common Mistakes of Potential Importers

1. Failure to develop sufficient knowledge of the import process, including import regulations, before starting the business.
2. Insufficient knowledge of the product to be imported.
3. Insufficient knowledge of the costs involved in obtaining, importing, and marketing a product.
4. Neglecting to seek quality products at the lowest possible price.
5. Failure to maintain a good working relationship with suppliers, banks, customs brokers, and other intermediaries.
6. Inability to develop an appropriate price structure.
7. Insufficient knowledge of the market.
8. Insufficient working capital.
9. Unwillingness to modify products to meet regulations or consumer preferences.
10. Failure to invest sufficient time and effort in developing the business.

INTERNATIONAL SOURCING

The outsourcing of products and services to external suppliers continues to expand, as firms search for ways to lower costs while improving their products to remain competitive. In 2019, the global market for outsourcing was estimated at US$92.5 billion, with a majority originating in the United States. Outsourcing is commonly used by firms in the areas of communications, computers, and semiconductors. Firms that outsource often realize cost savings and an increase in capacity and quality. In spite of its fast growth, outsourcing is frequently perceived to be poorly controlled, high in cost, and a drain on quality and service performance (for advantages and disadvantages, see International Perspective 17.5). A firm can undertake outsourcing under various arrangements.

INTERNATIONAL PERSPECTIVE 17.5

Advantages and Disadvantages of Outsourcing

Advantages	Disadvantages
1. Lower price	1. Difficulty in evaluating and selecting qualified suppliers
2. Higher-quality products (qualified suppliers)	2. Potential problems with quality and delivery times
3. Supply of products not available domestically	3. Political and labor problems

Advantages	Disadvantages
4. Advanced technology available from foreign sources	4. Paperwork and extra documentation as well as added costs such as freight, insurance import duties, cost of L/C, travel, marketing, etc.
5. Satisfy countertrade obligations	5. Currency fluctuations and payment problems
6. Improve international competitiveness	6. Harder to respond quickly to market changes

Wholly Owned Subsidiary

A firm may move production of parts or components to an affiliate established in a low-cost location abroad. The firm will then import the output as it is needed. For example, Sony outsources production of parts to its manufacturing plants located in China and other low-cost locations around the world.

Overseas Joint Ventures

A firm can import supplies made under a joint venture arrangement. For example, Fujitsu imports parts for its DRAMs production from its joint venture partner in Taiwan. Mitsubishi Electric and Toshiba have also contracted DRAM manufacturing to Taiwanese partners.

In-Bond Plant Contractor

A firm sends raw materials and components to be processed or assembled in a low-cost location by an independent contractor. No customs duty is imposed by the country where the goods are assembled (temporarily imported under bond) and when the products are re-exported to the home country, import duties are imposed only on the value added abroad. The most popular is the maquiladora, which allows U.S. or other foreign companies to combine their technology with low-cost labor in Mexico. The raw materials or components imported in bond and duty free are processed or assembled for eventual re-export. The maquiladora can also be established as a wholly owned operation of the foreign firm.

Contract Manufacturing

A company enters into a contract with a foreign supplier to import a given quantity of products according to specifications. The supplier manages the day-to-day operation of the production process and allows the importer to focus on other core activities. The contract will provide for assurance of quality and quality control. Nortel, a Canadian-based manufacturer of communications equipment, outsources nearly $1 billion worth of components to contract manufacturers abroad. Cisco uses contract manufacturers to reduce production cost and focus on research and development. Its products are mostly made by global manufacturers such as Flextronics and Jabil.

CHAPTER SUMMARY

Selecting products for importation	a. **Reactive Approach:** Selecting products without a proper assessment of long-term market needs. Products are found on the basis of market research, trade leads, foreign travel, or trade fairs and selected in terms of certain appealing characteristics such as quality, price, uniqueness, or popularity in the home market. b. **Proactive Approach:** Products are developed or designed for the market and intended to solve a given problem faced by consumers.
Steps taken before selecting the product and supplier	1. Purchase a sample of the promising item 2. Request inspection by customs to determine if there are any restrictions to entry of the product and establish the applicable duty 3. Check with a freight forwarder about shipping and insurance costs 4. Estimate the price and determine whether the product can be sold at a competitive price
Determinants of import volume	1. Per capita income 2. Population size 3. Price of imports denominated in foreign currency 4. Exchange rates 5. Price of domestic goods relative to imports 6. Price elasticity 7. Government restrictions, availability of foreign exchange
Selecting the Supplier: Important considerations	1. Product quality, brand name 2. Market appeal, minimum defects 3. Other supplier benefits: Timely delivery, warranties, after-sales service, reliability 4. Protection of intellectual property rights
Import marketing channels	1. Mass Markets 2. Fashion Markets 3. Regular Retail Market
Financing imports	1. Open account 2. Consignment 3. Documentary collection 4. Letter of credit

REVIEW QUESTIONS

1. How are products considered for importation?
2. What is contract manufacturing?
3. State some of the factors that determine import volume.
4. Explain the major steps involved in a typical import transaction.
5. What are some of the advantages of outsourcing?

REFERENCES

Deyak, T., Sawyer, W., and Sprinkle, R. (1993). A comparison of demand for imports and exports in Japan and the United States. *Journal of World Trade*, 27: 63–73.

Ghymn, K. (1983). The relative importance of import decision variables. *Journal of the Academy of Marketing Science*, 11: 304–312.

Grant, R. (2010). *Contemporary Strategy Analysis*. New York: John Wiley and Sons.

Lindert, P. and Pugel, T. (1999). *International Economics*. New York: McGraw-Hill.

Lutz, J. (1994). To import or to protect? Industrialized countries and manufactured products. *Journal of World Trade*, 28(4): 123–145.

Nelson, C. (2008). *Import/Export: How to Take Your Business Across Borders*. New York: McGraw-Hill.

Reinhart, C. (1995). Devaluation, relative prices, and international trade: Evidence from developing countries. *IMF Staff Papers*, 42: 290–312.

Sarmad, K. (1989). The determinants of import demand in Pakistan. *World Development*, 17: 1619–1625.

Shippen, B. (1999). Labor market effects of import competition: Theory and evidence from the textile and apparel industries. *Atlantic Economic Journal*, 27(2): 193–200.

Spiers, J. (2001). *How Small Business Trades Worldwide*. Seattle, WA: STC Press.

Warner, D. and Kreinin, M. (1983). Determinants of international trade flows. *Review of Economics and Statistics*, 65(1): 19–104.

Weiss, K. (2007). *Building an Import Export Business*. New York: John Wiley and Sons.

World Wide Web Resources

Finding Your Partners
Information on trade opportunities and partnerships:
www.sba.gov/content/state-trade-and-export-promotion-step-fact-sheet
www.agoa.gov/tradelinks/tradelinks.html
www.dmoz.org/Business/International_Business_and_Trade/Import_and_Export/Portals/
    Trade_Boards/

Learn How To Trade
U.S. Customs guide to importation and planning for growth:
www.unzco.com/basicguide/c2.html
www.cbp.gov/xp/cgov/trade/

Trade Shows
Information on international trade shows and conferences:
www.biztradeshows.com/
www.globalsources.com/TRADESHW/TRDSHFRM.HTM

Outsourcing
https://comparecamp.com/outsourcing-statistics/
www.statista.com/statistics/189788/global-outsourcing-market-size/

International Trade Closing Cases and Discussions

Maytag's Triad Strategy

Firm strategy plays an important part in determining the competitiveness of an industry in a global market. As governments embrace trade liberalization, local industries have become increasingly exposed to fierce competition from a growing array of international suppliers. Domestic producers of bulk appliances like dishwashers and refrigerators were largely insulated from foreign competition because of their size, which makes them expensive to ship across the ocean. However, low labor and production costs added to declining transportation costs has enabled many Asian appliance makers such as China's Haier Group and South Korea's LG Electronics to increase their U.S. market share. They are also opening plants in Mexico and neighboring countries to save on shipping.

Maytag had to adjust to the new competition through global sourcing and collaborative supply chain networks. In the case of dishwashers, its triad strategy entails sourcing the motors from suppliers in China, producing wire harnesses in Mexico, and assembling the parts in Jackson, Tennessee.

Dispensing certain activities across the transnational value chain to lower costs and gain competitive advantage is considered a successful global business strategy. This approach allows U.S. companies to share the risk with suppliers and to choose foreign companies with the best product lines or services.

Maytag selected certain suppliers (of motors for dishwashers) from China largely due to their low prices. However, it decided to make the wire harness in Mexico because they tend to be different in each model and sudden shifts in demand require proximity to the market.

Questions

1. Would you advise Maytag to produce motors for the dishwashers in Mexico in view of the latter's proximity to the U.S. market?
2. Would you advise Maytag to lobby the government for higher tariffs on imports of motors and/or wire harnesses to help them to produce them in the United States (for the domestic and export market)?

CHAPTER 18

The Entry Process for Imports

LEARNING OBJECTIVES:

18.1 Describe the entry process for imports
18.2 Learn about the various types of entry
18.3 Learn about liquidation of entry, protests, and petitions
18.4 Learn about the harmonized code
18.5 Understand the different methods of customs valuation
18.6 Learn about rules of origin and marking requirements

International Trade in Practice

Tariff Classification and Entry of Goods

Tariff classification is the process by which the correct tariff code for imported products is determined. Such classification is important to establish rates of duty and determine import restrictions and preferential duty for customs. The structure is based on the international harmonized commodity description and coding system administered by the World Customs Organization in Brussels, Belgium. The first six digits are the same worldwide.

Example: Fresh or chilled onions: HS code: 0703.10.10
07(HS chapter): Edible vegetables and certain roots and tubers; 03 (HS heading): Onions, shallots, garlic and other alliaceous vegetables, fresh or chilled; 10 (HS subheading): Fresh or chilled onions and shallots; 10 (country specific divisions): Fresh or chilled onions.

Classification rulings: U.S. Customs issues binding advance rulings in connection with the importation of merchandise. In cases where the importer or customs broker requests such a ruling, U.S. Customs requires complete description of the goods, a sample of the product, intended use of the product, any drawing, and similar particulars. Such rulings reduce the chance of noncompliance and ensures that imported merchandise will arrive without unnecessary delays.

Example of mushroom imports to the United States: Importing mushrooms poses certain challenges. First, identifying the correct HS code is not that easy as there are over a dozen HS codes for mushrooms that are preserved in different conditions. Importers or their customs brokers may be well advised to request the correct tariff classification ruling on the type of mushroom they intend to import into the U.S. market. Secondly, importing mushrooms is subject to permits and certificates by the U.S. Department of Agriculture. Furthermore, mushrooms that are intended for resale and public consumption are subject to FDA requirements and inspection. Thirdly, once the correct HS code is ascertained, it is important to establish the tariff rate applicable to the product. In general, a combination of the shipment weight and overall value is used to determine the import duty.

All goods entering the United States are subject to certain customs procedures regardless of their value or dutiable status. Duties accrue upon the imported merchandise on arrival of the vessel within the customs port (or on arrival of the merchandise within U.S. Customs territory for other means of transport). The making of an entry is generally required within five working days after arrival of the importing vessel or aircraft. "Entry'" is the act of filing the necessary documentation with the customs officer to secure the release of imported merchandise. If entry is not made within fifteen calendar days (after arrival of the goods), the goods are placed in a warehouse at the risk and expense of the importer. They may be sold at public auction if entry is not made within six months from the date of importation. Goods subject to depreciation (perishables) and explosive substances may be sold earlier (International Perspective 18.1).

Goods may be entered by the owner, purchaser, his authorized regular employee, or by a licensed customs broker. When the goods are consigned to "order," the bill of lading, properly endorsed by the consignee, may serve as evidence of a right to make entry. An air waybill may be used for merchandise arriving by air. A non-resident consignee has the right to make entry but any bond taken in connection with the entry shall have a resident corporate surety (in the case of a carnet, a resident guaranteeing association). A foreign corporation in whose name a product is entered must have a resident agent at the place where the port of entry is located.

In most cases, entry is made by a person (firm) certified by the carrier bringing the goods to the port of entry. The person (firm) entering the goods is considered the "owner" for customs purposes. The carrier issues a "carrier's certificate" stating that the consignee named in the document is the owner or consignee of the goods. In certain cases, entry may be made by means of a duplicate bill of lading or a shipping receipt (in the latter case, entry must be made by actual consignee or duly authorized agent). Where the goods are not imported by a common carrier, entry is made by the importer who possesses the goods at the time of arrival.

The importer or agent pays the estimated duty at the time of making entry even though customs has not yet liquidated the entry (i.e., final assessment of duty has not been made). Imported goods are not legally entered until after the shipment has arrived within the port of entry, delivery of merchandise has been authorized by customs, and estimated duties have been paid. It is the responsibility of the importer to arrange for examination and release of the goods. The required documentation can now be transmitted electronically to customs. U.S. Customs is in the process of moving toward a new paperless system in which importers can file their entries from a single location and clear shipments in hours instead of days (see International Perspective 18.4 for automated services).

U.S. Customs and Border Protection (CBP) processed 36 million trade entries and collected about $72 billion in tariffs, taxes, and user fees in 2019. Additional revenues accrue from confiscations of cash allegedly involved in money laundering, penalties for violations of import quotas, and so forth (www.cpb.gov). Furthermore, the President ordered safeguard actions under Section 201 of the U.S. Trade Act (Escape clause) that provides for safeguard actions or temporary relief to domestic producers that are adversely impacted by a surge in imports. Pursuant to this, the President placed tariffs on washing machines and parts as well as solar panels. This generated duties of over $2 billion in 2019. Section 232 (aluminum and steel) and section 301 duty assessments on China and EU goods provided additional revenue of almost $72 billion in 2019 (www.cpb.gov). Section 232 of the Trade Expansion Act, 1962 authorizes the President to place restrictions on imports that threaten national security while Section 301 of the Trade Act (1974) allows the President to take appropriate actions against countries that unjustifiably restrict U.S. commerce.

Besides U.S. Customs Service, importers should contact other agencies when questions regarding particular commodities arise. Questions with respect to imports of products regulated by the Food and Drug Administration (FDA), for example, should be forwarded to the nearest FDA district office. Similarly, the respective federal agencies should be consulted whenever an imported product is subject to their regulatory regimes.

THE ENTRY PROCESS

Filing Entry Papers

The entry process requires the filing of the necessary documents to enable customs to determine whether the merchandise may be released from its custody, as well as for duty assessment and statistical purposes. Both of these processes can be accomplished electronically via the Automatic Broker Interface Program. Entry documents generally consist of 1) an entry manifest (Form 7533) or application and special permit for immediate delivery (Form 3461), 2) a commercial invoice (or pro forma invoice when the commercial invoice cannot be produced), 3) a bill of lading, air waybill, or other evidence of right to make entry, 4) a packing list, if appropriate, and 5) other documents necessary to determine the admissibility of the merchandise. This may include information to determine whether the imported merchandise bears an infringing trademark. If the goods are to be released from customs on entry documents, an entry summary for consumption must be filed. An entry summary includes the entry package returned that allows for release of merchandise and other forms (Form 7501) (see International Perspective 18.2 for different types of entry).

Release of Merchandise and Deposit of Estimated Duty

Once the complete entry is made by filing with customs (i.e., the declared value, classification, and rate of duty applicable to the merchandise as well as an entry summary for consumption), the product is released by customs and the estimated duty deposited. A bond must be posted before filing the entry summary to guarantee payment of duties or taxes upon the final assessment of duties or other fees by customs (liquidation of entry). Bonds are required for almost all formal entries, and may be required for some informal entries and temporary importation under bond entries. There are also bonds covering the activities of warehouse proprietors, carriers, etc.

If goods are to be released upon entry, an entry summary for consumption must be filed and estimated duties deposited at the port of entry within ten working days of the goods' entry. Immediate release of a shipment can be obtained through a special permit (Form 3461) prior to arrival of the goods. Carriers participating in the Automated Manifest System can receive conditional release authorizations after leaving the foreign country and up to five days before landing in the United States. Upon approval by customs, shipments are released expeditiously after arrival of the merchandise. However, the entry summary must be filed and estimated duties deposited within ten working days after release. Immediate delivery release is allowed for certain types of goods: articles for a trade fair, shipment consigned to an agency of the U.S. government, tariff quota merchandise (in some cases, merchandise under absolute quota), or merchandise arriving from Canada or Mexico (when approved by the bond director and the bond is on file). In cases where articles subject to different rates of duty are packed together, the commingled articles shall be subject to the highest rate of duty applicable to any part of the commingled lot. However, the consignee or agent can segregate the merchandise to allow customs to ascertain the appropriate duty (within thirty days after notice by customs of such commingling).

A bond is different from a carnet because the latter serves as a customs entry document and as a customs bond. Carnets are ordinarily acceptable without posting further security. Institutions that issue carnets or guarantee the payment obligation under carnets must be approved by customs. In cases where a carnet is not used, a bond is usually required to secure a customs transaction. A single entry bond application is made by the importer or designated person to secure the entry of a single customs transaction, while a continuous bond application is made for multiple transactions. Such application is made to the port director. A single-entry bond is generally for the value of the merchandise plus duties, taxes,, and fees. Customs bonds are (usually 10 percent of the duties, taxes, and fees paid by the importer during the previous thirteen months) valid until cancelled either by the importer or surety. In lieu of a bond, an importer may pledge cash, savings bonds, or treasury notes. Bonds and/or cash are held until one year after an importation is liquidated (or in the case of transportation under bond, the importer demonstrates that the merchandise was either exported or destroyed properly). Customs bonds can be terminated by sending a letter to the port where the bond was originally registered and takes effect ten days after the

TABLE 18.1 CBP Bond Requirements

TYPE OF BOND	BOND REQUIREMENTS
Single Transaction Bond	
a. Basic single entry (for general goods)	Value + duty
b. Quota or visa entries	3 x value
c. Temporary importation	2 x estimated duty
d. Entries requiring compliance with other federal agencies	3 x value
e. Goods unconditionally free of duties	10 percent of value
f. Autos	3 x value
g. Antidumping/countervailing duties	Established by CBP
Continuous Bond	
a. Basic entries	10 percent of annual estimated duties for the next calendar year and rounded up to the next $10,000 It shall not be less than $50,000.
b. Goods conditionally free of duties	10 percent of duty applicable if the merchandise is dutiable.
c. Goods unconditionally free of duties	0.5 percent x annual estimated import value

request is received (sureties are required to send a request to customs and principal and this takes effect thirty days after receipt).

Bonds may be secured through a resident U.S. surety company, a resident and citizen of the United States, or in the form of cash or other government obligations. The list of corporations authorized to act as sureties on bonds and the limits of their bonds is published by the Treasury Department. If individuals sign as sureties, customs often requires two sureties on a bond to protect the revenue and ensure compliance with the regulations. There are also other requirements that individuals have to meet in order to act as sureties: U.S. residency and citizenship, evidence of solvency and financial responsibility, and ownership of property that could be used as security within the limits of the port where the contract of suretyship is approved. The current market value of the property, and so on, less any debts, and so on, must be equal to or greater than the amount of the bond. In the event of default by the importer, the surety and importer are liable to pay liquidated damages to customs (Serko, 1985) (Table 18.1).

INTERNATIONAL PERSPECTIVE 18.1

Avoiding Errors in Invoicing

Any inaccurate or misleading representation or omission of required information in an invoice presented to customs pertaining to an entry may result in delays in the release of merchandise or claims against the importer (unless he/she can establish due diligence). The invoice should reflect the real nature of the transaction. All invoices must include the following information:

- Description of port of entry and detailed description of merchandise, that is, grade, quality, quantity, marks, and numbers (for product and/or packages as the case may be) under which the product is sold.
- Description of the name of the actual seller, importer, place, and date of sale. It should also include the purchase price in the currency of sale. In the event that the product is shipped other than in pursuance of a purchase agreement, the invoice must state the value which the owner or shipper would have received in the ordinary course of trade.
- All charges included in the invoice price including commissions, insurance, etc. as well as any rebates or drawbacks allowed upon exportation of the merchandise. It should also state the value of any materials supplied by the importer.
- Any discounts as well as charges incurred by seller or consignee to deliver the merchandise to buyer and not just the FOB price.

INTERNATIONAL PERSPECTIVE 18.2

Types of Entry

Entry for Consumption: This is the most common type of entry. Merchandise that is not held for examination is released under bond. Even in cases where examination is required (e.g., to determine value, dutiable status, proper markings, or whether shipment contains prohibited articles), certain packages are designated for examination and the rest of the shipment is released under bond.

Entry for Warehouse: Imported goods may be placed in a customs-bonded warehouse and payment of duties is deferred until the goods are removed for consumption. No duty is payable if they are re-exported or destroyed under customs supervision. Goods may be manipulated, sorted, or repackaged in the bonded warehouse for eventual consumption or export. In this case, the duty payable is for the manipulated or new product at the time of withdrawal. Goods may remain in a bonded warehouse for up to five years from the date of importation.

Entry for Transportation in Bond: Merchandise may be entered for transportation in bond without appraisement to any other port of entry designated by the importer. Only an entry for consumption is accepted if more than a year has elapsed since the date of original importation (Customs Form 7512).

Informal Entry: Under this category are commercial entries valued at under $2,500 and household and personal effects, and tools of trade. It does not require the same formalities as consumption entry and is also liquidated at entry.

Mail entry: Merchandise that is imported by mail. No entry is required on duty-free merchandise not exceeding $2,000 in value. There is also no need to clear shipments for imports of under $2,000 (e.g., a parcel delivered by letter carrier). For merchandise whose value exceeds $2,000, formal entry (consumption entry) is required. For mail entry of certain products such as furs, leather, and footwear, the limit is $250.

Temporary Importation Under Bond: Certain types of goods that are not imported for sale (or sale on approval) are admitted without payment of duty, under bond, for exportation within one year (which could be extended up to three years upon application to the port director) from the date of importation. This generally includes merchandise imported for repair, articles used as models, samples, animals and poultry imported for breeding, etc. The ATA carnet can be used for this purpose.

Drawback Entry: A refund of 99 percent of all customs duties is allowed under certain conditions: 1) if the imported material is exported in the same condition as when imported or when destroyed under customs supervision within three years of the date of importation, or 2) if the imported merchandise is used in the manufacturing process and exported within five years from the date of importation.

Liquidation, Protests, and Petitions

Liquidation is the final ascertainment of the duties and drawback accruing on an entry by customs. Liquidation is required for all entries of imported merchandise except the following: temporary importation bond entry, transportation in bond, and imports that are subject to immediate exportation. The liquidation procedure involves determination of the value of imports, ascertainment of their classification and applicable rate of duty, as well as computation of the final amount of duty to be paid. Customs will then establish whether any additional (excess) duty has to be paid (refunded) to the importer, and notify such liquidation to the importer, consignee, or agent by posting a public notice. A formal entry is liquidated when an entry appears on the bulletin notice of liquidation posted in customs.

It is also important to note the following:

- *Limitation on liquidation*: If imported merchandise is not liquidated within one year from the date of entry, it is considered liquidated at the rate and amount of duty stated at the time of entry.
- *Voluntary reliquidation by customs*: Customs could reliquidate any entry within ninety days from the date of notice of the original liquidation.
- *Liquidation for informal, mail, and baggage entries*: The effective date of liquidation for such entries is the date of payment of estimated duties upon entry of merchandise or the date of release by customs under free duty or permit for immediate delivery (Rossides, 1986).

Conversion of Currency

The date of exportation of the goods is the date used to determine the applicable rate of exchange for customs purposes.

Liquidation is not final until any protest that has been filed against it has been decided. If an importer disagrees with the liquidation of an entry, a protest may be filed in writing within ninety days after the date of notice of liquidation. The protest could be with respect to any one or more of the following: the appraised value of the merchandise, classification, duties and other charges, the exclusion of a product from entry, or the refusal to reliquidate an entry. If a protest is denied by the district director, the importer can appeal to the Court of International Trade. The parties have a right to further appeal to the Court of Appeals for the Federal Circuit and from there to the highest court in the country, the Supreme Court of the United States. An importer can also request further review of the protest other than that provided by the district director. If the protest is denied by the latter, the matter is forwarded for review by the regional commissioner.

Any interested party could file a petition with the secretary of the treasury if the individual or group believes that the appraised value, classification, or rate of duty for an imported merchandise is not correct. The term "interested party" includes manufacturers, producers, wholesalers, or trade unions in the United States.

THE HARMONIZED CODE (HS CODE)

The HS code is a harmonized commodity description and coding system that is used for classifying traded products. The Harmonized System was developed under the auspices of the World Customs Organization (WCO), with the active participation of governments and private organizations. Since entering into force on January 1, 1988, the HS has been partially amended every four to six years to bring the HS nomenclature in line with the current international trade patterns, technological progresses, and customs practices. It is used by over 200 countries and customs or economic unions, representing about 98 percent of world trade.

The major benefits of adopting the Harmonized System are as follows:

- The HS Code will be in line with the tariff determination procedures of most countries of the world (in the United States, it is called the Harmonized Tariff Schedule or HTSUS).
- It facilitates the shipment and documentation of merchandise and creates a uniform and familiar system for exporters shipping to other countries.
- Such uniformity in classification and coding across countries simplifies the conduct of international trade negotiations and increases the accuracy of international trade statistics.

The HS Code classifies goods according to their "essential character" or, in the case of apparel, on the basis of the fiber of chief weight. It is a detailed classification system containing approximately 5,300 headings and subheadings organized into ninety-nine chapters and twenty-one sections (Tables 18.2 and 18.3). The six digits can be broken down into three parts. The first two digits (HS-2) identify the chapter in which the goods are classified. For example, 09 = coffee, tea, mate, and spices. The next two digits (HS-4) identify headings within that chapter, for example, 09.02 = tea, whether or not flavored. The next two digits (HS-6) are even more specific (subheadings). For example, 09.02.10 means green tea (not fermented). The HS Code up to the 6-digit level is followed internationally and is common to all countries.

As in the example below (Table 18.2), lentils are coded as 071340 in Turkey, United States, and Canada. However, countries add more digits (United States, S. Korea, EU, Canada add 4 additional digits [a total of 10 digits]; Turkey 6 more digits; India 2 more digits; Japan 3 more digits) to suit their national statistical and trading needs.

TABLE 18.2 Classification of Lentils under the HS Codes of Turkey, the United States, and Canada

	Turkey	United States	Canada
HS Code	0713.40	0713.40	0713.40
Seeds for sowing	0713.40.00.00.11	0713.40.10.00	0713.40.00.10
Green	0713.40.00.00.12	0713.40.10.10	0713.40.00.91
Red	0713.40.00.00.13	0713.40.10.30	0713.40.00.92
Other	0713.40.00.00.19	0713.40.10.80	0713.40.00.99

Goods imported are subject to duty or duty-free status in accordance with their classification under the HTSUS. Duty-free status, for example, is available under certain conditional exemptions provided in column 1 of the tariff schedule. Column 2 is intended for countries that do not qualify for the most-favored-nation (MFN) duty rate, and imports under this category are subject to the highest rate (Table 18.3). In cases in which the correct classification is not certain or the product falls under more than one classification, it is important to resort to the body of interpretative rules provided under the HTSUS or seek a binding tariff classification ruling from customs which can be relied on before placing or accepting orders. Although the average tariff rate in the United States is now around 5 percent, some imports are subject to high tariffs, such as watch parts (151.2 percent) and some shoe imports (67 percent). In certain cases, it is also possible for customs to reverse its classification even after the product has been imported and used. The customs service reversed its decision on imports of muffin mix toppings in 1996 and informed the importer to pay $750,000 penalty for violating the U.S. sugar quota (the decision was, however, reversed for the second time). In another case, imports of large antique red telephone booths were blocked on the grounds that the product was actually a steel product restricted by import quotas (Bovard, 1998). Thus, one cannot overemphasize the importance of obtaining expert opinion, seeking an advance ruling by customs, or establishing reliable procedures on the correct description and classification of a given merchandise before importation.

It is also important to note that the term HTSUS is used for imports and the classification is managed by the Office of Tariff Affairs and Trade Agreements within the International Trade Commission (ITC). When exporting from the United States, the system of classification is called Schedule B and managed by a different agency: the U.S. Census Bureau. The HTSUS and Schedule B are identical up to the 6-digit level but may vary at the level of the commodity code.

CUSTOMS VALUATION

Even though an imported item may be classified and given a rate of duty expressed as a percentage of the item's value, difficulty may arise in determining the value for customs purposes. In 1979, the United States adopted the customs valuation system that was the result of the Tokyo Round negotiations of the GATT. Valuation of a product is important because most imported products are subject to tariffs based on the percentage of the value of the import (ad valorem rate). It also helps countries to maintain accurate and comparable records of their international trade transactions (International Perspective 18.3).

TABLE 18.3 Harmonized Tariff Schedule of the United States

Heading/ Subheading	Stat. Suffix	Article Description	Units of Quantity	Rates of Duty		
				General	Special	2
4902		Newspapers, journals, and periodicals, whether or not illustrated or containing advertised material: appearing at least four times a week				
4902.10.00	00		Kg	Free	Free	Free
4902.90		Other:				
4902.90.10	00	Newspaper supplements printed by a gravure process	No	1.6%	Free (A,CA,E, IL, J MX)	25%
4902.90.20	20		Free	Free		
		Other: Newspapers appearing less than four times a week	Kg			
	40	Other business and professional journals and periodicals	No			
	60	Other (including single issues tied together for shipping purposes	No			

CA= Canada (import from Canada), A=GSP countries, MX= Mexico, E= Caribbean Basin countries, IL= Israel, J= Andean Preference Pact

Rates of Duty
General: GATT members and others obtaining such status by a bilateral agreement;
Special: Imports from countries accorded special duty treatment i.e., Canada, Mexico, GSP countries.
2. Countries not friendly to the United States: Libya, North Korea, etc.

Imported merchandise is appraised on the basis, and in the order, of the following:

1. Transaction value
2. Deductive value
3. Computed value

The Transaction Value

Transaction value is the invoice price of the goods as they enter the United States. In determining transaction value, the price actually paid or payable will be considered without regard to its method of derivation. The value includes various costs that enhance the goods' value to the importer: packing costs, sales commissions, and royalties. It also includes any direct or indirect items provided by the buyer free of charge or at a reduced cost for use in the production or sale of merchandise for export to the United States. In short, the transaction value is the price actually paid or payable for imported merchandise, excluding international freight, insurance, and other CIF charges. Transaction value cannot be used in the following situations:

- In cases in which the transaction value cannot be determined (proceeds of subsequent sales, etc.) or is not acceptable (related-party transactions).
- In cases involving restrictions on the sale or use of the product.

Example 1: A foreign shipper sold merchandise at $1,500 to a U.S. buyer. The seller subsequently increased the price to $1,650. The invoice price is $1,500.00 because that was the price agreed and actually paid by the importer. The merchandise should be appraised at $1,500 because the latter was the price actually paid by the buyer—the transaction value.

Example 2: DM, Incorporated, a firm located in Miami, Florida, purchased 10,000 barrels of crude oil from a Venezuelan oil company, Soto, Incorporated, for $250,000. The price consists of $200,000 for the oil and $50,000 for ocean freight and insurance. Soto would have charged $210,000 for the oil. However, since it owes DM $10,000, Soto charged DM only $200,000 for the oil. The transaction value is $210,000, that is, the sum of ($200,000 + $10,000), excluding CIF charges of $50,000 for ocean freight and insurance.

If the transaction value cannot be determined, the transaction value of an identical merchandise or, in the absence of the latter, the transaction value of a similar merchandise (commercially interchangeable) will be used. The transaction value of identical and similar merchandise (ISM) will be used under the following circumstances:

The products (ISM) must have been sold for export to the United States at or about the same time as the merchandise being appraised.
Value must be based on sales of ISM at the same commercial level and substantially the same quantity as the sale of the merchandise being appraised.
The ISM must be produced in the same country and by the same person (if not available, by a different person) as the merchandise being appraised.
In cases involving two or more transaction values for ISM, the lowest value will be used as the appraised value of the imported merchandise.

Deductive Value

This method is used when the transaction value cannot be determined, such as sales between related parties. However, if the importer designates computed value as the preferred method of appraisement, the latter can be used as the next basis of determining value. Deductive value is essentially the resale price of an imported product, with deductions for commissions, profit and general expenses, transportation and insurance costs (from the country of export to the United States), import duties and taxes, and any cost of further processing after importation. The deductive value is generally calculated by starting with the unit price and making additions to (such as packing costs), and deductions from, that price (see International Perspective 18.3).

Example 1: Merchandise is sold to an unrelated person from a price list which provides favorable unit prices for purchases in larger quantities:

Total Quantity Sold	Unit Price ($)
65	90.00
50	95.00
40	100.00
25	105.00

In this example, the unit price used in determining deductive value is S90.00 since the greatest quantity is sold at that price.

Example 2: A foreign parent company sells parts to its U.S. subsidiary in Texas. The product is not sold to unrelated parties and there is no similar or identical merchandise from the country of production. The U.S. subsidiary further processes the product and sells to an unrelated buyer in Florida within 180 days after importation.

In this example, the merchandise should be appraised under deductive value, with allowances for profit and general expenses, freight and insurance, duties and taxes, and the cost of processing.

Computed Value

The computed value starts with the costs of the materials, labor, and overheads in producing the imported goods. Customs then adds profits and general expenses incurred by the producer (based on average estimates for similar goods in the same country) as well as the prorated value of any materials supplied by the buyer free of charge or at reduced price and packing costs (U.S. Department of Commerce, 2003).

Example: Suppose under the previous Example 2, the U.S. importer requested the shipment to be appraised under computed value. The merchandise is appraised using the company's profit and general expenses if not inconsistent with sales of merchandise of the same class or kind.

If none of the previous methods can be used to appraise the imported merchandise, the customs value is based on a value derived from one of these methods, reasonably adjusted or administered flexibly. If an identical or similar product, for example, is not available in the exporting country, customs could appraise an identical or similar product from a third country to determine value.

INTERNATIONAL PERSPECTIVE 18.3

Unit Price in Deductive Value

One of three prices is used based on time and condition of sale:

- If the merchandise is sold in the condition as imported at or about the date of importation of the merchandise being appraised, the unit price used is the one at which the greatest quantity of the product is sold.
- If the merchandise is sold in the condition as imported, but not sold at or about the date of importation of the merchandise being appraised, the unit price used is the one at which the greatest quantity of the merchandise is sold before the ninetieth day after the date of importation.
- If the merchandise is not sold in the condition as imported and not sold before the close of the ninetieth day after the date of importation of the merchandise being appraised, the unit price used is the one at which the greatest quantity (after processing) is sold before the eightieth day after the date of importation. An amount equal to the value of the further processing is deducted from the unit price in arriving at the deductive value. This method cannot be used if the further processing destroys the identity of the merchandise.

RULES OF ORIGIN AND OTHER MARKING REQUIREMENTS

Imported articles are to be marked with the name of the country of origin to indicate to the ultimate purchaser the name of the country in which the product was manufactured. The ultimate purchaser is generally the last person in the United States who will receive the article in the form in which it was imported.

Country-of-origin determination is important because imports are subject to selective tariffs and non-tariff barriers depending on the origin of the merchandise. Country of origin is the country of manufacture, production, or growth. Most imports, for example, from Canada and Mexico, enter duty free, whereas those from other nations are subject to a higher tariff, a quota, or even an import ban (e.g., Cuba and North Korea). Customs uses the "substantial transformation test" to determine the country of origin of a product that is made up of components or materials from several different countries. The country of origin is determined to be the one where the product was substantially transformed into its current state (Buonafina and Haar, 1989).

Markings must be legible and located in a conspicuous place, where they can be seen with a casual handling of the merchandise. They should be capable of remaining (permanent) on the article during transportation or handling. In the case of certain articles for which marking is not required, such as artworks, lumber, sugar, and so forth, their containers must be marked to indicate the English name of the country of origin. There are also special marking requirements for certain articles, for example, watches, surgical instruments, knives, razors, steel, pipes, and vacuum containers. However, marking is not required for imports not intended for sale (personal use items), products used for further processing, crude substances, or items that are incapable of being marked or cannot be marked without injury or prohibitive expense. Other articles not required to be marked with the country of origin include articles valued at no more than $200 that are passed without the filing of a customs entry, articles brought into a foreign trade zone or a bonded warehouse for immediate exportation, certain coffee, tea, and spice products, etc. Notwithstanding the exemption, the containers must be marked to show the country of origin of such articles (19 CFR 1304).

INTERNATIONAL PERSPECTIVE 18.4

Automated Services in the United States to Facilitate International Trade

- **Automated Broker Interface (ABI):** The ABI is a component of the U.S. Customs Service's Automated Commercial System that permits participants to electronically file required import data with customs. Participants in ABI include brokers, importers, carriers, port authorities, or independent service centers. Presently, over 96 percent of all entries are filed through ABI. This automated process speeds up the release of merchandise. Entry summaries are electronically transmitted, validated, confirmed, corrected, and paid. Participants are also informed of current information. Participants can request quota status, visa requirements, entry or entry summary status. Filers are able to pay for multiple entries with one payment transaction.
- **Automated Clearing House (ACH):** The Customs ACH is an electronic payment option that allows participants to pay customs fees, duties, and taxes electronically. Participants' banks must belong to the National Clearinghouse Association. The accuracy and speed of ACH results in a higher volume of transactions.
- **Automated Export System (AES):** The AES is a joint undertaking between the Bureau of Export Administration, U.S. Customs, and other federal agencies intended to ensure compliance with U.S. export regulations and improve trade statistics. Export information is collected electronically and edited immediately, and errors are detected and corrected at the time of filing. The AES is a nationwide system operational at all ports and for all methods of transportation. It has been implemented in phases since 1995.
- **Automated Manifest System (AMS):** This is a cargo inventory control and release notification system. It interfaces with other systems such as ABI to allow for faster identification and release of low-risk shipments. It speeds the flow of cargo and entry processing and provides participants with electronic authorization of cargo release prior to arrival. It also facilitates the intermodal movement and delivery of cargo.
- **AMS paperless master in-bond participants:** This program is designed to take advantage of the detailed information available within the AMS to control the movement and disposition of master in-bond shipments from the custody of the ocean carrier at the port of unloading to the same carrier's custody at the port of destination. The AMS process tracks and records such merchandise.
- **Cargo Selectivity:** This system is used to sort high-risk cargo from low-risk cargo and to determine the type of examination required. It accepts data transmitted through ABI and compares it against established criteria.

CHAPTER SUMMARY

Entry of imports	Entry is the act of filing the necessary documentation with customs to secure release of imported merchandise. *Accrual of Duties on Imports* 1. On arrival of the vessel: Upon arrival of vessel within the U.S. Customs territory. 2. Arrival of merchandise: Upon arrival of merchandise within the U.S. Customs territory (for other means of transport). *Who May Enter the Goods* Owner, purchaser, authorized regular employee, or a licensed customs broker. *Documentation Required to Enter Merchandise* Entry manifest, commercial invoice, pro forma invoice, packing list, and other necessary documents. *Release of Merchandise* After complete entry is made, product is released by customs and estimated duty paid. A bond must be posted to guarantee payment of duty upon final assessment of duty. A bond may be secured through a resident surety company, resident, citizen, or posted in the form of cash or other government obligations. *Liquidation and Protests* 1. Liquidation: This involves the final ascertainment of the duties and drawback accruing on an entry by customs. 2. Protests: If an importer disagrees with the liquidation of an entry, it is possible to file a protest in writing with the district director within ninety days after notice of liquidation. The decision can be appealed to the Court of International Trade, the Court of Appeals for the Federal circuit, and the Supreme Court of the United States.
Harmonized Tariff Schedule of the United States (HTSUS)	The HTS is a commodity description and coding system that is used by many countries. It classifies goods according to their essential character.
Customs valuation	Imported merchandise is appraised on the basis and in order of the following: 1. The transaction value: Invoice value of the goods as they enter customs. 2. The deductive value: Resale price of imported merchandise with deductions for profit and general expenses. 3. The computed value: Cost of materials, labor, and overheads in producing the imported product plus profits and general expenses incurred by the producer and value of any items supplied by buyer.
Rules of origin and other marketing requirements	Marking requirements: Every imported article must be legibly marked with the English name of the country of origin unless otherwise indicated.

REVIEW QUESTIONS

1. When do duties accrue upon imported merchandise?
2. What is entry of goods? Who may enter the goods?
3. Explain the difference between a single-entry bond and a continuous entry bond.
4. What happens to merchandise that is not liquidated within one year from the date of entry?
5. Discuss the advantages of HTSUS.
6. Briefly describe computed value.
7. Why do importing countries require certificates of origin?
8. Describe some of the automated services at U.S. Customs?
9. What is liquidation of entry?
10. Transaction value cannot be used in certain circumstances. Discuss.

Minicase 18.1

A U.S. makeup retailer imports lipstick from an unrelated Mexican company that uses the below-identified materials and costs for materials used in the assembly of one tube of lipstick. In Mexico, the company assembles the materials into a finished product (a tube of lipstick packaged for retail sale). Upon the importation, the retailer, who is also the importer of record, intends to sell the lipstick for "cost + 20%."

Part No. (PN)	Description	Cost	Country of Origin
1.	Plastic tube base	$0.05	Mexico
2.	Plastic tube cover	$0.05	Mexico
3.	Plastic swivel base	$0.05	Canada
4.	Metal shell	$0.05	China
5.	Metal collar	$0.05	China
6.	Small round mirror that attaches to bottom of PN 1	$0.05	U.S.
7.	Lipstick mass	$0.55	France
8.	Packaging material	$0.10	U.S.

1. What is the per unit entered value?
2. What is the country of origin for the retail package?

REFERENCES

Bovard, J. (1998). Your partner: The Customs Service. World Trade (September): 48–49.

Buonafina,M. and Haar, J. (1989). *Import Marketing*. Lexington, MA: Lexington Books.

Rossides, E. (1986). *US Import Trade Regulation*. Washington, DC: The Bureau of National Affairs.

Serko, D. (1985). *Import Practice*. New York: The Practising Law Institute.

U.S. Department of Commerce (2003). *Importing into the United States*. Rocklin, CA: Prima Publishing.

World Wide Web Resources

Information on the importation of goods to the United States/ U.S. Customs rules and regulations: www.cbp.gov/xp/cgov/import/infrequent_importer_info/internet_purchases. xml

http://cbp.customs.gov/linkhandler/cgov/toolbox/publications/trade/iius.ctt/iius.pdf

Information on tariffs and related matters, including the HTSUS: www.usitc.gov/

Publications of U.S. Customs: entry of goods, classification, and valuation of merchandise: www.customs.ustreas.gov/xp/cgov/toolbox/publications/

International Trade Closing Cases and Discussions

1. Deemed Liquidation by Customs

Koyo Corporation of the United States (Koyo) imported roller and ball bearings for resale in the United States. At the time of entry, antidumping duty orders issued by the U.S. Department of Commerce (Commerce) were in effect. The orders required duty deposits to cover estimated antidumping duties between 48 and 74 percent ad valorem. Liquidation of the entries was suspended due to the ensuing litigation. The importers (Koyo) were successful and the rates were substantially lowered.

In view of the successful outcome for Koyo in the litigation, Commerce issued instructions to U.S. Customs to liquidate the entries at lower rates. Customs did not comply with Commerce's instructions. When Koyo contacted customs (one year later) about the liquidation of its entries, customs found these entries to have been "deemed liquidated" at the original higher antidumping duty rate.

Koyo took the case to the U.S. Court of International Trade (CIT) protesting the liquidations (after its initial protest was denied by customs). The issue is whether the deemed liquidations claimed by customs were justified under existing rules. The requirements for deemed liquidation following antidumping proceedings are that: 1) The suspension of liquidation that was in place must have been removed; 2) Customs must have received notice of the removal of the suspension; and 3) Customs must not liquidate the entry at issue within six months of receiving such notice.

The "deemed liquidation" provision was added to customs law in 1978 to place a limit on the period within which importers would be subject to the prospect of liability for a customs entry and to terminate the government's cause of action for the entry in question.

The court stated that Congress intended to encourage prompt liquidation and did not intend customs not to obey its instructions and thereby retain funds to which it no longer had valid claim. It ordered customs to re-liquidate the entries at the appropriate duty rates, as instructed by Commerce and refund the duties owed with interest to Koyo (2004 U.S. App; Fed. Circ, 2004).

Questions

1. Do you agree with the decision on prompt liquidation?
2. Conduct Internet research to examine the reasons why Congress introduced the provision on "deemed liquidation."

2. Product Classification

Better Home Plastics Corp. (BHP) imported shower curtain sets, which consisted of an outer textile curtain, inner plastic magnetic liner and plastic hooks. While the textile curtain is semi-transparent and decorative, the inner liner also matches the curtain and adds to the set's decorative appearance. The sets are sold to retailers at prices ranging from $5.00 to $6.00.

U.S. Customs classified the merchandise under HTSUS 6303.92.0000 at a rate of duty of 12.8 percent ad valorem. BHP protested that classification, stating that the merchandise should have been classified under HTSUS 3924.90.1010 (by the set's inner plastic liner) with a prescribed duty of 3.36 percent ad valorem. According to the General Rules of Interpretation, when goods are classifiable under two or more headings such as textile curtain and inner plastic liner, customs must classify the merchandise based on the heading which provides the most specific description (rule of relative specificity). This rule may not apply in cases where both headings are regarded as equally specific and each refers only to part of the items within the set.

In cases where the rule of relative specificity does not apply, merchandise can be classified by the component which gives their essential character (the essential character test).

BHP contends that the essential character test must be applied to classify the merchandise on the basis of its inner plastic liner while customs believes that the essential character of the product is embodied in the textile curtain because a) the liner is used for a short time when someone uses the shower while the curtain is employed throughout the day; b) consumers buy the product because of the decorative function of the outer curtain (not the inner plastic liner); and that c) the plastic liner is usually replaceable at one-third to one-fourth of the price of the set.

Questions

1. Do you agree with the position of BHP? Why/why not?
2. What is the essential character test?

CHAPTER 19

Import Relief to Domestic Industry

LEARNING OBJECTIVES:

19.1 Describe the notion of unfairly traded imports

19.2 Learn about import relief under the WTO

19.3 Learn about the difference between fairly traded versus unfairly traded imports

19.4 Learn about U.S. antidumping and countervailing duty rules

19.5 Understand the U.S. antidumping and countervailing duty proceedings

19.6 Learn about other trade remedies

International Trade in Practice

Dumping and Government Subsidies Pertaining to U.S. Imports of Utility Scale Wind Towers from Canada, Indonesia, South Korea, and Vietnam

A petition was filed by the Windtower Trade Coalition whose members are producers of wind towers in Texas and Wisconsin. In July 2019, the coalition filed antidumping (AD) petitions on imports of certain utility scale wind towers from Canada, Indonesia, Korea, and Vietnam and countervailing duty (CVD) petitions on imports of certain utility scale wind towers from Canada, Indonesia, and Vietnam. The U.S. anti-dumping law imposes special tariffs to counteract imports that are sold in the United States at less than "normal value." The U.S. countervailing duty law imposes special tariffs to counteract imports that are sold in the United States with the benefit of foreign government subsidies.

For AD duties or CVD to be imposed, the U.S. government must determine not only that dumping and/or subsidies are occurring, but also that there is "material injury" (or threat thereof) by reason of the dumped and/or subsidized imports. Importers are liable for any potential AD duties or CVD imposed. In

TABLE 19.1 Dumping and Subsidy Margins

Country	Dumping margin (%)	Subsidy margin (%)	Import value (US$) (2019)
Canada	4.94	1.18	56,642,010
Indonesia	5.90	5.90	108,790,263
Korea	5.41		78,660,914
Vietnam	63.80	2.84	106,111,843

addition, these investigations could impact purchasers by increasing prices and/or decreasing supply of certain utility scale wind towers (Table 19.1).

The United States International Trade Commission (USITC)determined that an industry in the United States is materially injured by reason of imports of utility scale wind towers from Canada, Indonesia, Korea, and Vietnam, provided for in subheadings 7308.20.00 and 8502.31.00 of the Harmonized Tariff Schedule of the United States (HTSUS), that have been found by the U.S. Department of Commerce (Commerce) to be sold in the United States at less than fair value (LTFV), and to be subsidized by the governments of Canada, Indonesia, and Vietnam. The AD/CVD orders will remain in effect for a minimum of five years, and there is an opportunity each year for duty rates to increase through the annual administrative review process.

Commerce directed U.S. Customs and Border Protection (CBP) to assess (upon further instructions by Commerce) AD duties and CVD for all relevant wind towers from Canada, South Korea, Indonesia, and Vietnam that are entered or withdrawn from warehousing for consumption on or after December 13, 2019 (the date of publication of preliminary determinations).

The acceleration in globalization witnessed over the last two decades and the corresponding increased exposure to competition from low-price producers in China and other developing nations have created a new economic environment. Since production costs—especially those that are wage-related—cannot be infinitely reduced, the main way for manufacturing firms in those economies to position themselves in domestic and international markets is to focus on offering upgraded and differentiated rather than "mundane" labor-intensive products. However, in an effort to increase market share, many producers and their governments in advanced countries are resorting to unfair trade practices. For example, farmers around the developing world face unfair competition from highly subsidized producers of cotton and dairy in advanced countries.

IMPORT RELIEF UNDER THE WTO

The WTO's most-favored-nation (MFN) principle provides for equal treatment of goods and services from other member countries. This principle of non-discrimination, however, is subject to certain exceptions:

a. Unfair imports
  • Anti-dumping duties to offset dumping (selling at an unfairly low price).
  • Countervailing duties to offset export subsidies.

b. Fairly traded imports
   - Emergency measures to limit imports temporarily, designed to "safeguard" domestic industries.

Unfairly Traded Imports

Anti-Dumping Actions

The WTO's Anti-Dumping Agreement governs the application of anti-dumping measures by WTO member countries. A product is considered to be "dumped" if it is exported to another country at a price below the normal price of a like product in the exporting country. Anti-dumping measures are unilateral remedies (the imposition of AD duties on the product in question) that the government of the importing country may apply after a thorough investigation has determined that the product is, in fact, being dumped, and that sales of the dumped product are causing material injury to a domestic industry that produces a like product. Its substantive requirements provide for the calculation of export price and normal value as a basis for establishing dumping margins (the difference between export price and normal value). Export price is considered to be the price when sold to unrelated buyers in the importing country without including shipping charges. If the product is exported from a non-market economy country, it provides for the use of "constructed price."

The WTO agreement also sets forth rules for determining whether dumped imports are causing injury to a domestic industry that produces a like product. Injury is defined to mean material injury itself, the threat of material injury or material retardation in the establishment of a domestic industry. It is important to establish that the dumped imports are a cause of injury to domestic industry. The WTO provides rules and procedures for initiating an anti-dumping investigation. Dumping disputes may be submitted to the WTO Dispute Settlement Body (DSB) for resolution. It may also review the final AD order of administrative agencies for consistency with the agreement. Anti-dumping duties are applied on all imports of the subject merchandise as long as necessary to counteract dumping that is causing the injury.

Countervailing Duty Actions

The WTO's Subsidies Agreement provides rules for the use of government subsidies and for the application of remedies to address subsidized trade that has harmful commercial effects. These remedies can be pursued through the WTO's dispute settlement procedures, or through a CVD investigation which can be undertaken unilaterally by any WTO member government. A subsidy is a benefit by a government to a domestic firm in the form of a direct transfer of funds (a potential transfer such as a loan guarantee) or foregone government revenue such as a tax credit or the purchase or provision of goods. The WTO allows certain types of government subsidies such as domestic subsidies used to fund social programs, finance R&D, and support firms to meet one-time costs of environmental requirements. A subsidy granted by a WTO member government is prohibited by the Subsidies Agreement if it is contingent on export performance or on the use of domestic over imported goods. These prohibited subsidies are commonly referred to as export subsidies and import substitution subsidies (Czako, Human, and Miranda, 2003).

A subsidy granted by a WTO member government is "actionable" under the Agreement (again, certain exceptions are made for agricultural subsidies) if it "injures" the domestic industry of another country, or if it causes "serious prejudice" to the interests of another country. Serious prejudice can arise in cases where a subsidy impedes or displaces another country's exports or increases the market share of the subsidizing country. Every WTO member is required to notify the WTO Subsidies Committee each year of any subsidy (as defined by the Subsidies Agreement) that it is granting or maintaining within its territory.

Fairly Traded Imports

The WTO's Safeguards Agreement establishes rules for the application of safeguard measures by WTO member countries. A safeguard is a temporary import restriction (for example a quota or a tariff increase) that a country is allowed to impose on a product if imports of that product are increasing so as to cause, or threaten to cause, serious injury to a domestic industry that produces a similar or directly competitive product. Under the WTO rules, member countries must conduct an investigation before they can apply a safeguard measure, and they must make a formal determination that imports of the product are significantly impairing or threatening to impair a domestic industry. They are only temporary (applied for up to four years but can be extended to eight years) and must be applied on a non-discriminatory basis and removed as conditions warrant. The WTO encourages countries imposing safeguards to compensate exporting nations by reducing tariffs on other products (Trebilcock and Howse, 2005; Folsom, 2018).

U.S. IMPORT RELIEF TO DOMESTIC INDUSTRIES

The U.S. trade policy is based on combating unfairly traded imports. There are regulations in place to provide relief to domestic producers that are adversely affected by imports that benefit from government subsidies in home countries or are dumped at low prices in the U.S. market. The U.S. rules are largely consistent with the WTO.

Antidumping and Countervailing Duties

Antidumping and countervailing duty laws in the United States have been subject to several changes over the years; the most recent amendments were to implement the Uruguay Round Agreements of the GATT. An important effect of the agreement is that it has reduced the discretion previously available to the administrating authorities by imposing strict statutory time limits. In the case of an antidumping or countervailing duty petition, for example, domestic authorities are required to make an initial determination within twenty days after the petition is filed. Similar time limits are imposed on the determination of injury. The U.S. Court of International Trade has taken the position that the WTO panel rulings do not have a binding effect (and are merely persuasive) on U.S. court decisions on such matters (Folsom, Gordon, and Spinogle, 2005).

Antidumping or countervailing duties are statutory remedies that cannot be vetoed by the president except by negotiation of an international trade agreement.

Such an agreement may, for example, take the form of voluntary export restraints to restrain the flow of the offending goods to the U.S. market.

It is important to describe the terms that are often used in the analysis of unfair trade practices, that is, dumping, subsidies, and material injury.

Dumping

Dumping is defined as selling a product in the United States at a price that is lower than the price for which it is sold in the home market in the ordinary course of trade (certain adjustments are made for differences in the merchandise, quantity purchased, or circumstances of sale). In the absence of sales or sufficient sales of a like product in the domestic market of the exporting country, dumping may be measured by comparison 1) with a comparable price of a like product sold in a third country or 2) with the cost of production in the country of origin plus a reasonable amount for administrative, selling, and other costs and for profits (constructed value). Selection of a third country is often based on the similarity of merchandise to the one exported to the United States, volume of sales (the country with the largest volume of sales), and similarity of market in terms of organization and development to that of the United States. In calculating constructed value, transactions with related parties that do not fairly reflect the usual market price, as well as sales that are made at less than the cost of production, are disregarded. In cases in which the economy of the home market is state-controlled and does not reflect the market value of the product, foreign market value can be determined based on, in order of preference, 1) the price at which such or similar merchandise produced in a non-state-controlled economy is sold either for consumption in that country or another country, including the United States, or 2) the constructed value of such and similar merchandise in a non-state-controlled economy country. Where the price comparison requires a conversion of currencies, such conversion is made using the rate of exchange on the date of sale.

A major problem with the application of such methods is that the surrogate market economy country selected for comparison may be inappropriate (in terms of its level of economic development) or its producers may not be willing to furnish the information necessary to determine constructed value (Czako, Human, and Miranda, 2003). (See International Perspective 19.1.)

Subsidies

There is no agreed definition of subsidies anywhere in the GATT or domestic law. However, it is reasonable to infer from the list of practices that are considered as subsidies that a subsidy is a preferential benefit given by the government to domestic producers. The benefit could be in the form of income or price support of any direct or indirect financial contributions (e.g., grants, loans, tax credits, loan guarantees, etc.).

Export subsidies are benefits intended to increase exports; domestic subsidies are granted on a product regardless of whether it is exported or consumed at home. Governments provide domestic subsidies to achieve certain socioeconomic goals, such as optimum employment or location of industries in depressed regions, that could not be attained by the sole efforts of the private sector. Although domestic subsidies may increase the subsidizing country's trade flow, they do not attract international condemnation as export subsidies.

It is important to review the rules with respect to permitted or actionable subsidies. If an actionable subsidy is found in a country that is a signatory to the GATT Subsidies Code and that subsidy causes injury to a domestic industry, a CVD is imposed on the subsidized imported product. Proof of injury is not required if the subsidized import comes from a country that is not party to the Subsidies Code or similar agreement. A CVD is imposed to offset the subsidy, that is, equal to the net amount of the subsidy (Trebilcock and Howse, 2005; Folsom, 2018).

The rules and practices on actionable subsidies and non-actionable subsidies (non-specific subsidies, subsidies for R&D, etc.) are consistent with the WTO rules.

Proof of Injury and Remedies

In both AD and CVD investigations, it is important to establish causation: material injury, threat of material injury, or retardation of a U.S. industry producing similar products because of the importation of subsidized and dumped products. Imports do not have to be the sole or even major cause of injury. "Like products" are defined as products which are "like" or in the absence of such "most similar in characteristics and uses" to the foreign product under investigation.

Typically, the USITC considers the collective impact of all imports of a product from a given country in arriving at its injury determination. However, in CVD investigations, there is no injury determination for imports from countries that are not signatories of the Subsidies Code or an equivalent arrangement with the United States, unless the goods are entered duty free.

In determining whether there is injury to a U.S. industry, the ITC will consider import volumes, price effects, and impact on domestic producers of like products as well as all other relevant economic factors that have a bearing on the domestic industry. Domestic industry impact analysis considers the effect of allegedly dumped or subsidized imports on the development and production of the domestic industry, employment, and utilization of plant capacity in the relevant industry. Threat of material injury can be found, for example, if lost sales indicate a threat to future sales, production, and profit. Price undercutting is not a per se basis for a finding of injury if the demand for the product is not price sensitive. Lost sales to the domestic industry have traditionally served as an important element of injury (Czako, Human, and Miranda, 2003). Injury may be shown even in cases involving an improvement in the condition of the industry or a decrease in import volume. The ITC's determination of threat of material injury is made on the basis of evidence that the threat is real and the actual injury imminent and not based on "mere conjectures and suppositions" (19 U.S. Code 1677).

Once it is established that foreign merchandise is being sold in the United States at less than fair market value and injury to domestic industry is established, an AD duty or CVD is imposed on the product (i.e., an amount by which the foreign market value exceeds the United States price of the merchandise). The causation factor can be satisfied if the dumped or subsidized imports contribute even minimally to injury of the domestic industry. A correlation between dumped/subsidized imports and alleged injury is not required for an affirmative injury determination.

The cumulation doctrine is also allowed in determining material injury in dumping or subsidy cases. This means that the effect of dumped and/or subsidized imports from two or more countries of like products (that compete with each other and with domestic products) can be assessed to determine injury to domestic industry. This encourages petitioners to name as many countries as possible. Similarly, if a subsidy is shown to exist and to cause material injury or threat thereof to U.S. industry, then a duty equal to the subsidy (CVD) is imposed. In the case of agricultural products, injury could still be established even though the prevailing market price is at or above the minimum support price. This is intended to insure that injury analysis is not distorted by the beneficial effects of government assistance programs (Trebilcock and Howse, 2005).

ANTIDUMPING AND COUNTERVAILING DUTY PROCEEDINGS

Antidumping and countervailing duty investigations are conducted either on the basis of a petition filed with Commerce through the International Trade Administration (ITA) and the ITC on behalf of a domestic industry or by Commerce upon its own initiative. In the latter case, Commerce must notify the ITC. In a CVD investigation, the ITC plays an active role only when the foreign government conferring the subsidies has entered a trade agreement such as the Subsidies Code or a similar arrangement with the United States (USITC, 2008). The procedural steps of a typical investigation are shown in Table 19.2.

Initiation of Investigation by Commerce

Once a petition is filed or an investigation started on the initiative of Commerce (ITA), the ITC begins to investigate material injury, or threat of material injury, etc. to the domestic industry. In the case of a petition, Commerce determines within twenty days whether to initiate or terminate the investigation based on whether the petition adequately alleges material injury or threat thereof with sufficient information

TABLE 19.2 Antidumping and Countervailing Duty Investigations

Day	Event
0	Petition filed
20	Decision on initiation
45	Preliminary Injury Determination by ITC*
AD: 160	Preliminary Determination by ITA
CVD: 85	Preliminary Determination by ITA
AD: 235	Final Determination by ITA*
CVD: 160	Final Determination by ITA*
AD: 280	Final Injury Determination by ITC
CVD: 205	Final Injury Determination by ITC*
AD: 287	Publication of Order
CVD: 211	Publication of Order

Note: AD = Antidumping duty; CVD = Countervailing duty; *If the determination is negative, the investigation is terminated.

supporting the allegations, and whether the petition has been filed by or on behalf of the industry (domestic producers or workers supporting the petition must account for at least 25 percent of total production and more than 50 percent of production of those supporting or opposing the petition). In the event that the 50 percent requirement is not met, Commerce must poll the industry or rely on other information to determine if the required level of support for the petition exists. In order to establish a standing to file a petition on behalf of an industry, it is common practice for various producers to file as co-petitioners, as co-petitioners with unions or trade associations; petitioners can also secure letters of support from non-petitioning members of the domestic industry, unions, or trade associations.

If Commerce (ITA) determines to initiate an investigation, it will begin to establish whether there is a subsidy or dumping in the U.S market and the commission continues its investigation on injury to domestic industry.

Preliminary Phase of ITC's Investigation

Within forty-five days after a petition is filed or an investigation is begun by Commerce, the ITC makes its preliminary determination, that is, whether there is a reasonable indication of injury to the domestic industry. If the determination is negative, or the imports subject to the investigation are negligible, the proceedings terminate.

Preliminary Phase of Commerce's Investigation

If the ITC's determination is affirmative, Commerce makes its preliminary determination based on the information available at the time whether there is a reasonable basis to believe or suspect that a countervailable subsidy or sales at less than fair market value exists.

If commerce finds a reasonable basis, it estimates the dumping or subsidy margin within 140 and 65 days, respectively, of initiating an investigation. However, such deadlines can be extended if the petitioner requests or the case is extraordinarily complicated.

If Commerce's preliminary determination is affirmative, Commerce 1) suspends liquidation of the investigated merchandise subsequently entered into the United States or withdrawn from the warehouse, 2) requires bonds or cash deposits to be posted for each entry of the merchandise in an amount equal to the estimated net subsidy or dumping margin, and 3) continues the investigation. In addition, the ITC institutes a final investigation concerning injury, threat, or retardation. If Commerce's preliminary determination is negative, Commerce's investigation simply continues (USITC, 2006).

Final Phase of Commerce's Investigation

Within seventy-five days after its preliminary determination, Commerce makes a final determination as to whether a subsidy is being provided or sales at less than fair value are being made. If the final determination is negative, the proceedings end, and any suspension of liquidation is terminated, bonds or other security released, and deposits are refunded. Any party to the proceedings can request for a hearing before final determination by Commerce. If the final determination by Commerce is affirmative, the ITC will then make its determination on injury.

Final Phase of ITC's Investigation

The ITC makes its final determination with respect to material injury, threat thereof, or retardation of domestic industry because of sales at less than market value or subsidies. The investigations must be completed within 120 days after Commerce's affirmative preliminary determination (if Commerce's preliminary determination is affirmative) or within seventy-five days after Commerce's affirmative final determination (if Commerce's preliminary determination is negative).

Issuance of an Order

If the final determination of the ITC is affirmative, Commerce issues an AD duty or CVD order, usually within a week of ITC's determination. The order requires the deposit of estimated AD duty or CVD at the same time as other estimated customs duties pending calculation of the final AD or CVD. If the final determination by the ITC is negative, no AD duty or CVD is imposed, and any suspension of liquidation is terminated, bonds released, and deposits are refunded (USITC, 2006). If the petitioner alleges in an investigation the existence of critical circumstances, that is, massive entry of subsidized imports or imports sold at less than fair value in a relatively short period, Commerce's final determination, if affirmative, will include a retroactive suspension of liquidation for all unliquidated entries of merchandise entered into the United States, including those withdrawn from warehouse.

Suspension of Investigation

An investigation can be suspended prior to a final determination by Commerce if the parties (exporter or subsidizing government) involved agree to cease exports or eliminate the dumping margin or subsidy within a few months after suspension of the investigation. At the same time as it suspends a proceeding, Commerce must issue an affirmative preliminary determination. Suspensions are reviewed by the ITC to ensure the injurious effect of imports is eliminated by the agreement. If the ITC determines that the injurious effect is not eliminated, the investigation (if not yet completed) will resume.

Appeal of Determinations

Any interested party adversely affected by a determination by Commerce or ITC may appeal to the U.S. Court of International Trade. In the case of USMCA members, an interested party may appeal for a review by a binational panel set up under the agreement (Table 19.3).

TABLE 19.3 Imposition of AD/CVD Measures by Top Ten Users, 1995–2019

Antidumping Measures (No. Cases)		Countervailing Duty (No. Cases)	
India	(706)	USA	(160)
USA	(502)	EU	(42)
EU	(332)	Canada	(35)
Argentina	(267)	Australia	(16)
Brazil	(266)	Mexico	(11)
China	(232)	Brazil	(10)
Turkey	(199)	China	(8)
Australia	(168)	India	(7)
Canada	(160)	Peru	(7)
S. Africa	(141)	S. Africa	(5)

Source: WTO (2020)

INTERNATIONAL PERSPECTIVE 19.1

Antidumping Duties and Fair Trade

Antidumping duties are generally intended to prevent predatory pricing by foreign firms. By setting low prices in export markets, they drive domestic producers out of business. Once these firms have gained a controlling interest of the export market, they increase their price to recover their losses. Such economic theory behind antidumping rules is questionable because:

- Such actions are unlikely to escape the attention of governments in importing countries.
- Any subsequent increases in prices are likely to invite other exporters to enter the market, thus nullifying the firm's potential gains from market power. Thus, if firms are not certain about future gains from market power, they are not likely to take losses on their export sales.
- Setting different prices in different markets is not inconsistent with normal business practice, especially in imperfect competitive markets.

Existing regulations to establish dumping often lead to unfair and arbitrary outcomes since the standard set to evaluate import prices and injury are difficult to meet due to variations in accounting methods, difficulty in collecting price information, lack of transparency in decision-making processes, etc. Furthermore, the low burden of proof to establish material harm to domestic producers often leads to acceptance of bogus claims. In the United States, for example, only 17 percent of dumping claims were rejected by the authorities between 1980 and 1997.

For domestic industries which have the support of unions and politicians, even threatening to bring cases often leads foreign exporters to agree to a settlement rather than risk broader trade tension. Many exporters agree to voluntary export restraints. Such agreements if conducted with the consultation of domestic industry would amount to antitrust violations in many countries.

A study by the ITC indicates that the removal of outstanding antidumping (AD) and countervailing duty (CD) orders results in a welfare gain. While domestic companies and their workers receiving AD/CD protection earned $658 million more in profits and wages, terminating this protection would have increased overall American business profits and wages by $1.85 billion in industries that were not receiving such protection (USITC, 1995). The economic effects of AD/CVD orders are ranked third behind the Multi-fiber Arrangement restrictions and the Jones Act maritime restrictions in their net costs to the economy.

OTHER TRADE REMEDIES

Unfair Trade Practices in Import Trade

The ITC is authorized, upon the filing of a complaint or on its own initiative, to investigate alleged violations of section 337 of the Tariff Act of 1930 and to determine whether such violations exist. Section 337 prohibits 1) the importation of articles that violate a valid and enforceable U.S. patent, trademark, copyright, and so on, for which an industry exists or is in the process of being established in the United States and 2) unfair methods of competition by the importer or consignee that could adversely affect a U.S. industry (19 U.S. Code S.1337). The ITC's investigations also include gray-market imports. Gray-market goods are products that, authorized by the owner of production rights to be made and sold in one market, are diverted and sold in another, often unauthorized market. The problem with such goods in import trade is that they are often purchased at discounted prices abroad and imported into the United States, taking away the market from authorized dealers.

A large percentage of such cases involve patent infringement; others pertain to violation of other forms of intellectual property. Such actions can also be raised with the U.S. Patent and Trademark Office. The remedies for such violations include: a) a general or limited exclusion order that directs customs to deny entry of certain goods; b) a cease and desist order that enjoins a person from further violations.

These remedies may be ordered by the ITC in the case of imports infringing upon U.S. intellectual property rights without finding injury. Determinations by the ITC may be appealed to the U.S. Court of Appeal for the Federal Circuit).

Unjustified Foreign Trade Practices

Section 301 of the Trade Act of 1974 was introduced in order to seek open access to U.S. exports in foreign markets. It allows the U.S. government to impose trade sanctions on foreign countries that either violate trade agreements or engage in other unfair trade practices. It is applicable to the export of goods and services, investment practices, and intellectual property rights. Recent Section 301 cases include France's digital services tax on U.S. companies that provide digital services to French users. Section 301 investigations were also made in relation to China's practices pertaining to forced technology transfer, unfair licensing, and intellectual property policies.

Special 301 is another version of Super 301 applicable to intellectual property rights. Priority countries (countries that do not provide adequate protection for intellectual property rights) are identified for bilateral negotiations. A Special 301 investigation is similar to an investigation initiated in response to an industry Section 301 petition. Trade sanctions for noncompliance could be imposed in the event that the country declines bilateral consultations or fails to implement an agreement to open its market or provide adequate protection for U.S. intellectual property rights.

Import Interference with Agricultural Programs

The ITC conducts investigations at the direction of the president to determine whether imports interfere with or render ineffective any program of the Department of Agriculture. The ITC makes its findings and recommendations to the president, who may take appropriate remedial action, including the imposition of a fee or quota on the imports in question. However, fees or quotas may not be imposed on imports from nations that are members of the WTO (USITC, 2006).

Trade Adjustment Assistance

For companies and workers adversely affected by fairly traded imports, trade adjustment assistance is provided in the form of retraining or relocation assistance for workers or certain forms of technical and financial assistance to companies. The Department of Labor (adjustment assistance for workers) or Commerce (adjustment assistance for firms) makes an affirmative determination insofar as imports constitute an important contributing factor to declines in production and sales as well as loss of jobs in the affected industries. Such assistance could be pursued before or in tandem with escape clause proceedings.

The Escape Clause

Under Section 201 of the U.S. Trade Act, 1974, the ITC assesses whether U.S. industries are being seriously injured by fairly traded imports and can recommend to the president that relief be provided to those industries to facilitate positive adjustment to import competition. Relief could take the form of increased tariffs or quotas on imports and/or adjustment assistance for the domestic industry. Such relief is temporary and may be provided for up to five years, with one possible extension of not more than three years. Such actions can be appealed to the U.S. Court of International Trade, then to the Court of Appeals for the Federal Circuit and from there to the U.S. Supreme Court.

Recent escape clause cases include imports of solar panels as well as large resident washing machines (2018). The safeguard measures authorize increased duties and tariff rate quotas on solar panels while imposing tariff rate quotas on washing machines.

IMPORT RELIEF BASED ON NATIONAL SECURITY

The Tariff Act (19 U.S. Code S.1862) gives the president discretion to restrict imports that threaten national security (Section 232 of the Trade Expansion Act,

1962). Commerce makes findings and recommendations to the president who may order the imposition of a quota, fee, tariff, or other remedies. Investigations can be initiated based on an application of an interested party or agency, or self-initiated by Commerce. Based on Section 232 investigations, the U.S. president authorized the imposition of tariffs on imports of steel and aluminum in 2018 (25 percent on steel and 10 percent on aluminum).

Although such remedies are rarely invoked, they could conceivably be used by companies in some strategic sectors. Such remedies are available only if it is established that a strategically important industry is adversely affected by imports and that supplies may not be available during a crisis either from domestic or foreign sources.

CHAPTER SUMMARY

Dumping and subsidies	Dumping is the selling of a product in a foreign market at a price that is lower than the price for which it is sold in the home market. Subsidies are any benefit given by the government to domestic producers. Domestic subsidies are provided to achieve certain socioeconomic goals, such as optimum employment. Export subsidies are intended to promote exports. *Proof of Injury and Remedies* In both cases, remedies are subject to proof of injury of subsidized or dumped imports. Injury is generally established by considering import volumes, lost sales, and the impact on domestic producers of similar products. *Antidumping and Countervailing Duty Proceedings* 1. Initiation of investigation by commerce 2. Preliminary phase of ITC investigation 3. Preliminary phase of Commerce investigation 4. Final phase of investigation by Commerce 5. Final phase of investigation by ITC
Other categories of trade remedies	1. Unfair trade practices, s. 337 2. Unjustified foreign trade practice, s. 301 3. Import interference with agricultural programs 4. Trade adjustment assistance 5. The escape clause

REVIEW QUESTIONS

1. What is the difference between dumping and subsidies?
2. State the types of nonactionable subsidy.
3. What is to be established in every subsidy and dumping investigation?
4. Briefly describe the preliminary phase of an ITC investigation.
5. Describe the procedural steps in a typical antidumping or countervailing duty investigation.

6. What is the role of the USITC in import relief?
7. Explain the escape clause. Can it be applied at any time to protect domestic industry?
8. Describe Special 301.

REFERENCES

Czako, J., Human, J., and Miranda, J. (2003). *A Handbook on Antidumping Investigations*. New York: Cambridge University Press.

Folsom, R. (2018). *Principles of International Trade Law*. St. Paul, MN: West Academic.

Folsom, R., Gordon, M., and Spanogle, J. (2005). *International Business Transactions and Economic Relations*. St. Paul, MN: Thomson.

Trebilcock, M. and Howse, R. (2005). *The Regulation of International Trade*. New York: Taylor & Francis.

U.S. International Trade Commission (USITC) (1995). *The Economic Effects of Antidumping and Countervailing Duty Orders and Suspension Agreements, Investigation No. 332–344, Publication 2900*. Washington, DC: U.S. Government Printing Office.

U.S. International Trade Commission (USITC) (2010/2012). *Annual Report*. Washington, DC: U.S. Government Printing Office.

U.S. International Trade Commission (USITC) (2006). *Summary of Statutory Provisions Related to Import Relief*. Washington, DC: U.S. Government Printing Office.

U.S. International Trade Commission (USITC) (2008). *Antidumping and Countervailing Duty Handbook*. Washington, DC: U.S. Government Printing Office.

World Wide Web Resources

Information provided by the U.S. International Trade Commission on antidumping and countervailing: www.usitc.gov/trade_remedy/731_ad_701_cvd/index.htm

Abstract of the judicial review of ITC determinations: www.questia.com/PM.qst?a=o&d=5000248716

The Heritage Foundation antidumping laws: www.heritage.org/Research/TradeandForeignAid/BG906.cfm

Special 301 Report: www.ustr.gov/about-us/press-office/reports-and-publications/2012-2

International Trade Closing Cases and Discussions

1. Like Products and Dumping

A Chilean salmon exporter was accused of dumping salmon in the U.S. market at less than fair value. An antidumping petition was filed in 1997 by the Coalition for Fair Atlantic Salmon Trade. The U.S. Department of Commerce (ITA) initiated an AD duty investigation to determine whether Chilean exporters of Atlantic, fresh, farmed salmon were selling in the United States at less than fair market value to the detriment of the U.S. industry. The purpose of the investigation was to determine whether AD duties should be imposed on the subject merchandise when imported into the United States.

The ITA conducted an investigation in order to compare the price of the salmon sold in the United States with its "normal value" in Chile (home market). Since the product is not sold in the home market, the ITA based normal value on the price of the salmon sold in Japan. The exporter sold "premium" grade salmon in the United States while it sold "premium" and "super premium" grades in Japan. The ITA found that a) salmon industries do not recognize any grade higher than premium grade and all salmon in this range are graded equally; b) salmon graded as "super premium" are in fact premium grade and comparable in the marketplace. The ITA recognized that the exporter reported higher prices for sales of super premium grade salmon to Japan (sales of premium salmon to Japan covered a few months and involved relatively small quantities, thus insufficient to evaluate price differences). The practical consequences of the ITA's decision to classify the two grades of salmon (super premium and premium) as identical in physical characteristics was to impose a dumping margin of 2.23 percent on the Chilean exports of premium salmon in the United States.

Questions

1. Are the products sold in Japan and the United States identical for duty analysis?
2. Based on the information, do you think dumping has occurred in the United States?

2. Dominican Republic: Safeguard Measures on Imports of Polypropylene Bags and Tubular Fabric

On October 15, 2010, Costa Rica requested consultations (under the WTO) with the Dominican Republic concerning the provisional and definitive safeguard measures imposed by the Dominican Republic on imports of polypropylene bags and tubular fabric and the investigation that led to the imposition of those measures. Costa Rica was concerned about certain aspects of the safeguard measures and the underlying investigation. In particular, Costa Rica alleges that these measures appear to be inconsistent with the Agreement on Safeguards, and Article XIX:1(a) of the GATT 1994. The dispute settlement panel concluded its work and submitted its report in January 2012. The Panel concluded that the provisional and definitive duties are safeguards, since they have suspended the Dominican Republic's obligations under GATT Article I:1 (the MFN obligation), because certain origins, Colombia, Indonesia, Mexico, and Panama, were excluded from its application; and Article II:1(b) (since they have imposed a tariff surcharge, different from an ordinary customs duty, which was not set forth in the Dominican Republic's GATT Schedule). After concluding that GATT Article XIX and the Safeguards Agreement were applicable to this dispute, the panel addressed the substantive claims raised by the complainants.

The panel found that the Dominican Republic acted inconsistently with its obligations under the GATT 1994 and the Safeguards Agreement because the report published by the competent authorities failed to provide an explanation of the existence of unforeseen developments and of the effect of the obligations of the GATT 1994.

The panel found that the Dominican Republic acted inconsistently with its obligations under the Safeguards Agreement and the GATT, by excluding certain products from the definition of the domestic directly competitive product and certain producers of like or directly competitive products, for the purpose of defining the domestic industry. It also failed 1) to provide reasoned and adequate explanations with respect to the existence of serious injury and 2) to take all reasonable steps to exclude Thailand, as a developing country, from the application of the provisional and definitive safeguard measures.

Soon after the issuance of the report, the Dominican Republic lifted the safeguard measure that was the subject of this dispute, and established the MFN tariff at the level that was in place before the application of the above-mentioned safeguard.

Question

Is the Dominican Republic required to notify the definitive safeguard measure to exporting nations subject to the measures under the safeguard's agreement?

CHAPTER 20

Intellectual Property Rights

LEARNING OBJECTIVES:

20.1 Describe intellectual property
20.2 Learn about the importance of intellectual property rights for international trade
20.3 Learn about national and international protection of intellectual property
20.4 Learn about global e-commerce
20.5 Understand the role of the Internet in international trade
20.6 Learn about international regulation of electronic commerce

---

International Trade in Practice

Market-creating Innovations and International Trade

Most people generally understand the importance of institutions and infrastructure as a foundation for economic growth. However, the role of innovation in the context of a nation's economic performance has not been sufficiently acknowledged. Innovations are a process by which an organization transforms labor, capital, and other materials into products or services of greater value. The products or services do not have to be entirely new. They can be borrowed from one firm to another and then improved upon (Christensen, Ojomo, and Dillon, 2019). Studies show that the prosperity of an economy is directly correlated with the amount of know-how in the nation (Hausmann et al., 2014).

Not all innovations are created equal and different types of innovation impact organizations and economies in varying ways. Sustaining innovations are improvements on existing products and often target customers that seek better performance from a product or service. Specialty tires, for example, are intended for existing car-buying customers. They are not aimed at expanding the present market i.e., they do not expand or change the existing distribution channel since the product is sold to a relatively known segment of the population. It is an attempt to sell more products to the same customer base. Banks, for example, provide credit card or investment services to their existing customers (Christensen, Ojomo, and Dillon, 2019).

Efficiency innovations enable firms to enhance efficiency by using fewer resources. This includes use of new equipment that uses less labor and results in higher profits. In the United States, for example, the oil and gas extraction sector employed about 220,000 in 1980 and produced 8.6 million barrels of oil per day. By 2017, it used about 146,000 people and produced over 9.3 million barrels per day. Such innovations rarely create jobs and do not substantially increase the market for a given product or service.

Market-creating innovations aim at new markets by either making new products or services or improving existing products or services to make it affordable and accessible to new consumers. It generates more employment and greater sales opportunities. It has the largest impact on trade as new or improved products and services are sold in domestic and foreign markets. Firms invest in manufacturing products at home and overseas to take advantage of lower wages. This type of innovation is also associated with the creation of new sales and distribution channels.

Galanz, a Chinese microwave oven manufacturer initially targeted the underserved domestic market. In the early 1990s, there were fewer than one million microwave ovens in a country with a population of over one billion people. Microwave ovens were quite expensive and unaffordable to the average Chinese consumer, so existing demand was small. Galanz began to produce less expensive microwave ovens (through reducing marketing cost, increasing capacity utilization and R&D) and captured a substantial part of the domestic and global market (about 40 percent in 2014). Its annual sales are estimated at US$10 billion. It is a market-creating innovation with a positive impact on employment and incomes. It targets nonconsumption everywhere and caters to fill the gap with new orimproved goods and services.

Intellectual property rights (IPRs) are associated with patents, trademarks, copyrights, trade secrets, and other protective devices granted by the state to facilitate industrial innovation and artistic creation (Wolfhard, 1991; Keupp et al., 2010; Geringer, Mcnett, and Ball, 2020). The grant of exclusive property rights provides owners with personal incentives to make the most productive use of their assets and facilitates transfers by making possible a high degree of exchange. Intellectual property rights are one form of exclusive rights conferred by the state to promote science and technology. The issue of intellectual property has received wider attention compared to other property rights for the following reasons:

• The volume of trade in goods protected by IPRs is becoming increasingly significant as more countries produce and consume products that result from creative activity and innovation (Gadbaw and Richards, 1988; Denton, 2011; WTO, 2021).

• The globalization of markets has created opportunities for the production and/or sale of unauthorized copies to supply the newly generated demand.

The OECD report (2018) indicates a 154 percent increase in counterfeits traded internationally—from $200 billion in 2005 to $509 billion in 2016. Similar information collected by the U.S. Department of Homeland Security (DHS) between 2000 and 2018 shows that seizures of infringing goods at U.S. borders have increased tenfold, from 3,244 seizures per year to 33,810 (Homeland Security, 2020). E-commerce platforms represent ideal storefronts for counterfeits and provide powerful gateways for counterfeiters and pirates to engage large numbers of potential consumers.

WHAT ARE INTELLECTUAL PROPERTY RIGHTS?

Intellectual property rights are exclusive rights given to persons over the use of their creation for a given period of time. Such rights are customarily divided into various areas, as detailed in the following material.

Patents

A patent is a proprietary right granted by the government to inventors (and other persons deriving their rights from the inventor) for a fixed period of years to exclude other persons from manufacturing, using, or selling a patented product or from utilizing a patented method or process. At the expiration of the time for which the privilege is granted, the patented invention is available to the general public, or falls into public domain (Menell et al., 2020).

Patents may be granted for new and useful products as well as processes for the manufacture (or methods of use) of new or existing products. The basis for patent protection is promotion of innovative activity, dissemination of technical knowledge, and facilitation of transfer of technology. Even though patents are granted as a recognition of the concept of a natural right in inventions, they provide an incentive for the encouragement of inventions and the promotion of economic development. With the monopoly grant, the patent owner can divulge the invention to the public and still retain exclusive use of it for the period of the patent. At the end of the monopoly period, the patent becomes available for the unrestricted use of the public. Patent protection also encourages the transfer of technology through direct investment or licensing. In the United States, patents are valid for a period of twenty years from the filing date. Patent violations are generally referred to as patent infringement or piracy.

Trademarks

A trademark is a word, name, symbol, or device, or any combination of these used by a manufacturer or seller of goods to identify and distinguish the particular manufacturer's or seller's goods from goods made or sold by others (Ladas, 1975; Hodgson, 2020). In general, trademarks perform three functions. They:

1. Identify one seller's goods and distinguish them from goods sold by others.
2. Signify that all goods bearing the trademark come from a single source and are of an equal level of quality.
3. Serve as a primary instrument in advertising and selling the goods.

An important part of the advertising effort is to develop goodwill. Trademark rights can be acquired by registration or use (reputation). Registered marks are renewable. Once a trader acquires a reputation in respect of a mark, that is, an unregistered mark, it becomes part of that trader's goodwill and is protectible as a registered mark. Violation of trademarks consists of counterfeiting and other forms of infringement, such as advertising, sales, or distribution of goods bearing a similar mark (to that of the owner) that results in deception or confusion. Counterfeiting is the unauthorized use of a mark. In the United States, trademarks are valid for ten years from the date of registration.

Trade Secrets

A trade secret involves a formula, method, or technique that derives independent economic value from not being generally known or available to other persons who can obtain economic value from its disclosure or use (Kinter and Lahr, 1983; Menell et al., 2020). The historical roots of trade secrets protection can be traced to ancient China, where death by torture was prescribed for revealing the secret of silk-making to outsiders, and to ancient Rome, where enticing a competitor's servant to disclose business secrets was a punishable offense. In England, the movement of artisans to other countries was prohibited by a series of statutes aimed at preventing knowledge of British processes from reaching possible competitors in Europe and America, and employers sued would-be emigrants and those who tried to seduce them (Ashton, 1988). Violation of trade secrets includes acquisition of a trade secret by improper means or disclosure without the consent of the owner.

In most developed nations, however, protection is afforded through laws pertaining to contracts, criminal law, or torts, such as breach of confidence (Seyoum, 1993; Hannah, 2006). Protection of trade secrets does not expire after a set period of time, as in the case of other IPRs. The owner, in effect, has perpetual monopoly on the innovation. A large part of technology being developed now, perhaps with the exceptions of pharmaceuticals and specialty chemicals, does not get patented. Many high-tech innovations, such as aircraft and automobiles, and most low-tech innovations, such as detergents or food products, are not patented (Williams, 1983). In some countries, a formula might be patentable, while methods of production based on personal skills are not patentable. Patent protection also ends at some point, even if one is able to obtain and keep the patent. Thus, companies prefer to maintain new innovations as trade secrets and protect their technology by contract rather than by patent.

Copyrights

A copyright is a form of protection granted to authors of original works, including literary, dramatic, musical, artistic, and certain other intellectual works. The owner of the copyright has the exclusive right to reproduce, distribute, sell, or transfer the copyrighted work to other persons. In the United States, copyrights are protected for a minimum period of fifty years after the death of the author. Since 2014, the core copyright industries (i.e., business and entertainment software) have grown faster than the U.S. economy (5.23 percent versus 2.21 percent in 2017). The industry added $1.3 trillion to the U.S. economy, employed nearly 5 percent of the total private labor force and paid 39 percent higher than average U.S. wages. Furthermore, exports of

U.S. copyright products amounted to $191.2 billion in 2017 compared to $174 billion (electronics), $138.2 billion (agriculture) and $137 billion (chemicals) (IIPA, 2018).

INTELLECTUAL PROPERTY RIGHTS AND INTERNATIONAL TRADE

Besides trade policy, changes in the nature and location of consumer demand, and cost of inputs that shape trade flows, technology is increasingly recognized as an important driver of international trade. Similar to steamships and railroads that changed the economics of trading during the second industrial revolution, digital technology has enabled the efficient coordination of global value chains. Trade flows increased as firms and countries began to participate in production networks of specialized suppliers and assembly plants.

It is likely that the next generation of technologies will reshape trade and global value chains. Some technologies such as e-commerce and blockchains will reduce transaction and logistics costs (WTO, 2021). Other technologies such as digital platforms connect buyers and sellers, lowering the costs of research and coordination (Brynjolfsson and McAfee, 2017). They facilitate payments, travel, learning, labor services, and other activities. This will enable small and medium-sized businesses to directly reach overseas customers. It is estimated that e-commerce could spur US$1.3 to 2.1 trillion in global incremental trade by 2030 by increasing trade in manufactured goods (McKinsey Global Institute, 2017). This development also underscores the rising importance of services, which have been growing faster than goods trade for some time. Miroudet and Cadestin (2017) show that about a third of the value of traded goods comes from embedded services in production, design, marketing, distribution, and other related services. Thus, appropriate regulation of IPRs, data flows, and the quality of digital infrastructure are likely to emerge as new sources of comparative advantage (WTO, 2021) (Table 20.1).

An important feature of IPRs is their exclusiveness and territorial dimension. This means that a patent holder or licensee is the person solely entitled to manufacture and market the patented product within a given territory of the state in which the patent is granted. The exclusive and territorial character of such rights is capable of creating obstacles to both the free movement of goods and competition. For example, a patent or trademark owner in country A may be entitled to block the importation of a product legally manufactured in country B by its own licensee or subsidiary. Although such restrictive use of IPRs interferes with free trade, the grant of monopoly rights is considered an acceptable trade-off to encourage research and the diffusion of new knowledge and technology. In short, free trade between countries as a result of an agreement such as USMCA, EU, or WTO does not preclude prohibitions or restrictions on imports, exports, or goods in transit justified on the grounds of the protection of IPRs.

Several issues pertaining to IPRs have important implications to the conduct and growth of international trade. They are as follows.

The Growth of Trade in Counterfeit Goods

The globalization of markets, the increased demand for new products, and the nearly prohibitive R&D costs to develop such products have created incentives for

TABLE 20.1 New Technologies and Potential Impact on Trade

Technology	Benefits	Impact on world trade

Internet of things
  E-commerce
  Blockchain
  Automated
  document
  processing
	Reduces transaction costs. Reduction in trade costs can lead to increased trade.	The reduction of transaction costs is likely to lead to US$4.7 trillion in goods trade by 2030.

Artificial *intelligence* *Automation* *3D printing*	Changes in production processes. As labor costs become less important, production can be moved closer to consumer markets. Adidas is moving its fully automated production plant to the United States and Germany. Call centers could be staffed by virtual agents, thus reducing the global market for business process outsourcing.	This could lead to a reduction in goods trade by US$4 trillion by 2030 as production moves closer to consumers.
Electric cars *Renewables* *Digital goods*	New goods. For example, solar and wind are less tradable than oil or coal. The wide use of electric cars will reduce trade in vehicle parts (they have fewer parts compared to international combustion engines). Also shifts from physical goods to streaming and leasing services.	This could lead to about a US$310 billion reduction in goods trade by 2030 due to changes in composition and tradability of goods.

Source: McKinsey Global Institute (2019)

the unauthorized use of IPRs. For example, counterfeiting (false labeling for sale in export markets) has spread from strong brand-name consumer goods to a variety of consumer and industrial goods. Related violations include copyright and patent infringement, and unfair competition. There is still a widespread manufacture, sale, and export of counterfeit goods. For example, China and Hong Kong accounted for about 80 percent of counterfeits (rings, purses, headphones, sunglasses) that were seized at U.S. Customs in 2020 (CBP, 2020) (International Perspective 20.1).

Lack of Adequate Protection for IPRs in Many Countries

An important contributing factor to trade in counterfeit/pirated goods is the lack of adequate protection and effective enforcement of IPRs in many countries.

Furthermore, some new technologies do not fit within any of the existing types of intellectual property. For example, in many developing countries, the protection of computer software, biotechnology, and semiconductor chips remains unclear.

For example, inadequate and ineffective protection of copyright (including online piracy) continues to be a significant problem in Russia, damaging the market for legitimate content. There is limited enforcement by local authorities. Jail sentences for piracy are rare and authorities do not conduct surprise inspections or seize/confiscate equipment (USTR, 2020).

Piracy of IPRs as a Trade Barrier

Given the fact that counterfeit/pirated goods displace those of legitimate producers, such action distorts international trade and has the long-term effect of reducing trade in technology-intensive goods. Piracy leads to the misallocation of resources by diverting trade from legitimate producers to pirates. Trade experts believe that elimination of piracy abroad of U.S. intellectual property could easily wipe out a majority of the U.S. trade deficit.

PROTECTION OF INTELLECTUAL PROPERTY

Protection Under Domestic Laws

Most countries have domestic laws to protect IPRs. In the United States, Section 337 of the Tariff Act of 1930 authorizes the International Trade Commission (ITC) to institute an investigation into the importation of articles that may infringe U.S patents, trademarks, or copyrights. If the ITC determines that a violation exists, the U.S. Customs Service is then charged to enforce an exclusive order, that is, to stop the article from entering the United States or, upon a subsequent violation, the property may be seized and forfeited to the U.S. government. Since 1972, over 500 individual cases of alleged IPR violations have been filed against non-U.S. firms in forty countries. Over 70 percent of these section 337 cases were decided in favor of the complainant (Chiang, 2004). Unlike antidumping and countervailing cases where domestic injury must be proved, the U.S. Department of Commerce does not play a role in such cases.

Section 301 of the 1974 U.S. Trade Act contains significant measures to ensure trade compliance. It allows the United States to apply trade sanctions on countries that impose an unjustifiable burden on or restrict U.S. commerce. These include but are not limited to denial of fair and equitable market opportunities such as denial of most-favored-nation (MFN) treatment to U.S. goods and services, lack of adequate and effective protection of IPRs (including those that are members of TRIPs), export targeting, and denial of workers' rights. A section 301 investigation may be commenced by the U.S. Trade Representative's Office (USTR) or any interested party that files a petition with the USTR. The USTR must conclude its investigation within a certain period after initiation of an investigation. It may authorize retaliatory action against the foreign country.

Special 301 focuses on unfair IPR practices. The Special 301 Provision of the 1988 Omnibus Trade and Competitiveness Act requires the USTR to identify (by April 30 of each year) countries that fail to provide adequate protection and enforcement for IPRs or deny fair and equitable market access to persons that rely on IPR protection. The USTR classifies countries that fail to provide adequate protection or enforcement into the following three categories (see also International Perspective 20.2):

- Countries under Priority Watch List: Countries the policies or practices of which have the greatest adverse impact (actual or potential) on the relevant

U.S. products, and are not engaged in good faith negotiations to address these problems;

- Countries under Watch List: Countries with serious IPR deficiencies but are not yet placed on the priority watch list;
- Countries under Section 301 Monitoring: Countries that are monitored for implementation of certain agreements or memoranda of understanding on IPR.

Countries under Priority Watch List

U.S. Customs has the authority to exclude the importation of imports that violate IPRs. Intellectual property rights (patents, trademarks, etc.) subject to protection have to be registered with the U.S. Patent and Trademark Office. Customs monitors imports to prevent the importation of violating articles based on the IPR owner's request or on U.S. Custom's initiative. Customs regulations establish the authority for trademarks, trade names, and copyright to be recorded with customs; to seize counterfeit articles that violate IPRs; and to restrict the importation of gray-market imports. The port director has the authority to demand the redelivery of violating articles and to claim liquidated damages in the event of failure to redeliver the goods. Customs also monitors importations of articles (for a fee) on a nationwide basis and reports to the patent holder the names and addresses of importers of infringing goods.

The USTR is required to initiate a Section 301 investigation within thirty days after identification of a priority foreign country. If negotiations are not successful within six to nine months, the USTR may retaliate against the exports of the country by withdrawing trade agreement concessions and imposing duties or other restrictions on imports. In this category are countries whose protection and enforcement of IPRs warrants close monitoring and resolution. The 2020 list of countries under this category includes Argentina, Chile, China, India, Ukraine, and Venezuela.

INTERNATIONAL PERSPECTIVE 20.1
Some Red Flags for IPRs

- Importer is known to buy infringing goods and has a history of enforcement actions for IPR violations
- Merchandise is shipped in small quantities on informal entries
- Merchandise is imported from sources (countries and/or vendors) with IPR problems
- Company documents show IPR identifier but the company does not have a license agreement with the owner of the IPR
- Invoices with no model or catalogue numbers and merchandise without lot numbers, factory codes, expiration dates, or dates of manufacture
- Payment term is cash on delivery rather than letter of credit
- Shipment is under-insured
- Vague or unusual shipment terms, unusually high or low value for the merchandise

INTERNATIONAL PERSPECTIVE 20.2

Protection and Enforcement of Intellectual Property Rights

Argentina: A key deficiency in the legal framework for patents is the unduly broad limitations on patent-eligible subject matter. Argentina rejects patent applications for categories of pharmaceutical inventions that are eligible for patentability in other jurisdictions, including in the United States. Additionally, to be patentable, Argentina requires that processes for the manufacture of active compounds disclosed in a specification be reproducible and applicable on an industrial scale. Another ongoing challenge to the innovative agricultural chemical and pharmaceutical sectors is inadequate protection against the unfair commercial use, as well as unauthorized disclosure, of undisclosed test or other data generated to obtain marketing approval for products in those sectors. There are also long delays for innovators seeking patent protection in the market. There is inadequate enforcement of IPRs and widespread sale of counterfeit goods and services. It is on the priority watch list for 2020.

 Algeria: Algeria remains on the Priority Watch list in 2020. Algerian law bans an increasing number of imported pharmaceutical products and medical devices in favor of local products. There is a lack of protection against the unfair commercial use, as well as unauthorized disclosure, of test and other data generated to obtain marketing approval for pharmaceutical products. Its inadequate patent protection and enforcement efforts have given rise to widespread piracy and counterfeiting.

 Bolivia: Bolivia remains on the Watch List in 2020. High levels of piracy and counterfeiting persist, and there is a continued need to improve criminal and civil IPR enforcement. There is inefficient prosecution of IPR violations, and limited coordination among Bolivian enforcement authorities. Limited resources are allocated for enforcement of such violations.

 Thailand: Counterfeit and pirated goods continue to be readily available, both in physical markets and online. Other U.S. concerns include inadequate copyright legislation and enforcement, backlogs in pending pharmaceutical patent applications, and widespread use of unlicensed software in both the public and private sectors. There are also lengthy civil IP enforcement proceedings and low civil damages, and extensive cable and satellite signal theft. There are concerns regarding legislation that allows for content quota restrictions for films. The United States encourages Thailand to provide an effective system for protecting against the unfair commercial use, as well as unauthorized disclosure, of undisclosed test or other data generated to obtain marketing approval for pharmaceutical and agricultural chemical products.

Source: U.S. Trade Representative (USTR), 2020

Countries Under Watch List

This category includes a list of countries that warrant special attention because they maintain certain practices or barriers to market access for intellectual property products that are of particular concern. The 2020 list includes Bolivia, Brazil, Canada, Ecuador, Egypt, and Vietnam.

Countries under Section 301 Monitoring

A Special 301 investigation is similar to an investigation initiated in response to an industry Section 301 petition (unfair foreign trade practices), except that the maximum time for the latter is shorter (in cases involving violation of TRIPs) than other Section 301 investigations. Special 301 is potentially an effective tool to protect U.S. IPRs abroad because it allows the administration to use a variety of trade sanctions (e.g., removal of GSP or MFN status) against a priority foreign country. However, its implementation has been sporadic and inconsistent over the years. For example, certain countries with gross violations of IPRs are not added under the priority country list and in some cases, when identified, sanctions are not imposed. Russia was classified under the "Watch List" category for many years in spite of its rampant black markets in videocassettes, films, music, and so forth. India was classified under the "Priority Foreign Country" category several times; however, no sanctions were imposed even though there was no resolution of the problems through bilateral negotiations.

INTERNATIONAL AND REGIONAL PROTECTION

The Paris Convention

The Paris Convention is used in connection with two separate treaties: 1) international protection of industrial property; and 2) international copyright protection (the Universal Copyright Convention). The Paris Convention is administered by the World Intellectual Property Organization (WIPO), whose mission is to promote the protection of intellectual property throughout the world and whose membership includes over 130 countries.

The Paris Convention for the Protection of Industrial Property

This convention was concluded in 1883 and has gone through various revisions. It applies to industrial property in the widest sense, including patents, trademarks, trade names, and so on. The treaty sets forth three fundamental rules:

1. *National treatment*: The principle of national treatment provides that nationals of any signatory nation shall enjoy in all other countries of the convention the advantages that each nation's laws grant to its own nationals.
2. *Right of priority*: The right of priority enables any resident or national of a member country to apply for protection in any other member state of the convention within a certain period of time (twelve months for patents and six months for trademarks and industrial designs) after filing the first application in one of the member states to the treaty. These later applications will then be regarded as if they had been

filed on the same day as the first application. A major advantage of this is that applicants wishing protection in multiple countries need not file all applications at the same time but have six to twelve months from the first application to decide in which countries to apply for protection.

3. *Minimum standards*: The convention lays down minimum standards common to all member countries.

The Universal Copyright Convention

This convention (1952, revised in 1971) establishes the national treatment standard and minimum rules common to all member countries. It also allows countries to set formalities or conditions for the acquisition or enjoyment of copyright in respect of works first published in its country or works of its nationals wherever published.

The Patent Cooperation Treaty

The Patent Cooperation Treaty (PCT) allows for a single application and a worldwide search for novelty in all member countries; that is, a search is made in one of the designated offices based on a single application without the need to file applications in all other member states. The application with the search report will be forwarded to the countries where the applicant seeks patent protection. Although such a system eliminates duplication of filing and patent examination in each patent office of a member country, each country retains full jurisdiction to grant or refuse a patent in accordance with its own domestic legislation. The PCT has been signed by 133 countries and regional patent bodies such as the European Patent Office (EPO) and the African Regional Industrial Property Organization (ARIPO).

Trade-related Aspects of IPRs (TRIPs)

The developed countries criticize the intellectual property conventions administered by WIPO because their minimum standards are considered insufficient and they contain no provisions for dispute settlement. Member states retain broad discretion in granting IPRs. Existing multilateral treaties fail to protect the most basic rights: Certain fields of patentable technologies such as pharmaceuticals, biotechnology, agricultural chemicals, and copyrightable documents including educational materials have been excluded from protection in many countries. Some countries limit patentability to the process (not the product), and/or limit the duration of patent protection.

Detractors contend that the deficiencies in the protection of IPRs distort international trade and reduce the value of concessions negotiated in various rounds of trade negotiations. The Intellectual Property Committee (IPC), a cross-industry organization of large multinational corporations notes that:

> Inadequate international protection of intellectual property has become a major cause of distortions in the international trading system . . . it is both appropriate and necessary for intellectual property issues to be dealt with under international trade rules.

> (Gad, 2003 p.676)

Negotiations led to the adoption of the Uruguay Round Agreement on Trade-Related Aspects of Intellectual Property (TRIPs) in 1994. The agreement established multilateral obligations for the protection and enforcement of IPRs and provided a dispute settlement mechanism under the World Trade Organization (WTO).

The TRIPs agreement covers almost all forms of intellectual property including patents, trade and service marks, industrial designs, trade secrets, and layout designs of integrated circuits.

The three fundamental features of the agreement are:

1. *Standards:* The agreement sets out minimum standards of protection to be provided by each member country. It provides broader protections for IPRs by granting MFN treatment for all signatories. It also requires members to comply with existing agreements such as the Paris Convention and the Berne Convention for the protection of literary and artistic works. It further supplements additional obligations on matters where the pre-existing conventions are silent or inadequate.
2. *Enforcement:* The TRIPs agreement lays down domestic procedures and remedies for the enforcement of IPRs.
3. *Dispute settlement:* The agreement makes disputes between WTO members subject to the WTO's dispute settlement procedures. It also authorizes trade sanctions against noncompliant nations.

Regional Conventions

The major regional agreement in the area of IPRs is the European Patent Convention (1973), which under a single application may result in the grant of a European patent valid in all member countries. It is a centralized patent-granting system administered by the European Patent Office (EPO) in Munich, Germany, on behalf of member countries. A similar regional organization is the African Regional Intellectual Property Organization (ARIPO), located in Harare, Zimbabwe. The ARIPO was established in 1976 to grant regional patents having effect in all designated member countries.

GLOBAL E-COMMERCE: SELLING IN A NETWORKED ECONOMY

Information and communication technologies are leading to a hyper-connected world where people and businesses can communicate with each other instantly. It is introducing new business opportunities by improving efficiency and productivity and generating new products and services (World Economic Forum, 2012). It is also profoundly changing the dynamics of economic growth similar to that achieved with the advent of railways and electricity.

The global online population is increasing at a rapid pace: The number of global Internet users increased from 2.4 billion in 2012 to 4.8 billion in 2020 (Internetworldstats.com). Asia has the largest number of Internet users accounting for 52.2 percent of the global online population, followed by Europe (15 percent) and North America (7 percent). In 2020, Africa evidenced the largest increase in Internet usage since 2000 (12,441 percent), followed by the Middle East (5,527 percent), and Latin America and the Caribbean (2,489 percent) (Table 20.2).

TABLE 20.2 World Internet Usage

Region	Population 2020	Population % of World	Internet Users, June, 2020	Internet Penetration % Population	Growth Internet Use 2000–2020	% Internet Users
Africa	1,340,598,447	17.2	566,138,772	42.2	12,441	11.7
Asia	4,294,516,659	55.1	2,525,033,874	58.8	2109	52.2
Europe	834,995,197	10.7	727,848,547	87.2	592	15.1
Middle East	260,991,690	3.3	184,856,813	70.8	5527	3.8
N. America	368,869,647	4.7	332,908,868	90.3	208	6.9
Latin America & Caribbean	654,287,232	8.4	467,817,332	71.5	2489	9.7
Oceania/ Australia	42,690,838	0.5	28,917,600	67.7	279	0.6
World	**7,017, 846,922**	**100**	**4,833,521,806**	62	1239	100

Source: Internetworldstats.com

Global E-Commerce

The size of global e-commerce (which includes business-to- business and business-to-consumer transactions) was estimated at $20 to 26 trillion in 2018 with 1.45 billion shoppers worldwide. There are already a number of stories about business successes with global online sales. A producer of draperies and other goods from New York, for example, sells her products as far away as S. Africa, Turkey, and Saudi Arabia. Women entrepreneurs in Guyana are selling hand-woven hammocks to consumers in different parts of the world via the Internet. Global business-to-business e-commerce has also been successful in a number of industries. Websites such as E-steel, COVISINT, Commercx are linking buyers and sellers of steel, car parts, and plastics, respectively, and facilitating greater volumes of cross-border trade (Freund and Weinhold, 2004).

The Internet and International Trade

Many studies show the positive effects of the Internet on international trade. The Internet reduces search costs (the cost of matching buyers and sellers) as well as the costs of finding agents, distributors, or retailers. Local distribution costs, including wholesale and retail margins, are estimated to be about 55 percent ad valorem tariff for the United States and 40 percent for other countries (Anderson and Van Wincoop, 2004). The Internet enables direct links in the supply chain. It also allows direct sales to the consumer without using intermediaries. Brynolfsson et al. (2003) show that increased product variety through electronic markets can be a significant source of consumer surplus gain. This is because online retailers are able to provide a large number of products for sale without regard to warehouse space. For example, the number of book titles available at Amazon.com is 57 times greater than the stock of books in any large bookstore. Internet retailers have unlimited "virtual inventory" and can offer a wider range of products and services to consumers than brick and mortar retailers. The Internet platform also allows firms to learn far more information about consumer preferences (search engines, website visits, terms used to search for information, etc.) and thus tailor advertisements that are targeted to specific market segments at relatively low cost.

Freund and Weinhold (2004) show that the reduced transaction costs arising from the Internet help increase the volume of international trade. The positive effects of the Internet are larger for developing countries than advanced nations. This is partly because the latter countries have developed the requisite infrastructure and networks to access to world markets. The new platform thus reduces the importance of past linkages on current trade. The Internet is likely to have a greater effect on the volume of trade in services (rather than goods) because of the intrinsic nature of services.

In spite of the rapid increase in global e-commerce, there are still a number of challenges to overcome.

- *Logistics and payment issues*: Even though the Internet provides easy access to global goods and services, shipping and distribution to different corners of the world can be difficult. The Internet does not eliminate challenges pertaining to transportation, distribution, tariff and non-tariff barriers, as well as payment and financing. Some businesses may not have acquired the core capabilities for exploiting electronic banking: technical and business dynamic capabilities such as managing customer relationships and integrating physical and virtual channels etc.
- *Return rates can be high*: Consumers cannot touch and see the physical product and may have a different impression when they actually see the product. Furthermore, the cost of shipping and tariffs may make the product less competitive. Some estimate that international return rates for goods ordered online can be as high as 80 percent.
- *Customer trust:* The biggest challenge to online commerce is ensuring customer trust. The threat of online scams, credit card fraud, and similar problems may make customers reluctant to use online stores.
- *Limited ICT readiness in many developing countries*: In many developing countries, the level of ICT readiness is still quite low because of an insufficient development of ICT infrastructure. This makes it difficult to access a good part of this market online.

TRADING ONLINE

The website is the main tool of communication in the online market and it is thus important to invest sufficient resources on building an attractive website with good content (some importers also use e-bay, Amazon, and Craiglist to market their products). It has to be fully functional (with the ability to upload images and accept payments), present up-to-date information, load quickly and be customer-friendly. If you are not familiar with web designing, you can always hire a web designer. Besides interactivity (interaction between the site and user), other attractive features of a website include personalization (advice, product selection), notification of product availability, newsletters, search capability (from the home page) as well as clear notification of shipping, tax, and other charges.

You can market your website through Google, Facebook, blogs or Youtube. It is also important to note the following pertinent issues:

- Register your domain name: It is good to pick and register a domain name that people can easily remember.
- Hosting the website: There are a number of web-hosting companies that operate for a modest annual fee. Make sure they offer technical support.
- Promoting your website: You can promote the site by enhancing its ranking through website optimization. You can also use social media such as Facebook and Youtube as well as search engines such as Google and Yahoo.

INTERNATIONAL REGULATION OF E-COMMERCE

The emergence of new technologies raises issues about the extent to which a balance has to be maintained between government regulation to protect the consumer and self-regulation. In 1997 the Clinton administration outlined a framework for global e-commerce and underlined the need for regulation and negotiation of international agreements on electronic commerce. It states:

> In some areas, government agreements may prove necessary to facilitate electronic commerce and protect consumers . . . Where government inter-vention is necessary to facilitate electronic commerce, its goal should be to ensure competition, protect intellectual property and privacy, prevent fraud, foster transparency, support commercial transactions and facilitate dispute resolution (principle 3).

> (White House, 1997)

The framework also emphasizes the need to avoid undue restrictions, recognize the unique qualities of the Internet and support and enforce a predictable, minimalist, consistent, and simple legal environment for commerce on a global basis.

The United Nations Commission on International Trade Law

The United Nations Commission on International Trade Law (UNCITRAL) adopted a model law on electronic commerce in 1996 that is acceptable to states with different economic and social systems. The model has been adopted by several countries and influenced the development of uniform e-commerce laws in the United States and Canada.

The UNCITRAL model law is based on the following basic principles.

Functional Equivalence

The model law attempts to extend the same level of recognition to electronic documents as corresponding paper documents with respect to concepts such as "writing," "signature," or 'originals." In cases where the law requires information to be in writing, that requirement is satisfied by an electronic message if the information is accessible to be used for subsequent reference.

In order to ensure that a message that was required to be authenticated should not be denied legal recognition because it was not done in a manner peculiar to paper documents, the model law establishes general conditions under which electronic documents would be considered as authentic, credible. and enforceable in the case of signature requirements. The only requirement to be met in the case of electronic documents is that it identifies the originator and confirms that the originator approved the content of the message.

Certain international trade documents such as insurance certificates or quality or inspection certificates are usually only accepted if they are "original" to reduce instances of alteration which would be difficult to detect. The model law sets minimum requirements for acceptance of electronic documents: a) if there exists a reliable assurance as to the integrity of the information from the time when it was first generated in its final form and b) information is being capable of being displayed to the person to whom it is to be presented.

Technology Neutrality

The rules should provide equal treatment to paper-based and electronic transactions. They should neither require nor assume a particular technology. It also extends similar treatment to different electronic transactions such as telex, email, or electronic data interchange (EDI).

Party Autonomy

The model law recognizes the primacy of party agreement on whether and how to use e-commerce techniques. It also allows the parties to determine the security level appropriate for their transactions.

Part two of the model law deals with specific uses of e-commerce such as EDI messages as substitutes for transport documents. The transfer of any right or obligation that is to be conveyed by paper documents can be equally conveyed by electronic means provided a reliable method is used to transfer them.

Other International Initiatives on E-commerce

Other initiatives at the international level include:

- *UNCITRAL Model Law on Electronic Signatures (2001)*: This model law establishes criteria of technical reliability for the equivalence between electronic and hand-written signatures as well as basic rules of conduct that may serve as guidelines for assessing duties and liabilities for the signatory, the relying party, and trusted third parties intervening in the signature process.
- *United Nations Convention on the Use of Electronic Communications in International Contracts (2005)*: The Electronic Communications Convention aims at facilitating the use of electronic communications in international trade by assuring that contracts concluded and other communications exchanged electronically are as valid and enforceable as their traditional paper-based equivalents. The Convention applies to all electronic communications exchanged between parties whose places of business are in different states when at least one party has its place of business in a contracting state (Article 1). It may also apply by virtue of the parties' choice. Contracts concluded for

personal, family, or household purposes, such as those relating to family law and the law of succession, as well as certain financial transactions, negotiable instruments, and documents of title, are excluded from the Convention's scope of application (Carr and Stone, 2010).

- *International Chamber of Commerce (ICC) Guidelines on E-Commerce (1997 and 2001)*: The ICC sets out best practices for adoption by businesses in order to promote trust in e-commerce by focusing on issues such as authentication, certification, public key certificates, and record keeping (Carr and Stone, 2017).

Regional Initiatives on E-commerce

Initiatives at the regional level include:

- *EU Directive on E-Commerce (2000)*: The Directive sets up an Internal Market framework for electronic commerce, which provides legal certainty for business and consumers alike. It establishes harmonized rules on issues such as the transparency and information requirements for online service providers, commercial communications, electronic contracts, and limitations of liability of intermediary service providers (Carr and Stone, 2017).
- *EU Directive on E-Signatures (1999)*: This Directive establishes the legal framework at European level for electronic signatures and certification services. The aim is to make electronic signatures easier to use and help them become legally recognized within the member states.

CHAPTER SUMMARY

Intellectual property rights (IPRs)	Intellectual property rights are associated with patents, trademarks, copyrights, trade secrets, and other protective devices granted by the state to facilitate industrial innovation and artistic creation.
Major issues pertaining to IPRs and international trade	1. The growth of trade in counterfeit goods. 2. Lack of adequate protection and enforcement of IPRs in many countries. 3. The long-term effect of piracy on trade in technology-intensive goods.
U.S. classification of countries that do not provide adequate protection of IPRs	1. Priority Watch List: Countries that do not provide adequate protection to IPRs and whose policies have the greatest adverse impact on U.S. commerce. 2. Watch List: countries that warrant close monitoring and resolution.
Regional/ international protection	*International Protection* The Paris Convention, the Universal Copyright Convention, the Patent Cooperation Treaty, trade-related aspects of IPRs (TRIPs) agreement. *Regional Protection* The European Patent Convention, the African Regional Industrial Property Organization.

Global e-commerce	The volume of global e-commerce was estimated at $26 trillion in 2018. The global online population was estimated at 4.83 billion in 2020. The Internet reduces search costs (the cost of matching buyers and sellers) as well as the costs of finding agents, distributors, or retailers. The reduced transaction costs arising from the Internet help increase the volume of international trade. The positive effects of the Internet are larger for developing countries than advanced nations. Some of the challenges of online trade include logistics and payment issues, customer trust, and limited ICT readiness in many developing countries. The website is the main tool of communication in the online market.
International regulation of e-commerce	• The UNCITRAL Model Law on Electronic Commerce (1996) • UNCITRAL Model Law on Electronic Signatures (2001) • United Nations Convention on the Use of Electronic Communications in International Contracts (2005) • International Chamber of Commerce (ICC) Guidelines on E-Commerce (1997 and 2001)

REVIEW QUESTIONS

1. What is the importance of IPRs to international trade?
2. What are patents? What are the advantages of providing an exclusive (monopoly) right to patent holders?
3. What is the importance of trademarks?
4. Discuss some of the reasons why some inventions are not patented.
5. Explain why piracy of IPRs is a trade barrier.
6. Discuss the level of protection and enforcement of IPRs in Japan and China.
7. What is the right of priority under the Paris Convention?
8. What are the three fundamental principles of the TRIPs agreement?
9. What are some of the challenges of online trade?
10. How do you promote a website?

REFERENCES

Anderson, E. and van Wincoop, E. (2004). Trade Costs. *Journal of Economic Literature*, 42(3): 691–751.

Ashton, T. (1988). *The Industrial Revolution*. London: Oxford University Press.

Brynolfsson, E., Hu, J., and Michael, D. (2003). Consumer surplus in the digital economy: Estimating the value of increased product variety at online booksellers. *Management Science*, 49(11): 1580–1596.

Brynjolfsson, E. and McAfee, A. (2017). *Machine, Platform, Crowd: Harnessing our Digital Future*. New York: Norton & Company.

Carr, I. and Stone, P. (2017). *International Trade Law*. London: Routledge.

Chiang, E. (2004). Determinants of cross-border intellectual property rights enforcement: The role of trade sanctions. *Southern Economic Journal*, 7(2): 424–440.

Christensen, C., Ojomo, E., and Dillon, K. (2019). *The Prosperity Paradox*. New York: Harper Collins.

Customs and Border Protection (CBP) (2020). Intellectual property rights. www.cbp.gov

Denton, A. (2011). *Intellectual Property Rights in Today's Digital Economy*. Discussion Paper. Geneva: ITU.

Freund, C. and Weinhold, D. (2004). The effect of the Internet on international trade. *Journal of International Economics*, 62(1): 171–189.

Gad, M. (2003). Impact of multinational enterprises on the multilateral rule-making: The pharmaceutical industry and the TRIPs Uruguay Round negotiations. *Law & Business Review of the Americas*, IX(4): 667–674.

Gadbaw, M. and Richards, T. (1998). *Intellectual Property Rights*. Boulder, CO: Westview Press.

Geringer, J. M., McNett, J. M., and Ball, D. (2020). *International Business*. New York: McGraw-Hill.

Hannah, D. (2006). Keeping trade secrets secret. *MIT Sloan Management Review* New York, 47(3): 17–20.

Hausmann, R., Hidalgo, C., Bustos, S., Coscia, M., and Simoes, A. (2014). *The Atlas of Economic Complexity: Mapping Paths to Prosperity*. Boston, MA: MIT Press.

Hodgson, C. (2020). Registered Trademarks: *The Business Owner's Essential Guide to Brand Protection*. New York: Brandaid Press.

Homeland Security (2020). *Combating Trafficking in Counterfeit and Pirated Goods. Report to the President of the United States*. Washington, DC: USGPO.

International Intellectual Property Alliance (IIPA) (2018). *Copyright Industries in the US Economy*. Washington, DC: IIPA.

Keupp, M., Beckenbauer, A., and Gassman, O. (2010). Enforcing intellectual property rights in weak appropriability regimes. *Management International Review*, 50: 109–130.

Kinter, E. and Lahr, J. (1983). *An Intellectual Property Law Primer*. New York: Clark Boardman.

Ladas, S. (1975). *Patents, Trademarks and Related Rights: National and International Protection*. Cambridge, MA: Harvard University Press.

McKinsey Global Institute (2017). *Jobs Lost, Jobs Gained: Workforce Transitions in a Time of Automation*. New York: McKinsey.

McKinsey Global Institute (2019). *Globalization in Transition: The Future of Trade and Value Chains*. New York: McKinsey.

Menell, P. S., Lemley, M. A., Merges, R. P., and Balganesh, S. (2020). *Intellectual Property in the New Technological Age*. New York: Clause 8 Publishing.

Miroudet, S. and Cadestin, C. (2017). *Services in Global Value Chains: From Inputs to Value Creating Activities*. Trade Policy Paper 197. Paris: OECD.

OECD (2018). *Governance Framework to Counter Illicit Trade*. Paris: OECD.

Seyoum, B. (1993). Property rights versus public welfare in the protection of trade secrets in developing countries. *The International Trade Journal*, 3: 341–359.

United States Trade Representative (USTR) (2020). *Special 301 Report*. Washington, DC: GPO.

White House (1997). *A Framework for Global Electronic Commerce*. Washington, DC: White House.

Williams, L. (1983). Transfer of technology to developing countries. *Federal Bar News and Journal*, 30: 266–267.

Wolfhard, E. (1991). International trade in intellectual property: The emerging GATT regime. *University of Toronto Faculty of Law Review*, 49: 106–151.

World Economic Forum (2012). *The Global Information Report*. Geneva: WEF.

World Trade Organization (WTO) (2021). *The Future of World Trade: How Digital Technologies Are Transforming Global Commerce*. Geneva: WTO.

World Wide Web Resources

Patents and intellectual property: http://members.tripod.com/~patents2/
Intellectual property mall: www.ipmall.info/
Intellectual property: Copyrights, trademarks, and patents: www.brint.com/IntellP.htm
Global Internet usage data: www.internetworldstats.com/stats.htm
UNCITRAL model law on e-commerce: www.uncitral.org/uncitral/uncitral_texts/electronic_commerce/1996Model.html
UNCITRAL model law on electronic signatures: www.uncitral.org/pdf/english/texts/electcom/ml-elecsig-e.pdf

International Trade Closing Cases and Discussions

1. Patents and Access to Life-saving Drugs

Under the Uruguay Round Agreement (1995), the jurisdiction of WTO was extended to the protection of IPRs. The agreement covers a wide range of subjects including patents, copyrights, and trade secrets. It allows trade sanctions against countries that fail to abide by the agreement. As regards the protection of pharmaceutical products, the agreement (Trade-Related Aspects of Intellectual Property Rights, or TRIPs) attempts to strike a balance between the short-term benefits of providing life-saving drugs and the long-term objective of encouraging technological innovation. TRIPs imposes the following obligations on member countries: 1) protection of product or process patents for at least twenty years from the date the patent application was filed, 2) nondiscrimination: members cannot discriminate between different fields of technology, places of invention, or whether the products are imported or locally produced, 3) compulsory licensing: governments are allowed to license someone to produce the patented product or process without the consent of the patent owner. A number of conditions must be met: a license must have been attempted unsuccessfully by the owner under reasonable terms (unless there is a national emergency), payment of adequate remuneration, non-exclusion of license.

Many developing countries were concerned with the potential implications of TRIPs for protecting public health. This issue gained world attention when a number of South African drug companies challenged the legality of the newly enacted legislation, which allowed for compulsory licensing of patented pharmaceuticals. The U.S. government also threatened to issue a compulsory license order against Bayer AG unless the company made significant quantities of capsules available (at a lower price) to victims of anthrax. Member countries agreed to interpret the TRIPs agreement in a way that supports public health by promoting access to existing drugs and the creation of new medicines. They also agreed to extend exemptions on pharmaceutical patent protection for the least developed countries until 2016.

The TRIPs agreement states that compulsory licensing can only be used to supply the domestic market. This means that a) countries that produce under compulsory license would be unable to export the drug; b) countries that do not have the manufacturing capability could not import it for domestic consumption. In August 2003 WTO members agreed to make it possible for countries to import cheaper generics made under compulsory licenses if they are unable to manufacture the medicines themselves.

Questions

1. Does TRIPs balance the interests of drugs companies with that of consumers in developing countries?
2. What are your suggestions that would be acceptable to both parties?

2. Intellectual Property Rights and International Trade

Intellectual property rights are exclusive rights given by the government to creators of new products, services, and processes. They include patents, trademarks, know-how, and copyrights. With the globalization of national economies, IPRs are playing an important role in global trade as many products incorporate technology-intensive components. Industries that depend on patent protection include chemicals, pharmaceuticals, aerospace, electronics, and semi-conductors. Copyright-based industries include movies, books, data processing, and recording industries. Businesses in retail, transportation, and other sectors also depend on IPRs such as know-how and trademarks.

In the United States, IPR-related activities account for about 75 percent of GDP growth and 60 percent of total U.S. exports. In addition, IPR-intensive industries contribute positively to the U.S. economy through productivity gains and other spillover effects.

In 2018, domestic sales by research-based pharmaceutical companies that are members of Pharmaceutical Researchers and Manufacturers of America (PhRMA) reached an estimated $225 billion, while sales abroad by PhRMA member companies totaled about $110 billion. The intellectual property industries contribute positively to the overall U.S. trade balance through royalties and licensing fees. Rights holders may authorize the use of technologies, trademarks, and entertainment products that they own to entities in foreign countries, resulting in revenues through royalties and license fees. In 2018, U.S. receipts from cross-border trade in royalties and license fees (relating to patent, trademark, copyright, and other intangible rights) totaled $129 billion. During the same year, U.S. payments of royalties and license fees to foreign countries amounted to $56 billion. Industrial processes, computer software, and trademarks accounted for the bulk of U.S. international trade in intangible assets.

Advances in information and technology and declining costs of transportation and communications, spurred by globalization, have fundamentally changed information and trade flows. Such changes have created new markets for U.S. exporters, but at the same time, have been associated with the proliferation of counterfeiting and piracy on a global scale.

TABLE 20.3 Seizure of Counterfeit Goods by U.S. Customs

Year	Number of seizures	Estimated retail value (US$ billion)	2019 Products (%)		Country of origin	2019 %	2019 Mode of transport	
2010	20,000	1.56	Watches/		China	66.00	Express	57%
2011	25,000	1.10	Jewelry	15	Hong Kong	26.00	Mail	33%
2012	23,000	1.23	Apparel	14	Turkey	1.00	Cargo	7%
2013	24,000	1.75	Handbags	13	Vietnam	0.90	Others	3%
2014	22,500	1.22	Footwear	12	Pakistan	0.80		
2015	28,000	1.37	Electronics	10	Singapore	0.70		
2016	32,000	1.40	Personal		Dominican			
2017	34,000	1.16	care	6	Rep.	0.60		
2018	33,810	1.42	Consumer		India	0.60		
2019	27,599	1.55	products	4	South Korea	0.40		
			Computers	1	Netherlands	0.30		
			Automotive/		Others	3.00		
			Aerospace	1				
			Others	17				

Source: CBP (2020)

Several factors contribute to the growing problem of IPR infringement:

- While the costs and time for research and development are high, IPR infringement is associated with relatively low costs and risks and a high profit margin. It takes a drug company about ten to fifteen years of research and development to create a new drug. PhRMA member companies, for example, collectively spent an estimated $1 trillion on R&D (domestic and abroad) in 2018. In contrast, drug counterfeiters can lower production costs by using inexpensive, and perhaps dangerous or ineffective, ingredient substitutes.
- The development of technologies and products that can be easily duplicated, such as recorded or digital media, has also led to an increase in counterfeiting and piracy. Increasing Internet usage has contributed to the distribution of counterfeit and pirated products.
- Civil and criminal penalties are often not sufficient deterrents for piracy and counterfeiting. The United States is especially concerned with foreign IPR infringement of U.S. intellectual property. Compared to foreign countries, IPR infringements levels in the United States are estimated to be relatively low.

According to the Organization for Economic Cooperation and Development (OECD), world trade in counterfeit and pirated goods was estimated to amount to about $509 billion in 2016. In the United States, the estimated domestic retail value of IPR-related seizures is estimated at $1.5 billion in 2018. Of all U.S. trading partners, China continues to account for the majority of counterfeits intercepted at the U.S. border. Other top trading partners from which IPR-infringing goods were seized include Hong Kong, Turkey, Vietnam, and Pakistan.

Question

Do you think counterfeiting improves the welfare of poor countries?

Trading Opportunities in Selected Countries

A.1 TRADING OPPORTUNITIES IN AFRICA AND THE MIDDLE EAST

Egypt

Country Profile

> **Population:** 104,124,440
> **Exports:** $23.3 billion
> **Major Exports:** crude oil and petroleum products, fruits and vegetables, cotton, textiles, metal products, chemicals, processed food
> **Export Partners:** UAE, Italy, United States, United Kingdom, Turkey, Germany, India
> **Imports:** $59.78 billion
> **Major Imports:** machinery and equipment, foodstuffs, chemicals, wood products, fuels
> **Import Partners:** China, UAE, Germany, Saudi Arabia, United States, Russia
> **Trade as % GDP:** Exports 18.9%; Imports 29.4%
> **Currency and Exchange Rate:** 18.05 Egyptian pounds (EGP) per U.S. dollar
> **GDP (official exchange rate):** $236.5 billion
> **GDP per capita:** $12,700
> **External Debt:** $77.47 billion

FOREIGN IMPORT POLICIES

- *Entry of goods*: The Egyptian government requires that every component of a product be inspected regardless of the compliance history of the product, country of origin, exporter, shipper, or importer. All imports must comply with either Egyptian standards or one of the international organizations standards to which Egypt is affiliated: International Organization for Standardization (ISO), International Electrotechnical Commission (IEC), and/or Codex Alimentarius.

- *Tariffs and taxes*: Egypt's average most-favored-nation (MFN) applied tariff rate was 19.1 percent in 2018 (latest data available). Egypt's average MFN applied tariff rate was 63 percent for agricultural products and 11.8 percent for non-agricultural products in 2018. Egypt has a simple average World Trade Organization (WTO) bound tariff rate of 36.6 percent.

  Egypt raised tariffs on 5,791 products. It also reduced tariffs on several medicines and imported natural gas vehicles and eliminated duties on electric cars.

  Egypt maintains high tariffs on a number of critical U.S. export products. Egypt's tariff on passenger cars with engines of 1,600 cubic centimeters (cc) or less is 40 percent, and its tariff on cars with engines of more than 1,600 cc is 135 percent. Tariffs on processed and high-value food products, including poultry, meat, apples, pears, cherries, and almonds range from 20 percent to 30 percent. There is a 300 percent tariff on alcoholic beverages for use in the tourism sector plus a 40 percent sales tax. The tariff on alcoholic beverages for use outside the tourism sector ranges from 1,200 percent on beer to 1,800 percent on wine and 3,000 percent on sparkling wine and spirits. There is a 46 percent tariff on foreign movies which are also subject to sales taxes and box office taxes higher than those for domestic films.

- *Non-tariff barriers*: Importers must have a registered import card and the card must be present during import transactions. All import transactions require a letter of credit that must be issued by an officially registered bank. The Egyptian government conducts inspections for quality control and arbitrary testing procedures that discriminate against foreign products. Motion pictures are subject to screen quotas. Other non-tariff barriers exist in the following industries and services: banking, investing, telecommunications, express delivery services, digital trade, social media, and media outlets.

- *Intellectual Property Rights Protection (IPRs)*: According to a 2019 U.S. special report, Egypt remains on the U.S. Watch List. While Egypt has taken steps to improve IPR enforcement, concerns remain, with the widespread use of pirated and counterfeit goods, including software, music, unlicensed satellite TV broadcasts, and videos. Intellectual property law in Egypt conforms to international standards and provides recourse for infringements. Egypt is a member of the World Intellectual Property Organization (WIPO) and a signatory to the Paris, Madrid, and Bern Conventions. Patent protection is valid for twenty years from the date of application.

- *Documentation requirements*: Import license, permits, certificate of international quality, certificate of origin, commercial invoice. Documents needed for smart phones which require National Telecommunications Regulatory Authority (NTRA) approval include a catalog of technical specifications and a full copy of the customs certificate. Goods under International Air Transport Association (IATA) Special Provision A67 require the following documents: Material Safety Data Sheet and a Non-Dangerous Goods declaration letter.

- *Distribution and sales channels*: Foreign firms must be registered to make sales directly within Egypt. Most foreign firms rely on Egyptian companies for wholesale and retail distribution. Many consumer goods retailers import their own supplies directly due to high wholesaler markups. Foreign firms can form a distributorship and allow Egyptian companies to form a separate company that will act as importer or agent. The Egyptian importer or agent will then handle marketing within Egypt.

BEST EXPORT PROSPECTS

Leading sectors for U.S. exports and investments are:

- Information and communications technology (ICT) and digital economy
- Infrastructure
- Medical equipment supplies
- Oil and gas equipment
- Renewable energy
- Safety and security
- Water and environment
- Electrical power systems
- Agriculture
- Education and training

EXPORTING FROM EGYPT

Major impediments to exporting from Egypt (in order of importance) are: Technical protocols abroad, unsuitable production technology and skills, access to imported inputs at competitive prices, access to trade finance, high cost or delays caused by domestic transportation, hard to meet quality/quantity requirements of buyers, tariff barriers abroad, high cost or delays caused by international transportation, identifying potential markets and buyers, rules of origin requirements, burdensome customs procedures at foreign borders.

IMPORTATION TO EGYPT

Major impediments to importation to Egypt (in order of importance) are: Tariffs and non-tariff barriers, burdensome import procedures, cost and delays due to domestic and foreign transportation, corruption on the border, unsuitable telecommunications infrastructure, crime theft, and domestic technical protocols.

Ethiopia

Country Profile

Population: 108,113,150

Exports: $3.23 billion

Major Exports: coffee, oil seeds, edible vegetables, khat, gold, flowers, live animals, raw leather products, meat products

Export Partners: Sudan, Switzerland, China, Somalia, Netherlands, United States, Germany, Saudi Arabia, United Kingdom

Imports: $15.59 billion

Major Imports: machinery, aircraft, metal, metal products, electrical materials, petroleum products, motor vehicles, chemicals, fertilizers

Import Partners: China, Saudi Arabia, India, Kuwait, France
Trade as % GDP: Exports: 7.9%; Imports: 20.8%
Currency and Exchange Rate: 25 birr (ETB) per U.S. dollar
GDP (official exchange rate): $80.87 billion
GDP per capita: $2,200
External Debt: $26.05 billion

FOREIGN IMPORT POLICIES

- *Entry of goods*: Customs clearance time is on average twenty-one days or less. Goods must be collected within fifteen days or a 20 percent tax will be charged as a penalty.
- *Tariffs and taxes*: In Ethiopia there is a weighted average tariff of 9.7 percent. The tariff rate ranges from 0–9.7 percent. As part of government trade reforms over the last five years the tariff bans have been reduced from over thirty to only five. While there are no quantitative import restrictions nor import quotas, foreign exchange regimes administered by the National Bank of Ethiopia may deter imports. Imports into Ethiopia are subject to an excise tax, surtaxes, and a 15 percent value-added tax (VAT).
- *Non-tariff barriers*: The Ministry has the power to restrict and/or limit imports and exports.
- *Intellectual Property Rights (IPR) Protection*: IPR enforcement is unpredictable in Ethiopia. Ethiopia is not a WTO member, which means it is not a member of the Agreement on Trade-Related Aspects of Intellectual Property Rights (TRIPs). However, Ethiopia is a member of WIPO and has shown an interest in strengthening its IPR regime.
- *Documentation requirements*: Agency agreement, bank permit, bill of lading or airway bill, certificate of origin, commercial invoices, customs import declaration, foreign exchange authorization, import license, insurance certificate, packing list, tax identification number (TIN) certificate, pre-shipment inspection clean report of findings, transit document, VAT certificate.
- *Distribution and sales channels*: Use of a local agent is required for most types of business. Direct marketing of foreign products in Ethiopia requires a local agent or distributor. Foreign companies can open a representation or project office in Ethiopia to promote and support sales of their products through their local agents or distributors.

BEST EXPORT PROSPECTS
Leading sectors for U.S. exports and investments are:

- Aviation
- Road and railways
- Agro-processing
- Energy
- Healthcare
- Agriculture
- Education

EXPORTING FROM ETHIOPIA

Major impediments to exporting from Ethiopia (in order of importance) are: Difficulties in meeting quality and quantity requirements of buyers, access to trade finance, inappropriate production technology, inappropriate production skills, access to imported inputs at competitive prices, burdensome procedures at foreign borders, high cost or delays caused by international transportation, rules of origin requirements abroad, corruption at foreign borders, technical requirements and standards abroad, tariff barriers abroad.

IMPORTATION TO ETHIOPIA

Major impediments to importing Ethiopia (in order of importance) are: High cost of delays due to domestic transportation, burdensome import procedures, tariffs and non-tariff barriers, border corruption, inappropriate telecommunication infrastructure, domestic technical requirements and standards, crime and theft, high cost or delays due to international transportation.

Ghana

Country Profile

Population: 29,340,248
Exports: $13.84 billion
Major Exports: oil, gold, cocoa, timber, tuna, bauxite, aluminum, manganese ore, diamonds, horticultural products
Export Partners: India, UAE, China, Switzerland, Vietnam, Burkina Faso
Imports: $12.65 billion
Major Imports: capital equipment, petroleum, foodstuffs
Import Partners: China, United States, United Kingdom, Belgium, India
Trade as % GDP: Exports: 36%; Imports: 35.4%
Currency and Exchange Rate: 4.385 cedis (GHC) per U.S. dollar
GDP (official exchange rate): $47.02 billion
GDP per capita: $4,700
External Debt: $22.14 billion

FOREIGN IMPORT POLICIES

- *Entry of goods*: Majority of imports are subject to inspection upon arrival, which causes delays and increases costs. Erratic application of customer and other import regulations, lengthy clearance procedures, and corruption are frequently reported by importers. Ghana ports suffer from congested roads and lack a functioning rail system to transport freight. This creates long waits for ships to berth at cargo terminals and for containers to be transported out of the ports.
- *Tariffs and taxes*: Ghana's average MFN applied tariff rate in 2018 was 11.9 percent. For agricultural goods, the average applied tariff is 15.4 percent, and for non-agricultural products it is 11.3 percent. Along with other Economic Community of West African States (ECOWAS) countries, Ghana

adopted a common external tariff (CET) with five bands. The five tariff bands are: zero percent duty on essential social goods (e.g., medicine); 5 percent duty on essential commodities, raw materials, and capital goods; 10 percent duty on intermediate goods; 20 percent duty on consumer goods; and 35 percent duty on goods that the Ghanaian government elected to afford greater protection (e.g., rice, poultry). Ghana imposes a 0.2 percent levy on imports from outside African Union (AU) member states to fund its contribution to the AU.

- *Non-tariff barriers*: Ghana requires a registration certificate for imports of food, cosmetics, pharmaceuticals, and agricultural goods. The government has limited the number of import permits issued for corn, poultry, and poultry products. In 2018 the State Minister of Agriculture halted the issuance and renewal of poultry import permits for local traders. Ghana has a ban on tilapia and the importation of excavators. Importers are confronted by a variety of fees and charges in addition to tariffs.

- *IPR protection*: IPR enforcement in Ghana is weak. Delays in infringement proceedings discourage IP rights holders from filing new claims in local courts. In 2016 Ghana launched its national IP policy and strategy in an effort to encourage innovation and investment.

- *Documentation requirements*: Invoice, Material Safety Data Sheet or Non-Dangerous Goods declaration letter for goods under IATA Special Provision A67. Packing list, Ministry of Health certificate, certificate of analysis and Form A2 for shipments of medicine.

- *Distribution and sales channels*: Distribution channels include wholesalers, retail outlets, and agents. It is not legally required to use an agent, but it is highly recommended.

BEST EXPORT PROSPECTS

Leading sectors for U.S. exports and investments:

- Agriculture
- Construction and infrastructure
- Mining industry equipment
- Oil and gas
- Cosmetic industry
- Real estate
- Automotive sector
- Energy
- Healthcare
- Franchising
- Education and training

EXPORTING FROM GHANA

Major impediments to exporting from Ghana (in order of importance) are: Access to trade finance, identifying potential markets and buyers, difficulties in meeting quality requirements of buyers, access to imported inputs at competitive prices, high cost or delays caused by domestic transportation, inappropriate production technology and skills, burdensome procedures at foreign borders, technical requirements and standards abroad, tariff barriers abroad, high cost or delays caused by international transportation, corruption at foreign borders, rules of origin requirements abroad.

IMPORTATION TO GHANA

Major impediments to importing to Ghana (in order of importance) are: Tariffs and non-tariff barriers, burdensome import procedures, corruption at the border, domestic technical requirements and standards, high cost or delays due to international transportation, high cost or delays due to domestic transportation, crime and theft, inappropriate telecommunications infrastructure.

Israel

Country Profile

Population: 8,675,475

Exports: $58.67 billion

Major Exports: machinery, equipment, cut diamonds, agricultural products, chemicals, textiles, and clothing

Export Partners: United States, Hong Kong, China, Belgium

Imports: $68.61 billion

Major Imports: raw materials, military equipment, investment goods, rough diamonds, fuels, grain, consumer goods

Import Partners: United States, China, Switzerland, Germany, United Kingdom, Belgium, Netherlands, Turkey, Italy

Trade as % GDP: Exports: 29.4%; Imports: 29%

Currency and Exchange Rate: 3.06 new Israeli shekels (ILS) per U.S. dollar

GDP (official exchange rate): $350.7 billion

GDP per capita: $36,400

External Debt: $88.66 billion

FOREIGN IMPORT POLICIES

- *Entry of goods*: Under the 1995 US–Israel FTA, greater market access allowed. As of January 10, 2018, U.S. exporters no longer require a hard copy of the "Green Form" also known as the certificate of origin. Instead U.S. exporters are required to print and sign a declaration as to origin on the invoice or on a letterhead document.
- *Tariffs and taxes*: Agricultural goods entering into Israel face high tariffs and a complicated TRQ system unless they enter duty free under WTO, FTA, or Agreement on Trade in Agricultural Products (ATAP) provisions. Under the 1985 US–Israel FTA, the United States and Israel agreed to a phased tariff reduction, ending with the complete elimination of duties on all products by January 1, 1995.
- *Non-tariff barriers*: In April 1998 Israel notified its customs valuation legislation to the WTO but has not responded to the WTO Checklist of Issues describing how the Customs Valuation Agreement is being implemented.

Israel's regulatory bodies often adapt standards developed by Israeli regulators or European standards organizations rather than international standards. This excludes some U.S. products from the market and increases cost to certain U.S. exports to Israel.

- *IPR Protection*: Israel is a signatory to the WIPO Copyright Treaty and the WIPO Performances and Phonograms Treaty. However, it has not ratified either. Israel lacks adequate protection against the unfair commercial use, as well as unauthorized disclosures, of undisclosed test or other data generated to obtain marketing approval for biologic pharmaceuticals. Israel lacks patent term restoration to compensate for marketing approval delays for pharmaceuticals. In 2018 Israel's Knesset passed amendments to the country's copyright enforcement law in an effort to strengthen IPR protection.
- *Documentation requirements*: Commercial invoice, declaration of goods, a detailed description of goods, catalog with technical information, any other relevant information, sample of material/product, lab testing results, authorizations from institutes/authorized government agencies, import licenses, and pre-ruling request form.
- *Distribution and sales channels*: Using an agent or distributor in Israel is not required but highly recommended to help maintain an aggressive and active presence in the country.

BEST EXPORT PROSPECTS

Leading sectors for U.S. exports and investments are:

- Agriculture
- Design and construction
- Energy
- Environmental technologies
- ICT
- Safety and security

EXPORTING FROM ISRAEL

Major impediments to exporting from Israel (in order of importance) are: Identifying potential markets and buyers, access to imported inputs at competitive prices, high cost or delays caused by domestic transportation, rules of origin requirements abroad, high cost or delays caused by international transportation, burdensome procedures at foreign borders, tariff barriers abroad, access to trade finance, technical requirements and standards abroad, inappropriate production technology and skills, difficulties in meeting quality and/or quantity requirements of buyers, corruption at foreign borders.

IMPORTATION TO ISRAEL

Major impediments to importation to Israel (in order of importance) are: Tariffs and non-tariff barriers, burdensome import procedures, domestic technical requirements and standards, high cost or delays caused by international transportation, high cost or delays caused by domestic transportation, corruption at the border, inappropriate telecommunications infrastructure, crime and theft.

Kenya

Country Profile

Population: 53,527,936
Exports: $5.792 billion
Major Exports: tea, horticultural products, coffee, petroleum products, fish, cement, apparel
Export Partners: Uganda, Pakistan, United States, Netherlands, United Kingdom, Tanzania, UAE
Imports: $15.99 billion
Major Imports: machinery and transportation equipment, oil, petroleum products, motor vehicles, iron and steel, resins, and plastics
Import Partners: China, India, UAE, Saudi Arabia, Japan
Trade as % GDP: Exports: 12%; Imports: 21.4%
Currency and Exchange Rate: 102.1 Kenyan Shillings (KES) per U.S. dollar
GDP (official exchange rate): $79.22 billion
GDP per capita: $3,500
External Debt: $27.59 billion

FOREIGN IMPORT POLICIES

- *Entry of goods*: Kenya is a member of the Common Market for Eastern and Southern Africa (COMESA) free trade area and the East African Community (EAC). Kenya ratified the European Union–EAC Economic Partnership Agreement (EAP) in 2016 and ratified the African Continental Free Trade Agreement, which came into force on May 20, 2019 and became operational on July 1, 2020.
- *Tariffs and taxes*: As of 2018 Kenya's average applied tariff rate for all products was 13.5 percent, 20.3 percent for agricultural products and 12.4 percent for non-agricultural products. Kenya has bound 16.4 percent of its tariff lines to the WTO, with a simple average WTO-bound tariff rate of 94.5 percent. The EAC Customs Union's Common External Tariff includes zero percent duty for raw materials, 20 percent duty for processed or manufactured inputs, and 25 percent duty for finished products. Products and commodities deemed "sensitive" receive ad valorem rates above 25 percent, 60 percent for most milk products, 50 percent for corn and corn flour, 75 percent for rice, 60 percent for wheat flour, 100 percent for sugar and 50 percent for textiles. The 2019 Finance Bill amends the Income Tax Act by taxing income accrued through a digital marketplace. The VAT Act of 2013 reduced the number of VAT-exempt items from 400 to 27.
- *Non-tariff barriers*: In 2017, the EAC introduced the EAC Elimination of Non-Tariff Barriers Act, which is under review by Kenya and other EAC partner states.
- *IPR Protection*: IPR continues to pose a challenge to rights holders; However, in 2020 the Government of Kenya created the Intellectual Property Bill

that attempts to tighten control around IP enforcement. The bill formed the Intellectual Property Office of Kenya (IPOK), which includes three agencies: the Kenya Copyright Board (KECOBO), the Kenya Intellectual Property Institute (KIPI), and the Anti-Counterfeiting Agency (ACA).

*   *Documentation requirements*: To import into Kenya an importer has to hire a clearing agent who will process electronically the import documentation through Kenya Customs on the Simba 2005 system and clear the goods on the importer's behalf. Documentation requirements include: an Import Declaration Form (IDF), Certificate of Conformity (CoC) from a Pre-Export Verification of Conformity (PVoC) agent for regulated products, Import Standards Mark (ISM) when applicable, pro forma invoices, bill of lading, and packing list.

*   *Distribution and sales channels:* Kenya has no laws or policies requiring the retention of a local agent or distributor by U.S. or other foreign companies exporting to Kenya. However, generally speaking it is highly advisable for a foreign company to retain an agent or distributor who is resident in Kenya.

BEST EXPORT PROSPECTS

Leading sectors for U.S. exports and investments are:

*   Agribusiness
*   Design and construction
*   Electrical power systems
*   Healthcare and medical devices
*   Information, communications, and technology (ICT)
*   Aircraft and aircraft parts
*   Education

EXPORTING FROM KENYA

Major impediments to exporting from Kenya (in order of importance) are: Difficulties in meeting quality and quantity requirements of buyers, access to trade finance, identifying potential markets and buyers, tariff barriers abroad, high cost or delays caused by domestic transportation, corruption at foreign borders, technical requirements and standards abroad, burdensome procedures at foreign borders, access to imported inputs at competitive prices, inappropriate production technology and skills, rules of origin requirements abroad, high cost or delays caused by international transportation.

IMPORTATION TO KENYA

Major impediments to importation to Kenya (in order of importance): Tariffs and non-tariff barriers, corruption at the border, burdensome import procedures, high cost or delays caused by domestic transportation, crime and theft, domestic technical standards and technical requirements, inappropriate telecommunication infrastructure.

Nigeria

Country Profile

Population: 214,028,302
Exports: $1.146 billion
Major Exports: petroleum, cocoa, rubber
Export Partners: India, United States, India, Spain, China, France, the
  Netherlands
Imports: $32.67 billion
Major Imports: machinery, chemicals, transport equipment, manufactured
  goods, food, live animals
Import Partners: China, Belgium, United States, South Korea, United Kingdom
Trade as % GDP: Exports: 15.5%; Imports: 17.5%
Currency and Exchange Rate: 323.5 nairas (NGN) per U.S. dollar
GDP (official exchange rate): $376.4 billion
GDP per capita: $5,900
External Debt: $40.96 billion

FOREIGN IMPORT POLICIES

- *Entry of goods*: Nigeria adopted a destination inspection policy for imports where all imports are inspected on arrival into Nigeria. The Nigerian Trade Hub serves as an information portal for traders and allows them to classify their imports/exports, estimate freight charges and applicable duty, and find information on clearing processes. Nigeria has a Single Window Portal which allows online access to needed documentation and submission of the documentation. The portal provides a way to track submission transactions and make electronic payment of fees.
- *Tariffs and taxes*: As of 2016 Nigeria's average MFN applied tariff rate was 12.1 percent, 15.7 percent for agricultural products and 11.5 percent for non-agricultural products. Nigeria has bound 20.1 percent of its tariff lines to the WTO, with a simple average WTO-bound tariff rate of 120.9 percent. Nigeria applies five tariff bands that include: zero percent duty on essential goods, five percent duty on essential commodities, raw materials, and capital goods, 10 percent duty on intermediate goods, 20 percent duty on consumer goods and 35 percent duty on certain goods that Nigerian government elected to afford greater protection, The CET was slated to be fully harmonized by 2020 but some ECOWAS member states have maintained deviations from the CET beyond the January 1 deadline.
- *Non-tariff barriers*: The Nigerian government uses bans and quotas to achieve self-sufficiency in certain commodities. In 2015 the Central Bank of Nigeria imposed a series of restrictions that prohibited the use of official foreign exchange to import forty-one product categories including rice, meat, poultry, vegetable oil, and a number of steel products.
- *IPR Protection*: IPR enforcement is lacking. There is a variety of government measures and policies that require or pressure companies to give up their IP as the price of market entry. In an attempt to prevent and criminalize online

fraud, the Federal Government of Nigeria signed the Cybercrime bill into law. Efforts to update copyright and industrial property laws have been stalled in the legislative process.

- *Documentation requirements:* SONCAP Certificate, Material Safety Data Sheet or Dangerous Goods declaration letter for goods under International Air Transport Association (IATA) Special Provision A67, bill of lading, commercial invoice exit note, duly completed form "M," packing list, single goods declaration, product certificate, certificate of origin.
- *Distribution and sales*: Products are generally exported to Nigeria through local agents and distributors.

BEST EXPORT PROSPECTS

Leading sectors for U.S. exports and investments are:

- Agribusiness
- Agriculture
- Aviation and defense
- Construction
- Education and training
- Electricity and power systems
- Franchise
- Healthcare
- Media and entertainment industry (Nollywood and Nigerian music)
- ICT
- Logistics
- Oil, gas, and mining
- Safety and security

EXPORTING FROM NIGERIA

Major impediments to exporting from Nigeria (in order of importance): Access to trade finance, inappropriate production technology and skills, difficulties in meeting quality and/or quantity requirements of buyers, access to imported inputs and competitive prices, high cost or delays caused by domestic transportation, inappropriate telecommunications infrastructure.

IMPORTATION TO NIGERIA

Major impediments to importation to Nigeria (in order of importance) are: Burdensome import procedures, correction at the border, tariffs and non-tariff barriers, high cost or delays caused by domestic transportation, crime and theft, domestic technical requirements and standards, high cost or delays caused by international transportation, inappropriate telecommunications infrastructure.

South Africa

Country Profile

Population: 53,527,936
Exports: $94.93 billion

Major Exports: gold, diamonds, platinum, other metals, minerals, machinery and equipment

Export Partners: China, United States, Germany, Japan, India, Botswana, Namibia

Imports: $89.36 billion (2017 est.)

Major Imports: machinery, equipment, chemicals, petroleum products, scientific instruments, foodstuffs

Import Partners: China, Germany, United States, Saudi Arabia, India

Trade as % GDP: Exports: 29.9%; Imports: 29.6%

Currency and Exchange Rate: 13.67 rand (ZAR) per U.S. dollar

GDP (official exchange rate): $349.3 billion

GDP per capita: $13,600

External Debt: $156.3 billion

FOREIGN IMPORT POLICIES

- *Entry of* goods: South Africa has a complex import process that requires an importer to register with Customs South Africa (Customs SA), a division of the South African Revenue Service, to obtain an importer's code.
- Tariffs and taxes: As of 2018, South Africa's average MFN applied tariff rate was 7.7 percent, 8.7 percent for agricultural products and 7.6 percent for non-agricultural products. South Africa has bound 94.3 percent of its tariff lines to the WTO with a simple average WTO-bound tariff rate of 19.2 percent, 39.1 percent for agricultural products and 15.7 percent for non-agricultural products. The maximum WTO-bound tariff rate for industrial products is 50 percent, and 597 percent for agricultural products. In February 2019 the South African Minister of Finance announced a 5 percent increase in sugar tax on sweetened beverages from 2.1 cents to 2.21 cents per gram of sugar content that exceeds 4 grams per 100ml.
- Non-tariff barriers: The Department of Trade and Industry (DTI) prohibits imports of goods of a specified class or kind unless the products are imported in accordance with a permit issued by the International Trade Administration Commission (ITAC).
- IPR Protection: South Africa has a well-developed IPR enforcement environment.
- Documentation requirements: Bill of lading—one negotiable and two non-negotiable copies are required. A Declaration of Origin Form DA59, four copies and one original commercial invoice, insurance certificate for sea freight, three copies of packing list, import licenses, import permit.
- Distribution and sales channels: The distribution and sales channels within South Africa vary depending on the type of imported equipment and/or product; However, the following traditional sales channels are found: wholesalers, retail organizations, consumer retail, franchises, after-sales agents, agents, distributors, and legal agents. Certain exports are also distributed through branches or subsidiaries.

BEST EXPORT PROSPECTS

Leading sectors for U.S. exports and investments are:

- Franchise
- Education
- Travel and tourism
- Automotive
- ICT
- Green building technologies
- Medical devices
- Rail infrastructure
- Mining equipment
- Aerospace
- Port logistics
- Pollution control equipment
- Agriculture
- Electricity power systems and renewable energy

EXPORTING FROM SOUTH AFRICA

Major impediments to exporting from South Africa (in order of importance) are: inappropriate production technology and skills, high cost or delays caused by domestic transportation, tariff barriers, identifying potential markets and buyers, burdensome procedures at foreign borders, access to imported inputs at competitive prices, access to trade finance, high cost or delays caused by international transportation, difficulties in meeting quality and/or quantity requirements of buyers, technical requirements and standards abroad, foreign border corruption, rules or origin requirements abroad.

IMPORTATION TO SOUTH AFRICA

Major impediments to importation to South Africa (in order of importance) are: Burdensome import procedures, tariffs and non-tariff barriers, high cost or delays caused by domestic transportation, high cost or delays caused by international transportation, crime and theft, domestic technical requirements and standards, border corruption, inappropriate telecommunications infrastructure.

A.2 TRADING OPPORTUNITIES IN THE AMERICAS

Argentina

Country Profile

Population: 45,479,118

Exports: $48.45 billion

Major Exports: soybeans/soybean derivatives, petroleum, gas, vehicles, corn, wheat

Export Partners: Brazil, United States, China, Chile

Imports: $63.97 billion

Major Imports: machinery, vehicles, petroleum, natural gas, organic chemicals, plastic
Import Partners: Brazil, China, United States, Germany
Trade as % GDP: Exports: 17.3%; Imports: 15.1%
Currency and Exchange Rate: 16.92 Argentine pesos (ARS) per U.S. dollar
GDP (official exchange rate): $637.6 billion
GDP per capita: $20,900
External Debt: $214.9 billion

FOREIGN IMPORT POLICIES

- *Entry of goods*: Argentina requires a license for imports. Licenses are managed through the Comprehensive Import Monitoring System. Detailed information about goods is submitted electronically through this system and reviewed by the Argentine government agencies' "Single Window System for Foreign Trade," whereby all formalities or procedures with regard to foreign trade are conducted under one administrative unit to enhance efficiency.
- *Tariffs and taxes*: As of 2018 Argentina's average MFN applied tariff rate was 13.6 percent, 10.3 percent for agricultural products and 14.2 percent for non-agricultural products. Argentina has bound 100 percent of its tariff lines to the WTO, with a simple average WTO-bound tariff rate of 31.8 percent. On December 23, 2019 Argentina raised the rate of statistical tax, a fee charged on imported goods for consumption, to 3 percent.
- *Non-tariff barriers*: Argentina imposes bans on many capital goods, self-propelled agricultural machinery, retreaded tires, used or refurbished medical equipment, automotive parts, and remanufactured goods. Argentina requires compliance with strict conditions on those used capital goods that may be imported.
- *IPR protection*: To receive IPR protection under Argentina Law, a patent or trademark must be registered in Argentina. A trademark or patent registered in the United States will not protect against unauthorized use in Argentina.
- *Documentation requirements*: Certificate of origin, import license, Material Safety Data Sheet or Non-Dangerous Goods declaration letter, Declaración Jurada Anticipada de Importación (Declaration of Anticipated Imports). Dangerous goods require a Government Agency Certificate.
- *Distribution and sales channels*: Sales and distribution in Argentina can be handled by a distributor or overseas suppliers. Smaller firms buy through intermediaries. Equipment is sold through sales agents or trade fairs and consumer goods through supermarkets or hypermarkets.

BEST EXPORT PROSPECTS

Leading sectors for U.S. exports and investments:

- Energy, oil, and gas
- Renewable energy
- Education and training
- Medical technology
- Agriculture

- ICT
- Agricultural machinery and irrigation equipment and parts and components

EXPORTING FROM ARGENTINA

Major impediments to exporting from Argentina (in order of importance) are: Access to imported inputs at competitive prices and trade financing high cost or delays caused by domestic transportation, inappropriate production technology and skills, tariff barriers abroad, burdensome procedures at foreign boarders, difficulty with identifying potential markets and buyers, difficulty meeting quality and/or quantity requirements of buyers, technical requirements and standards abroad, foreign border corruption, high cost or delays caused by international transportation, rules of origin requirements abroad.

IMPORTATION TO ARGENTINA

Major impediments to importing to Argentina (in order of importance) are: Burdensome import procedures, domestic technical requirements and standards, tariffs and non-tariff barriers, corruption at the border, high cost or delays caused by international/domestic transportation, domestic technical requirements and standards, inappropriate telecommunication infrastructure, crime and theft, inappropriate telecommunications infrastructure.

Brazil

Country Profile

Population: 211,715,973
Exports: $217.2 billion
Major Exports: transport equipment, iron ore, soybeans, footwear, coffee, automobiles
Export Partners: China, United States, Argentina, Netherlands
Imports: $153.2 billion
Major Imports: machinery, electrical equipment, transport equipment, capital goods, chemical products, oil, electricity
Import Partners: China, United States, Argentina, Germany
Trade as % GDP: Exports: 14.3%; Imports: 14.7%
Currency and Exchange Rate: 3.19 reals (BRL) per U.S. dollar
GDP (official exchange rate): $2.055 trillion
GDP per capita: $15,600
External Debt: $547.4 billion

FOREIGN IMPORT POLICIES

- *Entry of goods*: Import license is required for most products. Importers must register with the Foreign Trade Secretariat (SECEX), a branch of the Ministry of Economy.
- *Tariffs and taxes:* As of 2018 Brazil's average MFN applied tariff rate was 13.4 percent, 10.1 percent for agricultural products and 13.9 percent for

non-agricultural products. Brazil has bound 100 percent of its tariff lines to the WTO with a simple average WTO-bound tariff rate of 31.4 percent, 35 percent for non-agricultural products and 55 percent for most agricultural products. Brazil has a very complex domestic tax system.

- *Non-tariff barriers*: Brazil imposes import bans on used consumer goods and blood products. However, SECEX Ordinance 23/2011 establishes an exceptions list of more than twenty-five categories of approved used goods. Brazil has both automatic and non-automatic import licensing requirements.
- *IPR protection*: Brazil remains on the USTR Special 301 Watch List due to high levels of counterfeiting, piracy, and the approximately ten-year delay in the patent examination process.
- *Documentation requirements*: Certificate of origin, health certificate and declaration, Material Safety Data Sheet, Non-Dangerous Goods declaration letter. Several imported products require permission by Brazilian authorities that regulate the entry and commercialization of those goods. Some goods require an import license and that license requires approval from one or more of sixteen authorities. The licenses must be requested by a branch of the Ministry of Economy before the shipment and customs clearance.
- *Distribution and sales channels*: Distribution and/or sales are handled by local agents, distributors, import houses, trading companies, and by subsidiaries and branches of foreign firms.

BEST EXPORT PROSPECTS

Leading sectors for U.S. exports and investments are:

- Energy
- Agriculture
- Education and training
- Services in education
- Franchising
- Travel and tourism
- Infrastructure
- ICT
- Healthcare
- Defense, aviation, and security

EXPORTING FROM BRAZIL

Major impediments to exporting from Brazil (in order of importance) are: Access to imported inputs at competitive prices and trade financing, high cost or delays caused by domestic transportation, inappropriate production technology and skills, tariff barriers abroad, burdensome procedures at foreign borders, difficulty with identifying potential markets and buyers, difficulty meeting quality and/or quantity requirements of buyers, technical requirements and standards abroad, foreign border corruption, high cost or delays caused by international transportation, rules of origin requirements abroad

IMPORTATION TO BRAZIL

Major impediments to importing to Brazil (in order of importance) are: Tariffs and non-tariff barriers, burdensome import procedures, high cost or delays caused by international/domestic transportation, domestic technical requirements and standards, corruption at border, inappropriate telecommunication infrastructure, crime and theft.

Canada

Country Profile

Population: 37,694,085
Exports: $423.5 billion
Major Exports: motor vehicles, parts, industrial machinery, aircraft, telecommunications equipment, chemicals, plastics, fertilizers, wood pulp, timber, crude petroleum, natural gas, electricity, aluminum
Export Partners: United States, China
Imports: $442.1 billion
Major Imports: machinery and equipment, motor vehicles, parts, crude oil, chemicals, electricity, durable consumer goods
Import Partners: United States, China, Mexico
Trade as % GDP: Exports: 31.6%; Imports: 33.3%
Currency and Exchange Rate: 1.308 Canadian dollars (CAD) per U.S. dollar
GDP (official exchange rate): $1.653 trillion
GDP per capita: $48,400
External Debt: $1.608 trillion

FOREIGN IMPORT POLICIES

- *Entry of goods*: Canada has a Canada Border Service Agency (CBSA) eManifest program. eManifest requires carriers, freight forwarders, and importers in all modes of transportation to transmit cargo, conveyance, house bill/supplementary cargo, and importer data electronically to the CBSA prior to loading in the marine mode and prior to arrival by air, rail, or highway mode.
- *Tariffs and taxes*: Canada eliminated tariffs on all eligible industrial and mot agricultural products imported from the United States under the terms of the USMCA. Duty-free shipments apply for de minimis shipments.
- *Non-tariff barriers*: Canada uses a supply management system with a regime that involves production quotas, producer marketing boards to regulate price and supply and tariff rate quotas (TRQs) for imports.
- *IPR protection*: To receive IPR Protection in Canada, a patent or trademark must be registered in Canada. A trademark or patent registered in the United States will not protect against unauthorized use in Canada.
- *Documentation requirements*: Commercial invoice, customs coding Form B3, cargo control document, bill of lading, permits, certificates, examinations, standard business invoice (for mail order shipments).
- *Distribution and sales channel*: The following traditional distribution and/or sales channels are found in Canada: wholesalers, retail organizations, consumer retail, franchises, after sales agents, agents and distributors, and legal agents. The distribution chain varies depending on the type of imported product and/or equipment.

BEST EXPORT PROSPECTS

Leading sectors for U.S. exports and investments are:

- Aerospace and defense
- Agriculture
- Automotive
- Defense equipment
- Energy
- ICT
- Medical devices
- Education and training

EXPORTING FROM CANADA

Major impediments to exporting from Canada (in order of importance) are: Identifying potential markets, access to trade finance, burdensome procedures at foreign borders, tariff barriers abroad, rules of origin requirements abroad, technical requirements and standards abroad, high cost or delays caused by international transportation, access to imported inputs at competitive prices, inappropriate production technology and skills, high cost or delays caused by domestic transportation, corruption at foreign borders, difficulties in meeting quality and/or quantity requirements of buyers.

IMPORTATION TO CANADA

Major impediments to importing to Canada (in order of importance) are: Burdensome import procedures, tariffs and non-tariff barriers, domestic technical requirements and standards, high cost or delays caused by international/domestic transportation, inappropriate telecommunication infrastructure, corruption at border, crime and theft.

Chile

Country Profile

Population: 18,186,770
Exports: $69.23 billion
Major Exports: copper, fruit, fish products, paper and pulp, chemicals, wine
Export Partners: China, United States, Japan, South Korea, Brazil
Imports: $61.31 billion
Major Imports: petroleum, petroleum products, chemicals, electrical equipment, telecommunications equipment, industrial machinery, vehicles, natural gas
Import Partners: China, United States, Brazil, Argentina, Germany
Trade as % GDP: Exports: 28.2%; Imports: 28.6%
Currency and Exchange Rate: 653.9 Chilean pesos (CLP) per U.S. dollar
GDP (official exchange rate): $277 billion
GDP per capita: $24,600
External Debt: $183.4 billion

FOREIGN IMPORT POLICIES

- *Entry of goods*: Licensing is used as a means of gathering statistical information and not to control imports. Imports must be marked with the country of origin. Packaged goods must be labeled to show quantity, ingredients, and other important features.
- *Tariffs and taxes*: There has been a US–Chile Free Trade Agreement (FTA) since January 1, 2004. Tariffs on 90 percent of U.S. exports to Chile were eliminated. Since January 1, 2015 all trade between the United States and Chile has been duty free. There is a 6 percent uniform tariff for products not of U.S. origin. There is a 15 percent tax on certain imported "luxury goods" and all imports are subject to the same 19 percent value-added tax (IVA) imposed on domestic goods.
- *Non-tariff barriers*: There are no restrictions on the types or amounts of goods that can be imported into Chile, nor are there any requirements to use the official foreign exchange market; However, importers and exporters must report their imports and exports transactions to the Central Bank.
- *IPR protection*: Chile remains on the USTR's Special 301 Priority Watch List. Chile suffers from weak patenting procedures and inadequate trade secret protection.
- *Documentation requirements*: Commercial invoice, certificates of origin, bills of lading, freight insurance, packing lists, special permission certificates, sanitary and phytosanitary certificates (for agricultural products).
- *Distribution and sales channels*: Distribution and sales are handled through local agents or distributors. Corporations legally established in Chile can form a local branch or subsidiary office to handle distribution and sales under their own company name.

BEST EXPORT PROSPECTS

Leading sectors for U.S. exports and investments are:

- Healthcare
- Telecommunications
- Automotive parts
- Construction
- Mining and minerals
- Agriculture
- Agricultural machinery and equipment
- Travel and tourism
- Energy
- Energy efficiency
- Education and training

EXPORTING FROM CHILE

Major impediments to exporting from Chile (in order of importance) are: Identifying potential markets, access to trade finance, inappropriate production technology and skills, tariff barriers abroad, high cost or delays caused by international transportation, access to trade finance, difficulties in meeting quality and/or quantity requirements of buyers, technical requirements and standards abroad, high cost or delays caused by domestic transportation, burdensome procedures at foreign borders, rules of origin requirements abroad, access to imported inputs at competitive prices, corruption at foreign borders.

IMPORTATION TO CHILE

Major impediments to importing to Chile (in order of importance) are: High cost or delays caused by international transportation, burdensome import procedures, domestic technical requirements and standards, high cost or delays caused by domestic transportation, tariffs and non-tariff barriers, inappropriate telecommunications infrastructure, crime and theft, corruption at the border.

Colombia

Country Profile

Population: 49,084,841
Exports: $39.48 billion
Major Exports: Petroleum, emeralds, coffee, nickel, flowers, bananas, apparel
Export Partners: United States, Panama, China
Imports: $44.24 billion
Major Imports: Industrial equipment, transportation equipment, consumer goods, chemicals, paper products, fuels, electricity
Import Partners: United States, China, Mexico, Brazil, Germany
Trade as % GDP: Exports: 15.9%; Imports: 22.2%
Currency and Exchange Rate: 2,957 Colombian pesos per U.S. dollar
GDP (official exchange rate): $314.5 billion
GDP per capita: $14,400
External Debt: $124.6 billion

FOREIGN IMPORT POLICIES

- *Entry of goods*: To import into Colombia the following basic steps must be followed: Buy and fill out import registration form; customs inspection of merchandise when necessary; complete the "Andean Customs Value Declaration"; complete the import declaration; go to an authorized financial entity and pay the import duties, VAT, surcharges, and other fees; make arrangements with a financial entity to pay for the imported goods; obtain approval from the Ministry of Commerce, Industry and Tourism for the import registration form or import license; request cargo manifest; and obtain import permits if required. Documents must be kept for a period of no less than five years.
- *Tariffs and taxes*: The US–Colombia Trade Promotion Agreement (CTPA) entered into force on May 15, 2012 with the first tariff reductions occurring immediately and subsequent tariff reductions occurring on January 1 of each year. Consumer and industrial products from the United States are duty free under the CTPA as of January 1, 2021. The ninth round of tariff reductions took place on January 1, 2020. Almost 70 percent of U.S. agricultural

exports became duty free at entry into force of the CTPA and duties of most other U.S. agricultural goods phase out over a period of five to twelve years.
- *Non-tariff barriers*: Buyers of new trucks are required to pay a registration fee equivalent to 15 percent of the value of the new truck. The fee can be avoided by scrapping an old truck, which entitles them to a scrapping certificate that waives the fee. As of March 2020 Colombia has not ratified the WTO Trade Facilitation Agreement (TFA) but it is expected to do so.
- *IPR protection*: IP must be registered in Colombia to receive protection under local Law. Colombia has a Patent Protection Highway (PPH) agreement with the United States and continues to provide effective protection and enforcement of IPR and to implement its obligations under the CTPA.
- *Documentation requirements*: Import registration form, product description, tariff classification, Andean Custom Value Declaration, import declaration, import license, cargo manifest, import permits, import declaration form, pro forma invoice, letter of credit, draft bill, registration as national (local) producer, export offer and determination of origin, certificate of origin, commercial invoice, textile visa, phytosanitary certificates, and export declarations.
- *Distribution and sales channels*: Distribution and sales can be handled through agents, distributors, wholesalers selling directly to the public, department stores, or superstores. Some large manufacturing companies import directly or open purchasing offices and warehouses in the United States and contact suppliers and manufactures through the Internet.

BEST EXPORT PROSPECTS

Leading sectors for U.S. exports and investments are:

- Automotive
- Education
- Agriculture
- Design, construction, and infrastructure development
- Travel and tourism
- ICT
- Defense
- Oil and gas
- Processed food and beverages
- Medical equipment
- Electric power and renewable energy systems

EXPORTING FROM COLOMBIA

Major impediments to exporting from Colombia (in order of importance) are: High cost or delays caused by domestic transportation, inappropriate production technology and skills, access to imported inputs at competitive prices, technical requirements and standards abroad, identifying potential markets and buyers, difficulties in meeting quality and/or quantity requirements of buyers, tariff barriers abroad, access to trade finance, burdensome procedures at foreign borders, rules of origin requirements abroad, high cost or delays caused by international transportation, corruption at foreign borders.

IMPORTATION TO COLOMBIA

Major impediments to importing to Colombia (in order of importance) are: Burdensome import procedures, high cost or delays caused by domestic transportation, tariffs and non-tariff barriers, domestic technical requirements and standards, high cost or delays caused by international transportation, corruption at the border, crime and theft, inappropriate telecommunications infrastructure.

Mexico

Country Profile

Population: 128,649,565
Exports: $409.8 billion
Major Exports: manufactured goods, electronics, vehicles, auto parts, oil, oil products, silver, plastics, fruits, vegetables, coffee, cotton, silver
Export Partners: United States, Canada
Imports: $420.8 billion
Major Imports: metalworking machines, steel mill products, agricultural machinery, electrical equipment, automobile parts, aircraft, aircraft parts, plastics, natural gas, oil
Import Partners: United States, Canada, China, Japan
Trade as % GDP: Exports: 39.1%; Imports: 39.1%
Currency and Exchange Rate: 18.26 Mexican pesos (MXN) per U.S. dollar
GDP (official exchange rate): $1.151 trillion
GDP per capita: $19,900
External Debt: $445.8 billion

FOREIGN IMPORT POLICIES

- *Entry of goods*: On July 2016, Mexico ratified the WTO Trade Facilitation Agreement (TFA); However, U.S. exporters continue to express concerns about Mexican customs administrative procedures and insufficient prior notification of procedural changes, inconsistent interpretation of regulatory requirements at different border posts and uneven border enforcement of Mexican standards and labeling rules.
- *Tariffs and taxes*: On January 29, 2020 the United States-Mexico-Canada Agreement (USMCA) was implemented. The USMCA modernizes and rebalances U.S. trade relations with Mexico and Canada to benefit American workers and businesses and reduces incentives to outsource by providing strong labor and environmental protections, innovative rules of origin, and revised investment provisions.
- *Non-tariff barriers*: Mexico has established an import licensing system for many imports, which include, but are not limited to footwear, clothing, textile goods, and steel.
- *IPR protection*: Enforcement of IPRs remains weak in spite of the existence of adequate laws to protect such rights in Mexico.
- *Documentation requirements*: Mexican importers must register with the Official Register of Importers. Importers must also apply to the Secretariat

of Finance and Public Credit (SHCP) to be listed in Mexican sector registries. Mexico requires a completed "Pedimento" for all commercial crossings, a commercial invoice (in Spanish), a bill of lading, documents showing a guarantee of payment of additional duties for undervalued goods, a proof of origin certification, and, if applicable, documents demonstrating compliance with Mexican product safety and performance regulations. If importing steel products shipments must include the invoice and complete supplier information.

- *Distribution and sales channels*: Main channels in Mexico are local manufacturers and other large buyers, distributors, sales agents, and branches or subsidiaries of foreign manufacturers.

BEST EXPORT PROSPECTS

Leading sectors for U.S. exports and investments are:

- Aerospace
- Agribusiness
- Agriculture
- Automotive industry
- Construction
- Cosmetics
- Education and training
- Electricity
- Environmental technologies
- Healthcare products and services
- Internet and IT services
- Mining and minerals
- Oil and gas
- Packaging machinery industry
- Plastics and resins
- Renewable energy
- Safety and security
- Telecommunications equipment
- Textiles
- Transportation infrastructure equipment and services
- Travel and tourism

EXPORTING FROM MEXICO

Major impediments to exporting from Mexico (in order of importance) are: Identifying potential markets and buyers, access to trade finance, inappropriate production technology and skills, technical requirements and standards abroad, difficulties in meeting quality and/or quantity requirements of buyers, high cost or delays caused by domestic transportation, access to imported inputs and competitive prices, tariff barriers abroad, burdensome procedures at foreign borders, rules of origin requirements abroad, high cost or delays caused by international transportation, corruption at foreign borders.

IMPORTATION TO MEXICO

Major Impediments to Importing to Mexico (in order of importance) are: Burdensome import procedures, corruption at the border, crime and theft, domestic technical requirements and standards, high cost or delays caused by domestic transportation, tariffs and non-tariff barriers, inappropriate telecommunications infrastructure, high cost or delays caused by international transportation.

A.3 TRADING OPPORTUNITIES IN ASIA AND OCEANIA

Australia

Country Profile

Population: 25,466,459
Exports: $231.6 billion
Major Exports: iron ore, coal, gold, natural gas, beef, aluminum ores, wheat, meat, wool, alumina, alcohol
Export Partners: China, Japan, South Korea, India, Hong Kong
Imports: $221 billion
Major Imports: motor vehicles, refined petroleum, telecommunication equipment and parts, crude petroleum, medicaments, goods vehicles, gold, computers
Import Partners: China, United States, Japan, Thailand, Germany, South Korea
Trade as % GDP: Exports: 24.1%; Imports: 21.6%
Currency and Exchange Rate: 1.29 Australian dollars (AUD) per U.S. dollar (2021 est.)
GDP (official exchange rate): $1.38 trillion
GDP per capita: $50,400
External Debt: $1.714 trillion

FOREIGN IMPORT POLICIES

- *Entry of goods*: The Australian Customs and Border Protection Service has sole jurisdiction to clear imports. Local importers are responsible for obtaining formal customs clearance for goods. Customs does not require companies or individuals to hold import licenses, but importers may need to obtain permits to clear the goods.
- *Tariffs and taxes*: Goods entering Australia may incur duty, goods and services tax (GST), and/or additional charges. Customs duty rates vary and depend on type of goods and country of origin. Under the AUSFTA tariff arrangement 99 percent of U.S.-origin goods enter Australia duty free. The importer is still responsible for applicable GST payments. From July 2018, GST of 10 percent applies to sales of low-value imported goods to consumers.
- *Non-tariff barriers*: Products that are considered to pose a potential public danger (drugs, steroids, and weapons) as well as food, plants, and animals are restricted or quarantined due to photosanitary concerns. Australia still has in place some standards that restrict product entry. Government procurement policy lacks transparency and tends to favor local companies. Export subsidies are provided to manufacturers of autos and components.

- *IPR protection*: Australia generally provides strong IPR protection and enforcement through legislation that criminalizes copyright piracy and trademark counterfeiting.
- *Documentation requirements*: The following are the minimum document requirements: Customs entry or Informal Clearance Document, airway bill or bill of lading, invoice, and import permit.
- *Distribution and sales channels*: Distribution and sales channels include agents, wholesalers, and manufactures' representatives.

BEST EXPORT PROSPECTS

Leading sectors for U.S. exports and investments are:

- Building and construction
- Agriculture
- Education and training
- Cybersecurity
- Aerospace
- Smart grid
- Automotive parts
- Mining
- Travel and tourism
- Defense
- Medical devices

EXPORTING FROM AUSTRALIA

Major impediments to exporting from Australia (in order of importance) are: Identifying potential markets and buyers, high cost or delays caused by international transportation, access to imported inputs at competitive prices, tariff barriers abroad, high cost or delays caused by domestic transportation, burdensome procedures at foreign borders, technical requirements and standards abroad, rules of origin requirements abroad, inappropriate production technology and skills, difficulties in meeting quality and/or quantity requirements of buyers, corruption at foreign borders, access to trade finance.

IMPORTATION TO AUSTRALIA

Major impediments to importing to Australia (in order of importance) are: High cost or delays caused by international transportation, burdensome import procedures, high cost or delays caused by domestic transportation, tariffs and non-tariff barriers, domestic, technical requirements and standards, inappropriate telecommunications infrastructure, crime and theft, corruption at the border.

China

Country Profile

Population: 1,349,015,977
Exports: $2.49 trillion

Major Exports: electrical machinery, computers, telecommunications equipment, apparel, furniture, textiles

Export Partners: United States, Hong Kong, Japan, South Korea

Imports: $2.14 trillion

Major Imports: electrical machinery, integrated circuits, other computer components, oil, mineral fuels, optical equipment, medical equipment, metal ores, motor vehicles, soybeans

Import Partners: South Korea, Japan, United States, Germany, Australia

Trade as % GDP: Exports: 18.4%; Imports: 17.3%

Currency and Exchange Rate: 7.76 Renminbi yuan per U.S. dollar

GDP (official exchange rate): $12.01 trillion

GDP per capita: $18,200

External Debt: $1.598 trillion

FOREIGN IMPORT POLICIES

- *Entry of goods*: China has reduced tariffs, importing licenses, and quotas on almost all major imports. All products sold in China must be marked and certain imported commodities must be inspected and certified to be in compliance with compulsory national standards. Food labeling standards were recently implemented.
- *Tariffs and taxes*: As of 2018 China's average MFN applied tariff rate was 9.8 percent, 15.6 percent for agricultural products and 8.8 percent for non-agricultural products. China has bound 100 percent of its tariff lines to the WTO, with a simple average WTO-bound tariff rate of 10 percent. Its highest WTO-bound tariff rate is 65 percent for certain agricultural goods. As of 2018 China imposed tariffs ranging from 15 percent to 25 percent on a range of agricultural, steel, and aluminum products.
- *Non-tariff barriers*: Significant non-tariff barriers still exist in China, which include, for example, regulations that set high thresholds for entry into services sectors such as banking, insurance, and telecommunications; selective and unwarranted inspection requirements for agricultural imports; and the use of questionable sanitary and phytosanitary and technical barriers to trade measures.
- *IPR protection*: Intellectual property theft is widespread in China. However, major steps have recently been undertaken to protect and enforce IPR in China.
- *Documentation requirements*: CITES Certificate, import/export declaration form, Material Safety Data Sheet or Non-Dangerous Goods declaration letter, packing list, commercial invoice, waybill, certificate of origin, original invoices, importer/exporter customs registration code, China compulsory certification, quarantine certification, import license, China inspection and quarantine, sanitation certificate, certificate of origin, examining report, veterinary and plant inspection, automatic import license, pre-loading inspection certificate, import certificate, phytosanitary certificate from origin.
- *Distribution and sales channels*: Companies that handle export/import trade must be approved by the central government. Importation is generally made through local sales agents, international trading companies, or Chinese firms

with regional or national networks. Various sales techniques are used such as advertisement, direct mass mailing to end users, trade fairs, and exhibitions.

BEST EXPORT PROSPECTS

Leading sectors for U.S. exports and investments are:

- Technology and ICT
- Oil and gas
- Pharmaceuticals
- Medical devices
- Environmental technology
- Education and training
- Construction and green building
- Automotive industry
- Machinery
- Aviation
- Agricultural industry
- Rail and urban rail
- Travel and tourism

EXPORTING FROM CHINA

Major impediments to exporting from China (in order of importance) are: Technical requirements and standards abroad, identifying potential markets and buyers, burdensome procedures at foreign borders, tariff barriers abroad, access to imported inputs at competitive prices, access to trade finance, high cost or delays caused by international transportation, inappropriate production technology and skills, difficulties in meeting quality and/or quantity requirements of buyers, high cost or delays caused by domestic transportation, rules of origin requirements abroad, corruption at foreign borders.

IMPORTATION TO CHINA

Major impediments to importing to China (in order of importance) are: Tariffs and non-tariff barriers, burdensome import procedures, high cost or delays caused by international transportation, domestic technical requirements and standards, high cost or delays caused by domestic transportation, corruption at the border, inappropriate telecommunications infrastructure, crime and theft.

India

Country Profile

Population: 1,326,093,247
Exports: $304.1 billion
Major Exports: petroleum products, precious stones, vehicles, machinery, iron and steel, chemicals, pharmaceutical products, cereals, clothing
Export Partners: United States, UAE, Hong Kong, China
Imports: $452.2 billion

Major Imports: crude oil, precious stones, machinery, chemicals, fertilizer, plastics, iron, steel

Import Partners: China, United States, UAE, Saudi Arabia, Switzerland

Trade as % GDP: Exports: 18.7%; Imports: 21.4%

Currency and Exchange Rate: 65.17 Indian rupees (INR) per U.S. dollar

GDP (official exchange rate): $2.602 trillion

GDP per capita: $7,200

External Debt: $501.6 billion

FOREIGN IMPORT POLICIES

- *Entry of goods*: India has steadily replaced licensing and discretionary controls over imports with deregulation and simpler import procedures. Most import items fall within the scope of India's EXIM Policy regulation of Open General License, which means that they are deemed to be freely importable without restrictions and without a license, except that they are regulated by the provisions of the EXIM Policy or any other law.
- *Tariffs and taxes*: As of 2018 India's simple average MFN applied tariff rate was 17.1 percent, 38.8 percent for agricultural products and 13.6 percent for non-agricultural products. India has bound 74.3 percent of its tariff lines to the WTO, with a simple average WTO-bound tariff rate of 50.8 percent. In 2018 Indian implemented a 10 percent social welfare surcharge on imports, except certain products exempted pursuant to an official customs notification.
- *Non-tariff barriers*: India has three categories of products that maintain various forms of non-tariff regulations which are: Items that are banned or prohibited and are denied entry into India (e.g., animal tallow, fat, and oils), restricted items which require an import license (e.g., livestock products and certain chemicals), and "canalized" items (e.g., pharmaceuticals and corn under a tariff-rate quota) imported only by government trading monopolies and subject to cabinet approval.
- *IPR protection*: Protection and enforcement of trademarks, patents, and copyrights remain weak. There is no statutory protection of trade secrets and businesses must rely on contract law to secure sensitive information exchanged between parties.
- *Documentation requirements*: Import declaration in the prescribed bill of entry format, ex-factory invoice, freight, insurance certificates, import licenses, letter of credit, bill of sale.
- *Distribution and sales channels*: India uses a three-tier structure of re-distribution which includes stockists, wholesalers, and retailers. It is advised that companies establish a branch office or subsidiary in India or appoint an agent, a representative, or a distributor. Appointment of an agent, representative or distributor is required for some industries such as pharmaceutical drugs or cosmetics.

BEST EXPORT PROSPECTS

Leading sectors for U.S. exports and investments are:

- Aerospace and defense
- Environmental technology

- Energy
- Education services
- ICT
- Healthcare and medical equipment
- Travel and tourism
- Mining and mineral processing equipment
- Safety and security
- Chemical industry
- Agriculture

EXPORTING FROM INDIA

Major impediments to exporting from India (in order of importance) are: Corruption at foreign borders, high cost or delays caused by domestic transportation, burdensome procedures at foreign borders, difficulties in meeting quality and/or quantity requirements of buyers, identifying potential markets and buyers, access to imported inputs at competitive prices, access to trade finance, high cost or delays caused by international transportation, technical requirements and standards abroad, tariff barriers abroad, inappropriate production, technology and skills, rules of origin requirements abroad.

IMPORTATION TO INDIA

Major impediments to importing to India (in order of importance) are: High cost or delay caused by domestic transportation, crime and theft, corruption at the border, tariffs and non-tariff barriers, burdensome import procedures, high cost or delay caused by international transportation, inappropriate telecommunications infrastructure, domestic technical requirements and standards.

Indonesia

Country Profile

Population: 267,026,366
Exports: $168.9 billion
Major Exports: mineral fuels, animal fats, vegetable fats, palm oil, electrical machinery, rubber, machinery parts, mechanical appliance parts
Export Partners: China, United States, Japan, India, Singapore, Malaysia, South Korea
Imports: $150.1 billion
Major Imports: mineral fuels, boilers, machinery, mechanical parts, electric machinery, iron, steel, foodstuff
Import Partners: China, Singapore, Japan, Thailand, Malaysia, South Korea, United States
Trade as % GDP: Exports: 18.4%; Imports: 18.9%
Currency and Exchange Rate: 13,385 Indonesian rupiahs (IDR) per U.S. dollar
GDP (official exchange rate): $1.015 trillion
GDP per capita: $12,400
External Debt: $344.4 billion

FOREIGN IMPORT POLICIES

- *Entry of goods*: The Government of Indonesia requires extensive documentation prior to allowing the importation of goods. Since 2013 food products are required to have Indonesian language labeling.
- *Tariffs and taxes*: As of 2018 Indonesia's average MFN applied tariff rate was 8.1 percent, 8.6 percent for agricultural products and 8.0 percent for non-agricultural products. Indonesia has bound 96.3 percent of its tariff lines to the WTO, with a simple average WTO-bound tariff rate of 37.1 percent. Luxury goods, imported or locally produced, may be subject to a luxury tax of up to 200 percent and applied tax rates range from 10 percent to 75 percent.
- *Non-tariff barriers:* Exporters to Indonesia must comply with numerous and overlapping import licensing requirements that impede access to Indonesia's market. Under Minister of Trade Regulation 70/2015, all importers must obtain an import license as either an importer of goods for further distribution (API-U) or an importer for their own manufacturing (API-P), but importers are not permitted to obtain both types of license.
- *IPR Protection*: Indonesia has failed to provide effective protection and enforcement of IPR laws and remains on the USTR Special 301 Priority Watch List for IPR protection.
- *Documentation requirements*: Minimum requirements include pro forma invoice, commercial invoice, certificate of origin, bill of lading, packing list, and insurance certificates.
- *Distribution and sales channels*: Distribution is handled through agents, distributors, and other intermediaries; However, due to carrying charges associated with warehousing, finding a stocking distributor can be a problem. Corruption among custom agents makes the use of offshore warehouses more attractive.

BEST EXPORT PROSPECTS

Leading sectors for U.S. exports and investments are:

- Education and training
- Agriculture
- Telecommunications
- Medical equipment
- Aviation
- Power generation

EXPORTING FROM INDONESIA

Major impediments to exporting from Indonesia (in order of importance) are: High cost or delays caused by domestic transportation, technical requirements, and standards abroad, identifying potential markets and buyers, high cost or delays caused by international transportation, inappropriate production technology and skills, difficulties in meeting quality and/or quantity requirements of buyers, corruption at foreign borders, access to imported inputs at competitive prices, access to trade finance, tariff barriers abroad, rules of origin requirements abroad, burdensome procedures at foreign borders.

IMPORTATION TO INDONESIA

Major Impediments to Importing to Indonesia (in order of importance) are: Corruption at the border, tariffs and non-tariff barriers, high cost or delays caused by domestic transportation, domestic technical requirements and standards, burdensome import procedures, high cost or delays caused by international transportation, crime and theft, inappropriate telecommunications infrastructure.

Japan

Country Profile

Population: 125,507,472
Exports: $688.9 billion
Major Exports: motor vehicles, iron products, steel products, semiconductors, auto parts, power generating machinery, plastic materials
Export Partners: United States, China, South Korea, Hong Kong, Thailand
Imports: $644.7 billion
Import Partners: China, United States, Australia, South Korea, Saudi Arabia
Trade as % GDP: Exports: 18.5%; Imports: 18.3%
Currency and Exchange Rate: 111.1 yen (JPY) per U.S. dollar
GDP (official exchange rate): $4.873 trillion
GDP per capita: $42,900
External Debt: $3.24 trillion

FOREIGN IMPORT POLICIES

- *Entry of goods*: To import into Japan, goods must be declared to the Director-General of Customs and obtain an import permit after necessary examination of the goods. Certain items (i.e., hazardous materials, animals, plants, perishables, and high value articles) may require a Japanese import license. Import quota items also require an import license.
- *Tariffs and taxes*: As of 2018 Japan's average MFN applied tariff rate was 4.4 percent, 19.3 percent for agricultural products and 2.5 percent for non-agricultural products. Japan has bound 99.7 percent of its tariff lines to the WTO, with a simple average WTO-bound tariff rate of 4.7 percent.
- *Non-tariff barriers*: While tariffs are generally low, Japan does have non-tariff barriers that impede or delay the importation of foreign products into Japan, such as: standards unique to Japan (formal, informal, de facto, or otherwise) effectively shutting out new entrants in the market; official regulations that favor domestically produced products and discriminate against foreign products; licensing powers in the hands of industry associations with limited membership; cartels (both formal and informal).
- *IPR protection*: To receive IP protection under Japanese Law, a patent or trademark must be registered in Japan. A trademark or patent registered in the United States will not protect against unauthorized use in Japan.
- *Documentation requirements*: Import declaration form (C-5020), permits, import license, certificate of origin, commercial invoice, packing list, original signed bill of lading or airway bill.

• *Distribution and sales channels*: Limited space and a dense urban population have contributed to the consolidation of Japan's sales and distribution
channels, which include small retail stores and wholesalers that are required to
deliver smaller amounts of product more frequently. Japanese culture prefers
a less efficient distribution system, doing business via face-to-face contact.
Japanese existing distribution and sales systems still bear the traces of the keiretsu systems, where businesses are linked by cross shareholdings to establish
a robust corporate structure.

BEST EXPORT PROSPECTS

Leading sectors for U.S. exports and investments are:

• Travel and tourism
• Cyber security
• Cloud computing
• Liquefied natural gas
• Pharmaceuticals
• Healthcare IT
• Agriculture
• Nuclear decommissioning and decontamination
• Aircraft and related parts, equipment and services
• Education and training
• Defense procurement
• Semiconductors
• Renewable energy

EXPORTING FROM JAPAN

Major impediments to exporting from Japan (in order of importance) are: Tariff barriers
abroad, technical requirements and standards abroad, identifying potential markets and
buyers, rules of origin requirements abroad, high cost or delays caused by international
transportation, access to imported inputs at competitive prices, burdensome procedures
at foreign borders, difficulties in meeting quality and/or quantity requirements of
buyers, high cost or delays caused by domestic transportation, inappropriate production
technology and skills, corruption at foreign borders, access to trade finance.

IMPORTATION TO JAPAN

Major impediments to importing to Japan (in order of importance) are: Tariffs and
non-tariff barriers, domestic technical requirements and standards, burdensome
import procedures, high cost or delays caused by international transportation, high
cost or delays caused by domestic transportation, inappropriate telecommunications
infrastructure, corruption at the border, crime and theft.

Thailand

Country Profile

Population: 68,977,400
Exports: $235.1 billion

Major Exports: automobiles, automobile parts, computers, computer parts, jewelry, precious stones, polymers of ethylene I primary forms, refined fuels, electronic integrated circuits, chemical products, rice, fish products, rubber products, sugar, cassava, poultry, machinery, machinery parts, iron, steel, steel products

Export Partners: China, United States, Japan, Hong Kong, Vietnam, Australia, Malaysia

Imports: $203.2 billion

Major Imports: machinery, parts, crude oil, electrical machinery, electrical parts, chemicals, iron products, steel products, electronic integrated circuits, automobile parts, jewelry, silver bars, gold bars, computers, computer parts, electrical household appliances, soybean, soybean meal, wheat, cotton, dairy products

Import Partners: China, Japan, United States, Malaysia

Trade as % GDP: Exports: 59.7%; Imports: 50.6%

Currency and Exchange Rate: 34.34 baht per U.S. dollar

GDP (official exchange rate): $455.4 billion

GDP per capita: $17,900

External Debt: $132 billion

FOREIGN IMPORT POLICIES

- *Entry of goods*: Import licenses are required for twenty-six categories of items. Licenses are required for the import of many raw materials, petroleum, industrial, textiles, pharmaceuticals, and agricultural products. Imports not requiring licenses must comply with applicable regulations of concerned agencies, including extra fees and certificate of origin requirements.
- *Tariffs and taxes*: As of 2017 Thailand's average MFN applied tariff rate was 9.6 percent, 24 percent for agricultural products and 7.3 percent for non-agricultural products. Thailand has bound 75.2 percent of its tariff lines to the WTO, with a simple average WTO-bound tariff rate of 27.9 percent. Thailand applies import tariffs of 80 percent on motor vehicles, 60 percent on motorcycles and certain clothing products, 54 percent to 60 percent on distilled spirits, and 10 percent on most pharmaceutical products.
- *Non-tariff barriers*: Importing licenses are required for the importation of many raw materials, petroleum, industrial machinery, textiles, pharmaceuticals, and agricultural items. Thailand imposes domestic purchase requirements on importers of several products subject to tariff-rate quotas, including soybean and soybean meal.
- *IPR protection*: Thailand's IPR protection continues to improve and in December 2017, the USTR moved Thailand off the Special 301 Priority Watch List.
- *Documentation requirements*: Import/export license, customs import/export entry form, commercial invoice, packing list, bill of lading or airway bill, letter of credit, authorization from relevant agencies, certificate of origin.
- *Distribution and sales channels*: Distribution and sales should be conducted through a Thai importer, local agent, distributor, or manufacturers' branch office. Day-to-day bidding for routine government tenders is only permitted through local agents, distributors, or manufacturers' branch offices.

BEST EXPORT PROSPECTS

Leading sectors for U.S. exports and investments are:

- Telecommunications
- Medical equipment
- Education services
- Personal care and beauty products
- Aviation
- Defense and security

EXPORTING FROM THAILAND

Major impediments to exporting from Thailand (in order of importance) are: Identifying potential markets and buyers, tariff barriers abroad, technical requirements and standards abroad, difficulties in meeting quality and/or quantity requirements of buyers, access to imported inputs at competitive prices, inappropriate production technology and skills, high cost or delays caused by international and/or domestic transportation, burdensome procedures at foreign borders, access to trade finance, rules of origin requirements abroad, corruption at foreign borders.

IMPORTATION TO THAILAND

Major impediments to importing to Thailand (in order of importance) are: Burdensome import procedures, tariffs and non-tariff barriers, high cost or delays caused by international transportation, corruption at the border, high cost or delays caused by domestic transportation, domestic technical requirements and standards, inappropriate telecommunications infrastructure, crime and theft.

Vietnam

Country Profile

Population: 98,721,275
Exports: $214.1 billion
Major Exports: clothes, shoes, electronics, seafood, crude oil, rice, coffee, wooden products, machinery
Export Partners: United States, China, Japan, South Korea
Imports: $202.6 billion
Major Imports: machinery, equipment, petroleum products, steel products, raw materials for clothing, electronics, plastics, automobiles
Import Partners: China, South Korea, Japan, Thailand
Trade as % GDP: Exports: 106.8%; Imports: 103.6%
Currency and Exchange Rate: 22,425 dong (VND) per U.S. dollar
GDP (official exchange rate): $220.4 billion
GDP per capita: $6,900
External Debt: $96.58 billion

FOREIGN IMPORT POLICIES

- *Entry of goods*: Vietnam implemented the WTO Customs Valuation Agreement through the 2006 Customs Law and related regulations, which improved its customs valuation process. Despite this positive step U.S. exporters continue to have concerns about other aspects of the customs clearance process, citing inefficiency, unclear rules and regulations, red tape, and corruption as the most common issues. The United States continues to work with Vietnam to monitor implementation of the WTO Customs Valuation Agreement.

- *Tariffs and taxes*: In 2018 Vietnam's average MFN applied rate was 9.5 percent, 16.5 percent for agricultural products and 8.4 percent for non-agricultural products. Vietnam has bound 100 percent of its tariff lines to the WTO, with a simple average WTO-bound tariff rate of 11.7 percent. Import licensing is also required on goods such as medical diagnostic devices and twenty-four medical treatment devices.
- *Non-tariff barriers*: Vietnam implements non-tariff barriers that include import bans and restrictions of some products including certain children's toys, second-hand consumer goods, and used parts for vehicles.
- *IPR protection*: Vietnam is a member of the WTO and WIPO. However, their IP enforcement mechanisms still need improvement. Vietnam remains on the Watch List in the USTR Special 301 Report.
- *Documentation requirements*: CITES certificate, health certificate and declaration, chemical analysis (CA) or Material Safety Data Sheet, Non-Dangerous Goods declaration letter, packing list, import certificate, import license, invoice, inventory list.
- *Distribution and sales channels*: Vietnam requires companies to own import licenses. If a company does not have an import license it is required to work through a licensed trader. With import rights a foreign-invested company can be the importer of record and sell its imported products to distributors, licensed wholesalers, or retailers, but not to the final consumer. Vietnam reserves the import rights for several product categories for state-owned companies.

BEST EXPORT PROSPECTS

Leading sectors for U.S. exports and investments are:

- ICT
- Power generation
- Education and training
- Franchising
- Aviation
- Defense
- Agribusiness
- Environmental and pollution control equipment and services
- Healthcare

EXPORTING FROM VIETNAM

Major impediments to exporting from Vietnam (in order of importance) are: Identifying potential markets and buyers, tariff barriers abroad, technical requirements and standards abroad, difficulties in meeting quality and/or quantity requirements of buyers, access to imported inputs at competitive prices, inappropriate production technology and skills, high cost or delays caused by international and/or domestic transportation, burdensome procedures at foreign borders, access to trade finance, rules of origin requirements abroad, corruption at foreign borders.

IMPORTATION TO VIETNAM

Major impediments to importing to Vietnam (in order of importance) are: Burdensome import procedures, tariffs and non-tariff barriers, high cost or delays caused by international transportation, corruption at the border, high cost or delays caused by domestic transportation, domestic technical requirements and standards, inappropriate telecommunications infrastructure, crime and theft.

A.4 TRADING OPPORTUNITIES IN EASTERN EUROPE

The Czech Republic

Country Profile

Population: 10,702,498
Exports: $144.8 billion
Major Exports: manufactured equipment, transport equipment, raw materials, fuel, chemicals
Export Partners: Germany, Slovakia, Poland, France, United Kingdom, Austria, Italy.
Imports: $134.7 billion
Major Imports: machinery equipment, transport equipment, raw materials, fuels, chemicals
Import Partners: Germany, Poland, China, Slovakia, Netherlands, Italy
Trade as % GDP: Exports: 75.5%; Imports: 69.4%
Currency and Exchange Rate: 23.34 koruny (CZK) per U.S. dollar
GDP (official exchange rate): $215.8 billion
GDP per capita: $35,500
External Debt: $205.2 billion

FOREIGN IMPORT POLICIES

- *Entry of goods*: The Czech Republic is a member of the EU. When products enter the EU, they need to be declared to customs according to their classification in the Combined Nomenclature (CN). The CN document is updated and published every year.
- *Tariffs and taxes*: U.S. exports to the EU enjoy an average tariff of 3 percent. The standard VAT rate is 21 percent. The first reduced VAT rate of 15 percent is charged for selected goods, such as food. The second reduced VAT rate of 10 percent applies mainly to books and medicines.
- *Non-tariff barriers*: Import licenses are required on sugar, coal, explosives, and firearms. The Czech Republic is a member of the EU and has harmonized its standards based on European and international norms.
- *IPR protection*: IPRs are generally adequately protected in the Czech Republic.
- *Documentation requirements*: Certificate of origin, declaration of conformity, import license, Material Safety Data Sheet, inventory list, commercial invoice.
- *Distribution and sales channels*: Foreign products are generally sold through agents and distributors.

BEST EXPORT PROSPECTS

Leading sectors for U.S. exports and investments are:

- Automotive parts and equipment
- Agricultural sector
- Education and training
- Pet and veterinary
- Medical equipment
- Energy
- Cosmetics/toiletries

EXPORTING FROM THE CZECH REPUBLIC

Major impediments to exporting from the Czech Republic (in order of importance) are: Identifying potential markets and buyers, technical requirements and standards abroad, tariff barriers abroad, access to trade finance, inappropriate production technology and skills, access to imported inputs at competitive prices, difficulties in meeting quality and/or quantity requirements of buyers, rules of origin requirements abroad, high cost or delays caused by international transportation, burdensome procedures at foreign borders, corruption at foreign borders, high cost or delays caused by domestic transportation.

IMPORTATION TO THE CZECH REPUBLIC

Major impediments to importing to the Czech Republic (in order of importance) are: Domestic technical requirements and standards, burdensome import procedures, tariffs and non-tariff barriers, high cost or delays caused by international transportation, inappropriate telecommunications infrastructure, high cost or delays caused by domestic transportation, crime and theft, corruption at the border.

Poland

Country Profile

Population: 38,282,325

Exports: $224.6 billion

Major Exports: machinery, transport equipment, intermediate manufactured goods, food, live animals

Export Partners: Germany, Czech Republic, United Kingdom, France, Italy, Netherlands

Imports: $223.8 billion

Major Imports: machinery equipment, transport equipment, intermediate manufactured goods, chemicals, minerals, fuels, lubricants

Import Partners: Germany, China, Russia, Netherlands, Italy, France, Czech Republic

Trade as % GDP: Exports: 55.8%; Imports: 50.5%

Currency and Exchange Rate: 3.748 zlotych (PLN) per U.S. dollar

GDP (official exchange rate): $524.8 billion

GDP per capita: $29,600

External Debt: $241 billion

FOREIGN IMPORT POLICIES

- *Entry of goods*: Poland is a member of the EU. When products enter the EU, they need to be declared to customs according to their classification in the Combined Nomenclature (CN).
- *Tariffs and taxes*: The duty rates applied to imports into Poland typically range between 0 percent (e.g., books) and 17 percent (e.g., Wellington boots). Some products, such as laptops, mobile phones, digital cameras and video game consoles, are duty free. Certain goods may be subject to additional duties depending on the country of manufacture, for example bicycles made in China carry an additional (anti-dumping) duty of 48.5 percent.
- *Non-tariff barriers*: Export subsidies to state-owned enterprises, product certification, and approval procedures that are not in line with international standards, domestic content requirements for goods purchased by the government are some of the non-tariff barriers in Poland. Import quotas apply to some agricultural products. Certificates are required for red meat and poultry products.
- *IPR protection*: Although adequate laws exist for the protection of IPRs, enforcement remains weak and has allowed for a certain degree of trademark and copyright infringement. A recent report (USTR, 2020) highlights online copyright piracy and inconsistent law enforcement by the courts and police.
- *Documentation requirements*: Certificate of origin, declaration of conformity, import license, Material Safety Data Sheet or Non-Dangerous Goods declaration letter, health certificate, commercial invoice, inventory list.
- *Distribution and sales channels*: Distribution and sales are handled by Polish agents or distributors.

BEST EXPORT PROSPECTS

Leading sectors for U.S. exports and investments are:

- Defense
- Advanced manufacturing
- Agriculture
- Green building products
- Environmental technologies
- Infrastructure and intelligent transportation systems
- Agricultural machinery and equipment
- Education
- Digital technologies

EXPORTING FROM POLAND

Major impediments to exporting from Poland (in order of importance) are: Identifying potential markets and buyers, technical requirements and standards abroad, difficulties in meeting quality and/or quantity requirements of buyers, rules of origin requirements abroad, access to trade finance, burdensome procedures at foreign borders, access to imported inputs at competitive prices, high cost or delays caused by international transportation, tariff barriers abroad, inappropriate production technology and skills, corruption at foreign borders, high cost or delays caused by domestic transportation.

IMPORTATION TO POLAND

Major impediments to importing to Poland (in order of importance) are: Burdensome import procedures, tariffs and non-tariff barriers, domestic technical requirements and standards, high cost or delays caused by international and domestic transportation, inappropriate telecommunications infrastructure, corruption at the border, crime and theft.

The Russian Federation (Russia)

Country Profile

Population: 141,722,205
Exports: $353 billion
Major Exports: petroleum, petroleum products, natural gas, metal, wood and wood products, chemicals, civilian manufactures, military manufactures.
Export Partners: China, Netherlands, Germany, Belarus, Turkey
Imports: $238 billion
Import Partners: China, Germany, United States, Belarus, Italy, France
Trade as % GDP: Exports: 28.3%; Imports: 20.8%
Major Imports: machinery, vehicles, pharmaceutical products, plastic, semi-finished metal products, meat, fruits, nuts, optical instruments, medical instruments, iron, steel
Currency and Exchange Rate: 58.39 Russian rubles (RUB) per U.S. dollar
GDP (official exchange rate): $1.578 trillion
GDP per capita: $27,900
External Debt: $539.6 billion

FOREIGN IMPORT POLICIES

- *Entry of goods*: Food and agricultural exports to Russia from the United States are not currently possible due to Russian counter-sanctions.
- *Tariffs and taxes*: Russia became a member of the WTO in August 2012, lowering the average bound tariff rate on industrial and consumer goods to 2.8 percent in 2017. Value-added tax (VAT) is generally 20 percent for most goods, work, and services. A 10 percent rate applies to certain food products, children's goods, certain medical and pharmaceutical products, pedigree, livestock and certain books and periodicals.
- *Non-tariff barriers*: Non-tariff barriers in Russia include bans on certain food and agricultural imports from countries such as Australia, Canada, the EU, Norway and the United States. Russia has a simplified licensing regime.
- *IPR protection*: Companies need to ensure that their IP is registered in Russia for rights to be enforceable under Russian law; However, Russia remains on the USTR's Special 301 Priority Watch List and continues to have substantial IPR violations.
- *Documentation requirements*: Government registration certificates (sanitary-epidemiological control), declaration of conformity, Material Safety Data Sheet, documents showing business registration number, contract between shipper and consignee.

- *Distribution and sales channels*: Distribution and sales are handled through Russia's well-organized distribution channels and distribution organizations.

BEST EXPORT PROSPECTS

Leading sectors for U.S. exports and investments are:

- Construction and infrastructure
- Cosmetics and perfumery ingredients
- Agricultural equipment
- Pharmaceuticals
- Medical equipment
- Information technologies
- Food processing and packaging
- Education and training
- Cosmetics and perfumery finished goods

EXPORTING FROM RUSSIA

Major impediments to exporting from Russia (in order of importance) are: Inappropriate production technology and skills, high cost or delays caused by international transportation, technical requirements and standards abroad, difficulties in meeting quality and/or quantity requirements of buyers, burdensome procedures at foreign borders, identifying potential markets and buyers, high cost or delays caused by international transportation, tariff barriers abroad, access to trade finance and/or imported inputs at competitive prices, rules of origin requirements abroad, corruption at foreign borders.

IMPORTATION TO RUSSIA

Major impediments to importing to Russia (in order of importance) are: Tariffs and non-tariff barriers, burdensome import procedures, high cost or delays caused by international and domestic transportation, corruption at the border, domestic technical requirements and standards, inappropriate telecommunications infrastructure, crime and theft.

A.5 TRADING OPPORTUNITIES IN WESTERN EUROPE

Denmark

Country Profile

Population: 5,869,410
Exports: $113.6 billion
Major Exports: wind turbines, pharmaceuticals, machinery, machinery instruments, meat, meat products, dairy products, fish, furniture, design
Export Partners: Germany, Sweden, United Kingdom, Norway, China, Netherlands
Imports: $94.93 billion
Major Imports: machinery, equipment, raw materials, semi manufactures for industry, chemicals, grain, foodstuffs, consumer goods

Import Partners: Germany, Sweden, Netherlands, China, Norway, Poland
Trade as % GDP: Exports: 55.9%; Imports: 49.1%
Currency and Exchange Rate: 6.586 Danish kroner (DKK) per U.S. dollar
GDP (official exchange rate): $25.6 billion
GDP per capita: $50,100
External Debt: $484.8 billion

FOREIGN IMPORT POLICIES

- *Entry of goods*: Denmark applies no unliteral trade barriers against the United States. Once goods have cleared customs in one EU country, they may circulate freely within the Union.

- *Tariffs and taxes*: Denmark has historically maintained a no-barrier policy and often takes the lead in the international fight against non-tariff barriers. Denmark is a member of the EU and has the best record of all EU countries regarding implementation of Single Market Directives. Duties typically vary from 5 percent to 14 percent on industrial goods. A value-added tax (VAT) of 25 percent is applied on a non-discriminatory basis to all goods and almost all services sold in Denmark.

- *Non-tariff barriers*: Most goods may enter Denmark free from restrictions. Import licenses, issued by the Ministries of Industry, Agriculture or Fisheries are required only for a limited range of items. Import licenses are required for agricultural products and textiles, as well as products originating in specified countries.

- *IPR protection*: There is adequate protection for IPRs in Denmark. The work is protected when it is created. No formal registration is necessary.

- *Documentation requirements*: Certificate of origin, declaration of conformity, import license, Material Safety Data Sheet, Non-Dangerous Goods declaration letter, health certificates, commercial invoice, inventory list.

- *Distribution and sales channels:* Methods of distribution vary from product to product. Capital goods, commodities, and industrial raw materials are handled by non-stock sales agents. High-tech and specialized products are handled by fully owned subsidiaries.

BEST EXPORT PROSPECTS

Leading sectors for U.S. exports and investments are:

- Franchising
- Travel and tourism
- Green building products
- Drugs and pharmaceuticals
- Computer software and information technologies
- Medical technology and dental equipment
- Oil and gas field machinery
- Agriculture
- Renewable energy products
- Education

EXPORTING FROM DENMARK

Major impediments to exporting from Denmark (in order of importance) are: Identifying potential markets and buyers, technical requirements and standards abroad, access to trade finance, tariff barriers abroad, burdensome procedures at foreign borders, rules of origin requirements abroad, inappropriate production technology and skills, high cost or delays caused by international transportation, corruption at foreign borders, access to imported inputs at competitive prices, difficulties in meeting quality and/or quantity requirements of buyers, high cost or delays caused by domestic transportation.

IMPORTATION TO DENMARK

Major impediments to importation to Denmark (in order of importance) are: Tariffs and non-tariff barriers, burdensome import procedures, domestic technical requirements and standards, high cost or delays caused by international transportation, inappropriate telecommunications infrastructure, high cost or delays caused by domestic transportation, crime and theft, corruption at the border.

France

Country Profile

> **Population:** 67,848,156
> **Exports:** $549.9 billion
> **Major Exports:** machinery, transport equipment, aircraft, plastics, chemicals, pharmaceutical products, iron, steel, beverages
> **Export Partners:** Germany, Spain, Italy, Belgium, United Kingdom
> **Imports:** $601.7 billion
> **Import Partners:** Germany, Belgium, Netherlands, Italy, Spain, United Kingdom, United States, China
> **Trade as % GDP:** Exports: 31.8%; Imports: 32.8%
> **Major Imports:** machinery and equipment, vehicles, crude oil, aircraft, plastics, chemicals
> **Currency Exchange Rate:** 0.885 euros (EUR) per U.S. dollar
> **GDP (official exchange rate):** $2.55 trillion
> **GDP per capita:** $44,100
> **External Debt: $5.6 trillion**

FOREIGN IMPORT POLICIES

- *Entry of goods*: When products enter the EU, they must be declared to customs according to their classification, which can be found in the Combined Nomenclature (CN) database, updated yearly.
- *Tariffs and taxes*: U.S. exports to the EU receive an average tariff of 3 percent.
- *Non-tariff barriers:* Non-EU imports of manufactured goods are subject to rates between 4.2–17.3 percent ad valorem, while raw materials enter with higher tariff rates. Most agricultural imports from non-EU countries are covered by the CAP and are subject to variable levies.

- *IPR protection*: To receive IP protection under French law, a patent or trademark must be registered in France. A trademark or patent registered in the United States will not protect against unauthorized use in France.
- *Documentation requirements*: health certificates, permit, import license, certificate of origin, declaration of conformity, Material Safety Data Sheet.
- *Distribution and sales channels*: Sales agents, branches, and subsidiaries are often used to import into France. Distributors also import foreign goods for resale.

BEST EXPORT PROSPECTS

Leading sectors for U.S. exports and investments are:

- Travel and tourism
- Computer services and software
- Ecommerce
- Education services
- Additive manufacturing
- Agriculture
- Civil aircraft and aviation
- Cosmetics
- Medical devices
- Textiles
- Telecommunications
- Computers and peripherals

EXPORTING FROM FRANCE

Major impediments to exporting from France (in order of importance) are: Identifying potential markets and buyers, access to imported inputs at competitive prices, burdensome procedures at foreign borders, tariff barriers abroad, access to trade finance, technical requirements and standards abroad, rules of origin requirements abroad, high cost or delays caused by international transportation, inappropriate production technology and skills, difficulties in meeting quality and/or quantity requirements of buyers, high cost or delays caused by domestic transportation, corruption at foreign borders.

IMPORTATION TO FRANCE

Major impediments to importation to France (in order of importance) are: Domestic technical requirements and standards, tariffs and non-tariff barriers, burdensome import procedures, high cost or delays caused by international and/or domestic transportation, inappropriate telecommunications infrastructure, corruption at the border, crime and theft.

Germany

Country Profile

Population: 80,159,662
Exports: $1.434 trillion

Major Exports: motor vehicles, machinery, chemicals, computer and electronic products, electrical equipment, pharmaceuticals, metals, transport equipment, foodstuffs, textiles, rubber, and plastic products

Export Partners: United States, France, China, Netherlands, United Kingdom, Italy, Austria, Poland, Switzerland

Imports: $1.135 trillion

Major Imports: machinery, data processing equipment, vehicles, chemicals, oil and gas, metals, electric equipment, pharmaceuticals, foodstuffs, agricultural products

Import Partners: Netherlands, China, France, Belgium, Italy, Poland, Czechia, United States, Austria, Switzerland

Trade as % GDP: Exports: 47.0%; Imports: 41.1%

Currency and Exchange Rate: 0.885 euros (EUR) per U.S. dollar

GDP (official exchange rate): $3.701 trillion

GDP per capita: $50,800

External Debt: $5.326 trillion

FOREIGN IMPORT POLICIES

- *Entry of goods*: Germany is a member of the EU and relies on several of the EU's policies and regulations on imported goods. Preferences are given to EU associate members, developing countries, and EFTA members. When products enter the EU, they need to be declared to customs according to their classification in the Combined Nomenclature (CN).
- *Tariffs and taxes*: The duty rates applied to imports into Germany typically range between 0 percent (e.g., books) and 17 percent (e.g., Wellington boots). The standard VAT rate for importing items into Germany is at minimum 17 percent. The standard VAT rate is 19 percent and a reduced 7 percent VAT rate applies to some consumer goods and everyday services.
- *Non-tariff barriers*: Prohibitions and restrictions are applicable in certain areas such as firearms and ammunition (weapons of riflemen, hunting weapons, prohibited items), fireworks, literature of unconstitutional content, pornography, food, narcotics, etc. Imports of certain agricultural products such as foodstuffs and textiles require specific import licenses. Some imports are subject to quantitative restrictions (e.g., meat) and/or the requirement for specific import licenses or confirmation that the manufacturer is licensed to export from the country of origin (e.g., apparel manufactured in developing countries). Specific import regulations may also apply to products under monopoly control (e.g., medicines).
- *IPR protection*: IPRs are generally well protected in Germany. However, the level of software piracy continues to be a source of concern.
- *Documentation requirements*: Health certificates, permit, import license, certificate of origin, declaration of conformity, Material Safety Data Sheet.
- *Distribution and sales channels*: Trade fairs are important tools for introducing new products and/or companies to the German market. Most imports to Germany move through import regional houses, wholesalers, and distributors. Direct sales are also common for machinery and equipment. Multinationals use branch offices (subsidiaries) to sell their products.

BEST EXPORT PROSPECTS

Leading sectors for U.S. exports and investments are:

- Smart cities
- Agriculture
- ICT
- Travel and tourism
- Healthcare
- Education and training
- Advanced manufacturing

EXPORTING FROM GERMANY

Major impediments to exporting from Germany (in order of importance) are: Burdensome procedures at foreign borders, tariff barriers abroad, rules of origin requirements abroad, identifying potential markets and buyers, high cost or delays caused by international transportation, corruption at foreign borders, technical requirements and standards abroad, access to imported inputs at competitive prices, access to trade finance, high cost or delays caused by domestic transportation, difficulties in meeting quality and/or quantity requirements of buyers, inappropriate production technology and skills.

IMPORTATION TO GERMANY

Major impediments to importation to Germany (in order of importance) are: Tariffs and non-tariff barriers, burdensome import procedures, domestic technical requirements and standards, high cost or delays caused by international and/or domestic transportation, crime and theft, corruption at the border, inappropriate telecommunications infrastructure.

Ireland

Country Profile

Population: 5,176,569

Exports: $219.7 billion

Major Exports: machinery and equipment, computers, chemicals, medical devices, pharmaceuticals, foodstuffs, animal products

Export Partners: United States, United Kingdom, Belgium, Germany, Switzerland, Netherlands, France

Imports: $98.13 billion

Major Imports: data processing equipment, other machinery and equipment, chemicals, petroleum and petroleum products, textiles, clothing

Import Partners: United Kingdom, United States, France, Germany, Netherlands

Trade as % GDP: Exports: 126.8%; Imports: 112.4%

Currency and Exchange Rate: 0.885 euros (EUR) per U.S. dollar

GDP (official exchange rate): $331.5 billion

GDP per capita: $73,200

External Debt: $2.47 trillion

FOREIGN IMPORT POLICIES

- *Entry of goods*: Ireland relies on several of the EU's policies and regulations on imported goods. Imports on farm products must follow regulations in accordance with the Common Agricultural Policy (CAP). All importers must fill in an intrastate declaration form before entering goods into Ireland (used to distinguish the country of origin of products based on EU states or non-EU states). Most duties are ad valorem, based on the GATT Valuation Code (CIF value).
- *Tariffs and taxes*: The duty rates applied to imports into Ireland typically range between 0 percent (e.g., books) and 17 percent (e.g., Wellington boots). The standard VAT rate for importing items into Ireland is 23 percent, with certain products, for example, newspapers and periodicals, attracting VAT at the reduced rate of 13.5 percent.
- *Non-tariff barriers:* Import licenses are required for a limited number of items including agricultural products. Phytosanitary certificates are also required for plants, some cut flowers, rooted plants and plant material, trees and shrubs. Imports of certain goods (including textiles, steel, footwear, ceramic products, toys, and porcelain and glass products) originating in certain non-EU countries are subject to either quantitative restrictions or surveillance measures. Imports from non-EU countries of products covered by the CAP may be subject to various charges.
- *IPR protection*: To receive IP protection under Ireland's law, a patent or trademark must be registered in Ireland. A trademark or patent registered in the United States will not protect against unauthorized use in Ireland.
- *Documentation requirements*: Declaration of conformity, import license, Material Safety Data Sheet.
- *Distribution and sales channels*: Agents, distributors, and representatives are used to import products into Ireland.

BEST EXPORT PROSPECTS

Leading sectors for U.S. exports and investments are:

- ICT
- Healthcare and medical devices
- Agriculture
- Education and training
- Travel and tourism
- Safety and security
- Oil and gas
- Cybersecurity
- Energy, power generation and smart grids

EXPORTING FROM IRELAND

Major impediments to exporting from Ireland (in order of importance) are: Identifying potential markets and buyers, access to trade finance, tariff barriers abroad, high cost or delays caused by international transportation, access to imported inputs at competitive prices, burdensome procedures at foreign borders, technical requirements and standards abroad, difficulties in meeting quality and/or quantity requirements of buyers, inappropriate production technology and skills, high cost or delays caused by domestic transportation, rules of origin requirements abroad, corruption at foreign borders.

IMPORTATION TO IRELAND

Major impediments to importation to Ireland (in order of importance) are: High cost or delays caused by international transportation, burdensome import procedures, domestic technical requirements and standards, high cost or delays caused by domestic transportation, inappropriate telecommunications infrastructure, tariffs and non-tariff barriers, crime and theft, corruption at the border.

Italy

Country Profile

Population: 62,402,659

Exports: $496.3 billion

Major Exports: engineering products, textiles and clothing, production machinery, motor vehicles, transport equipment, chemicals, foodstuffs, beverages, tobacco, minerals, nonferrous metals

Export Partners: Germany, France, United States, Spain, United Kingdom, Switzerland

Imports: $432.9 billion

Import Partners: Germany, France, China, Netherlands, Spain, Belgium

Major Imports: engineering products, chemicals, transport equipment, energy products, minerals and nonferrous metals, textiles and clothing, food, beverages, and tobacco

Trade as % of GDP: Exports: 31.6%; Imports: 28.5%

Currency and Exchange Rate: 0.885 euros (EUR) per U.S. dollar

GDP (official exchange rate): $1.939 trillion

GDP per capita: $38,200

External Debt: $2.44 trillion

FOREIGN IMPORT POLICIES

- *Entry of goods*: When products enter the EU they need to be declared to customs according to their classification in the Combined Nomenclature (CN).
- *Tariffs and taxes*: The duty rates applied to imports into Italy typically range between 0 percent (e.g., books) and 17 percent (e.g., Wellington boots). The standard VAT rate for importing items into Italy is 20 percent, with certain products, for example books, newspapers and magazines, attracting VAT at the super-reduced rate of 4 percent.
- *Non-tariff barriers:* Quotas are established on an EU basis for a range of goods such as textiles, agri-foods and steel and iron industry products. A particular certificate, "Titolo all'Importazione," must be requested from the Italian Ministry of Foreign Trade. Import licenses are required for a limited list of items and are issued by the Ministry of Foreign Trade. There are a number of Italian regulations and EU directives that prohibit certain foodstuffs, food colorings, drugs and narcotics, plant and animal products.

- *IPR protection*: To receive IP protection under Italian law, a patent or trademark must be registered in Italy. A trademark or patent registered in the United States will not protect against unauthorized use in Italy.
- *Documentation requirements:* Certificate of origin, CITES certificate, declaration of conformity, import license, Material Safety Data Sheet, health certificates, import permit, health permit, commercial invoice.
- *Distribution and sales channels*: Distributors transport consumer goods. Local agents who know the market generally handle promotion.

BEST EXPORT PROSPECTS

Leading sectors for U.S. exports and investments are:

- Education
- Automotive
- Natural gas
- Airport and ground support equipment
- Medical devices and technology
- Advanced manufacturing
- Agriculture
- Travel and tourism
- Pet products
- Education and training
- Cybersecurity
- Cosmetics and toiletries
- Biotechnology

EXPORTING FROM ITALY

Major impediments to exporting from Italy (in order of importance) are: Access to trade finance, identifying potential markets and buyers, burdensome procedures at foreign borders, access to imported inputs at competitive prices, tariff barriers abroad, high cost or delays caused by domestic transportation, corruption at foreign borders, inappropriate production technology and skills, difficulties in meeting quality and/or quantity requirements of buyers, technical requirements and standards abroad, high cost or delays caused by international transportation.

IMPORTATION TO ITALY

Major impediments to importation to Italy (in order of importance) are: Burdensome import procedures, tariffs and non-tariff barriers, domestic technical requirements and standards, high cost or delays caused by domestic transportation, inappropriate telecommunications infrastructure, high cost or delays caused by international transportation, crime and theft, corruption at the border.

The Netherlands

Country Profile

Population: 17,280,397
Exports: $555.6 billion

Major Exports: machinery, transport equipment, chemicals, mineral fuels, food, livestock, manufactured goods
Export Partners: Germany, Belgium, United Kingdom, France, Italy
Imports: $453.8 billion
Major Imports: machinery, transport equipment, chemicals, fuel, foodstuffs, clothing
Import Partners: China, Germany, Belgium, United States, United Kingdom, Russia
Trade as % GDP: Exports: 82.5%; Imports: 71.8%
Currency and Exchange Rate: 0.885 euros (EUR) per U.S. dollar
GDP (official exchange rate): $832.2 billion
GDP per capita: $53,900
External Debt: $4.063 trillion

FOREIGN IMPORT POLICIES

- *Entry of goods*: The Netherlands relies on several of the EU's policies and regulations on imported goods. Imports on farm products must follow regulations in accordance with the CAP.
- *Tariffs and taxes*: Import tariffs on manufactured goods from non-EU countries range from 0 percent (e.g., books) and 17 percent (e.g., Wellington boots). The standard VAT rate for importing items into the Netherlands is 21 percent, with certain products, for example books, newspapers and magazines, attracting VAT at the reduced rate of 6 percent.
- *Non-tariff barriers*: EU imports restrictions apply on certain imports. Quotas are established on an EU basis for a range of goods such as textiles, agri-foods, and steel and iron industry products.
- *IPR protection*: To receive IP protection under Netherlands law, a patent or trademark must be registered in The Netherlands. A trademark or patent registered in the United States will not protect against unauthorized use in The Netherlands.
- *Documentation requirements*: Certificate of origin, declaration of conformity, Material Safety Data Sheet, health certificate, import license.
- *Distribution and sales channels*: Distribution and sales are handled through importers, agents, and distributors. Certain consumer goods are imported directly by wholesalers and dealers or directly through department stores, retail cooperatives, consumer cooperatives, or other purchasing organizations.

BEST EXPORT PROSPECTS
Leading sectors for U.S. exports and investments are:

- Energy
- Automotive parts and service
- Equipment/accessories
- Healthcare products and services
- Advanced manufacturing
- Defense technology
- Franchising
- Recreational transportation
- Marine technology

- Software
- Agriculture
- Aircraft parts

EXPORTING FROM THE NETHERLANDS

Major impediments to exporting from the Netherlands (in order of importance) are: Identifying potential markets and buyers, access to trade finance, tariff barriers abroad, burdensome procedures at foreign borders, rules of origin requirements abroad, access to imported inputs at competitive prices, technical requirements and standards abroad, inappropriate production technology and skills, high cost or delays caused by international transportation, corruption at foreign borders, difficulties in meeting quality and/or quantity requirements of buyers, high cost or delays caused by domestic transportation.

IMPORTATION TO THE NETHERLANDS

Major impediments to importation to the Netherlands (in order of importance) are: Tariffs and non-tariff barriers, burdensome import procedures, domestic technical requirements and standards, high cost or delays caused by international and/or domestic transportation, crime and theft, inappropriate telecommunications infrastructure, corruption at the border.

The United Kingdom

Country Profile

Population: 65,761,117
Exports: $441.2 billion
Major Exports: manufactured goods, fuels, chemicals, food, beverages, tobacco
Export Partners: United States, Germany, France, Netherlands, Ireland, China, Switzerland
Imports: $615.9 billion
Major Imports: manufactured goods, machinery, fuels, foodstuff
Import Partners: Germany, United States, China, Netherlands, France, Belgium
Trade as % GDP: Exports: 31.5%; Imports: 32.7%
Currency and Exchange Rate: 0.7836 British pounds (GBP) per U.S. dollar
GDP (official exchange rate): $2.628 trillion
GDP per capita: $44,300
External Debt: $8.126 trillion

FOREIGN IMPORT POLICIES

- *Entry of goods*: Since leaving the EU, the United Kingdom has not yet adopted its own regime on tariffs and non-tariff barriers.
- *IPR protection*: The United Kingdom is a member of the WIPO and provides a high level of IPR protection. Enforcement is comparable to that in the United States.
- *Documentation requirements*: Certificate of origin, declaration of conformity, import license, Material Safety Data Sheet, health certificate, permit, veterinary inspection, shipping invoice.

- *Distribution and sales channels*: The distribution and sales channels of the United Kingdom are well developed and include wholly owned subsidiaries of foreign manufactures to independent trading companies that buy and sell on their own account. There are also independent resellers, sales agents, and stocking distributors who have contracts with the suppliers.

BEST EXPORT PROSPECTS

Leading sectors for U.S. exports and investments are:

- Defense equipment
- Travel and tourism
- Aerospace
- Agriculture
- Cyber security
- Medical equipment
- Education and training
- Smart grids

EXPORTING FROM THE UNITED KINGDOM

Major impediments to exporting from the United Kingdom (in order of importance) are: Identifying potential markets and buyers, access to trade finance, inappropriate production technology and skills, burdensome procedures at foreign borders, tariff barriers abroad, technical requirements and standards abroad, difficulties in meeting quality and/or quantity requirements of buyers, high cost or delays caused by international transportation, rules of origin requirements abroad, access to imported inputs at competitive prices, high cost or delays caused by domestic transportation, corruption at foreign borders.

IMPORTATION TO THE UNITED KINGDOM

Major impediments to importation to the United Kingdom (in order of importance) are: Domestic technical requirements and standards, high cost or delays caused by international transportation, burdensome import procedures, tariffs and non-tariff barriers, high cost or delays caused by domestic transportation, inappropriate telecommunications infrastructure, crime and theft, corruption at the border.

DATA	Year	Source(s)
Population	2020	CIA, *The World Factbook*
Exports		
Major Exports		
Export Partners		
Imports		
Major Imports		
Import Partners		
Currency and Exchange Rate		
GDP (official exchange Rate)		
GDP (per capita)		
External Debt		

DATA	Year	Source(s)
Trade as % GDP	2018	World Bank Database
Entry of Goods	2020	Office of the USTR, *2020 National Trade*
Tariffs		*Estimate Report on Foreign Trade Barriers*
Non-tariff Barriers		
Best Export Prospects	2020	Trade.gov
Distribution and Sales Channels		
IPR		
Documentation requirements		UPS.com
Major impediments to importation	2016	World Economic Forum, *The Global Enabling*
Major impediments to exportation		*Trade Report 2016*

Importing into the United States

IMPORTANT QUESTIONS

Section 1: Entry of Goods

1. Do I need a license to import goods into the United States?
2. What products are prohibited from importation?
3. What factors should be considered before importation?
4. What do you consider before importing goods through mail?
5. What are the specific requirements of a commercial invoice when clearing goods through customs?
6. What is consumption entry?
7. What is a formal entry and how do I file it?
8. What is general order merchandise?
9. Is Puerto Rico considered part of the customs territory of the United States?
10. Do the following items require an entry during importation?
    a. Articles exported from space within the purview of the Tariff Act of 1930.
    b. Domestic animals driven across a neighboring country by the owner for temporary pasturage and brought back within thirty days.
    c. Exported articles that are undeliverable (within forty-five days) and that are within the custody of the carrier or foreign customs service.
    d. Personal goods purchased while overseas.
11. What are some of the eligibility requirements for participation in the ABI program?
12. What is required of importers who are habitually late in paying bills to U.S. Customs?
13. Are there taxes or fees required to import goods into the United States other than customs duties?
14. Can a foreign company export to the United States without an importer of record in the U.S.?
15. If goods arrive at the port of Miami, can they be cleared at the port of Dallas (if the importer requires it)?

Section 2: Customs Bonds

1. When is a customs bond required?
2. How do you obtain a customs bond?
3. What are the two types of bond?
4. What are some of the ways in which a bond to ensure the exportation of merchandise may be cancelled?
5. Can a bond rider be used to terminate the bond?
6. What charges are supposed to be paid first on merchandise remaining in a bonded warehouse beyond the specified time?
7. What type of bond is used to indemnify the United States for detention of copyrighted material?

Section 3: Quota, Marking Requirements, and Trade Agreements

1. What is the difference between an absolute and a tariff quota?
2. Do most goods from USMCA countries enter duty free into the United States?
3. What countries are not eligible for normal trade relations (NTR) or most-favored-nation (MFN) duty rates?
4. What is a non-qualifying operation under USMCA?
5. What happens to imports that are not properly marked?
6. A shipment of beef valued at $5,000.00 is subject to a tariff quota. At the time of importation, a high tariff rate is in effect but a lower rate is soon expected. How can an importer take advantage of the lower rate?
7. When imported merchandise exceeds a tariff quota, the importer may not commingle the merchandise and classification with non-quota class goods. True or false?
8. What is the rate of duty on imports from GSP eligible countries?
9. A claim for preferential treatment under USMCA may be filed within one year from the date of importation of the goods. True or false?
10. What are the origin criteria for textiles and apparel products under USMCA?

Section 4: Value

1. What is value and what value is used for customs purposes?
2. What are the secondary bases of value if the transaction value cannot be use?
3. In establishing transaction value, what is to be included in the price?
4. What is an assist?
5. What should be excluded from transaction value?
6. What is the basis of appraisement for the following merchandise: A U.S. produce wholesaler imports avocados from Mexico on consignment. A few days after importation, the wholesaler sells the avocados (for $0.25 per avocado) to retailers and receives a 2 percent commission from the Mexican sellers. Customs has sufficient information to appraise the merchandise.
7. What is the transaction value of the shipment of 5,000 imported computer monitors with a per-unit price of $50 FOB? The manufacturer received from the importer, free of charge, design work produced in the United States and 5,000 U.S. originating modules to be incorporated in the production of the monitors. The costs are as follows: cost of acquiring design work: $10,000; cost

of transportation to place of production: $100.00; cost of acquiring modules: $75 each; cost of transportation of modules: $5,250.00

8. What is "identical merchandise"?

Section 5: Broker Compliance and Other Areas

1. Is a power of attorney required when a broker is acting as the importer of record?
2. When is a multiple country declaration required?
3. What rate of currency exchange should be used when foreign currency is converted?
4. What are the penalties for conducting customs business without a license? What are the penalties against any broker who a) continuously makes the same errors on a particular type of entry, b) does not have a working knowledge of customs operations to render valuable service?
5. What information should be on a bill of lading?
6. Is the commercial invoice required at the time of shipment?
7. How does the duty drawback claim work?
8. Are there laws governing labeling requirements for certain products?
9. Does an importer who sells merchandise to another company that exports it qualify for a duty drawback?
10. Does the firm qualify for a rejected merchandise drawback claim under the following conditions:
    a. A Miami firm imports 200 pounds of shrimp for its national network of seafood restaurants. When it opened the boxes, it found that they contained 200 pounds of pork.
    b. An importer of oranges finds thirty crates of unordered vegetables.
    c. A company in New York imports twenty cases of Argentine wine. There was a strike at the port and the wine was not unloaded for a few days. When the importer picked up the wines, they were frozen.

ANSWERS

Section 1: Entry of Goods

1. *Do I need a license to import goods into the United States?* No. However, for certain items such as food products, plant, animal and dairy products, prescription medications, etc. you may require a license or permit from various government agencies.
2. *What are some of the products that are prohibited from importation?* Certain narcotics, drug paraphernalia, counterfeit articles, obscene and immoral articles, as well as merchandise produced by convicts or through forced labor.
3. *What factors should be considered before importation?* It is important to verify whether an item is subject to quotas and other restrictions or permits, reduced rates of duty, marking of country of origin, as well as exclusive rights due to ownership of IPR by certain companies.
4. *What are the specific requirements of a commercial invoice when clearing goods through customs?* Description of the item, quantity, value (in foreign currency and U.S. dollars), country of origin, place of purchase, name and address of seller, and consignee.

5. *What do you consider before importing goods through mail?* Can the item be legally sent through the U.S. Postal Service, is the value less than $2,000.00 (since items valued at over $2,000.00 require a formal entry), and is the item subject to restrictions?

6. *What is consumption entry?* This is the most common type of entry and means imported goods that are intended for use in the United States or go directly into the commerce of the United States without any time or use restrictions. It may be formal or informal.

7. *What is a formal entry and how do I file it?* A formal entry is used for merchandise valued at over $2,000 and is supported by a surety bond to ensure payment of duties and compliance with customs regulations. The major difference between formal and informal entries is the bond requirement and liquidation process. As regards filing a formal entry, a) identify the port of entry, relevant product classification and tariff rate; b) find out if the products are subject to any special requirements (or if there are any special forms that apply) such as quota, visa, FDA, USMCA or GSP; c) ascertain the limit of liability for a customs bond. No more than a week before the expected arrival of the merchandise at the port or no later than ten days after arrival, fill out the appropriate forms (Form 5106, 7501, etc.), purchase a customs bond and submit to customs along with invoice, packing list, shipping documents, and a check. After processing, the merchandise may be subject for release or examination before release. The entry will be liquidated one year after release of merchandise. Until then, the bond or cash will be held as surety.

8. *What is general order merchandise?* Merchandise is considered general order merchandise when it is taken into the custody of the port director and deposited in the public stores or a general order warehouse at the risk and expense of the consignee for any of the following reasons: entry is not made within the time provided by customs regulations, entry is incomplete due to failure to pay the estimated duties, entry cannot be made for want of proper documents or other reasons, or merchandise is not correctly invoiced. The general order expires six months from the date of importation.

Such merchandise may be exported without examination or appraisement if the merchandise is delivered to the exporting carrier within six months of the date of importation. This merchandise may be entered within six months from the date of importation for immediate transportation to any port of entry designated by the consignee. After six months from the date of importation, entry for immediate transportation is allowed.

9. *Is Puerto Rico considered part of the customs territory of the United States?* Yes.

10. *Do the following items require an entry during importation:*
    a. *Articles exported from space within the purview of the Tariff Act of 1930?* No.
    b. *Domestic animals driven across a neighboring country by the owner for temporary pasturage and brought back after thirty days?* Yes.
    c. *Exported articles that are undeliverable (within forty-five days) and that are within the custody of the carrier or foreign customs service?* No.
    d. *Personal goods purchased while overseas?* Yes. Entries must be filed on a timely basis to avoid paying fees to the carrier and the bonded warehouse. Personal importations are generally cleared informally, that is, no bond is required. No duty is assessed if the goods are valued at less than $200. If the

goods are valued at more than $200, a duty as well as a processing fee will be assessed. Imports that require a permit from other government agencies are subject to a formal entry and the posting of a customs bond.

11. *What are some of the eligibility requirements for participation in the ABI program?* The basic eligibility requirements for participation are: the ability to demonstrate a reputable background and the basic skills for performing entry services; the ability to make a commitment for sending not less than 90 percent of entry/entry summary volume electronically; the ability to satisfactorily complete all of the qualification testing phases as outlined in the program; the ability to maintain operational standards for data quantity and quality; the ability to maintain timely updates.

12. *What is required of importers who are habitually late in paying bills to U.S. Customs?* The port director notifies the importer to file the entry summary with duties attached before release of merchandise.

13. *Are there taxes or fees required to import goods into the United States other than customs duties?* Yes. Here are some of them:
    a. Federal excise tax: importation of alcoholic beverages and tobacco
    b. Merchandise processing fee (MPF): Ad valorem fee of 0.21 percent for formal entries (minimum of $25.00 and maximum of $485.00). It is based on the value of merchandise being imported, not including duty, freight, and insurance. For informal entries, it ranges from $5.00 to $9.00 per shipment.
    c. Harbor maintenance fee (HMF): This is for merchandise transported by ship and is 0.125 percent of the value of the cargo. Goods arriving by ship are subject to both MPF and HMF.

14. *Can a foreign company export to the United States without an importer of record in the United States?* Yes. A resident agent, such as a broker in the state where the port of entry is located can enter goods on behalf of the corporation.

15. *If goods arrive at the port of Miami, can they be cleared at the port of Dallas (if the importer requires it)?* In general, entry must be filed at the first port of arrival. To clear goods in Dallas, however, an immediate transportation (IT) entry must be filed by a broker, carrier, or importer (that is bonded with customs). In Dallas, a consumption or warehouse entry must be filed for clearance from customs.

Section 2: Customs Bonds

1. *When is a customs bond required?* A customs bond is required for imported merchandise valued at over $2,000; goods subject to quota or visa restrictions, or other government requirements; transportation of cargo or passengers to the United States or domestic transportation of imported cargo from one state to another; when using bonded warehouse facilities for imported or exported goods.

2. *How do you obtain a customs bond?* Customs bonds are obtained through a surety licensed by the Treasury department. The list of licensed sureties is available online.

3. *What are the two major types of customs bond?* Continuous entry bond applications are made for multiple transactions while single entry bonds (SEBs) are used to secure the entry of a single customs transaction. Continuous bonds are 10 percent of duties paid for the last year; SEBs are generally in an amount

not less than the total entered value plus any taxes and duties. The minimum amount for SEBs is $100.

4. *What are some of the ways in which a bond to ensure the exportation of merchandise may be cancelled?* Listing of the merchandise on the outward manifest, inspector's certificate of lading, record of clearance of the vessel, production of a foreign landing certificate (when required by the port director).

5. *Can a bond rider be used to terminate the bond?* No. To be valid, a bond rider must be signed, sealed, witnessed, executed, and filed at the port of approval.

6. *What charges are supposed to be paid first on merchandise remaining in a bonded warehouse beyond the specified time?* Internal revenue taxes.

7. *What type of bond is used to indemnify the United States for detention of copyrighted material?* A single entry bond.

Section 3: Quotas, Marking Requirements, and Trade Agreements

1. *What is the difference between an absolute and a tariff quota?* When absolute quotas are filled, further entries are prohibited during the remainder of the quota period. While some quotas are allocated to specific foreign countries, others are global. If the quota is exceeded by quota entries, the commodity is released on a pro rata basis. Tariff quotas allow a certain amount of a commodity to be entered at a reduced tariff during the quota period. Quantities entered in excess of the quota for the period are subject to higher duty rates.

2. *Do most goods from USMCA countries enter duty free into the United States?* Yes. However, a proof of certificate of origin and/or country of origin marking on the goods is required. The manufacturer or seller of the goods should provide the importer with such a document.

3. *What countries are not eligible for normal trade relations (NTR) or most-favored-nation (MFN) duty rates?* Cuba and North Korea.

4. *What is a non-qualifying operation under USMCA?* Dismantling.

5. *What happens to imports that are not properly marked?* The goods are seized or a penalty issued.

6. *A shipment of beef valued at $5,000 is subject to a tariff quota. At the time of importation, a high tariff rate is in effect but a lower rate is soon expected. How can an importer take advantage of the lower rate?* A warehouse entry (type 21) can be filed and when the lower rate is effective, the merchandise can be withdrawn (type 32) and low duty paid.

7. *When imported merchandise exceeds a tariff quota, the importer may not commingle the merchandise and classification with non-quota class goods. True or false?* True.

8. *What is the rate of duty on imports from GSP eligible countries?* Zero.

9. *A claim for preferential treatment under USMCA may be filed within one year from the date of importation of the goods. True or false?* True.

10. *What are the origin criteria for textiles and apparel products under USMCA?* To be eligible for duty-free treatment, the yarn forward rule states that the yarn used to form the fabric must originate in a USMCA country.

Section 4: Value

1. *What is value and what value is used for customs purposes?* Value is the price paid or payable for goods. It includes selling commissions, assists, royalties, packing and proceeds. Duty is assessed on the price paid and does not include freight and insurance charges.
2. *What are the secondary bases of value if the transaction value cannot be used?* The secondary bases of value, in order of precedence are: transaction value of identical merchandise, transaction value of similar merchandise, deductive value, computed value.
3. *In establishing a transaction value, what is to be included in the price?* The packing costs incurred by the buyer; any selling commission incurred by the buyer; the value of any assist; any royalty or license fee that the buyer is required to pay as a condition of the sale; and the proceeds, accruing to the seller, of any subsequent resale, disposal, or use of the imported merchandise.
4. *What is an assist?* Items that the buyer of imported merchandise provides directly or indirectly, free of charge or at reduced cost, for use in the production or sale of merchandise (tools, dies, molds, engineering, development, artwork, design work, etc.) for export to the United States.
5. *What should be excluded from transaction value?* The cost, charges, etc. for transportation or insurance relating to the shipment of the goods to the United States; costs incurred for constructing, assembling, etc., or transportation of the goods after importation; and tariffs and taxes for which the seller is ordinarily liable.
6. *What is the basis of appraisement for the following merchandise: A U.S. produce wholesaler imports avocados from Mexico on consignment. A few days after importation, the wholesaler sells the avocados (for $0.25 per avocado) to retailers and receives a 2 percent commission from Mexican sellers. Customs has sufficient information to appraise the merchandise.* Deductive value.
7. *What is the transaction value of the shipment of 5,000 imported computer monitors with a per-unit price of $50 FOB? The manufacturer received from the importer, free of charge, design work produced in the United States and 5,000 U.S. originating modules to be incorporated in the production of the monitors. The costs are as follows: cost of acquiring design work: $10,000; cost of transportation to place of production: $100; cost of acquiring modules: $75 each; cost of transportation of modules: $5250.00.* The transaction value is $630,250.
8. *What is "identical merchandise"?* Identical in all respects to the merchandise being appraised; produced in the same country as the merchandise being appraised; or produced by the same person as the merchandise being appraised.

Section 5: Broker Compliance and Other Areas

1. *Is a power of attorney required when a broker is acting as the importer of record?* No. A CBP power of attorney executed by a partnership is valid for two years.
2. *When is a multiple country declaration required?* A multiple country declaration is required for merchandise that has been subject to manufacturing processes in more than one country.

3. *What rate of currency exchange should be used when foreign currency is converted?* The rate of exchange in effect on the date of exportation.
4. a.   *What are the penalties for conducting customs business without a license?* $10,000 for any one incident.
   b.   *What are the penalties against any broker who continuously makes the same errors on a particular type of entry?* $1,000.
   c.   *What are the penalties against a broker who does not have a working knowledge of customs operations to render valuable service?* $5,000.
5. *What information should be on a bill of lading?* Receipt of the goods, contract of carriage and commitment to deliver the goods at the designated port of destination to the holder of the bill of lading.
6. *Is the commercial invoice required at the time of shipment?* No. It is required at the time of entry.
7. *How does the duty drawback claim work?* Importers can get a refund of duty paid on imports when they are exported or destroyed. Proof of duty payment, export (bill of sale or air waybill) or destruction (witnessed by customs officer) is required. A drawback claim must be made within three years after the date of exportation. A post-importation NAFTA duty refund claim may be filed within one year after the date of importation of the goods.
8. *Are there laws governing labeling requirements for certain products?* Yes. Most textile, wool, and fur products, for example, must have a label or tag disclosing the fiber or fur content, importer, distributor, seller, country of origin, etc.
9. *Does an importer who sells merchandise to another company that exports it qualify for a duty drawback?* No.
10. *Does a firm qualify for a rejected merchandise drawback claim under the following conditions:*
    a.   *A Miami firm imports 200 pounds of shrimp for its national network of seafood restaurants. When it opened the boxes, it found that they contained 200 pounds of pork.* Yes.
    b.   *An importer of oranges finds thirty crates of unordered vegetables.* Yes.
    c.   *A company in New York imports twenty cases of Argentine wine. There was a strike at the port and the wine was not unloaded for a few days. When the importer picked up the wines, they were frozen.* No.

Trade Profiles of Selected Nations (2020) (US$ Million)

	Merchandise Trade		Services Trade		Trade (% of GDP)	
	Exports	Imports	Exports	Imports	Exports	Imports
Developed Countries						
Australia	270,923	221,564	69,168	70,228	24	22
Austria	179,021	184,964	74,555	63,534	56	52
Belgium	444,679	426,194	118,189	120,330	82	82
Canada	446,981	463,657	99,057	114,093	32	33
Denmark	110,779	97,824	74,320	71,075	56	49
Finland	73,463	73,643	34,013	35,928	40	40
France	569,727	651,128	287,084	262,821	32	33
Germany	1,489,152	1,234,454	335,249	362,973	47	41
Greece	37,887	62,309	44,957	21,130	37	37
Ireland	169,880	99,757	238,556	321,095	127	112
Italy	532,663	473,512	121,422	122,683	32	29
Japan	705,564	720,957	200,541	201,713	19	18
Netherlands	709,415	634,490	262,139	246,145	83	72
New Zealand	39,517	42,363	16,696	14,164	28	28
Norway	102,799	85,319	45,099	53,303	37	35
Spain	333,622	371,929	157,479	85,990	35	32
Sweden	160,575	158,762	76,197	73,643	47	44
Switzerland	313,934	277,830	119,597	103,761	66	53
United Kingdom	468,831	691,895	411,794	279,184	32	33
USA	1,643,161	2,567,445	853,270	564,276	12	15
High-Income Countries						
Chile	69,889	69,802	9,831	14,184	28	29
Korea	542,233	503,343	101,473	124,975	40	37
Kuwait	64,483	33,574	7,683	28,491	57	44
Malaysia	238,195	204,998	40,808	43,244	65	58
Mauritius	2,230	5,609	2,943	2,128	39	54

	Merchandise Trade		Services Trade		Trade (% of GDP)	
	Exports	Imports	Exports	Imports	Exports	Imports
Saudi Arabia	261,603	153,163	23,468	51,569	36	26
Singapore	390,763	359,266	204,509	198,819	174	146
Trinidad and Tobago	7,975	7,100	758	1,668	55	34
Middle-Income Countries						
Argentina	65,116	49,124	13,992	19,168	17	15
Botswana	5,233	6,564	821	877	34	41
Brazil	225,401	184,370	33,291	67,088	14	15
China	2,499,304	2,077,967	281,651	496,967	18	17
Colombia	39,460	52,703	9,756	13,496	16	22
Costa Rica	11,803	16,148	9,472	4,141	34	32
Egypt	28,993	70,919	24,253	20,153	19	29
Indonesia	167,497	170,727	30,872	39,323	18	19
Jamaica	1,586	6,339	4,300	2,623	38	51
Mexico	460,704	467,342	30,062	36,132	39	39
Peru	47,690	42,265	7,716	10,580	24	23
Philippines	70,927	112,909	40,972	27,389	28	40
Thailand	246,245	236,640	81,617	58,473	60	51
Turkey	180,836	210,343	64,130	26,813	32	30
Uruguay	7,680	8,246	4,454	4,060	22	19
Venezuela	17,190	5,830	772	6,884	17	31
Low-Income Countries						
Bangladesh	39,337	59,094	3,207	9,526	15	21
Ethiopia	2,761	14,554	4,536	4,151	8	21
Ghana	15,668	13,411	8,746	10,686	36	35
India	324,218	486,048	213,731	178,071	20	21
Kenya	5,839	17,655	4,390	3,440	12	21
Nigeria	62,531	55,257	4,485	38,854	16	18
Pakistan	23,334	50,349	4,217	8,835	10	20
Tanzania	4,967	8,601	4,104	1,882	15	17
Uganda	3,472	7,518	1,752	2,653	19	27
Vietnam	264,273	253,903	27,421	18,552	107	104
Zambia	7,047	7,225	1,014	1,473	35	35
Zimbabwe	4,269	3,500	394	695	19	31

Source: Adapted from the World Bank (2020). *World Development Indicators*. Washington, DC and World Trade Organization. *Trade Profiles 2020: Imports and Exports of Goods and Services* (% of GDP).

Applied, Weighted Mean Tariff Rates of Selected Countries (2014–2018)

Country	Year	Primary Products (%)	Manufactured Products (%)
Algeria	2018	9.8	10.0
Argentina	2018	1.8	8.6
Australia	2018	0.6	1.0
Brazil	2018	2.5	9.3
Cameroon	2014	11.1	14.2
Canada	2018	4.1	0.9
Chile	2018	0.5	0.5
China	2018	2.0	4.3
Colombia	2018	3.2	3.3
Egypt	2018	11.0	6.6
European Union	2018	1.5	1.8
Ghana	2018	14.7	8.9
India	2018	3.0	6.0
Indonesia	2018	2.3	1.9
Israel	2017	5.2	1.0
Korea (South)	2018	9.5	2.3
Malaysia	2016	3.5	4.3
Mexico	2018	0.6	1.4
New Zealand	2017	0.6	1.6
Nigeria	2016	8.3	8.7
Norway	2018	13.2	0.4
Peru	2018	1.3	3.0
Philippines	2018	4.5	1.3
Saudi Arabia	2017	9.5	3.8
Singapore	2018	0.8	0.0
Thailand	2015	5.7	2.9
Uganda	2018	14.3	6.2
USA	2018	1.7	1.6
Zambia	2018	.8	4.5

Source: Adapted from the World Bank (2020). *World Development Indicators*. Washington, DC: https://databank.worldbank.org/source/world-development-indicators

China: Import–Export Duties and Taxes

The following three types of tax are applicable to companies importing products from or exporting products to China:

1. Value-added tax;
2. Consumption tax; and
3. Customs duties.

VALUE-ADDED TAX FOR IMPORTED GOODS

From April 1, 2019, China's import VAT on imported goods has been lowered to either 9 percent or 13 percent, down from the previous 10 percent or 16 percent, according to the *Announcement of the State Taxation Administration (STA) on Deepening the Reform of VAT* (STA Announcement [2019] No. 39).

The 9 percent tax is available for certain goods that fall mainly within the categories of agricultural and utility items, while the 13 percent tax applies to other goods subject to VAT such as manufactured goods.

Taxable services provided by foreign entities or individuals in China are subject to 6 percent of VAT as before.

The import VAT can be calculated based on the following formula:

Import VAT = Composite Assessable Price × VAT Rate
= (Duty-Paid Price + Import Duty + Consumption Tax) × VAT Rate
= (Duty-Paid Price + Import Duty) / (1-Consumption Tax Rate) × VAT Rate

CONSUMPTION TAX FOR IMPORTED GOODS

China's consumption tax (CT) is imposed on companies and organizations who manufacture and import taxable products, process taxable products under consignment, or sell taxable products.

Imported products taxable under China's consumption tax include those that are harmful to one's health like tobacco or alcohol, luxury goods like jewelry and cosmetics, and high-end products, such as passenger cars and motorcycles.

For imported goods, the consumption tax varies depending on the type of product being brought into the country.

Calculating consumption tax can be done by using either the ad valorem method, quantity-based method, or the compound tax method. The formulas to compute the consumption tax are as follows:

- Ad valorem method

$$Consumption\ Tax\ Payable = Taxable\ Sales\ Amount \times Tax\ Rate$$

- Quantity-based method

$$Consumption\ Tax\ Payable = Taxable\ Sales\ Quantity \times Tax\ Amount\ per\ Unit$$

- Compound tax method

$$Consumption\ Tax\ Payable = Taxable\ Sales\ Amount \times Tax\ Rate + Taxable\ Sales\ Quantity \times Tax\ Amount\ per\ Unit$$

CUSTOMS DUTIES

Customs duties include import and export duties, with a total of 8,549 items taxed, according to the *Notice on the Tariff of Import and Export of PRC* (2020) (Tariff Commission Announcement [2019] No. 9).

Starting January 1, 2020, China has further adjusted parts of its customs duties, including MFN duty rates, temporary duty rates, conventional duty rates, etc., covering agricultural, medical, manufacturing, and information technology industries.

Import Duties

Duty rates on import goods consist of:

- General duty rates
- Temporary duty rates
- Most-favored-nation (MFN) rates
- Conventional duty rates
- Special preferential duty rates
- Tariff rate quota (TRQ) duty rates.

GENERAL DUTY RATES
General duty rates are applied to imported goods originating from countries or territories that are not covered in any agreements or treaties or are of unknown places of origin.

TEMPORARY DUTY RATES
China also sets temporary duty rates for certain imported goods in order to boost imports and meet domestic demand.

According to the *Notice on Adjustment Plan of Import Temporary Tax Rate in 2020* (Shui Wei Hui [2019] No. 50), starting January 1, 2020, China has implemented temporary tax rates on a total of 859 imported commodities, which are even lower than the MFN tariffs, including on raw materials of anti-cancer drugs, diapers, some frozen foods, and kaolin.

MFN DUTY RATES

Most-favored-nation rates are the most commonly adopted import duty rates. They are much lower than the general rates, which apply to non-MFN nations. They apply to goods:

- imported to China from WTO member countries;
- originating from countries or territories that have concluded bilateral trade agreements containing provisions on MFN treatment with China; and
- originating from China.

From July 1, 2020, MFN duty rates on 176 of 484 information technology products have been further reduced, including on medical diagnosis machines, speakers, and printers.

CONVENTIONAL DUTY RATES

Conventional duty rates are applied to imported goods that originate from countries or territories that have entered into regional trade agreements containing preferential provisions on duty rates with China.

So far, China has signed bilateral or multilateral free trade agreements with more than twenty countries or regions. Imported goods originating in these countries and regions will be subject to conventional duty rates, which are normally lower than the MFN duty rates.

From January 1, 2020, China has reduced conventional duty rates with New Zealand, Peru, Costa Rica, Switzerland, Iceland, South Korea, Australia, Georgia, and Asia-Pacific Trade Agreement countries. From July 1, 2020, China further reduced the conventional duty rate with Switzerland.

Except for the products to which mainland China has made special commitments in relevant international agreements, zero tariffs will be applied to all products originating in Hong Kong and Macao (please refer to the tariff list of the Ministry of Commerce).

SPECIAL PREFERENTIAL DUTY RATES

Special preferential duty rates are applied to imported goods originating from countries or territories with trade agreements containing special preferential duty provisions with China.

TARIFF RATE QUOTA DUTY RATES

Under tariff rate quota (TRQ) schemes, goods imported within the quota are subject to a lower tariff rate, and goods imported beyond the quota are subject to higher tariff rates.

For example, the TRQ rate for importing wheat products within the quota is as low as 1, 6, 9, or 10 percent—substantially lower than the MFN duty rate of 65 percent and the general duty rate, which is as high as 130 percent or even 180 percent.

Export Duties

Export duties are only imposed on a few resource products and semi-manufactured goods. From January 1, 2020, China continued to impose export tariffs or imposed provisional export duties on 107 export commodities with fixed and unchanged tax rates. Among them, the provisional export tax rate was canceled for 94 taxable items, such as fertilizer, apatite, iron ore, etc.

OTHER DUTY RATES

Considerably higher rates may be implemented according to Chinese regulations regarding dumping, anti-subsidies, and safeguard measures. Retaliatory tariffs could also be applied to goods originating from countries or regions that violate trade agreements.

Over the course of the U.S.–China trade war, China has imposed retaliatory tariffs on US$185 billion worth of U.S. goods, including beef, lamb, pork, vegetables, juice, cooking oil, tea, coffee, refrigerators, and furniture, among many others.

DUTY RELIEF FOR KEY TECHNICAL EQUIPMENT

At the end of 2019, China released the *Catalog of State-supported Key Technical Equipment and Products* (2019 version) and the *Catalog of Imported Key Components and Raw Materials of Key Technical Equipment and Products (*2019 version), which took effect on January 1, 2020.

Importing certain key components and raw materials or exporting certain key technical equipment and products listed in the catalog to eligible Chinese domestic enterprises is exempt from import VAT and customs duties.

DUTY PAYING VALUE FOR IMPORTED GOODS

The amount of import taxes and customs duty payable is calculated based on the price or value of the imported goods. This value is called the duty paying value (DPV).

The DPV is determined based on the transacted price of the goods—that is, the actual price directly and indirectly paid or payable by the domestic buyer to the foreign seller, with certain required adjustments.

The DPV includes transportation-related expenses and insurance premiums on the goods prior to unloading at the place of arrival in China. Import duties and taxes collected by customs are excluded from DPV.

CALCULATING IMPORT–EXPORT TAXES AND DUTIES PAYABLE

Import Duties

Import taxes and duties payable can be calculated after determining the DPV and the tax and tariff rates of the goods. Similar to consumption tax, customs duties are also computed either on an ad valorem basis, quantity basis, or compound formula. The formulae are:

- Ad valorem basis:

$$Duty\ payable = DPV\ x\ Tariff\ rate$$

- Quantity-based:

$$Duty\ payable = Quantity\ of\ imported\ goods\ x\ Amount\ of\ duty\ per\ unit$$

- Compound formula:

$$Duty\ payable = DPV\ x\ Tariff\ rate + Quantity\ of\ imported\ goods\ x$$
$$Amount\ of\ duty\ per\ unit$$

Import taxes and duty payable should be calculated in RMB using the benchmark exchange rate published by the People's Bank of China.

Export Duties

The tax base for export duties is the same as import duties—that is, the DPV.

The DPV for export duties is based on the transacted price: the lump sum price receivable by the domestic seller exporting the goods to the buyer.

Export duties, freight-related expenses, and insurance fees after loading at the export spot, and commissions borne by the seller, are excluded.

U.S. Trade Profile

TABLE F.1 U.S. International Trade in Goods and Services, 2014–2019

	2014	2015	2016	2017	2018	2019
TRADE BALANCE						
Trade, total	-484,184	-491,261	-481,169	-513,791	-579,937	-576,865
Goods	-749,917	-761,868	-749,801	-799,343	-880,301	-864,331
Services	265,733	270,607	268,632	285,552	300,364	287,466
EXPORTS						
Export, total	2,392,268	2,279,743	2,237,923	2,387,391	2,540,383	2,528,262
Goods	1,635,563	1,511,381	1,457,393	1,557,003	1,676,950	1,652,437
Services	756,705	768,362	780,530	830,388	863,433	875,825
Travel	180,265	192,602	192,868	193,834	196,465	193,315
Transportation	90,687	84,434	81,779	86,342	196,465	193,315
Charges for the use of intellectual property	116,380	111,151	112,981	118,147	118,875	117,401
Other business services	132,240	141,421	152,089	167,270	177,261	189,441
Financial services	119,933	114,951	114,762	128,035	132,240	13,698
Government goods & services	19,693	20,087	18,777	19,924	21,949	22,555
Maintenance & repair services	17,978	19,847	21,587	23,239	27,948	27,868

TABLE F.1 Cont.

	2014	2015	2016	2017	2018	2019
IMPORTS						
Import, total.	2,876,412	2,771,004	2,719,093	2,901,243	3,119,320	3,105,126
Goods	2,385,480	2,273,249	2,207,195	2,356,345	2,557,251	2,516,767
Services	490,932	497,755	511,898	544,898	562,069	588,359
Travel	96,248	102,664	109,155	117,972	126,008	134,594
Transportation	99,810	99,557	92,391	96,515	106,303	107,458
Charges for the use of intellectual property	37,562	35,178	41,974	44,405	43,933	42,733
Other business services	90,716	95,119	100,505	106,991	107,834	113,584
Financial services	32,770	32,594	32,672	26,649	39,249	40,350
Government goods & services	24,236	21,531	21,503	22,047	22,975	24,083
Maintenance & repair services	6,732	8,084	7,595	6,796	7,133	7,823

Source: Bureau of Economic Analysis, U.S. Department of Commerce, U.S. International Trade in Goods and Services, Release October 6, 2020.

TABLE F.2 U.S. Exports and Imports with Selected Countries, 2018–2020 US$ Million)

Country	U.S. Exports			U.S. General Imports		
	2018	2019	2020	2018	2019	2020
Total	1,665,689	1,643,161	924,252	2,537,729	2,497,532	1,493,770
Argentina	9,908	8,152	3,891	5,822	4,917	2,861
Australia	25,334	25,990	15,338	10,081	10,845	10,185
Austria	3,564	5,709	2,163	13,573	13,162	7,244
Belgium	31,410	34,726	18,492	17,176	20,164	13,125
Brazil	39,409	42,853	22,577	31,214	30,844	14645
Canada	299,732	292,633	163,112	318,521	319,428	172,157
Chile	15,312	15,728	8,496	11,385	10,393	6,854
China	120,289	106,447	69,564	539,243	451,651	262,681
Colombia	15,114	14,747	7,991	13,753	14,166	6,965
Costa Rica	6,470	6,219	3,821	4,891	5,147	3,404
Cote d'Ivoire	310	279	141	1,249	924	689
Czech Rep.	3,003	2,791	1,888	4,993	5,525	3,543
Denmark	2,608	3,195	2,150	8,857	11,010	7,840
Ecuador	5,903	5,536	2,832	6,738	6,954	3,824
Egypt	5,052	5,484	3,219	2,480	3154	1,453
El Salvador	3,391	3,369	1,674	2,510	2,480	1,124
Ethiopia	1,308	1,014	434	445	572	343
Finland	1,881	1,768	1070	7162	6,384	2,979
France	36,589	37,718	18,504	52,443	57,593	28,642
Georgia	478	769	295	190	153	92
Germany	57,758	60,112	37,261	125,784	127,507	73,097
Ghana	769	840	523	581	943	476
Greece	1,084	11442	944	1606	1513	871
Honduras	5,594	5,440	2,567	4,693	4,824	2,417
Hong Kong	37,311	30,783	15,258	6,274	4,735	6,757
Hungary	1,750	1,914	1,386	5,063	5,310	3,208
Iceland	670	555	196	430	483	268
India	33,191	34,288	17,125	54,282	57,694	31,043
Indonesia	8,171	7,733	4850	20,829	20,147	13,218
Iran	426	77	27	70	1	3
Iraq	1,312	1,190	498	11,872	7,025	2,622
Ireland	10,745	9,058	6,149	57,450	61,895	42,847
Israel	13,709	14,405	6,806	21,777	19,508	10,019
Italy	22,844	23,839	13,264	54,699	57,264	31,145
Japan	75,149	74,377	43,243	142,242	143,566	75,144
Jordan	1,581	1,483	883	1,814	2,170	1,210
Kenya	365	402	243	643	667	381
Korea, South	56,310	56,539	34,690	74,244	77,470	48,661
Kuwait	2,974	3,171	1,454	2,974	1,418	506
Morocco	3,000	3,496	1,516	1,553	1,583	794
Netherlands	48,561	51,108	29,848	24,513	29,719	17,705
New Zealand	4,060	3,948	2,069	4,188	4,114	2,953
Nicaragua	1,629	1,652	886	3,580	3,884	2,283

TABLE F.2 Cont.

Country	U.S. Exports			U.S. General Imports		
	2018	2019	2020	2018	2019	2020
Nigeria	2,687	3,200	1,901	5,616	4,610	931
Norway	5,424	3,894	1,881	6,785	6,511	2,577
Panama	6,733	7,534	3,860	420	452	237
Paraguay	2,257	2,108	728	131	162	93
Peru	9,695	9,668	4,846	7,886	6,144	3,308
Philippines	8,716	8,642	5,182	12,592	12,778	6,975
Poland	5,358	59554	3,347	8,013	8,377	5,775
Portugal	1,573	1,716	914	3,886	3,894	2,607
Qatar	4,428	6,457	2,212	1,571	1,695	796
Russia	6,658	5,785	3,065	20,851	22,260	11,055
Saudi Arabia	13,597	14,486	7,243	24,066	13,405	6,965
Senegal	289	197	160	127	131	63
Singapore	32,881	31,218	18,167	26,524	26,398	21,554
Slovakia	289.3	389	223	4,160	5,149	2,446
Slovenia	322	344	141	847	963	815
South Africa	5,531	5,368	2,932	8466	7,800	7,509
Spain	13,064	15,208	8,787	17,209	16,787	10,337
Sri Lanka	871	390	245	2,669	2,749	1,583
Sweden	4,471	4,368	3,250	10,992	12,130	7,948
Switzerland	22,172	17,896	10,733	41,091	44,644	55,237
Taiwan	30,480	31,294	19,918	45,732	54,253	38,108
Tanzania	332	333	157	97	130	92
Thailand	12,520	13,299	7606	31,863	33,447	23,944
T. & Tobago	2,118	2,801	1,676	3,672	3426	1595
Tunisia	597	461	259	649	470	384
Turkey	10,254	10,033	6,952	10,308	10,631	7,005
Uganda	88	104	65	69	80	58
Ukraine	2,487	2,355	1,211	1,352	1,296	827
United Kingdom	66,455	69,078	38,511	60,697	63,219	32,535
Uruguay	1,384	1,617	895	508	519	380
Venezuela	6,074	1,289	684	13,194	1,933	110
Vietnam	9,676	10,861	6,619	49,159	66,630	48,979
Zambia	195	99	49	190	83	32
Zimbabwe	34	40	30	75	47	21

Source: U.S. Census Bureau, 2020, www.census.gov/foreign-trade/balance/index.html

TABLE F.3 U.S. Exports and General Imports by Selected Standard International Trade Classification (SITC) Commodity Groups, 2018–2020 (US$ Million)

Selected Commodity	US Exports			US General Imports			US Trade Balance		
Unit indicator	2018	2019	2020	2018	2019	2020	2018	2019	2020
Total Balance of Payment Basis (2)	970,474	1,100,813	920,816	1,461,063	1,682,866	1,491,370	–490,589	–582,053	–570,554
Total Census Basic (2)	965,598	1,094,383	918,034	1,449,353	1,669,627	1,482,512	–483,755	–575,244	–564,478
Manufactured goods (3)	673,845	753,066	622,717	1,242,329	1,442,571	1,306,618	–568,484	–689,505	–683,901
Agricultural commodities (3)	82,799	89,862	87,026	77,036	89,085	90,333	5,763	777	–3,307
Food and Live Animals	60,359	66,607	66,071	66,871	78,107	79,816	–6,512	–11,500	–13,745
Live animals other than fish	424	558	506	1,545	1,939	1,813	–1,121	–1,381	–1,307
Meat and preparations	11,092	12,574	12,856	5,590	6,549	7,078	5,502	6,025	5,778
Dairy products and birds' eggs	2,862	3,282	3,817	1,240	1,536	1,516	1,622	1,746	2,301
Fish and preparations	2,748	3,159	2,575	12,520	14,390	13,838	–9,772	–11,231	–11,263
Cereals and preparations	15,046	14,907	15,418	5,930	7,017	7,564	9,116	7,890	7,854
Vegetables and fruit	12,563	14,348	13,436	22,463	25,812	26,391	–9,900	–11,464	–12,955
Sugars, preparations, and honey	1,155	1,276	1,159	2,781	3,116	3,458	–1,626	–1,840	–2,299
Coffee, tea, cocoa, and spices	1,694	1,958	1,721	7,891	9,195	9,102	–6,197	–7,237	–7,381

(continued)

TABLE F.3 Cont.

Selected Commodity	US Exports			US General Imports			US Trade Balance		
Unit indicator	2018	2019	2020	2018	2019	2020	2018	2019	2020
Feeding stuff for animals	7,353	7,936	8,165	1,955	2,222	2,361	5,398	5,714	5,804
Miscellaneous edible products	5,423	6,610	6,418	4,956	6,333	6,696	467	277	−278
Beverages and Tobacco	**3,955**	**3,978**	**3,641**	15,005	18,472	17,091	−11,050	−14,494	−13,450
Beverages	3,085	3,292	3,003	13,849	17,100	15,861	−10,764	−13,808	−12,858
Tobacco, manufactures	871	686	638	1,156	1,371	1,230	−285	−685	−592
Crude Materials Except Fuels	**45,960**	**48,829**	**42,798**	22,048	23,826	21,187	**23,912**	**25,003**	**21,611**
Hides, skins, and fur skins, raw	965	746	572	41	33	36	924	713	536
Oil seeds and oleaginous fruits	10,975	11,961	9,802	692	708	766	10,283	11,253	9,036
Crude rubber	1,615	1,564	1,208	1,896	2,180	1,647	−281	−616	−439
Cork and wood	4,724	4,259	3,793	5,452	4,949	5,302	−728	−690	−1,509
Pulp and waste paper	5,250	5,804	4,946	2,152	2,544	1,949	3,098	3,260	2,997
Textile fibers, including waste	6,136	6,119	5,389	793	921	764	5,343	5,198	4,625
Crude fertilizers	1,803	1,842	1,494	1,904	2,092	1,810	−101	−250	−316
Metalliferous ores and metal scrap	12,522	14,319	13,567	5,378	6,243	5,124	7,144	8,076	8,443
Crude animal vegetable materials	1,971	2,214	2,027	3,740	4,155	3,786	−1,769	−1,941	−1,759

Mineral Fuels and Lubricants	**107,286**	**128,510**	**102,205**	136,556	139,155	81,517	−29,270	−10,645	20,688
Coal, coke, and briquettes	7,324	7,354	4,184	497	598	523	6,827	6,756	3,661
Petroleum products and preparations	84,430	101,459	77,957	129,114	131,064	75,956	−44,684	−29,605	2,001
Gas, natural and manufactured	15,334	19,364	19,930	5,612	6,214	3,796	9,722	13,150	16,134
Electric current	198	333	134	1,334	1,279	1,242	−1,136	−946	−1,108
Animal and Vegetables Oils	**1,586**	**1,573**	**1,966**	4,116	4,112	4,335	−2,530	−2,539	−2,369
Animal oils and fats	395	488	604	161	236	241	234	252	363
Fixed vegetable fats	1,035	933	1,160	3,821	3,704	3,923	−2,786	−2,771	−2,763
Animal or vegetable fats, processed	156	152	202	134	172	172	22	−20	30
Chemicals and Related Products	**121,040**	**142,069**	**129,536**	150,916	180,923	185,900	−29,876	−38,854	−56,364
Organic chemicals	22,042	24,466	21,482	30,718	33,815	34,215	−8,676	−9,349	−12,733
Inorganic chemicals	6,736	7,206	6,780	6,847	8,217	6,659	−111	−1,011	121
Dyeing, tanning, and coloring materials	4,515	4,906	4,206	2,583	2,916	2,770	1,932	1,990	1,436
Medicinal and pharmaceutical products	27,128	35,839	33,198	69,300	88,974	97,681	−42,172	−53,135	−64,483
Essential oils and resinoids	9,678	11,276	10,271	9,778	11,119	10,479	−100	157	−208
Fertilizers	1,794	2,193	1,893	3,846	4,856	3,672	−2,052	−2,663	−1,779
Plastics in primary forms	21,219	24,251	21,430	10,401	10,976	9,087	10,818	13,275	12,343

(continued)

TABLE F.3 Cont.

Selected Commodity	2018	2019	2020	2018	2019	2020	2018	2019	2020
Unit indicator	US Exports			US General Imports			US Trade Balance		
Plastics in nonprimary forms	8,231	9,104	8,110	6,899	7,869	7,608	1,332	1,235	502
Chemical materials and products	19,697	22,827	22,166	10,545	12,179	13,729	9,152	10,648	8,437
Manufactured Goods by Material	**66,127**	**70,907**	**59,313**	161,869	176,134	158,082	**-95,742**	**-105,227**	**-98,769**
Leather and leather manufactures	550	545	347	839	871	662	-289	-326	-315
Rubber manufactures (4)	5,529	6,404	4,994	12,952	15,324	12,308	-7,423	-8,920	-7,314
Cork and wood manufactures	1,197	1,287	1,101	7,532	7,465	7,277	-6,335	-6,178	-6,176
Paper and paperboard	9,455	9,952	9,085	10,008	11,570	10,204	-553	-1,618	-1,119
Textile yarn, fabrics	7,305	8,179	6,376	17,325	20,230	28,969	-10,020	-12,051	-22,593
Nonmetalic mineral manufactures (4)	7,869	8,021	6,988	28,428	30,146	19,856	-20,559	-22,125	-12,868
Iron and steel	8,994	8,283	6,471	23,655	23,133	15,565	-14,661	-14,850	-9,094
Nonferrous metals	9,855	10,428	9,598	27,791	28,104	27,816	-17,936	-17,676	-18,218
Manufactures of metals	15,371	17,807	14,352	33,338	39,290	35,425	-17,967	-21,483	-21,073
Machinery and Transport Equipment	**300,985**	**338,887**	**263,445**	605,649	703,031	591,365	**-304,664**	**-364,144**	**-327,920**

Power-generating machinery (4)	20,561	24,400	19,553	42,884	53,391	41,338	-22,323	-28,991	-21,785
Specialized industrial machinery	29,463	30,310	28,000	31,908	39,477	31,976	-2,445	-9,167	-3,976
Metalworking machinery	3,113	3,281	2,379	6,614	7,498	6,019	-3,501	-4,217	-3,640
General industrial machinery	35,839	41,161	34,753	64,032	74,098	63,732	-28,193	-32,937	-28,979
Office machines	11,329	11,865	10,520	78,179	82,328	86,682	-66,850	-70,463	-76,162
Telecommunications equipment (4)	11,943	13,228	10,484	86,797	94,584	84,079	-74,854	-81,356	-73,595
Electrical machinery (4)	46,792	53,030	49,161	107,878	123,182	114,321	-61,086	-70,152	-65,160
Road vehicles	69,921	81,028	57,677	166,758	202,910	142,415	-96,837	-121,882	-84,738
Transport equipment (4)	72,024	80,583	50,917	20,599	25,563	20,803	51,425	55,020	30,114
Miscellaneous Manufactured Articles	**72,887**	**83,858**	**68,703**	224,287	268,063	247,114	**-151,400**	**-184,205**	**-178,411**
Prefabricated buildings	1,424	1,607	1,245	8,239	9,011	7,674	-6,815	-7,404	-6,429
Furniture (4)	3,660	4,031	2,910	30,905	34,007	29,707	-27,245	-29,976	-26,797
Travel goods	410	448	310	6,494	7,177	5,229	-6,084	-6,729	-4,919
Apparel and clothing accessories	1,769	2,177	1,477	51,102	63,033	49,464	-49,333	-60,856	-47,987
Footwear	536	764	505	15,349	18,580	13,522	-14,813	-17,816	-13,017
Scientific and controlling equipment (4)	29,238	33,865	30,382	34,985	42,487	39,539	-5,747	-8,622	-9,157
Photographic equipment	3,825	4,385	3,871	8,620	10,005	7,718	-4,795	-5,620	-3,847

(continued)

TABLE F.3 Cont.

Selected Commodity / Unit indicator	US Exports			US General Imports			US Trade Balance		
	2018	2019	2020	2018	2019	2020	2018	2019	2020
Miscellaneous manufactured articles	32,024	36,581	28,004	68,593	83,763	94,260	-36,569	-47,182	-66,256
Miscellaneous Commodities	**38,990**	**41,738**	**39,268**	62,036	77,805	96,056	-23,046	-36,067	-56,788
Special transactions	5,606	6,684	5,836	45,163	59,310	54,233	-39,557	-52,626	-48,397
Coin, including gold coin	123	134	190	457	573	1,303	-334	-439	-1,113
Coin, other than gold	4	10	31	12	15	15	-8	-5	16
Gold, nonmonetary	13,107	11,335	11,732	6,007	5,401	29,380	7,100	5,934	-17,648
Low value estimate	20,150	23,576	21,480	10,397	12,505	11,124	9,753	11,071	10,356
Re-Exports	**146,422**	**167,429**	**140,942**	(X)	(X)	(X)	(X)	(X)	(X)
Manufactured goods (3)	139,069	160,124	135,410	(X)	(X)	(X)	(X)	(X)	(X)
Agricultural commodities (3)	2,892	3,221	3,181	(X)	(X)	(X)	(X)	(X)	(X)

SYMBOL
X Not applicable.

Notes
X = Not applicable
(1) Free alongside ship basis.
(2) Total exports including re-exports (exports of foreign merchandise).
(3) Manufactured Goods is based on the North American Industry Classification System (NAICS) and Agricultural Commodities is based on the Harmonized System commodities specified by the U.S. Department of Agriculture definition. All other commodity detail is based on the SITC.
(4) Export statistics for certain commodity classifications related to the aircraft industry are subject to suppression and have been aggregated in a manner that prevents the disclosure of confidential information.

Source: U.S. Census Bureau (2020). www.census.gov

Export Credit Agencies in Selected Countries

CANADA: EXPORT DEVELOPMENT CORPORATION

The Export Development Corporation (EDC) is Canada's official export credit agency wholly owned by the Canadian government but operating autonomously. It provides financing and risk management services to Canadian exporters and investors with offices hosted all around the world.

The EDC is financially self-sustaining and operates like a commercial institution. Its treasury and risk management strategies enable it to assist Canadian exporters without relying on tax dollars. The EDC raises funds by charging fees for its services and interest on its loans, as well as issuing debt in capital markets.

The EDC is governed by a board of directors with fifteen directors from the private sector, appointed by the Minister for International Trade with the approval of the governor. The chair and president of the board are appointed by the governor in Council. Products and services offered by the EDC include insurance, financing for Canadian companies and for their foreign customers, bonding solutions, as well as information on opportunities in international markets.

The EDC has facilitated more than 1.5 trillion Canadian dollars in exports and foreign investments by Canadian companies. In 2019 nearly 17,000 Canadian companies were aided in expanding their business into international markets. Of those companies 86 percent were small to medium-sized businesses and they facilitated more than 102 billion Canadian dollars in global business.

In 2017 the EDC created a Canadian development finance institute, a subsidiary of the EDC, FinDev, the core mandate of which is to support inclusive private sector growth and sustainability in developing markets.

The EDC's mission is to: Support and develop, directly or indirectly, Canada's export trade and Canada's capacity to engage in that trade, and to respond to international business opportunities. In March 2020, the EDC's mandate was temporarily extended to help non-exporting Canadian companies face the financial challenges caused by the Covid-19 pandemic. Due to the global health crisis the EDC will support and protect Canadian businesses, whether they sell internationally or within Canada.

The EDC offers the following products.

Export Financing

- **Buyer Financing:** Provides flexible financing arrangement with flexible term payments instead of cash up-front.
- **Direct Lending:** Provides direct financing to companies or foreign affiliates through a secured loan.
- **Structured and Project Finance:** Provides financing for large-scale projects with multiple parties involved with an internationally focused project finance team.
- **Purchase Order Financing:** Provides financing to cover up to 90 percent of the purchase order amount.

Insurance

- **EDC Credit Insurance:** Covers up to 90 percent of losses against the risk of non-payment due to a variety of events, with Select Credit Insurance providing short-term coverage on an as-needed basis, or Portfolio Credit Insurance to provide ongoing coverage for active exporters.
- **Performance Security Insurance:** Covers 95 percent of losses if a customer wrongfully calls a letter of guarantee or if exporter is unable to meet obligations due to specific political risks.
- **EDC Advance Payment Insurance (CapEX):** Covers up to 90 percent of a company's financial losses due to a supplier's inability to fulfill shipping obligations or return required advanced payments made before shipping.

Guarantee Programs

- **EDC Business Credit Availability Program (BCAP) Guarantee:** A partnership between EDC and approved financial institutions across Canada to help businesses of all sizes, sectors, and regions address the financial impacts of Covid-19 and improve cash flow to cover business operating costs.
- **Export Guarantee Program:** Provides guarantees to financial institutions to encourage them to extend financing to businesses.
- **Account Performance Security Guarantee:** Provides a 100 percent guarantee to an exporter's financial institution for any bonds posted for the company. Issues letters of guarantee to financial institution as collateral without putting up cash or credit.
- **Foreign Exchange Facility Guarantee (FXG):** Secures exchange rate without putting up capital and protects margins.
- Surety Bonds

CHINA: EXIM BANK AND SINOSURE

There are two major state-owned institutions that provide export credit in China: Exim Bank, China's official export credit agency and Sinosure, China's Export and Credit Insurance Corporation.

Exim Bank was founded in 1994 and has already become the world's largest export credit agency. Its services include export credits, guarantees, and concessional loans, which are an important part of China's foreign aid. Even though the institution does not publish lending figures, U.S. officials estimate that it finances more exports than the export credit agencies (ECAs) of the Group of Seven industrialized nations combined. *The Financial Times* estimates that in 2009 and 2010, China Exim Bank (along with China Development Bank) lent over US$110 billion to other developing countries, which is more than that lent by the World Bank during the same period. China's Exim Bank is not bound by OECD guidelines.

China's Exim Bank finances the construction of dams, particularly in Africa and Southeast Asia. Its hydropower projects include Kamchay (Cambodia), Mphanda Nkuwa (Mozambique), Merowe (Sudan), and Yeywa (Burma), as well as other dams in Albania, Cambodia, Guinea, Laos, Malaysia, Mozambique, Nepal, the Republic of Congo, Zambia, and elsewhere.

In August 2007 China's Exim Bank issued *Guidelines for Environmental and Social Impact Assessments of the China Export and Import Bank's (China EXIM Bank) Loan Projects*. These guidelines are an improvement over the Bank's 2004 environmental policy, which was released to the public in April 2007 (International Rivers, 2013).

Sinosure was established in 2001, the year China joined the WTO, and is China's sole provider of export insurance. Along with China's Exim Bank, Sinosure is at the forefront of China's export boom, providing competitive financing to exporters and buyers of Chinese goods and services. In 2009, for example, the institution insured US$116 billion-worth of exports worldwide.

Sinosure provides a great number of commercial and political risk insurance products to exporters and buyers of Chinese goods and services, such as short-, medium-, and long-term export credit insurance. In such cases, there is 95 percent cover for commercial and political risk, with maximum repayment over ten years for 85 percent of the value of exported goods and services. The institution also provides investment insurance products and has started selling bonds and guarantees (CC Solutions, 2012).

China's official system of export financing is supplemented by lending from commercial banks controlled or owned by the government as well as quasi-government agencies. The China Development Bank, for example, extends loans for special projects which are included in China's official economic plans. The ultimate goal is to produce national champions able to compete on a global scale (Tucker, 2012).

From 2005 to 2008, China supported more than 3 percent of its merchandise exports with financing assistance, while the United States supported only 1 percent of its merchandise with export credit assistance during the same period. China issued over $203 billion in new medium- and long-term export credit financing between 2006 and 2010), an amount four times that invested by the United States in absolute dollars, and ten times more as a share of GDP.

China is not a member of the OECD, but it is blamed for providing aggressive export credit financing (Ezell, 2011; Tucker, 2012). Its export financing program in Africa has particularly drawn much criticism from the Western world (Bosshard, 2010; Brautigam, 2009). The United States and China agreed to negotiate export credit deals, with a goal of concluding an agreement by 2014 (Palmer, 2012).

FRANCE: COMPAGNIE FRANÇAISE D'ASSURANCE POUR LE COMMERCE EXTÉRIEUR (COFACE) AND AGENCE FRANÇAISE DE DÉVELOPPEMENT

France has two companies that provide credit export agency services, The Compagnie Française d'Assurance pour le Commerce Extérieur (COFACE) for credit insurance and Agence Française de Développement (AFD) for financing.

The Compagnie Française d'Assurance pour le Commerce Extérieur (COFACE) was founded in 1946 as France's official export credit agency. It was subsequently privatized by the government and continued as a commercial enterprise. Currently, COFACE is a fully owned subsidiary of Natixis (which is a subsidiary of BPCE Group). It facilitates state guarantees for exports by French corporations and provides other international support for exporters. It also manages public export guarantees for the government.

As a worldwide leader in credit insurance, COFACE offers companies protection against the risk of financial default of their domestic and foreign clients. In addition to its private sector activities, COFACE manages a separate account for state export credits and reports to the Ministry of Finance, which takes decisions on the largest and most important transactions.

Agence Française de Développement, The French Development Agency, is a specialized public financial institution that implements policy defined by the French Government. It is the main operator of French cooperation policy, therefore combining the functions of development bank and implementing agency for France's official development assistance policy. The mission of the AFD is to fight poverty and promote sustainable development.

Export Financing

According to the OECD (2020):

> The AFD offers the following financial instruments of which can be used to finance export credits: Subsidies, Guarantees, Shareholdings, and all forms of commercial loans. AFD can provide guarantees for operations that make it possible to reduce the risk to issuing bonds in local currencies. Coverage is provided for political risks or State's non-fulfillment of obligations.

Insurance Products

Insurance products provided by COFACE include:

- **TradeLiner Credit Insurance:** Protects against non-payment due to bankruptcy, late payment, natural disasters, political issues such as war or currency transfer restrictions.
- **TopLiner Credit Insurance:** Coverage for high-priority or highly profitable development projects. It is designed to provide coverage for buyers in situations where the insured company has received a guarantee with an amount less then requested or no guarantee at all. TopLiner Credit Insurance will provide supplemental coverage for the development project.

- **Single Risk Credit Insurance:** Provides protection to companies and financial institutions against foreign commercial and political risks. Single Risk Credit insurance provides five unique contract solutions: political risk guarantee, export and domestic guarantee, import guarantee, financing guarantee, investing guarantee.

Insurance policies issued by COFACE are always conditional (compensation is paid only if damage occurs as a result of one of the risks covered) and the proportion covered is always less than 100 percent.

GERMANY: EULER HERMES

A Hermes cover is an export credit guarantee (ECG) by the German Federal Government that protects German companies against non-payment of foreign debtors. In 1949, the system of Hermes covers was introduced as an alternative for exporters unable to find private insurance. Hermes guarantees allow exporters coverage against economic and political risks.

The guarantees are managed by Euler Hermes, a credit insurance company (lead management) and PricewaterhouseCoopers. The Federal Government appointed and authorized those companies to make and receive all declarations of export credit guarantees on their behalf.

Decisions on matters of principle and underwriting of large export transactions are made by an inter-ministerial committee with representatives from the German Federal Ministry of Economics and Technology, Federal Ministry of Finance, German Foreign Office and the Federal Ministry of Economic Cooperation and Development. Hermes cover has a mission to protect businesses against the risks involved in export transactions (OECD, 2020).

Export Financing

The Kreditanstalt fur Wiederaufbau (KfW) IPEX-Bank is one of many specialist banks focused on export and project financing in Germany. In 2014, KfW successfully lobbied for the KfW IPEX-Bank to remain under national supervision on the grounds that its parent group is in the ownership of the German government; the bank had originally been on a list of twenty-four German lenders that were among 128 banks across the eurozone deemed significant enough to be supervised directly by the European Central Bank.

Insurance

FEDERAL EXPORT CREDIT GUARANTEES

Short-, medium-, and long-term ECGs (supplier and buyer credit risk cover), whole turnover policies, and pre-shipment risk are all handled by Euler Hermes on behalf of the Federal Government.

- **Whole Turnover policy light (APG Light):** offers small and medium-sized export companies supplying goods/services to several buyers in various countries an easily manageable tool for safeguarding trade receivables with a credit period of up to four months. It offers protection against payment default if the foreign buyer fails to make payment within six months after the due date (protracted default).

- **Whole Turnover Policy (APG):** offers exporters supplying goods/services to several buyers in various countries an easily manageable tool for safeguarding trade receivables with a credit period of up to twelve months.
- Cover includes protection against payment default, particularly due to buyer insolvency or non-payment of receivables within six months after due date (protracted default), adverse measures taken by foreign governments or warlike events, non-conversion/transfer of local currency amounts, confiscation of the goods due to political circumstances and contract frustration due to political circumstances.
- **Manufacturing Risk Cover** safeguards the production costs invested in the performance of an export transaction. It offers protection against a discontinuation of production, particularly due to the insolvency of the foreign buyer, the cancellation of the contract or the occurrence of other fundamental contract violations, adverse measures taken by foreign governments or warlike events, embargo measures taken by the Federal Republic of Germany or third countries participating in the export transaction, as well as non-payment of cancellation fees or non-fulfillment of the claim to partial repayment after legitimate cancellation of the contract by the buyer.
- **Supplier Credit Cover** safeguards amounts receivable due to a German exporter under a single export transaction with short, medium, or long repayment terms.
- It offers protection against payment default due to the insolvency of the foreign buyer, adverse measures taken by foreign governments or warlike events, non-conversion/transfer of local currency amounts, confiscation of the goods due to political circumstances or contract frustration due to political circumstances, as well as non-payment within six months after due date (protracted default).

INVESTMENT GUARANTEE SCHEME

Guarantees granted by the Federal Republic of Germany to protect German entrepreneurs from political risk, losses due to non-payment, wars, civil unrest, lack of hard currency in the buyer's country, payment default by the customer, and insolvency. The budgetary responsibility for this guarantee scheme lies with the German government.

JAPAN: JAPAN BANK FOR INTERNATIONAL COOPERATION (JBIC) AND NIPPON EXPORT AND INVESTMENT INSURANCE (NEXI)

The Japanese government has two separate state-owned institutions to provide export financing and insurance services in Japan: Japan Bank for International Cooperation (JBIC), which acts as Japan's ECA, and Nippon Export and Investment Insurance (NEXI), which administers investment insurance activities for Japan.

The JBIC was established on October 1, 1999 through a merger between Japan Export–Import Bank (JEXIM) and the Overseas Economic Cooperation Fund (OECF). It is a public financial institution with a mission to secure natural resources, ensure competitiveness of Japanese companies, respond to disruptions in the international economy, and improve the environment.

Nippon Export and Investment Insurance (NEXI) was formed on April 1, 2001 under the jurisdiction of the Ministry of Economy, Trade and Industry (METI). Its mission is to contribute to Japan's economy by anticipating changes in the market, responding to customer needs, and conducting insurance business by covering risks that arise in international transactions but are not covered by regular commercial insurance (GAO, 2012).

The following export products are offered by JBIC and NEXI.

Export Financing

Japan Bank for International Cooperation (JBIC): Provides the following types of export loan to overseas importers and financial institutions to support financial exports of Japanese machinery, equipment, and technology:

- **Buyers' Credit (B/C):** A direct loan to a foreign importer for financing the import of Japanese machinery, equipment, or use of Japanese technical services.
- **Bank-to-Bank Loan:** A direct loan to a foreign financial institution for financing Japanese imports of machinery, equipment, or use of Japanese technical services.

Insurance

Nippon Export and Investment Insurance (NEXI): As a trade and investment insurance administrative agency of the Japanese Government, NEXI looks to enhance Japanese companies' international business. Its policies cover up to 97.5 percent for political risks and 95 percent for commercial risks. The Japanese Government is responsible for reinsuring insurance agreements underwritten by NEXI and bound by OECD consensus. NEXI insurance products for exports include:

- **Export Credit Insurance:** Covers losses sustained by Japanese companies unable to export goods due to war, revolution, import restriction/prohibition, terrorism, natural disaster, or bankruptcy of the foreign business. This insurance also covers losses suffered from an exporter's inability to collect receivables after shipment of goods or services for the reasons mentioned above.
- **Export Credit Insurance for SMEs and AFF Sector:** Exclusively supports export activities of Japanese small and medium-sized enterprises (SMEs) and organizations related to agriculture, forestry, and fisheries (AFF).
- **Trade Insurance for Standing Orders from Specific Buyers:** Covers transactions with a buyer or buyers to which a Japanese exporter repeatedly supplies products.
- **Export Bill Insurance:** Covers losses suffered by a Japanese commercial bank that negotiates documentary bills of exchange drawn without a letter of credit for export payments. This includes losses that may be sustained when

the bank is unable to collect money because of nonpayment of the bill caused by war, revolution, prohibition of foreign currency exchange, suspension of remittance, natural disaster, or bankruptcy of the foreign importer

- **Comprehensive Export Insurance with Simplified Procedure:** Insurance for companies that continually and repeatedly export to a number of buyers.
- **Prepayment Import Insurance:** Covers losses sustained by Japanese importers who paid for goods in advance as per the contract terms but could not receive the goods on the due date and could not receive a refund because of war, revolution, prohibition of foreign currency exchange, suspension of remittance, natural disasters, bankruptcy, or delay in the performance of obligations by the counterparty.
- **Buyers' Credit Insurance: Direct credit** Buyer credits and bank-to-bank loans are extended to foreign governments, foreign banks, foreign corporations, and international or regional agencies. In the case of buyer credits and bank-to-bank loans, JBIC carries the risk itself for its portion of the financing. For the bank-financed part, however, NEXI insurance is in principle required.
- **Overseas Investment Insurance:** Covers losses suffered by a Japanese company with a subsidiary or joint venture in a foreign country when the subsidiary or joint venture is forced to discontinue business due to war, terrorism, natural disasters, and/or unavoidable catastrophes (OECD, 2020).
- **Overseas Untied Loan Insurance:** Insurance for loans of business funds or bond purchase.
- **Investment and Loan Insurance for Natural Resources and Energy:** Covers risks linked to overseas resource development projects. With lower premium rates and a wide range of risk coverage this insurance provides senior loans as well as subordinated loans and investments

Guarantee Programs

Japan Bank for International Cooperation not only provides export financing for Japanese companies but also has a guarantee facility for Japanese companies that borrow, to finance the import of aircraft and other manufactured products. It also provides Counter-Guarantees for Export Credits.

When Japanese companies export machinery and equipment jointly with foreign companies, JBIC provides a counter-guarantee for the guarantee provided by the foreign company's country's ECA.

UNITED KINGDOM: EXPORT CREDITS GUARANTEE DEPARTMENT (ECGD)

UK Export Finance (UKEF) is the operating name of the Export Credits Guarantee Department (ECGD), the United Kingdom's ECA. Its mission is to: "Ensure that no viable UK export fails for lack of finance or insurance, while operating at no net cost to the taxpayer" (Gov.UK, 2020). The ECGD was awarded the best global ECA in 2019 and is the longest-running ECA in the world.

Established in 1919, the powers of the ECGD stem from the Export and Investment Guarantees Act of 1991. The ECGD tries to benefit the U.K. economy by providing guarantees, insurance, and reinsurance, to U.K. firms to invest internationally and win business for exporters of U.K. goods and services.

Underwriting of long-term loans to support the sale of capital goods and for the export of aircraft, bridges, machinery, and services, is the largest activity of the ECGD.

Underwriting services are provided by some large financial institutions, such as banks, insurance companies, and investment houses, guaranteeing payment in case of damage or financial loss, and accepting the financial risk for liability from such guarantee.

The ECGD is required by government to run its credit insurance operations to generate sufficient reserves on a slightly better than break-even basis. It offers the following products and services.

Export Finance

- **Buyer Credit Facility:** Provides a guarantee to a bank making a loan to an overseas buyer, so that capital goods, services, and/or intangibles can be purchased. This facility enables the exporter to receive payment up front as though it was a cash contract, while the buyer can access extended repayment terms. The loan is typically repaid over a period of two years or longer by the buyer while the exporter receives payment via the credit facility as amounts fall due under the export contract. Buyer Credit has the following additional features: an export refinancing facility, local currency financing, and lines of credit.
- **Direct Lending Facility:** Under the Direct Lending Facility the exporter is paid as if it has a cash contract. UK Export Finance (UKEF) provides loans within an overall limit of 8 billion pounds to overseas buyers, allowing them to finance the purchase of capital goods and/or services from U.K. exporters. The funding is provided at a fixed rate of interest, based on the applicable Commercial Interest Reference Rate (CIRR) set by the OECD or the cost of U.K. Government funds (national/loans fund rates) if higher.
- **Supplier Credit Financing Facilities:** Supplier Credit Financing Facilities include the Supplier Credit Loan Facility and Supplier Credit Bills and Notes Facility. The Supplier Credit Loan Facility covers a loan to an overseas buyer to finance the purchase of goods and/or services from a U.K. exporter, for loans typically below 5 million pounds. The Supplier Credit Bills and Notes Facility covers payments due under bills of exchange or promissory notes purchased by a bank from a U.K. exporter.

Insurance

- **Export Insurance Policy:** Covers up to 95 percent of exporters' losses in the event of nonpayment under an export contract. It covers costs incurred if the exporter contract is terminated because the buyer defaults before the goods are delivered or fails to pay due to political, economic, or administrative events.
- **Bond Insurance Policy:** Protects U.K. exporters against demands for payment under a bond or a counter-guarantee that is either unfair or caused by political events.

- **Overseas Investment Insurance (OII):** Insurance that covers investors against losses on overseas investments due to political risks.

Guarantee Programs

- **Bond Support Scheme:** Provides partial guarantees up to 80 percent of the value of the bond to banks. This helps exporters meet demand for contract bonds and allows banks to release the cash needed to sure the bond for the exporter to use as working capital. There is no maximum value for each bond and no maximum or minimum term for a guarantee.
- **Export Development Guarantee (EDG):** Helps U.K. exporters access high-value loan facilities for general working capital or capital expenditure purposes that do not need linkage to a specific export contract. They provide partial guarantees covering up to 80 percent of the risk to lenders for a maximum repayment period of five years.
- **Export Working Capital Scheme:** Helps U.K. exporters access working capital finance for specific export-related contracts. To cover the credit risks associated with export working capital facilities for both pre- and post-shipment, partial guarantees are provided to cover up to 80 percent of the risk to lenders. There is no minimum or maximum value for the working capital facility.

REFERENCES

Bosshard, P. (2010). The Real Story of China in Africa. www.internationalrivers.org/blogs/227/the-real-story-of-china-in-africa

Brautigam, D. (2009). *China, Africa and the International Aid Architecture*. Abidjan, Ivory Coast: Africa Development Bank Working Paper No. 107.

CC Solutions (2012). Understanding ECAs: Chinese Export Credit Agencies. http://ccsolutionsblog.blogspot.com/2012/04/understanding-ecas-chinese-export.html

Ezell, S. (2011). *Understanding the Importance of Export Credit Financing to U.S. Competitiveness*. Washington, DC: The Information Technology & Innovation Foundation.

Government Accountability Office (GAO) (2012). Export Finance: Challenges Facing the US Export–Import Bank. Washington, DC: GAO.

Gov.uk (2020). www.gov.uk/government/organisations/uk-export-finance/about

International Rivers (2013). China Exim Bank. www.internationalrivers.org/campaigns/china-exim-bank

OECD (2020). Export credit agencies. www.oecd.org/mena/competitiveness/ismed-export-credit-agencies.htm

Palmer, D. (2012). U.S.–China agree to negotiate export credit deal. *Reuters*, February 14: 5.

Tucker, A. (2012). *Export Assistance and the China Challenge*. Washington, DC: US–China Economic and Security Review Commission.

United States Trade Representative (USTR) (2020). *National Trade Estimate Report on Foreign Trade Barriers*. Washington, DC: USTR.

A Brief Comparison of Cargo Conventions

	Hague Rules	Hague–Visby Rules	Hamburg Rules	Proposed Rotterdam Rules
Contract of carriage	Contract of carriage applies only to contracts of carriage covered by a bill of lading (BL) or any similar document of title, insofar as such document relates to the carriage of goods by sea.	Same as Hague rules	Contract of carriage by sea includes carriage by some other means.	The contract shall provide for carriage by sea and may provide for carriage by other modes of transport in addition to the sea carriage.
Which voyages are covered	No provision	Rules apply to every bill of lading relating to the carriage of goods between ports in two different states if: 1) BL issued in a contracting state (CS), 2) carriage from a CS, or 3) contract of carriage expressly applies rules.	Rules apply if 1) BL issued in a CS, 2) carriage from or to CS, 3) BL expressly provides for its application.	Rules apply if any one of the following places is located in a CS: (a) The place of receipt; (b) The port of loading; (c) The place of delivery; or (d) The port of discharge. Receipt and delivery must be in different states.
Carrier's period of responsibility	"Carriage of goods" covers the period from the time when the goods are loaded on to the time they are discharged from the ship.	Same as Hague Rules	Covers the period during which the carrier is in charge of the goods at the port of loading, during the carriage, and at the port of discharge.	The period of responsibility of the carrier begins when the carrier or a performing party receives the goods for carriage and ends when the goods are delivered.

	Hague Rules	**Hague–Visby Rules**	**Hamburg Rules**	**Proposed Rotterdam Rules**
Carrier's duty of care	The carrier shall be bound before and at the beginning of the voyage to exercise due diligence to: *a)* Make the ship seaworthy; *b)* Properly man, equip, and supply the ship; *c)* Make the holds, refrigerating and cool chambers, and all other parts of the ship in which goods are carried, fit and safe for their reception, carriage, and preservation. Also carrier must properly and carefully load, handle, stow, carry, keep, care for, and discharge goods.	Same as Hague Rules	Carrier, his servants, or agents must take all measures that could reasonably be required to avoid the event causing loss and its consequences.	To carry the goods to the place of destination and deliver them to the consignee; to properly and carefully receive, load, handle, stow, carry, keep, care for, unload, and deliver the goods. Before, at the beginning of, and during the voyage by sea, carrier is to exercise due diligence to: *(a)* Make and keep the ship seaworthy; *(b)* Properly crew, equip, and supply the ship and keep the ship so crewed, equipped, and supplied throughout the voyage; *(c)* Make and keep the holds and all other parts of the ship fit and safe for their reception, carriage, and preservation.
Liability of carrier	"Goods" does not include live animals and deck cargo. Carrier's defenses include act, neglect, or default of the master, mariner, pilot, or the servants of the carrier; fire unless caused by carrier, accidents of the sea, act of god, war, riots, strikes, saving or attempting to save life or property at	Same as Hague Rules	Carrier must prove he, his servants or agents took all measures that could reasonably be required to avoid the occurrence and its consequences.	Must either show absence of fault on the part of the carrier or its crew. Carrier's defenses include act of God, accidents, war, terrorism, civil war, quarantine restrictions, strikes, fire on the ship, latent defects not

	Hague Rules	**Hague–Visby Rules**	**Hamburg Rules**	**Proposed Rotterdam Rules**
	sea, waste from inherent defect, insufficient packing, latent defects. Any other cause arising without the actual fault or privity of the carrier, or without the fault or neglect of the agents or servants of the carrier, but the burden of proof shall be on the person claiming the benefit of this exception.			discoverable by due diligence, act or omission by shipper, inherent defect, quality, or vice of the goods, insufficiency of packing or marking, saving or attempting to save life or property at sea.
Burden of proof	Rules not specific on this issue.	Rules not specific on this issue.	Carrier must prove that reasonable steps to avoid loss were taken unless damage is caused by fire.	Claimant to prove that loss, damage or delay took place during carrier's period of responsibility. Carrier to prove that cause or one of the causes of the loss, damage, or delay is not attributable to its fault or the fault of any performing party, master, or crew of ship, employees, etc.
Limits of liability for goods lost or damaged	£100 ($500) per package or unit unless value declared and inserted in the BL.	2 SDRs per kg or 666.67 SDRs per package.	2.5 SDRs per kg or 835 SDRs per package.	875 SDR per package or other shipping unit or 3 SDRs per kg of gross weight subject of claim, whichever is higher, unless value declared.
Limits of liability for goods delayed	No provision.	No provision.	2.5 x freight payable on goods delayed, subject to upper limit of total freight on all goods or amount of limitation if goods have been lost or destroyed.	2.5 times freight payable for goods delayed, not to exceed limit for total loss.

	Hague Rules	Hague–Visby Rules	Hamburg Rules	Proposed Rotterdam Rules
Upper or lower limit by agreement	Upper limit allowed if recorded in BL. Lower limit allowed in special circumstances.	Same as Hague Rules.	Upper limit allowed if recorded in BL. No specific right to agree lower limits.	Upper limit allowed if agreed between carrier and shipper. Except in "volume contracts," terms which limit liability of carrier will be void.
Statement in BL	Prima facie evidence of accuracy.	Prima facie evidence in hands of shipper, conclusive in hands of third party such as consignee to whom the BL is transferred in good faith.	Prima facie evidence of statement in hands of shipper (whether shipped or received BL). Conclusive in hands of third party who relies on statements. If freight is payable by holder of the BL failure to state this is evidence that no freight is payable.	Prima facie evidence of the carrier's receipt of the goods as stated. Proof to contrary not admissible where contract is negotiable or nonnegotiable but requires it be surrendered for delivery and the document is in the hands of a consignee/third party acting in good faith.
Duties of shipper with regard to info supplied to carrier	Shipper is deemed to guarantee accuracy of statement as to weight and quantity of cargo. Shipper to indemnify carrier for loss resulting from errors.	Same as Hague Rules	Same as Hague Rules	Shipper is deemed to have guaranteed the accuracy of the information provided.
Notification and consequences of failure to notify carrier of damage etc.	Notice of loss or damage must be given in writing to the carrier or his agent on day of delivery, or within 3 days where damage is latent. Failure to notify is prima facie evidence of delivery of goods in condition described in BL.	Same as Hague Rules	Notice of loss or damage to be given in writing to carrier by the working day following delivery to consignee or within 15 days of delivery where damage is latent.	Notice of loss of or damage to goods to be given at time of delivery or within 7 working days after delivery if damage not apparent.

	Hague Rules	Hague–Visby Rules	Hamburg Rules	Proposed Rotterdam Rules
			Notice of delay must be given within 60 days of delivery. Carrier must give notice of complaint to shipper within 90 days of delivery. Failure to notify is prima facie evidence of delivery of goods in condition described in BL. If complaint not made in the case of delay within 60 days, carrier is exempted from liability.	Notice of loss or damage due to delay to be given within 21 consecutive days of delivery. Need not give notice if joint inspection by receiver and carrier. Failure to give notice raises presumption that goods delivered in same condition as described in the contract particulars. It does not affect the right to claim compensation for loss or damage nor does it affect the allocation of the burden of proof.
Limitation of action	Suit must be brought within 1 year of delivery or date delivery should have taken place.	Same as Hague Rules. Indemnity actions may be brought after 1 year; the period for commencing suit to be determined by local law but not to be less than 3 months after claim settled or suit served.	Litigation or arbitration to be commenced within 2 years from date of delivery of goods or the last day upon which the goods should have been delivered. Indemnity proceedings may be commenced after this period (at least 90 days from date of commencement of action against carrier must be allowed).	Two years after delivery or when goods should have been delivered. An action for an indemnity can be brought within the later of time allowed under local law, or 90 days after claimant settled with primary claimant or was served with process, whichever is earlier.

	Hague Rules	**Hague–Visby Rules**	**Hamburg Rules**	**Proposed Rotterdam Rules**
Place to commence proceedings	No specific provision.	No specific provision.	Shipper may sue in court of a) principal place of business of carrier; b) place contract was made; c) port of loading or discharge; d) place of arrest of vessel. This may be challenged by the carrier if he submits to one of the other jurisdictions and provides security for the claim.	Domicile of carrier, the place of receipt or delivery under the contract, port of loading or port of discharge. Or agreed jurisdiction between shipper and carrier. Agreed jurisdiction will be "exclusive" under certain circumstances, including volume contracts.

Countries that Are Members of Cargo Conventions

Hague Rules	Hague–Visby Rules	Hamburg Rules
Algeria, Angola, Argentina, Aruba, Australia, Bahamas, Bangladesh, Belize, Bolivia, Brazil, Brunei, Bulgaria, Colombia, Congo (DR), Cuba, Dominica, Estonia, Fiji, Ghana, Grenada, Guinea Bissau, Guyana, India, Iran, Israel, Ivory Coast, Jamaica, Madagascar, Malaysia, Malta, Mauritius, Monaco, Mozambique, Pakistan, Panama, Papua New Guinea, Philippines, Portugal, St. Kitts and Nevis, Sao Tome, Seychelles, Slovenia, Solomon Islands, Somalia, Timor, Trinidad & Tobago, Turkey, Tuvalu, U.S.A.	Argentina, Australia, Bahrain, Belgium, Bermuda, Canada, China, Croatia, Denmark, Ecuador, Finland, France, Germany, Greece, Hong Kong, Iceland, India, Indonesia, Ireland, Israel, Italy, Japan, Kuwait, Latvia, Lithuania, Mexico, Montserrat, Netherlands, New Zealand, Norway, Oman, Poland, Portugal, Qatar, Russia, Singapore, South Africa, South Korea, Spain, Sri Lanka, Sweden, Switzerland, Taiwan, Thailand, Tonga, Turks & Caicos, Ukraine, UAE, U.K., Venezuela, Vietnam	Albania, Australia, Austria, Barbados, Bolivia, Botswana, Burkina Faso, Burundi, Cameroon, Canada, Chile, China, Colombia, Czech Rep., Dominican Rep., Egypt, Gambia, Georgia, Guinea, Hungary, Iraq, Jordan, Kazakhstan, Kenya, Lebanon, Lesotho, Liberia, Malawi, Morocco, Nigeria, Paraguay, Romania, Senegal, Sierra Leone, Slovakia, Syria, Tanzania, Tunisia, Uganda, Ukraine, Venezuela, Zambia

Freight Calculations

AIR FREIGHT: CONVERSION TABLE

Physical Weight and Linear Measurements

- *Conversion from pounds to kilos: multiply by 0.4536*
- *Conversion from kilos to pounds: multiply by 2.2046*
- *Conversion from metric tons to kilos: multiply by 1,000*
- *Conversion from inches to centimeters (cm): multiply by 2.54*
- *Conversion from centimeters to inches: multiply by 0.453592*

Dimensional Weight (Volume Weight)

For every shipment, physical weight is compared to dimensional weight and the *higher of the two* is used to determine the shipment cost. The International Air Transport Association (IATA) standard is based on 6,000 cubic centimeters per one kilogram:

Example: length (cm) x width (cm) x height (cm)/6000 = volume kilos

length (inches) x width (inches) x height (inches)/366 = volume kilos
length (inches) x width (inches) x height (inches)/166 = volume pounds

One pallet with the following dimensions: 150 kg and 122 x 102 x 127 cms:

Weight: 150 kg or 122 x 102 x 127/6000 = 263.40 volume kilos

One pallet with the following dimensions: 150 kg and 48 x 40 x 50 inches:

Weight: 150 kg or 48 x 40 x 50/366 = 262.30 volume kilos

One pallet with the following dimensions: 150 kgs and 48 x 40 x 50 inches

Weight: 150 kgs or 48 x 40 x 50/166 = 578.31 volume pounds

SEA FREIGHT: CONVERSION TABLE

Physical Weight and Linear Measurements

- *Conversion from pounds to kilos: multiply by 0.4536*
- *Conversion from kilos to pounds: multiply by 2.2046*
- *Conversion from metric tons to kilos: multiply by 1,000*
- *Conversion from long ton to pounds: multiply by 2,240*
- *Conversion from short ton to pounds: multiply by 2,000*
- *Conversion from inches to centimeters: multiply by 2.54*
- *Conversion from centimeters to inches: multiply by 0.453592*
- *Conversion from meters to feet: multiply by 3.281*

Dimensional Weight (Volume Weight) (1,000 Kilos or One Cubic Meter)

Weight is calculated in kilos or cubic meters

- *Conversion from cubic meters to cubic feet: multiply by 35.3145*
- *Conversion from cubic feet to cubic inches: multiply by 1,728*
- *Conversion from cubic meters to cubic centimeters: multiply by 1,000,000*
- *Conversion from volume kilos to cubic meters: multiply by .006*

Example: *One pallet with the following dimensions: 150 pounds and 45 x 45 x 60 inches*
Actual weight: 1500 lbs or 1500/2.2046 = 680 kilos
Volume: 45 x 45 x 60 /1728 = 70.30 cubic feet; 70.30/5.32 = 1.99 cubic meters; one cubic meter is equivalent to 1000 kilos. Thus, freight will be based on volume.

Sample Export Business Plan
Donga Michael Export Company

EXECUTIVE SUMMARY

Donga Michael is a newly created export company located in Fort Lauderdale, Florida. The company started its operation in September 2019. It exports computers and parts to the Republic of South Africa. Trade in computers between the United States and South Africa has been growing at a faster rate over the last few years. The company intends to supply high-quality computers to the business sector and later to schools and universities.

South Africa is the largest computer market for the United States in Sub-Saharan Africa. Every year, it imports computer peripherals, accessories, and ICT goods worth over US$7.3 billion. With the end of apartheid and the lifting of sanctions, South Africa is open for trade and investment. The development of a black professional and business class and the building of infrastructure facilities to enable all South Africans to participate in the economic life of the country provide enormous business opportunities for U.S. exporters of information technology. Even though there is strong price competition in the computer sector, Donga Michael will focus on the upper end of the consumer market. Donga Michael's competitive advantages over existing companies include a coordinated marketing program, prompt delivery and services, as well as a professional image and expertise in the North American market.

President and founder George Hunat brings a wealth of experience to the firm. Vice President Alice Munroe also has extensive marketing experience. The estimated required investment is $200,000. Mr. Hunat will invest $40,000 of his own personal funds in the business. Ms. Munroe will invest $35,000, while $80,000 will be borrowed from a local bank. The balance of $45,000 is solicited from a venture capitalist who will acquire 37.5 percent of the corporation stock.

The company intends to become a major player in the South African market in the next five years capturing about 30 percent of the computer market. After this objective is realized, the company intends to explore export opportunities in Zimbabwe, Zambia, and Kenya.

GENERAL INDUSTRY AND COMPANY

The South African computer market is valued at over $7 billion and is changing its focus from mainframes to personal computers (PCs) and PC-based networks. The increasing processing power coupled with decreasing prices for PCs is also boosting demand for laptop computers and peripheral equipment, including printers and storage devices. Opportunities exist for sales of computers, peripherals, and accessories, as South African manufacturing and service companies seek to become more competitive in the domestic and global marketplaces. Presently, about four U.S. companies sell computer hardware to the South African market. Local manufacture of PCs remains negligible, and there is an increasing demand for established computer brand-name products. Donga Michael intends to bring such products into the market at competitive prices to help regain the market share lost during the sanctions period. With closer economic relations between South Africa and other African countries, the South African market will become the beachhead from which exports could be made to neighboring states, such as Zimbabwe, Zambia, Kenya, Tanzania, and Uganda. An encouraging development pertaining to the industry is the revision of U.S. controls on computer exports in. The 2018 regulations eliminate or significantly ease controls on computer exports to most countries of the world, except those designated as terrorist states. There are no U.S. restrictions on computer products and accessories that Donga Michael plans to export to South Africa. A problem that plagues the industry in the short term, however, is the shortage of trained manpower to manage the complex and interconnected networks proliferating everywhere.

Donga Michael is a newly created export firm that is incorporated as a Chapter S corporation in the state of Florida. The company will market digital ABD machines with central processing input–output units, parts and accessories, laptop and notebook computers, networking software, and software for computer-aided design and electronic design automation. The products need not be adapted for the South African market except for the different voltages (i.e., 100v). George Hunat and Alice Munroe comprise the two partners of the firm and also manage the company as president and vice president, respectively.

TARGET MARKET

South Africa has a gross domestic output of $350 billion and a per capita income of $13,600 (as of 2017) and the second-largest economy in Sub-Saharan Africa. It possesses a modern infrastructure, supporting an efficient distribution of goods to major urban centers throughout the region and well-developed financial, legal, and communications sectors. Its economic growth has been in the range of 3 to 3.5 percent over the last five years. However, with favorable economic conditions and a stable political climate, it is likely to register higher rates of growth, estimated at 5 to 10 percent in the next few years and beyond. This is critical to offset high unemployment rates. Present efforts to revamp the educational system, boost economic productivity, and provide access to basic services to all South Africans present opportunities for U.S. companies to export computers and other information technology.

Total U.S. merchandise exports to South Africa in 2019 amounted to $5.4 billion. The South African information technology market is the twentieth-largest in the world and constitutes one of the top ten emerging markets that are being targeted by international computer companies. The base of installed PCs is slightly over one million, and indications are that 84 percent of the top information technology users are investing in client-server systems. Information and communications technology spending is likely to grow from $13 billion to $20 billion in the next few years. The U.S. market share for computer peripherals was estimated at about 25 percent in 2019 amounting to about $50 million. A couple of reasons account for the continual expansion of the market for computer peripherals and accessories:

1. Because the country has ended its isolation and instituted a democratic political system for all South Africans, there is a significant inflow of foreign investment. For example, in 2019, the country attracted over US$4.6 billion in foreign direct investment. The government plans to attract US$100 billion in foreign investment by 2023. This creates business opportunities for exports of computers and information technology.
2. The black middle class has experienced faster growth since the end of the apartheid system. Hence, this emerging professional and business class will soon be a big consumer market.

In terms of market access, there are no restrictions or quotas on computer peripheral imports to South Africa. These imports are, however, subject to a 10 percent ad valorem tariff and a 14 percent value-added tax. There are no non-tariff barriers such as prior deposits or foreign exchange restrictions.

There is fierce competition in the South African market. Acer Africa is the top PC assembler and distributor, followed by Mustek electronics and IBM. Third-country suppliers from the Far East, Britain, France, Germany, and Italy are also present. Donga Michael should focus on the upper end of the consumer market for use by the business sector. In spite of the relatively high prices compared to the competition, discerning firms know the value of quality products and would be favorably disposed to buying U.S.-made computers and parts. U.S.-branded peripherals have high status in South Africa.

MARKETING PLAN AND SALES STRATEGY

Donga Michael Inc. intends to target the middle-to upper-level business firms that are in the process of using computers for various office functions, such as finance and accounting, word processing, electronic communication, and presentations. It should later begin to focus on high schools, universities, and research centers by entering into a supply agreement with the government. The company can establish retail outlets in major cities, and since it represents a well-known brand, it can have a marketing advantage.

Donga Michael can also promote sales by participating in computer trade exhibitions, advertising, and carefully managed public relations programs, such as sponsorship of special events, charitable donations to social causes, and so on.

MANAGEMENT AND ORGANIZATION

The company is managed by George Hunat, founder and president, and Alice Munroe, vice president and director of sales and marketing. George Hunat has an MSc in

TABLE K.1 Ownership Structure

Partners	Capital	Ownership Share	Salary/month
George Hunat	$40,000 (20%)	33.33%	$3,500
Alice Munroe	$35,000 (18%)	29.16%	$3,000
Bank loan	$80,000 (40%)	-----	
Venture capital	$45,000 (23%)	37.50%	

TABLE K.2 Forecasted Balance Sheet (Liabilities)

Liabilities	Year 1 ($)	Year2 ($)	Year3 ($)	Year4 ($)
Accounts payable	150,000	220,000	230,000	150,000
Long-term debt	80,000	50,000	40,000	22,000
Retail earnings		220,000	200,000	400,000
Total liabilities and capital	**230,000**	**490,000**	**470,000**	**572,000**

TABLE K.3 Financial Plan: Donga Michael Export Company Forecasted Year-End Income Statements

	Year1	Year2	Year3	Year4
Sales	$120,000	$1,120,000	$3,980,000	$5,200,000
Less cost of goods sold	30,000	350,000	600,000	1,350,000
Commission	10,000	120,000	200,000	420,000
Delivery	32,000	60,000	98,000	150,000
Total variable expenses	**72,000**	**530,000**	**898,000**	**1,920,000**
Less fixed expenses				
Rent	10,000	10,000	10,000	10,000
Advertising	15,000	22,000	25,000	60,000
Travel	20,000	25,000	27,000	20,000
Utilities	7,000	7,500	7,700	8,000
Wages	25,000	38,000	45,000	45,000
Misc.	15,000	18,000	22,000	25,000
Total fixed expenses	**92,000**	**120,500**	**136,700**	**168,000**
Net income	**(44,000)**	**469,500**	**2,945,300**	**3,112,000**

computer engineering from Emory University in Atlanta, Georgia. Since graduation in 1995, he has worked as director of logistics for a multinational firm in San Diego, California (1995–2014), and later joined a successful computer export firm in Silicon Valley, California, as export manager (2014–2018). He has extensive experience in computer sales, marketing, and logistics operations. Alice Munroe received a BA in computer systems from Texas A&M in 1997 and has since worked as a marketing manager for a communications firm in New York.

Donga Michael will employ six people and a clerk. The employees will be trained to handle distribution, storage, transportation, and marketing of Donga

TABLE K.4 Forecasted Year-End Balance Sheet (Assets)

Assets	Year 1 ($)	Year 2($)	Year 3 ($)	Year 4 ($)
Cash	$40,000	$165,000	$600,000	$750,000
Accounts receivable	420,000	500,000	700,000	850,000
Inventory	100,000	150,000	160,000	220,000
Other	320,000	400,000	500,000	650,000
Less depreciation	15,000	25,000	30,000	45,000
Total assets	**865,000**	**1,190,000**	**1,930,000**	**2,425,000**

Michael's computer products. Two of the employees will be sent to South Africa to handle marketing and distribution. They will also recruit and train South African employees who will handle the retail outlets in major urban centers. For the first few years, the retail outlets will be located in Johannesburg, Pretoria, and Cape Town.

The employees and clerk will be paid hourly at $10.00 and $8.00 per hour, respectively. The capital structure and salary level for the president and vice president are as shown in Table K.1. Future increases in salary will be based on sales performance.

LONG-TERM DEVELOPMENT PLAN

Donga Michael plans to show steady progress over the next five years, becoming one of the largest retailers of computers and parts in South Africa. It plans to capture 20 percent of the market by the year 2025 (see Tables K.2–4).

The marketing staff will be increased as more sales are generated. Additional sales distribution outlets will be established in other urban areas. After five years, the company plans to expand to Zimbabwe, Zambia, and Kenya. Additional bank financing will be secured to finance the expansion.

Sample Import Business Plan
Otoro Import Company

EXECUTIVE SUMMARY

Otoro Imports is a spice importing and marketing corporation established in June 2019. It is located in Los Angeles, California, and specializes in the importation and marketing of high-quality spices at competitive prices. The company also provides certain programs to educate and inform distributors, retailers, and consumers about the use and health benefits of spices.

The United States is the world's largest spice importer and consumer. With the increased ethnic diversity of the population, strong U.S. dollar, and limited domestic production, there is greater demand for and affordability of such foods. The industry is dominated by a small number of companies. Otoro intends to import three types of spices: black and white pepper, paprika, and cinnamon, products showing fast growth in domestic demand.

The management team includes Davie Lee, president, and Howard Tzu, vice president. They both have extensive experience in the spice industry. The company has hired four full-time employees and a clerk. It will hire additional employees as the need arises. The company will market the imports through its retail outlets in California, Florida, and New York and through outside distributors in other states. Its future plan includes expansion to Canada and Mexico and maintaining a substantial presence in the U.S. market, by 2025, probably controlling about 25 percent of the market.

GENERAL DESCRIPTION OF INDUSTRY AND COMPANY

Otoro Imports intends to import spices from various countries for sale and distribution in the United States. Besides the importation and marketing of high-quality spices, Otoro intends to provide education programs to its distributors and retailers about the various types of spices, their uses, and their health benefits. As sales volume increases, the company also plans to hold free public seminars to inform and educate the North American consumer about the benefits and usage of various spices. The company aims to be known as the premier spice importing and marketing firm in North America. Its development goals are for steady expansion, with profitability by the second year.

The United States is the world's largest spice importer and consumer. Per capita consumption totaled 3.5 pounds in 2018 and it is likely to grow in the next few years. A number of factors contribute to the growing demand for spices in the United States. First, the growth of ethnic populations has caused a surge in the use of the spices common to their different cultures. According to the U.S. census, the Asian and Hispanic populations grew to 22.8 and 10 million, respectively, between 2010 and 2020. Second, ethnic foods have become increasingly popular in the United States. Nowadays, it is rare to see a typical shopping center without an ethnic restaurant. There is also a trend toward the use of spices to compensate for less salt and lower fat levels in foods.

The industry is dominated by a small number of companies that process and market imported or domestically produced spices. For example, McCormick/Schilling accounts for about 37 percent of the U.S. retail market. Given the trend toward mergers in most sectors, there is a possibility of mergers and acquisitions in the spice industry resulting in fewer, larger firms.

Otoro intends to import high-quality spices at competitive prices. It ensures importation of top-quality spices by maintaining constant communication with foreign producers and stationing a quality control specialist at most export locations to determine and advise on quality before importation into the United States. Importation from Indonesia, India, and China of seven of the most popular spices in the United States (vanilla beans, black and white pepper, capsicums, sesame seed, cinnamon, mustard, and oregano) is planned over the next five years because of their comparative advantages in climate, soil, and labor costs.

The seven products to be imported make up about 75 percent of U.S. spice imports (see Table L.1). There has been a marked increase in spice imports since 2000. The country imported spices estimated at US$282 million in 2018. Otoro will import three products during the first two years: black and white pepper, paprika, and cinnamon.

Presently, there are no restrictions on the importation of spices into the United States. However, food safety regulations require the treatment of spices to kill insects and microorganisms that thrive under tropical conditions.

TARGET MARKET

Otoro intends to operate retail outlets in the major metropolitan centers of California (Los Angeles, San Diego, and San Jose), Florida (Jacksonville, Miami, and Tampa), and New York (New York City, Buffalo, and Rochester). In other states, the products will be marketed through distributors. Major customers include restaurants, fast-food chains, and individual consumers.

Imports have played an important role in the American diet by providing needed spices throughout the year and by moderating retail prices during times of shortages or other disruptions in domestic production. The United States produces a limited supply of spices—garlic, onions, mustard, ginger, and capsicum pepper—and

TABLE L.1 U.S. Spice Imports

PRODUCT	BRIEF PROFILE
Vanilla beans	Imports average over $70 million a year. Major suppliers include Comoros, Madagascar, and the Pacific Islands. Mainly used for ice cream.
Black and white pepper	Imports average over $60 million a year for black pepper and about $12 million for white pepper. Major suppliers are Brazil, India, and Indonesia. Used as seasoning for food.
Capsicum and paprika peppers	Capsicum peppers are mainly imported from China, India, Mexico, and Palestine. Paprika is imported from Hungary, Morocco, and Spain. Total imports amount to over $62 million a year.
Mustard seed	Import value averages at $138 million a year. There is some domestic production. Most imports come from Canada.
Cassia and cinnamon	Widely used for doughnuts. Most imports come from Indonesia. Import value averages at about $30 million a year.
Oregano	Mostly used for pizza. Imported from Mexico and Turkey. Annual imports average about $14 million a year.
Sesame Seed	Used in the fast-food sector. Imported from Guatemala, El Salvador, and Mexico. Import value averages about $45 million a year.

its average annual exports were estimated at $42 million in 2018. However, the U.S. import share of total domestic consumption stands at about 87 percent (as of 2018), and thus, there is heavy reliance on foreign suppliers. The volume of spice imports grew substantially in the past decade. The major suppliers include Canada, China, India, Indonesia, and Mexico. India supplied the largest share during the last few years.

A number of factors contribute to steady growth and expansion of spice imports in the United States:

- Given the current per capita consumption, total domestic use of spices is likely to increase by over $300 million over the next few years.
- The increased ethnic diversity of the U.S. population will lead to more consumption of spices.
- Because domestic production of spices is limited in volume and variety, the United States will continue to import over 90 percent of its domestic spice needs.
- The increased value of the U.S. dollar in relation to the currencies of our major exporters, such as Indonesia, as well as low U.S. tariffs for spice imports, is likely to increase the availability and affordability of such foods.
- Foreign producers have increasingly adapted new production technologies to meet the necessary safety and quality standards of U.S. consumers and have also enhanced the popularity of imported spices

There is strong competition from established companies in the industry that sell natural as well as artificial substitutes. However, Otoro's competitive advantage will be in the supply of high-quality spices at competitive prices. Furthermore,

TABLE L.2 Ownership Structure

Partners	Capital ($)	Ownership share (%)	Salary/month
David Lee	350,000	58.33	4,000/month
Howard Tzu	250,000	41.67	3,000/month
Bank Loan	150,000	-----	-------

TABLE L.3 Otoro Imports: Projected Income Statement

	Year 1	Year 2	Year 3
Total net sales	$450,000	$800,000	$1,500,000
Cost of goods sold	150,000	350,000	650,000
Gross profit	**300,000**	**450,000**	**850,000**
Expenses			
Utilities	35,000	40,000	60,000
Postage	2,000	3,000	4,500
Warehouse	86,000	100,000	250,000
Transportation	40,000	55,000	100,000
Rent	85,000	85,000	85,000
Miscellaneous	60,000	75,000	100,000
Total expenses	**308,000**	**358,000**	**599,500**
Net profit (loss) before tax	**(8,000)**	**92,000**	**250,500**

current and future needs cannot be met by the existing competition, and Otoro wants to position itself as an important supplier of black and white pepper, paprika, and cinnamon. Industry sources also indicate that these three products will constitute the fastest growing spice import groups in the U.S. market.

MARKETING PLAN AND SALES STRATEGY

Otoro will invest sufficient resources to achieve improvements in quality and reliability. It is important to find a suitable manner of presentation (e.g., bags, baskets, tins, etc.) that is timesaving and attractive to customers. The product will be marketed at a low price to be competitive in the market. Promotion includes participation in food shows and advertising.

MANAGEMENT AND ORGANIZATION

The company is managed by its founder, David Lee (president), and Howard Tzu (vice president). They both worked as managers for a reputable spice trading firm in Las Vegas, Nevada. Four people will be hired during the first phase of operation to clear imports from customs, transport the goods, and warehouse the shipments. The employees and a clerk will be paid $10.00 and $7.00 per hour, respectively. The capital structure and salary levels for the president and vice president are as shown in Table L.2.

TABLE L.4 Start-Up Expenses for the First Six Months

Item	Range ($)
Supplies	1,000 to 2,000
Insurance	400 to 600
Rent	2,000 to 2,500
Utilities	400 to 600
Furniture, etc.	3,000 to 5,000
Licenses/taxes	500 to 200
Advertising	3,000 to 4,000
Professional services	5,000 to 8,000
Salaries	200,000 to 240,000
Inventory	350,000 to 500,000
Operating capital	5,000 to 8,000
Total start-up expenses	**570, 300 to 770,900**

LONG-TERM DEVELOPMENT PLAN

Otoro intends to be a major retailer and distributor of natural spices, capturing about 25 percent of the U.S. market by 2025. In the next five years, expansion plans will be focused on Canada and Mexico. Additional borrowing may be required to finance expansion (Tables L.3 and L.4).

Export Sales Contract
(Basic Clauses)

1. **PRICES**
   A. Prices include the following costs:
      (i) Seller's usual inspection and factory tests
      (ii) Seller's usual packing (or containerizing if applicable) for export
      (iii) Freight by Seller's usual means to alongside vessel at the point of export designated by Seller (but not the cost of insurance or charges for pier handling, marshaling, lighterage, and heavy lifts). Insurance to cover the inland shipment shall be arranged by Seller at Buyer's expense if Seller is arranging for the export shipment pursuant to Article 3 . . .
   B. Unless otherwise stated, prices are quoted in Canadian funds.
2. **TAXES, DUTIES, AND EXCHANGE RATES**
   A. Prices quoted include all applicable Canadian taxes except for sales, use, excise, value-added, and similar taxes. If sales, use, excise, value-added, or similar taxes are levied against the Seller, the Buyer shall reimburse the Seller upon presentation of invoices therefor. However, where a refund of such taxes may be applied for, the Seller, if promptly furnished by the Buyer with evidence of exportation, will apply for a refund. If the Buyer has reimbursed the Seller, the Buyer shall be credited with the refund.
   B. Prices quoted do not include Canadian import duties. All rights in drawback of customs duties paid by the Seller belong to and shall remain in the Seller. At the Seller's request, the Buyer shall provide documents and assistance necessary to process the Seller's drawback claims, failing which, the Buyer shall reimburse the Seller for such import duties. Such reimbursement shall be payable upon presentation of Seller's invoice therefor.
   C. Prices quoted herein are based upon the prevailing rates for taxes and freight at the date of the Proposal and, with respect to the purchase price of goods to be bought by the Seller in foreign countries, on duty and exchange rates current at the date of the Proposal. Any increase or decrease in these rates or the imposition of any new duties or taxes between the date of the Proposal

and the date of payment by the Seller will be paid by the Buyer, upon presentation of Seller's invoices therefor, or will be credited to the Buyer.

D. Any taxes, duties, fees, charges, or assessments of any nature levied by any governmental authority other than of Canada in connection with this contract, whether levied against the Buyer, against the Seller or its employees, or against any of the Seller's subcontractors or their employees shall be for the Buyer's account and shall be paid directly by the Buyer to the governmental authority concerned. If the Seller, its subcontractors, or the employees of either are required to pay any such taxes, duties, fees, charges, or assessments in the first instance or as a result of the Buyer's failure to comply with any applicable laws or regulations governing the payment of such levies by the Buyer, the amount of any such payment so made shall be reimbursed by Buyer, payable upon presentation of Seller's invoice therefor.

3. **PAYMENT**

A. Payment shall be made in Canadian dollars at Toronto, Canada, as follows:

   (i) On all orders of ten thousand dollars ($10,000) or less, payment in full shall be made simultaneously with the giving of the order.

   (ii) On orders of over ten thousand dollars ($10,000), payment shall be made through a Letter of Credit to be established by the Buyer at its expense (including any bank confirmation charges). All Letters of Credit shall be in favor of and acceptable to the Seller, shall be maintained in sufficient amounts and for the period necessary to meet all payment obligations, shall be irrevocable and issued or confirmed by a Canadian chartered bank in Toronto within fifteen days after the date of this contract, shall permit partial deliveries, and shall provide for pro rata payments, payable upon presentation of Seller's invoices and Seller's certificate of delivery FOB factory or of delivery into storage with cause therefor.

B. If the Buyer fails to fulfill any payment obligation, the Seller may suspend performance (and any costs incurred by the Seller as a result thereof shall be paid by the Buyer, payable upon presentation of invoices therefor) or may complete performance if Seller deems it reasonable to do so. Seller shall be entitled to an extension of time for performance of its obligations equaling the period of Buyer's nonfulfillment, whether or not the Seller elects to suspend performance. If such nonfulfillment is not rectified by the Buyer promptly upon notice thereof, the Seller may, in addition to its other rights, terminate this contract, and the Buyer shall pay to the Seller its charges for termination, payable upon presentation of Seller's invoice therefor and determined according to the TERMINATION CHARGES clause.

4. **DELIVERY, TITLE, AND RISK OF LOSS**

A. Except as stated in paragraph C below, Seller shall deliver the goods FOB factory. Partial delivery shall be allowed. Any delivery dates given are approximate and are based upon prompt receipt by Seller of all information necessary to permit Seller to proceed with work without interruption.

B. Title and risk of loss and damage shall pass to the Buyer on delivery.

C. If the goods or any part thereof cannot be delivered when ready due to any cause referred to in the EXCUSABLE DELAY clause, the Seller may place such goods into storage (which may be at the place of manufacture). In such event:

(i)   seller's delivery obligations shall be deemed fulfilled and title and risk of loss and damage shall pass to Buyer,

(ii) any amounts payable to the Seller on delivery shall be payable upon presentation of Seller's invoices and its certification as to such cause, and

(iii) all expenses incurred by the Seller, including, but not limited to, all expenses of preparation and shipment into storage, handling, storage, inspection, preservation, and insurance shall be for Buyer's account and shall be payable upon Seller's presentation of invoices therefor.

5. **EXCUSABLE DELAY**

A. The Seller shall not be in breach of any of its obligations under this contract where failure to perform or delay in performing any obligation is due, wholly or in part, to:

(i)   a cause beyond its reasonable control;

(ii) an act of God, an act or omission of the Buyer or of any governmental authority (de jure or de facto), wars (declared or undeclared), governmental priorities, port congestion, riots, revolutions, strikes or other labor disputes, fire, flood, sabotage, nuclear incidents, earthquake, storm, epidemic; or

(iii) inability due to a cause beyond the Seller's reasonable control to obtain necessary or proper labor, materials, components, facilities, energy, fuel, transportation, governmental authorizations or instructions, material or information required from the Buyer. The foregoing shall apply even though any such cause exists at the time of the order or occurs after the Seller's performance of its obligations is delayed by another cause.

B. The Seller will notify the Buyer of any failure to perform or delay in performing due to a cause set out in paragraph A and shall specify, as soon as practicable, when the obligation will be performed. Subject to paragraph C, the time for performing the obligation shall be extended for the period lost due to such a cause.

C. Where the period lost is at least sixty days and the parties have not agreed upon a revised basis for performing the obligation, including the adjustment of the prices, then, either party may, upon thirty days' written notice, terminate this contract, whereupon the Buyer shall pay to the Seller termination charges determined in accordance with the TERMINATION CHARGES clause.

6. **TERMINATION CHARGES**

A. In the event that this contract is terminated by the Seller pursuant to any of its terms, the termination charges payable by the Buyer shall be calculated as follows:

(i)   material, labor, and indirect expenses committed or incurred to date of termination;

(ii) all costs incurred in the execution of the termination;

(iii) reasonable profit on (i) and (ii) herein above cited;

(iv) the greater of 10 percent of the unbilled portion of the contract price or the unrecoverable, ongoing, fixed costs and expenses due to discontinuities in operation plus loss of reasonable anticipated profit; and

(v) interest at the rate of 1.5 percent per month on the amount of the claim as cited in (i) to (iv) inclusive, if the termination charges are not paid as invoiced.

B. The termination charges shall be payable upon presentation of Seller's invoice therefor.

7. **EXPORT SHIPMENT**

If the Seller agrees to make export shipment, all fees and expenses, including, but not limited to, those covering preparation of consular documents, consular fees, storage, marine insurance (including war risk, if available) and other insurance, ocean freight, and Seller's then current fees for such services shall be payable by the Buyer upon presentation of invoices therefor. Unless otherwise instructed by the Buyer, the Seller shall prepare consular documents according to its best judgment but without liability for fines or other charges due to error or incorrect declarations.

8. **GOVERNMENT AUTHORIZATIONS**

The Seller shall, without any assumption of liability therefor, apply for an export permit on behalf of the Buyer where a permit is required by law. In the event that an export permit is denied or revoked, the Buyer shall have the right to elect to terminate the contract subject to the payment to the Seller of termination charges determined according to the TERMINATION CHARGES clause. The Buyer shall be responsible for obtaining any import permit, exchange permit, or other governmental authorization required by the law of the country of importation.

9. **NUCLEAR USE**

The goods sold are not intended for nor shall they be used for or as any part of any activity or process involving any use or handling of any radioactive material, including any nuclear material (as that term is defined in the Nuclear Liability Act of Canada). If the goods or any part thereof are used by the Buyer contrary to the aforesaid, the Buyer shall provide, at its own expense, insurance and indemnity satisfactory to the Seller protecting the Seller and all of its subcontractors and suppliers from all loss, expense, damages, costs, or liability of every kind, whether in contract or in tort (including negligence), and the Seller may terminate this contract. Upon such termination, the Buyer shall pay to the Seller termination charges determined according to the TERMINATION CHARGES clause.

10. **PATENTS**

A. The Seller shall, if notified promptly in writing and given authority, information, and assistance, defend, at its own expense, any suit or proceeding brought against the Buyer so far as based on a claim that the goods, or any part thereof, sold under this contract infringe any patent of Canada, and the Seller shall pay all damages and costs awarded therein against the Buyer. In the event that the goods, or part thereof, are in such a suit held to constitute an infringement and use of the goods, or part thereof, is enjoined for the intended use, the Seller shall, at its expense and option:

(i) procure for the Buyer the right to continue using the same;

     (ii)   replace the same with non-infringing goods or part thereof;

     (iii) modify the same so as to eliminate infringement; or

     (iv) remove the same and refund the purchase price (less reasonable depreciation for any period of use) and any transportation costs and installation costs paid by the Buyer.

B. The preceding paragraph shall not apply to any goods, or any part thereof, manufactured to the Buyer's design. As to such goods, or part, the Seller assumes no liability whatsoever for infringement.

C. The rights and obligations of the parties with respect to patents or any other industrial property rights are solely and exclusively as stated herein, and the foregoing states the entire liability of the Seller for patent infringement.

11. WARRANTIES

A. The Seller warrants to the Buyer that the goods manufactured by the Seller will be free from defects in material, workmanship, and title and will be of the kind and quality described in the contract.

B. If a failure to meet any of the foregoing warranties, except as to title, appears within one year from the date of shipment or within one year after completion of installation, if the latter is supervised by or performed by the Seller, and provided that completion of installation is not unreasonably delayed by the Buyer, then the Buyer shall not be entitled to terminate or rescind this contract, but the Seller shall correct any such failure by either, at its option, repairing any defective or damaged part or parts of the goods or by making available, FOB Seller's plant or other points of shipment, any necessary repaired or replacement part or parts. Where a failure cannot be corrected by the Seller's reasonable efforts, the parties shall negotiate an equitable adjustment in price. In the event of a failure to meet the warranty as to title, the Buyer shall not be entitled to elect to terminate or rescind this contract but the Seller shall correct such failure. The foregoing sets out the Seller's sole obligation for failure to comply with the foregoing warranties. The Seller shall have no obligation whatsoever and the Buyer shall have no right to make a claim against the Seller in respect of the failure to meet any of the foregoing warranties, except as to title, which appears after the one-year period set out in this clause.

C. The obligations set forth in this clause are conditional upon:

     (i)   proper storage, installation (except where installation is supervised by or performed by the Seller), use, maintenance, and compliance with any applicable recommendations of the Seller; and

     (ii) the Buyer promptly notifying the Seller of any defect and, if required, promptly making the goods available for correction.

D. There is no warranty whatsoever with respect to goods normally consumed in operation or that have a normal life shorter than the warranty period set out in this clause.

E. With respect to goods not manufactured by the Seller (except for integral parts of the goods sold, to which the warranties given in this clause shall apply), the Seller gives no warranty whatsoever, and only the warranty, if any, given by the manufacturer shall apply.

F. The foregoing is exclusive and in lieu of all other warranties and conditions, regardless of whether they be oral, written, express, or implied by statute, including the implied conditions of reasonable fitness for purpose, merchantability, and correspondence with description.

12. **LIMITATION OF LIABILITY**

A. In no event, whether as a result of a breach of contract or a tort (including negligence), shall the Seller be liable to the Buyer for:

   (i)   loss of profit or revenue, loss of use, cost of capital, downtime costs, cost of substitute goods, facilities, services or replacement power;

   (ii) property damage external to the product and loss arising out of such damage;

   (iii) special or consequential damages; and

   (iv) any of the foregoing suffered by a customer of the Buyer.

B. Except as may be provided in the PATENTS clause, in no event, whether as a result of a breach of contract or a tort (including negligence) shall the liability of the Seller to the Buyer exceed the price of the goods, or part thereof or to the service, which gives rise to the claim.

C. If the Buyer transfers title to or leases the goods sold hereunder to, or otherwise permits or suffers use by, any third party, Buyer shall obtain from such third party a provision affording Seller and its suppliers the protection of paragraph A.

D. If the Seller furnishes Buyer with advice or other assistance that concerns the goods supplied hereunder or any system or equipment in which any such goods may be installed and which is not required pursuant to an express term of this contract, the furnishing of such advice or assistance is done without any assumption of responsibility or liability therefor, and the Buyer shall not institute a claim in contract or in tort (including negligence) arising out of or in any way connected therewith.

13. **GENERAL**

A. Unless otherwise stated in this contract, the goods shall be installed by and at the expense of the Buyer.

B. The delegation or assignment by the Buyer of any or all of its duties or rights without the Seller's prior written consent shall be void.

C. No waiver, alteration, or modification of any of the provisions of this contract shall be binding on the Seller unless it is in writing and signed by a duly authorized representative of the Seller.

D. Any goods sold shall comply with federal and provincial laws and regulations applicable to the manufacture, packing, and shipment of such goods as of the date of the Seller's Proposal and shall comply with any amendments thereto that may have come into effect prior to the time such goods are shipped, provided that the price and, if necessary, delivery shall be equitably adjusted to compensate the Seller for having to comply with such amendments.

E. The invalidity, in whole or in part, of any of the foregoing clauses will not affect the remainder of such clauses or any other clauses in this contract.

F. Any reference to "goods" in this contract shall, where the context requires, be a reference to a single chattel personal or to a part of such single chattel personal.

G. No trade usage or course of dealing will be binding on the Seller unless specifically referred to in the contract.

H. This contract and any amendments thereto shall be governed in all respects including, but not limited to, validity, interpretation, and effect, by the laws of the Province of Ontario and of Canada.

EXHIBIT A   PRICE ADJUSTMENT CLAUSE (Manufacturing Only)

All prices stated herein are subject to adjustments, upon completion of this agreement, for changes in labor and material costs. Such adjustments, involving increases or decreases in the prices stated herein, are to be determined in accordance with the following:

1. LABOR

A. For the purpose of adjustment, the proportion of the price representing labor is accepted as 50 percent thereof.

B. The above amount accepted as representing labor will be adjusted for changes in labor cost. Such adjustment will be based upon the Index Numbers of the *Average Hourly Earnings in the Electrical Industrial Equipment Manufacturing Industry,* published monthly by Statistics Canada.

2. MATERIAL

A. For the purpose of adjustment, the proportion of the price representing material is accepted as 40 percent hereof.

B. The above amount accepted as representing material will be adjusted for changes in material costs. Such adjustment will be based upon the *Combined Index of Wholesale Prices for Iron and Non-Ferrous Metals Groups* (excluding gold), or any similar mutually agreed-upon index published monthly by Statistics Canada.

The averages of the monthly indices for labor and material referred to above for the period from a date six months preceding shipment to date of shipment of order under this agreement will be computed separately, and percentage increases or decreases will be established for labor and material by comparison with corresponding indices in effect at the time this proposal was made in the month of _____.

The adjustments for changes in labor and material will be obtained by applying the respective percentages of increase or decrease to the amounts covering labor and material as specified above, and the results will be accepted as an increase or decrease in the aforementioned price.

If Field Construction is involved, refer for Price Adjustment Clause for Field Labor to_____ on page_____.

EXHIBIT B PRICE ADJUSTMENT PROVISIONS

Upon completion of the work, the total contract price for the apparatus to be supplied under this contract shall be subject to an increase or decrease due to fluctuation in the cost of material and/or labor. Adjustments shall be determined in accordance with the following, and the results shall be accepted as an increase or decrease in the Contract price.

1. **LABOR**
   A. For the purpose of adjustment, the proportion of the contract price representing labor is accepted as 50 percent.
   B. The amount so accepted as representing labor will be adjusted for changes in labor costs. Such adjustment will be based upon Table 18 "Average Hourly Earnings, Machinery—Except Electrical, Canada" as shown in *Employment Earnings and Hours*, published monthly by Statistics Canada. An average of those published monthly/hourly earnings for the period from a date six months before complete shipment to the date complete shipment of the apparatus is made from the Company's works will be calculated, and the percentage increase or decrease will be calculated by a comparison with such published hourly earnings for the month during which the Company's tender was submitted. The adjustment for changes in labor costs will be obtained by applying such percentage of increase or decrease to the amount representing labor above mentioned.

2. **MATERIAL**
   A. For the purpose of adjustment, the proportion of the contract price representing material is accepted as _____ percent hereof.
   B. The amount so accepted as representing material will be adjusted for changes in material costs. Such adjustment will be based upon Table 2 "General Wholesale Index—Iron Products (1,935 – 39 = 100)" as shown in *Industry Price Indexes*, published monthly by Statistics Canada. An average of those published indexes for the period from the date six months before complete shipment to the date complete shipment of the apparatus is made from the Company's works will be computed, and the percentage increase or decrease will be calculated by a comparison with such published index for the month during which the Company's tender was submitted. The adjustment for changes in material costs will be obtained by applying such percentage of increase or decrease to the amount representing material above mentioned.

3. **SUBCONTRACT**
   To carry out this contract, the Company will purchase the components or material listed below, which may increase or decrease in price due to increases or decreases in the cost of labor or material. The Purchaser shall reimburse the Company the amount of any increase and the Company shall credit the Purchaser the amount of any decrease due to such adjustment from date of submission of the Company's tender.

EXHIBIT C   PRICE ADJUSTMENT CLAUSE (Field Labor Only)

Prices stated herein applicable to construction or assembly of the equipment provided, at the Purchaser's site, are subject to adjustments upon completion of this agreement for changes in labor costs. Such adjustments, involving increases or decreases in the prices stated herein, are to be determined in accordance with the following:

1. **FIELD LABOR**

   A. For the purpose of adjustment, the proportion of the price representing labor is accepted as _____ percent thereof.
   B. The above amount accepted as representing labor will be adjusted for changes in labor cost. Such adjustment will be based upon the *Average Hourly Earnings in the Construction Industry, Other Engineering Group* published monthly by Statistics Canada, for the area of _____ _____.

   The monthly average hourly earnings for labor referred to above for the period of construction under this agreement will be computed separately, and percentage increases or decreases will be established for labor by comparison with corresponding average hourly earnings in effect at the time this proposal was made in the month of _____ _____.

   The adjustments for changes in labor will be obtained by applying the respective percentage of increase or decrease to the amounts covering labor as specified above, and the result will be accepted as an increase or decrease in the aforementioned price.

Sample Distributorship Agreement

This Distributorship Agreement is entered into this ____day of _____between ABC 2 Company, hereinafter referred to as "Company," having its principal place of business at Naples, Florida, and XYZ Company of Mexico City, Mexico, hereinafter referred to as "Distributor."

1. **DEFINITIONS**
   A. Product(s): Product or products refers to products manufactured or marketed by the company, that including spare parts which are listed in Exhibit A. Exhibit A is subject to change by mutual agreement of the parties.
   B. Territory: Territory shall mean the geographical area designated under Exhibit B. Exhibit B may be revised from time to time by mutual agreement of the parties.
   C. Contract year: Contract year shall mean the period commencing January 1 and ending on December 31. The first contract year shall commence as of the date of this contract, and subsequent years shall commence on January 1 thereafter.
   D. Trade terms: Trade terms such as FOB, CIF, etc., shall be interpreted according to the latest version of International Chamber of Commerce (ICC) Rules.
   E. Purchaser: Purchaser shall mean a purchaser of goods for consumption and not for resale as a distributor.
2. **APPOINTMENT AND ACCEPTANCE**
   A. Company hereby appoints Distributor as the sole importer–distributor of products in the territory and Distributor accepts such appointment.
   B. Company shall not appoint any third person to import, sell, or otherwise deal with products in the territory during the time when the agreement is in effect.
3. **TERM OF THE AGREEMENT**
   The term of this agreement shall be from _____ to _____ unless sooner terminated or further extended as hereinafter provided.

4. **MINIMUM ANNUAL PURCHASES**

   Distributor shall purchase from Company during the contract year such minimum dollar or unit amount of products as specified in Exhibit C attached thereto. Minimum sales for subsequent periods shall be specified in an addendum to this agreement. Should no agreement be reached between the parties, the minimum annual sales for the new contract year shall be deemed to be _____ percent of the minimum annual sales for the preceding contract year.

5. **PRICES FOR THE PRODUCTS**

   A. Company reserves the right to establish or revise at its sole discretion, from time to time, upon thirty days, prices and terms of its sales of products to distributor, including the right at any time to issue new price lists and to change the prices, terms, and provisions therein contained. The price to be paid by the Distributor, excluding spare parts, shall be the price quoted on the Company's current international price list, less a discount of 12 percent.

   B. Company shall provide an additional discount of 3 percent when Distributor takes responsibility at the company's request to service products during the guarantee period. Company shall provide replacement parts free of charge to Distributor during the guarantee period.

   C. Distributor shall bear the cost of freight, insurance, and duties for such parts. Distributor shall make no charge for the replacement parts to customer.

   D. After the end of the guarantee period, spare parts shall be sold to Distributor at the company's current international price, less a discount of 20 percent.

6. **PAYMENTS TO DISTRIBUTOR FOR DIRECT SALES**

   A. Where the Company sells products direct to a customer, the Company shall pay Distributor such commission as is agreed between the parties. In the event that no specific commission is agreed, company shall pay Distributor 8 percent of the net selling price for the products.

   B. Any sums earned by Distributor shall be paid by Company thirty days after receipt by the Company of payment for any such order, provided that no such sums shall be payable by the Company to Distributor in respect of any orders received by the Company after termination of this agreement, except where orders are accepted from potential customers within six months after termination of this agreement and at the time of termination the Distributor has provided the Company with a written list of such potential customers, including evidence to show potential customer's communication and intent to buy the products.

7. **GOVERNMENT LICENSES AND PERMITS**

   The Company shall secure the necessary licenses and permits for the sale and export of the products. It is also incumbent on the Distributor to obtain the necessary licenses and permits required for purchase and importation of the products.

8. **INTELLECTUAL PROPERTY RIGIITS**

   A. The Distributor shall not remove or obliterate any marks or symbols affixed on the goods without the written permission of the Company. A small label bearing the words "supplied by" together with the name and address of the Distributor, shall be applied to the goods.

   B. The Distributor shall advertise the goods solely under the trademarks of the Company. However, it shall not act in any manner, whether by advertising or other means, that might adversely affect the validity of any intellectual property rights belonging to the Company.

C. The Distributor shall, at all times, do all in its power to protect the Company's intellectual property rights and shall ensure that the same remain connected only with the products as defined in this agreement and as the Company may indicate from time to time.

D. The Distributor shall notify the Company in writing as soon as it becomes aware of any infringements of the latter's intellectual property rights in the territory. The Distributor shall bring an action to prevent infringement of such rights at the Company's expense. However, the Company shall not be liable for any infringement caused by the actions of the Distributor.

9. **WARRANTY AND LIABILITY**

A. The Company guarantees that products sold to Distributor are free from defects in material and workmanship and agrees to reimburse all costs of repairs, including reasonably necessary related labor charges, or, at Company's option, to replace any or all defective products within the period of such warranty.

B. The period of the warranty shall extend for one year after the date of sale to the customer for products and ninety days from the date of sale to customer for parts. The Company shall not be liable for the acts or defaults of the Distributor, its employees, or its representatives.

10. **UNDERTAKINGS BY THE DISTRIBUTOR**

A. Distributor agrees to be responsible for supplying or making arrangements for supplying all necessary service to products in the territory, and this includes using its best efforts to provide the best possible service for all owners of products. The Distributor shall hire an adequate number of technicians in order to provide such services promptly.

B. Distributor shall purchase and maintain such volume and assortment of parts as may be necessary to satisfy the service needs of customers.

C. Distributor shall use its best efforts to promote the sales of the goods in its territory as well as maintain adequate staff of salespeople to carry out such responsibility.

D. If at any time during the continuance of this agreement, the Distributor shall become entitled to any development, improvement, or invention relating to any of the products, the Distributor shall give notice in writing to Company and grant to the Company a first option to acquire rights with respect to such invention.

E. The Distributor shall spend a reasonable sum each year on promoting the product in the territory. The Company may make a contribution toward such costs.

F. The Distributor shall assist the Company to produce sales literature in the language of the territory and also provide the Company any sales literature prepared by it relating to the products.

G. The Distributor shall provide Company detailed reports of sales every ninety days, general market information in the territory, and suggestions for any improvements in December of each year.

H. The Distributor shall refrain from purporting to act as an agent of the Company unless otherwise specified in the agreement. In addition, Distributor shall not make any contracts binding the company, warehouse, or advertise the goods outside its territory as well as get involved in the manufacture, production, sale, or advertising of competing goods in the territory.

I. The Distributor shall not transfer or assign the benefit of this agreement to any third party without the prior written consent of the Company.

11. UNDERTAKINGS BY THE COMPANY

The Company agrees to undertake the following responsibilities:

A. Assist the Distributor in advertising the goods by providing the necessary advice and literature as it considers reasonably sufficient to promote the goods in the territory.

B. Support the Distributor in its sales and technical efforts by paying regular visits to the territory of experienced personnel. In the event that a technician is sent to assist the Distributor, the Distributor shall be responsible for traveling expenses to and from the territory, all local traveling expenses, accommodation, and reasonable subsistence costs in the territory.

C. Provide the Distributor with maintenance and servicing instructions and other documentation as well as information on technical changes that are necessary and relevant in connection with the products. The Company may provide appropriate training to suitable qualified technicians of the Distributor that is necessary to install, maintain, or service the products. The parties will determine in due course where the training will take place as well as matters pertaining to expenses.

12. TERMINATION

This agreement may be terminated by a written instrument duly executed by the parties if any of the following situations arise:

A. Either party commits any breach of contract and in the case of a breach capable of being remedied, the party does not remedy the same within sixty days after receipt of notice in writing of such breach.

B. Either party becomes insolvent or goes into liquidation or has a receiver appointed in respect of all or a substantial part of its business.

C. Payment of any sum remains unpaid to either party for a period of thirty days after the due date.

The innocent party may forthwith, by notice in writing, terminate this agreement. Any such termination shall be without prejudice to the rights of the parties accrued up to the date of termination. Neither party will be responsible, by reason of termination of this agreement, to the other for compensation or damages on account of any loss of prospective profits on anticipated sales or on account of expenditures, investments, leases, or other commitments relating to the business or goodwill of either party.

Within thirty days after the termination or expiration of this agreement, Company may, at its option, repurchase from Distributor, at the latter's net warehouse cost, any or all products and/or parts that are commercially usable or salable as well as any usable advertising or promotional materials. Distributor shall return any packaging or promotional materials that were provided by Company free of charge. Distributor shall cease all use of the name and trademark of Company.

13. **FORCE MAJEURE**

    The occurrence of certain events that make the continuance of this agreement impossible, such as riots, government restrictions, or other events outside the reasonable control of the party, shall not constitute a breach of this agreement.

14. **AGREEMENT AND INTERPRETATION**

    A. This agreement and its annexes constitute the whole of the agreement between the Company and Distributor with respect to the products. No variation, alteration, or abandonment of any of its terms shall have effect unless made in writing by the Distributor or its duly authorized representative and by the Company or its duly authorized representative.

    B. This agreement shall be construed in accordance with U.S. law.

    C. The illegality or invalidity of any part of this agreement shall not affect the legality or validity of the remainder thereof.

    D. The headings are for reference purposes only and shall not affect the interpretation of this agreement.

LIST OF EXHIBITS

A. Products

B. Territory

C. Minimum annual purchases

D. Price list

E. Initial order

F. Intellectual property rights

Signed for ABC Company by	Signed for XYZ distributor by
In the presence of	In the presence of

Sample Sales Representative Agreement

MEMORANDUM OF AGREEMENT entered into in duplicate, this ---------- day of ---------.

BETWEEN:	duly incorporated under the laws of Canada, having its head office and principal place of business at Toronto, Province of Ontario (hereinafter referred to as party of the first part [PFP].
AND:	a body politic and corporate, having its head office and place of business in -------(hereinafter called the Sales Representative).

WITNESSETH THAT in consideration of the premises and of the mutual covenant and agreements hereinafter contained, the parties hereto agree each with the other as follows:

PFP hereby engages the Sales Representative to provide services in accordance with the terms and conditions of this Agreement for the sale of proprietary products (hereinafter called Equipment) listed in the Schedule attached hereto and made an integral part hereof to markets in _____(hereinafter called Served Market).

1. **TERRITORY**
   The geographical area (hereinafter called Territory) in which the Sales Representative shall undertake the responsibilities specified in this Agreement is
   _____.

2. **TERMS AND SCOPE**
   The term of this Agreement shall be from _____ to _____
   _____ unless sooner terminated as hereinafter provided. The provisions of this Agreement shall govern all transactions between PFP and the Sales Representative unless otherwise agreed to in writing by the duly authorized representatives of both parties.

3. **COMPANY RESPONSIBILITIES**
PFP agrees that during the term of this Agreement, it will, subject to and in accordance with the terms and conditions herein expressed:

A. keep the Sales Representative advised of new products, sales plans, and objectives with respect to Equipment for Served Market Customers in the Territory;

B. support the sales efforts of the Sales Representative by furnishing printed commercial and technical data and information and other publications that PFP may have available from time to time for export distribution; and

C. pay a commission as provided in Article 5 hereof on orders for Equipment received and accepted by PFP from Served Market Customers in the Territory as a result of the effort of the Sales Representative. As used in this Agreement, the terms "order" or "orders" include contracts for Equipment with Served Market Customers in the Territory executed by PFP.

4. **SALES REPRESENTATIVE RESPONSIBILITIES**
The Sales Representative agrees that during the term of this Agreement, it will, subject to the terms and conditions herein expressed:

A. maintain an adequate sales organization and use its best efforts to assist PFP in the sale of Equipment to Served Market Customers in the Territory;

B. maintain active contacts with Served Market Customers in the Territory;

C. keep PFP fully informed of all governmental, commercial, and industrial activities and plans that do or could affect the sale of Equipment to Served Market Customers in the Territory;

D. provide market information to PFP on Served Market Customers' and competitors' activities;

E. recommend improvements to sales plans, assist in developing strategy, and clarify the Equipment requirements of Served Market Customers in the Territory;

F. as requested, transmit proposals and technical data to Served Market Customers in the Territory, interpret customer inquiries, requirements, and attitudes, and assist in contract negotiations. (All proposals so transmitted will contain terms and conditions of sale substantially in accordance with PFP's Standard Terms and Conditions of Sale, a copy of which is attached hereto and is subject to change by PFP from time to time. No proposal shall be transmitted to a Served Market Customer unless terms and conditions of sale are approved by PFP or the Standard Terms and Conditions of Sale are incorporated in such proposal); and

G. perform such liaison services with Served Market Customers in the Territory as PFP may from time to time direct relative to any order(s) awarded to PFP from the supply of Equipment, including assistance in the resolution of any claims or complaints of such Customers arising out of PFP's performance of said order(s).

5. **COMPENSATION**
A. As compensation to the Sales Representative for services rendered here-under, PFP agrees to pay the Sales Representative a commission on the

following orders for PFP's proprietary equipment from Served Market Customers in the Territory during the term of this Agreement:

    (i)   Orders that are forwarded by the Sales Representative.

    (ii)   Orders that the Sales Representative has specifically identified to PFP being forthcoming directly from a Served Market Customer in the Territory when, in the absolute judgment of PFP such commission may be warranted by the effort used by the Sales Representative resulting in said orders.

B.   The commission, based on the net sale price (FOB factory), will be paid in accordance with the Schedule(s) (__) attached hereto and made an integral part of this Agreement.

C.   Said commission shall be disbursed in Canadian dollars to the Sales Representative within thirty days subsequent to the payment for the Equipment delivered to the Served Market Customer in accordance with the terms of payment established and accepted in the contract between PFP and the Served Market Customer.

D.   No commissions will be paid on the value of technical, construction, installation, or similar services, nor on the value of insurance, bonds, interest, ocean freight, or other charges that may be included in the PFP's invoice to a Served Market Customer.

E.   It is understood that if an order should be rescinded, revoked, or repudiated by a Served Market Customer for reasons beyond PFP's control or by PFP for breach of contract or by either party for force majeure causes, or it becomes invalid or inoperative due to any governmental regulation, the Sales Representative shall not be entitled to a commission with respect to such order, except pro rata to the extent of any amounts PFP may have received and retained as payment for Equipment delivered to a Served Market Customer.

F.   It is further understood that no compensation, by way of commission or otherwise, shall be due the Sales Representative in connection with an order on which a commission would otherwise be payable, if as to such an order:

    (i)   any applicable governmental law, rule, or regulation prohibits or makes improper the payment of any commission, fee, or other payment to a Sales Representative;

    (ii)   any Served Market Customer makes it a condition that no commission, fee, or payment be made to a Sales Representative; or

    (iii) any action has been taken by the Sales Representative in violation of its commitments set forth in Article 6, paragraphs C and D.

6.   **RELATIONSHIP OF PARTIES AND CONTROLLING LAWS**

Λ.   PFP may assign the installation and commissioning portion of its contract to the Sales Representative but, except as aforesaid, this Agreement and any rights hereunder are nonexclusive and non-assignable, and any assignment by one party without the prior written consent of the other party shall be void. The Sales Representative is an independent contractor to PFP. It is understood that the Sales Representative or its agents, subsidiaries, affiliates, and employees are in no way the legal representatives or agents of PFP for any purpose whatsoever and have no right or authority to assume or create, in writing or otherwise, any obligation of any kind, expressed or implied, in the name of or on behalf of PFP. PFP reserves the right to determine in its sole discretion the acceptability of any order, any provisions thereof, or any condition proposed by the customer and shall in no way be obligated to bid, quote to, or negotiate with any Served Market Customer.

B. This Agreement and any services hereunder are subject to and shall be governed by all the applicable laws and regulations of Canada; the rights and obligations of the Sales Representative as well as those of PFP under or in connection with this Agreement shall be governed by such laws and regulations and by the law of the Province of Ontario, Canada.

C. The Sales Representative agrees to comply with the law applicable to the performance of its obligations under the terms of this Agreement. Without limitation to the foregoing, the Sales Representative will comply fully with the export control laws and regulations of the Canadian Government with respect to the disposition of products and the printed commercial and technical data and information and other publications supplied by PFP. Further, the Sales Representative agrees that it will not pay, nor will it make any offer or commitment to pay, anything of value (either in the form of compensation, gift, contribution, or otherwise) to any employee, representative, person, or organization in any way connected with any Customer, private or governmental, where such payment is contrary to applicable law, including the laws of Canada and the laws of the country in which the Sales Representative provides services under this Agreement.

D. With respect to any transaction arising under this Agreement, it is specifically understood and agreed that neither the Sales Representative nor its employees or representatives shall receive any payments in the nature of a rebate or similar benefit paid directly or indirectly by the Customer, nor shall any employee or representative of PFP receive any such payment paid directly or indirectly by the Sales Representative or by the Customer.

7. **EXPIRATION, RENEWAL, TERMINATION**

A. This Agreement shall automatically expire at the end of the term specified in Article 2 hereof unless specifically renewed prior thereto by mutual consent given in writing by the parties hereto.

B. This Agreement may be terminated prior to the completion of the term specified in Article 2 hereof:

(i)   by mutual consent given in writing by the parties hereto;

(ii) by either party at will, with or without cause, upon no less than sixty days' notice in writing by registered mail, cable, or personal delivery to the other party; or

(iii) by PFP upon one day's similar notice in the event the Sales Representative attempts to assign this Agreement or any right hereunder without PFP's prior written consent; there is a change in the control or management of the Sales Representative that is unacceptable to PFP; the Sales Representative ceases to conduct its operations in the normal course of business; a receiver for the Sales Representative is appointed or applied for or it otherwise takes advantage of an insolvency law; the Sales Representative represents other parties whose representation, in PFP's opinion, involves a conflict with the Sales Representative's obligations hereunder; or the Sales Representative breaches this Agreement or acts in any manner deemed by PFP to be detrimental to the best interest of PFP. The foregoing events shall without limitation be deemed to be cause for termination by PFP.

8. **OBLIGATIONS UPON EXPIRATION OR TERMINATION**

In the event that an order from any Served Market Customer in the Territory for the supply of Equipment is accepted by PFP prior to the date of expiration or termination of this Agreement, the obligations assumed by both parties hereunder with respect to any such order shall continue in force until fully performed. In the event this Agreement expires or is terminated, and within _____ from the date of such expiration or termination an order from a Served Market Customer in the Territory for the supply of Equipment is accepted by PFP and is implemented within said period by financial arrangements acceptable to PFP, the Sales Representative's rights to commission payments will be fully protected, provided such purchase order is awarded in the sole opinion of PFP as a result of services performed by the Sales Representative prior to the effective date of expiration or termination. Such acceptance of an order from, or the sale of any Equipment to, a Served Market Customer after the expiration or termination of this Agreement shall not be construed as a renewal or extension hereof, but the obligations undertaken in this Article 8 shall survive such expiration or termination.

9. **PRIVATE INFORMATION**

   A. The Sales Representative shall maintain in confidence and safeguard all business and technical information that becomes available to it in connection with this Agreement, the information being either of proprietary nature or not intended for disclosure to others. This obligation shall continue for five years after expiration or termination of this Agreement.

   B. Knowledge or information of any kind disclosed by the Sales Representative to PFP shall be deemed to have been disclosed without obligation on the part of PFP to hold the same in confidence, and PFP shall have full right to use and disclose such information, subject to the approval of the Sales Representative, whose approval shall not be withheld without proper cause and without any compensation to the Sales Representative beyond that specifically provided by this Agreement.

10. **COMPANY TRADEMARKS AND TRADE NAMES**

The Sales Representative agrees that it will comply at all times with the rules and regulations furnished to the Sales Representative by PFP with respect to the use and ownership of trademarks and trade names; it will express and identify properly the "Authorized Sales Representative" relationship with PFP for Equipment; it will not publish or cause to be published any statement, nor encourage or approve any advertising or practice that might mislead or deceive any parties or might be detrimental to the good name, trademark, goodwill, or reputation of PFP or its products. The Sales Representative further agrees upon request to withdraw any statement and discontinue any advertising or practice deemed by PFP to have such effect.

11. **LIMITATION OF LIABILITY**

Neither party to this agreement shall have liability to the other with respect to the claims arising out of, in connection with, or resulting from this agreement, whether in contract, tort (including negligence of any degree), or otherwise except as provided under the terms of this agreement.

12. **RELEASE OF CLAIMS**

In consideration of the execution of this Agreement by PFP, the Sales Representative hereby releases PFP from all claims, demands, contracts, and liabilities, if any thereby, as of the date of execution of this Agreement by the Sales Representative, except indebtedness that may be owing founded upon a written contract.

13. **FAILURE TO ENFORCE**

The failure of either party to enforce at any time or for any period of time the provisions hereof in accordance with its terms shall not be construed to be a waiver of such provisions or of the right of such party thereafter to enforce each and every provision.

14. **NOTICES**

Any notice, request, demand, direction, or other communication required or permitted to be given or made under this agreement or in connection therewith shall be deemed to have been properly given or made if delivered to the party to whom it is addressed, or by registered mail, telegram, cable, or telex addressed as follows: _____

15. **EXECUTION AND MODIFICATION**

A. This Agreement constitutes the entire and only agreement between the parties respecting the sales representation to the Served Market of Equipment specified herein.

B. This Agreement wholly cancels, terminates, and supersedes any and all previous negotiations, commitments, and writing between the parties with respect to Equipment. No change, modification, extension, renewal, ratification, rescission, termination, notice of termination, discharge, abandonment, or waiver of this Agreement or any of the provisions hereof; nor any representation, promise, or condition relating to this Agreement shall be binding upon PFP unless made in writing and signed by duly authorized personnel of PFP,

IN WITNESS WHEREOF, this agreement has been executed by both parties.

Trade Documents

COMMERCIAL INVOICE

Export References:		
Invoice No:		
Exporter Name and Address:	*Ultimate Consignee/End User Name and Address:* Contact:	*Sold To Name and Address:*
Intermediate Consignee/ Consigned to:	*Notify Party Name and Address:*	*Date of Shipment:* *AWB/BL Number:* *Currency:* *Letter of Credit Number:*
Conditions of Sale and Terms of Payment: *Freight:* *Title Transfer:* *Payment Terms:*	*Transportation:* *Via:* *From:*	*Total Number of Packages:* *Total Net Weight (kgs):* *Total Gross Weight (kgs):*

Line No.	Item Number, Harmonized Number, Product Description	Country of Origin	Quantity	Unit Price	Total Price
	Additions to be charged to customer including freight charges, these details are contract and trade term dependent.				
	Total				

Please Note: *These commodities, technology, or software were exported from the United States in accordance with the Export Administration Regulations. Diversion contrary to U.S. law prohibited.*

Authorized Signature:	**Company:**
Name:	**Title:**

CERTIFICATE OF ORIGIN

Shipper/exporter (name and address including zip code):	Booking/shipment number:	B/L or AWB number:
	Export references:	
Consignee (name and address):	Forwarding agent (name and address - references):	

Intermediate consignee/notify party (name and address):	Point (state and country) of origin:		
	Domestic routing / export instructions:		
Pre-carriage by: / **Place of receipt:**			
Exporting carrier: / **Port of loading/export:**	Transportation method:		
Foreign port of unloading (vessel and air only):	Place of delivery by on-carrier:	Containerized (vessel only): YES NO	
Container No. / Seal No. / Marks and Numbers:	Number of Packages:	Description of commodities, Model/Serial number, harmonized number, country of origin	Gross weight (kg):	Measurement CBM/CUFT

The undersigned_____(Owner or Agent), does hereby declare for the above named shipper, the goods as described on the above date and consigned as indicated and are products of the United States of America. Dated at_____on the_____ day of   . Sworn to before me this_____day of_____,_____.

Signature of Owner or Agent

The_____, a recognized Chamber of Commerce under the laws of the State of_____, has examined the manufacturer's invoice or shipper's affidavit concerning the origin of the merchandise, and, according to the best of its knowledge, finds that the products named originated in the country named above.

Secretary_____

Export References:		Expiration Date:	
Exporter Name and Address:	Ultimate Consignee Name and Address:	Sold To Name and Address:	
Intermediate Consignee/ Consigned to:	Notify Party Name and Address:	Date of Shipment: AWB/BL Number: Currency: Letter of Credit Number:	
Conditions of Sale and Terms of Payment: Freight (please mark): Pre-paid__Collect___ Title Transfer Occurs At: Payment Terms:	Transportation Via: From:	Total Number of Packages: Total Net Weight (kgs): Total Gross Weight (kgs):	
Item Number, Product Description, Tariff Classification Number, Country of Origin	Quantity	Unit Price	Total Price

Please Note: These commodities, technology, or software were exported from the United States in accordance with the Export Administration Regulations. Diversion contrary to U.S. law prohibited.

Authorized Signature:	Company:	
Name:	Title:	
Date:	E-mail:	Telephone Number(s) Voice: Facsimile:

FORMAL QUOTE

A quotation is one of the first steps in an export transaction. It is a response to an inquiry received from a potential buyer (or a U.S. representative of the foreign entity) or a proactive marketing step of a U.S. based company.

   If a quotation is sent to a foreign company that is not familiar with the company or products, the description should be very specific and detailed, more so than if the buyer were domestic. Along with the description, there are other items that should be included, such as:

1. Seller's name and address
2. Potential buyer's name and address
3. Buyer's reference – inquiry number if noted
4. Prices of items: per unit and extended
5. Weights and dimensions of quoted products
6. Discounts, if applicable
7. Terms of sale or Incoterms used (include geographical delivery point)
8. Terms of payment
9. Validity of quotation
10. Estimated shipping date
11. Estimated date of arrival

When quoting a price, it is beneficial to give a potential buyer some options of trade terms selection. Incoterms are very effective when presenting pricing options to the potential buyer. For some very large foreign companies, it is more convenient and cost-effective to negotiate their own freight rates and organize their own shipments, so they may prefer EXW or F-terms. On the other hand, there may be other buyers that would prefer the seller to organize the movement, thereby preferring the C-terms or even the D-terms.

This template includes instructions to the buyer regarding the seller's conditions for a letter of credit. If you will not be paid under a letter of credit, please delete these instructions from your template.

Template: Formal Quote

SELLER/EXPORT COMPANY   Street Address
                                              City, State Zip Code USA

                                              Quotation number:
                                              Dated: Month Day, Year
                                              Page 1 of 5

FORMAL QUOTATION

Customer Name
Address

Subject: Your request for quote for Product.
                        Our Reference No.:

Currency: USD
Trade Term: Subject to Incoterms® 2010

Model No.	Description	Quantity	Unit Price	Extended Price
	Tariff Classification Country of Origin			
	Export Packing/Crating: Inland Freight: **Total Incoterms® Rule City, State, Country**			

TERMS AND CONDITIONS OF SALE:

Payment Terms: Payable in U.S. Dollars by wire transfer of funds prior to shipment of order or by an *acceptable* letter of credit. Instructions are attached for opening a letter of credit.

Terms of Sale: Buyers may choose any of the above trade terms (Incoterms® 2010) that are in bold print, then submit a purchase order with your selection. When submitting a purchase order, please state the appropriate Incoterms® Rule indicating the "named place" and followed by the words: "... *per Incoterms® 2010.*"

Transfer of Title: Occurs at .
Validity of offer: (insert number) calendar days from date of quote.
Shipment Date: (insert number) weeks after receipt of payment or acceptable letter of credit.
Export Control: Please be advised, this order may be subject to an export license.

SELLER/EXPORT COMPANY

QUOTATION NUMBER:

Dated: Month Day, Year
Page 2 of 5

SHIPPING INFORMATION:

(Estimate only; may vary at time of shipment)

ITEM	PART NUMBER	QUANTITY (PIECES)	INVENTORY AVAILABILITY	GROSS WEIGHT (LBS) EACH	TOTAL GROSS WEIGHT (LBS)	CUBIC FEET (PER PIECE)	TOTAL CUBIC FEET

TOTALS

Total chargeable weight for ocean shipping:

RECOMMENDED MODE OF SHIPMENT:

EXPORT INFORMATION:

Origin of Goods:

HS No.:

The receipt of your purchase order will signify acceptance with the terms and conditions of this quotation. Please use Seller/Export Company quotation number when placing your order.

If changes to this offer are needed, please request a revised quote.

Destination Control Statement:

These commodities, technology or software will be exported from the United States in accordance with the Export Administration Regulations. Diversion contrary to U.S. law prohibited.

For Seller/Export Company:

> **IMPORTANT!**
>
> In compliance with United States federal law, the Destination Control Statement (DCS) is to be entered on the invoice, the bill of lading, air waybill, or other export control document that accompanies the shipment from its point of origin in the United States to the ultimate consignee or end-user abroad. The Export Administration Regulations specify when it is mandatory.

SELLER/EXPORT COMPANY   **QUOTATION NUMBER:**

Date: Month Day, Year
Page 3 of 5

LETTER OF CREDIT REQUIREMENTS

Customer Name
Address

Subject: Your request for quote
               Our Reference number:

If a letter of credit is issued, below are the terms and conditions acceptable to Seller/Export Company If any of these requirements are unacceptable, please contact Ms. George with alterations so an agreement can be reached. This will eliminate unnecessary costs and delays later due to amendments on the letter of credit.

1. Please open the letter of credit by SWIFT; opening letters of credit by mail may delay the order process by 2-4 weeks.

2. The credit shall be drawn in irrevocable form and subject to "Uniform Customs and Practice for Documentary Credits" International Chamber of Commerce Publication Number 600.

3. The letter of credit is to be advised and confirmed by any U.S. owned bank, preferably at the counters of (insert bank's name). Seller/Export Company's bank may be the advising/confirming if the customer does not already have a bank for this purpose. Banking information for letters of credit are as follows:

Seller/Export Company	Quotation number:
	Date: Month, Day, Year
	Page 4 of 5

4. The credit shall be payable at the counters of any U.S. Bank.
5. The letter of credit shall show as The Beneficiary:

> **Seller/Export Company**
> **Street Address**
> **City, State Zip Code USA**

6. The letter of credit shall be payable in U.S. Dollars at sight of draft and documents and in the amount specified in the order.
7. The following documents will be provided for this transaction. Please avoid the requirement for any other documents without prior agreement by us.

   a. Commercial Invoice at value per the agreed order subject to Incoterms® 2010 (insert trade term and location). 1 original and 3 copies.
   b. Packing List in 1 original and 3 copies.
   c. The transport document as follows:

> **For Air Freight:**
> **Clean** Air Waybill consigned to the issuing bank designating "notify applicant."
> - Air consolidator's air waybills shall be allowed.
> - Marked freight collect or prepaid, as agreed in the order.
> **For Ocean Freight:**
> **Clean** on Board Multimodal Ocean Bill of Lading consigned "to order" of shipper.
> - NVOCC bills of lading shall be allowed.
> - Marked freight collect or prepaid, as agreed in the order.

8. The port of export (for air or for ocean) shall be specified as "any USA port/airport."
9. The entry port at destination.
10. Transshipment allowed.
11. Partial shipments shall be allowed, if agreed upon in the order.

SELLER/EXPORT COMPANY   **QUOTATION NUMBER:**

Dated: Month Day, Year
Page 5 of 5

12. The expiration date on the letter of credit shall not be less than (insert number) days after the issuance of the transport document (air or ocean bill of lading).
13. The letter of credit shall not be transferable.
14. *All* banking charges incurred inside and outside the beneficiary's country are for the account of the applicant (customer). **Note**: this includes all charges related to amending the letter of credit as well as confirmation fees (must be specified in writing within the credit).
15. Please describe the product as follows:
16. Letter of credit must be in English.
17. No boycott, restrictive trade practices, or discriminatory provisions will be allowed in the letter of credit.

TIPS:

- Use a multi-modal Incoterms® 2010 rule associated with a location or port/airport (CPT foreign ocean port of entry).
- Specify "transport document" rather than ocean bill of lading or air waybill, in case the method of transportation changes.

INDEX

Printed in the United States
by Baker & Taylor Publisher Services